THE PSEUDEPIGRAPHAL LETTERS TO THE THESSALONIANS

THE PSEUDEPIGRAPHAL LETTERS TO THE THESSALONIANS

Marlene Crüsemann

Translated
by

Linda M. Maloney

t&tclark

NEW YORK • LONDON • OXFORD • NEW DELHI • SYDNEY

T&T CLARK
Bloomsbury Publishing Plc
50 Bedford Square, London, WC1B 3DP, UK
1385 Broadway, New York, NY 10118, USA

BLOOMSBURY, T&T CLARK and the T&T Clark logo are trademarks of
Bloomsbury Publishing Plc

Originally published in German as *Die Pseudepigraphen Briefe an die Gemeinde in Thessaloniki*, © 2010, W. Kohlhammer GmbH, Stuttgart.

First published in Great Britain 2019

The translation of this work was funded by Geisteswissenschaften International – Translation Funding for Work in the Humanities and Social Sciences from Germany, a joint initiative of the Fritz Thyssen Foundation, the German Federal Foreign Office, the collecting society VG WORT and the Börsenverein des Deutschen Buchhandels (German Publishers & Booksellers Association).

A catalogue record for this book is available from the British Library.

A catalogue record for this book is available from the Library of Congress

ISBN: HB: 978-0-5676-8332-8
ePDF: 978-0-5676-8333-5
ePUB: 978-0-5676-8335-9

Typeset by RefineCatch Limited, Bungay, Suffolk
Printed and bound in Great Britain

CONTENTS

PREFACE

This book is an updating of my doctoral dissertation, *Die Briefe nach Thessaloniki und das gerechte Gericht. Studien zu ihrer Abfassung und zur jüdisch-christlichen Sozialgeschichte,* submitted to the University of Kassel in 1999 and published in microfiche.

I thank first of all Professor Dr. Dr. h.c. †Luise Schottroff, my esteemed teacher, Doctor-Mother and dear friend, for her encouragement, support, and advocacy over many years, for the unrestricted freedom to do research she granted me from the very beginning, and for many rich hours of shared work, life, and celebration. I dedicate this book to her with all my heart and much gratitude.

Also I sincerely thank Professor Dr. Claudia Janssen for her stimulation and encouragement in numerous projects and assignments, especially in the area of our New Testament working group, "Die Paulinen," together with Luise Schottroff.

For our conversations and the helpful contacts he arranged, I am grateful to Professor Dr. Jürgen Ebach, as I am to Professor Dr. Klaus Wengst for his magnanimous support and for the new opportunities he opened up for me.

Sincere thanks to the editors of the New Testament Section of the *Beiträge zur Wissenschaft vom Alten und Neuen Testament*, Professor Dr. Reinhard von Bendemann and Professor Dr. Marlis Gielen, for accepting this book into the series and, especially, for the labor of reading the text with great care and for the valuable questions and suggestions they offered for the development of the argumentation.

I thank the W. Kohlhammer Publishing House and its theological editor, Dr. Jürgen Schneider, for the friendly accommodation given to me, and Dr. Florian Specker of the editorial office for his care and responsiveness at all times in connection with technical and substantive matters.

Many thanks also to Hauke Christiansen for his initiatives in rescuing electronic data, to Ute Ochtendung for her devoted, knowledgeable, and careful preparation of the final copy, and to Sebastian Stüwe for his friendly technical assistance.

I thank the Geschwister Boehringer Ingelheim Stiftung für Geisteswissenschaften sincerely for their extremely generous contribution to the printing costs.

I also thank my theological friends Rosi Becker-Ubbelohde, Karin Greifenstein, Dr. Ursula Hardmeier, and Dr. Hanne Köhler: we are trusted companions to one another on the way, some of us since our student days. For her friendship and affection I thank Elisabeth Hölscher, who inspires me and gives me wings again and again.

Thank you to my "salon" friends in Bielefeld: Berthild Boueke-von Waldthausen, Brunhild Hilf, Ruth Matthes, Dr. Heide Schorlemmer, and Erika Stückrath for many years of shared life and literature. And I am very grateful to Karin Röstel-Reglinski and Elisabeth Umierski, my school friends, for their strong devotion, for our old and renewed friendship.

I am especially deeply grateful to my partner in marriage, Professor Dr. Frank Crüsemann, who not only endured our conversations about the First Epistle to the Thessalonians over the years but also encouraged and supported me constantly with diverse practical assistance all the way to reading the page proofs and preparing the index. "Thank you" also to our son Max Crüsemann, who, despite the pharmaceutical-chemical focus of his profession, knows how to value his mother's theological work.

And I want to thank very particularly my sister Ilse-Marie Cohrs for her presence to me from our childhood and youth and for our mutuality in remembering our brother Heiner Cohrs (1957–1984) and our parents Ilse Cohrs (1928–1986) and Erich Cohrs (1929–2008). I am also grateful for her ever-fresh interest in my theological texts; it means so very much to me.

Marlene Crüsemann
Bielefeld, Spring 2010

FOREWORD TO THE ENGLISH EDITION

My heartfelt thanks to all who have labored on the English translation of this book and brought it to fruition. Prof. Dr. h.c. Martin Rumscheidt of Ottawa saw to it, by his devoted and ongoing efforts, that the project got underway, bringing it to a publisher and even obtaining endorsements for the work. His enthusiasm and wide-ranging work gave me enormous joy and fill me with the deepest gratitude.

I am grateful to Professor David J. A. Clines of Sheffield for his willingness to publish the work with Sheffield Phoenix and for his vote to approve; I am deeply grateful also to Prof. Dr. Dr. h.c. Athalya Brenner of Tel Aviv and Amsterdam for her positive vote. Thanks are due also to Nicola Oster of Kohlhammer publishers for her work on the application for financial support for the translation.

My gratitude goes to the Fritz Thyssen Stiftung, the VG Wort, the Börsenverein des Deutschen Buchhandels, and the Foreign Office for their financial awards in support of the translation. I am likewise grateful to the personnel at Bloomsbury Publishing and Bloomsbury Academic for their work to bring the book to publication.

In particular I thank the translator, the Rev. Dr. Linda M. Maloney, for her splendid and impressive work, to which she has applied so much care and scholarly ability.

Marlene Crüsemann
Bielefeld, August 2017

Chapter 1

INTRODUCTION

"Is it a Letter? Is it a letter at all? I think not."

—After Reich-Ranicki's parody of Hape Kerkeling

"Test everything; hold fast to what is good."

—1 Thessalonians 5:12

1.1 The Two Letters to Thessalonica

The first letter to the church in Thessalonica is a peculiar writing; the more often one reads it, the stranger it appears. The following study is the fruit of a multi-year reading process; it seeks to invite readers into what may turn out to be an adventurous journey: through the idiosyncrasies of this first, and then also the second letter to Thessalonica. This also involves trying out a new proposal about the relationship between the two letters. That relationship presents a profile unique within the New Testament. We need only recall that, ever since William Wrede's pioneering work[1] and its precursors, 2 Thessalonians has been widely assumed to be a pseudepigraphical writing that copies and at the same time modifies 1 Thessalonians, a genuine letter of Paul. This would mean that, decades after the genuine correspondence, someone took up the pen to communicate further news, in a new situation but with almost the same means, apparently to the same church, though now most likely made up of considerably younger (?) members. Perhaps it is this long hiatus separating the two letters that lets many English-speaking interpreters maintain the authenticity of 2 Thessalonians.[2]

1. William Wrede, *Die Echtheit des zweiten Thessalonicherbriefs untersucht* (1903); see 6.1 below.

2. E.g., the commentaries by Ernest Best, *Thessalonians* (1977); F. F. Bruce, *1 & 2 Thessalonians* (1962); I. Howard Marshall, *1 & 2 Thessalonians* (1983); Charles A. Wanamaker, *Thessalonians* (1990); Abraham J. Malherbe, *Thessalonians* (2000); Gregory K. Beale, *1–2 Thessalonians* (2010); Ivor H. Jones, *Thessalonians* (2005); Ben Witherington III, *1 & 2 Thessalonians* (2006); Gordon D. Fee, *Thessalonians* (2009), and to some extent Robert Jewett, *The Thessalonian Correspondence* (1986); Todd D. Still, *Conflict at Thessalonica* (1999); Colin R. Nicholl, *From Hope to Despair* (2004).

But a text with "false" information about authorship is not uncommon in the New Testament canon; quite the contrary. Of its twenty-seven writings, only seven letters of Paul are currently considered unquestionably authentic, meaning that the person named in the prescript is indeed the author of the writing insofar as such an indication can be found therein. Most others are said to be anonymous or pseudonymous writings.[3]

So when this study reopens the discussion of the "inauthenticity" of the first letter to the Thessalonians as well, it is not a revolutionary claim within the framework of the whole New Testament. But, given the current scholarly status of 1 Thessalonians, such an undertaking evokes accusations of *lèse majesté* and impertinent sacrilege.[4] That is because this brief letter is generally considered Paul's first, and as such the oldest New Testament text. The high esteem accorded this text has risen phenomenally among New Testament scholars in recent decades.[5] This first written apostolic statement is said to be an "experiment in Christian writing,"[6] that is to say, the prototype of the entire genre of apostolic letters. Accordingly, Paul here invents the form best suited for his own communication with his churches. His subsequent, thematically more sublime letters then build on this primal form and in a sense develop from it. Thus 1 Thessalonians constitutes the basis for Pauline exegesis,[7] and

3. For this see the introductions to the Pauline letters by, e.g., Hans Conzelmann and Andreas Lindemann, *Arbeitsbuch zum Neuen Testament* (2010), 203–50; Udo Schnelle, *Einleitung in das Neue Testament* (1994), 61–182; Stefan Schreiber, "Briefliteratur im Neuen Testament" (2008), 260–64, etc.

4. A "widely shared consensus has emerged in twentieth-century scholarship that 1 Thessalonians is an undisputedly authentic letter . . . no one in the current scholarly debate doubts its authenticity" (Jewett, *Thessalonian Correspondence*, 3). D. Edmond Hiebert's remarks may be regarded as *communis opinio*: all objections to the authenticity of 1 Thessalonians are, according to him, "inadequate or even baseless," and serve instead as arguments for its genuineness. The letter is said to document a degree of reality that no forger could have produced, and no persuasive explanation has yet been offered for its character if it is pseudepigraphical. Pauline authorship shortly after his stay in Thessalonica, when he founded the community, is held to be reasonable and logical. The vocabulary, style, and content are held to be clearly Pauline (Hiebert, *1 & 2 Thessalonians* [Chicago: Moody Bible Institute, rev. 3d. 1992], 29).

5. As documented, e.g., in the seminar papers published as *The Thessalonian Correspondence*, ed. Raymond F. Collins and Norbert Baumert (1990), an entire book containing nearly 300 pages of bibliography on the Thessalonian letters; Jeffrey A. Weima and Stanley E. Porter, *An Annotated Bibliography of 1 and 2 Thessalonians* (1998); and the reports on research by Collins, "Recent Scholarship" (1984); Earl J. Richard, "Contemporary Research" (1990); Stanley E. Porter, "Developments in German and French Thessalonians Research" (1999); and Stefan Schreiber, "Früher Paulus mit Spätfolgen" (2007).

6. Helmut Koester, "1 Thessalonians—Experiment in Christian Writing" (1979), 33–44.

7. Hence it is possible, e.g., for Raymond F. Collins's book, entitled *The Birth of the New Testament* (1993), with the subtitle *The Origin and Development of the First Christian Generation*, to be almost entirely an exegesis of 1 Thessalonians.

for that of the entire New Testament and church history. "The oldest written document of Christianity lies before us in 1 Thessalonians; we stand at the beginning of (earliest) Christianity's literary history."[8]

Yet a critical examination still raises doubts about the historical classification of 1 Thessalonians. Among other questions, my study asks whether 1 Thessalonians is an *early* letter of Paul, a letter of *Paul*, and, finally, a *letter* at all. The following unusual features of the text give rise to these questions:

- the nearly pervasive structuring of authorship in the first person plural, which departs from the usual pattern;
- the extremely anti-Jewish passage in 2:14–16, which raises the question whether it can be regarded as an interpolation within the text;
- the fact that chapters 1–3 speak only of events that took place very shortly before the letter was written,[9] all aspects of which would be known to the congregation and be fresh in their memory, something the authors also acknowledge frequently;
- the fact that, on closer analysis, the material situation of this epistolary communication is obscure;
- finally, for example, the passage in 4:13–17 concerning the resurrection of the dead, which culminates in a reception like that for an ancient ruler rather than in the eschatological victory of Jesus over the power of death.

These and other questions posed to the text have led me to a new interpretation of the most important parts of 1 Thessalonians, which makes up the principal section of this study. But because the two epistles to Thessalonica are canonically linked, and because I have become convinced that only an interpretation of both together in terms of their interrelatedness (which becomes apparent when the two letters are read together) can best do justice to the unique character of each writing, the final chapter proposes a new answer, based on their content, to the question of their relationship to each other.

8. Stefan Schreiber, "Der erste Thessalonicherbrief" (2008), 384–96, at 384.

9. Cp. the common assumption of the situation in which 1 Thess was written, as formulated by Wilhelm Bornemann, *Die Thessalonicherbriefe* (1894), 39: "the first letter to the Thessalonians is the first letter Paul wrote to the believers in Thessalonica after his unwilling separation from the Thessalonian community, written immediately after his reunion with Timothy, who had been sent from Athens to Thessalonica, thus probably in Corinth, about six months after the foundation of the Christian community in Thessalonica. It is true that the immediate occasion, the return of Timothy and his report on the conditions in Thessalonica, which Paul had been longing to receive, is not addressed immediately at the beginning of the letter, as one might expect, but only in the middle of the letter (3:6), so that the content of the letter is divided into two sections, temporally speaking."

1.2 The Dimensions of Early Christian Social History

Social-historical exegesis of New Testament texts must attend fundamentally to three dimensions of life in early Christian congregations that also represent the potential areas of social conflict. These are bundled together and addressed in Galatians 3:28. For me that text is a constant reminder of this social-historical "trinity";[10] it is a hermeneutical summons to take into account the three focal points of early Christian times. It reminds us that in the congregations women and men, Jews and non-Jews, free and non-free, and therefore also poor and non-poor human beings tried to shape life together in a new way. The areas of conflict that emerged as a result are implicitly and explicitly present in every New Testament text. Social-historical exegesis, as a matter of principle, has to keep these three conflict levels in mind at all times. Methodologically speaking, feminist exegesis of the New Testament oriented to liberation theology has developed this most thoroughly by centering its attention on the life and work of Jewish and non-Jewish early Christian women.[11]

However, when analyzing a text it is appropriate to determine the foci of one's primary examination of those three social dimensions in accordance with its situation. In the case of the letters to Thessalonica and the description of their individual characteristics and interrelatedness, I judge the appropriate focus to be on the Jewish/non-Jewish dimension in the question of the common life of people of pagan and Jewish origin in the Christian congregations. The basis for a new, overall view of these texts is to be found here.

Hence in this case the feminist dimension does recede into the background somewhat, although a feminist perspective is still presupposed in principle. Several sections of feminist reflection, as well as corresponding aspects, will be presented in some of the detailed exegetical examinations. To date, feminist interpretations of 1 Thessalonians have been based on the traditional understanding of the letter, which this study seeks to alter fundamentally. A new view of the two Thessalonian letters, together with their relationship, will be forged through the analysis of their Jewish-Christian dimension (see below), and not in the first instance through a feminist analysis such as has been both possible for and fundamental to the exegesis of 1 Corinthians.[12] It has been lamented on several occasions that the two letters to the Thessalonians yield only meager clues about the existence of women

10. Cp. Marlene Crüsemann, "Unrettbar frauenfeindlich" (1996), 199–223 (abbreviated English version: *JSNT* 79 [2000]: 19–36).

11. Luise Schottroff, *Lydia's Impatient Sisters* (1995); eadem, "Toward a Feminist Reconstruction" (1998), 178–253 in Luise Schottroff, Silvia Schroer, and Marie-Theres Wacker, eds., *Feminist Interpretation* (1998).

12. Antoinette Clark Wire, *The Corinthian Women Prophets* (1990); Luise Schottroff, "1 Corinthians: How Freedom Comes to Be" (2012), 718–42.

and their lives in the congregations of that city.[13] In my view this is closely related to the pseudepigraphical character of the text.

Only the reference to σκεῦος (vessel) in 1 Thessalonians 4:4 might throw a bit of light on real women, in the context of the topic of sexuality and, possibly, of marriage. Non-feminist exegesis to a large extent has read "vessel" here as a "euphemism" for women.[14] This requires feminist critique, particularly in view of the relevant history of reception.[15] Several variants of the second classic rendering have more recently been proposed for σκεῦος: "body"[16] (as in the Greek perception

13. Judith L. Hill, "Establishing the Church of Thessalonica" (1990), 201–13, detects indirect references to women and postulates their existence in the congregation (see esp. 212–13); similarly, Lone Fatum, "1 Thessalonians" (1994), 250–62; Mary Ann Beavis, "2 Thessalonians" (1994), 263–71; Jutta Bickmann, "1 Thessalonians" (2012), 810–20; Marlene Crüsemann, "2 Thessalonians" (2012); Christine Gerber, *Paulus und seine "Kinder"* (2005), 251–52 n. 3.

14. Basic to this interpretation was Christian Maurer, art. σκεῦος, *TDNT* 7: 358–67; similarly, e.g., Traugott Holtz, *Der erste Brief an die Thessalonicher* (1986), 156–59; Herbert Ulonska, "Christen und Heiden" (1987), 210–18; Renate Kirchhoff, *Die Sünde gegen den eigenen Leib* (1994), 31–32. A variant of this reading is the interpretation of the expression τὸ ἑαυτοῦ σκεῦος κτᾶσθαι in the sense that it refers to marriage and must therefore mean "take his own wife," e.g., Hans Baltensweiler, "Erwägungen zu I. Thess. 4,3–8" (1963); O. Larry Yarbrough, *Not Like the Gentiles* (1985); Norbert Baumert, "Brautwerbung" (1990); Luise Schottroff, "Frauen und Geld im Neuen Testament" (1991), 25–56, at 30–32; Trevor J. Burke, *Family Matters* (2003), 185–93; Jones, *Thessalonians* (2005), 49–54; Witherington, *Thessalonians* (2006), 109–16; Eckart D. Schmidt, *Heilig ins Eschaton* (2010), 252–76. Matthias Konradt, "Εἰδέναι ἕκαστον ὑμῶν τὸ ἑαυτοῦ σκεῦος κτᾶσθαι" (2001): 128–55, and *Gericht und Gemeinde* (2003), calls for τὸ ἑαυτοῦ σκεῦος κτᾶσθαι to be interpreted as "a euphemism for sexual congress with one's own [female] partner" (*Gericht*, 102 n. 466) and thus more or less durative for marriage; see the critique of that position in Schmidt, *Heilig ins Eschaton*, 271ff. Judith Hill, "Establishing the Church," 201–13, sees it as addressing both sexes and suggests reading the expression inclusively, as a paraenesis on "how to 'acquire' his (or her) own spouse" (p. 209).

15. Schottroff, "Frauen und Geld" (1991), 30ff.; eadem, "Sozialgeschichtliche Bibelauslegung zu 1 Thess 4,1–8" (1992): 500–1.

16. Cp., e.g., Martin Dibelius, *An die* Thessalonicher (1925; 1937), 21, who rejects "supposed" rabbinic examples of the reading "woman/wife" (also against these, Gerhard Jankowski and Ton Veerkamp, "Was ist sexistisch?" (1992): 3–24; they advocate the translation "gain something for himself"); Michael McGehee, "A Rejoinder" (1989): 82–89; Dieter Lührmann, "Beginnings" (1990), 237–49; George P. Carras, "Jewish Ethics and Gentile Converts" (1990), 306–15, who sees an adoption of a Jewish expression here; Earl J. Richard, *Thessalonians* (1995), 198–99; Jutta Bickmann, "1 Thessalonians" (2012), 810–20, at 810, 817–18; Todd D. Still, "Interpretive Ambiguities" (2007): 207–19, at 215–16; Eduard Verhoef, "1 Thessalonians 4:1–8" (2007): 347–63, at 355–56.

of the body as the "vessel" of the soul)[17] or also as a term for the male member.[18] As I see it, the phrase τὸ ἑαυτοῦ σκεῦος κτᾶσθαι means to say that one ought to keep watch on one's own body in a dangerous sexual sphere and keep it holy, in the sense of practicing abstinence.[19] There were many impressive contrary positions on this subject in Greco-Roman cities, given the omnipresent prostitution. In view of its androcentric nature, this admonition is presumably addressed primarily to men, but it may also have been understood in the course of its reception as an ethical exhortation to women. A critical feminist history of the interpretation of 1 Thessalonians 4:4 would indeed be a welcome contribution in future.[20]

1.3 Jewish-Christian Social History

What contours do the letters to the congregation in Thessalonica reveal for the relationship between Jewish and non-Jewish people inside and outside the congregation? How do these fit into the current models of early Christian history?

Moreover, what does "Jewish" or "Christian" mean? Here it is essential to point out the preliminary nature of these concepts and, especially, the lack of precision in the predicate "Christian" in general in many exegetical and historical treatises.[21] It is astonishing how little attention is generally paid to the dubious nature of current concepts. While it is still possible lexically to fix the term "Jew"

17. This fits well with the anthropological concept in 1 Thess 5:23, which sounds more like Greek than Hebrew-Jewish anthropology: "spirit"/πνεῦμα, "soul"/ψυχή, and "body"/σῶμα; cp. A. M. Festiguère, "La trichotomie de 1. Thess. 5,23 et la philosophie grecque," *RSR* 20 (1930): 385–415.

18. E.g., J. Whitton, "A Neglected Meaning" (1982); Solomon K. Avotri, "Possessing One's Vessel" (1991); Torleif Elgvin, "To Master His Own Vessel" (1997); Paul-Gerhard Müller, *Thessalonicher* (2001), 172–73: "this is thus not a description of an ideal Christian marriage but of the disciplined shaping of male sexuality" (p. 173); Gordon D. Fee, *Thessalonians* (2009), 145–50. J. Edward Ellis, *Paul and Ancient Views* (2007) remains determinedly undecided; see his pp. 1–17, 160–70.

19. Marlene Crüsemann, "Gefässe der Ehre" (1998); similarly Gregory K. Beale, *Thessalonians* (2010), 155–213.

20. To my knowledge there exists only one monograph on the passage, Avotri's dissertation, "Possessing One's Vessel" (1991): see n. 18 above. But see now the work on sanctification and sanctity in 1 Thessalonians by Eckart D. Schmidt, *Heilig ins Eschaton* (2010), 102–325 (on 1 Thess 4:1–8).

21. A particular *curiosum* in this sense is, for example, Ernest Best's translation of 1 Thess 1:1 (in his *Thessalonians* [1972], 60): ἐκκλησία is rendered as "Christian community," which, together with the following ἐν ... Ἰησοῦ Χριστῷ, doubles "Christian" and seems over-determined. The commentary speaks of "Christian" as an adjective (p. 61), making it unclear to readers who do not know Greek that it is not in the text.

unambiguously to some extent in the New Testament,[22] the situation becomes utterly sketchy when it comes to the presumed counterpart: "Christian." This fact alone, and the corresponding picture in Acts, make it abundantly plain that simple antithetical models are misleading.

The first and almost singular time the word "Χριστιανοί/Christians" occurs in the New Testament is in Acts 11:26,[23] where it designates congregations; it is introduced and explained as a new name for the "μαθηταί/disciples" in Antioch. Just before that, Acts says explicitly that the congregation in that city consisted initially of Jewish and then increasingly of Greek members (vv. 19–21). Here the problems with seemingly unambiguous concepts used to make distinctions become readily apparent, for by no means does this designation indicate that a non-Jewish group is involved. On the contrary, it is explicitly acknowledged as an original "offspring" of the Jerusalem congregation and its envoy Barnabas (vv. 22–24). What was the Antiochene congregation's self-understanding? That must first be established. There is nothing to suggest that the "Jews" among the Χριστιανοί subsequently defined themselves as non-Jews.[24] For example, according to Acts 21:39 and 22:3 Paul still speaks of himself in Jerusalem as "a Jewish person," "a Jewish man" who, in addition, speaks to the people in Hebrew, which is

22. Ἰουδαῖος is attested more than 190x in the NT (cp. Horst Kuhli, art. Ἰουδαῖος [1981], 474; James D. G. Dunn, "The Question of Anti-Semitism" [1992], 182–87, where he lists 194 instances on p. 182 but includes a self-identified Jewish follower of Christ; see only Acts 16:20; Gal 2:13).

23. Otherwise only in Acts 26:28 and 1 Pet 4:16. For historical discussion of Acts 11:26 see esp. Helga Botermann, *Das Judenedikt* (1996), 142–67 (with bibliography); Klaus Wengst, *"Freut euch"* (2008), 70–74. Cp. Luise Schottroff, "Zur historische Einordnung" (1997), 21; Gerhard Schneider, art. Χριστιανός (1983), 1145–47; and Rudolf Pesch, *Die Apostelgeschichte (Apg 1–12)* (1986), ad loc.; Jacob Jervell, *Die Apostelgeschichte* (1998), ad loc.; Hubert Frankemölle, *Frühjudentum und Urchristentum* (2006), 31. For the theme of "Christian community and synagogue association in Antioch" on the basis of Acts 11:19–26 see also Karl-Wilhelm Niebuhr, "'Judentum' und 'Christentum'" (1994), 226–28.

24. On this see esp. Elias Bickermann, "The Name of the Christians" (1949; 1986), in which he reads "Christians" as a self-designation or proper name for what was "still a Jewish movement" (p. 195), one that expressed its official belonging to the Anointed One, the messianic king and his rule; cp. Luise Schottroff, "Zur historische Einordnung" (1997), 21–22. Niebuhr, "Judentum," also includes the Χριστιανοί among the synagogal community of Antioch (p. 227); similarly Botermann, *Judenedikt* (1996), 144–67, esp. 165–67: "for me, it is simply unimaginable that a whole group could have decided 'to withdraw from the synagogal community.' In any case, they would not have ceased to be Jews if they had been Jews from birth" (p. 166). Cp. Martin Hengel and Anna Maria Schwemer, *Paulus zwischen Damaskus und Antiochien* (WUNT 108; Tübingen: Mohr Siebeck, 1998), 340–50; Klaus Wengst, *"Freut euch"* (2008), 70–71; Christian Strecker, art. "Judentum/Christentum" (2009), 282: "designation for a specific Jewish group."

emphasized twice (Acts 21:40; 22:2).[25] Moreover, we must ask to what extent the Greek followers of Jesus in Antioch, living together with Jewish women and men in community, still saw themselves as people living a Jewish life, in one way or other, as the result of their confession of Jesus, the Jewish Messiah.[26] In particular, the assent of the Jerusalem congregation is suggested by the flexibility in its discussion concerning dietary laws (Acts 11:1–18).

We know that the concept of "Christianity/Χριστιανισμός" appears for the first time outside the New Testament in the writings of Ignatius of Antioch (at the beginning of the second century CE). By using this concept Ignatius establishes Christianity as an explicit opposite to "Judaism/Ιουδαϊσμός" (*Ign. Magn.* 10:1, 3; *Ign. Phil.* 6:1; *Ign. Rom.* 3:3). His intent was to dissuade the congregations in those cities from practicing a Jewish way of life. "It is absurd to profess Christ Jesus, and to Judaize. For Christianity did not embrace Judaism, but Judaism Christianity, that so every tongue which believes might be gathered together to God" (*Ign. Magn.* 10:3). Thus the concept of "Christianity" was developed in the church's early history as an anti-Jewish polemical concept, and Christianity becomes a "model of separation" from Judaism: "It first emerges, in other words, when the church defines itself as anti-Jewish, and is accordingly only the church of the gentiles [*Völkerkirche*]; as a result, it [sc. Christianity] immediately becomes a counter-concept to 'Judaism.'"[27] Since the concept and, to a large extent, its derivatives are not found in the New Testament, it follows that it does *not* (yet) advocate the renunciation of the Jewish way of life, but instead that the Jewish followers of Christ maintain their Jewish identity and their membership in the Jewish people as a matter of course.

Therefore the New Testament's use of language already indicates that the word "Christians," in its character as an undifferentiated collective term, is unsuitable for describing the origin and composition of the groups it designates in exegetical and especially in historical literature.[28] In particular, the assumption that there is a confrontational encounter of "Jews against Christians" (and vice versa) in the New

25. For the image of Paul in Acts see esp. Jacob Jervell, *The Unknown Paul* (1984).

26. For the Jewish way of life of communities in Acts cp. Ivoni Richter Reimer's social-historical study, *Women in the Acts of the Apostles* (1995), and fundamentally Luise Schottroff, *Lydia's Impatient Sisters* (1994) and her "'Gesetzesfreies Heidenchristentum" (1996), 227–45.

27. Klaus Wengst, "Christliche Identitätsbildung" (1998): 99–105, at 102; cp. Frankemölle, *Frühjudentum* (2006), 27–36; Daniel Boyarin, "Semantic Differences" (2007); Steve Mason, "Jews, Judaeans, Judaizing, Judaism" (2007), 470–76.

28. Cp., by analogy, the beginnings of a critical confrontation with the concept of "Hellenists" by Wolfgang Reinbold, "Die 'Hellenisten'" (1998); he concludes that the word is not suitable for use as a *terminus technicus* in New Testament scholarship and, in view of the state of the sources, ought to be avoided altogether (p. 101), because it "all too often provokes much too slippery contrasts" (p. 102).

Testament is highly misleading.[29] On the one hand, careful attention must be paid to the relevant concepts in individual writings; these should be adopted and elucidated. On the other hand, a more useful social-historical terminology needs to be developed for more general questions regarding early Christian times. A good beginning here would be a more circumspect use of the terms "Jewish Christians"[30] or "Christians from among the nations" ["gentile Christians"]. This means, for example, that one does not speak, as is generally customary, of the postulated "Jewish-Christian opponents"[31] of Paul without making it clear that the apostle himself would have to be designated a Jewish Christian.[32]

Beyond this, the development of alternative designations, such as the constructive proposal by Ekkehard and Wolfgang Stegemann, who speak of "messianic communities" and "messianic Jews,"[33] is a positive sign. But what about their decision to apply those terms only to congregations in the land of Israel and automatically to count the followers of Jesus in the countries of the Jewish diaspora as "sociologically . . . no longer belong[ing] to (diaspora) Judaism"?[34] Should that

29. "Jews and Christians do not appear as paired opposites in the New Testament" (Niebuhr, "Judentum," 218), though he considers it anachronistic to regard the New Testament "as belonging to Judaism."

30. For the problem and history of the term "Jewish Christians," cp., e.g., Carsten Colpe, "Das deutsche Wort 'Judenchristen'" (1978); expanded version: *Das Siegel der Propheten* (1990), 35–58; Annette Yoshiko Reed, "'Jewish Christianity'" (2003), 189–96; 230–31; John G. Gager, "Did Jewish Christians See the Rise of Islam?" (2003); James C. Paget, "The Definition of the Terms" (2007); for a subtler perception of "Gentiles," and "Jews," and "Christians" in the New Testament see also the proposals in Reinhard Feldmeier and Ulrich Heckel, eds., *Die Heiden* (1994) as well as the relevant essays in the 2007 collection edited by Skarsaune and Hvalvik, *Jewish Believers in Jesus*: Richard Bauckham, "James and the Jerusalem Community"; Donald A. Hagner, "Paul as a Jewish Believer—According to His Letters"; Reidar Hvalvik, "Paul as a Jewish Believer—According to the Book of Acts"; idem, "Named Jewish Believers Connected with the Pauline Mission"; idem, "Jewish Believers and Jewish Influence in the Roman Church until the Second Century"; Peter Hirschberg, "Jewish Believers in Asia Minor according to the Book of Revelation and the Gospel of John."

31. Luise Schottroff presented a thoroughgoing critique of the concept of Paul's "opponents" in his letters, using 1 Corinthians as a basis, in her "1 Corinthians: How Freedom Comes to Be" (2012); cp. eadem, "A Feminist Hermeneutic of 1 Corinthians" (1998).

32. Cp., e.g., Donald A. Hagner, "Paul as a Jewish Believer," who writes: ". . . his Christian faith was not the nullification of his former Judaism as much as it was its fulfillment. . . . And in that new reality Paul, the apostle of Christ to the Gentiles, found the meaning and culmination of his Jewish identity" (p. 120); Reidar Hvalvik, "Paul as a Jewish Believer": "The Paul of Acts is 'without exception a law-abiding Jew'" (p. 151, citing Stephen G. Wilson, *Luke and the Law*, SNTSMS 50 [Cambridge: Cambridge University Press, 1983], 68.

33. Ekkehard and Wolfgang Stegemann, *The Jesus Movement* (1999), 355. The fundamental NT concept of *ekklēsia* (ibid., 262–64) does not in and of itself contribute to clarity with regard to the composition of the communities.

34. Ibid., *passim*.

be accepted as plausible without detailed proof? They themselves counter their own position by putting heavy emphasis on the practice of the Torah,[35] which, according to Paul (Rom 3:27–30), applies also to non-Jewish people, in a "charismatically" flexible frame of reference, as well as the respective self-definitions of the communities.[36] The most serious objection, however, is the questionable legitimacy of simply denying the Jewish members of these communities their sociological affiliation with Judaism, their identity, and their concomitant experience of continuity.

A feminist social history that refuses to regard religion as essentially something that belongs to men and that asks, for example, "What does it mean for a non-Jewish woman to become a Christian? What does it mean for a Jewish woman to become a Christian?"[37] will not make male circumcision the principal criterion for membership in a religion. From this perspective the idea of an everyday Christian life without the Torah cannot be maintained and has to be understood more as a traditional hermeneutical postulate, a "concept of gentile Christianity free from the law,"[38] and not as the result of detailed social-historical investigation.

Furthermore, more recent historical investigations stress that ancient Judaism in the late centuries BCE and the early ones CE was not yet an entity to be delimited and defined with precision.[39] Its rites of admission took their form only gradually and were modified any number of times, particularly in view of the growing number of women converts.[40] For that reason we sometimes find

35. On this see, e.g., Peter von der Osten-Sacken, "Das Verständnis des Gesetzes" (1989); Peter J. Tomson, *Paul and the Jewish Law* (1990); Karin Finsterbusch, *Die Thora als Lebensweisung* (1996); Luise Schottroff, "Gesetzesfreies Heidenchristentum" (1996); eadem, "'Wir richten die Tora auf'" (2003); Klaus Wengst, *"Freut euch,"* 208 and elsewhere; Luise Schottroff, "Die Theologie der Tora" (2010); Marlene Crüsemann, "Heisst das" (2010); for Matthew see also Hubert Frankemölle, "Die Tora Gottes" (1998), esp. 276ff.; Martin Vahrenhorst, *"Ihr sollt überhaupt nicht schwören"* (2002), 234–48; Matthias Konradt, "Die vollkommene Erfüllung" (2006); Peter Fiedler, *Matthäusevangelium* (2006), 19–24 and elsewhere; for Luke and Acts: Matthias Klinghardt, *Gesetz und Volk Gottes* (1988); Marlene Crüsemann and Frank Crüsemann, "Das Jahr, das Gott gefällt" (2000); Kerstin Schiffner, *Lukas liest Exodus* (2008), 297–319.

36. Stegemann and Stegemann, *The Jesus Movement*, esp. 339, 353–54.

37. Luise Schottroff, "Gesetzesfreies Heidenchristentum," 232ff. See also the methodologically groundbreaking essay by Bernadette Brooten, "Frühchristliche Frauen und ihr kultureller Kontext" (1985).

38. See esp. Luise Schottroff, *Lydia's Impatient Sisters*; eadem, "Toward a Feminist Reconstruction," 201–6; eadem, "Gesetzesfreies Heidenchristentum"; Claudia Janssen, art. "Heidenchristentum" (1997), 47–49.

39. Cp., e.g., Shaye J. D. Cohen, "Crossing the Boundary" (1989); James D. G. Dunn, *The Partings of the Ways* (1991), 143ff.; Tessa Rajak, "The Jewish Community" (1992); Martin Goodman, "Jewish proselytizing" (1992); Hubert Frankemölle, "Die Entstehung des Christentums" (1998), 30–31; idem, *Frühjudentum* (2006), 27ff. Judith Lieu, *Christian*

references to "Judaisms," intended better to do justice to the variety of Jewish forms of life and corresponding stages of transition.[41] Archaeological evidence in particular shows that affiliation with Judaism permitted diverse degrees of closeness accompanied by emphasis on essential adherence to Judaism. For example, a Jewish inscription in the theater of Miletus from Roman times shows that "God-fearers," that is, people from among the nations who had not in the full sense converted, might explicitly be called "Jews."[42]

In addition, we may point to just one example of the monumental inscriptional evidence for Judaism: the marble column at Aphrodisias in Asia Minor (probably from the beginning of the third century CE), with the longest Jewish inscription in antiquity known to date.[43] It names 125 persons, sponsors of the local synagogue,

Identity (2004) shows the extent to which "Christian" identity, "Judaism," and "Christianity" were social and literary constructs in the first centuries CE (cp. esp. 1–26, 298–316); Daniel Boyarin, *Border Lines* (2004). Mason, "Jews, Judaeans" (2007) emphasizes the ethnic connotations of the concept of Ἰουδαῖοι κτλ. and opts essentially for the translation "Judaeans" (see his summary on pp. 510–12).

40. Shaye J. D. Cohen, "The Rabbinic Conversion Ceremony" (1990), esp. 185–86; 193ff.; Judith Lieu, "Circumcision, Women and Salvation" (1994); cp. Barbara H. Geller-Nathanson, "Toward a Multicultural Ecumenical History" (1993).

41. Cp., e.g., Jacob Neusner, William S. Green, and Ernest Frerichs, eds., *Judaisms and their Messiahs* (1987); Ross Shepard Kraemer, "On the Meaning of the Term 'Jew'" (1989), 36–37; Martin Goodman, *Mission and Conversion* (1994), 38ff.; Martina S. Gnadt, "Gospel of Matthew" (2012), 607; Robert A. Kraft, "The Weighing of the Parts" (2003); Peter Fiedler, *Matthäusevangelium* (2006), 23–24.

42. *CIJ* II, 748. Adolf Deissmann, *Light from the Ancient East* (1927; 1978), 447, plate 82, published this inscription, one of the first on Jewish seats: Τόπος Εἰουδέων τῶν καὶ Θεοσεβίον, which he translates "Place of the Jews, who are also called God-fearing." He understands "God-fearing," however, as an "appellation of the Jews" (p. 447); likewise, among others, Bernd Wander, *Gottesfürchtige und Sympathisanten* (1998), 105–10. But the relationship could also be regarded as the reverse, since Ross S. Kraemer, in her study of the inscriptional record of the concept of Ἰουδαῖοι, concludes that it was often adopted by non-Jews affiliated with Judaism as a self-designation for themselves and their children. They call themselves proselytes, followers of the Jews (Kraemer, "On the Meaning of the Term 'Jew,'" summary on pp. 52–53).

43. Joyce Reynolds and Robert Tannenbaum, *Jews and God-Fearers* (1987); the text of the inscription is on pp. 5–7. Cp. Shaye J. D. Cohen, "Crossing the Boundary," 32–33; Helga Botermann, "Griechisch-Jüdische Epigraphik" (1993); Bernd Wander, *Trennungsprozesse* (1994), 178ff.; M. P. Bonz, "The Jewish Donor Inscriptions" (1994); Stegemann and Stegemann, *The Jesus Movement*, 256–57; Helga Botermann, *Judenedikt* (1996), 163 n. 526; Bernd Wander, *Gottesfürchtige* (1998), 121–28, and elsewhere; Steve Mason, "Jews, Judaeans," 479. The text of the Aphrodisias inscription, with a German translation, can be found in the appendix to Wander's book on pp. 235–39; an English translation is available in Lawrence H. Schiffman, ed., *Texts and Traditions* (1998), 197–98.

who probably supported a project in the form of a soup kitchen for the poor. Nearly half of those persons are called "God-fearers/Θεοσεβεῖς"; they have Jewish as well as non-Jewish names. Yael, the only woman named in the inscription, is close to the top of the list; she may well have been the president of the synagogue.[44] What was the everyday practice of individual persons and groups of different origins that accompanied such public profession of affiliation with the synagogue and its care for the poor? We may assume that, besides proselytes, "God-fearers" of non-Jewish birth also identified themselves with Judaism, that they perhaps also supported projects other than this one, and in so doing complied with the Torah's commandments in many ways. And is it really unthinkable that followers of Christ were among them? This question is in line with that of the religious practice of Lydia, presumably a God-fearer, who worshiped God in the Jewish manner, along with other women in Philippi (Acts 16:13–15).[45] What would lead one to conclude that her participation in the life of the synagogue ended after Paul brought her to profess her faith in the Jewish messiah Jesus?

Thus many historical sources indicate that, contrary to the view that it set itself off and differentiated itself sharply from the world around it, Judaism was distinguished by the fact that, irrespective of origin, those attracted to it declared themselves in various ways as adherents of Judaism. Feminist social history is particularly sensitive to the shifting boundaries of membership in the individual religious communities and has developed inclusive historical models accordingly. Within this framework Christianity can be seen as a form of Judaism. On the basis of the relevance of women's history, Luise Schottroff presents an inclusive model of the relationship between "Christianity" and "Judaism" in New Testament times:

> The history of Jewish Christian and gentile Christian women (as well as that of the men in both groups) in the first and into the second century is . . . part of the history of Judaism in the Diaspora and in the Jewish homeland. The gentile Christian people were part of the large group of Jewish proselytes/God-fearers. They opted for the God of Israel, for the Jewish way of life in different forms, and they made the messiah Jesus the center of their relationship with God. They were on the margins of the Jewish people or belonged within it—from their own perspective, that of Rome, and that of the Jewish and Jewish-Christian congregations. There were conflicts between Jewish and Jewish-Christian people

44. The name Jael, with the title προστάτης / "president, patron," in the 9th line of the inscription, is unmistakably to be identified as a woman's name, as Bernadette Brooten has shown in "Jael προστάτης" (1991); see also her "The Gender of Ιαηλ" (1990). The complicated maneuvers undertaken in some of the previously-cited literature (e.g., Reynolds and Tannenbaum, *Jews and God-fearers*, 101) to try to read a masculine name here are not persuasive.

45. On this see Richter Reimer, *Women in the Acts of the Apostles*, 91–161.

> from the very beginning, but those conflicts were in themselves no clear indication of a definitive separation at this point.[46]

In contrast, the paradigm of the relationship of Judaism and Christianity in the first two centuries CE still dominant in our exegetical literature puts the separation at the center.

1.3.1 The Still-Dominant Paradigm of the "Separation of Jews and Christians" and Some Alternatives

It does make a difference which approach one associates with a "Jewish-Christian social history." Some see it more as a "social history of Christianity as one Jewish group among others" while others speak of "a social history of Jews and Christians (more in the sense of non-Jews)." The latter concept appears to lurk unacknowledged or to be silently presupposed in most historical studies as well as in the formulation of one of the core subjects in early Christian history: the "separation" or "parting of the ways of Jews and Christians," of "synagogue and church." This question has become virtually a central notion of history, the paradigm *per se* for early Jewish-Christian relations. History cannot get around this question, but using a model of conflict and division easily leads one to imagine a nearly inevitable and unstoppable process of separation, of two blocs drifting apart. Depending on how it is interpreted, the beginning of this process of separation is dated to around 70 CE,[47] or to the Bar Kochba revolt in 135 CE,[48] or as beginning already in the days of Paul,[49] in which case what is essentially Christian is regarded as something that from a very early time was distinctly different from and competing with Judaism.[50]

46. Luise Schottroff, "Gesetzesfreies Heidenchristentum," 236. For Christianity or "the Jesus movement" as a "renewal movement within Judaism" see Elisabeth Schüssler Fiorenza, *In Memory of* Her (1983), 105–59; Luise Schottroff, *Lydia's Impatient Sisters* (1995), "a [Jewish] liberation movement within the Pax Romana" (p. 9); and, e.g., Martin Hengel, "Das früheste Christentum" (1997); Frankemölle, *Frühjudentum* (2006), 29: "The Jesus group was one of the many reform groups in early Judaism."

47. This was dominant in earlier research; cp., e.g., Samuel G. F. Brandon, *The Fall of Jerusalem* (1951); and see the overview in Wander, *Trennungsprozesse* (1994), 36ff.

48. Thus, e.g., Gerd Theissen, *The New Testament* (2012); James D. G. Dunn, *Partings of the Ways* (2006), esp. 238ff.; Luise Schottroff, "Gesetzesfreies Heidenchristentum" (1996), 240ff.

49. Thus, e.g., François Vouga, *Geschichte des frühen Christentums* (1994), 171–72 for the community in Rome. It appears that he regards the known house churches in Rome as the indication of a separation of these congregations made up of "Jewish and Gentile Christians" from "the synagogue."

50. Hans Conzelmann, *Gentiles, Jews, Christians* (1992), for example, gives a historical summary of these conflicts under the subtitle "First Experiences of Christians with Jews" (p. 249–89), thus suggesting a fundamental distinction between the two groups from the

The reasons for this may lie in the theology of the particular interpreter, but often also in the unreflective terminology we complained about earlier. For example, two relevant studies show indirectly how relatively useless the seemingly clear concepts of "separation," "Jews," and "Christians" are for describing historical relationships in the first century CE.

> Bernd Wander, for one, does not want to consider this history in too one-dimensional a way and prefers instead to speak of "processes of separation" in the plural in order to be clear about the multiplicity of possible courses.[51] He briefly reflects on the problem in relation to established concepts (pp. 39–40) and gives preference to the more accurate, differentiating designation "followers of Christ" over "Christians." He also does without a "working hypothesis of a separation of Jews and Christians" (pp. 50, 277). But since his historical examination of the Acts of the Apostles begins with the gospels' reports of the execution of Jesus, the layout of his book and its title, *Trennungsprozesse zwischen Frühem Christentum und Judentum im 1. Jh. n. Chr.* (Processes of Separation Between Early Christianity and Judaism in the First Century CE) suggests, irrespective of all partial results, that a separation between "Judaism" and "Christianity" began, more or less, with Jesus' death, a "historical benchmark in an emergent alienation between Jews and followers of Christ" (p. 277). Because of his terminology, which ultimately is insufficiently clarified, this results—surely contrary to the author's intention—in an extremely early dating of the parting of ways. On the other hand, it demonstrates in exemplary fashion that focusing early Christian-Jewish history in the first century on the phenomenon of "separation" does more to confuse than to clarify.
>
> This is evident also in James D.G. Dunn's *The Parting of the Ways Between Christianity and Judaism*,[52] a forward-looking study fully aware of the problematic, inasmuch as it perceives the unified statement of the New Testament writings to be that they themselves are intended to be representative of Judaism—that is, what they regard as the true Judaism (p. 231). Hence there can be no talk of a separation between "Judaism" and "Christianity." Accordingly, the really tense debate occurs at several bifurcations of different forms of "Jewish Christianity" seeking to find their place within Judaism as a whole. Thus the decisive and difficult question of the rupture between "mainstream Christianity

beginning. For the questionable nature of this separation theme see Stegemann and Stegemann, *The Jesus Movement*. They, however, augment the usual chronological ("pre-sociological") schema with a spatial separation between the Jewish Jesus movement in the land of Israel and non-Jewish communities in the Diaspora (pp. 253–54) (see above).

51. Wander, *Trennungsprozesse* (1994), with summary on pp. 276–89; see the other page citations in the text.

52. Dunn, *Partings of the Ways* (2006), with summary on pp. 230ff., and discussion of the concept of the "Jew" (pp. 143ff.). A corresponding analysis of "Christian" is lacking. See further page citations in the text.

and Jewish Christianity" (pp. 233, 239) arises only in the post-New Testament time of the second century CE. Only that break must be judged irreversible; it is to be dated to the second revolt under Bar Kochba in 135 CE (p. 243). Dunn concludes his study by emphasizing his continuing conviction of the abiding Jewish character of Christianity (p. 258).

Besides the general lack of precision in its concepts, the shortcoming of "separation research"[53] is that it locates the Jewish-Christian relationship in the first centuries CE exclusively within that category. This causes the history of conflict in early Christian times to be presented and interpreted solely as a history of separation and suggests that the historical process thus described was largely inevitable and necessary. But new approaches in research have in the meantime caused the current "separation" scheme to lose some of its significance in face of the fundamental question of how the relevant entities define themselves and/or are defined from the outside.

Thus Judith M. Lieu focuses on the meaning of "Christian identity" in the context of the Jewish and Greco-Roman environment in the first centuries CE. Among the main conclusions of her work are therefore that the boundaries of identity were fluid, and that such boundaries and self-definitions are correspondingly evanescent. This makes it difficult to go on speaking baldly about separations and separation-processes between "Judaism" and Christianity."

> Yet this must lead us to ask ... if Judaism and Christianity (if not already Christians and Jews) are implicated in the construction of each other, then how can we speak of a parting between them? *Conceptually*, the existence of the one is predicated upon that of the other. Which does not mean, of course, that there were not those who understood themselves as Christians without reference to the Jews, and, even more so, those who understood themselves as Jews without reference to the Christians. For ... the actual dynamics of relationship with real "others" are always fluid and unpredictable. Indeed, if we recognize the possibility of other patterns of relationship with "the other," or of other ways of maintaining multiple identities, whether or not hierarchically structured, we may find ourselves challenging the binary construction of Jew v. Christian. It is for all these reasons that we not only can but must say that in many situations Jews and Christians behaved as if there were no rigid boundaries to separate them, *and* that "Jews" and "Christians" shared a common culture, *and* that Judaism and Christianity are reciprocally exclusive—so long as reciprocal exclusivity is not taken to mean a necessary reciprocal antagonism, and so long as this opposition is as open to negotiation and mediation as all others.[54]

53. For more on this see, e.g., Hennecke Gülzow, "Soziale Gegebenheiten" (1990); Gerd Theissen, "Judentum und Christentum" (1991); Dunn, ed., *Jews and Christians* (1999), including the essay by Andrew Chester, "The Parting of the Ways" pp. 239–313; also the essays in Daniel Marguerat, ed., *Le déchirement* (1996).

54. Judith Lieu, *Christian Identity* (2004), 307. Emphasis in original.

Therefore, since such a true-to-life model includes the possibility that one person might belong at the same time to several identity-providing ethnic and religious groups, one's preferred self-understanding or the value one ascribes to different identities in the course of one's life can also change, sometimes in response to appellations applied by outsiders:

> "Christian," "Jewish," "Greek," "Roman," may not be "the same sort of thing"; indeed, none of them is only one sort of thing. They are not necessarily mutually incompatible, although they may on occasion be so constructed. There were, no doubt, those who could claim more than one of these labels—again suggesting a hierarchy of identities—and those who would refuse such a claim. Yet neither are any of them intrinsically oppositional, although this, too, is how they can be constructed.[55]

It is, indeed, possible that such theories and models of Jewish-Christian separation or coming together in antiquity may point to the conclusion that in a certain sense the ways never parted as unambiguously as hitherto assumed. There is an anthology dealing with early Christian and early Jewish history entitled *The Ways that Never Parted*. The contributors' primary concern is to identify the traditional concept of two monolithic religious entities as literary and historical fiction and to replace it with more appropriate analyses.[56]

The task of a solid, complete presentation of these relationships and debates is to determine the location of every individual source and of every writing within this Jewish-Christian or early Christian history. This study attempts to do so in relation to the two epistles to Thessalonica.[57] Only on such a basis can a complete picture of life in togetherness and in separateness at that time, a comprehensive social history with better circumscribed categories, be established. I seek to show that the general classification "separation/separation processes" and the concomitant understanding that these progressed unstoppably can comprehend neither the "Jewish-Christian" interactions nor the possible social

55. Ibid., 309–10. The distinguishing attributions in works by ancient writers and theologians, assigning writings to the opposing groups, which are thereby declared heretical, are the focus of Daniel Boyarin's study, *Border Lines* (2004).

56. Becker and Reed, eds., *The Ways That Never Parted* (2007); see esp. the Introduction, and in the same volume Paula Fredriksen, "What 'Parting of the Ways?,'" Daniel Boyarin, "Semantic Differences," Robert Kraft, "The Weighing of the Parts," Andrew S. Jacobs, "The Lion and the Lamb," Martin Goodman, "Modeling the 'Parting of the Ways,'" with a number of graphic representations of different "partings" theories; Reed, "Jewish Christianity . . . in the Pseudo-Clementines," Alison A. Salvesen, "A Convergence of the Ways?" and John G. Gager, "Did Jewish Christianity see the Rise of Islam?"

57. For exegesis of the letter to the Ephesians with this focus see the study by Eberhard Faust, *Pax Christi et Pax Caesaris* (1993).

processes moving in every direction. Such a classification is too one-sided and is misleading when it presents the separation as a historical necessity. This must be demonstrated here.

1.4 About this Study

The main part of this study is the exegesis of First Thessalonians. Methodologically, the usual procedure in the exegetical literature is to describe the characteristic features of that epistle by emphasizing where it agrees with (other) epistles by Paul or by smoothing out differences. The contrary procedure, namely, highlighting the contradictions, is less often pursued, but it will sometimes be followed here. I foreground the interpretation of the letter "out of itself" and examine it as an individual and independent composition. What I mean particularly is that individual exegetical questions are not to be answered immediately with details from the other Pauline epistles; rather, I will seek to show and take into account how they differ, for that is what reveals the characteristic and strange nature of 1 Thessalonians among or over against the Pauline writings.

The study is structured as follows: Every chapter seeks to present a conceptual advance in the examination of the two epistles' characteristics and in how they relate to each other. In addition, each chapter seeks to discern the evidence for challenging the authenticity of both writings while indicating their significance within the framework of a Jewish-Christian social history. My intermediate conclusions are briefly recapitulated in the transitions between sections and chapters.

The ideas about judgment found in the Thessalonian letters constitute one of their focal points. Current research on early Christian and apocalyptic conceptions of judgment still leaves something to be desired.[58] As I see it, the most important deficit is a targeted exegesis of every individual New Testament writing on the subject of "judgment." This is in part a deficiency in studies on "judgment in Paul"[59] in which verses of his writings are discussed at random without a thorough examination of one individual writing on the topic. That will be undertaken

58. Cp. the deficits listed by Egon Brandenburger, "Gerichtskonzeptionen" (1993), and Karlheinz Müller, "Gott als Richter" (1994).

59. Cp., *inter alia*, Lieselotte Mattern, *Das Verständnis des Gerichtes* (1966); Ernst Synofzik, *Die Gerichts- und Vergeltungsaussagen* (1977); Wolfgang Beilner, "Weltgericht und Weltvollendung" (1994); Matthias Klinghardt, "Sünde und Gericht" (1997); Ulrich Luz, "Neutestamentliche Lichtblicke" (2003); and the methodological reflections by Karlheinz Müller, "Gott als Richter" (with bibliography), including a critique of the common positing of a contrast, in this connection, between Christian eschatology or apocalyptic and Jewish-apocalyptic ideas of judgment (pp. 25ff.). Differently Nicola Wendebourg, *Der Tag des Herrn* (2003), who works without any such constructed contrast.

here for 1 Thessalonians and, in connection with it, for 2 Thessalonians as well.[60] Social-historical exegesis is our best tool for this task.

The concept of a divine judgment, and the fears and hopes associated with it in early Christian times, need to be understood in relation to the corresponding traditions of Israel as expressions of more or less marginalized groups and apocalyptic circles. The hope for a divine and judging intervention in the events of the world, and the related possibility that a law different from that of political oppression will prevail and the respective enemies be judged both have their *Sitz im Leben* among people shaped by resistance to imperial ideas and world domination.[61] The task of describing and understanding a text's concept of judgment and the group that holds that concept includes description of the locus of the respective activities of resistance. In his examination of what is said about judgment in 1 Corinthians in light of conceptions of judgment in the Old Testament and in early Jewish apocalyptic, David W. Kuck concludes that in early Judaism "a belief in God's judgment can serve to define one group over against another group or provide identity and encouragement in the face of a threat. Will the group maintain courage and loyalty of its members and its distinctiveness under pressure?"[62] So it is these very self-definitions, as well as statements about conflicts, hopes, and proclamations of God's judgment that groups make over against others that form the basis for social-historical examination of early Christian texts. This will be considered in what follows in connection with the two epistles to the Thessalonian congregation. Again and again we will see that the social-historical profile and character of both letters can be described and, indeed, decoded on the basis of these group statements. Here the issue of Jewish, pagan, Jewish-Christian, and pagan-Christian groups, and who is assigned to each of them, is the primary key, so to speak, to the Thessalonian correspondence.

When, after many years of studying 1 Thessalonians, one reaches the conclusion that "there is something wrong with this letter," as Henning Paulsen once put it,[63] one is alerted to the numerous peculiarities of the text that make it something special within the Pauline corpus and the New Testament. The following examination brings the evidence together in sequence; the chapter on 1 Thessalonians 2:14–16, containing the single reference to the Ἰουδαῖοι, is only the point of departure. All subsequent chapters, as well as and in particular the last

60. On this see also the study by Matthias Konradt, *Gericht und Gemeinde* (2003), 23–196, who has essentially confirmed my analysis of the structure of the idea of judgment in 1 Thessalonians: cp. Marlene Crüsemann, "Die Briefe nach Thessaloniki" (1999), 14–67, 187–244, 274–83. For the idea of judgment in 1 Corinthians see Konradt, *Gericht und Gemeinde*, 197–471; this is followed by sketches of the topic in the other Pauline letters.

61. The basic work here is by Luise Schottroff, "Die Gegenwart in der Apokalyptik" (1983; 1990), and Jürgen Ebach, "Apokalypse" (1985).

62. David W. Kuck, *Judgment and Community Conflict* (1992), 94.

63. Correspondence with the author.

chapter on the relationship of 1 and 2 Thessalonians, are to be seen as a progressive investigation into the possibly pseudepigraphical character of the first letter. We will have to keep saying "possibly" because no one can say "how it really was" until, for example, newly discovered writings or other archaeological evidence allow for more unambiguous conclusions. But in face of the fact that historical criticism today accepts only seven of the thirteen New Testament writings that name Paul as the author or co-author as indubitably authentic letters of Paul, the question of what criteria make a New Testament text a Pauline text arises again and again. Even the option of the Pauline authorship of 1 Thessalonians is a hypothesis, since its author(s) appear(s) throughout almost exclusively in the plural (cf. 3:1). I am persuaded that a critical reading of 1 Thessalonians raises such questions constantly, and that they demand a new openness on the part of biblical scholarship to discussion of this epistle's problems. This book develops the view that the problems of 1 Thessalonians are best resolved in terms of a presumption of its inauthenticity; I therefore want to encourage readers to be or become attentive to the peculiar traits of this unique New Testament writing as well as to its equally unique relationship to its twin, 2 Thessalonians. One may well expect that an intensive discussion of the view developed here will stimulate further arguments for or against such an altered reading of 1 Thessalonians.

When I took up the discussion of the inauthenticity of 1 Thessalonians again and worked out my thesis in tandem with study of the second epistle to the congregation in Thessalonica, I found that no completely new ground had to be trodden. Rather, I was able to refer to the results of many angles of interpretation and numerous individual observations from studies quite far apart both in method and in time. I simply rearranged (some might say disarranged) them. This confirmed my experience that in working out one's own inescapably time-conditioned exegetical judgment there is essentially no position or individual view belonging to other scholars that must be utterly jettisoned or deemed "false" in view of their partial conclusions or observations. One of the happy aspects of philological and exegetical work with texts is that texts tame all attempts at capriciousness through the resistance that comes from their enduring literary existence. The other fortunate circumstance is that it always allows one to reflect on and appreciate the insights individual exegetes have gained from their work with these texts, independently of one's own theory. This raises the hope that the present study and its possible reception may not be completely foreign to this experiential context.

Chapter 2

"THE JEWS" AS ENEMIES: 1 THESSALONIANS 2:14–16

The central and most complex statement in 1 Thessalonians about the fate of a specific group of people in relation to another group within the horizon of divine judgment is the section in 2:14–16 on the actions of "the Jews" in relation to "us" and God's judgment on "them." This is a focal point, if not the central one, for any question about the contribution of the correspondence with Thessalonica to a Jewish-Christian social history.[1] In what follows, this text will be examined for clues to the author's self-definition and the corresponding definitions of other social groupings. Associated with this is the question of locating 1 Thessalonians in the context of social and political conflicts in the *Imperium Romanum* in the first century C.E.

2.1 A First Look at the Text of 1 Thessalonians 2:14–16

The passage in 2:14–16 appears as part of the opening section of 1 Thessalonians, which makes up approximately the first half of the letter, from 1:2 to 3:13, in the form of a second thanksgiving beginning at 2:13. Thus 1 Thessalonians manifests a special letter form within the *Corpus Paulinum*, as Paul-Gerhard Müller has accurately described it: the "development of 1 Thess [following the prescript in 1:1] is unique among the genuine Pauline letters insofar as the theme of thanksgiving

1. This is also where Todd D. Still's investigation begins (*Conflict* [1999], 24–45). He proposes to use the question of possible social conflicts in the community at Thessaloniki as a key to the exegesis of the two letters to that place ("The Impact of Intergroup Conflict on the Thessalonian Congregation," 268–86). Still regards 2 Thess as authentically Pauline (pp. 46–60). He concludes, among other things, that Paul had been driven out of Thessalonica by a group of Jews who did not belong to the Christ community, while the community itself was being attacked verbally, socially, and perhaps even physically by their pagan fellow townspeople, and that Paul was reacting to this with 1 Thess 2:14–16 (see his summary on pp. 287–90). His study also includes a chapter on social-scientific theories of deviance and group conflict (pp. 83–124). See also Philip F. Esler, "Keeping It in the Family" (2000), 145–84, at 162–73, where he distinguishes "ingroups and outgroups" in Thessalonica (p. 166).

begins in 1:2, is taken up again in 2:13, is deepened in 3:9, and is only brought to a conclusion in 3:13. For that reason many interpreters have seen the whole section, 1:2–3:13, as essentially the proemium of the letter; because of its extended length it in fact constitutes the letter's first section. No other New Testament letter other than Ephesians (1–3) contains such an extended proemium."[2] The second thanksgiving in 1 Thessalonians, which begins in 2:13, gives thanks for the community's reception of the word of God. That this is about the word of God as distinct from human words is made clear by the reference to imitating the fate of the communities in Judea, who for its sake also suffered at the hands of their fellows (as the effect of the word of God is described in 2:14). There follows, in vv. 15–16, one of the most radical anti-Jewish statements in the New Testament, concluding with a pronouncement of judgment in v. 16c.

Thus, being introduced only formally by the recapitulation of the epistolary thanksgiving in 2:13, this passage is unmediated in its content as well as in its polemical harshness.[3] Previously 1 Thessalonians had seemed altogether harmonious, beginning with an extended, descriptive thanksgiving for the exemplary reception of the preaching in Thessalonica (1:2–10), followed by an equally extensive recapitulation of the successful work of the missionaries (2:1–12). There is a constant emphasis on the loving relationship of all with one another. The story of apostolic success is dampened only slightly by some scattered references to "persecution" (1:6) and "suffering" (2:2) without any mention of details of circumstances or causes. In addition, there is nothing that could be thought to refer to "Judaism" even in the broadest sense, or to be a discussion of Jewish scriptural interpretation or way of life within the horizon of early Christian daily life. For example, 1 Thessalonians contains not a single demonstrated

2. Paul-Gerhard Müller, *Thessalonicher* (2001), 44, with reference to Dibelius, *Thessalonicher* (^{3}1937), *ad loc.*; Philipp Vielhauer, *Geschichte* (1975), 84–85. For the structure and opening section of 1 Thessalonians see also Paul Schubert, *Form and Function* (1937), 16–27; Thieme, "Struktur" (1963); Traugott Holtz, *Der erste Brief an die Thessalonicher* (1986), 29–32; Schnider and Stenger, *Briefformular* (1987), 42–59; Johanson, *Brethren* (1987), 61ff.; Lambrecht, "Thanksgivings" (1990/2000); idem, "A Structural Analysis" (2000); Bickmann, *Kommunikation gegen den Tod* (1998), 103–46; Haufe, *Thessalonicher* (1999), 7ff.; Abraham J. Malherbe, *Thessalonians* (2000), 78–81; Gerber, *Paulus und seine "Kinder"* (2005), 254–55; Schreiber, "Der erste Thessalonicherbrief" (2008), 384–87; David Luckensmeyer, *Eschatology* (2009), 47–74; Eckart D. Schmidt, *Heilig ins Eschaton* (2010), 110–25, and many others. Thus 1 Thessalonians clearly consists of two major halves: chaps. 1–3 and 4–5. This obvious twofold division is found in no other Pauline letter, but does appear in deutero-Pauline texts such as Ephesians, 2 Thessalonians, and also Colossians; on this see Gerd Theissen, "Zur Entstehung des Christentums aus dem Judentum," (1988), who concludes from this finding that 1 Thessalonians provided the formula for the deutero-Pauline author.

3. For the impression that the rhetorical tone is interrupted within the context see Roberts, *Images* (1992), 153ff.; for the character of an excursus within the overall progression see Kraus, *Das Volk Gottes* (1996), 149.

scriptural quotation nor any reference to the author or authors' belonging to the Jewish people. And yet here suddenly there is a compact and altogether negative statement about "the Jews," together with a renewal of the motif of suffering:

(2:14) Ὑμεῖς γὰρ μιμηταὶ ἐγενήθητε, ἀδελφοί, τῶν ἐκκλησιῶν τοῦ θεοῦ τῶν οὐσῶν ἐν τῇ Ἰουδαίᾳ ἐν Χριστῷ Ἰησοῦ, ὅτι τὰ αὐτὰ ἐπάθετε καὶ ὑμεῖς ὑπὸ τῶν ἰδίων συμφυλετῶν καθὼς καὶ αὐτοὶ ὑπὸ τῶν Ἰουδαίων,

(2:15) τῶν καὶ τὸν κύριον ἀποκτεινάντων Ἰησοῦν καὶ τοὺς προφήτας καὶ ἡμᾶς ἐκδιωξάντων, καὶ θεῷ μὴ ἀρεσκόντων, καὶ πᾶσιν ἀνθρώποις ἐναντίων,[16] κωλυόντων ἡμᾶς τοῖς ἔθνεσιν λαλῆσαι ἵνα σωθῶσιν, εἰς τὸ ἀναπληρῶσαι[4] αὐτῶν τὰς ἁμαρτίας πάντοτε.

ἔφθασεν[5] δὲ ἐπ' αὐτοὺς ἡ ὀργὴ εἰς τέλος.

(2:14) For you, brothers and sisters, became imitators of the churches of God in Christ Jesus that are in Judea, for you suffered the same things from your own compatriots as they did from the Jews,

[15] who killed both the Lord Jesus and the prophets, and drove us out; they displease God and oppose everyone [16] by hindering us from speaking to the Gentiles so that they may be saved. Thus they have constantly been filling up the measure of their sins; but God's wrath has overtaken them totally.[6]

4. Cp. Matt 23:32; *Barn.* 5:11; *Gos. Pet.* 5(17).

5. First aorist of φθάνω, a frequent verb in Greek. Blass/Debrunner/Rehkopf §101 n. 82 and Bauer/Aland (1708 *ad loc*) translate ("reach") here, as late Greek, but give the same verb in 1 Thess 4:15 as "precede," its principal meaning in classical Greek; NRSV follows (cp. Beda Rigaux, *Thessaloniciens* [1956], 452). Liddell/Scott (1927), however, also read it with prepositions as: "'come' or 'arrive' first"; anticipate." BAGD (1) "come before, precede," with reference to 1 Thess 4:15; (2) "arrive, reach" with reference to 1 Thess 2:16, as well as Matt 12:28 *par.* Luke 11:20. See these Synoptic parallels with ἐπ': "the kingdom of God has come to you," ἔφθασε ἐφ' ὑμᾶς. This describes an event that has already happened in the present context, emphasized by the aorist (cp. esp. Fitzer, "φθάνω" [1974], 87–92), as also in T.Levi 6:11, an almost literal correspondence: ἔφθασε δὲ (ἐπ') αὐτοὺς ἡ ὀργὴ τοῦ Θεοῦ εἰς τέλος: the wrathful judgment strikes the inhabitants of Shechem and they are killed; but "it is applied to the enemies of the Jews and not to themselves" (Best, *Thessalonians* [1972], 122); for the parallel in T.Levi 6:11 see most recently esp. Lamp, "Is Paul Anti-Jewish?" (2003), and Luckensmeyer, *Eschatology* (2009), 159–60; cp. 2.4.3 n. 179 below. The translation "has already come" corresponds to the inherent content of the verb in the sense of an earlier or previous arrival of an event. The authors of 1 Thessalonians are in any case familiar with that meaning, as 4:15 shows. But according to Liddell/Scott the additional preposition emphasizes the "previous" nature of an event; cp. Matt 12:18 *par.*; for more on this see below at 2.5.2.

6. NRSV. For this translation of εἰς τέλος see Rigaux, *Thessaloniciens* (1956), 453; cp. the list of current possibilities in Theissen, "Judentum und Christentum" (1991), 338n15: (1) substantively, as "end" of history, i.e., for example, "until the end"; (2) adverbially, either quantitatively with the meaning "completely, entirely," or temporally in the sense of "finally." In any case the definitive character of the statement is clear; see below at 2.5.2.

This listing of the supposed misdeeds of "the Jews," extending from the killing of the Lord Jesus through all kinds of misanthropy to putting obstacles to the mission to the Gentiles, and thereby drawing the eschatological judgment of wrath upon themselves, has been differently perceived and evaluated in research to date. The principal impulse to calling Pauline authorship into question is usually the incompatibility with what Paul says in Rom 11:25–32 about the ultimate salvation of all Israel, as well as his subtle expressions within the overall context of Romans 9–11.[7] This chapter was rediscovered in the course of the beginnings of Christian-Jewish dialogue after the Shoah, and its theological weight has been increasingly acknowledged.[8] This is always accompanied by serious perplexity and a more critical attention to 1 Thessalonians.[9]

2.2 *Positions Taken by Scholars Over Time*

In what follows the principal trends in exegesis, their varied evaluations, and their general assessment of 1 Thess 2:14–17 will be reviewed. The most important positions will be listed according to the way in which they emphasize one or another solution to the problem of the text. However, we are often presented with a combination of arguments, so that some authors belong under a number of headings and a "clean" division is not always possible.[10] Still, we will make an effort at it, in the interests of clarity.

7. "Romans 9–11 does not *end* with 'wrath': there is its greatest difference from 1 Thess 2:15f" (Simpson, "Problems," *HBT* 12/1 [1990]: 42–73, at 59); see also his overall comparison with Rom 9–11 on pp. 46–62; cp. Penna, "L'évolution de l'attitude" (1986), 411ff.

8. On this see, e.g., Klappert, "Traktat für Israel" (1981), and the corresponding hermeneutical foundation and development, e.g., by Wengst, "*Freut euch*" (2008).

9. Cp., e.g., the initiative of Birger A. Pearson, "1 Thessalonians 2:13–16: A Deutero-Pauline Interpolation," *HTR* 64 (1971), 79–94, who, while he does not count himself among the actual participants in the "dialogue," refers to it and intends to work with it both historically and exegetically in his critique of 1 Thess 2:13–16; see also Ekkehard Stegemann, "Zur antijüdischen Polemik in 1 Thess 2,14–16" (1990): 54–64, who makes cleaning up the contradiction to Romans 11 the criterion for the genuineness of the Thessalonians passage (57).

10. See, for example, the article by Raymond Collins, "A propos" (1979/1984), who in opposition to the thesis of interpolation applies nearly all subsequent reasoning in favor of Pauline authorship. The fullness of cited positions and their relativizing solutions contrasts with a more or less complete absence of any evident personal interpretation or profile by Collins himself; see similarly Donald A. Hagner, "Paul's Quarrel with Judaism" (1993), 130–36, and Luckensmeyer, *Eschatology* (2009), 115–72.

2.2.1 No problem

Many interpreters do not see any major problem in holding the content of this section to be Pauline or in reconciling it with other statements by Paul.[11] Both older and more recent exegetes argue on the basis of, on the one hand, the character and temperament of the apostle: "P. loves to characterize the persons of whom he speaks—in love and hate; he simply cannot be objective."[12] Or else they say, as does Gordon D. Fee, that the passage is simply "too Pauline" and hence must be explained in terms of Paul's own experiences of suffering: "Thus scholarly integrity demands that one come to terms with the passage as having been written by one for whom its immediate context has touched a raw nerve regarding his own treatment by fellow, but non-believing, members of the Jewish community."[13]

On the other side, it is said that particular traits of the Jewish people play a role here. These interpretations, which must be categorized as explicitly anti-Jewish, are more rare, but were still appearing in Germany after 1945. For example, the text is commented without any evidence of historical distance or a trace of hermeneutical reflection. Precisely the intention to remain on a theological plane and formulate in a transparent spirit proves in this case very consequential. The general agreement with the radical judgments conveyed by the text is enriched with some particular anti-Jewish associations. "The Jews," those "misanthropes" and "original persecutors" quickly become "the Jew" as such, who, however, has already "brought God's wrathful judgment down upon himself."[14] But even when a stronger historical argument is presented, predicates are applied and used in a present sense, apparently as timeless: Jews are "always troublemakers," their being cut off is a sign of the anticipated "final execution of judgment."[15] Ernst Bammel, who explains the final statement of v. 16 in terms of the Claudian edict (49 C.E.), speaks of the "destruction of God's opponents" and writes that "the Jews were hindering the arrival of the new hour," proved themselves to be "enemies of God"; their own hour was "truly in the past," as was their "opportunity to relieve themselves of the burden of their sins."[16] The "'complete elimination' of the Jewish people" lurks between the

11. Typical of such positions is Rigaux's: one cannot deny a person like Paul the ability to write both Romans 11 and 1 Thessalonians 2 (*Thessaloniciens* [1956], 436).

12. Ernst von Dobschütz, *Die Thessalonicher-Briefe* (Göttingen: Vandenhoeck & Ruprecht, 1909), 111.

13. Gordon D. Fee, *The First and Second Letters to the Thessalonians* (NIC; Grand Rapids and Cambridge: Eerdmans, 2009), 91.

14. Heinrich Schlier, *Der Apostel und seine Gemeinde* (1972), 40–41.

15. Albrecht Oepke, *Briefe* (1962), 163. The 1936 commentary, with its National Socialist categories such as "Judaized" or "popular ideal" (163–64) was reprinted unchanged in 1962.

16. Ernst Bammel, "Judenverfolgung" (1959), 307–8. The expression "Jewish persecution" [*Judenverfolgung*] in the title was intended (in 1959!) to be read as a subjective genitive.

lines.[17] Such a free and willing move beyond the vocabulary of 1 Thessalonians seems, after the *Shoah*, alienating, to say the least.[18] Nor does the pericope give Rudolf Pesch any difficulties, since he sees the Jews as in any case identified with Satan (2:18): "The Satan who had hindered [Paul] was, according to Acts 17:10–15, the Jews from Saloniki who had driven him out of Beroea";[19] Ernst von Dobschütz's judgment is similar: "but the Satan prevented him, scarcely through illness or anything like that, but through Jewish stalking."[20]

It is still quite current to harmonize the text with Romans 11; the tendency is to say that the two texts ultimately say the same thing. This implicitly assumes a reading of Romans 9–11 that is extremely critical of Israel, as demonstrated, for example, by Raymond F. Collins.[21] He cites with approval the position of Bent Noack,[22] according to which Paul, before the statements in Rom 11:25ff., had presented his highly pessimistic view of Israel's fate. Collins concludes from this that the content of 1 Thess 2:14–16 belongs on the same theological level. The inconsistency lies within Romans, and not between it and 1 Thessalonians: "The expression in Rom of his pessimism about the fate of the Jews is not radically different from the thought of 1 Thess 2:13–16."[23] Likewise Traugott Holtz, who employs especially crass expressions for Israel and Judaism that are apparently not thought of as time-conditioned, concludes that the two texts agree in their substance: "For not only 1 Thess 2:16 but also Rom 9–11 reveal not the least doubt that the members of the synagogue who reject the gospel of Jesus Christ are subject to the judgment."[24] Rudolf Hoppe's thesis, that we find ultimately

17. Ibid., adopting a quoted expression by Heinrich Ewald (p. 308 n. 7).

18. Similarly Traugott Holtz, *Thessalonicher* (1986), ad loc., who assumes a Pauline fit of rage (p. 110). Verse 16c is said to be his own addition to a received tradition: "The Jews, by their deeds, are gathering destruction to themselves," the "Jews hostile to Christ are working out their eschatological rejection" (p. 107). Paul is said to be describing "the Jews, with unheard-of acerbity, as notorious murderers and persecutors of the messengers of God" (p. 111), and "we have no reason to call" his outburst "utterly wrong" (p. 112); despite every criticism of anti-Judaism in the church's history there yet remains "God's 'no' to the post-Christ way of Israel, a path of disobedience to their own God" (p. 113).

19. Pesch, "Entdeckung" (1984), 47.

20. Von Dobschütz, *Thessalonicher-Briefe* (1909), 14, and frequently.

21. Collins, "A propos" (1979/1984), 98; similarly 103; cp., *inter alia*, Karl P. Donfried, *Paul and Judaism* (1984), 252–53; Weatherly, "Authenticity" (1991), 89–90, and in general these positions and others collected by Carol J. Schlueter that hold for the consistency of 1 Thess 2:14–17 with Romans 11 (*"Filling Up"* [1994], 54–62).

22. Noack, "Current and Backwater" (1965).

23. Collins, "A propos," 127–28.

24. Holtz, "The Judgement on the Jews and the Salvation of All Israel. 1 Thes 2,15–16 and Rom 11,25–26," in *The Thessalonian Correspondence*, ed. Raymond F. Collins (BETL 87; Leuven: Brill, 1990), 284–94, esp. 123–31; the quotation is on p. 130.

the same statement about the overcoming of all resistance to the proclamation in 1 Thess 2:13–16 and in Rom 11:1–10, as proof of the power and effectiveness of the Gospel, aided by the motif of the murder of the prophets, does not enter into discussion of the contradiction between 1 Thess 2:16c[25] and Rom 11:26: how can the judgment of destruction and the certainty of all Israel's salvation be reconciled?

2.2.2 Apostolic wrath and rhetoric

Many of the positions thus named, and those that follow, also include positing a spontaneous eruption of anger on the part of Paul.[26] Some of them center on this idea, combining it with corresponding psychological speculations. Significant among these is the interpretation by Samuel Murrell:[27] according to him, the occasion is the apostle's rage at Jewish persecution and hostility that continued to make his life difficult, as attested by Acts and Galatians, but experienced also in Thessalonica. Paul is said to have been a man with faults who did not always maintain political correctness; the latter Murrell considers to be the unspoken measure applied by many exegetes, whom he therefore calls censorious "paulinists." Paul, as a human being, could speak in anti-Jewish terms like any other: "He was every bit like we are."[28] The passage in 1 Thess 2:14–16 and other such passages are said to reveal this human side very clearly. In Murrell's case it is remarkable that, besides his too-emphatic psychologizing of the text, he particularly attempts to interpret the words of 2:14–16 by using the argument of humanity. It appears that he himself has no critical standard to resort to, while he makes the critique and judging ability of other exegetes almost laughable. On the whole, according to Murrell, this is a piece of hyperbolic rhetoric, a popular rhetorical artifice in the first century.[29]

Carol J. Schlueter's dissertation on 1 Thess 2:14–16 also concludes that Paul is making use of a rhetorical figure, a "hyperbole" exaggerated by "polemic."[30] She thus positions herself within a prominent trend in scholarship by locating and analyzing 1 Thessalonians against the background of the genres of ancient

25. Hoppe, "Der Topos der Prophetenverfolgung" (2004), does say that this is not about the whole Jewish people but only the "Jews who try to hinder the gospel about the salvation of the Gentiles" (p. 542); still, 2:15–16 "might be understood collectively" (p. 543). For a comparison with Romans 11 see also Jacques Buchhold, "1 Thessaloniciens 2.13–16," *Théologie Évangelique* 6 (2007): 229–40, esp. 239–40.

26. E.g., Weiss, *Das Urchristentum* (1917), 214 [English: *Earliest Christianity* (1959), 466]; Coppens, "Diatribe antijuive" (1975), 94: "a holy anger"; Holtz, *Thessalonicher* (1986), 110ff.

27. Samuel Murrell, *The Human Paul* (1994), 169ff., 175ff.

28. Ibid., 177.

29. Ibid., summary on 183.

30. Carol J. Schlueter, *"Filling Up"* (1994), esp. 65–123, 186–98.

rhetoric.[31] Schlueter defines as hyperbole the consequences of the negative statements in 1 Thess 2:15–16, which, as amplification, are meant to prepare the way for the climax in v. 16c, which she compares to texts from Quintilian and Cicero.[32] This polemic is said, however, to function to define the opponents anew. It is true that the Jews appear as a great evil, but the accusation against them is supposed to legitimate any and every kind of resistance to anything that causes the righteous to suffer. In the present case it is their "own people" [NRSV: compatriots] (συμφυλεταί) who are the opponents.[33] This serves to build up the identity of those addressed, in that, from a divine perspective (so to speak), a clear distinction is drawn between two categories of people: "them" and "us." Carol Schlueter says, by way of excuse, that the statement "the Jews displease God" is a standard accusation in Jewish literature,[34] without seeming to recognize that authors such as Josephus and Philo quote anti-Jewish writings for the sole purpose of refuting such accusations.[35] The subsequent listing and discussion of other polemic outbursts in the Pauline letters, for example in 2 Corinthians 11, are supposed to show, in order to relativize the fact, that Paul revealed his natural bent for polemics in many other debates. In doing so he is said to have turned equally against "Jews" and "Christians," something that scholars have not adequately acknowledged by noting only the anti-Jewish sayings. Thus 1 Thess 2:14–16 is said to represent Paul's polemical attitude toward the Jewish people at an early stage of his career.[36]

On the whole, this attempt to interpret the passage exclusively as a rhetorical figure means that the form of the statements interprets their content and thus relativizes it.

31. See the works of rhetorical analysis and interpretation of 1 Thessalonians by Jewett, *Thessalonian Correspondence* (1986); Johanson, *Brethren* (1987); Hughes, *Early Christian Rhetoric* (1990); Olbricht, "Aristotelian Rhetorical Analysis" (1990); Wanamaker, *Thessalonians* (1990); Wuellner, "Argumentative Structure" (1990); Schoon-Janssen, *Umstrittene "Apologien"* (1991), 14–65; Hester, "Invention" (1996); Chapa, "Is First Thessalonians a Letter of Consolation?" (1994); Smith, *Comfort One Another* (1995); Walton, "What has Aristotle to do with Paul?" (1995); Hoppe, "Der erste Thessalonicherbrief" (1997); Witherington, *1 and 2 Thessalonians* (2006); and see the overview in Hans-Josef Klauck, *Die antike Briefliteratur* (1998), 284–92, as well as the critical evaluation by Stefan Schreiber, "Früher Paulus" (2007), 267–84.

32. Schlueter, *"Filling Up"* (1994), 111ff.

33. Ibid., 120ff. For an important observation on the effective functionalizing of "the Jews," see below at 2.4.3.

34. Ibid., 122.

35. See 2.4.1 below.

36. Schlueter, *"Filling Up"* (1994), 124–63, summary on 162–63. Paul-Gerhard Müller represents a similar position as regards content in a hermeneutically reflective essay ("Judenbeschimpfung und Selbstverfluchung bei Paulus" [1989]): Paul, he says, resorts to anti-Jewish polemic as an expression of inner-Jewish critique and an allusive self-cursing, something that can be found *in nuce* in his other letters.

2.2.3 *Explanations in terms of tradition history*

The observation that vv. 15–16 contain a large number of expressions characterized as non-Pauline points to the inclusion of traditional material, something that might serve as an explanation that would excuse Paul,[37] who would therefore not be responsible for the original formulation. Odil Hannes Steck has proved influential in this regard: he worked out a traditional "deuteronomistic prophetic saying" on the subject of the violent fate of Israel's prophets; he sees this as having been adopted in 1 Thess 2:15–16, expanded to include the death of Jesus.[38] According to Steck the non-Pauline elements include ἀποκτείνειν for the killing of Jesus, the idea of the violent fate of the prophets, ἐκδιώκειν, "persecute intensively," the adjective "hostile," and the expressions ἀναπληροῦν τὰς ἁμαρτίας / "fill up the measure of sins," φθάνειν ἐπὶ τίνα / "come to someone," and εἰς τέλος / "finally, completely." Thus Paul has adopted an already-formulated statement within a broader context. In particular, the sequence of killing the prophets, killing of Jesus, hindering the mission to the Gentiles, and final judgment represents a parallel to Mark 12:1–9, the parable of the wicked tenants. This produces a radical, though historically unclear, understanding of the judgment pronounced on the Jewish people at each point: the wrath "consists in the fact that the Jews as such will be deprived, indeed are already deprived of their election and promise."[39] Synoptic parallels for the material, especially Matt 23:29–36, have already been recognized in the past, from time to time,[40] and must be examined alongside others in their particular formulation,[41] but it is only Steck's assignment of the passage to a "deuteronomistic prophetic statement" that gives 1 Thess 2:15–16 an overall biblical flair. Together with the drastic formulation as a rejection of the Jews also given to the passage, it has gained many followers. Ingo Broer has dedicated particularly intensive and extensive attention to the interpretation of 1 Thess 2:14–16 from this point of view.[42] He emphasizes the

37. Decidedly to the contrary: Hans-Heinrich Schade, *Apokalyptische Christologie* (1981), 128, and Ingo Broer (including in "'Antisemitismus'" [1983], 70).

38. Odil Hannes Steck, *Israel* (1967), 274–78.

39. Ibid., 277.

40. Cf., e.g., J. Bernard Orchard, "Thessalonians and the Synoptic Gospels" (1938), 20–23; Reinier Schippers, "Pre-Synoptic Tradition" (1966), 227–34, esp. 232–34; Pearson, "1 Thessalonians 2:13–16" (1971), 92ff.; Bruce C. Johanson, "1 Thess 2,15–16: Prophetic Woe-Oracle with ἔφθασεν as Proleptic Aorist" (1995), 523ff.; Michael A. Rydelnik, "Was Paul Anti-Semitic?" (2008), 64–65; Luckensmeyer, *Eschatology* (2009), 149–50. Critically on this point: Tuckett, "Synoptic Tradition?" (1990), 165ff.

41. On this, see below at 2.4.2.

42. Broer, "'Antisemitismus'"; idem, "'Der ganze Zorn'" (1990); idem, "Antijudaismus" (1991), 326–32; idem, "Die Juden" (1992), 8–12. Following Steck, *Israel*, the tradition-historical shaping of 1 Thess 2:14–16 is also emphasized by Dieter Zeller, "Christus, Skandal und Hoffnung" (1979), 256–78, at 258–59; Schade, *Apokalyptische Christologie* (1981), 126ff.; Lüdemann, *Paulus und das Judentum* (1983), 22ff.; Bickmann, *Kommunikation gegen den Tod* (1998), 196ff.; Hoppe, "Der Topos" (2004), esp. 540ff. and elsewhere.

compositorial activity and intention with which Paul makes use of biblical-prophetic traditions as well as pagan elements of polemic against the Jews, and gives a special rhetorical flourish to the statement about judgment thus conveyed: Paul "would see this judgment in the removal of the fundamental preference for the Jews over all others. Election and promise are taken from them; the distinction between Jew and Gentile no longer exists; the Jews are reduced to the level of all humanity."[43] But as an "example of inner-Jewish polemic" this is ultimately meant as a means to move Israel to convert to Christ, and in this sense it can scarcely be seen as contrary to Romans 11.[44] Even though Broer's emphatic style, especially the anything-but-clinical tone of the theological vocabulary of destruction he has drawn from the text, seems questionable and alienating, his studies contain important individual insights to which we will return.

2.2.4 *Interpolation*

Following some ancient and more modern interpreters who have explained 1 Thess 2:13–16, or parts thereof, as an interpolation from the period after the fall of Jerusalem and the destruction of the Temple in 70 C.E.,[45] the thesis has been presented recently and most impressively by Birger A. Pearson.

43. Broer, "'Der ganze Zorn,'" 157.

44. Broer, "'Antisemitismus,'" 87ff.; idem, "'Der ganze Zorn,'" 157ff. See also Holtz, "The Judgement on the Jews" (1990), who asserts that 1 Thess 2:16 (!) and Romans 9–11 "in material agreement" say to the members of the "synagogue" who reject Jesus Christ that they have "fallen under judgment" (130).

45. See the overviews of research on and discussion of the interpolation thesis by, among others, Carl Clemen, *Die Einheitlichkeit der paulinischen Briefe* (1894), 14ff.; Collins, "A propos," 126ff.; George E. Okeke, "1 Thessalonians 2.13–16" (1980/81), 127–28; Jewett, *Thessalonian Correspondence*, 37ff.; Broer, "'Der ganze Zorn'"; Schlueter, *"Filling Up"* (1994), 25–38; Still, *Conflict* (1999), 24–45; Luckensmeyer, *Eschatology* (2009), 161–67. Albrecht Ritschl (["Zu 1 Thess 2,16c]," [1847]: 1000; cp. Nestle-Aland[27], ad loc.) was the first to regard 2:16c as interpolated (a view he later revised: see his *Die christliche Lehre von der Rechtfertigung und Versöhnung* [1889], 2:142ff.). He was followed by Rudolf Knopf, *Das nachapostolische Zeitalter* (1905), 139; Paul W. Schmiedel, *Die Briefe an die Thessalonicher und an die Korinther* (1892), 21, who adds 2:15–16, as does Walter Schmithals, "Die historische Situation der Thessalonicherbriefe" (1965), 89–157, at 131. [See the English translation in idem, *Paul and the Gnostics* (Nashville: Abingdon, 1972), 127.] Verses 14–16 are regarded as a gloss by, among others, Hippolyte Rodrigues, *Les seconds chrétiens: Saint Paul* (1876), 225ff. (noted by Clemen, *Einheitlichkeit*, 14); Samuel G. F. Brandon, *The Fall of Jerusalem and the Christian Church* (1951), 92–93. Albert Loisy extends the interpolation to 2:1–16 and other longer sections of 1 Thess (*Les Livres du Nouveau Testament* [1922], 135ff.), as do Karl G. Eckart, "Der zweite echte Brief" (1961): 30–44; Ebba Refshauge, "Literærkritiske overvejelser til de to Thessalonikerbreve" (1971): 1–19, summary on p. 18; and Christoph Demke, "Theology and Literary Criticism in 1 Thessalonians" (1996):

Pearson bases his plea for the interpolation of vv. 13–16 in the letter on historical, theological, and form-critical arguments. He sees the finality of divine wrath against the Jews formulated in 2:16c in a clear aorist, something that in this massive degree could be connected to the destruction of Jerusalem in 70 C.E.[46] Verse 15 contains a clear allusion to the typical Gentile denunciation of Judaism as "misanthropic," which cannot be considered Pauline, any more than the assertion that the Jews killed Jesus, something that is more at home in the time when Acts was written. In contrast, Paul himself in 1 Cor 2:8 calls the "rulers of this age," that is, forces outside Judaism, responsible for the death of Jesus; in addition, v. 16 contradicts Rom 11:26.[47] The reference to persecution of Jewish-Christian churches by their fellow Jews in Judea would, if it were genuine, be the only passage that mentions such a persecution before the outbreak of the Jewish war against Rome. But there were none in that period. Likewise, the community in Thessalonica could not have been the victim of a systematic persecution during the apostolic period. The *mimesis* terminology here does not, as elsewhere, refer to imitation of Paul, but rather to imitation of Jewish-Christian communities. It is a secondary extension of the *mimesis* motif in 1:6.[48] Finally, referring to the pioneering work of Paul Schubert,[49] Pearson offers a form-critical argument for the interpolation, because a striking and anomalous second thanksgiving begins at 2:13; with this, vv. 13–16 interrupt a genuine connection between 2:1–12 and 2:17–3:6.[50]

According to Pearson the interpolator's method was to select key words from the broader context of the letter, such as "imitation," and use them in a different sense in order to give the impression of Pauline authorship. The motivation is said to be a general encouragement of the Gentile-Christian community by suggesting a connection with the identical fate of Christians in Palestine who were suffering persecution, thus establishing a "united front" of all Christians against all Jews.[51] This is said to be indicated also by the material in Matthew 23–24, similar in its tradition history and corresponding to the actual common historical situation after the destruction of the Temple. Pearson thinks that this is when the decisive break between church and synagogue took place, so that the suffering Matthean community could be made a model for the community in Thessalonica.[52]

194–214, accessible at https://depts.drew.edu/jhc/demke.html. We should add here those who dispute the authenticity of the whole letter, e.g., Karl Schrader, *Der Apostel Paulus* (1836), vol. 5, and F. C. Baur, *Paulus, der Apostel Jesu Christi* (1873), 2: 94ff. [English: *Paul the Apostle of Jesus Christ: His Life and Works, His Epistles and Teachings* (Peabody, MA: Hendrickson, 2003)]; see also below at 4.1.

46. Pearson, "1 Thessalonians 2:13–16," (1971), 81–83.

47. Ibid., 83–86.

48. Ibid., 86–88.

49. Schubert, *Form and Function* (1939).

50. Pearson, "1 Thessalonians 2:13–16," 88–91.

51. Ibid., 91.

52. Ibid., 92–94.

This combination of historical and theological anomalies and their general incompatibility with Paul's positions has caused a number of exegetes to adopt Pearson's thesis, or at least to acknowledge these seriously anti-Jewish features of the text in order to explain them in some other way, as we will see below. Among those who follow Pearson in positing an interpolation are Hendrikus Boers, Gerhard Krodel, Helmut Koester, Daryl Schmidt, Franz Laub, Jouette M. Bassler, and Earl J. Richard.[53] According to Richard the theology of vv. 14–16, inserted in the letter as a marginal gloss, cannot be associated with Paul:

> The theology of these verses is un-Pauline in tone, content, and overall treatment of Israel and represents a later generation's misreading of polemical texts, particularly from Matthew and Luke-Acts, in the context of a Hellenistic anti-Jewish perspective. The difficulties of the early Church are laid at the feet of the dispersed nation of Israel. Verses 15–16 indeed constitute an unrelenting condemnation of all Jews, an attitude with which the Church will do battle throughout the centuries.[54]

It is worth noting that in recent exegesis German-language research as a whole is more inclined to affirm the unity of the letter and seeks by all means to integrate 2:14–16, while a critical number of English-speaking scholars seem more prepared to accept that these verses are an interpolation.

2.2.5 Theory of development

A general acknowledgment of 1 Thessalonians as Paul's first writing to a congregation makes it possible to evaluate the "word on the Jews," among other elements of its content, as an early expression or lapse on the part of the apostle in this "objectively archaic form of 1 Th"[55] that was later overcome and has little representative value. In particular Gerd Lüdemann's thesis, according to which 1 Thessalonians originated as early as 41 C.E. and thus about ten years earlier than

53. Hendrikus Boers, "The Form Critical Study" (1976): 140–58, at 151ff.; Gerhard Krodel, "2 Thessalonians," (1978), 73–96, at 77ff.; Helmut Koester, "I Thessalonians: Experiment in Christian Writing," (1979), 33–44, at 38; Darryl D. Schmidt, "1 Thess 2:13–16: Linguistic Evidence for an Interpolation," (1983): 269–79; Franz Laub, *1. und 2. Thessalonicherbrief* (1985), 21–22; Jouette M. Bassler, "I and II Thessalonians," (1989), 311–18, at 314; Earl J. Richard, *First and Second Thessalonians* (1995), 17ff., 119–27. See also the recipients of the interpolation thesis listed in Frank D. Gilliard, "The Problem of the Antisemitic Comma" (1989): 481–502, at 495n5, including John G. Gager, *The Origins of Anti-Semitism* (1983), 255–56, as well as Bernhard Bonsack, "Literarkritische Kapricen" (1988), 180–90, at 184–85, 190, and Leander E. Keck, "Images of Paul in the New Testament," (1989): 341–51, at 345.

54. Richard, *First and Second Thessalonians* (1995), 18.

55. Schade, *Apokalyptische Christologie* (1981), 173.

has previously been supposed,[56] provides broad room for relativization. Lüdemann himself attributes the different Pauline attitudes in 1 Thess 2:14–16 and Romans 11 to the differing situations of the two texts, brought about by *historical* development: "In 1 Thess 2,14ff the Gentile mission (and thus Gentile Christianity!) is under threat; Rom 11:25–26 reflects the danger of a contemporary elimination of Jewish Christianity. Basic to both letters is the theological axiom of a church made up of Jews and Gentiles."[57]

A personal development on the part of Paul himself is often postulated. Thus Dieter Zeller traces it essentially to a difference in Paul's assessment of the salvation-historical situation. While 1 Thess 2:14–16 condemns the hindrance of the Gentile mission in prophetic style, Paul later experienced a new "prophetic word-event" concerning the ultimate fate of Israel, a "gift of the Spirit" that brought about a "reversal," as documented by Romans 11.[58] John C. Hurd posits that in an early apocalyptic phase of his development Paul was captive to a specific black-white thinking. In making use of later ecclesial anti-Judaistic expressions in this phase "he was ahead of his time in expressing a historical-theological anti-Judaism."[59]

John W. Simpson's extensive investigation, which rejects the idea of interpolation, proceeds in essence from the position that there must have been a development in Paul up to the time of Romans 9–11. In my opinion he does not convincingly explain how and why that could have come about.[60] Romano Penna had taken a similar position previously: a great deal happened between the two extremes of 1 Thessalonians and Romans, and Paul's attitude toward Israel had shifted from severity to sympathy.[61] Simon Légasse also admits, after having affirmed 1 Thess 2:14–16 as an original element of the letter and developed the unexampled radicality of its content within the New Testament, that it is not easy to draw a

56. Lüdemann, *Paulus, der Heidenapostel*, vol. 1; see the overview of the chronology on 272–73.

57. Lüdemann, *Paulus und das Judentum* (1983), 42; similarly Okeke, "1 Thessalonians 2.13–16" (1980/81), 132ff., and Udo Schnelle, *Wandlungen im paulinischen Denken* (1989), 77ff., 85ff. However, 1 Thess 2:14–16 in no way attests to the unity of the church "made up of Jews and Gentiles," even if one takes into account Greek-Christian communities' imitation of Jewish-Christian ones (Lüdemann, *Paulus und das Judentum*, 24). The same notion of imitation attests to an ethnic separation and, in fact, no Jewish-Gentile communion in the individual local churches (see 2.4.3 below).

58. E.g., Dieter Zeller, "Christus" (1979), 257ff., 267ff., summary at 275ff.n273.

59. John C. Hurd, "Paul Ahead of His Time" (1986), 21–36, at 36.

60. Simpson, "Problems" (1990), esp. 46–62. A more intensive turn of the later Paul toward Jerusalem in connection with the delivery of the collection (pp. 46–49) and the intervening growth of the Gentile mission are not sufficient explanation for the attitude behind 1 Thess 2:14–16.

61. Romano Penna, "L'evolution de l'attitude" (1986), with summary on 419ff., and 390–97 on 1 Thess 2:14–16.

line of development from there to Romans 11. He only hints that a new spirit must have come upon Paul, or that particular circumstances in the Jewish community must have moved him to a theological attitude more friendly to Israel.[62]

The idea of developments has an advantage with regard to the exegesis of the anti-Jewish polemic in 1 Thessalonians: it allows one to work out the hard sayings in the texts—for example, the complete contrast with Romans 9–11—with relative clarity[63] without too quickly assuming apostolic relativizing in the course of things. On the other hand, in that way the teeth of the earlier statement are drawn by the later, which thus becomes Paul's final and thus binding word to Israel—on the whole, an advantageous theological position. Nevertheless, in my opinion there has thus far been no convincing description of such a fundamental development and its causes. Basically, the texts resist any biographical harmonization, and in these interpretations they still stand irreconcilably alongside one another.

Consequently, declining to offer an explanation, and a general perplexity at the severity of 1 Thess 2:14–16 such as Wolfgang Kraus reveals in his study on the people-of-God theme in Paul, seem more honest.[64] Kraus sees in the adoption of traditional elements of deuteronomistic prophetic speech, pagan polemic against Jews, and especially the idea of an eschatological mass of sin—which is used in 1 Thessalonians, counter to tradition, against the Jewish people[65]—and also in the announcement of eschatological judgment what practically amounts to a revocation of Israel's election and its status as people of God: "With this Paul in fact put the Jews who were persecuting the community on the same level with the Gentiles . . . unlike in Rome, Paul here considers the possibility that Israel might lose its character as people of God altogether and be surrendered to divine wrath, something that otherwise was thought possible only for the Gentiles."[66] Kraus sees no possibility of softening the severity of the statement; there remains no explanation for it except to say that 1 Thessalonians represents a "document of early Pauline theology."[67]

62. Simon Légasse, "Paul et les Juifs" (1997): 572–91, at 572, 590–91.

63. See, e.g., Schnelle, *Wandlungen* (1989), 85: "The apostle's position toward Israel has changed radically. 1 Thessalonians 2:14–16 is irreconcilable with Rom 11:25–26, so that we must speak of a revision of Paul's attitude"; Penna, "L'évolution de l'attitude" (1986), 411ff.: "two extreme points, two utterly divergent moments" (p. 419).

64. Wolfgang Kraus, *Volk Gottes* (1996), 148–55; on 1 Thessalonians as a whole see pp. 120–55. Likewise Otto Michel, "Fragen zu I Thessalonicher 2,14–16" (1967), 50–59, at 58–59, emphasizes the acerbity of the statements without venturing an explanation that might serve to downplay it.

65. On this see below at 2.4.3 and 2.5.2.

66. Kraus, *Volk Gottes*, 153.

67. Ibid., 155.

2.2.6 Relativizing the most severe statements

Due either to necessity or to interest in understanding the text ultimately as stemming from Paul (whether necessarily or because of a desire to do so), or because of a recognition of how difficult that is in light of its content, there have been a number of different suggestions for relativizing the hardest sayings.

The escape route that says not all Jews can be intended, but only those who have in fact made themselves guilty of the listed deeds, is represented by, among others, Frank D. Gilliard.[68] His goal was to delete the orthographic comma after τῶν Ἰουδαίων between 1 Thess 2:14 and 15 from Greek text editions and translations, since in any case it appears only in late medieval manuscripts. Without a comma it is said to be impossible that all Judaism is accused. Rather, what results is a restrictive, relativizing sequence of statements in which Paul has quite distinct Jewish groups in view, each of which he considers individually.[69] He thus discovers at least five different groups corresponding to the following negative statements: Jews who killed Jesus and the prophets; Jews who persecuted; Jews who did not please God, etc. It remains a difficulty for this solution that Ἰουδαίων appears with the article, whereas the word could better be interpreted in this sense without it, and that at the end of 2:16c it is said that wrath will come on "them" (αὐτοὺς), without any differentiation. With or without the comma, we have here an extreme buildup of negative attributes that are applied to Jewish people. Willi Marxsen's relativizing solution is restricted to seeing only those Jews who persecuted the missionaries and hindered the mission to the nations as being accused. It is of them alone that it is said that they are the enemies of all.[70] Here the problem remains that with "killing the prophets" the text takes up a motif that applies to the history of Israel and thus more probably to the whole Jewish people.[71] As regards

68. Gilliard, "Antisemitic Comma" (1989); see the further text-critical development of this thesis by Christian B. Amphoux, "1 Th 2,14–16" (2003): 85–101.

69. Gilliard, "Antisemitic Comma," 498ff.; so also, following Gilliard's thesis, e.g., Malherbe, *Thessalonians* (2000), 169, 174ff.

70. Willi Marxsen, *Der erste Brief an die Thessalonicher* (1979), 49ff.; Penna, "L'évolution de l'attitude" (1986), 395; see also the position of Weatherly, "Authenticity" (1991), 84ff., who likewise presents a very particular understanding of οἱ Ἰουδαῖοι; Légasse, "Paul et les Juifs" (1997), 577ff.; idem, *Les épîtres aux Thessaloniciens* (LD 7; Paris: Cerf, 1999), 141–65; Amphoux, "1 Th 2,14–16" (2003), who accuses only the Jerusalem high priests and sees them as condemned (100–101); Jeffrey S. Lamp, "Is Paul Anti-Jewish? (2003), 410–11, 422ff.; Hoppe, "Der Topos" (2004), 542–43, 548; or Fee, *Thessalonians* (2009), 89–103, who sees only inhabitants of Judea who had shown themselves hostile to Jesus and the Christian communities as falling under Paul's indictment.

71. For this reason Gilliard again argues that here the text is only speaking of "Christian" prophets, since προφήτας belong to Jesus and should be translated "his prophets" (Gilliard, "Paul and the Killing of the Prophets in 1 Thess 2:15" [1994]: 259–70, esp. 264ff.)

the use of the article τῶν in 2:15, it can also be shown grammatically that all the reproaches are meant to apply to *all* "Jews."[72]

Willi Marxsen is also among the exegetes who recognize that the statements about Jewish persecutors are essential parts of a parallel structure that, in fact, aims toward statements about "Gentile" persecutors: "But exegetical interest should not fixate on these words and ideas as such; rather, we should notice what statements they serve. Only then can the statement be applied to the situation in Thessalonica."[73] Still, we must express a fundamental doubt about whether this represents a weakening of the anti-Jewish content of the pericope, as will be discussed below.[74]

Michael A. Rydelnik grounds his position that the Pauline anti-Jewish reproaches in 1 Thess 2:14–16 are directed not to the whole people Israel but only to their political leadership ("Jewish leaders") with the reference to the communities "in Judea" in v. 14, who were not among the Jewish persecutors.[75] He then argues by means of statements in the gospels that attribute the initiative for the killing of Jesus solely to the leading class of Jews (John 11:47–53; Luke 23:2; Matt 27:20; Mark 15:11); besides, in Matthew 23 it is only the Pharisees who are condemned, not the whole people. This, he says, is true also of 1 Thess 2:14–16. But that is questionable in itself because the language of this text, as we will discuss, is distinct from that of other supposed parallels in the New Testament; in addition, Rydelnik does not discuss the adoption of pagan anti-Jewish expressions about atheism and misanthropy in 2:15.[76]

Another possible means of weakening the anti-Jewish content of the passage is to refer to the proclamation of wrath in 2:16c. Various attempts have been made to see the aorist of φθάνω, ἔφθασεν, "is (already) come," as temporally modified, so that there need not be an announcement of a judgment that has already arrived, or the "wrath" need not be understood as final judgment. Martin Dibelius, for example, supposes that Paul is alluding to the "stubbornness of the people of God," and so speaks in "prophetic style," saying "that the beginning of the end has already arrived."[77] Recently the supposition of a definitively "prophetic" aorist, whereby the judgment becomes more an announcement and anticipation of it, with the aorist actually representing a future form,[78] has shifted to the idea of a "proleptic" and

72. Eduard Verhoef, "Die Bedeutung des Artikels τῶν in 1 Thess 2,15" (1995): 41–46.

73. Marxsen, *Thessalonicher* (1979), 50.

74. See below at 2.4.3 for this and similar positions by Johanson, *Brethren* (1987), 96ff.; Weatherly, "Authenticity" (1991), 88–89; Peter Wick, "Ist I Thess 2,13–16 antijüdisch?" (1994): 9–23, at, 19ff.

75. Rydelnik, "Was Paul Anti-Semitic?" (2008), 63–67.

76. On this, see below at 2.4.1 and 2.4.2.

77. Martin Dibelius, *Thessalonians* (2d ed. 1925), 11. Légasse, "Paul et les Juifs" (1997), 584–91, also argues for an anticipation of the wrath and thus a mere warning of judgment.

78. Adolf Hilgenfeld, "Die beiden Briefe" (1862), 237–38; von Dobschütz, *Thessalonicher-Briefe* (1909), 114–15. See also, *inter alia*, Hagner, "Paul's Quarrel" (1993), 132; Georg Geiger, "1 Thess 2,13–16" (1986), 157.

also a "gnomic" or "complexive" aorist. Bruce Johanson develops his thesis of a "proleptic" aorist by setting 1 Thess 2:14–16 alongside prophetic texts, thus seeking to understand the passage as a kind of Old Testament "woe": wrath is (yet) to come. He points out that the Hebrew imperfect and perfect forms used in the corresponding texts appear most times in the Septuagint as future, and also as aorists, which is why he calls the latter a "proleptic" aorist.[79] But in doing so Johanson ignores the fact that a text such as Hab 2:15–17 is different, for the very reason that there Israel itself is addressed in the second person as "thou," while 1 Thess 2:14–16 condemns "the Jews" in the third person and an eventual turning back is not in view.[80] So Hab 2:16 can in fact be read as an announcement of judgment, which does not seem to be the case with the pronouncement of judgment in 1 Thess 2:16, thanks to the chosen form (3d person plural), and the aorist should instead be seen as a past form. Ekkehard W. Stegemann speaks of a "complexive" or "gnomic" aorist, expressing a constantly recurring, typical process or a repeated experience. He believes that in this way the "wrath" referred to is seen to represent a punishment within history for the temporarily erring Jewish people and not an eschatological judgment.[81]

2.2.7 Historicizing and harmonizing comparisons with Acts 17

While a part of scholarship emphasizes the contradictions between Acts 16–18 and 1 Thessalonians,[82] assigning unconditional priority to the letters of Paul as historical sources,[83] another part is interested in harmonizing the letter with the narratives in Acts,[84] upgrading the historical value of the latter. Basically, this accomplishes a kind of leveling of the different information in the two sources. The essential differences are: (1) According to 1 Thess 1:1–3:1 Paul, Silvanus, and Timothy are missionizing together in Thessalonica, while from Acts 16:25 to 17:14 Timothy's name is omitted and Paul and Silas/Silvanus appear to be the primary actors; (2) 1 Thess 3:1–3 says that Timothy is being sent from Athens to Thessalonica,

79. Bruce Johanson, "1 Thessalonians 2:15–16" (1995), esp. 525ff.

80. Weatherly, "Authenticity" (1991), 90–91, regards the expression as idiomatic and therefore (?) sees this as an immediately impending judgment rather than one that has actually arrived, and thus also a hint of the possibility of repentance and an agreement with Rom 9–11; Rydelnik, "Was Paul Anti-Semitic?" (2008), 66–67 has a similar solution, reading here a prophetic prediction of the catastrophe of 70 C.E., the definitive end (εἰς τέλος).

81. Ekkehard W. Stegemann, "Zur antijüdischen Polemik in 1 Thess 2,14–16," (1990), esp. 59ff.; similarly, e.g., Chantal Reynier, "Le thème de la colère" (2004), 281–95, at 285–89, esp. 287; see the discussion below at 2.5.2.

82. See, e.g., Ernest Best, *Thessalonians* (1972), 131–32; Marxsen, *Thessalonicher* (1979), 13–14.

83. See only Gerd Lüdemann, *Paulus, der Heidenapostel* 1 (1983), 35–36; 45ff.

84. See as early as Theodor Zahn, *Einleitung* (1906), 145ff. [English: *Introduction to the New Testament* (1909), 207–15]; von Dobschütz, *Thessalonicher-Briefe* (1909), 13ff.

while according to Acts 17:13–14; 18:5 Timothy and Silas remain in Beroea while Paul travels alone to Athens and only meets the other two again in Corinth; (3) the wording of 1 Thessalonians gives no explicit indication that there are Jewish people in the congregation, while according to Acts 17:4 it seems that only Jewish persons and the Greek "God-fearers" (σεβόμενοι) who define themselves as Jewish are attracted to the community; the unrest and expulsion of the missionaries are brought about by a different group of adherents of the synagogue, while 1 Thess 2:14 speaks of pressure from "people of the land" (συμφυλετῶν) whose Jewish identity is questionable.

Rainer Riesner's study[85] is one of the best-grounded attempts at harmonizing Acts and 1 Thessalonians as a whole. He makes a particular effort to shape the last-mentioned difference into a unified historical picture. According to Riesner the weighty anti-Jewish diatribe in 1 Thess 2:14–16 should be explained against the background of the conflict related in Acts 17:5–10. The Jews of Thessalonica had stirred up the mob there against the apostle and 2:14–16 is a Pauline reaction to his forced flight from the community brought about by the Jews. Hence the word συμφυλέτης must also and particularly refer to Jewish citizens. "The account in Acts is able to illuminate the apostle's experience here and to make his shockingly harsh manner of expression at least historically comprehensible."[86]

Riesner has to deal with the finding that, according to Acts 17, the majority of the community itself, or at least a significant part of it, had to consist of Jewish men and women; there is no indication of this in 1 Thessalonians. Acts, on the other hand, does not mention any "Gentile Christians." Hence he harmonizes by identifying the "God-fearers" in Acts, who according to the text were members of the synagogue community, with those addressed in 1 Thessalonians, now apparently (again) genuinely Gentile Christian people who at the same time, because they had "formerly had contact with the synagogue" are supposed to embody the vanishing or already vanished *Jewish* element of the Christian community in 1 Thessalonians.[87] Here, as in the discussion of other shortcomings of 1 Thessalonians, it is striking that Riesner's method tends to presume what is absent *e silentio* or to insert it from other sources because, in his opinion, on the basis of historical and chronological presumptions it simply *must* exist.[88] Nevertheless, this attempt to describe the composition of the community and the role of the

85. Rainer Riesner, *Die Frühzeit des Apostels Paulus* (1994), esp. 297–365. [English: *Paul's Early Period: Chronology, Mission Strategy, Theology*, trans. Doug Stott (Grand Rapids: Eerdmans, 1998)].

86. Riesner, *Paul's Early Period*, 352–54, at 353; for further discussion and the concept of συμφυλέτης see below at 2.4.3.

87. Ibid., 348–49, at 349.

88. See, e.g., his remarks on the absence of a doctrine of justification or a theology of the cross or baptism in 1 Thess, which, however, must be implicitly present because Paul certainly would have taught them in Thessalonica and simply sees no reason to address them here (ibid., 398–99).

God-fearers is an important indicator of the fundamental problematic of early Christian social history: how, in particular, should we define the status of the "God-fearers," who in their own self-concept may well have wanted to be, or were, associated with the synagogue, whereas in the exegetical literature, as in this case, it is often implicitly assumed as a matter of course that as members of the messianic Christian community they must have been subjected to a thorough process of de-Judaizing, so that their option for Judaism was more or less automatically annulled by their confession of Christ? That, in fact, is the question, and it must be put in its social-historical context in the relevant texts, discussed, and answered in each case. The same is true of the question of the self-understanding and enduring membership of messianic Jewish men and women and proselytes in the people Israel.[89]

2.3 *Part of the letter or interpolation?*

The following exegesis attempts to understand 1 Thess 2:14–16 first and primarily in the narrower and wider contexts of the letter. An interpretation that primarily starts with other Pauline texts on the subject of Israel and Judaism and then devotes itself to 1 Thess 2:14–16 as an early form of his thought and tries to discover bridges that will unify his statements often results in prematurely watering down the text and producing a methodologically problematic apologetics. While this is useful when done with a concomitant intent to avoid the worst anti-Jewish aspects of the history of interpretation,[90] it is not very enlightening as regards the unique contours of 1 Thessalonians. However, we must first ask

89. For an exclusively Jewish composition of the Thessalonian community and a corresponding integration of the God-fearers according to Acts 17:4, see the commentary on Acts by Jacob Jervell, *Die Apostelgeschichte* ([17]1998), 433ff. Overall and for the subject of God-fearers in the "Jewish-Christian" social-historical problematic, see above at 1.3. For a harmonization of the information in 1 Thess with Acts 17 see, *inter alia*, the positions of George Milligan, *St. Paul's Epistles to the Thessalonians* (1908; repr. 1953), 29; Rigaux, *Thessaloniciens* (1956), 443; Légasse, "Paul et les Juifs" (1997), 396n20; Still, *Conflict* (1999), 61–82; David Alvarez Cineira, *Die Religionspolitik des Kaisers Claudius* (1999), 260–90, who reads the statement about judgment in 1 Thess 2:16c as a Pauline reaction to the Edict of Claudius (pp. 281–86); Markus Bockmuehl, "1 Thess 2,14–16 and the Church in Jerusalem" (2001), 18–31, also takes this position with reference to the Edict; and see esp. Mikael Tellbe, *Paul Between Synagogue and State* (2001), 86–96, 105–15: "My conclusion then is that Paul explicitly refers to opposition from certain Jews in Thessalonica, and that 1 Thess. 2:15–16 on this point generally concurs with Luke's account of Jewish opposition in Acts 17:1–14" (p. 108). Nicholas H. Taylor, "Who persecuted the Thessalonian Christians?" (2002) 784–801, esp. 795–98, has a similar argument.

90. Thus, e.g., Geiger, "1 Thess 2,13–16" (1986), 156–57.

whether 2:14–16 can be regarded in any way as an integral part of the letter, or whether it must be understood to be a foreign body, a later interpolation. For we must firmly emphasize the uniqueness of this speech about "the Jews" within the Pauline corpus,[91] so that the possibility of a later insertion seems likely and altogether plausible. Walter Schmithals, who considers the idea of an interpolation, gives reasons for it in terms of an important question posed by Paul W. Schmiedel: "Why this powerful critique of the Jews when the persecution had come from the Gentiles? Can the one-time persecutor speak this way? The 'antisemitism' of this passage contradicts everything Paul says elsewhere about his attitude toward his ancestral people. Can Paul already be saying that the *Jews* crucified Jesus, when the tradition rightly makes the Romans responsible for the crucifixion? Can v. 16b be understood in any other way that as *vaticinium ex eventu* of the catastrophe of the year 70?"[92]

The difficulties in seeing these verses as words of Paul that Birger A. Pearson has worked out rest, argumentatively speaking, primarily on theological and historical grounds[93] that should not be overlooked and must rank high in considering how to interpret this section. They result from comparisons with other Pauline texts, and that is important for the overall interpretation but is insufficient for literary-critical operations. Their justification must first be based methodologically on traces in the manuscript tradition and contradictions in the overall context of the

91. Matters are clearly different in, for example, 2 Cor 3, which a number of contemporary scholars regard as an anti-Jewish exposition by Paul. But in 2 Cor 3 the old covenant is not simply equated with the Old Testament, with an independent new covenant alongside it. With echoes of the new covenant in Jer 31 and an inspired interpretation, a midrash on Exod 34, Paul anchors what he says about the new covenant in Scripture, the Old Testament; on this see Dierk Starnitzke, "Der Dienst des Paulus" (1999): 193–207; Frank Crüsemann, *Das Alte Testament als Wahrheitsraum des Neuen* (2011), 5.3.γ. (bibliography). It should be kept in mind that Exod 32–34 already speaks of two covenants: a first with fatal consequences and then a new covenant of God with Moses and Israel that gives new life and a future. Moses, who speaks directly with God in the Tent of Meeting (Exod 34:34; 2 Cor 3:16), thus becomes a prototype for the ever-renewed possibility of turning to God and a model for the community and for Israel as a whole (Marlene Crüsemann, "Der Gottesname im Neuen Testament" [2007], 18). So 2 Cor 3 cannot be called an anti-Jewish text. Nor does it speak of "the Jews," but of the "sons and daughters of Israel" (τοὺς υἱοὺς Ἰσραήλ, 2 Cor 3:7, 13); for the insertion of "Israel" in the quotation of Exod 34:34 in 2 Cor 3:16 by the Luther revision of 1984—against Luther himself (1545)—as well as the significance of that citation and the recognizable character of the divine name here, see Crüsemann, "Der Gottesname" (2007). In contrast, we must above all maintain that there is not a single OT quotation in 1 Thess, to say nothing of an exegesis of scripture.

92. Walter Schmithals, "Die historische Situation" (1965), 131n212; see Schmiedel, *Die Briefe an die Thessalonicher* ([2]1892), 21.

93. See 2.2.4 above.

writing under examination. Since textual criticism tells us nothing that would call the inclusion of this section into question,[94] there remains the literary-critical question: are there fundamental tensions and contradictions within the nearer and broader context that can be adduced to show a later interpolation? Or, to the contrary, are the verses not so anchored in the overall text that removing them from this context seems altogether arbitrary? On the basis of 1 Thessalonians alone, what speaks against the inclusion of this anti-Jewish outburst? To put it in sharper terms: the clash with the content of a text like Rom 11:26 can, in fact, only be a decisive argument for the secondary character of 1 Thess 2:14–16 if a comparable statement about the salvation of Israel, or at least a hint of it, can be found within the larger context of the writing under investigation, that is, within 1 Thessalonians itself. That is not the case. On the basis of 1 Thessalonians alone there is nothing to be said against the authenticity of these verses. Whether that must mean that they are therefore authentically Pauline is something that remains to be investigated.

The lack of any content out of harmony with the context is seen, first, from the fact that there are no other statements about Israel and Judaism in 1 Thessalonians, not even Jewish-Christian themes regarding theology and observance. But that does not mean that therefore we can easily remove the text, for 1 Thess 2:(13), 14–16 is solidly anchored in the context of the letter. Thus it seems logical to conclude that talk about "the Jews" is an apparently altogether foreign body within a writing that appears to have only non-Jewish addressees (1:9). The geographical note ἐν τῇ Ἰουδαίᾳ ("in Judea") is analogous to other place-determiners in 1 Thessalonians: ἐν τῇ Μακεδονίᾳ καὶ ἐν τῇ Ἀχαίᾳ (1:7, 8; cp. 4:10), which fits with the inclination and method of 1 Thessalonians in naming Roman provinces. Talk about God's "wrath" (ὀργή; 2:16) is part of the ordinary vocabulary of the letter (1:10; 5:9), as is the motif in 2:15 of "pleasing God" (ἀρέσκειν θεῷ; 2:4; 4:1). It cannot be asserted that these and other keywords in the context are used in this pericope in a different way in order to give the text a "Pauline" flavor, as, for example, Pearson thinks.[95] Rather, they contribute to the consistency of the overall text in form and content.[96]

This is shown especially by the application of the idea of imitation; here we can best discern the original location of the passage, because the statement that the members of the community in Thessalonica had imitated the communities in Judea (μιμηταὶ ἐγενήθητε, 2:15), like the imitation mentioned in 1:6 (μιμηταὶ ἡμῶν

94. In v. 15 some textual witnesses add ἰδίους before προφήτας, whereby the prophets are more clearly located within Israel's history; one ms. of the Vulgate eliminates the climax in v. 16c.

95. Pearson, "1 Thessalonians 2:13–16" (1971), 91.

96. See 5.4 below on the location of 1 Thess 2:14–16 within the context of all the apocalyptic sayings about judgment in 1 Thess, as well as the social-historical connection of the motif of misanthropy with the theme of persecution (see 2.5.1 below).

ἐγενήθητε), is in the aorist indicative[97] and therefore both differ from the otherwise consistent usage in the Pauline letters, where it is demanded in the imperative (μιμηταί μου γίνεσθε, 1 Cor 4:16; 11:1; cp. Phil 3:17).[98] This unique feature of 1 Thessalonians is underscored by the analogously used and content-equivalent *typos* model in 1:6, which declares the community in Thessalonica to be an already-existing model (τύπος) for others. The idea of whole communities as models, and their imitation by other communities, is an idea formulated, within the New Testament, only in 1 Thessalonians, aided by the mimesis motif; in fact, it ties 2:14 closely to its context. In addition, the argument of the piling up of un-Pauline words says little in favor of an interpolation[99] in a letter that tends, in every part, to use expressions that are uncommon for Paul and, in fact, for the New Testament as a whole. This begins with "entry" (εἴσοδος)[100] and the unusual expression ἔμπροσθεν τοῦ θεοῦ (κυρίου) ("before God"), not used in a spatial sense;[101] it continues with the piling up of *hapax legomena* and "non-Pauline" expressions in 2:1–12,[102] up to θεοδίδακτοι ("taught by God") and "living quietly" (ἡσυχάζειν) in 4:9–11,[103] or ἀπάντησις, the "meeting" with the Lord (4:17), to mention only a few. Finally, the repetition of the thanksgiving in 2:13–16 can scarcely be adduced as indicating the beginning of a secondary passage when thanks are given a third time in 3:9 and the whole letter is characterized by apparently unmotivated

97. Broer correctly asserts this in his dialogue with Pearson ("Antisemitismus," 1983, 65–69, at 68–69); see also the table of linguistic agreements between 1 Thess 1:2–10 and 2:13–16 in Hurd, "Paul Ahead of His Time" (1986), 29, and how Johanson, *Brethren*, points out a broad chiastic structure in this area (cp. esp. 149, and see below). See also Michel, "Fragen" (1967), 50ff., and Coppens's objections to Pearson ("Une Diatribe antijuive" [1975], 90–95); Lüdemann, *Paulus und das Judentum* (1983), 25ff.; Donfried, *Paul and Judaism* (1984), 244ff.; Légasse, "Paul et les Juifs" (1997), 576; Hoppe, "Der Topos" (2004), 539ff., and, for discussion of the interpolation thesis, Schlueter, *"Filling Up"* (1994), 25–38; Bockmuehl, "1 Thess 2,14–16" (2001), 5–17; Taylor, "Who persecuted the Thessalonian Christians?" (2002), 785–89; Buchhold, "1 Thessaloniciens 2,13–16" (2007) 230ff. John W. Simpson's article, "Problems" (1990), is in large part a focused argument against Pearson (esp. from 49 onward).

98. For more on the idea of imitation and its role in the interpretation of 1 Thess 1–2, see below at 3.3.4.

99. Thus, e.g., Richard, *Thessalonians* (1995), 119–27.

100. Found in the Corpus Paulinum only in 1 Thess 1:9; 2:1. The degree to which this keyword is associated with the structure and content of 1 Thess 1–3 is treated by Seyoon Kim, "Paul's Entry (εἴσοδος)" (2005): 519–42; see idem, "Structure and Function" (2006), 170–88—though he does not make a point of the uniqueness of the term εἴσοδος.

101. Exclusively in 1 Thess 1:3; 2:19; 3:9, 13. Otherwise Paul regularly uses ἐνώπιον τοῦ θεοῦ / κυρίου: Rom 3:20; 14:22; 1 Cor 1:29, and frequently; see Demke, "Theology and Literary Criticism" (1996).

102. On this, see further below at 3.3.3.

103. See below at 3.3.2.

repetitions, such as the constant reference to the previous knowledge of those addressed ("as you know"; καθὼς οἴδατε, 1:5; 2:1, 2, 5, 11, and frequently).[104]

The solid integration of the pericope in its immediate and broader context is underscored by the rhetorical and linguistic study by Bruce C. Johanson, who has produced a methodological proof of the unity of 1 Thessalonians as a well-conceived composition with a ring structure and parallelisms in its detailed as well as its macro structure.[105] For 2:13–16 he demonstrates its embeddedness within 1:2–2:12 through an existing chiastic structure (which he describes as A B B′ A′).[106] The keywords εὐχαριστοῦμεν τῷ θεῷ, ἐδέξασθε . . . λόγον, μιμηταὶ ἐγενήθητε, and ὀργή in 2:13, 14, 16 correspond with like terms in 1:2, 6, 10, thus forming the external clamp for the system. In contrast, the attempt by Daryl Schmidt to demonstrate linguistic evidence for an interpolation does not succeed because, methodologically, he makes too much use of strong passages in other Pauline letters[107] instead of giving primary attention to the context of 1 Thessalonians, as is his stated intention.[108] Thus overall we may say that 1 Thess 2:(13), 14–16 is in its language an integral part of the text as a whole. Besides, there is no reason for literary-critical operations based on possible contradictions in content within the context.

2.4 *Exegesis of 1 Thessalonians 2:14–16: A Triply Anti-Jewish Text*

The fact that because of its embeddedness in the context there is no reason to eliminate 1 Thess 2:14–16 as a foreign body does not, however, mean, methodologically speaking, that the anti-Jewish features of the texts must by all means be relativized if we are still to regard it as Pauline. That cannot be the primary motive for exegesis; we must first attempt to understand the given text, even in its possibly radical nature.[109] It is only in a second step that we may consider how it can accord with other Pauline expressions and positions. The conclusion of the following exegesis will be that the text contains a cumulative threefold composition of anti-Jewish statements.

104. See below at 3.3.1.

105. Johanson, *Brethren* (1987), 59–153, with summary on 169ff.

106. Ibid., 94–98, 169–70 on 2:13–16, and especially the overview on p. 149; cp. Karl P. Donfried, "Paul and Judaism" (1984), 246–47, and the "ABA pattern" in Hurd, "Paul Ahead of His Time" (1986), 28ff., the semantic analysis of Bickmann, *Kommunikation gegen den Tod*, (1998), 156–214, esp. 166ff., and also the overview in Buchhold, "1 Thessaloniciens 2,13–16" (2007), 231.

107. Daryl D. Schmidt, "Linguistic Evidence" (1983), 274ff.

108. For an argument with Schmidt see also Johanson, *Brethren* (1987), 171; Simpson, "Problems" (1990), 49ff., 52ff.; Weatherly, "Authenticity" (1991), 91–98.

109. This has been attempted repeatedly by those who favor its authenticity; e.g., see the sharp expressions in Broer, "'Antisemitismus'" (1983), and Holtz, *Thessalonicher* (1986), 96–113; idem, "The Judgement on the Jews" (1989), and the contrasting, sympathy-evoking bewilderment of Kraus, *Volk Gottes* (1996), 148–55. (See above at 2.2.1, 2.2.2, and 2.2.5.)

2.4.1 Elements of ancient pagan anti-Judaism

This is the only place in the New Testament where both the familiar anti-Jewish motifs of antiquity have found entry.[110] The assertions in 2:15 that "the Jews" do not please God (θεῷ μὴ ἀρεσκόντων), and are hostile to all people (πᾶσιν ἀνθρώποις ἐναντίων) can be recognized as clear allusions to the accusations of atheism and misanthropy or apanthropy, frequently encountered in Greco-Roman authors and laid at the doorstep of the Jewish people,[111] and that have been thoroughly addressed and discussed by scholars.[112] The two motifs are closely entwined thematically, since they are the external reflection of two aspects of Jewish faith with closely connected origins: faith in the one God means living according to God's Torah, which implies turning away from the ancient deities and their cultic worship. Israel's monotheism is denounced as "atheism," and the corresponding shape of the whole way of life according to Torah as "misanthrophy" with regard to

110. One of these motifs, supposed Jewish misanthropy, may appear in Matt 5:43; on this see Gerhard Dautzenberg, "Mt 5,43c und die antike Tradition" (1988), 47–77, but in my opinion it cannot be placed on the same level as the direct expression in 1 Thess. Klaus Haacker also sees a certain affinity to pagan anti-Judaism in Gal 4:21–5:2; 5:12; Phil 3:2 ("Elemente des heidnischen Antijudaismus" [1988], 404–18, at 412ff., 415ff.)

111. For the beginnings, in the third century B.C.E., with Hecataeus of Abdera (for which see Berndt Schaller, "Hekataios von Abdera" [1963]), the documentation for the centuries-long anti-Jewish utterances of Greco-Roman authors is found above all in the collection of sources, with commentary, by Menachem Stern, *Greek and Latin Authors on Jews and Judaism* (1974–1984), which replaces the older collection by Reinach, *Textes d'auteurs grecs et romains relativs au Judaïsme* (1895; repr. 1963). Cp. the corresponding listing of sources and discussion in Wilhelm Nestle, "Odium humani generis" (1927); Isaak Heinemann, art. "Antisemitismus" (1931), 19ff.; J. H. Lewy, "Die Epoche des Zweiten Tempels" [1942], *FrRu* 24 (1972), 22–26; Yehoshua Amir, "Die Stellungnahme" (1975); idem, "Das jüdische Paradox" (1985); Jan N. Sevenster, *Roots of Pagan Antisemitism* (1975), 89–144; Menachem Stern, "The Jews in Greek and Latin Literature" (1976); Hans Conzelmann, *Heiden, Juden, Christen* (1981), 43–120; Nicole Bickhoff-Böttcher, "Das Judentum in der griechisch-römischen Welt" (1984), 130–73; Hans-Peter Stähli, "Judenfeindschaft" (1987), 141–46; Dautzenberg, "Mt 5,43c" (1988), 58–64; Peter Schäfer, *Judeophobia* (1997), esp. 15–118.

112. On this see, e.g., Martin Dibelius, *Thessalonicher* ([3]1937), 12, 34ff.; Michel, "Fragen" (1967), 56ff.; Pearson, "1 Thessalonians 2:13–16" (1971), 83; Broer, "'Antisemitismus"' (1983), 79ff.; Holtz, *Thessalonicher* (1986), 105–6; Paul-Gerhard Müller, "Judenbeschimpfung" (1989), 63–64; idem, *Thessalonicher* (2001), 145; Ekkehard Stegemann, "Zur antijüdischen Polemik in 1 Thess 2,14–16" (1990), 54; Simpson, "Problems" (1990), 56–57; Kraus, *Volk Gottes* (1996), 150–51; Matthias Konradt, *Gericht und Gemeinde* (2003), 81ff., and above all Haacker, "Elemente" (1988), 406–12. It is true that Schlueter says almost nothing about this section in her book (*"Filling Up"* [1994]); the same holds for Weatherly, "Authenticity" (1991); Fee, *Thessalonians* (2009), 94–100, and above all Malherbe, *Thessalonians* (2000), 170, speak firmly against a reception of pagan anti-Jewish polemic in 1 Thess 2:15.

those outside; therefore these accusations often appear together and in the eyes of the non-Jewish world were seen more or less as the essence of Jewish existence.

It is worth noting that the two motifs also appear together in 1 Thess 2:15. This matches up with the thematically stereotypical and at the same time redundant use of language, something documented, for example, in Diodorus Siculus, an author from the first century B.C.E. In the course of an account of the siege of Jerusalem by Antiochus VII Sidetes, he depicts friends and advisors of the king as describing and denouncing the difference between Judaism and the nations in terms of the Jews' halakhic way of life and their monotheism.[113] They urge genocide to completely eliminate the Jews (τὸ γένος ἄρδην ἀνελεῖν τῶν Ἰουδαίων), because they regard all people as their enemies (πολημίους ὑπολαμβάνειν πάντας), and say they are unbelievers and are hated by the gods (ἀσεβεῖς καὶ μισουμένους ὑπὸ τῶν θεῶν); that is why they were rightly expelled from Egypt (1). Further variations on the charge of misanthropy follow: that "the Jews" in Jerusalem had made hatred of humankind (μῖσος τὸ πρὸς τοὺς ἀνθρώπους) their tradition (2). In the course of the narrative Diodorus adopts this label as "objective": Moses is said to be the originator of the misanthropic and lawless (μισάνθρωπα καὶ παράνομα) Jewish customs (3), and these laws are hostile to foreigners (μισόξενα) (4).

Another example can be found in Apollonius Molon, a writer from Asia Minor (1st c. B.C.E.), in whose work one finds anti-Jewish remarks almost everywhere, as Josephus remarks in summarizing his attitude: "... he sometimes reproaches us as atheists, and man-haters, (ὡς ἀθέους καὶ μισανθρώπους), and sometimes hits us in the teeth with our want of courage ..."[114] Apion, a Greek author of Egyptian origins (first half of the first century C.E.) with considerable influence on the intellectual and educated classes, against whom Josephus directed his apology for Judaism primarily for that reason,[115] is said to have been influenced by Apollonius and Poseidonius, who "accuse us for not worshiping the same gods whom others worship" (*quare nos eosdem deos cum aliis non colimus*).[116] In that connection Apion adduces the motif of misanthropy in the form of a legend of ritual murder by a Greek supposedly imprisoned in the Jewish Temple, who was to be slaughtered, "fulfilling a law of the Jews which [the servants in the Temple] must not tell him" (*legem ineffabilem Iudaeorum*) whereby an oath was sworn "that they would ever be at enmity with the Greeks" (*ius iurandum facere ... ut inimicitias contra Graecos haberent*).[117]

113. Diodorus Siculus, *Bibliotheca Historica* XXXIV–XXXV, 1:1–5. Stern, *Authors* I (1974), 154–55; see Dautzenberg, "Mt 5,43c" (1988), 62–63; Werner Stenger, *"Gebt dem Kaiser, was des Kaisers ist ... !"* (1988), 99.

114. Josephus, *Contra Apionem* II, 148, in *Works* (1987); Stern, *Authors* I (1974), 154–55; see Dautzenberg, "Mt 5,43c" (1988), 61n65.

115. See Stern, "The Jews in Greek and Latin Literature," (1976), 1115–16.

116. Josephus, *C.Ap.* II, 79. Stern, *Authors* I (1974), 409–10.

117. Josephus, *C.Ap.* II, 95. Stern, *Authors* I (1974), 410ff.; see Dautzenberg, "Mt 5,43c" (1988), 63–64.

The depiction of the Jews and their religion in Tacitus, *Histories* V, then forms "the great pool into which flow smoothly all the streams of hatred for Jews in antiquity."[118] "Tacitus describes the Jews as a band of lawbreakers who pursue their mischief in the Roman state . . . as the enemy in one's own house who is destroying the foundational structure of the Roman way of life: the family."[119] The special peril of Judaism, according to Tacitus, was the growing number of its proselytes, who on converting to Judaism separated from their own families. At the beginning of his remarks on the successful campaign of Titus and Vespasian against Jerusalem, Tacitus makes some general remarks about the character of the Jewish people: "the Jews are extremely loyal toward one another, and always ready to show compassion, but toward every other people they feel only hate and enmity" (*sed adversus omnes alios hostile odium*). The proselytes are taught, as the first commandment, "to despise the gods" (*contemnere deos*), "to disown their country, and to regard their parents, children, and [siblings] as of little account" (*parentes liberos fratres vilia habere*).[120] Tacitus thereby brings together in the shortest possible compass a compact summary of both motifs, with misanthropy doubled by being specially attributed to a supposed catechesis for proselytes. Menachem Stern sees precisely here the parallels to misanthropy in 1 Thess 2:15.[121] From the time of the Jewish revolt against Trajan we then find four instances in the papyri of the phrase οἱ ἀνόσοι Ἰουδαῖοι ("the impious Jews"), "which also appears to have been a common epithet used against Jews at that time."[122]

These few examples already show the dispersion in time and place of anti-Jewish motifs and the monotony of their content, even in the face of flexible choices of words here and there. This matches the way they are used in 1 Thess 2:15 with the verb ἀρέσκω, "(dis)please" and the adjective ἐναντίος, "hostile."[123] The former could most certainly be considered Pauline usage.[124] Romans 8:8 appears at first to be a parallel formula, though far broader in scope: "those who are in the flesh cannot please God" (θεῷ ἀρέσαι οὐ δύνανται), were it not that the statement in 1 Thess 2:15, "[the Jews] . . . displease God" (θεῷ μὴ ἀρεσκόντων) has preempted it by applying divine judgment to one ethnic group and establishing its final character.[125] Thus already in 1 Thess 2:15 this is about determining a judgment

118. Amir, "Das jüdische Paradox" (1985), 119.

119. Lewy, "Epoche" (1942/1972), 24.

120. Tacitus, *Hist.* V, 5,1–2. English translation at http://penelope.uchicago.edu/Thayer/E/Roman/Texts/Tacitus/Histories/5A*.html. Stern, *Authors* II (1980), 17–88 (on *Hist.* V, 1–13).

121. Stern, *Authors* II (1980), 39; see ibid., 39ff. for texts of ancient expressions of suspicion about Jewish separation through the food laws and other regulations in the Torah.

122. Amir, "Das jüdische Paradox" (1985), 119; *CPJ* II, 157, ll. 43, 49–50; 158a col. 6, l. 14; 438 l. 4; 443 col. 2, ll. 4–5; see Dibelius, *Thessalonicher* (^{3}1937), 35.

123. Use of ἐναντίος is in the form of an abbreviated participle; to ἐναντίων should be added ὀντῶν.

124. Rom 8:8; 15:1, 3; 1 Cor 7:32, 33, 4; 10:33; Gal 1:10.

125. Thus also Broer, "'Antisemitismus'" (1983), 80–81.

from God's perspective. That sheds light on the fact that 2:16 must also be about the proclamation of a definitive judgment, something that is occasionally denied in order to rescue the text for Paul.[126] The incorporation of the pagan motif of ἀσέβεια, the Jews' supposed atheism, is accomplished by its being almost invisibly "Christianized" in that here the text does not speak, as elsewhere, of gods and goddesses, but of the one God, without the use of any further identifying predicates, so that, content-wise, it arrives at a statement very similar to the one cited above from Diodorus: μισουμένους ὑπὸ τῶν θεῶν, "hated by the gods." The adjective ἐναντίος ("hostile") is found nowhere else in Paul and ensures that the motifs of "atheism" and "misanthropy" are presented here in an unmistakable allusion whose concentration is thoroughly compatible with the anti-Judaism of a Tacitus.

Thus 1 Thess 2:15 is "undoubtedly to be regarded as a 'borrowing' of the words of Gentile anti-Judaism, which must have been recognizable as such to the readers of this letter."[127] In the first century labeling someone as having "hatred of the human race" was not a mere harmless epithet in common use, nor was it a purely intellectual and inconsequential play on words; it could at any moment be used as an accusation within a political trial,[128] and thus implies criminal behavior. Cicero regarded *odium humani generis*, "hostility to the community" as a crime against the state:

> There are some also who, either from zeal in attending to their own business or through some sort of aversion to their fellow-men (*odio quodam hominum*), claim that they are occupied solely with their own affairs (*suum negotium agere dicant*), without seeming to themselves to be doing anyone any injury. But while they steer clear of the one kind of injustice (*iniustitia*), they fall into the other: they are traitors to social life (*deserunt enim vitae societatem*), for they contribute to it none of their interest, none of their effort, none of their means.[129]

126. Thus, e.g., Ekkehard Stegemann, "Zur antijüdischen Polemik in 1 Thess 2,14–16" (1990), 57ff.; see above at 2.2.6 and below at 2.5.2.

127. Haacker, "Elemente" (1988), 408.

128. As is true in the accusation of misanthropy documented in Esth 3:8 in the form of separation from other peoples: in the context of the events at the Persian court narrated there it serves as the spark for political persecution of Diaspora Judaism, intended to end in a genocide (Esth 3:13).

129. Cicero, *De officiis* I, 29. English translation at http://penelope.uchicago.edu/Thayer/E/Roman/Texts/Cicero/de_Officiis/1B*.html. See Antonie Wlosok, *Rom und die Christen* (1970), 20–21, also on the translation and the movement from Greek μισανθρωπία to the expression *odium humani generis* (p. 20), as previously pointed out by Eduard Zeller, "Das odium generis humani der Christen" (1891): 356–67. Stenger, *"Gebt dem Kaiser, was des Kaisers ist . . . !"* (1988), 106, adduces this Ciceronian definition as the juridical background in his discussion of the trial for ἀσέβεια of Flavius Clemens and his wife Domitilla by Domitian (Dio Cassius 67, 14, 1–3; Suetonius, *Domitilla* 10–15). The accusation of "living like a Jew," that is, misanthrophy and atheism, brought about the execution of Flavius Clemens and the banishment of Domitilla. See Stenger, 105–8; Giorgio Jossa, *Jews or Christians?* (2006), 142–43.

During the Neronian persecution a similar accusation was hurled at the Christians in Rome in connection with the burning of the city (*odio humani generis convicti sunt*), for which they were executed in 64 C.E., as Tacitus reports.[130] It is clear from his account (44,3) that because of the origins of this "most mischievous superstition (*exitiabilis superstitio*)" and Christ, the one responsible for it, in "Judea, the first source of the evil (*per Iudaeam, originem eius mali*)," Christianity was to be regarded as a Jewish sect,[131] and the "Christiani" were therefore to be attacked as Jews. It is obvious that from Rome's perspective the persecution and indictment of Jewish and Christian persons who were suspected of not being completely loyal to the state, as far as indictment and sanctions were concerned, was, in the first century C.E., one and the same process as persecution of Christians and Jews, and thus cannot be distinguished phenomenologically.[132]

Similarly, the accusation of atheism as a crime against official religion (ἀσέβεια) was, as early as the ἀσέβεια trials in Greek democracy, most prominent of which was that of Socrates, a means to be used against enemies of the state (at that time these were philosophers).[133] Under the Roman emperors there was "no [need] that there be armed or even public propagandistic activities against Roman rule; in given circumstances one could for the most trivial reasons be charged with 'crimen laesae maiestatis' (ἀσέβεια / *impietas*)," and capital punishment could result.[134] The reign of Domitian in particular brought with it an avalanche of accusations of *lèse majesté*, especially in connection with the institution of the *fiscus Judaicus*, more intensely activated under his rule; this was a department responsible for collecting the special tax on Jews that was imposed after the destruction of the Jerusalem

130. Tacitus, *Annales* XV, 44, 2–4. For interpretation, philological and historical discussion see esp. Wlosok, *Rom und die Christen* (1970), 7–26; Paul Keresztes, "The Imperial Roman Government and the Christian Church" (1979), 247–57 (with bibliography); also Helga Botermann, *Das Judenedikt des Kaisers Claudius* (1996).

131. *Ann.* 44, 3. Wilhelm Nestle, "*Odium humani generis*" (1927), 91–93; Luise Schottroff, "Die Gegenwart in der Apokalyptik der synoptischen Evangelien" (1983), 85. Botermann, *Judenedikt*, 182, writes that the "derivation from the Jewish criminal Christus, the source of the evil in Judea, and the accusation of *odium humani generis*, which was an anti-Jewish *topos*" create the impression that Tacitus saw the "Christiani" as a part of Judaism.

132. Schottroff, "Gegenwart," esp. 82–86.

133. On this see Wilhelm Nestle, "Asebieprozesse," (1950), 735–40; Erich Fascher, "Der Vorwurf der Gottlosigkeit" (1963), 78–96.

134. Wolfgang Stegemann, *Zwischen Synagoge und Obrigkeit* (1991), 233; ibid. on Dio Cassius, who referred to *lèse majesté* as ἀσέβεια (e.g., 68,1,2; 70,9.2) and the punishment for the *crimen laesae maiestatis* beginning with Augustus (234); see Schottroff, "Gegenwart," 84, and on the whole subject Theodor Mommsen, *Römisches Strafrecht* (1899; repr. 1955), 537–94, esp. 537ff.; for the imperial cult and the tightening of the laws regarding *lèse majesté* under Domitian see also Marlis Gielen, *Tradition und Theologie neutestamentlicher Haustafelethik* (1990), 424ff.

Temple, for the support of the temple of Jupiter in Rome. This reappropriation of the original Temple tax was put in place as a means of humiliating the Jews.[135] It appears that under Domitian the "Jewish way of life" and *lèse majesté* were seen as more closely associated, as a note in Dio Cassius (68,2) suggests: from the time of Nerva, Domitian's successor, "it was no longer permitted to accuse anyone of *lèse majesté* (ἀσεβείας) or a Jewish way of life (Ἰουδαϊκοῦ βίου)." In Wolfgang Stegemann's estimation this means that "the accusation of living like a Jew was placed on a level with *lèse majesté*," that it became a matter of "a close material association,'"[136] and that this became a dangerous combination of accusations for Jewish, Jewish-Christian, and Gentile Christian people.[137] The crimes of ἀσέβεια, atheism, and *odium humani generis* should be placed on the same level; all were instruments of denunciation and accusation.[138] "In the first century officials did not set these accusations and inquisitions against Jews and Christians in motion of themselves; they came about only as a result of *delatio* / denunciation.... The role of these accusations or denunciations in the daily life of the Roman Empire seems to have been substantial."[139]

The fundamental danger of these anti-Jewish labels, which lies in the ever-present possibility that they could be used for denunciation, caused Philo and Josephus to make broad attempts to refute them, and especially to describe the

135. For the *fiscus Iudaicus* see, among others, M. S. Ginsburg, "*Fiscus Judaicus*" (1930/31); Wolfgang Pöhlmann, "Die heidnische, jüdische und christliche Opposition gegen Domitian" (1966), 247–306; Paul Keresztes, "The Jews, the Christians, and the Emperor Domitian" (1973); idem, "The Imperial Roman Government" (1979), 258ff.; Edith Mary Smallwood, *Jews under Roman Rule* (²1981), 371ff.; L. A. Thompson, "Domitian and the Jewish Tax" (1982); Bickhoff-Böttcher, "Das Judentum" (1984), 275–302; Stenger, *"Gebt dem Kaiser, was des Kaisers ist . . . !"* (1988), 79–113; Helmut Schwier, *Tempel und Tempelzerstörung* (1989), 317ff.; Günter Stemberger, "Die Juden im Römischen Reich" (1990), 15ff.; Martin Goodman, "Nerva, the 'fiscus Judaicus' and Jewish Identity," (1989); idem, *Mission and Conversion* (1994), 121ff.; Wolfgang Stegemann, *Zwischen Synagoge und Obrigkeit* (1991), 221ff.; 244ff.; 278ff.; Jossa, *Jews or Christians?* (2006), 138–44, and now the study by Marius Heemstra, *The Fiscus Judaicus and the Parting of the Ways* (2010), which primarily studies the role of the *fiscus* within Jewish-Christian social history as a major factor in the "parting of the ways"; see also below at 6.3.3. n. 116.

136. Stegemann, *Zwischen Synagoge und Obrigkeit* (1991), 244.

137. For this set of problems see, among the sources in n. 127a, only Keresztes, "The Jews" (1973), which illustrates the controversial nature of the charge in the example of the consul Flavius Clemens and his wife Domitilla, who were accused of "atheism" and of practicing "Jewish customs" (Dio Cassius 67,14,1–2), precisely on the question whether they are to be regarded as "Christian" (thus Keresztes, 7ff.) or "Jewish" (thus, e.g., Bickhoff-Böttcher, "Das Judentum," 121ff.

138. See Schottroff, "Gegenwart," 84–85.

139. Ibid., 84.

philanthropic features of the Torah,[140] which deliberately includes strangers and extends even to animals belonging to others, in fact, even those of enemies (Exod 23:4–5).[141] Philo directly addresses assertions that Israel is misanthropic: "But these men have established these enactments with reference to human beings, but this lawgiver of ours, going beyond them all, extends his humanity even to brute beasts, in order that . . . we being accustomed to practise all the things ordained in his laws, may display an excessive degree of humanity, abstaining from pursuing any one, or even from annoying them in retaliation for any annoyance which we have received at their hands . . ."[142] In light of this exemplary Jewish argumentation against unbridled accusations of misanthropy it is difficult to read 1 Thess 2:15 as part of an "internal Jewish" conflict, as is sometimes suggested in order to make the text seem less difficult.[143] For, whoever wrote it, it refers to evil accusations of non-Jewish origin; moreover, these are now uttered before a completely non-Jewish-Christian forum, as is clear from 1 Thess 1:9: the community has turned from idols to the living and true God, and accordingly would not have belonged formerly to a synagogue congregation.[144]

Overall we must conclude that "Misanthropy and atheism were . . . in Roman opinion only two sides of one and the same coin and ultimately led to a crime against the state."[145] Thus what we have in 1 Thess 2:15 is nothing less than "a reason for persecution of Jews by Roman authorities," in that "the Jews" are accused of

140. The major works are Josephus, *Contra Apionem*; Philo, *In Flaccum* and *Legatio ad Gaium*; for an extended illustration of this strategy of refutation and description of Judaism for non-Jewish people, using Josephus, *Contr. Ap.*, as an example, see Christine Gerber, *Ein Bild des Judentums* (1997); see also Günther Baumbach, "Antisemitismus II" (1978), 119–22, and Dautzenberg, "Mt 5,43c" (1988), 65–77.

141. These dimensions of the Torah have also been repeatedly overlooked in the course of its centuries-long defamation by Christians, especially Protestants. The task of valuing them and introducing a positive Christian reception of the content of the Torah remains largely unfulfilled thus far. (See the work of Frank Crüsemann, *The Torah. Theology and Social History of Old Testament Law* [Edinburgh: T & T Clark, 1996], as well as his *Maßstab: Tora. Israels Weisung für christliche Ethik* [Gütersloh: Chr. Kaiser/Gütersloher Verlagshaus, ^{2}2004]).

142. Philo, *Virtues* 140, in *Works* (1993), 654. Thus Dautzenberg, "Mt 5,43c," 72–73; see ibid., 69ff., for a general treatment of Philo's "On Philanthropy," ΠΕΡΙ ΦΙΛΑΝΘΡΩΠΙΑΣ, *Virt.* 51–168; for Philo's strategy for refuting the charge of misanthropy see also Naoto Umemoto, "Juden, 'Heiden' und das Menschengeschlecht," (1994), 22–51, at 43–47.

143. Thus, e.g., Broer, "'Antisemitismus'" (1983), 87ff.; P.-G. Müller, "Judenbeschimpfung" (1989); Hagner, "Paul's Quarrel" (1993), 134; Wick, "I Thess 2,13–16," (1994), 19ff.

144. For 1 Thess 1:9 as a motif in conversion preaching addressed to pagan people see below at 3.3.4 n. 90 and 5.2.4 n. 111.

145. Stenger, "'*Gebt dem Kaiser, was des Kaisers ist . . . !*'" 100.

"disloyalty to the Roman state."[146] Here lies the key to a social-historical and political analysis of 1 Thessalonians in light of the relationship between Jewish and non-Jewish groups within the Christian communities.[147]

2.4.2 *A key New Testament assertion: "The Jews killed Jesus."*

The motif of Jews' "misanthropy" and lack of favor before God, drawn from the pagan anti-Jewish arsenal, are surrounded in 1 Thess 2:15–16 by accusations that derive from the history of Israel and of Jesus as well as the contemporary mission to the Gentiles: they killed Jesus and the prophets and "drove us out";[148] they prevented "us" from speaking to non-Jewish people (ἔθνεσιν) to save them. With this the accusation of misanthropy is applied to the current mission to the Gentiles by means of the grammatical construction[149] and thus made concrete; it is hard to see this as defusing the situation.[150]

It is impossible to find anywhere in the New Testament, in Paul's writing or elsewhere, an apodictic statement identical to the formulation in 1 Thess 2:15: "the Jews, who killed . . . the Lord Jesus" (τῶν Ἰουδαίων, τῶν καὶ τὸν κύριον ἀποκτεινάντων Ἰησοῦν), a fact that can be quickly established. As a rule it is the opposite that is asserted: "Nonetheless, the statement that the Jews had killed Jesus appears frequently in the New Testament. That is the case above all in the missionary speeches in Acts, but it is also—at least in what quickly comes to mind—the basic idea of the parable of the wicked vinedressers in Mark 12:1–9 *par.*"[151] Statements like these obscure the fact that a lexical comparison can produce no real verbal parallels.

For Paul we must assert, first of all, that he otherwise never speaks of "the Jews" (οἱ Ἰουδαῖοι) with the article, in a pejorative sense; indeed, he primarily speaks of "Jews" in general without using the article. The most frequent form is the contrast of "Jews" and "Greeks" or "nations" (Ἕλλην / Ἕλληνες / ἔθνη): Rom 1:16; 2:9, 10;

146. Luise Schottroff, "Antijudaismus im Neuen Testament" (1984), in eadem, *Befreiungserfahrungen* (1990), 222–23; here she assumes the Pauline authorship of the text; see eadem, "Gegenwart" (1983 / 1990), 84–85.

147. See the social-historical framework above in 1.4 and the beginning of this second chapter.

148. For plural authors ("us") see 3.1 below. According to Bauer / Aland, ἐκδιώκω, "drive out," "sharply persecute" (in the NT otherwise only at Luke 11:49 in some mss.) is here, strangely enough, in the aorist, that is, "the Jews drove us out." This shifts the persecution of the missionaries to the time of Jesus' execution; see Dibelius, *Thessalonicher* (^{3}1937), 12.

149. The "hindering" of the Gentile mission is a present participle subordinated to the previous negative statements; see Haacker, "Elemente" (1988), 410.

150. Thus, e.g., Michel, "Fragen" (1967), 57; Marxsen, *Thessalonicher* (1979), 50; Kampling, "Skizze," 1993), 212, on this motif in ancient church authors (see n. 169 below; Légasse, "Paul et les Juifs" 581ff.

151. Holtz, *Thessalonicher* (1986), 104; similarly Simpson, "Problems" (1990), 56.

3:9, 29; 9:24; 10:12; 1 Cor 1:22, 23, 24; 10:32; 12:13; Gal 3:28.[152] One of these passages in particular, 2 Cor 11:24, where Paul speaks of mistreatment by Jews, does not say that "the Jews" beat him, but "Jews," and here that can only mean "some Jews," that is, members of Jewish judicial institutions, not the people as a whole. Only three times does Paul use the article in connection with Ἰουδαῖος, but in two of those instances the sense is altogether positive. In Rom 3:1 he asks in the singular about the advantage of "the Jews" (τοῦ Ἰουδαίου), with the prompt response: "Much, in every way!" (v. 2). In 1 Cor 9:20 the subject is how to win Jewish people for his gospel, how to be "a Jew" or "Jewish" in relation to "the Jews." Here, within the sentence, the article is used once and then omitted; nothing bad is said about the "Jews." Moreover, for Paul the Jewish people who have become "Christian" clearly continue to be "Jewish": for when, third, it is said in Gal 2:13 that "the other Jews" (οἱ λοιποὶ Ἰουδαῖοι) with Peter behaved hypocritically, the reference is certainly to Jewish-Christians and thus by no means the whole (rest of the) people. Such a negative statement about "the Jews" as a people, especially in the form of such a cumulative series as in 1 Thess 2:15–16, is found nowhere in Paul's other writings. Besides, Paul otherwise does not place the guilt or the principal responsibility for Jesus' death on "the Jews." Apart from the fact that, when speaking of Jesus' death, he always speaks of "dying" (ἀποθνῄσκω) rather than "killing" (ἀποκτείνω) (e.g., Rom 5:6, 8; 8:34; 14:9, 15; 1 Cor 8:11; 15:3; 2 Cor 5:14; Gal 2:21)[153] or "the cross" (σταυρός) or "crucifying" (σταυρόω) (1 Cor 1:17, 23; 2:2, 8; 2 Cor 13:4; Gal 3:1; 5:24; 6:12, 14; Phil 2:8), he attributes responsibility for Jesus' execution to "the rulers of this world" (τῶν ἀρχόντων τοῦ αἰῶνος τούτου), 1 Cor 2:8, that is, the world power Rome, corresponding to the historical facts.[154]

Besides this, the parable of the "wicked tenants" (Mark 12:1–9 *parr.*) does not literally say that "the Jews" killed Jesus, either in the course of the parable itself or on the level of narrated reception. Those who want to seize Jesus and who apply the parable to themselves (12:12) are, on the basis of 11:27, only the chief priests, scribes, and elders, not the whole nation.[155] Anyone who wants to see in 1 Thess 2:15–16 elements of a "deuteronomistic prophetic speech" analogous to the one in

152. Other instances in Paul without the article: Rom 2:17, 28, 29; 2 Cor 11:24; Gal 2:14. For the use of the article with "names of nations" as a whole see Blass/Debrunner/Rehkopf §262, though in my opinion the missing article before "Jews" in Paul's usage mainly indicates the significance of a unique difference between them and other nations in the sense of "people like the Jews / Greeks . . . ," as the authors suppose is the case only for the names of non-Jewish nations.

153. Also 1 Thess 4:14; 5:10.

154. See Gerd Theissen and Annette Merz, *Der historische Jesus* (1998), 388–414 [English: *The Historical Jesus* (1998), 467–69, at 469].

155. On this see esp. Willy Schottroff, "Das Gleichnis von den bösen Weingärtnern" (1996), 40–41; in the context of the parable the "leading classes" of the Jews are warned; cp. Luise Schottroff, *The Parables of Jesus*, trans. Linda M. Maloney (Minneapolis: Fortress Press, 2006), 15–28, esp. 22–23; Tania Oldenhage, "Spiralen der Gewalt" (2007), 352–66.

Mark 12:1–9[156] must also emphasize that Mark 12 does not speak explicitly of "the Jews," as is the case in 1 Thess 2:14–16. The motif of killing the prophets appears in the gospels only in the course of speeches addressed to particular Jewish groups and institutions. Thus in Matt 23:34 and Luke 11:47 the address is to scribes and Pharisees; in Luke 13:34 Jesus laments over Jerusalem and its inhabitants.[157] Matthew 23:32 does *not* say that "the Jews" have "filled up the measure" (πληρώσατε τὸ μέτρον) of their "ancestors,"[158] as could easily be asserted in light of its similarity to 1 Thess 2:16 (εἰς τὸ ἀναπληρῶσαι αὐτῶν ἁμαρτίας). Rather, the accusation again falls on the scribes and Pharisees, only a part of Israel. Another important difference from other passages such as Gen 15:16; Dan 8:23 (Theodotion and LXX); 2 Macc 6:14, and even Matt 23:32 is that only in 1 Thess 2:16 is it said that the mass of sins, and precisely the mass of Israel's sins, has in the meantime been quantitatively (more than) filled up.[159]

The often-asserted analogies to 1 Thess 2:15–16 in the "mission discourses" of Acts prove to be very much weaker versions of the accusation of having killed Jesus. First, it is important to note that these are for the most part critical but at the same time recruiting sermons "within Judaism, with the goal of repentance and return."[160] Peter's Pentecost sermon, in which he tells the "people of Israel" (Acts 2:22) that "you crucified and killed [Jesus] by the hands of those outside the law" (2:23; cp. 2:36), has immediate success among the inhabitants of Jerusalem as a call to repentance, resulting in a mass baptism of three thousand persons (2:41) and the beginning of the common life of the first community (2:42–47). Then, in Peter's speech in the Temple, we find the reproach: "you killed the Author of life" (3:15) together with the admission that this was done out of ignorance and can be retrieved through penance and confession of Jesus as Messiah (3:17–20). In his persuasive narrative exegesis of Luke-Acts, Günter Wasserberg also emphasizes that "For Luke, the murder of Jesus is

156. See the table in Steck, *Israel* (1967), 276; and see above at 2.2.3.

157. The motif of killing the prophets in Rom 11:3 is a citation of Elijah's lament in 1 Kgs 19:10 (LXX), enhanced in Rom 11:4 with 1 Kgs 19:18 with reference to the "remnant" of the 7,000 who did not worship Baal. Here again it was not the whole people of Israel who murdered the prophets. Formulations like these, arbitrarily given the author's own meaning in statements about "the Jews as notorious murderers and persecutors of the messengers of God" and "Israel that murdered the prophets" (Holtz, *Thessalonicher* [1986], 111–12; cp. Riesner, *Paul's Early Period*, 352), or cited and generalized as being in agreement with the thought of 1 Thessalonians should just stop.

158. For the idea of an eschatological mass of sin in Judaism see Rainer Stuhlmann, *Das eschatologische Maß* (1983), 93–98, 103ff. on Matt 23:32.

159. Simpson, "Problems" (1990), 45. See Kraus, *Volk Gottes* (1996), 152: "Such acerbity is unique within early Jewish literature." Most exegetes miss the special character of the content of 1 Thess 2:16 in this regard; thus, e.g., Légasse, "Paul et les Juifs" (1977), 584–85.

160. Jürgen Ebach, "Antisemitismus," (1988), 500; cp. John R. Wilch, "Jüdische Schuld am Tod Jesu?" (1980), 236–49; Stephen H. Wilson, ed., *Anti-Judaism in Early Christianity. Vol. 2* (1986).

not unforgivable! The way to repentance lies open for the Jews, because God has raised Jesus and exalted him to God's right hand, in order to enable *Israel's* repentance for the forgiveness of sins. . . . Thousands of people come and are baptized" (Acts 2:41, 47; 4:4; 5;14–16).[161] Even in the face of what are certainly the harshest words in Stephen's speech, saying that those he addresses are "betrayers and murderers" of Jesus (προδόται καὶ φονεῖς ἐγένεσθε),[162] we must note that it is spoken to the Council (7:52). Nowhere in Acts is there a definitive statement that "the Jews killed Jesus" in connection with the proclamation or assertion of divine wrath without any possibility of repentance. To the very end it is about the "hope of Israel" (28:20), preached even by the imprisoned Paul, in chains before the Roman public and the Jews present in Rome.[163] In contrast, 1 Thess 2:14–16 represents an attitude that Earl J. Richard characterizes as ". . . contrary to the texts of Paul, Matthew, or Luke which foster hope for a repentant Israel, insist on its continued role as God's people, or leave open the door for a Jewish mission or more mysteriously for God's salvific activity . . . ."[164]

Even the Gospel of John, with its stereotypical remarks that "the Jews" (οἱ Ἰουδαῖοι) "sought to kill" Jesus (ἐζήτουν αὐτὸν . . . ἀποκτεῖναι, 5:16, 18; 7:1),[165] is unable to call the execution a Jewish deed, but must admit that "the Jews" themselves say to Pilate "we are not permitted to put anyone to death" (18:31). This matches the fact that the final judgment is issued by Pilate (19:16) and must be carried out by his soldiers (19:23).[166]

161. Günter Wasserberg, *Aus Israels Mitte* (1998), 213–32, at 214 (with bibliography).

162. Other statements on the killing of Jesus are found at Acts 4:10; 5:30; 10:29; 13:28.

163. For Acts 28:16–31 see, besides Jacob Jervell, *Apostelgeschichte* (1998), 622–31, especially Wasserberg, *Aus Israels Mitte*, 71–118, 352ff., with a clear critique (ibid., 95ff.) of Jervell and his modified thesis of rejection, which he produced despite all his efforts on behalf of a new, not-anti-Jewish understanding of Luke's work. For him the pericope is "a hermeneutical key for the overall understanding of Luke-Acts" (p. 114): "God's salvation from now on is for Jews and ἔθνη alike, but from of old the communication of God's salvation—as well as that of Jesus and his witnesses—comes first to Israel" (p. 115).

164. Richard, *1 Thessalonians* (1995), 127.

165. See, in the same sense, John 7:19, 20, 25; 8:37, 40; 11:53; cp. the references to Jesus' crucifixion and plans to kill him that run throughout John, esp. in David Granskou's overview ("Anti-Judaism in the Passion Accounts of the Fourth Gospel" [1986], 201–16). For the usage "the Jews" see esp. Klaus Wengst, *Bedrängte Gemeinde und verherrlichter Christus* (^{3}1990), esp. 55–74, 128–52, with the thesis that this way of speaking arose out of conflicts between Jewish-Christian communities and formative rabbinic Judaism at the time when the Fourth Gospel was being written, conflicts that were projected back to the time of Jesus; see idem, *Das Johannesevangelium*, 1 (2000), 21–28.

166. According to the Fourth Gospel as well, Jesus was executed by Pilate, that is, the Romans; for this and the tendency in Johannine exegesis to excuse and depoliticize Pilate see Luise Schottroff, "Die Schuld 'der Juden' und die Entschuldung des Pilatus" (1990), esp. 331–32, 334–43, 448ff.; see also Theissen and Merz, *Der historische Jesus* (1996), 394–98 [*The Historical Jesus*, 603–9]; Wengst, *Johannesevangelium* 2 (2001), 195–272.

Our preliminary conclusion must be that in 1 Thess 2:15–16 we "scarcely seem to be facing the nervous and excited reaction of Paul, e.g., in a situation of persecution . . . but a polemic against Jews that has been consciously adopted and stylized."[167] We are faced with an accumulation of anti-Jewish expressions unequaled in the New Testament. Nowhere else do we find allusions to two of the most common Jewish-hating *topoi* in the Greco-Roman world, tending toward the accusation of crimes against the state, nor is there any other place in the New Testament writings that simply says "the Jews killed Jesus." But the real innovation that characterizes the text consists in the melding of motifs from two different sources, namely, pagan- and Christian-motivated polemic against the Jews that also makes use of the inter-Jewish motif of the persecution and killing of the prophets. The nature of such a composition must not be underestimated and defanged, as Klaus Haacker emphasizes, for "the adoption of a jargon always also [contributes] to its spread . . . often even to the fixing of the implications of its content because of the plausibility of its new application." A high price is paid: "he [Paul] has here given new arguments to the existing anti-Judaism of antiquity and so became accessory to the survival of this anti-Judaism beyond antiquity and Greco-Roman paganism."[168] This translation is accomplished by 1 Thess 2:14–16 through a particular concentration of motifs, for which there is also no real parallel even in later times.

However, there are comparable texts from the church fathers, who occasionally combine their escalating sermons on supposed Jewish responsibility for the death of Jesus with accusations of atheism and misanthropy:[169] for example, Justin († ca. 165): "you slew the Christ . . . you hate and murder us" (*Dial.* 133,6);[170] "And a vast

167. Broer, "'Antisemitismus,'" (1983), 86.

168. Haacker, "Elemente" (1988), 411; for Richard, *1 Thessalonians* (1995), 18, this is evidence that the passage was composed later: "It is especially the accusation of 'hostility against the rest of humanity' which indicates non-pauline authorship."

169. Kampling, in his sketch of the historical exegesis of 1 Thess 2:14–16 ("Skizze," 1993), thinks that ancient church authors were not linking to "a pagan anti-Semitism" in their interpretation of this text, since they understood Jewish misanthropy solely in terms of obstruction of Christian preaching (p. 212). But did that kind of "Christianization," on the part of these authors and their readers mean that in actual fact no connection was or could be made with corresponding expressions from other sources? Is a general anti-Jewish accusation more honorable if it receives a "Christian" foundation? Or is it not instead true that in the process what is "Christian," now adorned accordingly, falls to the same Jew-hating level as the words of non-Christians? This question needs to be kept in mind for the entire exegesis of 1 Thess 2:14–16; see Haacker's arguments.

170. These are only a few quotations from Justin's endless anti-Jewish invective; for his polemic as a whole see Heinz Schreckenberg, *Adversus-Judaeos-Texte* (1982), 182–200; Schreckenberg's work collects excerpts from anti-Jewish polemic in ancient church and medieval sources in more than 500 closely-printed pages. For "Adversus-Judaeos" literature in the ancient church (and Middle Ages) see the collection by Ora Limor and Guy G. Stroumsa, *Contra Iudaeos* (1996), including Michael Mach on Justin's *Dialogue with Trypho*,

multitude in your nation are convicted of being of this kind, imbibing doctrines of bitterness and godlessness, but spurning the word of God" (*Dial.* 120,2); "But the highest pitch of your wickedness lies in this, that you hate the Righteous One, and slew Him; and so treat those who have received from Him all that they are and have, and who are pious, righteous, and humane" (*Apol. I*, 36; *Dial.* 136).[171] John Chrysostom also († 407), who blames the Jewish people massively for the murder of Christ,[172] calls them "enemies of God" (PG 48, 935, 937) and says repeatedly that "the Jews" are "godless" and "godlessness" belongs to them (PG 48, 850, 853, 869, etc.). Beyond all that, they are the "the common disgrace and infection of the whole world" (PG 48, 852).[173]

These few examples may suffice to show that 1 Thess 2:15–16 anticipates, in concentrated form, the language and content of the anti-Jewish writings of the ancient church's authors, and in this sense it must be called a piece of New Testament Adversus-Judaeos literature. We should again emphasize that here, as in the church fathers, what is presented is not *internal Jewish* polemic; in light of 1 Thess 1:9 the community addressed is to be seen as exclusively Gentile Christian, or at least is depicted that way from the author's perspective.[174] Likewise, in their "we" statements in 2:14–16 the authors do not include any Jewish people; these are clearly "they," a different group from their own.[175] Thus it emerges quite

with a focus on discovering traces of "Jewish believers" in ancient church authors; cp. Skarsaune, "The History of Jewish Believers in the Early Centuries" (2007), 745–81, esp. 749ff.: the function of anti-Jewish outbursts lies in the attempt to influence a broad local and temporal peaceful religio-social life of "Jews" and "Christians" together.

171. Schreckenberg, *Adversus-Judaeos-Texte*, 187, 197.

172. PG 48, 845, 847, 849, 850, 851, 852, 853, etc. Cp. Schreckenberg, *Adversus-Judaeos-Texte*, 322–23; ibid., 320–29 on Chrysostom's polemic against the Jews in general, and, making some further distinctions in the evaluation of Chrysostom's anti-Judaism, Adolf M. Ritter, "Chrysostomos und die Juden" (1990), with bibliography.

173. Schreckenberg, *Adversus-Judaeos-Texte*, 326–27.

174. A Jewish identity of the community addressed can usually be asserted only by including the events depicted in Acts 17; in the process, the contradiction to the actual information in 1 Thessalonians must be harmonized or ignored, as, for example, Gottfried Schimanowski has done quite clearly and in a few words ("Abgrenzung und Identitätsfindung" [1994], 300–1; see above at 2.2.7). That 1 Thessalonians is directed to a completely Gentile Christian community is emphasized, e.g., throughout by Jürgen Becker, "Die Erwählung der Völker" (1986), 82–101; in fact, he says that the letter is "quite consciously oriented to Gentile Christianity" (p. 97); see further below at 2.4.3 and 3.3.4.

175. "Surprisingly, 2:13–16 employs the language of pagan anti-Judaism without revealing the Jewishness of its purported authors" (Roberts, "Images" [1992], 154; Roberts tends to posit an interpolation but remains undecided; see 149–56). Richard, *1 Thessalonians* (1995), is convinced there is an interpolation: "The author is post-Pauline and is writing from a Gentile-Christian perspective which one should characterize as anti-Jewish" (p. 127); cp. Michel, "Fragen" 1967), 53.

unmistakably that here "an image of Judaism as an entity apart from one's own sphere of reference in faith and community"[176] is being projected; this will be developed below. In this way the text shows itself to be a deliberate and considered composition for a very particular purpose, which will now be explored.

2.4.3 Parallel structure and functional accusation: "The Jews" as example

These few verses, 1 Thess 2:14–16, give the impression of having been assembled out of all possible sources as the most negative things that could be said about Israel and Judaism. There are even elements that in their original context were actually aimed at Israel's enemies, but here they are reversed and applied to Judaism itself. This twisting of individual motifs results in a still further sharpening of the hostile attack on Judaism. For one thing, there is the idea of the mass of sins belonging to the nations; according to Gen 15:16 the Amorites have not yet filled it.[177] In contrast, 1 Thessalonians declares that the mass of Jews' sins is full, and in fact this "full"filment is going on constantly (πάντοτε, 2:16): the vessel has in a sense been filled to overflowing, to use a similar image.[178] We can observe the same reversal in comparison to the parallel text in Testament of Levi 6.11. Here, in almost the same words, God's wrath is applied to Judaism, whereas in t.Levi it falls on the non-Jewish inhabitants of Shechem: ἔφθασε δὲ (ἐπ') αὐτοὺς ἡ ὀργὴ τοῦ θεοῦ εἰς τέλος. As regards the meaning contained in 1 Thess 2:16c it is significant, independent of the question of literary dependence or the process of tradition of the formula, that t.Levi 6.11 uses a synonymous expression to refer to a real destruction, physical death in Shechem. So the statement, with these concepts, can mean something of that sort. Hence it seems likely that the choice of words in 1 Thessalonians does not exclude the possibility that the authors may have had in mind a thoroughly visible and historical event of judgment.[179] There is a method in the application of the technique of inversion in 1 Thessalonians that, for example, turns a statement about Israel's enemies back on Israel itself, because basically 2:14–16 is a single reversal, as we will show, for the purpose of masking the real statement on the surface. Finally, the *function*

176. Ebach, "Antisemitismus" (1988), 500.

177. See Stuhlmann, *Das eschatologische Maß* (1993), 93–98, 103ff. on 1 Thess 2:16 and Matt 23:32. Matthew's gospel applies the mass of sins to the scribes and Pharisees, or their ancestors (Matt 23:29–33), and calls in the imperative for fulfillment. Both the addressees and the form of the statement in 1 Thess deviate clearly from that; on this, see Simpson, "Problems" (1990), 45; Kraus, *Volk Gottes* (1996), 151ff.

178. See ibid.: "The real point of the expressions, however, lies in the reversal of the idea of an eschatological measure and its application to Israel" (p. 153).

179. See Ibid., 152–53; for the comparison between 1 Thess 2:16c and t.Levi 6.11 the most recent extensive treatment is in Lamp, "Is Paul Anti-Jewish?" 414–27; his thesis is that neither text announces the complete destruction of all members of the respective populations, "the Jews" or the inhabitants of Shechem (p. 427).

of the Jew-hating diatribe, which will now be described, reveals its third anti-Jewish dimension.

Once again we will begin our examination of the occasion and possible cause for this multi-dimensional short sermon "*adversus Judaeos*," whose acerbity could scarcely be surpassed, if at all, with Paul W. Schmiedel's question: "But why, after all, this vigorous diatribe against the Jews, if the persecution had come from the Gentiles (συμφ[υλετῶν])?"[180] That question brings us to a discussion of the strange demographic concept of community that underlies 1 Thess 2:14–16. With the aid of the idea of imitation,[181] first, a broad parallelization of far-distant communities is achieved (2:14): "For you, brothers and sisters, became imitators of the churches of God in Christ Jesus that are in Judea, for you suffered the same things from your own compatriots as they did from the Jews." Thus the "churches of God in Christ Jesus that are in Judea" (τῶν ἐκκλησιῶν τοῦ θεοῦ τῶν οὐσῶν ἐν τῇ Ἰουδαίᾳ ἐν Χριστῷ Ἰησοῦ)[182] and in Thessalonica, as well as their specific persecutors, "the Jews" and "your own compatriots," are on the same level. The suffering at the hands of their own people in Thessalonica corresponds to the suffering under "the Jews" in Judea. Here one should note the emphasis on "your own" (ἰδίων) compatriots, which explicitly underscores the common membership in one nation in that place,[183] and hence the difference from the people in Judea. This is thus, essentially, about distinguishing between Jewish and non-Jewish people.[184] In this way something amazing is expressed within the framework of the first early Christian era: Jewish congregations are at home in Judea and non-Jewish ones outside Judea, in this case in Greek Thessalonica. Correspondingly, "the Jews" are restricted to a particular region, namely, the province of Judea,[185] since on the basis of the parallel structure of the sentence they must be the "compatriots" of the congregations in Judea, where also the persecution that had fallen on the senders, "us," was localized (2:15, ἐκδιωξάντων, aorist participle). Thus the individual communities appear as ethnically homogeneous islands in a sea of burning hostility from the mass of their compatriots, also regarded as homogeneous masses. There seems to be no thought of congregations made up of Jews, Greeks, and Romans; otherwise the parallelism does not work. This is something altogether unknown in the world of Paul, and

180. Schmiedel, *Die Briefe an die Thessalonicher* (^{2}1892), 21.

181. On this see above at 2.3, and at greater length below at 3.3.4.

182. For this overburdened construction whereby the communities in Judea "are, in fact, of an indeterminate makeup," see Holtz, *Thessalonicher* (1986), 100. Otherwise Paul speaks of Christians in the land of Israel solely as the "church of God" (1 Cor 15:9; Gal 1:13) or the "churches of Judea that are in Christ" (Gal 1:22).

183. See von Dobschütz, *Thessalonicher-Briefe* (1909), 109–10.

184. See Pearson, "1 Thessalonians 2,13–16" (1971), 86, with reference to the corresponding commentary by Theodore of Mopsuestia.

185. For the inclination in 1 Thessalonians to introduce the names of Roman provinces see more below at 3.3.2. The geographical localization of "the Jews" presented here is addressed by, among others, Weatherly, "Authenticity" (1991), 85–86.

even of Acts, where, as we know, the people who made up the Jewish diaspora communities, for example in Greece (Acts 16:13–16; 17:10–16; 18:4–9) and in Thessalonica (17:1–9!), were part of the core of the growing Messianic Christian communities. Does the text of 1 Thessalonians say that there were no Jewish people in Thessalonica, or does it not consider them worthy of mention?

> Since a complete absence of Jews among the population of this great Greek port city is not very probable historically,[186] there have been repeated attempts to show that the word συμφυλέται in 1 Thess 2:14 could describe both non-Jewish Greek and Jewish citizens. But that is only possible through a harmonization with Acts 17:1–9, according to which the successful preaching in the synagogue, and especially the conflict with "the Jews" narrated there, must be transposed to a time after 1 Thess 2:14–16 and then supports this interpretation.[187] In the NT συμφυλέτης is a *hapax legomenon*, and it is a very rare word in secular Greek. In 1 Thess 2:14 does it have the usual meaning of "fellow member of a [tribe, clan, nation]" (from φυλή, "tribe, clan") or "fellow-countryman/woman," also and particularly in the ethnic sense and, metaphorically, also with reference to membership in a societal level or class?[188] Christoph von Brocke's suggestion seems plausible: he sees in the συμφυλέται a reference to the city *phylae* of

186. Archaeological witnesses are confined to an inscription from the first century c.e. (CIJ I, 693d = IG X / 2,1 72), though its Jewish identity is not fully certain. See Charles F. Edson, *Inscriptiones Thessalonicae et viciniae* (Berlin: de Gruyter, 1972), 36; cp. Winfried Elliger, *Paulus in Griechenland. Philippi, Thessaloniki, Athen, Korinth* (Stuttgart: Katholisches Bibelwerk, 1987), 91–92; Christoph vom Brocke, *Thessaloniki: Stadt des Kassander und Gemeinde des Paulus. Eine frühe christliche Gemeinde in ihrer heidnischen Umwelt* (WUNT 2d ser. 125; Tübingen: Mohr Siebeck, 2001), 217; Jewish sarcophagi; a Samaritan inscription (CIJ $I^2$693a = IG X / 2,1 789) with the Aaronide blessing (Num 6:22–26) from the fourth century allows us to conclude to the existence there of a Samaritan synagogue, at least (Baruch Lifschitz and J. Schiby, "Une Synagogue samaritaine" [1968]; Riesner, *Paul's Early Period*, 343–49; vom Brocke, *Thessaloniki*, 222–23, as well as other individual inscriptions that may be identified as Jewish [vom Brocke, *Thessaloniki*, 223–32]).

187. Thus, e.g., Milligan, *Thessalonians* (1908), 29; Rigaux, *Thessaloniciens* (1956), 443; Riesner, *Paul's Early Period*, 352–54 (see 2.2.7 above), who speaks here of "ethnicity" (p. 352) and points for his thesis of συμφυλέται as a concept for mixed ethnicity to Helga Botermann, "Der Heidenapostel und sein Historiker" (1993), 83n55, and her assumption that this refers only to Jewish citizens. But that is not an exegesis of 1 Thess 2:14; it only discusses the Jewish identity of the communities according to Acts and the associated historical probability (74ff.) There follows only a generalized conclusion back to 1 Thess 2:14. Similarly arguing from Acts 17 are Mikael Tellbe, *Paul Between Synagogue and State* (2001), 107–15, and Taylor, "Who persecuted the Thessalonian Christians?" (2002), 789–93. Luckensmeyer, *Eschatology* (2009), 136–39, assumes that Jewish people were among the persecuting συμφυλέται and defines the concept on that basis.

188. Liddell / Scott, 1688.

Thessalonica, a form of Greek community organization that continued to flourish in Roman times.[189] These segments of the citizenry, also named and attested in inscriptions at Thessalonica, recruited from male full citizens; they excluded slaves and foreigners. Jewish inhabitants were not members there because in general they were not accorded full citizenship rights, and besides, they tried to avoid the associated participation in pagan religious cults.[190] According to this theory 1 Thess 2:14 conveys that the non-Jewish community in Thessalonica was being persecuted by the Greek, non-Jewish population.[191]

So if the text, in contrast to Acts 17:5–10, assumes a non-Jewish hostile atmosphere in the city, we may also assume the presupposition of a non-Jewish makeup of the congregation, at least as far as the overwhelming majority or the authors' image of them is concerned. Favoring this, besides 1 Thess 2:14, is the "turning" of those addressed from "idols" to "the living and true God" in 1:9. The statement there could, certainly, not sustain such a conclusion all by itself, as 1 Cor 12:2 and Gal 4:8–9 show; in that case we would have to suppose that Corinth and the Galatian communities had a completely non-Jewish membership. But the echo of 1 Thess 1:9 in the ethnic parallelism of 2:14 shows that the underlying idea is consistent and includes a geographic separation between Jews and non-Jews. On the level of the congregation as depicted we can thus perceive the beginnings of a separate local and national church, something that cannot be reconciled either with the testimony of Acts or with the congregational reality that underlies the Pauline texts.

Paul, after all, continues to call Jews who have become "Christians" "Jews" (Gal 2:13–15), and in addressing the recipients of his letters he refers to Jewish missionaries and relatives who are at home in the communities outside the land of Israel. Thus, for example, Paul greets Andronicus and Junia, then resident in Rome (Rom 16:7), as συγγενεῖς, members of the Jewish people, as well as the συγγενής Herodion (Rom 16:11). From the place where Romans was composed (probably Corinth)[192]

189. Vom Brocke, *Thessaloniki* (2001), 155–66, following and contradicting Holtz, *Thessalonicher*, 102.

190. Vom Brocke, *Thessaloniki* (2001), 162–65, with reference, among others, to Karl Leo Noethlichs, *Das Judentum und der römische Staat* (1996), 34.

191. See, in addition, Gottlieb Lünemann, *Thessalonicher* (1850/1867), 63 ("the sharp contrast" between συμφυλετῶν and Ἰουδαίων must "be an exclusive one," underscored by the "added ἰδίων"); von Dobschütz, *Thessalonicher-Briefe* (1909), 109–10; Michel, "Fragen" (1967), 51–52, and the brief discussion of it in Roberts, "Images" (1992), 151 ("the Thessalonians … have been rejected by their own people"), as well as Johanson, *Brethren* (1987), 98; Still, *Conflict* (1999), 224–27; Craig Steven de Vos, *Church and Community Conflicts* (1999), 157–58; Konradt, *Gericht* (2003), 26–27; 88ff.: "There is no indication in the text to support the thesis that the Jews were the real inciters of the conflicts" (89n388).

192. See Schnelle, *Einleitung* (1994), 135.

the Jewish συγγενεῖς Lucius, Jason, and Sosipater send greetings (Rom 16:21). These few notes alone testify to the community of life of Jewish and non-Jewish people in the congregations associated with Paul.[193] If, on the other hand, Israelites who do not believe in Christ also remain συγγενεῖς, members of the same people (Rom 9:3), it follows that ethnic belonging—or, more precisely, enduring membership in Judaism—runs across all temporary confessional boundaries and is not touched by them. For that reason the division of 1 Thess 2:14 into Jewish-Christian communities who dwell with the "Jews" persecuting them in Judea and those living in the purely Greek community at Thessalonica, under pressure from their Greek "compatriots," must be said to be unusual for the epoch of the early Pauline communities. Moreover, the general opinion is that 1 Thessalonians is the first apostolic letter directed to one of those early, recently-founded Greek communities. At the same time it is striking that there is no material expression of the ties between the communities in Macedonia and Achaia and those in the land of Israel; 1 Thessalonians makes no mention of the collection for the poor in Jerusalem.

What, then, is the function of this parallelization of 1 Thess 2:14 with regard to the overall statement of these verses? If the pressure exerted by "the Jews" in Judea was like the pressure from compatriots in Thessalonica, this suggests a comparison also between the characteristics listed. The overwhelmingly negative description of "the Jews" as persecutors implies that we have here an indirect statement about pagan persecutors—indeed, that a vocal accusation could be raised against them. A veiled invective against the real local enemies is presented in the form of a public accusation against "the Jews." As a result, the "Jews" receive a kind of "metaphorical" blow. We see here an important intentional moment in the composition: the congregation addressed is to be consoled in a situation of persecution and be given an account of the fate they can expect to befall their persecutors. The more definitive the statement of judgment presented, the more comprehensive such a consolation would be. This central significance of the parallel structure of statements for the interpretation of the section has been advanced by a few exegetes to date.

Christoph Demke had already formulated this idea very clearly and pointed to a typifying stylization of "the Jews": The "viewpoint that . . . extends the thought is that the righteous judgment of God over the example of oppressors, the Jews, has been fulfilled, which signifies comfort for [all those] who, following the example of the suffering Judean communities, are still being persecuted. Their oppression will also bring forth judgment. We have to do, therefore, with a contemporary event . . .

193. For an understanding of the Christian congregations outside Israel as "messianic communities in the Jewish diaspora" and therefore communities living as Jews, see Luise Schottroff, *Lydia's Impatient Sisters* (1995), "Christianity of Gentile Women and Men, or Messianic Communities in the Jewish Diaspora?" pp. 11–14, and eadem, "'Gesetzesfreies Heidenchristentum'" (1996), 227–45, at 227–37.

that is also generally addressed in 2 Thess."[194] Such a severe instrumentalization of the Jewish people would be scarcely imaginable as coming from Paul's pen, which is why most authors attempt to soften it, arguing that such an "improper" use of Jew-hating ideas is not genuine anti-Judaism. Thus Willi Marxsen thinks that the "purpose" of such statements about "the offenders" should be taken into account, as well as the "positive sense" thus attained: "Thus the Thessalonians are to understand that what has happened to them is part of the end-time events. There is even a positive sense in that. It is true also of the Thessalonians' fellow citizens that they 'do not please God' and 'are hostile to all people.' This knowledge can help the community ... to live with the persecution."[195] The functional attribution of misanthropy to the pagan persecutors is an important finding that calls for further interpretation.[196]

Apart from Bruce Johanson and John Weatherly, who follow Marxsen,[197] Peter Wick in particular has worked out, in a way that advances the argument, the parallel structure and consolatory function of 1 Thess 2:14–16, which represents part of that same function in the overall context of 1 Thessalonians: "So all attacks on the Jews, through v. 16, serve to help the Thessalonians to understand their acute situation and to put it in context: a situation that they—obviously—are not suffering because of the Jews, but from their own people (v. 14). This phrase, 'from your own people,' represents a reference point for everything that follows, to v. 16."[198] What

194. Demke, "Theology and Literary Criticism" (1996), 3.2.3. Available at https://depts.drew.edu/jhc/demke.html (without pagination). Demke applies the text, as part of what he regards as the extensive post-apostolic passage (see below at 3.3.1), to the destruction of Jerusalem. "The post-apostolic author would then comfort persecuted Gentile Christians (v. 14b) precisely by affirming that the hoped for retribution ... has already been carried out on the prototype of persecutors, the Jews" (3.2.3). Michel, "Fragen" (1967), 50ff., had already suggested the motif of imitation.

195. Marxsen, *Der erste Brief an die Thessalonicher* (1979), 50. Add to this that, according to Marxsen, it does not apply to all Jews but only to those who persecuted the missionaries and congregations (48ff.); on this, see above at 2.2.5.

196. See 2.5 below.

197. Johanson, *Brethren* (1987), 96ff.; Weatherly, "Authenticity" (1991), 88–89; see also Schlueter, *"Filling Up"* (1994), 120–21 (see above, 2.2.2). Noteworthy also is Wilhelm Bornemann's remark on 2:16 (*Thessalonicherbriefe* [1894], 11): "This righteousness before God is also a consolation for the believers in Thessalonica."

198. Peter Wick, "1 Thess 2,13–16" (1994), 19–20 (regrettably without reference to his predecessors). But I cannot agree with his assertion that "the purpose of this pericope and of the Thessalonian letter is not anti-Jewish" (23); see below in 2.5. The thesis proposed by Wick (and the others) has been taken up and developed contextually by Konradt, *Gericht* (2003), 88–93 (as previously by Marlene Crüsemann, "Die Briefe nach Thessaloniki und das gerechte Gericht," Diss. Kassel 1999, 52–67).

is announced is said to be a purely temporal judgment,[199] and that is given a consolatory function, "which is why their Gentile (!) persecutors will also not escape punishment. This shows all the more how dangerous it is to interpret verse by verse, without taking into account that every verse is a subordinate part of a larger unit of meaning."[200] But this "larger unit of meaning" offers Wick room for the broadest possible relativizations that, among other things, are intended even to lead to a resolution of the contradiction to Romans 11.[201] If, in addition, one asks about the social-historical implications and consequences of such a "unit of meaning," what emerges, besides its deliberately-aimed anti-Jewish points, is an astonishing ignorance of the lives and fate of Jews.

2.5 Social-historical considerations on the function of the anti-Jewish statements

Thus if the accusation against "the Jews" is not central to the passage, but instead its purpose is to console the addressees, it would be wrong to call this an anti-Jewish outburst. That would be the possible relativization to be offered by those who perceive a governing paraenetic function here. Nevertheless, the fact remains that the text speaks in explicitly negative terms about Jewish people; the foreground of the statement does not simply disappear as soon as its background is illuminated. In what follows we will inquire more deeply into the meaning of such a foregrounded caricature in terms of its actual social implications.

2.5.1 Resistance through denunciation: who are the misanthropes?

The play on current anti-Jewish slogans in which the accusation of misanthropy has an especially important role is not softened by the notion that someone else is the real target. The text can certainly be read as refined political camouflage, concealed political critique to protect its authors and addressees, if the intention is to avoid speaking openly against the real persecutors and persecuted. In that sense Bruce Johanson has described—probably correctly, in my opinion—the protective function of the concealed accusation when he says that an attack on Jews was less

199. With reference to Ekkehard Stegemann, "Zur antijüdischen Polemik in 1 Thess 2,14–16" (1990); on this, see above at 2.2.5 and below at 2.5.

200. Wick, "1 Thess 2,13–16," 20.

201. Légasse, "Paul et les Juifs" (1997), 591n71, criticizes the tendency of Stegemann and especially Wick to harmonize 1 Thess 2:14–16 with Rom 9–11 and thus to overlook the fact that 1 Thess speaks of an eschatological judgment. He calls this (in French) an "abuse of the texts" and a "poor service to a good purpose." Without wanting to share in this overdrawn polemic we must nevertheless see that the greatest exegetical ingenuity is still insufficient to explain away the radicality of 1 Thess 2:14–16.

dangerous than one directed at pagan persecutors, "in case the letter fell into the wrong hands."[202] But at the same time it cannot be emphasized too strongly or plainly that the text also declares the foreign, unique Jewish people, all too easy to denounce as "misanthropic" in their surroundings, to be enemies. Hence the consequences of such a statement must be considered. Even if we allow that Paul, in the course of an epistolary attack of rage, utters such denunciations as an internal Jewish critique, and besides that he simply wants to console his community,[203] the explicit political message still exists, as Luise Schottroff has written with acuity, in words that bear repeating: such vocabulary is nothing less than "a reason for a persecution of Jews by Roman authorities" as it accuses "the Jews" of "disloyalty to the Roman state."[204] The fact that the accusation of misanthropy can be part of the indictment in political trials[205] lends a denunciatory character to the expressions in 1 Thess 2:15. It gives the impression of constructing a front, in union with state and society, against "a-social elements." This impression is certainly enhanced in that these accusations are fleshed out with newer and specifically "Christian" reproaches such as the murder of Christ and the prophets. This makes it more plausible that the enemy thus denounced is in fact common to all those concerned.

Two possible effects are associated with this: the excusing of one's own group and an attempt at a truthful identification of the local persecutors.

If the congregation in Thessalonica had itself been accused of misanthropy, this accusation would shift attention instead to those known to be thus characterized, namely, the Jews, in the sense that they are the real enemies, as the whole world knows. We find indications in 1 Thessalonians that the congregation there had to deal with comparable attacks. There is a certain connection between allusions to sufferings and oppressions thus experienced and references to people's possible or actual displeasure at the "word" of the Gospel that gives the congregation its identity, something we find in a number of passages in 1 Thessalonians.

First of all, there is the appearance of the missionaries[206] themselves, who had previously suffered (προπαθόντες) in Philippi and been mistreated (ὑβρισθέντες, 2:2), in order then to preach in Thessalonica as well a Gospel that is meant to please God alone and not humans (οὐχ ὡς ἀνθρώποις ἀρέσκοντες ἀλλὰ θεῷ, 2:4). It can be assumed that the experience of displeasing people indicates

202. Johanson, *Brethren* (1987), 97. For the social conflict situation of the Thessalonian community with its pagan neighbors see Still, *Conflict* (1999), 228–67. Still emphasizes the conflict fields in the Greco-Roman context involving family, religion, and government, in all of which the Christians were located in a subversive position (251–67).

203. Wick, "1 Thess 2,13–16" (1994), 19–23.

204. Luise Schottroff, "Antijudaismus im Neuen Testament," 222–23.

205. See above at 2.4.1.

206. For the methodological consequences of understanding the grammatical authorial plural as genuine, see below at 3.1.3.

consequences that were experienced as repression of a minority. The same ideas are part of the profile of 1 Thess 2:13–16. It is significant that in particular the verb ἀρέσκω in 2:4 is the same verb chosen for the reference to the accusation of atheism in 2:15. There is thus a play on words linking the Jew-hating expression and possible sufferings experienced from social hostility in connection with the attempt to please God, that is, the experience that this confession of God is accompanied by social hostility. For the chain of anti-Jewish expressions, which also touches in a central way on the sufferings in Thessalonica (ἐπάθετε, 2:14), is also introduced with a remark that the proclaimed "word" is that of God and not of humans (οὐ λόγον ἀνθρώπων, 2:13). That effect is explicitly evident in the suffering of hostile social actions from one's immediate political neighborhood, one's "own people" (2:14–16), which can be described as confrontation with people who "oppose everyone" (ἀνθρώποις ἐναντίων, 2:15). Therefore we should assume a deliberate combination of the concepts of "not pleasing" or "pleasing" (ἀρέσκω), "suffering" (παθεῖν) and the associated choice between "God" (θεός) and "humans" (ἄνθρωποι) with the same theological-social agglomeration of conflicts.

But the surface of the text contains a massive accusation of guilt directed at "the Jews." On the one hand they have nothing to do with the God-pleasing Gospel because they are precisely the ones who "do not please God," and besides, they are the true enemies of humankind because they are hostile to "all" (πᾶσιν; 2:15), both the missionaries whom they persecute and a greater number of people, namely, "all," the public in general. Inasmuch as the indicated possible and actual alienation from other people associated with the acceptance of the Gospel (2:4, 13) is connected with the supposedly misanthropic and God-not-pleasing "Jews" (2:14–16), it appears that we have here a shifting of public aggression. It is not the Christ-believers in Thessalonica who are putting themselves outside the social context but in fact a different group, the Jews.

The fact that this Christian community itself must continue to expect accusations of misanthropy is further indicated, indirectly but clearly, from the ethical principles of the warning in 1 Thess 4:1–8 and their probable consequences. Again it is a matter of "pleasing God" (ἀρέσκειν θεῷ, 4:1), and again it is about a possible social affront in which belonging to God or to humans plays a role: "whoever rejects this rejects not human authority (οὐκ ἀνθρώπων ἀθετεῖ) but God (ἀλλὰ τὸν θεὸν), who also gives his Holy Spirit to you" (4:8).[207] This may represent either an internal rejection of the paraenesis within the community or one from without, and would affect those who live according to it. Ultimately the separation from further social life is formulated as a positive ideal and goal. What is promoted

207. The concrete ethical question primarily involves avoiding πορνεία (4:3), which, as a practice of "sacralization" (4:4, 7), opens a broad field of potential conflict with the pagan (4:5) Greco-Roman world; on this see Marlene Crüsemann, "Gefässe der Ehre" (1998), 518–20; for the pericope see 1.2 above.

is living "quietly" (ἡσυχάζειν),[208] working with one's own hands,[209] "so that you may behave properly toward outsiders (τοὺς ἔξω) and be dependent on no one" (4:11–12). One who preaches such ideals need not be surprised later by socially-conditioned enmities, for if we compare this to Cicero's definition, cited above (*De off.* 1, 29),[210] of "aversion to fellow humans" (*odium hominum*), a disdain for common social life shown through separation (*deserunt enim vitae societatem*), consisting of an assertion that one need only be concerned with one's own affairs (*suum negotium agere dicere*), the community itself could scarcely avoid being accused of a crime against the state. Because of its practices it has to fear such accusations at any time. Thus its defense consists, on the one hand, in pointing away from itself to another group that appears dangerous to the state: "the Jews" are denounced as the real enemies of the state, which, after all, should be precious to everyone.

On the other hand, the skillfully parallelizing construction of 1 Thess 2:14–16 is intended to turn the accusation of misanthropy and inability to please God back at the local persecutors. If Jewish oppressors can be thus characterized on the basis of their aggression against the congregations in Judea, the same applies to the local "compatriots." The hidden message is then: besides these, the real misanthropes are your immediate and present opponents, because they are oppressing the community of the true God. They are the real atheists, for they do not please our God, who is the only one, while their gods are idols (1:9).[211] The statement is thus

208. The verb ἡσυχάζειν, "be quiet, live quietly" (ἡσυχία is also used in 2 Thess 3:12), as we know, is found in the NT epistolary literature in connection with the ethical ideals of the late-NT Pastoral Epistles: "a quiet life," ἡσύχιος βίος (1 Tim 2:2), or the "silence" (ἡσυχία) imposed on women along with the prohibition of teaching (1 Tim 2:11, 12). For ἡσυχία in 1 Tim 2:11–12 as a concept of Orders that tries to impose on women the "renunciation of any position on their own part and acceptance of a purely receptive attitude" see Ulrike Wagener, *Die Ordnung des 'Hauses Gottes'* (1994), 97ff., at 98. Luise Schottroff prefers to translate ἡσυχία as "conformity" (*Anpassung*) to express the comprehensive subjection demanded by this "encompassing law for women" (*Lydia's Impatient Sisters* [1995], 74, 70). In 1 Tim 2:2 what is aimed at is, in essence, "a quiet and peaceable life" (ἤρεμον καὶ ἡσύχιον βίον) "in all godliness and dignity" (ἐν πάσῃ εὐσεβείᾳ καὶ σεμνότητι), subject to the king and all rulers; on this see, overall, the exegesis and location of 1 Tim 2:9–3:1 in Annette Merz, *Die fiktive Selbstauslegung des Paulus* (2004), 268–375, esp. 279–88: ἡσυχία "is a virtue of the politically subordinated who are content with their assigned position and do not seek to advance" (280). I do not see a warning to keep the Sabbath commandment in 1 Thess 4:11 as does Schimanowski, "Abgrenzung," 302–11.

209. On this, see below at 3.3.3 n. 43.

210. For Cicero's *De officiis* 1, 29 as a legal basis in trials for *asebeia* see above, 2.4.1 n. 129.

211. The same reversal of the charge of atheism is probably present in Eph 2:12, where former "pagans" are called ἄθεοι because they lived far from the Jewish-Christian God (see Fascher, "Der Vorwurf der Gottlosigkeit"[1963], 103; Eberhard Faust, *Pax Christi et Pax Caesaris* [1993], 105ff.)

not uttered openly, or apparently dare not be spoken openly in this acerbic form,[212] but it emerges for the addressees on the basis of the parallel structure of the phrases. This is the first indication that 1 Thessalonians is a deliberately composed subversive writing. The fact that the opposing local forces also represent the communal and state officialdom of the Roman Empire, as well as its representatives and protagonists, seems probable when it is read with 1 Thess 5:3. "Their" saying, "there is peace and security" (εἰρήνη καὶ ἀσφάλεια) quotes a slogan of the *Pax Romana* (*pax et securitas*),[213] which identifies the outsiders and opponents as partisans of Rome.

The suspicion of misanthropy and atheism to which the community itself is apparently exposed is thus turned back on the regional aggressors by means of a denunciatory instrumentalizing of Jews. Accordingly, the third anti-Jewish dimension of the text is that members of the Jewish people are stylized as a negative example for likewise negative statements about third parties and are made a negative, evil model—in this case as "type and prototype of the persecutor," a classic anti-Jewish figuration frequently used in Christian sermons.

Gerhard Rau, in his investigation of twentieth-century Lutheran sermons, has described this functionalization of Judaism for paraenetical purposes in the (Gentile) Christian church precisely as an anti-Jewish mechanism:

> Within the context of world history the Jewish people and their fate were thus reinterpreted into a means, both genetic and pedagogical in nature, for advancing the history of Christianity in evolutionary fashion. In other words: the preachers are not talking about Jews at all; their theme is quite different: the Christian personality, the German people, or Western culture. The "Jewish Question" is related to and intertwined with the particular theme in such a way that it is instrumentalized, serving a demonstrative function within objective categories for something else.[214]

Likewise, 1 Thessalonians uses Jews for purposes of demonstration in this sense, namely, to illustrate the fate of "persecutors of Christ[ians]," in that beneath the surface the text is not speaking of "the Jews" themselves but of the situation of Gentile Christians and those who oppress them. The pedagogical intent is to

212. On the other hand, 4:5 should apparently be regarded as a a less specific and therefore public accusation of atheism: "the Gentiles who do not know God" (τὰ ἔθνη τὰ μὴ εἰδότα τὸν θεόν). It does not occur here in the context of persecution and prophecy of the destruction of enemies and appears more generalized. Whether one can see it as adopting "typical Jewish polemic toward the Gentiles" (thus Wick, "I Thess 2,13–16," 21ff.; see Holtz, *Thessalonicher*, 160), depends on how one sees the forum within which it is spoken and the question of authorship as well. In any case, this phrase scarcely mitigates the anti-Judaism in 2:14–16.

213. See further below at 5.3.1.

214. Gerhard Rau, "Die antijüdisch-antisemitische Predigt" (1980), 31.

convey consolation and instill confidence. But the result is the full development of an anti-Jewish model that will last for ages.

Thus in the very first letter to the community in Thessalonica we can perceive a decipherable social-historical situation such as Gerd Theissen describes, using the example of the passion account, for what he regards as a late stage of the process of Jewish-Christian separation: "But they [the Christians] could not publicly express the aggressive feelings against the powerful Romans arising with every repression. So they were turned against a nearby minority that found it difficult to defend itself against accusations (and who had now and then fingered Christians), but who were made responsible in a completely disproportionate way for the Christians' difficulties."[215] Here in 1 Thessalonians both were taken up and expressed as one: aggression against "Jews" and aggression against Rome.

2.5.2 Jewish catastrophe and judgment in 1 Thess 2:16 as a sign of hope for the Christian community, presented as non-Jewish

The contrast between "we" on the one hand and "the Jews" on the other linguistically unites the author and those addressed in a non-Jewish group identity. That is in turn intensified in that the condemned persecutory activity of the Jews in 2:16 seems to be extended to "us," that is, the missionaries to the Gentile peoples. In any case, "the Jews" are outside, and they are stricken by a judgmental divinely-authored event. This climax in v. 16 is the rhetorical goal of the pericope and thus constitutes, in a sense, the pinnacle of anti-Judaism. Something definitive is being demonstrated on "the Jews." To what extent does that affect the whole Jewish people? In the context of attempts to reconcile the text with Pauline authorship a number of possible ways in which the invective could be aimed only at a certain anti-Christian segment of Judaism have been suggested.[216] In that case it would be directed only at those Jews who had killed Christ or the Christian prophets,[217] and the "wrath" would fall only on them. But the very adoption of the motif of murdering the prophets clearly signals that this is about the whole history of Israel and thus all of Israel itself.[218] Moreover, it is part of a series of statements written as a dictum about a third party, contains no appeal to repentance, and thus, unlike Acts 2:36, for example, shows no invitational or pastoral intent.[219]

215. Theissen, "Zur Entstehung" (1988), 185.

216. Thus, e.g., W. D. Davies, "Paul and the People of Israel" (1978), 8; Marxsen, *Thessalonicher* (1979), 48ff.; Gilliard, "Antisemitic Comma" (1989); Légasse, "Paul et les Juifs" (1997), 577ff.; Amphoux, "1 Th 2,14–16" (2003); Fee, *Thessalonians* (2009), 89–103; see above at 2.2.6.

217. Thus esp. Gilliard, "Paul and the Killing of the Prophets" (1994); see 2.2.6 above.

218. On this see Dieter Zeller, "Christus" (1979), 259; Broer, "'Antisemitismus'" (1983), 74ff.

219. See Schade, *Apokalyptische Christologie* (1981), 128–29: The deuteronomistic sayings of the prophets adduced in 1 Thess 2:15–16 are shorn of their traditional, original function in the preaching of repentance.

A relativizing of the key statement, which arises less from the linguistic evidence than from the need to claim it as Pauline, is involved also in the discussion of the aorist ἔφθασεν. As such, an aorist in 2:14–16 is nothing unique, as the forms ἀποκτεινάντων and ἐκδιωξάντων show. But the assertion that wrathful judgment has already fallen on "the Jews" goes beyond everything said about them previously. Then there is no way of avoiding a reading of ὀργή to mean God's act of judgment, as attested by the corresponding use of the concept in 1 Thess 1:10; 5:9.[220]

But while 1:10 speaks of the coming wrath (τῆς ὀργῆς τῆς ἐρχομένης), according to 2:16 it has already happened—if we take the aorist literally, along with all the corresponding statements in the passage. Hence an attempt has been made to see here a prophetic[221] or complexive or gnomic aorist expressing a repeatedly occurring or tangible event. This last is the thesis of Ekkehard W. Stegemann, who thus considers it possible to see ὀργή not as the last judgment but as one of many "divine punishments within history, chastising judgments . . . whose function is precisely to preserve against the judgment of destruction at the end."[222] This retains the temporal aspect of the verb form, which is not the case if one supposes a prophetic aorist; the latter must "somehow" go against the time-sequence and assert that a future event is already present. The gnomic aorist solution could therefore point a way to avoid the extreme interpretation according to which Judaism has been subjected to the eschatological judgment of retribution, hence an act of divine rejection. That would be the sharpest contradiction to Rom 11:26.

Still, 1 Thess 2:16 must be interpreted primarily in connection with the whole text of 1 Thessalonians, and in that context, precisely in the connection between 1:10 and 5:9, it is apparent that ὀργή means nothing else than God's decisive and final judgment.[223] In fact, in 2:16 ὀργή is given a further qualification beyond the other passages by the expression εἰς τέλος, "complete, total," as though it were intended to forestall any interpretations that would make light of the definitive character of this ὀργή. This usage defines the "wrath" as *the* judgment and makes it impossible, in my opinion, to introduce any relativization through a reductive interpretation that would make it an event within history among many others, or

220. See Konradt, *Gericht* (2003), 59–93; 174ff.: "Paul thus links to traditional language about the ὀργή (1:10; 2:16; 5:9), where in each case the reference is to God's eschatological act of destruction" (187); for this connection see also 5.2.4 below, and 5.3 and 5.4 as well.

221. E.g., von Dobschütz, *Thessalonicher-Briefe* (1909), 116–17; cp. Légasse, "Paul et les Juifs" (1997), 587–88, and see above at 2.2.6.

222. Ekkehard W. Stegemann, "Zur antijüdischen Polemik in 1 Thess 2,14–16" (1990), 58; for the "gnomic aorist" see pp. 59ff.

223. See also Gerd Lüdemann, *Paulus und das Judentum* (1983), 24; Holtz, *Gericht* (1989), 121–22. For the concept and judgment type of ὀργή as a judgment of destruction in the Bible and particularly in the NT see Egon Brandenburger, "Gerichtskonzeptionen im Urchristentum und ihre Voraussetzungen" (1993), 22–23; 26ff., and also Konradt, *Gericht* (n. 220 above).

by a futurizing of the aorist ἔφθασεν, which is quite clear as it stands. The motif of the over-full mass of sin enhances the impression that this is about a long-overdue and definitive divine act of judgment that besides, contrary to tradition, is turned against Israel in extreme fashion: "Traditionally, the wrath against Israel is always limited in time. Here, in contrast, it appears that God punishes εἰς τέλος, that is, completely. In that case God is acting toward Israel as God has traditionally acted against the Gentiles."[224]

The concepts chosen in 1 Thess 2:16c are mutually reinforcing in their radicality, for the verb φθάνειν, through its fundamental meaning, "anticipate," contains *per se* the tendency to be applied to events that in fact are happening ahead of time. Given the use of φθάνειν in 1 Thess 4:15, that can certainly "play into" 2:16.[225] The valencies of environment that more narrowly define the verb also point in that direction: in a participial construction the meaning "anticipate" is clear,[226] and the preposition ἐπί introduces the element of surprise:[227] that is, the wrath comes to "the Jews" "first" and "surprisingly." Thus there is no need of the aorist to achieve the unusual assertion that "the Jews" are faced with a surprising and premature judgment of wrath. Still, the equivalent use of the aorist ἔφθασεν in Matt 12:28 (par. Luke 11:20) also shows that it can refer to an event of eschatological nature that has already happened in the present: the reign of God has come![228]

Accordingly, 1 Thess 2:16c should be translated: "But the [divine] wrath has already [surprisingly] come upon them totally."[229] The inbreaking of the divine judgment on "the Jews" is stated as a fact; in this we must agree with Traugott Holtz: "As in 1:10, ὀργή is the final judgment that falls on God's enemies to their destruction. It has—according to this statement—already broken upon the Christ-hating Jews. The aorist is not a prophetic way of speaking that anticipates the

224. Kraus, *Volk Gottes* (1996), 152. Cp. Broer, "'Antisemitismus'" (1983), 82–83; in critique of Ekkehard Stegemann also Broer, "Die Juden im Urteil der Autoren des Neuen Testaments" (1992), 2–33, at 9ff.

225. See 2.1 n. 3 above, and Blass-Debrunner-Rehkopf §101,82; 414,7.

226. I am grateful to Prof. Dr. Jens-Uwe Schmidt of Bielefeld for this point; cp. also Bornemann, *Thessalonicher-Briefe* (1894), 116–17.

227. Ernst Synofzik, *Die Gerichts- und Vergeltungsaussagen bei Paulus* (1977), 119n35.

228. Okeke, "1 Thessalonians 2.13–16" (1980/81), 130; Simpson, "Problems" (1990), 45–46. We should also note φθάνειν in Ezra 3:1; Neh 7:73 (= 8:1); Song 2:12 (LXX) for Hebrew [נגע] with the meaning "has come"; see Roger D. Aus, "Relevance" (1976), 261n40 (cp. Fitzer, "φθάνω, κτλ," 90). The same Hebrew verb is used in *Pesikta Rabbati* 36 in connection with the messianic birthpangs in the statement: "The time of the redemption has come" (see Aus, "Relevance").

229. For the usual translations of εἰς τέλος see Rigaux, *Thessaloniciens* (1956), 453, and 2.1 n. 4 above. The option "totally" is chosen here rather than the "completely, wholly" ordinarily used [NRSV: "at last"]. In any case it underscores something definitive, the finality of the "wrath" (see Pearson, "1 Thessalonians 2:13–16" [1971], 82–83).

future in order to depict the certainty of its arrival; it names an event that has already happened."[230]

From a social-historical point of view this saying and its rhetorical function are the climax of a self-rescue at the expense of the Jews. The judgment that has already fallen on "the Jews" constitutes proof for the certainty that their fate will come upon the pagan persecutors as well. What is important is not primarily the hypothetical identification with a historical event but again the function of the statement in the overall fabric of the text. A catastrophe for Judaism, described as definitive, is represented as a necessary punishment for their persecutory actions toward Christian communities. This constitutes also a prophecy of the certain end of the "pagan" persecutors and oppressors. The prophetic dimension of the texts is precisely not about the wrath that will fall on Judaism but on vengeance for the acts of non-Jewish forces. Wrath will come to them as it has already come upon "the Jews."[231]

In this way the eschatological judgment of wrath on "the Jews" becomes a *sign of hope* for "Christian" communities—more precisely, congregations defining themselves as "Gentile Christian"—as they will experience relief from their own (different) enemies. Hence we may suppose that the people thus addressed would be able to identify the wrath with a current catastrophic event happening to the Jewish people that would serve as assurance for their own consolation, for the consolatory function and the prophecy of the eschatological destruction of their own enemies depend in a certain sense on a vivid presence of the event of judgment, a historical verification. One would expect a concrete "ruin" (ὄλεθρος, 5:3) that would come upon outsiders, among whom would be the persecutors. Thus whatever may have been indicated by these words as an event of judgment happening to the Jews, they demonstrate a general and calculating coldness: the judgment on Jewish people serves as a consolation for a "Gentile Christian" community. Here we find formulated a Christian "separation" from the fate of the Jewish people, "the Jews" as such, understood as final. This means a separation in space and time of the eschatological judgment for the different groups and nations.[232] These words not only anticipate God's decree of judgment on a part of humanity; it is proclaimed as accomplished. In contrast, the judgment on a part of the Gentiles, namely, the persecuting "compatriots," exists in the form of a concealed prophecy, but the actual carrying-out of the words remains in the future. This stated and prophesied stepwise realization of God's judgment describes, in essence,

230. Holtz, *Thessalonicher* (1986), 108; for a critique of Holtz's anti-Judaism, whereby he apparently regards the content of 1 Thess 2:14–16 as the timelessly-valid word of God on Judaism, adding a crass expression (see 2.2.1 n. 18 above), see Ekkehard Stegemann, "Zur antijüdischen Polemik in 1 Thess 2,14–16," 55–56.

231. "This judgment applied to 'the Jews' in 2:14–16 is something the addressees may and should 'apply' to *their* opponents: they, too, are displeasing to God and will reap the fruits of their behavior" (Konradt, *Gericht*, 93).

232. See further below at 5.4.

the uniqueness of the concept of judgment in the first letter to the community in Thessalonica. The exegesis of 1 Thess 4:13–5:11 will augment it and make it more precise,[233] while the exegesis of 2 Thessalonians 1–2 will show how 2 Thessalonians contradicts it with its own, alternative conception of history.[234]

Since 1 Thess 2:14–16 is part of the genuine constitution of the overall text, we must now inquire more closely about who wrote it. For the common opinion that 1 Thessalonians is the earliest letter of the apostle Paul, such a question is irrelevant. But in the next chapter I will show that, in light of the information given about the letter's authorship within 1 Thessalonians itself, the answer must at least be essentially different. First of all, we must maintain that 2:14–16, with its overall distance from the Jewish self-understanding and way of life, must give us pause when we posit Jewish authorship of such statements. The perceptible identity visible in these statements about the author's own and other groups, in fact, points rather to a non-Jewish identity, because "the Jews" are neither "we" nor "you," and besides, they are presented purely for the purpose of demonstration in service to a hoped-for condemnation of real opponents. Can we even imagine that this passage, and thus possibly the whole of 1 Thessalonians, could come from a non-Jewish hand, since other parts of the letter are increasingly being interpreted by exegetes precisely as Jewish thought and tradition? The admonitions to maintain "holiness" (ἁγιασμός) from 1 Thess 4:3 onward, or the motif of "election" (ἐκλογή) in 1:4 in reference to the addressees are quite often used in the course of interpretation as proof of Paul's Jewish background.[235]

Yet, depending on how one defines the genre—genuine Pauline letter or deutero-Pauline composition—the question of the point of contact or place in the chain of tradition will receive a different answer: what, in the case of authenticity, is explained by recourse to the OT and Jewish terminology in biographical terms—Paul as a Benjaminite and Pharisee (Phil 3:5–6)—is instead, on the level of Pauline pseudepigraphy, part of a general Christian paraenesis, as is usually said of the deutero-Pauline parallel texts to 1 Thess 4:3–8. In other words: a direct derivation of the paraenesis of 1 Thess 4:3–8 from the OT and Jewish ethics, such as is occasionally discussed, depends on the assumption that 1 Thessalonians is the first and oldest Pauline writing. If that assumption becomes questionable, one will also have to define the tradition-historical provenance of the admonitions

233. See chap. 5 below.

234. See chap. 6 below.

235. Thus, e.g., by Karin Finsterbusch, *Die Thora als Lebensweisung für Heidenchristen* (1996), 108–84, on 1 Thess 4:1–8 passim; Reinhard von Bendemann, "'Frühpaulinisch' und/oder 'spätpaulinisch'?" *EvTh* 60 (2000), 223–26; Martin Vahrenhorst, *Kultische Sprache in den Paulusbriefen* (2006), 115–39. E. D. Schmidt, *Heilig ins Eschaton* (2010), on the contrary, sees the holiness concept in 1 Thess not so much as a link to Jewish content as a redefinition of the cultic for an independent "third identity" (413) of the pagan Christian community. The word field of ἅγιος is known to have been significant for pagan cultic contexts as well; on this see Vahrenhorst, *Kultische Sprache*, 73–113.

differently, namely, as a common early Christian catalogue of ethics, on the same level of tradition as the deutero-Pauline parallel texts to 1 Thess 4:3–8, that is, Eph 4:17–19; 5:3–7; Col 3:5–18,[236] which represent a further development of Jewish-Christian paraenetic content.

A critical view of 1 Thessalonians will in any case note that 3:13 presents an extremely striking deviation from Paul's other usage regarding the "saints": this writing does not use the characteristic address and description ἅγιοι for the sisters and brothers in the community (e.g., in Rom 1:7; 16:2, 15; 1 Cor 1:2; 16:1, 15; 2 Cor 1:1; 13:12; Phil 1:1; 4:21, 22; Phlm 5, 7), but appears to regard the term as referring to angels[237] who will accompany Jesus at his parousia. The sisters and brothers in Thessalonica are never addressed as ἅγιοι, but rather ἀδελφοί (1:4; 2:1; 4:1, etc.). In the year 1836 this irritating finding caused Karl Schrader, in the midst of his commentary on 1 Thessalonians, to posit the inauthenticity of the letter from then on.[238] Similarly, the reference to the ἐκλογή in the community in 1:4 is remarkable in that it promises election to a pagan Christian community, whereas Paul otherwise speaks of ἐκλογή (election) only in the context of Romans 9–11, referring there to the election of Israel and Jacob (Rom 9:11; 11:5, 7, 28).[239] "Theologically, this is a stunning assertion. Paul is applying to a predominantly *Gentile* congregation election terminology that in his Jewish Bible is used exclusively of Israel."[240] To put it pointedly, we may ask: was it Paul who, in his very first letter, not only transferred Israel's election to a congregation of Gentiles but also uttered a definitive decree of destruction on Jewish people? In what follows, we need to pursue the peculiarities of 1 Thessalonians in more detail.

236. For a particular affinity between 1 Thess 4:3–6 and Col 3:5–18 and Eph 5:3–7 see Konradt, *Gericht* (2003), 119ff.; likewise, 1 Thess 4:3–6 points to "a series of points of contact with 1 Pet 1:14–17" (ibid., 126n578).

237. For the exegetical discussion of 1 Thess 3:13 and the different interpretations of the ἅγιοι (angels or the deceased), see E. D. Schmidt, *Heilig ins Eschaton* (2010), 334ff.

238. Schrader, *Der Apostel Paulus* 5 (1836), 23–24; see 4.1 below.

239. See, e.g., Eckart Reinmuth, "Der erste Brief an die Thessalonicher" (1998), 118 ("central key word of Jewish confession"), and Fee, *Thessalonians* (2009), *ad loc.* For an alternative, "profane" interpretation of ἐκλογή in 1 Thess 1:4 on the basis of expressions in papyrus letters see Andreas Bammer, "Erwählung inmitten einer multikulturellen Gemeindesituation" (2007).

240. Victor Furnish, "Faith, Love, and Hope: First Thessalonians as a Theological Document," in *The Impartial God.* FS *Jouette M. Bassler*, ed. Calvin J. Roetzel and Robert L. Foster (Sheffield: Sheffield Phoenix Press, 2007), 221–31, at 224 (emphasis in original).

Chapter 3

THE COMPOSITION OF THE FIRST LETTER TO THE COMMUNITY AT THESSALONICA

Now that we have achieved some clarity about the casual way in which the fate of the whole Jewish people is treated, with the intent of functionalizing it as a sign of hope for Thessalonica, we find ourselves confronted with a Paul who is more or less unknown to us, one who apparently expresses a complete separation of himself and of God from his own people: who, in fact, regards this separation from God as a judgment, and hence a positive sign with which to exhort Christians drawn from among the Gentiles. Paul's otherwise-documented humility (1 Cor 15:9; Gal 1:13; Phil 3:6) as a former *Jewish* persecutor of the messianic Jewish community is not in evidence here, rather the contrary. According to 1 Thess 2:15 it was "the Jews" (in Judea) who had persecuted *him*.[1] It seems as if, contrary to the uniform witness of his other letters and Acts (Acts 8:1–4; 9:1–9; 22:3–6; 26:9–12, and also 1 Tim 1:13!), Paul had stood on the side of the messianic communities from the beginning. His biography as a principal actor in the only known persecution of

1. The fact that Paul's own persecutory activity is not mentioned in 1 Thessalonians and that he appears solely on the side of the victims has thus far not occasioned any questioning among scholars, not even when they are writing a section on 1 Thess 2:14–16 on "Paul's persecution(s)" (Ingo Broer, "Antisemitismus" (1983), 77ff.). Thus, for example, the listing of the "Jewish Persecution of the Judaean Churches" from about 35 C.E. in Judea, by Markus Bockmuehl, "1 Thess 2,14–16" (2001), 20–24, contains not a single reference to the persecution undertaken by Paul himself. Rare is any remark like that of Dieter Zeller, "Christus, Skandal und Hoffnung" (1979), 258, who notes the "impersonal bitterness" with which "he [i.e., Paul] here speaks to the Gentile Christians about this people as if he himself did not belong to them. Indeed, he seems to have forgotten completely that he himself once persecuted the church in Judea." Cp. also Romano Penna, "L'évolution de l'attitude" (1986), 393–94. And yet Ferdinand Christian Baur had already remarked (*Paul the Apostle* 2 [1873; 2003], 87) that Paul could not report on the individual persecutions in Judea that come into the picture here without mentioning himself as a "principal actor." For Baur's fundamental objection to the genuineness of 1 Thessalonians, see chap. 4.1 below.

Christ-communities in the land of Israel in his time, and as a later defector,[2] does not enter the picture; after all, it would upset the schema of the argumentation. And yet 1 Thessalonians, as the oldest and first letter of the apostle, should have been closest in time to Paul's persecutions of the Jerusalem community among all the texts that refer to these events.[3] It is certainly puzzling that at this point in time in particular a cleaned-up version could be presented without being contradicted by elements in Paul's *vita*.

Theories of development that see in 1 Thessalonians a strictly anti-Jewish Paul who developed in the course of time to a theologian of redemption for Israel in the sense of Romans 11 can scarcely be sustained against such a background.[4] There would have to have been a number of mutations of his personality: chronologically, first a change of sides as he shifted from being the punishing arm of the synagogue to becoming part of the messianic community. This, as we have seen, is documented in 1 Corinthians, Galatians, and Philippians, which, in current opinion, are later than 1 Thessalonians and thus are more distant in time from the events, as well as the Pauline traditions in Acts and 1 Timothy. Then Paul would have had a rigorously anti-Jewish phase, essentially congruent with silence about his own actions as persecutor, but paradoxically to be found—only!—in his oldest text. Finally there came the "development" to a more friendly attitude toward Israel, culminating in the letter to the community in Rome, which, however, seems more like a zigzag course, a constant shifting of position that, besides, had to have been incongruently reported over time. But if the extreme statement about the "final wrath" on "the Jews" falls outside the chain of events thus sketched, the course of tradition about the image of Paul as persecutor would be clear, and a theory of development regarding his attitude to his people would be superfluous. All the theories of development find their indispensable basis in the first letter to Thessalonica, as becomes more and more obvious.[5] If it is irrelevant, then the proposed developments are relativized,

2. On this see, e.g., Martin Hengel, "Der vorchristliche Paulus" (1991), 268–91; Christian Dietzfelbinger, *Die Berufung* (1985); Alan F. Segal, *Paul the Convert* (1990); Richard L. Longenecker, ed., *The Road from Damascus* (1997); Peter von der Osten-Sacken, "Vom Saulus zum Paulus?" (2005); Klaus Wengst, *"Freut euch"* (2008), 69–100; Gerd Theissen, "Die Bekehrung des Paulus" (2010).

3. Hengel concludes on the basis of 1 Cor 15:8–11; 9:1; Phil 3:6 that these texts can only be understood against the background of older information received by the communities; thus "Paul [would have] informed all the communities he founded about his actions as a persecutor and his call" ("Der vorchristliche Paulus," 269). Not only does nothing in 1 Thessalonians allow us to conclude to any such communications: on the contrary, it presents Paul himself as the persecuted victim.

4. John W. Simpson in particular tries to demonstrate such a development ("The problems posed by 1 Thessalonians 2,14–15" [1990], 46–49), but without giving any adequate explanation of the definitive character of 1 Thess 2:14–16 as a starting point for the "development." Cp. 2.2.5 above.

5. On this see, e.g., Hans-Heinrich Schade, *Apokalyptische Christologie* (1981), 22: the basis for the idea of development in Pauline theology is found in 1 Thessalonians, which

also as regards many individual subjects such as have become fashionable in Pauline research. A much-simplified image of the apostle would remain.

Considering the fact that 2:14–16 cannot be separated from the letter as an interpolation, the question now arises: what was the date of such a final statement, as well as its function in the text as a whole? But first we must determine more precisely whether and why Paul should undoubtedly be regarded as the author of 1 Thessalonians. What does the letter itself say about his authorship?

3.1 Who Wrote 1 Thessalonians?

In general, that does not seem to be a question at all. On the contrary, it is assumed without discussion that this is a letter in which we clearly hear the voice of the apostle Paul. Paul's route, described therein, with the names of Philippi, Thessalonica, and Athens, in fact points (based on the information in Acts 16–18 and the sequence of events described there) to Paul's very first "European" period, that of the so-called second missionary journey, so that 1 Thessalonians must be regarded as the first canonical letter of Paul, and in fact the oldest writing in the New Testament. Virtually all chronological and exegetical works agree.[6] And yet if we compare the information about the sender with the unique stylistic features of the text itself we cannot avoid seeing "Paul, Silvanus, and Timothy" as the authors. First Thessalonians does not even assert that it is a letter of Paul; it presents itself as a Paul-Silvanus-Timothy letter.

3.1.1 Plural authorship: what we find in 1 Thessalonians

The first letter to Thessalonica, as far as the authorship is concerned, is written almost entirely in the first person plural. In only three places, namely, 2:18; 3:5; 5:27, do we find statements in the first person singular, that is, with "I."[7] This is an

lacks all Paul's principal theological concepts. The decisive developmental step as regards eschatology could exist only between 1 Thessalonians and 1 Corinthians, whereas afterward nothing comparable can be observed (summary on pp. 213ff.). See also Udo Schnelle, *Einleitung* (1994), 73: the particular character of 1 Thessalonians in contrast to all other Pauline letters can be traced to an early stage of Pauline thought. Thus one can only posit changes and developments in Paul; cp. idem, "Der erste Thessalonicherbrief" (1986), and see below at 4.3.

6. Cp. only Alfred Suhl, *Paulus und seine Briefe* (1975), 92ff.; 108ff.; 299ff.; Schade, *Apokalyptische Christologie*, 173–90; Robert Jewett, *A Chronology of Paul's Life* (1979); Schnelle, "Der erste Thessalonicherbrief," 207ff.; idem, *Einleitung*, 1–26; Karl P. Donfried, "1 Thessalonians, Acts and the early Paul" (1990); Rainer Riesner, *Paul's Early Period* (1998), 3–28; 233–35; 294–96; 342–70.

7. See also the informative table of all first-person-singular pronouns in the authentic and other "Pauline" letters in Eduard Verhoef, "Numerus, Sekretär und die Authentizität der

altogether unusual situation in the world of the Pauline letters, and is in no way comparable to the otherwise observable shift between "I" and "we" passages, as seen, for example, in 2 Corinthians.[8] In that letter the first chapter, written primarily in the first person plural, is followed by mainly "I" passages in the second chapter. Then, until 2 Corinthians 8, the "we" style dominates, and after chapter 9 shifts back to mainly "I" statements. In all the other letters the author's statements are couched primarily and throughout in the "I" form, as in Galatians, 1 Corinthians, and Philippians, or that form appears repeatedly in long segments, for example in Rom 1:1–16; 7:7–25; 9:1–3; 15:14–33. The letter to Philemon, Apphia, and their house community contains only twenty-five verses, but fifteen of them are in the "I" form. We may say, then, that a complete epistolary text containing only three "I" statements is completely foreign to the Corpus Paulinum.[9]

So it is "we" who are writing this text. Who exactly are those included? The prescript, 1 Thessalonians 1:1, introduces Paul, Silvanus, and Timothy as equals. Differently from all the other Pauline letters, here Paul is not given the title "apostle" or any other, and the same is true for the co-authors. Romans, 1 and 2 Corinthians, and Galatians all begin with Παῦλος ἀπόστολος and other appellations. The co-authors Sosthenes (1 Cor) and Timothy (2 Cor, Phlm) are regularly called "brother" (ἀδελφός); Paul is once referred to as the "prisoner" (δέσμος) of Christ Jesus (Phlm). In the letter to Philippi the two senders, Paul and Timothy, appear as equals, but not without a predicate: "slaves" (δοῦλοι) of Christ Jesus. The simple introduction "Paul, Silvanus, and Timothy," without any addition, characterizes only 1 Thessalonians, together with 2 Thessalonians, its literary dependent.[10]

Besides the almost universal plural forms, there is a prescript that presents a collective authorship without emphasis on any individual person. This corresponds to the fact that in 2:7 all three call themselves "apostles" (ἀπόστολοι) of Christ, and the same is true, as if it were a matter of course, throughout the narrative. The plural use of the title "apostle" at this point is especially striking, for two reasons: first, it emphasizes the equality of the named authors, with no position of primacy accorded to Paul. In addition, this makes it even more probable that 1 Thessalonians

paulinischen Briefe" (1995), 51: for example, Philippians has 54, 1 Corinthians 86, and even Philemon has 17, while 1 Thessalonians has only two; see the similar conclusion in Ernst von Dobschütz, "Wir und ich bei Paulus" (1932), 254, and cp. also Raymond Collins, "Paul, as seen through his own eyes" (1980/1984), 178–80: "Paul's Exceptional Use of the Singular Number" (p. 178).

8. For the authorial plural in 2 Corinthians see, e.g., Verhoef, "The Senders of the Letters" (1996); E.-M. Becker, "Schreiben und Verstehen" (2002), 153–54.

9. For discussion of grammatical number in all the Pauline letters see, e.g., Verhoef, "Numerus," and especially Samuel Byrskog, "Co-Senders, Co-Authors" (1996), as well as Eve-Marie Becker, *Schreiben und Verstehen* (2002), 149–55 ("Zur Diskussion der Co-Absenderschaft in den Paulus-Briefen"); Christine Gerber, *Paulus und seine 'Kinder'* (2003), 78–80 ("Wer ist Wir?"); see also below at 3.1.2.

10. Cp. 6.1 below.

is supposed to be written by a genuine plural, a real "we." It is not Paul alone whom the community is to emulate, as urged in 1 Cor 4:16; it is already following "our example" (1 Thess 1:6).[11] Even the peculiar formulation in 3:1, according to which someone remained "alone" in Athens, points in this direction: that "alone" (μόνοι) is likewise plural, remarkably enough, as is the saying about sharing in the "life" of the apostles: τὰς ἑαυτῶν ψυχάς (2:8). And even a passage in "I" form strengthens the impression that a genuinely plural authorship is intended throughout. In 2:18 Paul is deliberately distinguished from the collective by the expression ἐγὼ μὲν Παῦλος, "I, Paul," as the one who had more than once wanted to visit the community. The fact that one person is explicitly distinguished by name from a predominant "we" speaks in favor of his or her otherwise unquestioned belonging to the group. But that means that Paul is *also* part of the group; the group does not consist essentially of himself alone, as in the *pluralis maiestatis* or in the sense of a merely authorial plural.[12] Likewise, neither of the other two passages in "I" form indicates a false or formal plural elsewhere.

> In 3:5, similarly to 2:18, we find an emphasis on an "I" standing alone, strengthened by a καὶ: διὰ τοῦτο κἀγὼ μηκέτι στέγων ("when I could bear it no longer"). Then there is a repetition in the singular (ἔπεμψα) of the remark in 3:1–2 that for this reason Timothy is to be sent; in the previous passage the sending is in the first person plural: μηκέτι στέγοντες … ἐπέμψαμεν ("we could bear it no longer … and we sent"). This does not necessarily indicate "that even in the plural in v. 1 Paul was thinking only of himself."[13] On the contrary: it is precisely the correction of a possible misunderstanding about who had sent whom that reveals that the plural is elsewhere meant to be taken seriously; otherwise it would not require further clarification.[14] Verses 1–2 report that, because Timothy returned to Thessalonica, "we" remained "alone" in Athens. Since, as noted, this "alone," as μόνοι, is clearly plural, it must or should refer to Paul and Silvanus as having remained in Athens.[15] Since, according to the text, it is these two who sent Timothy, it is plausible to conclude from the sequence of events here discernible what is then more explicit in 3:5, that the intent is to place clearer emphasis on one of the senders, namely, Paul. Thus it seems that the singular is deliberately

11. For "imitation" and "model" see below at 3.3.4.

12. Thus especially Karl Dick, *Der schriftstellerische Plural* (1899); see further below at 3.1.2.

13. Traugott Holtz, *Der erste Brief an die Thessalonicher* (1986), 129.

14. See further below at 3.2.5.

15. So also Johann C. K. von Hofmann, "Der erste Brief Pauli an die Thessalonicher" (1869), 195; George Milligan, *St. Paul's Epistles to the Thessalonians* (1953), 37; Béda Rigaux, *Saint Paul: Les Épîtres aux Thessaloniciens* (1956), 467; Ernest Best, *A Commentary on the First and Second Epistles to the Thessalonians* (1972), 131; F. F. Bruce, *1 & 2 Thessalonians* (1982), 60–61, et al. (Cp. Holtz, *Der erste Brief*, 124 and n. 599). Holtz himself appears not to note the plural μόνοι and thinks that "undoubtedly" Paul and Silvanus were not together in Athens.

chosen in 3:5 because the plural of the "we" statements in 3:1–2—and analogously in the whole text—may represent a real group.

Finally, the singular is used for the emphatic exhortation in 5:27, equivalent to an order, that I would call the "command to transmit": "I solemnly command (ἐνορκίζω) you by the Lord that this letter be read to all [the brothers (and sisters)]!" Probably this "I" is intended again to refer to Paul, but since no name is given it really remains indefinite.

Thus what we find in the text leads us to the hypothesis that the first-person statements that are grammatically plural and are addressed to an audience must also indicate a plural authorship, that is, we are dealing with a deliberately "real" plural. These are also, obviously, combined with "we" statements that include both senders and audience, such as 4:17, or that apply to people in all the communities (for example, speaking of "God, our Father," as in 1:3). They all express a real "we." But in this letter the "we" of the authors in contrast to those addressed does not appear to represent a disguised Pauline "I."

3.1.2 Scholars' interpretations of this plural

The voices collected by Karl Dick on the interpretation of the first person plural in the Pauline letters, from early church exegesis to that of the nineteenth century,[16] reveal in passing that 1 Thessalonians in particular was often attributed to a plural authorship because the Thessalonian letters differ from the others in this respect. Of special interest is the judgment of Abraham Calov, according to whom Silvanus and Timothy really took part in the composition; we should conclude especially from 2:18 and 3:1 that a real plural is in evidence: "Paulus de se solo non amat in plurali loqui."[17] Johann Albrecht Bengel also decided clearly, in the case of 1 and 2 Thessalonians, that Silvanus and Timothy are to be regarded as co-authors with Paul.[18] Previously Johann Friedrich Köhler likewise applied the first person plural in 1 Thessalonians to Silvanus and Paul, who are said to have sent Timothy together. In support of this argument he adduces the plural τὰς ἑαυτῶν ψυχάς (2:8), the naming of Paul in 2:18, and the plurals in 3:1, 6, which are to be referred to both: "Thus the apostle wrote the letter not only in his own name, but also in that of his friend Silvanus, and very little appears in it that concerns him alone."[19]

A broader discussion then began in 1862 with Johann C. K. Hofmann. "The apostle had his two co-senders with him when he addressed the first letter to the

16. Dick, *Der schriftstellerische Plural*, 4–14.

17. "Paul does not like to speak of himself in the plural." Calov, *Biblia N.T. illustrata* (1719), 694, cited in Dick, *Der schriftstellerische Plural*, 7.

18. Quoted in ibid., 8; Bengel, *Gnomon N.T.* 3 (1877; 2004), commenting on 1 Thess 2:18; 3:1.

19. Köhler, *Versuch über die Abfassungszeit* (1830), 65ff.; the quotation is from p. 66. For Köhler's extremely late dating of 1 Thessalonians see below at 4.1.

community in Thessalonica, and so he did not write only in his own name but likewise in theirs. They were to receive it as the first written word of these three servants of Christ who had worked together in their founding, and thus it is understandable that Paul speaks in the first person plural."[20] It is true that this means primarily that Paul, as the person first named in the prescript, is supposed to have formulated the letter on behalf of the two others, but they are more than a mere entourage of the principal author who are named *pro forma*. Accordingly, despite a constant commentary in the style of "Paul thinks," "Paul writes," etc., Hofmann repeatedly points out that Paul "includes the others with himself, in the plural,"[21] and that the congregation had the whole group as "their preachers."[22]

Subsequent voices countering Hofmann include those of J. C. M. Laurent, who concludes that Paul is using the "*pluralis maiestaticus*," but out of modesty: consequently, the plural forms in 3:1–2 would refer to him alone;[23] then Paul Schmiedel, according to whom the doubling in 3:1, 5 in itself shows that Paul consistently speaks of himself in the plural but occasionally includes the others "*honoris causa*."[24] Friedrich Spitta, in contrast, emphasizes that the change in number must be heeded, and that it makes a difference whether the particular reference is to Paul alone or to two or three persons. He also concludes from the finding "that the letter, issued in the names of Paul, Silvanus, and Timothy, evidently comes from none other than Paul himself," who "undoubtedly" dictated it to Timothy, "the youngest of his companions."[25] Wilhelm Bornemann in turn reacted against Spitta, emphasizing the uncertainty created by the change in number with reference to the members of the authorial group. He allows for a genuine plural on the basis of the plural expressions τὰς καρδίας ἡμῶν ("our hearts") in 2:4, Χριστοῦ ἀπόστολοι ("[the] apostles of Christ") in 2:7, and τὰς ἑαυτῶν ψυχάς ("our life/lives") in 2:8,[26] all of them intended as self-references by the author.

Gustav Wohlenberg is similarly undecided and even self-contradictory, but he does make acute observations: while in the context of 2:18; 3:5 he admits in part to a genuinely plural usage he repeatedly refers explicitly in the commentary to the authors as "the letter-writers," and he takes the plural μόνοι in the reference to Athens in 3:1–2 seriously. On the other hand, without further basis he sees in "the linguistic usage . . . that Paul remains the principal person even in passages where the plural is used."[27] This corresponds to the uncertain remark in his exegesis of the prescript: ". . . wherever the first person plural is used in the letter we should refer the plural not to Paul alone but, if not to all three, then certainly to two, Paul and

20. Hofmann, "Der erste Brief," 147.

21. Ibid., 191.

22. Ibid., 159.

23. Laurent, *Neutestamentliche Studien* (1866), 117–18.

24. Schmiedel, *Die Briefe* (1892), 24.

25. Spitta, *Zur Geschichte und Literatur des Urchristentums* I (1893), 120ff., 122.

26. Bornemann, *Die Thessalonicherbriefe* (1894), 37ff., 53.

27. Wohlenberg, *Der erste und zweite Thessalonicherbrief* (1903), 6–7, 71ff.

Silas, though it is necessary to suppose that it is really Paul who is writing and to whom everything said about the writers primarily applies."[28]

Since Theodor Zahn's *Einleitung in das Neue Testament* appeared in 1897 we find here and there some relatively extensive discussions of "we" forms in Paul, with special reference to the Thessalonian correspondence. Zahn's thesis was that the "we" should be regarded as genuine throughout the Pauline letters.[29] His analysis of 1–2 Thessalonians provides the proper paradigm, and it is most thoroughly examined there.[30] He speaks unambiguously in favor of authorship by all three apostles: "Shortly before the composition of this letter, Timothy returned with cheering news to Paul, or rather, since the 'we' is retained in 1 Thess 3:6f., to Paul and Silvanus, whereupon this letter was sent to the Church in Thessalonica in the name of all three."[31] Throughout the letter "it is . . . impossible to draw a line further on beyond which the 'we' is shrunk to an 'I.' . . . Since the Church is represented as a single family made up of many children, the corresponding relation of the three missionaries to the Church can be compared to that of a nurse and again to that of a father, 1 Thess 2:7, 11; but in this very passage we are reminded by ὡς Χριστοῦ ἀπόστολοι, 2:7, that it is more than one person whose attitude is described."[32] Paul, as the principal, occasionally emerges from the "we" with an "I," as in 3:5; 5:27. The singular passage in 2:18 is said to make it absolutely clear that previously it was a genuine "we" who spoke.

Thereafter, in his brief commentary on 1 Thessalonians,[33] Zahn establishes a model of how an exegesis should look if it takes the plural number of supposed authors seriously. According to this it is always the "missionaries," the "founders of the community," and "the apostles" who console, admonish, and remind their sisters and brothers in Thessalonica. Only in his treatment of the more theological chapters 4 and 5 does Zahn fall back into the common usage, having "Paul" alone speak, despite the continued use of the plural—a step that seems involuntary, neither considered nor explained.

The treatment by Karl Dick is nothing but a confrontation, throughout, with Zahn's general thesis that every "we" in the Pauline correspondence should be read as a genuine plural. Dick, in contrast, opts in general to see his "authorial plural," nothing but a dressed-up singular drawn from "later Graecisim," in the Corpus Paulinum, although that need not necessarily apply to every "we."[34] With regard to 1 Thessalonians, the main support of Zahn's thesis, Dick tries to refute Zahn on

28. Ibid., 18.

29. The English is Theodor Zahn, *Introduction to the New Testament* (1909), here at I: 203, 210, 227–28, 307, 316–17, 439–42, 538–39; cp. Byrskog, "Co-Senders," 230 n. 2; E.-M. Becker, *Schreiben und Verstehen* (2002), 154–55.

30. Zahn, *Introduction*, I: 203, 207, 209–11.

31. Ibid., 205.

32. Ibid., 210.

33. Ibid., 215–24.

34. Cp. Dick, *Der schriftstellerische Plural*, 33ff. Donfried, "War Timotheus in Athen?" (1991), 191–92, also sees a "redactional plural" in 3:1–10.

every point. He says that we find an "authorial plural" throughout, with a single exception: the "we" statement in 2:18, which stands immediately before a statement by Paul in the singular and therefore must be seen as reflecting a different content.[35]

> Dick's counterarguments are unpersuasive; they pay too little attention to the priority of the existing text of 1 Thessalonians for its interpretation: for example, he says that the "we" of the three authors is not genuine because, according to Acts 16–17, Timothy was not present when the community in Thessalonica was founded and is only recommended at 1 Thess 3:2 as a quasi-unknown (but was he not just returning from there, according to 3:6?). The plural μόνοι in 3:1 is not accepted; it is said to stand for "Paul's complete isolation."[36] Supposedly Paul speaks in 2:1–12 of only one person, namely himself, while the plural ἀπόστολοι in 2:7 is said to refer to Christian apostles in general, but *not* to Timothy and Silvanus, since according to 1 Corinthians 9 they are to be regarded as helpers (though if anyone in 1 Thessalonians belongs among "the apostles" it is surely these two).

Thus 1 Thessalonians is the least appropriate place to ground the thesis of an authorial or redactional plural for genuine statements of Paul about himself. The text as we have it is shaped in such a way that we should much more probably assume a deliberate, genuine plural authorship. Hence even in older exegesis there was a significant discussion of this matter that must have influenced what followed.

However, since that time many studies have followed the path of applying all grammatical forms to the person of Paul alone, without further thought. One of the pioneers of that line was Ernst von Dobschütz in his commentary on Thessalonians. Referring to the authors named above, he argued against Dick that, because of the names of the senders, most of the statements must be referred to Paul, Silvanus, and Timothy as to both form and content. But it is not a full, genuine "we," since in other letters Paul uses the first person plural when he cannot be referring to anyone but himself. It should be seen as a plural "*humilitatis*"; here Paul is deliberately retreating behind his "office" and "missionary companions": "Thus we will most properly do justice to the feeling that dictated this 'we' to Paul's pen if we think primarily of him alone, and thereafter sometimes of this and sometimes of that category with which he feels himself in solidarity. His 'fellow authors' are then at most included, but they have no prerogative."[37]

35. Dick, *Der schriftstellerische Plural*, 56–83 on 1 Thessalonians as a whole; pp. 57, 85 on 2:18. According to Dick, Abraham Malherbe, *The Letters to the Thessalonians* (2000), also holds for the "authorial plural" on pp. 86–89, where he applies to Paul an analogy with Seneca's style ("literary or authorial plural," 88).

36. Dick, *Der schriftstellerische Plural*, 67. On Dick's thesis see also Milligan, *Thessalonians*, 131–32 and, more critically, Roller, *Das Formular der paulinischen Briefe* (1933), 169ff.

37. Von Dobschütz, *Die Thessalonicherbriefe* (1909), 67–68, at 68.

> In von Dobschütz's later essay devoted particularly to the shift in number, 1 Thessalonians serves as one of the many variants on the theory of Paul's "development": "Paul, as a Jew, thinks collectively, and as a devout Christian he feels individualistically."[38] On the one hand von Dobschütz maintains this kind of parallel, but on the other hand Christianity is ultimately accorded the higher value; the move is from a collectively-thinking Judaism to a more individual and thus supposedly more highly developed Christianity.[39] Otto Roller advocated a similar theory of development, seeing it as the unfolding of an increasing personal independence on the part of Paul; consequently, a kind of "self-realization" took place: "In the beginning the participation of his fellow senders was undisputed and dominant, but later it retreated in favor of the developing independence of the apostle, which in the last phase of his work steadily pushed his fellow workers into the background and finally eliminated them entirely, even from the superscriptions. His fellow workers had become helpers . . ."[40]

Martin Dibelius's judgment was similar to that of von Dobschütz; he saw Paul as an author who moved "without scruple from the communicative to the personal plural, and from there to the singular." The more rhetorical and hence impersonal statements in 1 Thessalonians 1–2 are said to be the expression of such a communicative plural in the sense of "we Christian missionaries in general."[41] Inasmuch as, in this way, the first-person number is seen as the expression of Paul's sensibility, depending on the moment, the plurals in the text can, on the one hand, be perceived and addressed, but on the other hand the appearance of a push toward an unconditional priority of the principal apostle is still asserted. In the process a feeling for the unique features of 1 Thessalonians was and is lost, as the broad current of research on the letter reveals. Béda Rigaux, for example, sees the smallest frequency of "I" and the greatest of "we" in the two letters to Thessalonica among all the Pauline letters, and hence the greatest disproportionality. But "we" is then said to be the expression of Paul's community consciousness and part of his paraenesis for the purpose of uniting believers in the one church.[42] Traugott Holtz also devotes a section to this striking situation but—so it appears—gives extremely short shrift to the authorial participation of the "fellow workers" in the letter. It seems from 3:1 that Paul alone is speaking, and 2:7, 11 are much too personal for a group statement: "Thus co-sender does not mean equal co-author." But Paul did discuss the content with them.[43]

38. Von Dobschütz, "Wir und ich bei Paulus" (1932), 253.

39. Ibid., 276; however, apart from the table on p. 254, the essay says nothing directly about 1 Thessalonians.

40. Roller, *Formular*, 172ff., 174. Cp. also the complicated, though not especially revealing tables on pp. 173, 176, 181, and 183.

41. Dibelius, *An die Thessalonicher* I (2d ed. 1925), 12, 11.

42. Rigaux, *Thessaloniciens* (1956), 77–80.

43. Holtz, *Der erste Brief an die Thessalonicher* (1986), 13–14, 35ff. The quotation is from p. 14.

Thus social considerations are found even among exegetes who otherwise have no affection for social-historical exegesis; at most, as in this case, they are inclined to social fantasy. That, however, appears to evoke a Paul with whom they can deeply identify.

* * *

Excursus: Remarks on the Exegetes' Fixation on Paul

It would be idle to speculate about how exegesis would have reacted if tradition had preserved the writings of an impressive woman apostle instead of, or alongside, Paul's. Would identification with her theological utterances be taken just as unquestioningly as the starting point for nearly every non-feminist interpretation? A critical history of interpretation that takes into account the over-hasty and unreflecting partisanship toward and identification with Paul on the part of male exegetes remains to be written. Only a few of them have recognized it as a source of theological and historical distortion: "The hermeneutical standpoint of interpreters of the Pauline letters . . . is, as a rule, an identification with the apostle's perspective. The matter-of-fact way in which Paul's opponents are labeled false teachers or heretics may be sufficient evidence for many. Such an intimate hermeneutical relationship certainly makes room for observations of particular tendentious expressions and statements in Pauline argumentation, but the primary attitude is one of understanding assent. This means, unavoidably, a one-sidedness in the hermeneutical process . . . ."[44]

Feminist exegesis, with its earth-shattering and groundbreaking reconstruction of early Christian history,[45] has also made an essential contribution to the demystification of the traditional idea of the opponents, which both implicitly and explicitly branded possible "female opponents" in particular. In the realm of Pauline exegesis we should note especially the work of Antoinette C. Wire, who reconstructs and focuses on the theology and practice of the Corinthian women prophets through the lens of Pauline rhetoric.[46] But without necessarily making Paul a conceptual opponent, it is possible to describe early Christian history "more objectively" in terms of feminist social history than non-feminist research has been able to do. What emerges is a more subtle image of Paul that brings to light his contradictory nature and hence his vulnerability to criticism[47] as well as his self-relativizing in expressions that otherwise have been seen as the only "correct"

44. Osten-Sacken, "Paulus und die Wahrheit" (1980), 117.

45. See the two standard works by Elisabeth Schüssler Fiorenza, *In Memory of Her* (1983), and Luise Schottroff, *Lydia's Impatient Sisters* (1995).

46. Antoinette C. Wire, *The Corinthian Women Prophets* (1990). For methodology see also Bernadette Brooten, "Frühchristliche Frauen" (1985).

47. Thus especially Luise Schottroff, "How Justified is the Feminist Critique of Paul?" (1985).

position against supposed opposing parties. Thus Luise Schottroff arrived at a new description of Paul's primary intention regarding the situation in Corinth: "The congregation is to recognize the structures of competition within its own ranks as something dangerous.... What Paul wants is to promote both recognition of and resistance against *structures* of competition rather than competitors and rivals.... [Paul] employs sharp criticism, but in doing so he does not claim special authority for himself."[48] This says that the Pauline letters reflect a multivocal process of discussion within which Paul's intent is to argue, to fight, and to convince by rhetorical means.[49] His letters are "expressions of the opinion of a member of a community. They are not, either in their own claims or in the expectations of other members of the community anything more than the expressions of opinion by other members of the community."[50] Overall, these texts should be understood as "in large part ... collective documents in which the voices of many women and men in the communities can also be heard. For example, Paul did not invent all the images of hope that he employs; he delivers to us the language of hope that was the source of life for many Jewish and Christian people of his time."[51]

In current descriptions of the personal relationships in 1 Thessalonians the still largely paulocentric "coworker" model plays a major role. The relevant work by Wolf-Henning Ollrog on Paul and "his coworkers"[52] does represent a major advance beyond the previously dominant, and pre-feminist, monolithic and solitary image of Paul in exegesis by elevating the many people who were associated with him. But the word "coworker" obscures the independence of many of those persons, the mutuality in their relationships, and Paul's consequent dependence on them as well. These are revealed, for example, in the predicates Paul applies to Prisca and Aquila (Rom 16:3) and in the address of the letter to Philemon (Phlm 1): "Paul did not see himself as the main bearer of the early Christian mission but as one among many."[53] We should therefore pose the fundamental question whether the New Testament's συνεργός μου in the Pauline writings is accurately represented by the modern word "coworker," with its connotations of subordination. It may be that such expressions as "together with whom I work," emphasizing

48. Luise Schottroff, "1 Corinthians: How Freedom Comes to Be" (1998; 2012), 720.

49. Cp. Luise Schottroff, "A Feminist Hermeneutic of 1 Corinthians" (1999), 209–11.

50. Ibid., 211.

51. Ibid. 212. On this see also Elsa Tamez, *The Amnesty of Grace* (1993; 2002), "Paul, a 'Plural Subject'"), who characterizes Paul as a "transindividual individual," a "collective author with a collective consciousness" on behalf of the suffering and struggling people linked with him (p. 48); see also Claudia Janssen, "Paulus. Grenzgänge zwischen Traditionen und Zeiten" (1999). For the state of research in feminist hermeneutics and exegesis of Paul, see Marlene Crüsemann, "Paulus" (2d ed. 2002).

52. Ollrog, *Paulus und seine Mitarbeiter* (1979); see also Ellis, "Paul and his Co-Workers" (1971).

53. Luise Schottroff, "Feminist Critique of Paul," 38; cp. Beavis, "2 Thessalonians" (1994), 265.

collegiality and mutuality, are more appropriate, as is suggested especially by Rom 16:3.[54]

To this point, despite all the previous discussions about coworkers and co-senders, and without reference to all the plural forms of expression in the text, only one principle dominates most commentaries on 1 Thessalonians: *solus Paulus*, as Eckhart Reinmuth, a follower of Holtz, has demonstrated: Paul dictated a letter, as the three singular forms indicate. *He*, as the sole author, names Silvanus and Timothy as co-senders. They are said to be secondarily included among the senders and in the letter's message by virtue of its being dictated.[55] The secretarial hypothesis thus presented adds a new facet to the elite image of Paul: he now appears as the "boss," and the mind's eye associates him with an office and a secretarial pool. Certainly there can be no doubt that Paul dictated the letter to Rome, at least (Rom 16:22). Closing greetings in his own hand may also point to that (1 Cor 16:21; Gal 6:11; Phlm 19). But whether the unique features of 1 Thessalonians and especially "we" in it are explained as the work of a secretary—that we may doubt.[56]

However, the lonely summit of paulocentrism has long been held by Karl Schrader. Even his translation generally renders the text's plurals in the singular.[57] Martin Dibelius himself falsified the text when he wrote an overview of the content made up of quotations in the "I" form as *vox Pauli*.[58]

* * *

54. For Romans 16 cp. Luise Schottroff, "Feminist Critique of Paul," 36–38. It is true that Ollrog emphasizes partnership and independence, but he nowhere questions the continual use of "coworkers" (cp. *Paulus und seine Mitarbeiter*, 69 n. 37; 162ff., and frequently elsewhere). In the translations in the *Bibel in gerechter Sprache* (3d ed. 2007) a non-hierarchical presentation of "coworking" and the corresponding translation of συνεργός are often addressed; cp. Rom 16:3, 9, 21; 1 Cor 3:9; 2 Cor 1:24; 6:1; 8:23.

55. Reinmuth, "Der erste Brief an die Thessalonicher" (1998), 109; similarly Marxsen, *Der erste Brief an die Thessalonicher* (1979), 53, and Hiebert, *1 & 2 Thessalonians* (2d ed. 1992), 38–39, who does also speak of "writers" and "joint authors." Rudolf Pesch, *Die Entdeckung des ältesten Paulus-Briefes* (1984), 20, even asserts without any argumentation that Paul was the sole author. Otto Merk, "1 Thessalonians 2:1–12" (2000), 106, says of the ἀπόστολοι in 1 Thess 2:7: "the plural form refers to Paul alone."

56. For a secretary and dictation, besides Bahr, "Paul and Letter Writing" (1966), see esp. E. R. Richards, *The Secretary in the Letters of Paul* (1991), who also supposes that 1 Thessalonians was written by a secretary, because of the "autograph postscript" and the fact of the "co-senders" (p. 189). Against the confusion of "coworkers" and "secretaries" see Verhoef, "Numerus" (1995), 56ff. Binder, "Paulus und die Thessalonicherbriefe" (1990) thinks that, starting with the prescript, Paul and Silvanus might have alternated in dictating the letter to one another (90); for a similar position see also Vouga, "Der Brief als Form" (1992); see n. 65 below.

57. Schrader, *Der Apostel Paulus* (1836), 3–8. For Schrader's special role in the history of scholarship see below, chap. 4.

58. Dibelius, *An die Thessalonicher* I, 1.

For some time now a number of English-language exegetes have advocated a more participatory line, which pays more attention to the special features of 1 Thessalonians, and its conclusions increasingly point to a more collective authorship. Although even these authors do not surrender the focus on Paul, in the content of their work they tend more to follow the lead of Zahn. The line began with George Milligan, who was inclined to the idea of a "literary plural," but because of the particular linguistic contours reckoned with a close and consistent "joint authorship" of 1 Thessalonians (and 2 Thess), and therefore asserted a "normal" use of the plural.[59] Still, that did not mean that Milligan spoke of "the authors" in his commentary.

Robert Scott, advocate of a modified theory of the spuriousness of the Thessalonian correspondence, in his book on the Pauline correspondence as a whole concluded unequivocally, on the basis of his own idiosyncratic theory, that 1 and 2 Thessalonians fall completely outside the Pauline framework[60] and belong to the post-apostolic period; he found the original clue leading to that conclusion in the threefold nature of the authorship.[61] He asserts that these letters make no claim to being the sole and immediate work of Paul, and that the idea that the introduction of the two co-authors is merely conventional could be called a conventional error. The second and third authors should be considered for the main authorship just as much as one may regard the letters as a committee production or see the naming of Paul as purely honorific. Finally, Scott attributes the actual writing of various sections of the letters to Silvanus and Timothy as late authors.

An essay by E. H. Askwith then asserts the use of a genuine plural, although as used by Paul, who on the one hand appears as partner in a common writing that in fact is his alone; on the other hand, Askwith sees no reason why Paul should say "we" when he means "I."[62] In his *Introduction* he at times regards Paul, Silvanus, and Timothy as common authors: the "writers of the Epistle."[63] The verdict of W. F. Lofthouse was similar: apart from the three passages in the singular we are dealing with a genuine plural in the sense that Paul speaks for all three, the "little band of evangelists as a whole."[64]

Edward G. Selwyn, in his commentary on 1 Peter, not only advocates the thesis that Silvanus was the chief author of 1 Peter but, referring to Milligan, also asserts his authorship of the Thessalonian letters. He says that 1 Thess 2:18; 3:5; 5:27 indicate

59. Milligan, *Thessalonians*, 131–32 (and xxxiv–xxxv).

60. Scott, *The Pauline Epistles* (1909), 12–13, 23–24, 125–26, 215–33, 266ff., 295ff. For more on Scott's thesis see below at 4.2.1.

61. Ibid., 220–21.

62. Askwith, "'I' and 'We' in the Thessalonian Epistles" (1911), 159.

63. Askwith, *Introduction to the Thessalonian Epistles* (1902), 25 and elsewhere.

64. Lofthouse, "'I' and 'We' in the Pauline Letters" (1955), 74 (only pp. 73–74 deal with 1 Thess); similarly Jones, *The Epistles to the Thessalonians* (2005), 4: "Then there is Paul himself, the main author of the letter, but choosing to write it in the name of all three of them."

Paul's special position and leadership and even seem shaped by his personal temperament, but the letter otherwise exhibits a calmer character. The "we" throughout is thus traceable to Silvanus and Paul together, since Timothy, as the youngest, would have taken a subordinate position.[65] Ernest Best also, in recapitulating the discussion of the authenticity of 1 Thessalonians in his 1972 commentary,[66] speaks of "joint authorship" or "plural authorship" several times, emphasizing the connection between number and the question of the letter's origins.[67] Even though he ultimately favors the secretarial hypothesis and attributes the statements in the singular to the addition of personal marginal and concluding notes, the language itself causes him to consider seriously whether Silvanus and Timothy might have formulated individual sections or the whole letter.[68] This even brings him to the cautious statement that his exegesis rests on the *assumption* of Pauline authorship.[69]

Frederick Fyvie Bruce shows what a commentary looks like when it consistently assumes multiple authorship. Here Timothy, and especially Silvanus, are understood to be "joint-authors." He bases this on what he sees as the undeveloped profile of Paul in the content of the two letters to Thessalonica. The consistent plural shows that this is a community effort to which Paul himself added only a few personal notes, perhaps when reading over the letter after its composition. In this way he gave affirmation to the letter as a whole, no matter who formulated the content in detail and was chiefly responsible for it. Accordingly, it is really all the founders who write to their community.[70] This conclusion leads to a consistent commentary employing the plural: the apostles/missionaries/senders remind, console, and admonish their community. Similarly, the liberation-theological commentary by Joel Antônio Ferreira speaks, consistently and as a matter of course, of "Paul, Silvanus, and Timothy" as the authors of the letter and of their common teaching.[71]

65. Selwyn, *The First Epistle of St. Peter* (1947), 9–17, esp. 15ff.; cp. the adoption of Selwyn's thesis by Vouga, "Der Brief als Form" (1992), 9, 56 n. 103.

66. For the whole question, see chap. 4 below.

67. Best, *Thessalonians*, 25–26; on the plural esp. 26–28.

68. This is based on the arguments by Scott, *Pauline Epistles*; Selwyn, *First Epistle of St. Peter*; Morton, *Christianity and the Computer* (1964), and others; see further discussion below in chap. 4. Whiteley, *Thessalonians* (1969), appears to have been so impressed by Morton that he considers Silvanus as the co-author most responsible for the actual writing, but for the commentary as a whole he prefers to maintain that in reality Paul was the author (pp. 16–18).

69. Best, *Thessalonians*, 26.

70. Bruce, *1 & 2 Thessalonians* (1982), xxxii–xxxiii, 5–8. Cp. the commentary on 2:18 (p. 55); 3:5 (pp. 61–62); 5:27 (p. 135).

71. Ferreira, *Primeira epístola* (1991), beginning with the Introduction (pp. 10–13), under the section title "A quem e por que escreveram Paulo, Silvano e Timóteo" (p. 11). The same procedure is followed, e.g., by van Houwelingen, "The Great Reunion" (2007).

This corresponds in part to the study by Mark D. Roberts, who compares the image of Paul in Acts 17 with that in 1 Thessalonians and develops a group-identity for the apostle in the letter. On the basis of 2:18 and 3:5 as insertions by Paul, the otherwise consistent plural is seen as authentic. If the "we" were really an "I," those remarks would have been superfluous.[72] This brings Roberts to some original conclusions: Paul is said to be the "player/coach of the apostolic team" (p. 178); in contrast to his "starring" role in Acts he is here a "co-star" (pp. 186–87). The use of jargon from the worlds of sport and film shows that Roberts is inclined to interpret the plural as a rhetorical one intended to project an image of Paul alone, whether or not Silvanus and Timothy contributed to the letter (p. 81). On the other hand, however, he emphasizes repeatedly that all three of them wrote (p. 91); hence he calls them "writers" and co-authors. There is no note of or reflection on this methodological contradiction between the clear description of the grammar and the implicit trend to focus everything on Paul alone. Still, this work represents a significant advance in the study of 1 Thessalonians beyond the general body of Pauline studies on the letter. Similarly, Günter Haufe, in his commentary on 1 Thessalonians, takes Paul to be the principal author but sees his coworkers as also authors of the letter: "As 'apostles of Christ' (2:7) involved in the founding of the community they also participated in the composition of the letter. Nothing prevents us from supposing that the content of the letter was prepared in the form of address by three persons."[73] Paul-Gerhard Müller comments on 1 Thessalonians similarly to F. F. Bruce before him, often basing his remarks on a threefold authorship and thus not considering Paul the sole sender. He sees the three as in constant "theological trialogue, pastoral consultation," so that the thoughts of all three apostles are to be found in the letter. It is necessary to value the contributions of Timothy and Silvanus much more highly than has been done previously; furthermore, "the named coworkers may have cooperated in dictating to the scribes and stenographers."[74] Regina Börschel emphasizes the equality of the missionaries, expressed in the style of 1 Thessalonians, although, based on the three passages in the first person singular, Paul is seen as having had the special position of the "significant other" in the eyes of the community as the "leading man" in its founding, the one who communicates the new faith.[75] Christine Gerber also honors the nearly consistent authorial plural in 1 Thessalonians and emphasizes that the letter places "scarcely any value on putting Paul himself in the

72. Roberts, *Images of Paul and the Thessalonians* (1992), 80–81. The exegesis of 1 Thessalonians 1–3 is on pp. 79–184 and the summary on pp. 185–96. See further page references in the text below.

73. Haufe, *Der erste Brief des Paulus an die Thessalonicher* (1999), 3; cp. Schreiber, "Der erste Thessalonicherbrief" (2008), 388.

74. Paul-Gerhard Müller, *Der Erste und Zweite Brief an die Thessalonicher* (2001), 78ff.; the quotation is on p. 79.

75. Börschel, *Konstruktion einer christlichen Identität* (2001), 125–37, at 137.

foreground as author or missionary." Hence she speaks occasionally in her exegesis of 1 Thessalonians of "several senders and missionaries."[76]

Finally, I will mention two recent essays on number in the Pauline letters, by Eduard Verhoef and Samuel Byrskog, both of which show that 1 Thessalonians has a special role within the Corpus Paulinum.[77] Verhoef is primarily concerned to engage with the secretarial hypotheses, showing that they are of no use either in answering questions of authenticity or for clarifying the differing usage of the first person. What is found in 1 Thessalonians "indicates that Timothy and Silvanus were really co-authors, and in the sense that the letter attests to the common body of thought developed through discussions."[78] Samuel Byrskog offers the most thorough overall treatment of the subject of "I and we in Paul." He cautions against assuming a literary plural in 1 Thessalonians, or any of the Pauline letters, because a comparison with Greco-Roman and Jewish letters suggests no such thing.[79] His finding with regard to 1 Thessalonians is that most instances of the first person plural include all the senders, or at least two of them. None of them gives any evidence that it is not a genuine plural. It is more difficult to say whether all three functioned as real authors, though the prescript suggests that they did. On the one hand, Paul is the main author; on the other hand, the equality of all three is emphasized. Thus 1 Thessalonians, according to Byrskog, is the only "Pauline" letter that we can call "collective" as a whole[80]—further evidence of the unique character of the text. This has methodological consequences for all those who consider 1 Thessalonians authentic and accord this first apostolic writing special importance for their exegesis.

3.1.3 Consequences for 1 Thessalonians: A "genuine" authorial plural

In summary, we have seen the following previous types of interpretation of the "we" in 1 Thessalonians:

1. "Literary plural," really a singular = Paul alone writes;
2. Genuine plural = Paul writes, but for himself; the group or the other apostles are only conceptually included;
3. Genuine plural = the three apostles write and appear as real authors; Paul is distinguished from the group, in a singular usage, in up to three places.

The structure of the text and the discussion have shown that the thesis of a purely literary plural has an extremely weak basis. Even Karl Dick had to seek for external

76. Gerber, *Paulus und seine 'Kinder'* (2005), 261–62 (quotation on pp. 262–63); 251–349 on 1 Thessalonians as a whole.

77. Verhoef, "Numerus" (1995), with pp. 55–58 on 1 Thessalonians; Byrskog, "Co-Senders" (1996), with pp. 236–38 on 1 Thessalonians. Cp. also the sparse remarks in Cranfield, "Changes of Person and Number in Paul's Epistles" (1982), 285–86.

78. Verhoef, "Numerus," 55.

79. Byrskog, "Co-Senders," 233ff., 236, 249.

80. Ibid., 238; cp. 249.

reasons to maintain it in the case of 1 Thessalonians. "We" does not mean a disguised "I," but should be translated and interpreted as a real "we."

There remains the possibility, chosen by nearly all those who read a genuine "we," to read the real plural only in a restricted sense. This position always presupposes that it is Paul alone who writes or is responsible for the content, and that in any case "we" is *his* inclusive choice of words or a means of expressing cooperation, as Lofthouse writes: "when he wrote 'we,' he was thinking of himself as one of a number."[81] But is that methodologically defensible? What, in that case, is the meaning of a grammatical structure that has Paul undoubtedly and explicitly speaking only in 2:18, but in such a way that the "we" previously used appears as a real *pars pro toto*? Apart from the undiscussed presupposition that Paul must be the real author in any case, in whatever way, there remains scarcely any basis for maintaining an implicit "I." When Paul's name is mentioned first, that does not mean that this is a letter *from Paul*, but only that it presents itself *also* and *perhaps especially* in the name of Paul.

The fact that, as far as authorship is concerned, 1 Thessalonians stands apart in its language has consequences for commentary in regard to usage as well. For even if one opts for the possibility of dictation, the "others" here are in any case more than "secretaries." The moment the one dictating says "we," the one writing is no longer a mere assistant but has already been elevated, by that expression, to the level of an author. Hence the best solution in view of the textual evidence is to assume a real and intentional authorial "we" by a number of persons, as Zahn recognized.

Methodologically, the conclusion follows that in commentary on and exegesis of 1 Thessalonians there *must* be a genuine plural authorship in view. According to its wording, 1 Thessalonians is a letter written by three authors to an early Christian community—that is, if we take its own statement and the grammatical findings seriously. Those who advocate for its relevance, in particular, should in future avoid expressions such as "Paul says, hopes, writes" etc., and instead treat the text as the product of teamwork and comment accordingly, when possible choosing statements that describe it in collective terms: the authors, apostles, missionaries desire, pray, hope.

How should we imagine the concrete circumstances of writing, then? The letter could have been written by all three simultaneously; it could have been dictated by Paul; it could have been discussed between Paul and the others; it could be an independent letter from Silvanus and Timothy, who included Paul by name; or it could have been written by one of the three after a mutual discussion. All these solutions are possible within the framework of the generally posited historical situation, shortly after the founding of the community. All the inconsistencies in the text, deviations from other Pauline letters that are explained, for example, by means of theories of development, and in particular the passage in 2:14–16, could be understood and resolved in light of a factual threefold authorship. Should we see it as the product of an inter-apostolic discussion and suppose that in its

81. Lofthouse, "'I' and 'We,'" 73.

formulation a Paul who otherwise thought differently could have bowed to the vote of the other two in the sense of an "imperative mandate"? If Paul is no longer the sole author, or perhaps only wrote some parts himself, there is a good deal of room for the unique features of 1 Thessalonians. And yet a seldom-noticed but really obvious special character of the letter is still not explained by such a proposal.

Consequently, we need to go a step further and examine the matter more closely in what follows—for a closer examination of the individual relationships and the conditions under which the letter was written raises further questions and doubts. Is this really an active exchange among senders, messengers, and community? What are the characteristics of authentic letter correspondence? This is important for our conclusions, since in the New Testament canon it is the letter form in particular that was used by pseudepigraphical authors for the presentation of fictitious documents.[82] A really obvious question will help us to talk about the authentic conditions for communication by letter: *Who conveys the letter to the addressees?*

3.2 *Who Conveys the Letter to the Addressees?*

This question about who transported the letter to its addressees is seldom, in fact almost never asked regarding 1 Thessalonians; accordingly, it is hardly ever

82. For pseudepigraphy in the New Testament as a whole see Speyer, "Religiöse Pseudepigraphie" (1965/66); idem, art. "Fälschung" (1969); idem, *Literarische Fälschung* (1971); idem, "Fälschung" (1972); Kurt Aland, "Das Problem der Anonymität und Pseudonymität" (1967); idem, "Noch einmal" (1980); Balz, "Anonymität und Pseudepigraphie" (1969); Rist, "Pseudepigraphy and the Early Christians" (1972); von Fritz, ed., *Pseudepigrapha I* (1972); Trilling, *Untersuchungen zum 2. Thessalonicherbrief* (1972), 133–55; Brox, *Falsche Verfasserangaben* (1975); idem, ed., *Pseudepigraphie* (1977, a collection of previous publications); Pokorný, "Das Problem der neutestamentlichen Pseudepigraphie" (1984); idem, art. "Pseudepigraphie" (1997); Meade, *Pseudonymity and Canon* (1987); Paulsen, art. "Pseudepigraphen II" (1992); Wolter, art. "Pseudonymität II" (1997); idem, "Anonyme Schriften" (1988); Kraft, "Pseudepigrapha in Christianity" (1994); Reinmuth, "Der zweite Brief" (1998), 190–202; Klauck, *Die antike Briefliteratur* (1998), 301–306; Standhartinger, *Studien zur Entstehungsgeschichte & Intention des Kolosserbriefs* (1999), 29–56; Baum, *Pseudepigraphie und literarische Fälschung* (2001); Frenschkowski, "Pseudepigraphie und Paulusschule" (2001); idem, "Erkannte Pseudepigraphie?" (2009); Zimmermann, art. "Pseudepigraphie" (2003); idem, "Unecht—und doch wahr?" (2003); E.-M. Becker, "Von Paulus zu 'Paulus'" (2009); and in particular the detailed critical history of research on early Christian pseudepigraphy by Martina Janssen, *Unter falschem Namen* (2003, with bibliography), and now the (additional) individual contributions in the collected volume edited by Jörg Frey, Jens Herzer, Martina Janssen, and Clare K. Rothschild (with Michaela Engelmann), *Pseudepigraphie und Verfasserfiktion in frühchristlichen Briefen* (2009, with bibliography).

answered. But it casts light on a major epistolary inconsistency in the document. It is also true that in the exegesis of the other authentic letters in the Corpus Paulinum the discussion and presentation of the real circumstances of their delivery plays an amazingly small role. But if we take these writings to be authentic and important means of communication among the communities, then the explicit and implicit information on their delivery has social-historical significance. Their casual nature and their necessity furnish a criterion for judging the existing relationships between sender(s) and addressee(s), as we will show. They can thus be pointers to a concrete *Sitz im Leben* of the letter in question, something that can be viewed as part of a more extensive communication and hence must demonstrate "authenticity."

In answering this question we will be less concerned with the many studies of the ancient letter formula,[83] the theory and hermeneutics of letters,[84] or form-critical studies of the New Testament letters,[85] as far as method is concerned,[86] and instead will focus more attention on information on the practice of transportation and reception of letters. Our perspective will be primarily social-historical and will attend to the conveyance of information through letters. However, in light of the general dearth or sporadic nature of discussion of this subject we have to say that broad swaths of New Testament scholarship[87] in general, and Thessalonians research in particular, have shown little interest in this material aspect of letter communication. Still, the scattered works on ancient postal practice as a basis for the study of the New Testament epistolary literature that are noted below do show what a wealth of source material is available to aid discussion of the letters in their *Sitz im Leben* of materially-conditioned communication.[88] Unlike the dominant form-critical comparison of different types of letters and parts of letters, an

83. For example, Koskenniemi, *Studien zur Idee* (1956); Thraede, *Grundzüge griechisch-römischer Brieftopik* (1970); White, *Form and Function* (1972); idem, "New Testament Epistolary Literature" (1984), 1730–39; Stowers, *Letter Writing* (1986); Probst, *Paulus und der Brief* (1991), 55–105.

84. For example, Malherbe, *Ancient Epistolary Theorists* (1988); Klauck, *Briefliteratur*, 148–80 (with bibliography); E.-M. Becker, *Schreiben und Verstehen*, 103–39.

85. For example, Roller, *Formular*; Schubert, *Form and Function* (1939); Doty, *Letters in Primitive Christianity* (1973); Berger, "Apostelbrief" (1974); White, "New Testament Epistolary Literature" (1984), 1739–56; Schnider and Stenger, *Studien zum neutestamentlichen Briefformular* (1987); Vouga, "Der Brief als Form"; Weima, *Neglected Endings* (1994); Murphy-O'Connor, *Paul, the Letter-Writer* (1995); Markus Müller, *Vom Schluss zum Ganzen* (1997).

86. On this see the instructive overview of research in Bickmann, *Kommunikation gegen den Tod* (1998), 5–31.

87. One early exception is Stirewalt, "Paul's Evaluation" (1969); see also the section in Klauck's textbook, *Briefliteratur*, 66–70.

88. Epp, "New Testament Papyrus Manuscripts and Letter Carrying" (1991), 36ff., emphasizes the social-historical value of papyrus correspondence; in terms of method for interpretation of the NT and the Pauline letters within the framework of the Salzburg

exegetical concentration on the information relating to the conveyance of the correspondence can make a major contribution to our assessment of the authenticity of letter communications. In the case of 1 Thessalonians this will lead us to serious doubts about that authenticity.

3.2.1 The conveyance of letters in antiquity

The transmission of private letters of all kinds in the Greco-Roman period lay exclusively in the hands of servants, slaves, relatives, and more or less passing acquaintances of the persons who wrote them. Detailed information can be found in the work of the journalist Wolfgang Riepl on "news in antiquity,"[89] which remains a standard work on the subject. Even a man of the upper class like Cicero (whose correspondence has been a central subject of analysis, together with other, primarily Roman sources)[90] had no opportunity to use a public or state-organized system for exchange of letters. The *cursus publicus* established by Augustus in the imperial period served "only the political and military purposes of the ruler."[91] Apart from that everyone who wanted "to send an oral or written communication, a commission, a letter, or a dispatch ordinarily had to send a personal messenger to the place, or await an opportunity to give the communication to a friend or guest, an acquaintance, a merchant, etc. who was traveling there" (Riepl, 242). This meant that letter-writers and recipients were highly dependent on temporary and shifting opportunities and circumstances for communication, as well as on the

research project "Analyse der Paulusbriefe vor dem Hintergrund dokumentarischer Papyri" see esp. Arzt, "Analyse" (1994); idem, "Ägyptische Papyri" (1997); Michael Ernst, ed., *Die Wüste spricht* (1996); Arzt-Grabner, *Philemon* (2003), 39–56 and *passim* (for the conveyance of letters see pp. 195, 215); for method in general, cp. Bammer, "Erwählung inmitten einer multikulturellen Gemeindesituation" (2007), 104ff.

89. Riepl, *Das Nachrichtenwesen des Altertums* (1913).

90. Ibid., 241–322, and 140ff. within the chapter on "Means and Speed of Spreading the News," 123–240, and frequently elsewhere; cp. Reck, *Kommunikation und Gemeindeaufbau* (1991), 106–10; for Cicero see also Richards, *The Secretary in the Letters of Paul* (1991), 7–10; Murphy-O'Connor, *Paul, the Letter-Writer*, 37–40; esp. Klauck, "Compilation of Letters" (2003), and Schmeller, "Cicerobriefe" (2004). Additionally on the subject of postal service see White, "Documentary Letter Tradition" (1982), 102–104; idem, *Light from Ancient Letters* (1986), 214–15; Casson, *Travel in the Ancient World* (1994), 219–25; and esp. Llewellyn, "Conveyance of Letters" (1994, with bibliography); Klauck, *Briefliteratur*, 66ff.; Kolb, *Transport und Nachrichtentransfer* (2000), 20–21, 27; E.-M. Becker, *Schreiben und Verstehen*, 53–54.

91. Riepl, *Die Nachrichtenwesen des Altertums*, 241 (see other page references in the text above); for the *cursus publicus* see pp. 241ff., 262ff.; see esp. Kolb, *Transport und Nachrichtentransfer*, 49ff., 93ff.; also Reck, *Kommunikation und Gemeindeaufbau*, 107–108 (with bibliography); Markus Müller, *Vom Schluss zum Ganzen*, 30–42 n. 70; Llewellyn, "Conveyance of Letters," 13–22 (with bibliography, as well as information on postal conveyance in the Persian Empire and in Ptolemaic Egypt on pp. 2–13).

persons entrusted with it. Cicero's letters are a rich source of information about the overwhelming significance of the people who carried letters. His remarks on the subject take up a great deal of space, which certainly sheds light on common experiences in the transmission of letters.

There is frequent complaint about the dearth of private messengers, usually the slaves of friends or family, and about the complete absence of such messengers, depending on where one was located. That is why, for example, Cicero called for help when he was exiled in Thessalonica (Riepl, 249): "Send me letter-carriers, that I may know what is going on and what you are all doing" (*Cic. fam.* 14,1,6); "Send slaves to me with letters as soon and as often as possible" (*Cic. Att.* 3,19). In other "urgent cases he sends letter-carriers to travel with those from whom he expects to receive news" (Riepl, 250). It was important to exploit the messengers' travel to and fro so that, in the course of a journey, new letters could be written and given to them to convey. A letter was thus quite often written because of an immediate opportunity to send it: "I am giving this letter to another man's letter-carriers, who are in a hurry to start; that, and the fact that I am about to send my own, accounts for its brevity" (*Cic. Att.* 11,17,1, in Riepl, 255). In this way messengers could be sent around among acquaintances to collect as many letters as possible, "but usually not to wait for letters to be written, which on the one hand would cost too much time and on the other hand would force the sender to write quickly and briefly" (Riepl, 256).[92]

So it often happened that packets containing many letters to different addressees were collected and distributed at the place of arrival or were redistributed or forwarded through intermediary places. Thus it could be that a single letter would pass through many hands or could be misdirected as part of a packet (Riepl, 252–53). But on the whole it was possible for members of the social elite to achieve a considerable speed and frequency of exchange of letters, as Eldon J. Epp has calculated and discussed in terms of the wealth of surviving Zenon papyri from the Ptolemaic period (3d c. B.C.E.) that contain dates and notes of receipt.[93]

Thus while members of the Roman upper classes maintained a relatively active exchange of letters among themselves, thanks to the work of well-trained and numerous slaves, the situation for the poorer classes was quite different. They had to depend solely on contacts with people traveling on business and on commercial caravans or wait for relatives and friends, and not miss their chance when someone was planning a trip.[94] That made them more dependent on timing and also on the ability to assess the trustworthiness of strangers as accurately as possible. It was immeasurably more difficult to maintain regular contact through letters. Private papyri found in Egyptian digs are especially important documentation of the letter

92. For the influence of the practical circumstances occasioned by the arrival of messengers on the composition of some of Cicero's letters see also Klauck, "Compilation of Letters," 328ff.

93. Epp, "New Testament Papyrus Manuscripts and Letter Carrying," 51ff.

94. White, "Documentary Letter Tradition," 103.

communications of "ordinary people."[95] We learn from the papyri, on the one hand, that the chance to send a letter with a traveler was gladly seized, so that the opportunity itself was the motivation for the letter, and was mentioned in it. Heikki Koskenniemi names this expression, increasingly more frequent in the course of centuries to the point of becoming a fixed convention of letter-writing, the ἀφορμή formula, after one of the concepts used in it.[96] Often a few such formulae sufficed to fulfill the main purpose of the letter, namely, to give a sign of life "in a land with a high death rate, great distances, and infrequent communication."[97]

Information about messengers and commissioning becomes more individualized and differentiated when it is primarily about an important message or its sending and an opportunity must be sought or cannot be carefully chosen because of urgency. Even though complaints about the dearth or inadequacy of opportunities for sending can be interpreted as excuses offered by lazy correspondents to their recipients,[98] there were often real difficulties in getting a letter underway. The Greek letter of a young recruit named Apollinarius,[99] for example, dictated to a scribe near Rome, to his mother, Taesion, in Karanis in Egypt, first mentions a previous letter to her from Cyrene that he had sent when he (finally) found someone traveling from there to his home town. He now asks her urgently to write to him right away. If she finds no one who is traveling to the place he names she should write to a certain Socrates, who will transmit the letter to her son. The Greek letter of the soldier Terentianus from Alexandria to his sister Tasoucharion mentions the delivery of goods.[100] The one bringing the letter is supposed to hand over a full basket as well. The sender asks his sister to see what is in it and write him about it; apparently this was a necessary means of checking the honesty of the messenger. She is to receive another delivery through Valerius, a

95. Some stages in the evaluation of these sources, so important for New Testament letters, are Deissmann, *Light from the Ancient East* (1927; 1978), esp. 143–246; Exler, *Form of the Ancient Greek Letter* (1923); Koskenniemi, *Studien zur Idee*; White, *Light from Ancient Letters* (for places and digs see 4ff.); Epp, "New Testament Papyrus Manuscripts and Letter Carrying," esp. 40–51; the whole NDIEC series, including esp. Llewellyn, "Conveyance of Letters," and the works of the Salzburg research project "Analyse der Paulusbriefe auf dem Hintergrund dokumentarischer Papyri," directed by Michael Ernst and Peter Arzt-Grabner (see n. 88 above).

96. Koskenniemi, *Studien zur Idee*, 77–87, esp. 82ff.; cp. Llewellyn, "Conveyance of Letters," 26–27.

97. Hengstl, *Griechische Papyri aus Ägypten* (1978), 216.

98. This is the tenor of Koskenniemi, *Studien zur Idee*, 64–67; Epp, "New Testament Papyrus Manuscripts and Letter Carrying," 47ff.; and Llewellyn, "Conveyance of Letters," 27–29, in each case with examples.

99. *p.Mich.* VIII, 490, 5–16, 2d c. C.E.; see White, *Light from Ancient Letters*, 161ff.; cp. Epp, "New Testament Papyrus Manuscripts and Letter Carrying," 50–51; Markus Müller, *Vom Schluss zum Ganzen*, 32.

100. *p.Mich.* VIII, 481, 5–12, early 2d c. C.E.; see White, *Light from Ancient Letters*, 176ff.

goldsmith, and she is to confirm receipt of that as well. This shows how even this presumably wealthy family had to worry about the reliability of messengers and was dependent on the services of traveling merchants familiar to them. Similar problems are revealed by the letter from Indike to her mistress Thaisous.[101] She is sending her a bread basket by the camel driver Taurinos and asks her lady in friendly and apparently urgent fashion to confirm its contents.

Did women also convey letters? Although Cicero's frequently-used technical term *tabellarius*[102] and other similar Latin and Greek terms such as γραμματηφόρος,[103] as well as the personal names of occasional letter-bringers, mainly suggest male messengers, we should naturally suppose that women carried and delivered letters from their owners or employers, their friends and relatives, when they traveled. In view of the ancient practice of postal delivery, references to women's journeys should always be regarded as reflecting opportunities for the delivery of letters. In the letter from the Egyptian laborer Hilarion of Alexandria to his pregnant wife Alis that Adolf Deissmann describes, in which he suggests, among other things, that in case she bears a daughter she should expose her, there is mention of a woman named Aphrodisias as a connection.[104] She has journeyed from Oxyrhynchos to Alexandria and brought Hilarion news from home; consequently she will probably bring his letter when she returns home. Within the New Testament letter corpus we have a sure reference to a letter-bearer in the person of Phoebe (Rom 16:1–2).[105]

These few examples from Greco-Roman private letters already signal the frequency of information about the conditions of their transmission and the delivery of other letters mentioned in them. Many more such letters show the same.[106] It is these witnesses to the public nature of the exchange of letters, the hope for an adequate experience of delivery and receipt and, connected with that, the next step in the ongoing communication that document the vitality of a correspondence, even if it consists of only a few lines as in the letter from Indike quoted above.

101. *p.Oxy.* II, 300, 1–5, end of the 1st c. C.E.; see White, *Light from Ancient Letters*, 146. On the problem of the reliability of messengers cp. Stirewalt, "Paul's Evaluation," 184ff. (at 185 n. 1), with reference to the correspondence of Plato's disciple Chion; see also Klauck, *Briefliteratur*, 68–69.

102. *Cic.fam.* 2, 7, 3; 2, 29, 1; 9, 15, 1; 14, 1, 6; 14, 18, 2; *Att.* 1, 18, and frequently; cp. Richards, *The Secretary in the Letters of Paul*, 7 n. 34.

103. Cp. Llewellyn, "Conveyance of Letters," 1–2 (on *p.Oxy.* LI 3623); 48ff.

104. *p.Oxy.* IV, 744; Deissmann, *Light from the Ancient East*, 154–55.

105. See below at 3.2.2.a.

106. Cp., besides many other examples, the collections in White, *Light from Ancient Letters* (e.g., BGU 137 on p. 89; *p.Mich.* VIII, 479,8–15, on pp. 175–76); Hengstl, *Griechische Papyri aus Ägypten* (e.g., *p.Oxy.* III 531 on p. 211; *p.Giss.* 69 on p. 337); and Stowers, *Letter Writing* (e.g., pp. 61ff., 72ff., 88, 110, etc.) and Llewellyn, "Conveyance of Letters" (BGU XIV, 2417 on p. 26); there is an extended discussion of sender information in the papyrus letters in Epp, "New Testament Papyrus Manuscripts and Letter Carrying," 43–51.

With regard to early Christian letters, to the extent that the manuscript tradition has actually preserved an authentic letter or exchange of letters it should likewise demonstrate the existence of a vital communicative situation. Given these examples, what should we expect to find in the case of the Pauline communities? Here again the reliability of messengers is an important factor; consequently, we may anticipate information about messengers and their reliability as a recommendation of them, as well as their plans, duties, and activities at the goal of their journey. If someone completely unknown delivers the letters, that would be mentioned not only in family letters but also and especially in those directed to communities. The required use of opportunities to and fro[107] could be especially appropriate for messengers sent by communities. The possibility of having something carried by another had to be exploited. Thus when people are mentioned who are en route to the addressee we may suppose that they are bringing something with them, primarily the letter but possibly also packages of goods (Phil 4:14, 18), and above all the great collection for Jerusalem (1 Cor 16:3; 2 Cor 8:16–24; 9:1–5).[108] Familial connection among communities, their members, and the apostles allows us to suppose that there was a great desire for further contacts and corresponding expressions of that desire as it concerned the concrete conditions of their immediate future.

3.2.2 Possible carriers of Paul's letters: Romans, 1 and 2 Corinthians, Philippians, Philemon

In view of the great difficulties and inconsistencies involved in clarifying the question of the conveyance of 1 Thessalonians and potential plans for other visits, to be described below, we are struck by the relative ease and probability with which such questions can be answered in the case of the other authentic Pauline letters. A vivid image of multiple, mutually cultivated relationships, by no means dominated by Paul, is visible to the attentive eye; it deserves an extended study, independent of the usual chronological reconstructions of Paul's journeys.[109] Here I must restrict myself to the information provided about the supposed bearers of the letters.

107. For the conditions of travel by road and by sea in the Roman period and the corresponding rates of speed see, e.g., Bruce, "Travel and Communication" (1992); Casson, *Travel in the Ancient World*, 115–218; 309–17; Kolb, *Transport und Nachrichtentransfer* (2000), 308–32.

108. For the "intermediate" tasks of those sent see Reck, *Kommunikation und Gemeindeaufbau*, 204–205; cp. Ollrog, *Paulus und seine Mitarbeiter*, 95–108; Mitchell, "Envoys in the Context of Greco-Roman Diplomatic and Epistolary Conventions" (1992).

109. See the work of Ollrog, *Paulus und seine Mitarbeiter* (for a critique of the "coworker" model see the excursus above at 3.1.2). For the "fabric of relationships" (Ollrog, 187) in Pauline communities see also Reck, *Kommunikation und Gemeindeaufbau*; Leutzsch, *Die Bewährung der Wahrheit* (1994), 29–30; Börschel, *Konstruktion einer christlichen Identität*, 191–95 ("Die Verknüpfung der Gemeinden"); using 2 Corinthians as an example: Marlene Crüsemann, "Das weite Herz" (2004), 357–72; eadem, "Trost, *charis* und Kraft der Schwachen" (2009), and fundamentally for the whole, Ehrensperger, *Paul and the Dynamics of Power* (2007).

Margaret Mitchell has provided an extensive treatment of the subject of messengers in the New Testament within the framework of the diplomatic and epistolary conventions of the Greco-Roman world. The question of messengers is touched on throughout but is not emphasized and answered as such. Paul's recommendations to the envoys and his self-recommendations, which Mitchell adduces in the cases of Galatians, 1 and 2 Corinthians, Romans, Philemon, and Philippians,[110] are not necessarily of equal significance to the naming of the current bearer of the letter, and that is not adequately discussed.[111] Hence, despite her materially rich presentation and accurate observations,[112] she does not contribute anything decisive to the means by which the Pauline letters were delivered.

M. Luther Stirewalt's essay is probably the only work to date that contains an extended discussion of the delivery of the Pauline letters.[113] He includes the occasional naming of co-senders in his consideration and thinks that Timothy most probably did not carry any of the letters, in particular none to and from Thessalonica.[114] The contrary is true for Titus, who is said to be the letter-carrier between Paul and Corinth. It is not altogether clear whether that applies to both the Corinthian letters, but it is certainly true of the second. Romans is also missing from the collection. The letter to Philippi is said to have been carried by Epaphroditus, the one to Colossae by Tychicus and Onesimus. An overview reveals the multiple reciprocal contacts to and from Corinth, as reflected in 1 Corinthians.[115] Thus Stirewalt concludes that, in comparison to the difficult conditions of ancient postal service, Paul was in a fairly comfortable situation because he always had at his disposal an adequate number of willing men (!) who were available for a variety of services, including the delivery of letters. On the whole, these relatively extensive observations, despite suggestive (though scarcely adopted) insights into the roles of messengers, do not seem to have been consistently thought through. In fact, it seems to me that the recoverable details in each of Paul's letters that are regarded as authentic offer a solid and clear picture from which 1 Thessalonians deviates significantly. For that reason I need to survey them sequentially below in terms of what they say about their conveyance.

110. Mitchell, "Envoys," 645ff.

111. Ibid., 652–53 n. 55.

112. See 3.2.4c below for a comparison between 1 Thess 3:6–9 and 2 Cor 7:5–10 (ibid., 653–61).

113. Stirewalt, "Paul's Evaluation," 186–90; cp. the further literature listed below in n. 121. Previously, Roller had attempted to evaluate "the remarks on messengers as evidence of authenticity" (*Formular*, 131–33, with overview on p. 132). He determines that both Thessalonian letters and Galatians (as the "earliest letters") have no information about the messengers, not even in 1 Thess 3:2, 5; in addition, he regards the Pastorals, Hebrews, and other letters as also Pauline, which greatly reduces the value of his investigation as far as "authenticity" is concerned.

114. Stirewalt, "Paul's Evaluation," 187.

115. Ibid., 189.

What kind of information in a New Testament letter points to its conveyance and the ones who carried it? If we suppose that it was within the realm of Christian practice for trustworthy, deserving persons known to one or both parties to undertake the communication of news and letters to other congregations insofar as they had to make the journey anyway or went for that specific purpose, we would expect that their names would appear somewhere, either within or on the margins of a (real) letter. There would be an explanation that these persons are about to begin a journey, a movement between sender and addressee, or have just completed one. Expressions like ἔπεμψα ("I have sent") indicate a real, current contact. The verb in the so-called epistolary aorist certainly describes a sending that is current to the sender: "The ancient letter-writer places [himself or herself] in the situation of the reader and thus writes, as here, 'I have sent,' even when thinking at the moment, at the time of writing, of a sending that has yet to happen, which we have to render in the present tense."[116] Verbs like ἀποστέλλω and πέμπω refer *per se* to the things and persons that are sent together with the letter; the latter, at least in the Hellenistic period, applies only to persons.[117] They also point directly to the person or persons bringing the letter. Finally, words of recommendation such as συνίστημι, "I commend," and remarks on characteristics and services of the one commended, together with requests that they be received and wishes concerning the attitude and behavior of the addressees toward the messenger(s) are important indicators. These accompanying words represent a kind of identity card for the traveler. At the same time they strengthen the relationship among all those involved, since by making the recommendation the senders have in a sense made part of the journey; they influence the encounter that will take place at the end of the journey, in their absence, and so can participate in it.

So in what follows we will look at the communication of letters of recommendation for messengers within the text of more comprehensive letters. The only text we have that can be characterized as entirely a letter of recommendation is Philemon.[118] We should note the combination of these elements:

116. Schweizer, *Der Brief an die Kolosser* (2d ed. 1980), 176; cp. BDR §334; Koskenniemi, *Studien zur Idee*, 189–90; Llewellyn, "Conveyance of Letters," 51 n. 9.

117. Koskienniemi, *Studien zur Idee*, 193–94, 196.

118. Cp. Kim, *Form and Structure of the Familiar Greek Letter of Recommendation* (1972), 123–28. Kim's remarks on texts of recommendation in the NT (pp. 119–42) are only partly useful for the question of messengers since he does not introduce the latter and so discusses recommendations independently of possible journeys. For the ancient social conventions of recommendation and letters of recommendation see White, "Documentary Letter Tradition," 95–96; Marshall, *Enmity in Corinth* (1987), 91–129; Reck, *Kommunikation und Gemeindeaufbau*, 112ff., and especially Leutzsch, *Die Bewährung der Wahrheit*, 18–26, 122–30, with bibliography. Leutzsch emphasizes that Christian letters of recommendation, unlike pagan ones, do not create new relationships; instead, they are intended to identify strangers who are already joined by the "relational concept of siblinghood" (p. 27).

- Names of contact persons and their relationship to the senders or recipients;
- Is there mention of a journey, a current contact between these persons and the addressees? Sender formulae and references to their activities at the place of arrival?;
- Petitions for reception and admonition to a particular attitude to the persons named (in the imperative); mention of their services as recommendation.

Acts 15:23–29 can serve as a model for the information about transmission that can be found within an early Christian community letter. This is the writing by which the conclusions of the Jerusalem authorities on the question of Torah observance by "Gentile Christians" are to be communicated to the congregations in Antioch and nearby. We may see this as the "earliest evidence for the composition of a community letter."[119] Two brothers, Judas and Silas, are chosen and sent with Paul and Barnabas, who, as the context shows, are apostles of these communities and therefore known to them. This is mentioned in the summary of the decree mentioned at the beginning (v. 22), together with their names, so that the process of communication is clear. Still, the quoted letter itself gives information about this, so that we are in a position to understand what is written there as a clear reference to those bringing the letter. They are distinguished by use of the vocabulary of sending: ἐκλεξαμένοις ἄνδρας πέμψαι πρὸς ὑμᾶς (v. 25); ἀπεστάλκαμεν (v. 27). With this they are also identified through the letter itself as contact persons who are making a present journey to the place where the addressees are located. The worthy engagement of their own lives for the name of the Lord Jesus Christ is mentioned as a recommendation for Judas and Silas (v. 26). The conclusion is that Paul, Barnabas, Judas, and Silas are to be regarded as the conveyers of this apostolic communication. As a final cross-check, vv. 30–33 show that they have delivered the letter and are able to give additional explanations and interpretations for it in Antioch.

Thus Acts 15:23–33 offers us a testable model for the veracity of information about messengers such as we find within the authentic New Testament letters themselves, since the narrative describes, from its own perspective, an event of the actual delivery of a letter. That has heuristic value for the Pauline letters, which are also supposed to have arisen from a real situation of epistolary communication.

119. Andresen, "Zum Formular frühchristlicher Gemeindebriefe" (1965), 233; for the historicity of the event cp. Klinghardt, *Gesetz und Volk Gottes* (1988), 207–24; Jervell, *Apostelgeschichte* (1998), 403ff., and above all Wehnert, *Die Reinheit des "christlichen Gottesvolkes"* (1997), 21–82, 239–75; for the epistolary character of the text see Klauck, *Briefliteratur*, 315–22. The model for early Christian community relationships and exchanges might be found in the practice of epistolary communication between Jewish Diaspora congregations and the authorities in Jerusalem. (On this see Shmuel Safrai, "Relations" [1974], and Alexander, "Epistolary Literature" [1986]; cp. esp. Andresen, "Zum Formular," and Taatz, *Frühjüdische Briefe* [1991], as well as Theissen, "Judentum und Christentum bei Paulus" [1991], 354ff.).

In light of Acts 15:23–29; 1 Cor 4:17–19a, and 1 Thess 3:1–5, Rudolf Pesch has outlined a messenger formula with the following components: (1) presentation of the messenger with the formula "I have sent" or something similar; (2) recommendation of the messenger and that person's qualifications; (3) description of the messenger's assignment. This is found also in Romans, 2 Corinthians, Philippians, Colossians, Ephesians, and Philemon.[120] This formula can be used to describe the messengers, much as in the following investigation: Phoebe (Rom); Timothy (1 Cor); Titus (2 Cor); Epaphroditus (Phil); Onesimus (Phlm),[121] but not the special situation of the first letter to Thessalonica if one does not agree with Pesch's strict hypothesis of divisions.[122] Thus it will be necessary to pay attention not only to the actual movements we can discern on the part of the emissaries but also to the situative openness of the whole writing: does it envision a continuation of the various relationships, and if so, in what way?

A. The Letter to the Community in Rome

In Romans 16:1–2, Paul recommends to the Roman community a woman otherwise unknown to them, named Phoebe: Συνίστημι δὲ ὑμῖν Φοίβην. She is introduced as deacon of the community in Cenchreae. Paul requests that she be received (αὐτὴν προσδέξησθε) in the Lord, as is fitting for the saints. There is also a petition that they support (παραστῆτε) her in her activities in every way. The commendation concludes with praise of Phoebe as patron and director/leader (προστάτις).[123] Paul's trusting relationship with her emphasizes that she is such for Paul as well.

Accordingly, Romans gives a number of indications about how it was delivered. The commendation of Phoebe and the request that she be received are a clear signal that she is about to travel to Rome. It is equally clear that she is not going on orders from Paul or anyone else; rather, the respectful way in which she is presented, as an independent missionary with a position of leadership, indicates that she is traveling for her own purposes. In all probability she is bringing the letter to the

120. Pesch, *Entdeckung*, 57–64, with the formula on p. 59.

121. There are only sporadic further listings of messengers in the exegetical literature, for example, Murphy-O'Connor, *Paul, the Letter-Writer*, 40–41 (1 & 2 Thess: strangers; 1 Cor: Stephanas and associates; 2 Cor: Titus; Rom: Phoebe; Col: Epaphras and associates; Gal: unknown); Llewellyn, "Conveyance of Letters," 51–54 (1 Cor: Timothy; 2 Cor: Titus and others; Col + Eph: Tychicus; Phil: Epaphroditus; Phlm: Onesimus; he asserts an absence of messengers for 1 and 2 Thess, Gal, and Rom). The only somewhat fuller listing is in Stirewalt, "Paul's Evaluation," 186–90; see above at 3.2.2.

122. And even in that case only for the first of the writings discussed; see further below at 3.2.4b.

123. For προστάτις with this meaning of leadership, and against the traditional idea of "helper, assistant," see Schüssler Fiorenza, *In Memory of Her*, 47–48, 169–72, 181–82; Luise Schottroff, "How Justified is the Feminist Critique of Paul?" 37–38; Markus Müller, *Vom Schluss zum Ganzen*, 214ff.; cp. also Brooten, "Jael προστάτις" (1991).

community in Rome that Paul has entrusted to her.[124] In addition we read of Paul's concrete plans to visit Rome (Rom 15:22–24), and there is an extended list of other contact persons linking Paul and the Roman community (16:3–15).

B. The first letter to the community in Corinth

At first glance there seem to be a number of persons and delegations who might have delivered 1 Corinthians. It appears from 1 Cor 1:11 that Paul has received current news from Corinth through Chloe's people; evidently they traveled from there to Ephesus, where he is staying at the time of writing (1 Cor 16:8). But we learn nothing of a possible return journey by these people.

Something similar is true for Stephanas, Fortunatus, and Achaicus, the delegation from the Corinthian community at whose arrival (παρουσία) Paul so clearly rejoices (16:17–18). Previously, Paul had baptized Stephanas and his household (1:16), his first converts in Achaia (16:15–16). There is an admonition to acknowledge their leadership, justified also by their διακονία for the saints. It is probable that Fortunatus and Achaicus are part of that community. Paul calls them contact persons in the fullest sense of the word: they take the place of the Corinthians in their absence and have refreshed (ἀνέπαυσαν, v. 18) not only his spirit but also that of those he addresses (!)—however we might imagine such a retroactive or anticipated harmony with people at a distance. Hence it is possible to translate this aorist also in the present:[125] "they refresh my spirit and yours," which, combined with the closing and admonitory imperative, "give recognition to such [persons]!" may certainly serve as a commendation and an indication that they will be returning home. So they are also possible bearers of the letter.[126]

Still, there are some factors that favor Timothy. It is said that he is on the way to Corinth at the time when the letter is written: "If Timothy comes . . ." (16:10), and his return to Ephesus is expected: ". . . so that he may come to me; for I am expecting him with the brothers [and sisters]" (v. 11). The admonitory imperative may be intended to ensure an anxiety-free sojourn in Corinth for Timothy as well as his being sent back (προπέμψατε) in peace. It is customary to read this, because of ἐὰν,

124. Thus also, e.g., Wilckens, *Der Brief an die Römer*, 1 (1978), 22; 3 (1982), 131–32; Markus Müller, *Vom Schluss zum Ganzen*, 215; Tamez, "Romans: A Feminist Reading" (2012), 699–700; Haacker, *Der Brief des Paulus an die Römer* (1999), 318–19 and elsewhere.

125. See the perfect passive ἀναπέπαυται of Titus by the Corinthians in 2 Cor 7:13, a statement about past events.

126. Thus also Schrage, *Der erste Brief an die Korinther* 1 (1991), 69, and Malherbe, "Did the Thessalonians write to Paul?" (1990), 254; idem, *The Letters to the Thessalonians*, 209–10 (which makes it all the more surprising that Malherbe neither asks nor answers the question of messenger[s] for 1 Thess). Bärbel Bosenius, who advocates for the unity of 2 Corinthians, pleads on the basis of 2 Cor 7; 12:18 for Titus as the bearer of 1 Corinthians (*Die Abwesenheit des Apostels* [1994], 16ff.). However, her acute reflections do not take into account the fact that there is no mention of Titus in 1 Corinthians itself.

"if,"[127] as also an announcement of the missionary's imminent passage through Corinth.[128] But in 4:17 there is a very casual remark within the argumentative context that Timothy has already been sent to Corinth (ἔπεμψα ὑμῖν Τιμόθεον), and he may be there when the addressees are reading the letter.[129] Since all the abovementioned criteria pointing to letter-bearers apply to him, and especially because both his journey to Corinth and his return are explicitly mentioned, the letter could preferably have been given to him. However, it remains important for the comparison we wish to make with 1 Thessalonians that the future travels of all possible bearers of the letter to Corinth are clearly stated. Stephanas, Fortunatus, and Achaicus come from Corinth and will now or at some point return there. Timothy's current and future "travel plans" between the partners in the letter exchange are also clearly evident in 16:10–11. Paul himself shares detailed dates and routes for his own coming in 16:3–9.

C. The Second Letter to the Community in Corinth

It is striking that in the second letter to the community in Corinth, despite all the hypotheses that divide the letter into separate writings,[130] the canonical text gives a relatively clear and simple answer to the question of its delivery. The letter neither contains plural and mutually contradictory dispatch formulas nor did a possible redactor leave the question of delivery unanswered. That answer could, of course, furnish another argument for the unity of the text:[131] Titus and his companions are clearly portrayed as the probable envoys. Titus has recently returned from Corinth

127. Or "when": conditional sentence with ἐὰν; see the options in BDR §§373, 373.

128. Cp. Conzelmann, *1 Corinthians* (1975), 296; Lang, *Die Briefe an die Korinther* (1986), 247.

129. Differently Lindemann, *Der Erste Korintherbrief* (2000), 380: Timothy is "not the bearer of the letter, since otherwise the admonition would be rather too late (the letter must be in Corinth before Timothy; 4:17 assumes nothing else)." If we read this as not an epistolary aorist, with, for example, Schrage (*Der erste Brief an die Korinther*, ad loc) and Stirewalt ("Paul's Evaluation," 187 n. 3), this would be speaking of a previous visit by Timothy; at the same time, however, 16:10–11 would have to be understood in the sense of something future. This is no more probable than that both represent a current contact. Pesch advocates for Timothy as the bearer of a part of the letter to Corinth (*Entdeckung*, 58–59). For hypotheses on the fragmentary nature of 1 Thessalonians, see further below at 3.2.4b).

130. For theories of the division and/or compilation of the letter cp., e.g., Thrall, *The Second Epistle to the Corinthians* 1 (1994), 3–49; Bieringer, "Teilungshypothesen zum 2. Korintherbrief" (1994); Grässer, *Der zweite Brief an die Korinther* 1 (2002), 26–35; E.-M. Becker, *Schreiben und Verstehen*, 3–19, 94–102; Schmeller, "Der zweite Korintherbrief" (2008), 332–38.

131. This position is advocated by, among others, Christian Wolff, *Der zweite Brief des Paulus an die Korinther* (1989); Bieringer, "Plädoyer für die Einheitlichkeit" (1994); Bosenius, *Abwesenheit des Apostels*; and Marlene Crüsemann, "Das weite Herz."

and his arrival is a consolation to the senders, Timothy and Paul; in addition, his report on the Corinthians' obedience to Paul has caused him to rejoice (2 Cor 7:6–16). The repeated statements about the mutuality of relationships and the description of the emotional effects on Paul, the other missionaries, the communities, and their members with regard to one another are remarkable. Paul apparently intends in this way to weave and solidify the network of connections among them.[132] This section is about the sorrow Paul has caused the community, the result of which is his consolation and joy in the return of Titus, whose spirit and mind were also consoled in Corinth (v. 7) and put at rest (v. 13).[133] It also speaks of Titus's profoundly moving recollection of the obedience "of all of you" and "how you welcomed him [ἐδέξασθε, v. 15] with fear and trembling." The context of remembering places this aorist in the past.

Second Corinthians 8 speaks of an imminent or actually occurring visit by Titus (see also 9:5; 12:17–18). The occasion is the completion of the great collection (8:10–11) for the "saints" (v. 4) in Jerusalem.[134] At the urging of Paul and Timothy (v. 6), and because of his own desire, he is now returning (ἐξῆλθεν, v. 17) to them. A "brother" designated by the community to bring the collection is being sent as well (συνεπέμψαμεν, v. 18) in order that Paul may be assured, on his return, of the correct administration of the whole business. Still a third brother is also being sent (συνεπέμψαμεν, v. 22). The concluding injunction to give these three, Titus and the messengers/apostles of the communities (ἀπόστολοι ἐκκλησιῶν), proof of their love (τὴν ἔνδειξιν ... ἐνδεικνύμενοι, vv. 23–24)[135] makes it clear that this is about a real visit, at which time 2 Corinthians can be delivered.

Overall, in comparison with 1 Thessalonians we can see that here, as in 1 Corinthians, we have information not only about the presumed emissaries but also about past and present journeys and details of those about to happen in the immediate future, revealing an active back-and-forth movement. Also, Paul speaks here about his third visit to the community in the near future (12:14–16; 13:1–2).

D. The Letter to the Communities in Galatia

According to Galatians 1:2b this letter is written "to the churches of Galatia." This is not merely an address: "The designation of the addressees consists solely of facts

132. For the network of relationships among Pauline communities as illustrated by 2 Corinthians see Luise Schottroff, "Sieg des Lebens" (1982); Frettlöh, "Der Charme der gerechten Gabe" (2001), 136–61; Ehrensperger, *Paul and the Dynamics of Power*, 63–80, 98–116; Marlene Crüsemann, "Trost, *charis*."

133. See n. 125 above.

134. For the collection and its function in a cycle of blessing, rescue, and multiple connections of the communities to one another see Georgi, *Remembering the Poor* (1992; on the "cycle" see pp. 149–51); Frettlöh, "Charme," 136–61; Marlene Crüsemann, "Trost, *charis*," 118–25.

135. Middle participle in an imperative sense; cp. BDR §468 n. 5; many mss. instead have the imperative ἐνδείξασθε.

and represents the letter as a circular."[136] Such a circular letter would scarcely have been delivered by just one person or delegation to several communities. We should instead suppose that each of the communities would have sent some of their members or given the letter to them when they were traveling for other purposes. For that reason Paul has no need to worry about details of its delivery. It therefore makes sense that neither names nor contact persons are mentioned in the letter to the communities in Galatia, nor is anything said about travels between the senders ("Paul . . . and all the members of God's family who are with me," Gal 1:1a, 2a) and the addressees; for the same reason the vocabulary of sending and commendation is also absent. As a result we can say nothing more in detail about the question of delivery of this letter.

E. The Letter to the Community in Philippi

Timothy is planning a future journey to Philippi; Paul hopes to send him soon (ἐλπίζω . . . Τιμόθεον ταχέως πέμψαι, 2:19, 23) to receive news from there. Paul himself has no concrete plans to visit (1:26–27; 2:24) because of his current imprisonment (1:12–14). The visitor at present, however, is Epaphroditus. He works and "soldiers" together with Paul and is also the messenger/apostle of the community. He came to Paul and Timothy with a gift of food from Philippi (4:14, 18), and Paul thinks it necessary to send him back (ἀναγκαῖον δὲ ἡγησάμεν . . . πέμψαι, 2:25) because he has been ill and the community was worried about him. The Philippians' concern for him in turn makes Epaphroditus long for his community, which is why Paul has sent him (ἔπεμψα, 2:28) so quickly, that the congregation may see him again and their happiness may be restored. It is again striking how precisely Paul describes the individual relationships, taking care in the process to present himself also as one who supports and encourages connections. The epistolary aorist in 2:25, 28 indicates the present state of the readers, following as it does after an imperative injunction to receive Epaphroditus (προσδέξεσθε, 2:29) "with all joy."

Epaphroditus, who comes from Philippi (2:25; cp. 4:18), therefore in all probability carries this letter with him.[137] His journeys, and those of Timothy, link Paul to the community in past, present, and the immediate future.

136. Vouga, *An die Galater* (1998), 18. Cp. Hans Dieter Betz, *Galatians* (1979), who, while he does not speak of a circular letter, refers to the closeness of these communities, probably not only in the geographic sense. "The fact that Paul writes to several churches raises the question of their organization. They must have been connected in some organizational way unknown to us" (p. 40), which would have created common means of communication among them.

137. Cp. Walter, "Der Brief an die Philipper" (1998), 14: "So Paul now sends him, restored to health, to Philippi (in place of Timothy, whom he probably had wanted to send) and gives him the letter to carry." For the question of possible partition and/or compilation of the letter see ibid., 17–20. As in the case of 2 Corinthians it is striking that Philippians, whether a unit or a compilation, also offers an uncomplicated and plausible answer to the question of its delivery, without any apparent duplications or riddles.

F. The Letter to Philemon, et al.

The slave Onesimus himself is to be regarded as bearer of the letter to Philemon, his household community, Apphia, and Archippus; the letter from Paul and Timothy is almost exclusively about him. This is apparent from vv. 10–16: beginning with a petition (παρακαλῶ) that is later made concrete, Paul immediately declares (1st person singular) that he "[is] sending him … back to you" (ἀνέπεμψα σοι).[138] The real purpose, however, seems to be to express a desire that the slave and brother, who had previously belonged to Philemon (v. 11), be returned once again to the sender.[139] But this must be decided freely by Philemon (v. 13–14), so that his arrival may be swiftly followed by his return, and then by another visit, perhaps together with Paul, who himself looks forward to visiting this house community if he is released (v. 22). Finally, the appeal for an appropriate reception of the visitor is not lacking: Philemon is asked to receive him (προσλαβοῦ αὐτὸν, v. 17) as a friend like Paul.

With this unforced explanation of its transmission the letter to Philemon also reveals the mutual paths between sender and receiver(s) in the past and present of the writing, but especially in the near future.

G. Conclusion: The Rule for Messengers

As a conclusion, I would formulate a "rule for messengers": *Whenever Pauline letters speak of messengers to the communities or from them it is clear who is envisioned as the bearer of the particular letter.* The letter to the Galatians is an exception because it says nothing about a correspondence in the sense of plans for journeys and movements between communities and senders, which allows us to conclude that it is a circular letter carried by a number of people. *But whenever Pauline letters mention the travels of messengers there is at least one section that points explicitly to one person as the real messenger who can bring the letter, or there is a clear indication, at least indirectly, of who is a contact person with the opportunity to convey the letter.* This means that the writings of Paul and other senders to individual communities and persons show themselves to be genuine letters that were actually sent, because actual contact persons are named in them. It seems surprising that, apart from all the discussions of hypotheses concerning the divisions and/or compilations of letters,[140] we can find a relatively simple and coherent answer to the question of the delivery of the other letters. It seems that even redactors kept the postal requirements in mind and, possibly, deleted contradictory doublings or were careful to retain notes about sending, as, for

138. Cp. Stuhlmacher, *Der Brief an Philemon* (1975), 40; Arzt-Grabner, *Philemon* (2003), 195, 215: "Paul now sends the slave Onesimus back to Philemon with the letter" (p. 215); Wengst, *Der Brief an Philemon* (2005), 42: "Equipped with Paul's letter to Philemon, Onesimus departs to return to his master."

139. Thus, among others, Ollrog, *Paulus und seine Mitarbeiter*, 101ff.

140. For 2 Corinthians and Philippians see nn. 130 and 137 above; in addition see Schenke and Fischer, *Einleitung* (1978), 102–23, 124–32, and the overview in Schnelle, *Einleitung*, 101ff., 164ff.; on the thesis that Romans 16 represents a separate letter or part of a letter see, e.g., Standhartinger, *Studien zur Entstehungsgeschichte*, 86–87.

example, the canonical 2 Corinthians shows. The overview presented, however, speaks more in favor of an overall integrity of the texts.

The question of bearers of the Pauline letters, scarcely ever posed,[141] thus helps us to answer a still more important one: based on these considerations, what are the marks of a community letter arising out of a genuine communicative situation? We find a network of multifarious and reciprocal contacts through the named contact persons involving some concrete plans for visits by the senders. That is, concrete information about the most recent past is conveyed, but in addition and especially about the immediate future because, as a rule, an intensive advancement of the relationships is anticipated.

3.2.3 Comparison with 1 Thessalonians 2:17–3:13: No Messenger and no Common Future?

The first striking observation is that, apart from the three senders, there is no other person mentioned by name in 1 Thessalonians, neither members of the community specially alluded to or greeted nor other persons from the place of origin who send greetings, and not even the names of particular persons in autobiographical passages like those in Galatians 1–2. This is something altogether unusual in the world of the Pauline letters and happens otherwise only in the related 2 Thessalonians. Even the Deutero-Paulines and the Pastorals include the names of other persons, at least in the greetings; Colossians and Ephesians contain the names of actual contact persons (Col 4:7–9; Eph 6:21–22),[142] and the tiny letter to Philemon has eight names beyond those of the senders. If, accordingly, people may be introduced at any point in pseudepigraphical writings to make them more believable (and preferably in a block at the end),[143] their absence within an authentic correspondence is unusual. The structuring of the lives and communications of the early communities was so bound up with the existence and work of individuals that mention of their names could become a kind of sermon on their services to the communities and what is owed to them (Romans 16), and without them it is scarcely possible to speak of the past (Gal 1:18–23). Likewise, the names of individuals from within the communities are substitutes for current and concrete relationships to Paul and the other apostles (1 Cor 1:11–16; Phil 4:2–3). In contrast, other persons known by name seem to play no part in the relationships to be maintained with the community in Thessalonica.

Thus the search for a contact person, and hence the probable carrier of the letter, only yields one of the named authors: Timothy. We may search for an answer to our

141. See n. 121 above.

142. For this reason Colossians, prior to Ephesians, is considered authentic correspondence, e.g., by Schweizer, *Der Brief an die Kolosser* (1976), even if it is not from Paul himself (see esp. pp. 23ff. and 175ff.)

143. See the Pastorals (2 Tim 4:10–15, 19–21; Titus 3:12–14); however, these are not the sign of an active correspondence, since contact persons (as defined by the criteria given above) are for the most part absent.

question in 1 Thess 2:17–3:13, which is usually regarded and interpreted as a unit[144] and where contacts with the community are listed. Here there are two mentions of sending Timothy back, as a substitute for Paul and Silvanus. In 3:2 we read: "we have sent (ἐπέμψαμεν) Timothy, our brother and coworker for God (συνεργὸν τοῦ θεοῦ)[145] in proclaiming the gospel of Christ, to strengthen and encourage you for the sake of your faith. . . ." The repetition, this time in the first person singular, then follows in 3:5: "For this reason, when I could bear it no longer, I sent (κἀγω μηκέτι στέγων ἔπεμψα) to find out about your faith. . . ." By analogy to the sender notes, for example in 2 Corinthians 8 or Philippians 2:25–30, we should be able to draw conclusions from these text passages about the real messengers, especially since there is a passing mention of the "coworker for God." If they were formulated correspondingly in the epistolary aorist these statements would mean an assignment to Timothy,[146] beyond his carrying the letter, to take care that the community continues to be built up and strengthened, and that those still in Athens would hear from people returning from there how things are with the Christ-believers in Thessalonica. Then we would have here a structure similar to the intended contacts in Philemon, for example.

And yet, oddly enough, we learn nothing here about the intended carrier of 1 Thessalonians. Neither the one "sending" nor the one sent can refer to the carrying of the letter. The process of a possible present and future beginning of contact is declared, more or less in the same breath, to have already been completed, because both the sender formulae refer to a past visit by Timothy that is only spoken about; hence they cannot be interpreted as epistolary aorists.[147] That this is intended as a retrospect is seen from the time of writing, as given in 3:6: "But Timothy has just now (ἄρτι) come to us from you, and has brought us the good news (εὐαγγελισαμένου)[148] of your faith and love." We find no follow-up about another visit by an emissary to Thessalonica. Thus also the promised journey of Timothy, based on the recommendation given him, fits seamlessly within the schema of reflection on the past that dominates at least half of 1 Thessalonians.[149] So does the non-mention of the actual transmission of the letter exclude its

144. Cp. Holtz, *Der erste Brief*, 113–14, and esp. Bickmann, *Kommunikation gegen den Tod*, 215–65, who succeeds by means of speech-act theoretical analysis in demonstrating the great value of this passage for the overall composition of 1 Thessalonians.

145. The high evaluation of Timothy as "coworker for God" (or "with God") is, as the *lectio difficilior*, and despite its more narrow attestation (D* 33b m* Ambst), to be preferred to the relativizing predications διάκονον τοῦ θεοῦ (a A P Ψ etc.), διάκονον τοῦ θεοῦ καὶ συνεργὸν ἡμῶν (D2 μ, etc.), or διάκονον καὶ συνεργὸν τοῦ θεοῦ (F G). This reading again emphasizes the equality of all the named authors of 1 Thessalonians.

146. This is advocated by Fee, *The First and Second Letters to the Thessalonians* (2009), 115; see more on this in the next section, 3.2.4.e.

147. On this see esp. Donfried, "War Timotheus in Athen?" 193ff., arguing against Pesch, *Entdeckung*; see below at 3.2.4.b.

148. See 3.3.4 below.

149. For 1 Thessalonians 1–2 from this point of view see 3.3.2 below.

transport by other, unnamed messengers? For the present, at any rate, we observe that since there is no mention of other travelers in the letter we cannot find a "messenger formula" like the one in the Pauline letters discussed above; the allusion to missionaries and their journeys contains nothing at all about their bringing the letter! The plea in 5:12 to acknowledge those who work in the community and its leaders (τοὺς κοπιῶντας ἐν ὑμῖν καὶ προϊσταμένους[150] ὑμῶν) can be seen as a commendation[151] of authorities but scarcely as a reference to messengers,[152] since apart from their naming there is no indication that such persons are traveling, nor is there any honoring of contact persons such as we find, for example, in 1 Cor 16:17–18. The letter, with its extensive remarks on the relationship between the apostles and the community,[153] at the same time remains hovering somewhere between them as a message that evidently is not to be materially communicated.

Further questions about the communicative situation present themselves. What form is a future meeting with the community supposed to take? What information about further contacts can we draw from the text? To begin with, it is again striking that past plans are discussed. The "orphaned" (ἀπορφανισθέντες, 2:17) senders have worked toward a renewed personal encounter and have wanted to come, Paul himself more than once, "but Satan blocked our way" (2:18). Instead, Timothy was then sent from Athens (3:1–3). But this summary of relatively concrete intentions to visit in the past has no equivalent regarding the near or more distant future, either with regard to other emissaries or to the authors themselves; the closing remarks in 3:10–11 are not at all about "plans for a visit" or anything of the sort, though overviews and form-critical summaries sometimes suggest as much. Such works are blatantly vague, as demonstrated especially by Robert W. Funk's schema of the "apostolic parousia," meaning apostolic arrival or presence. His overview of the corresponding passages in the Pauline letters and their characteristics makes no distinction with regard to the lapse of time: Thus the *retrospect* in 1 Thess 2:17–3:13, without being marked as such, is equivalent (no. 6 in Funk's summary) to the other notes on sending or visiting (nos. 1–5, 7–13), both *present and future* in the various versions: Rom 15:14–33; Rom 1:8–15; Phlm 21–22; 1 Cor 4:14–21; 16:1–11; 2 Cor 12; Phil 2:19–24; Gal 4:12–20 (also about an earlier visit); 2 Cor 9:1–5;

150. Those "in charge," the προϊστάμενοι or προεστῶτες, appear in the NT, apart from 1 Tim 3:4–5, otherwise only in Rom 12:8; 1 Tim 5:17; this is a sign of much-developed community structures. According to 1 Tim 3:4–5 the bishop is supposed already to have proved his qualities of leadership as patriarch and head of his own household before he leads the community. This set of concepts does not fit the situation of a still-mobile community of new converts in Thessalonica that is generally assumed.

151. Kim, *Form and Structure* (1972), 120ff., 129–30.

152. Thus apparently Schnider and Stenger, *Studien zum neutestamentlichen Briefformular*, 95.

153. On this see the further exegesis of 1 Thess 1:2–2:16 and 2:17–3:13 as a complex web of speech-acts in a "communicative community" in the major part of Bickmann's work (*Kommunikation gegen den Tod*, 156–265), and see below at 3.3.1.

8:16–23; Phil 2:25–30; 1 Cor 16:12.[154] No notice is taken of the fact that, among these, only 1 Thessalonians speaks of *previous movements of the "coworkers,"*[155] and accordingly 1 Thessalonians is repeatedly and deceptively described throughout the study as Paul's "announcement of his coming" ("so that he can announce his coming in advance"); indeed, it is said that 1 Thessalonians alone contains the complete set of parousia elements and is thus the prototype of the genre.[156]

This procedure uses form criticism to level out major differences among the letters; the result, for Funk, is that 1 Thess 3:2–3a is embedded in a sequence made up of the formulations of current and future dispatch of messengers in other letters (1 Cor 4:17; Phil 2:19–24, 25–30; 2 Cor 8:18–24, 9:3–5),[157] with the result that the unique temporal profile of 1 Thessalonians, precisely as regards the question of messengers, is leveled out and thus made unrecognizable. In this context Timothy appears as a messenger who is soon to be sent on his way.

Terence Y. Mullins makes the same mistake in his investigation of the "visit talk," the allusion to visits and language about intended visits. According to Mullins these plans are to be seen more as a theme than as a formal scheme in the Pauline letters; he adduces corresponding elements from private papyrus letters. However, he appears to be as oblivious as Funk, to whose "Parousia" article he refers, to the fact that most of the elements of the theme, such as concrete intentions to visit, obstacles to a visit in the near future, and the sending of a messenger are mentioned in 1 Thessalonians *only as recapitulation, in the past tense* (2:17b, 18; 3:2–5).[158] The "visit talk" in 1 Thessalonians appears significantly different from that in the other letters, which address future events from the point of view of the letter's situation (e.g., Rom 15:22–29). Much as with Funk, a formal comparison apparently invites the author to neglect the major peculiarity of 1 Thessalonians. On the other hand, John L. White notes that the section of thanksgiving beginning at 2:13, as a part of the *corpus* of the letter, appears, because of the particular situation of the letter, in the remarkable form of a retrospect.[159] Although he emphasizes that, differently from Paul's practice elsewhere, the statements are about the past, he neither excludes 1 Thessalonians from the form-critical pattern nor sees it as an occasion

154. Robert W. Funk, "The Apostolic Parousia" (1967), 253–54; cp. the overview in Schnider and Stenger, *Studien zum neutestamentlichen Briefformular*, 94–95.

155. Although Funk does adduce the category of retrospect for other parts of 2 Corinthians ("Apostolic Parousia," 251 n. 1, 254), the same does not seem to be true for him in 1 Thessalonians. For a critique of Funk, see Mitchell, "Envoys," 652 n. 58, who makes note of the fact that 1 Thess 3:2–3 is not a commissioning but a retrospect. Llewellyn, "Conveyance of Letters," 54, asserts to the contrary that Funk classifies 1 Thess 2:17–19 itself as a past "parousia," which is not the case.

156. Funk, "Apostolic Parousia," 260.

157. Ibid., 255–58; similarly Lambrecht, "Thanksgivings" (1990), 196–97 = "Thanksgivings" (2000), 150ff.

158. Mullins, "Visit Talk" (1973), 353–54.

159. White, *Form and Function*, 71, 122 n. 65.

for drawing different conclusions. It is true that Hendrikus Boers takes note of this,[160] but it does not prevent him from investigating and affirming 1 Thessalonians as a whole as a form-critical model for all the later Pauline letters, also as regards the "apostolic parousia" in 2:17–3:11.[161]

Add to this that 1 Thessalonians *lacks* the Pauline use of the expression παρουσία, "coming," for the presence of the apostle and other people, unlike 1 Cor 16:17; 2 Cor 7:6–7; 10:10; Phil 1:26; 2:12. Παρουσία is associated in 1 Thessalonians exclusively with the eschatological return of Jesus, and in that sense it is relatively frequent: 1 Thess 2:19; 3:13; 4:15; 5:23. The expression has this function for Paul otherwise only in 1 Cor 15:23—in itself a rather remarkable finding.[162]

Instead of a concrete announcement of a visit, what we find in 1 Thess 3:10–11 is only a vague request for prayers,[163] a "wishing"[164] without detail or planning: the senders beg day and night that they may see their community again in order to increase the content of their faith, and they leave it to God and "our Kyrios Jesus" to make a way for them. But if it is God alone who brings about a reunion, that means a refusal to undertake it on one's own initiative.[165] In modern terms this corresponds, however, to an "à Dieu," and thus an "adieu" in the truest sense, namely, a farewell (for now). It is thus appropriate that in the rest of the letter there is no whisper of a personal reunion between sender and addressees being envisioned; instead, the focus is on the encounter with Jesus Christ and his future. It is not the apostolic "parousia" but only the "parousia" of Jesus that the community should expect, so it seems.[166]

160. Boers, "The Form Critical Study of Paul's Letters" (1976), 150.

161. Ibid., 146ff., esp. 149–53. Boers finds a form-critical ground for seeing 2:13–16 as an interpolation (pp. 151–52); on this see above, chap. 2.2.4.

162. See 5.2.1 below, on 4:13–17; the fact that παρουσία, as the Pauline word for a visit to the community, is absent from 1 Thessalonians is not observed or noted by most exegetes: cp., e.g., Lambrecht, "Thanksgivings" (2000), 150ff.; Weima, "The Function of 1 Thessalonians 2:1–12," 117–18; Schoon-Janssen, "On the Use of Elements of Ancient Epistolography" (2000), 184ff. Differently E. D. Schmidt, *Heilig ins Eschaton* (2010), 198–202, with a corresponding critique, referring to the unusual finding regarding the concept of παρουσία in 1 Thessalonians (pp. 201–2).

163. For the genre "wish-prayer" see Holtz, *Der erste Brief*, 140ff. Ernst Synofzik places 1 Thess 3:10 within the genre element "expression of a wish to see the recipients of the letter" in the category of Pauline thanksgivings (*Die Gerichts- und Vergeltungsaussagen bei Paulus* [1977], 16–17). Thus 1 Thessalonians stands alongside the wishes in Rom 1:9–13; Phil 1:8; 2 Cor 1,12–16, and would not fall outside the category except that here everything is lacking that belongs to the concretion of the author's and others' desire to visit in the near future; cp. above at 3.2.2 (a-f).

164. This is Bickmann's description (*Kommunikation gegen den Tod*, 253–59) of this "expressive speech-act," as she calls it.

165. "In 2:17 Paul spoke of his own efforts to visit them; now he appears to leave the matter to God." (Best, *Thessalonians*, 147).

166. Cp. Klauck, *Briefliteratur*, 281.

Hence with the aid of the messenger question we can define the unique temporal and communicative profile of 1 Thessalonians: the mutuality of contact exists only in the narrated past. On the basis of the wording, actions relating to intentionally sought and realized efforts to make contact are excluded. Chapters 1 and 2 contain a long retrospective view of the founding visit as well as numerous attempts to come to the community again (2:17–19). The mission by Timothy as emissary to test the fidelity of the community (3:1–5) as well as his return with the wholly good news (3:6) are both in the past. It seems as if that was it. Nothing is said about a reciprocal back and forth in the letter's present time and, given the lack of plans for the future, there seems to be little prospect of it. This finding is altogether singular in contrast to what we find in other letters: a tangible network of relationships, more precisely defined as a network of narrated, intended, and implicitly determinable real contacts in all phases of time. It leads us to the hypothesis that therefore 1 Thessalonians does not reflect any authentic situation involving communication by letter but only attempts to depict such a thing. We need to press the question of messengers, and with it our hypothesis, in light of the existing exegetical literature.

3.2.4 Overview: How do the Circumstances of the Conveyance of 1 Thessalonians appear in Scholarly Research?

First we must again emphasize what an astonishing fact emerges from the review of multiple commentaries, monographs, and other secondary literature on 1 Thessalonians: scarcely anyone explicitly poses (much less discusses) the question of how 1 Thessalonians reached its addressees. That is possible on the one hand because the letter, as we have shown, says nothing on the subject and, despite the mention of contacts with the community, neglects to say anything about a meeting to be expected in the immediate *future*, something that contrasts with the other Pauline letters, which mention the movements of messengers. And yet, surprisingly, this has scarcely occurred to any researcher. In exegetical treatments especially of 1 Thess 2:17–3:5 all discussion focuses on the past contacts; no one emphasizes or is sufficiently clear about the fact that from the standpoint of the letter there is no consideration of anything but the past. Commentary style requires a constant reflection on past journeys, so that the time-levels are erased.[167] It seems simply to be forgotten that, besides the chronological reconstruction of the previous journeys of the apostles, and especially of Timothy, there is need for another return journey by some person to transmit 1 Thessalonians.[168] Consideration of deviations from the description in Acts 17–18 and corresponding

167. For this dominant perspective see, by way of example, the commentary in Holtz, *Der erste Brief*, 114–30 (e.g., pp. 126–27: "This actual purpose for sending Timothy is certainly clear in substance ... Timothy is to strengthen the community's faith ....")

168. Cp., e.g., Rigaux, *Thessaloniciens*, 42–62. Rigaux simply remarks briefly that Timothy was not the bearer of previous letters (p. 52).

efforts at harmonization[169] play a major role. Likewise, given the strong emphasis on the intimacy[170] of the relationship between apostle and community in exegesis, there is no correspondingly adequate reflection on the material bases for human relationships and their expression. At this point, then, we seem to observe a lack of attention to social-historical questions.

A. Older Interpretations

In addition, at present there is scarcely anyone who discusses the very complicated situation that appears if, for example, we take the information in the letter about the sending of Timothy (mentioned twice in 1 Thess 3:2 and 3:5) literally and try to interpret it as actually having occurred, as the older interpreters did. Thus, for example, Theodor Zahn[171] discusses, in connection with the unique plurals in 1 Thessalonians, a thesis of Johann C. K. Hofmann[172] and Friedrich Spitta,[173] who, in his opinion, read in 3:5 "that, after Paul and Silas together had dispatched Timothy from Athens to Thessalonica (3:2), Paul alone sent still another messenger thither," and that Silvanus also left Paul. The singular in 3:5 is thus taken seriously by Hofmann and Spitta and explained as the sending of an unnamed third messenger. In rejecting this thesis Zahn comes close to the messenger question. Silvanus could only have been sent to Macedonia: "In this case there would be a double sending in addition to the mission of Timothy (3:2),—the sending of Silas, which is nowhere mentioned, and that of an unnamed person supposedly referred to in iii.5." But Zahn thinks that Paul would not have been able to remain silent about these messengers and their names, as the sending of Timothy shows. "In the other event, however, the messenger could only have been the bearer of a letter, and the failure to mention the letter thus sent by him would be incomprehensible." The omission of an object for ἔπεμψα in 3:5 is unjustified; it is to be supplied from 3:1–2, "and both places refer to the same occurrence." Does this mean that Zahn thinks Timothy is the carrier of

169. Cp., e.g., Bornemann, *Die Thessalonicherbriefe*, 11ff., 29ff.; Dibelius, *An die Thessalonicher*, 27–28; Best, *Thessalonians*, 2ff.; Riesner, *Paul's Early Period*, 342–70; see also von Dobschütz, *Die Thessalonicherbriefe*, 14ff., 129ff.; he does make brief mention of the transportation of the letter on pp. 17–18.

170. See only Holtz, *Der erste Brief*, 116: between the Thessalonians and Paul, he says, there was a "solid unity of soul and spirit," Paul feels "devouring concern for the existence of the community" and "anxious longing for his young community."

171. Zahn, *Introduction* I, 209–11; the following quotations are from pp. 210–11.

172. Quoted by Zahn as Hofmann, *NT*, i, 205ff. (= Hofmann, "Der erste Brief Pauli an die Thessalonicher," 201ff. in the edition used here, from 1862).

173. Spitta, *Geschichte und Literatur* I, 115, 121 (really 121–22); similarly also Wohlenberg, *Der erste und zweite Thessalonicherbrief*, 7: Timothy was first sent from Athens. Then Silvanus and Paul went to Corinth. Wohlenberg refers 3:5 (without object) to another sending, this time of an unknown party "because Timothy resisted," "a rapid messenger" to Thessalonica, who was supposed to return more quickly. But Timothy got there before him with "happy news" (3:6).

1 Thessalonians? Since the community "might not hold out longer without the personal encouragement of its founders," for that very reason Paul himself could not bear it any longer (3:5) "and ... sent Timothy to Thessalonica." Nevertheless, we cannot conclude from this that Zahn sees Timothy as the bearer of the letter just written, since, if 3:5 has the same object as 3:1–2, we would still be hearing about the previous journey. Thus Zahn does not really ask the messenger question, but he does read accurately when he discusses the absence of an object in 3:5 and attends to the number in the sentences.[174] Still, he suggests tendentially and through silence that readers should see Timothy as the possible real bearer of the letter, since he thinks that Paul always names and commends his messengers.

In older interpretations the necessity of the delivery of the letter is mentioned at least occasionally: George Milligan asserts that there is no information about the delivery and that Paul must have entrusted the letter to a personal courier or a friend. Ernst von Dobschütz's thinking is much the same: "We do not know what opportunity Paul had to get the letter to Thessalonica. He did not have a postal service at his disposal. He was dependent on traveling brothers."[175]

B. Fragmentation Hypotheses

Another possibility for at least touching on the messenger question is offered by the various fragmentation hypotheses regarding the Thessalonian correspondence. They take the unique character of the text seriously, at least in part, even though their solutions are scarcely persuasive.

Rudolf Pesch has pointed most clearly to the aporias and unanswered questions presented by 1 Thessalonians against the background of the otherwise familiar practice of early Christian letter transmission.[176] "Certainly doubts may arise if we read the section in 1 Thess 2:17–3:5 carefully, supposing that Timothy has just come from Saloniki. ... Why does the apostle return to speaking about the sending of Timothy to Saloniki, as he does? Why, indeed, does he talk again at such length about his concern for the community he had left so suddenly, when, after all, Timothy has brought the best possible news from Saloniki? And finally, would Paul have let the opportunity escape to give Timothy a letter to Saloniki when he left Athens?" This last question, and thus the search for an earlier, still older letter of Paul, is said to be justified: "If we look through Paul's letters we see that whenever he sent one of his coworkers to one of his communities he always sent along a letter."

Pesch seeks by literary-critical means, and with precision, to identify that first letter, a commendation Paul is said to have given to Timothy to carry when he returned alone from Athens to Thessalonica. He considers contradictions and a number of doublings in the existing letter, such as the twofold thanksgiving in

174. See above at 3.1.

175. Milligan, *Thessalonians*, xxxviii and 130; von Dobschütz, *Die Thessalonicherbriefe*, 17–18.

176. Pesch, *Entdeckung*, 21–22.

1:2–7; 2:13–16, and singles out 1 Thess 2:1–12; 2:13–16; 2:17–3:5; 3:11–13; 4:1–8.[177] This solution has the advantage of discovering a messenger formula in 3:1–5 like those in the other Pauline letters (1 Cor 4:17–19; Phil 2:25–30, etc.).[178] As in those cases, so also in 1 Thess 3:2 an epistolary aorist, ἐπέμψαμεν, is said to describe an actual sending. The situation of restless longing and concern has a clear location, he says, whereas the praise of the already spreading activities of the Thessalonian community and their effects (1:2–10) seems more plausible from a later standpoint: why should anyone be concerned about the status of a community and greet the report of a necessary messenger so effusively if that community already has well-known missionary successes to display, if "in every place [their] faith in God has become known," and if "the people of those regions report about us what kind of welcome we had among you . . ." (1:7–9)?[179] In that case the second part of the letter would have been written at a later time, after Timothy's return with the very good news.[180] This, then, is an explanation for the contradictory situation in the letter that we have seen, and that Pesch calls double. The service rendered by those who hypothesize a division of the letter is to have recognized this situational contradiction and drawn conclusions from it, even though, in my opinion, they are not entirely correct or the only possible ones.[181]

177. Ibid., 39–64, with summary on pp. 65ff. The reconstructed text is on pp. 68–72 and a summary on pp. 113, 115. We should note that for Pesch this first letter is supposed to begin, of all things, with 2:13–16, the condemnation of "the Jews," which contains a thanksgiving, as required for the beginning of a letter. Pesch seems unbothered by the fact that this would make these the first words of Paul that were written and handed down to us. Murphy-O'Connor, *Paul, A Critical Life* (1996), advocates a similar fragmentation thesis that also places 1 Thess 2:13–16 at the beginning: "An originally independent letter, 2:13 to 4:2, with its own thanksgiving and conclusion, has been inserted into another letter constituted by 1:1 to 2:12 and 4:3 to 5:28" (pp. 102–29, quotation on p. 105), whereas 2 Thessalonians is a unit and stems from Paul (pp. 110–14).

178. Pesch, *Entdeckung*, 57–64. See above at 3.2.2.

179. But in fact the information in 1:7–9 does not fit much better in a letter of jubilation occasioned by the return of Timothy (3:6). What need would there have been of his news? Or is he also reporting on the successes spoken of in 1:7–9? (cp. Pesch, *Entdeckung*, 100); see further below at 3.3.

180. Ibid., 89–111.

181. Fragmentary hypotheses that take the situational contradiction into account include those of Schenke and Fischer, *Einleitung*, 65–75, esp. 67–71; earlier esp. Eckart, *Der zweite echte Brief* (1961), which sees a letter of recommendation in 1:1–2:12; 2:17–3:4; 3:11–13 that Timothy brought with him on his return (p. 43), because the situations in 3:1–5 and 3:6–8 are mutually exclusive (p. 34). Eckart thus suggests that there are two small genuine letters in 1 Thessalonians, to which were added some extensive non-Pauline passages such as 2:13–16; 4:1–8; 4:10b–12; 5:12–22 (p. 37). Kümmel, "Das literarische und geschichtliche Problem" (1965), with his comprehensive and apologetic polemic, makes light of Eckart because of his methodological weaknesses, but he smooths out justified questions posed to 1 Thessalonians and its epistolary situation, with much detail but without any questions of

Why does Pesch's thesis not seem acceptable?[182] Let me adduce only a few counterarguments:

- "Athens" is mentioned in 3:1 in such a way that it does not appear to be the location of the sender,[183] but according to Pesch the verse is part of the Athens letter.
- The existence of Philemon, with its brevity, speaks against the idea of a letter compilation that was undertaken because an existing letter would otherwise have been too short and "barren of content" or inconvenient for sending.[184]
- Precisely the doublets (thanksgiving, conclusion of the letter, etc.) speak against a compilation: why were they left in place, since the prescript and conclusion would likewise have been combined and reduced?
- Second Thessalonians shows that 1 Thessalonians is a unit; it is the model[185] to which 2 Thessalonians is oriented. The formal elements themselves were copied by the authors. So we also find two thanksgivings in 2 Thessalonians, in 1:3–5 and 2:13–15;[186] besides the letter-conclusion in 2 Thess 3:16–17 there is here again a kind of final remark, with 2:16–17 analogous to 1 Thess 3:13.[187]
- The manuscript tradition indicates the questionable nature of fragmentation hypotheses in general: "Either . . . the letters had previously not been exchanged between the various churches, and/or the compiler, after finishing

his own. Fuchs, "1 Thess 1,2–10" [1963/64], 300, in turn encourages Eckart not to abandon his theory in spite of all the criticism, but instead to insist on it, because he himself has serious doubts about 1 Thess 1–3). A newer version of the fragmentary letter hypothesis by Richard (*First and Second Thessalonians* [1995], 11–19) bypasses the contradiction mentioned above by trying to find the oldest first letter to the Thessalonians in 2:13–4:2, omitting 2:14–16, which are to be regarded as Gentile Christian interpolation. (The second letter, written later, is said to consist of 1:1–2:12 and 4:3–5:28.)

182. For the argument with Pesch cp. also Donfried, "War Timotheus in Athen?" 193–96.

183. Cp. Holtz, *Der erste Brief*, 15.

184. Pesch, *Entdeckung*, 113–14.

185. See only Wrede, *Die Echtheit des zweiten Thessalonicherbriefs untersucht* (1903), 4–17; and see further below at 6.1.

186. The two Thessalonian letters have this double thanksgiving in common, in contrast to all the Pauline letters; cp. Marxsen, *Der zweite Brief an die Thessalonicher* (1982), 21 n. 8 on this argument against fragmentation.

187. Pesch then has to posit also that 1 Thessalonians was available to the author of 2 Thessalonians as a complete composition (*Entdeckung*, 124ff.). But then it is not clear why these doublets should not in themselves constitute a ground for literary-critical operations such as, for example, Schmithals undertakes; he thus reconstructs four partial letters linked crossways by the compilers ("Die Thessalonicherbriefe als Briefkomposition" [1964], 308; cp. idem, "Die historische Situation der Thessalonicherbriefe" [1965], 153–54).

his work, was able to destroy all the originals. Otherwise one can hardly explain why in the manuscript tradition we possess not a single piece of evidence previous of the earlier text form."[188]

To return to Pesch's conclusions on the transmission of the letters: he determines that there was a messenger in the person of Timothy, at least for the first section of the letter he posits.[189] But then arises the question about the second letter he reconstructs: why is there no commendation or information about the transmission of the letter in this case? In light of the numerous doublets elsewhere, such an omission is striking. Hence the question of messengers remains, at least for the supposed second letter.

Pesch's posited solution to the transmission of the second partial letter—that the delegation from Macedonia mentioned in 2 Cor 11:9 is supposed to have taken it with them to Thessalonica[190]—is not persuasive. After all, he himself identified an actual messenger formula for his first partial letter in 3:1–5. Why, then, is there none for the second in a text that otherwise, in his opinion, is shaped around a great many doublets? The second in particular, which according to Pesch actually frames the first, should have been much more likely to use vocabulary of sending and commendation than did the first, and so it should appear in the reconstructed text as a whole. Why does the sending mentioned twice in 3:1 and 3:5 not correspond to the supposed second situation of the sending and arrival of Timothy? Pesch, contrary to his usual practice, does not even consider these passages as such, though they are the most striking doublet of all.[191] For him they are part of the first, "oldest" letter of Paul, as is the expression of the apostle's

188. Riesner, *Paul's Early Period*, 405. For the fundamental methodological problems of fragmentation hypotheses cp. also Schnelle, *Einleitung*, 95–96; for 1 Thessalonians see Klauck, *Briefliteratur*, 282ff.; Haufe, *Der erste Brief*, 5ff.; P.-G. Müller, *Der erste und zweite Brief*, 48ff.; Luckensmeyer, *The Eschatology of First Thessalonians* (2009), 123–27. E.-M. Becker, *Schreiben und Verstehen*, has presented a new theory about the compilation of Pauline letters, focused on 2 Corinthians, on the basis of the writing materials probably used, such as wax tablets or papyrus leaves, and the subsequent necessity of making copies very quickly and combining the various letters to individual communities (see esp. pp. 56–93). For the possibility and questionable nature of New Testament parallels to the compilation of Cicero's correspondence see Klauck, "Compilation of Letters," and Schmeller, "Cicerobriefe"; Schreiber, "Briefliteratur im Neuen Testament" (2008), 258ff.

189. Schenke and Fischer, *Einleitung* (1978), 68, 72 likewise see Timothy as the bearer of the first partial letter. Richard, *First and Second Thessalonians*, 31, does suppose a messenger *from* Thessalonica ("a messenger or Christian traveler who also provides news in the form of an oral report") who handed on the community's questions to the missionaries (see 4:3–8), but he fails to address the question of the transmission of partial letters "a" (1 Thess 2:13–4:2 [omitting 2:14–16] and "b" [1:1–2:12; 4:3–5:28]).

190. Pesch, *Entdeckung*, 20–21.

191. Ibid., 61.

concern, whereas only the joy about the "now"-returned Timothy in 3:6 belongs to the second partial letter.[192] But in particular the division of the supposed doublet would have to make sense if these are two "genuine" writings that were combined. If we resort to fragmentation hypotheses to resolve difficulties, for the most part we only create new questions that have no answers. The riddles of 1 Thessalonians cannot be solved in that way.

However, hypotheses of letter divisions like this one from Rudolf Pesch, as we have seen, do have the advantage of shining light on a major inconsistency in 1 Thessalonians. They make it clear that 2:17–3:5, with the failed plans for a visit described there, especially one by Paul, his concern and longing, and the notice of sending would all have been part of a single letter given to Timothy on a first return visit to Thessalonica. In the letter written "now," after his return (3:6), the situation so extensively described is already in the past, and we ask ourselves: what was the point of that whole summary of what has already happened? There is no occasion offered for the transmission of the whole of 1 Thessalonians or of the second partial letter as proposed by the fragmentation theory: there seems to be no messenger for the communication "now" written.

C. Other Proposals about Messengers, especially Timothy

One way of addressing the transmission of 1 Thessalonians indirectly, as we saw in Pesch's work, is to combine information from other letters. Alfred Suhl, Willi Marxsen, and Franz Laub conclude from 2 Cor 11:9 that the delegation from Macedonia mentioned there, consisting mainly of people from the Philippian community, returned to Paul in Corinth, the place where 1 Thessalonians was written. Timothy must have visited Philippi also on that occasion.[193] This seems to be an indirect attempt to clarify the notion that 1 Thessalonians could have been among the things conveyed by that delegation. But 1 Thessalonians itself says nothing of the sort; there are no related notes or recommendations to be found.

If anyone is suggested as a possible messenger, it is always Timothy. The first to point to him were probably Euthalius (ca. 450 C.E.) and Oecumenius (ca. 990 C.E.), who, commenting on the letter, wrote that Timothy was sent by Paul to carry 1 Thessalonians: ὁ ἀπόστολος πολλὰς θλίψεις παθῶν ἐν Βεροίᾳ καὶ ἐν Φιλίπποις τῆς Μακεδονίας καὶ ἐν Κορίνθῳ … ἀποστέλλει Τιμόθεον αὐτοὺς μετὰ τῆς ἐπιστολῆς ταύτης.[194]

It is sometimes assumed, without discussion, that Timothy was again the messenger: "This document was probably dictated in Corinth in the year 50 or the spring of 51, carried to Thessalonica by Timothy, and read there at worship."[195]

192. Ibid., 65ff.

193. Suhl, *Paulus und seine Briefe* (1975), 110 n. 6; Marxsen, *Der erste Brief an die Thessalonicher*, 14; Laub, *1. und 2. Thessalonicherbrief* (1985), 10.

194. According to Bornemann, *Die Thessalonicherbriefe*, 26; Bornemann himself rejects this idea (his sources are *Euthalius*, ed. Zacagnius [Rome, 1698], and Oecumenius, ἐξηγήσεις παλαιαί, ed. Morellio [Paris, 1630], 2 vol. fol., in Migne, *PL* 118, 119); ibid., 1.

195. Knoch, *1. und 2. Thessalonicherbrief* (1987), 15.

Robert Funk's overview of commendations of messengers indirectly suggests Timothy as the actual bearer by placing the sender-notices in 1 Thessalonians alongside the commendations of actual messengers in the other Pauline letters.[196] Margaret Mitchell also parallels 1 Thess 3:6–10 with the sending of the actual messenger Titus in 2 Cor 7:5–16.[197] She calls Timothy and Titus the "two-way-boys," that is, news-bearers constantly in motion back and forth; thus she must at least indirectly consider Timothy the messenger of 1 Thessalonians. But there is a major difference between 2 Corinthians and 1 Thessalonians: while it is clear from 2 Corinthians 8 that Titus really is revisiting the community and is to be regarded as one of the bearers of 2 Corinthians, no such information is found in 1 Thessalonians; the "two ways" here are entirely in the past![198] One of the few exegetes to make a brief reference to the absence of a bearer for 1 Thessalonians is Regina Börschel, in her monograph: "We cannot learn from 1 Thessalonians by whom the letter was taken to Thessalonica. It is improbable that one of Paul's colleagues, Silvanus or Timothy, traveled to Macedonia again and took the letter with him."[199] Most recently Gordon D. Fee has postulated an actual sending of Timothy as bearer of 1 Thessalonians, on the basis of 1 Thess 3:2, reading ἐπέμψαμεν there as an epistolary aorist: "Paul is going to send Timothy back to Thessalonica as the bearer of the present letter."[200] But the subsequent passage in 3:6 with its emphatic ἄρτι, "now!" speaks against this: the sending in 3:2, together with the double statement in 3:5, clearly points to the past, especially since in each case the same situation of abandonment is addressed as something the author(s) cannot bear (στέγοντες in 3:1; στέγων in 3:5). Now, according to 3:6 and the joyfully-greeted arrival of Timothy, this situation is explicitly something in the past; hence 3:2 cannot refer to a new sending.

Finally, we may point to works that, assuming 2 Thessalonians to be authentic, posit a later situation for the canonical first letter than for the second. They thus reverse the sequence of 1 and 2 Thessalonians;[201] some of them assume that 2 Thessalonians was then given to Timothy to carry to Thessalonica.[202] In this way

196. Funk, "Apostolic Parousia," 255ff.; see above at 3.2.3.

197. Mitchell, "Envoys," esp. 653ff. Cp. the parallelism between 1 Thess 2:17–20, 3:1–6 and the accounts of journeys and the sending of messengers in the Corinthian letters observed by F. C. Baur, *Die beiden Briefe an die Thessalonicher* (1855/1867), 347–49, something that for Baur speaks in favor of the non-genuine character of 1 Thessalonians.

198. See above at 3.2.2.c and 3.2.3.

199. Börschel, *Konstruktion einer christlichen Identität*, 206.

200. Fee, *The First and Second Letters to the Thessalonians*, 115; cp. above at 3.2.3.

201. Grotius, *Annotationes in Novum Testamentum* (1756/57), 693, 715ff.; F. C. Baur, *Die beiden Briefe*, 364ff.; Ewald, *Die Sendschreiben des Apostels Paulus* (1857), 16ff.; West, "The Order of 1 and 2 Thessalonians" (1914), as well as those mentioned in the next note. For discussion of this thesis see, e.g., Best, *Thessalonians*, 42ff.

202. Weiss, *Earliest Christianity* (1959), 827; Hadorn, *Die Abfassung der Thessalonicherbriefe* (1919), 116ff.; Manson, "St. Paul in Greece" (1952/53), 436ff., 446–47; Gregson, "A Solution of the Problems of the Thessalonian Epistles" (1966), 78ff.; Wanamaker, *The Epistles to the Thessalonians* (1990), 44–45, 126ff.

they assign a bearer for 2 Thessalonians, whose messenger vocabulary is to be found as a kind of retrospect in 1 Thessalonians, whereas in 2 Thessalonians, that is, the chronologically first letter carried by Timothy, nothing of the sort is mentioned. Apart from the fact that these theories are unsustainable because of the literary dependence of 2 Thessalonians on 1 Thessalonians,[203] here again the question of the transmission of canonical 1 Thessalonians remains open.

On the whole it seems that it is more fruitful to discuss the transport of undelivered letters, something that can be deduced from 1 Thessalonians,[204] than to give further thought to the delivery of the text we have before us.

D. Why Timothy in Particular cannot have been the real Bearer

As a conclusion to this overview of the delivery of 1 Thessalonians we must assert that it appears no one has clearly thought through the associated details in order to arrive at a consistent answer to the question of delivery.

So who brings 1 Thessalonians to the community? Those who are not willing from the outset to suppose, *e silentio*, something like unknown travelers[205] or to shape possible scenarios based on information in other letters[206] will be disturbed by the extended passage in 1 Thess 2:17–3:13. There is no mention of a return journey, and thus the arrival of a messenger; Paul himself does not even indicate any concrete plans to visit. According to the "messenger rule" developed above, mentions of movements on the part of coworkers always indicate the possibility for the actual conveyance of the letter in question. But Timothy's journeys as described in 1 Thess 3:1–7 are now in the past. Since other travelers are not mentioned, it also seems possible that he would undertake another journey to deliver 1 Thessalonians, which, as seen above, tends to be the opinion of some exegetes if they think about it at all. Another possibility is that the apostle here simply forgot to say anything about the transmission of the letter by means of unknown persons, even though other letters referring to correspondence never lack such information, especially when that section occupies so large a percentage of the content as in 1 Thessalonians. Or is there no thought of any real further relationship, so that references to it are not needed, the letter was not really delivered or even written in a situation of authentic epistolary dialogue, but was in fact "forged"?

203. See 6.1 below.

204. Thus Malherbe, "Did the Thessalonians write to Paul?" He posits both an earlier writing by Paul to Thessalonica and, following Harris, "A Study in Letter-Writing" (1898) and Faw, "On the Writing of First Thessalonians" (1952), a letter from the community to him, both conveyed by Timothy; cp. Malherbe, *The Letters to the Thessalonians*, 75ff., 197, 209, and frequently. Malherbe discusses the question of messengers and the delivery of canonical 1 Corinthians and Philippians at length (and answers it), as well as that of a previous letter *from* Thessalonica to Paul, but—astonishingly—without giving a single thought to the problem of the delivery of 1 Thessalonians ("Did the Thessalonians write to Paul?" 252–55; *Thessalonians*, 209ff.).

205. Thus Murphy-O'Connor, *Paul, the Letter-Writer*, 40.

206. See n. 193 above.

Still, 1 Thessalonians seems to suggest that Timothy was the contact person and the one responsible for messages. Then why would Timothy, as the only named messenger, not have delivered 1 Thessalonians as well? Of course, in that case one of the authors of the letter would also have been its bearer! Can we imagine that such a person would have expressed himself by writing a letter if he himself intended to visit the community again? We should consider that in 1 Thessalonians, given the nearly consistent plural authorship, Timothy appears to a great degree as an equally involved co-author.[207] What do we find in the other Pauline letters investigated? Are co-authors and supposed bearers of the letters identical in them?[208]

- The prescript of the letter to the community in Rome (Rom 1:1) names no author other than Paul, while Phoebe appears to be the bearer (16:1–2).
- The first letter to the community in Corinth was written by Paul and Sosthenes (1:1). Timothy (4:17; 16:10–11) and the delegation with Stephanas (16:17–18) are possible bearers.
- The second letter to the community in Corinth shows Paul and Timothy to be the authors (1:1). Titus, together with some "brothers," seems to have been tasked with its delivery, or with the transmission of partial letters (8:17–24; 9:5; 12:17–18).
- The letter to Galatia, written by Paul together with "all the members of God's family" who are with him (1:1–2), is a circular letter and thus requires no information regarding individuals who will carry it or about their several journeys.
- The letter to the community in Philippi is written by Paul and Timothy (1:1), and it seems that Epaphroditus delivered it (2:25–30).
- The letter to Philemon, Apphia, Archippus, and their household community was written by Paul and Timothy (v. 1) before Onesimus brings it with him (vv. 10–13).

We see from this summary that in Paul's letters the sender or co-sender is *never* identical with the bearer of the letter! This is not drawn from any knowledge of the practice of letter communication as such. After all, why should a person be introduced by name as a co-author of a letter if that person had no need to write because she or he, as messenger, expects personal contact in the near future and will have the opportunity to convey indirectly all the news of those remaining behind? Hence we can fill out the "rule for messengers": *In all cases of Pauline letters with named senders it is clear who is envisioned as the bearer of the actual letter. Co-senders and bearers are never the same person(s).*

The first letter to Thessalonica falls completely outside the postal pattern of the Pauline letters: despite the existence of notices about journeys and the vocabulary

207. Llewellyn, "Conveyance of Letters," notes the coincidence of the authorial plural with the absence of bearers of 1 and 2 Thessalonians.

208. See the section above on the delivery of Paul's letters (3.2.2).

of sending, we cannot discover a real bearer of the letter. On the other hand, however, it appears that Timothy is the only contact person with the community, but he can scarcely be considered as a real messenger because otherwise co-authors do not carry the letters they have no need to write when they have the opportunity to visit and engage in oral communication.[209] Thus in the case of 1 Thessalonians we are dealing with extremely unclear and questionable epistolographic conditions, namely, with a letter that was probably not sent. It appears that no consideration has been given to the real necessities and plausibilities of communication by letter in antiquity in general and of the Pauline correspondence in particular. Consequently, we are led to suspect that this is not an authentic epistolary communication.

3.2.5 The absence of a messenger and a narration of past events

Thus at present we have two bases for considering 1 Thessalonians questionable: the much-criticized and thus suspect and awkward passage in 2:14–16 with its social-historical statement, together with, in particular, the section in 2:17–3:13 whose immediacy and freshness are so often emphasized and that, as such, appears to reflect close, emotional, and authentic relationships.[210] And yet the authors are careless about the real demands of the letter's transmission, and in particular the characteristic conditions of communication among the early communities and their apostles.

The mention of a "double sending" of Timothy could be understood as a strategy of the real, pseudonymous author, and in that case it could be explained this way: At first, at 3:1–2, the writing is simply and almost entirely in the plural; even "alone" is, strikingly, expressed with the plural μόνοι. Then it was noticed that this could be confusing. A plural could mean that Timothy, as a co-sender of the letter, had dispatched himself, or it could appear too imprecise and create misunderstanding of the sequence to be described. So it is repeated in the singular in order now to describe a "real" sending of Timothy, though only at a time in the past. In correcting this mistake the author(s) apparently forgot the necessity of mentioning a messenger for the conveyance of 1 Thessalonians; the result is an even greater mistake. Alone among the Pauline letters thus far judged to be genuine, 1 Thessalonians thus violates the "rule for messengers," according to which an opportunity for delivery of the letter is always mentioned whenever a letter alludes to contact persons.

The often-emphasized heartfelt and emotional style says little in itself to contradict this: "It can be regarded from the outset as certain that in a purely fictive epistle in which a strong, personal vividness is associated with the fiction of an

209. Cp. Richards, who also denies that commercial secretaries had the additional task of carrying letters (*Secretary*, 7 n. 33); differently White, *Light from Ancient Letters*, 216.

210. "Paul's expressions seem inadequate for the purpose. He speaks effusively to his community, like a happy mother to her dear child. Indeed, spousal love speaks through him . . ." (Wohlenberg, *Der erste und zweite Thessalonicherbrief*, 68).

intimate relationship between the correspondents, we may well find a great deal more natural style and freshness than in a real, purely sober and businesslike letter to a recipient who is unfamiliar or even unknown."[211]

Rudolf Pesch's important observation that the extensively recapitulated concerns for the community in 1 Thess 3:1–5 really belong in a letter occasioned by those fears and not by their resolution through new information just received (3:6)[212] points to the motives of possible pseudepigraphical authors. It seems as if the apostolic sending of messengers and the corresponding journeys imitate the model of the "Greek" letters 1 and 2 Corinthians and Philippians in order to suggest a lively exchange. Measured against the material demands of genuine ancient epistolary communication, the letter reveals some serious mistakes. For the motif of the arrival of the joyfully-received messenger we may look especially to 2 Cor 7:6–16.[213] In 2 Cor 8:17–24 there is extensive discussion of a reciprocal exchange with the community in Corinth in the future, after the dispatch of the letter. There is no corresponding information in 1 Thessalonians, and consequently nothing about precisely this natural, matter-of-course exchange of repeated contacts that belongs to the real situation but seems so complicated from outside it. We may conclude from this that the text was not created *within* an authentic epistolary situation but pretends to it from *outside*, from a distance in time and space.

211. Koskenniemi, *Studien zur Idee*, 91. And yet many expressions of affection and closeness in 1 Thessalonians reveal themselves to be not so much original as conventional, and correspond to the common motifs of ancient letters of friendship. Cp., e.g., Schoon-Janssen, "On the Use of Elements of Ancient Epistolography."

212. Pesch, *Entstehung*, 21–22; cp. 3.2.4.b above. Revealing, and symptomatic of the confusion still caused (though unnoted) by 1 Thessalonians is, for example, Reinmuth's description of the reason for the letter ("On the situation presumed by the letter"): "When Paul wrote this letter he could not know whether the young community in Thessalonica would survive" (*Der erste Brief*, 105). That fits much better with the motive for the past mission of Timothy than with his joyfully-greeted return with good news (3:6), which is supposed to be the real reason for the writing of 1 Thessalonians. For the still greater disharmony with the situation in 1 Thessalonians see below at 3.3.1.

213. Cp. the analysis of the similarities between 1 Thess 3:6–10 and 2 Cor 7:5–16 in Mitchell, "Envoys," 651–62; Seyoon Kim, "Paul's Entry (εἴσοδος) and the Thessalonians' Faith" (2005), 538ff., and esp. F. C. Baur, *Die beiden Briefe*, 347ff., who regards 2 Cor 2:12 and 7:15–16 as the written model for 1 Thess 3:1–5: "but if . . . the same thing is related, even in the same words, we have a right to ask whether the one is not deliberately modeled on the other" (p. 349; cp. 4.1 below). Baur writes that in order to give an impression of the tender relationship of the apostle to a community similar to that in 1 and 2 Corinthians, the author of 1 Thessalonians included that also in his concept "without noticing the difficulty involved" (p. 348). That material difficulty now emerges clearly because of the lack of any reflection on the messenger question in 1 Thessalonians and the answers to it, which require a significant effort to produce.

Thus there is an attempt to suggest a lively exchange, but the content of the correspondence, especially beginning with 1 Thess 3:1–5, and the absence of conflicts between the letter partners in the text as a whole, shows the absence of the finest and most lively weaknesses in such an exchange, namely, that questions remain open, that there is a need to clarify and discuss differences of opinion that are on the table, and that an open process of relating can be perceived. Here, in contrast, the important questions about the survivability and fidelity of the community are scarcely posed before they are answered in a heartbeat by the attitudes and behavior of the community, always characterized as outstanding. The motive of presenting the community in Thessalonica as a model for all others thus clashes with the effort to depict an authentic communication. That motive dominates especially in the first chapters of the letter, but it is consistent throughout, as we will show.[214]

We get quite a clear picture if we read the passage in 1 Thess 2:17–3:13, as it now stands, as a historical overview in the form of a narrative of the last contacts between the apostles and the community, a kind of summary of their relationships, which can be described unreservedly as ideal, against the background of 1:2–2:12, the recollection of the equally ideal founding visit.[215] Thus almost nothing but the past is in view. No real future of those relationships will (or can) follow the "now" in 3:6, 8. This is to be regarded as the implicit honesty and truthfulness of the writing.[216] The supposed doublet in 3:11–13 can neither be seen as the conclusion of a letter fragment[217] nor is it without purpose; it closes the first major section of the letter, the account of the glorious past of the community and its founders in chapters 1–3. The opening section is thus also the major section, the body of the letter, which gives an explanation in terms of content for the unique feature of the letter, so often marveled at, namely, its extremely long opening section.[218] We must see it as one of the author's primary intentions that the past should be so extensively described: in that case it is not just a matter of recapitulating and redundantly

214. See 3.3.2 below ("The ideal community").

215. See further in the next section, 3.3.

216. On this see the exegesis of 4:13–17 and 5:10, below in 5.2.1 and 5.3.2.

217. Thus, e.g., Eckart, *Der zweite echte Brief*, 37.

218. "From a purely formal point of view a writing that consists only of an introduction and a conclusion is a monster—or a torso" (von Dobschütz, *Die Thessalonicherbriefe*, 26–27). For the problem of the extraordinary breadth of the introductory thanksgiving beginning in 1 Thess 1:2, see esp. the now-classic work of Schubert, *Form and Function*, 16–27 (and see there also, p. 7, the discussion in earlier exegesis); the difference from the other Pauline letters is especially evident, for in those other letters the opening thanksgivings occupy only a few verses (cp. ibid., 4ff.). From a form-critical point of view the "excessive length" (p. 17) of the opening extends it to 3:13, so that there is no real body of the letter, because the conclusion of the letter in the strictly formal sense begins at 4:1 with one of the customary phrases, λοιπὸν οὖν, ἀδελφοί. It necessarily follows that the thanksgiving is itself the main body of the letter (pp. 25–26). For the discussion since Schubert cp., e.g., Johanson, *To All the Brethren* (1987), 61ff., who then declares 1 Thess 1:2–5:24 to be the body of the

reciting the community's past, but instead of establishing it in this form as reality. That is what gives such a retrospect its necessity and weight. We must now further verify this possible function of the letter exegetically.

Thus in my opinion the epistolographic contours of 1 Thessalonians raise even more doubts about whether the historical Paul wrote this letter than does the anti-Jewish passage in 2:14–16. The most-frequent formulation in the authorial plural shows, to begin with, that even the letter itself does not assert that it was written by Paul alone. Authorship by the apostles Silvanus and Timothy in the period after the founding visit to Thessalonica is thus also within the realm of possibility, although the important moment of contact with messengers, the material transmission of the letter just written, and thus the immediate continuation of contact with the congregation are completely lacking in this letter. From this I arrive at the thesis that this letter was never sent. In this it clearly differs from the other genuine Pauline letters to individual local communities or persons. It must thus be regarded as more probably fictive than authentic. This suspicion can be supported by further observations within the text; those will be the subject of the remainder of this third chapter.

3.3 First Thessalonians 1–2 as Establishing the History of an Ideal Community and its Ideal Apostle

Again and again individual scholars remark how poorly the relieved cry in 1 Thess 3:6 because Timothy has finally brought good news about the continued existence of the community, which had caused so much concern to this point (3:5), accords with the laudatory statements in the first chapter of the letter, which praised the broad influence of a well-known community that had thereby become important for many others:[219]

> (1:7) so that you became an example (τύπος) to all the believers in Macedonia and in Achaia. (8) For the word of the Lord has sounded forth from you not only in Macedonia and Achaia, but in every place (ἐν παντὶ τόπῳ) your faith in God has become known, so that we have no need (μὴ χρείαν ἔχειν ἡμᾶς) to speak [about it]. (2) For the people of those regions report about us (ἀπαγγέλλουσιν) what kind of welcome we had among you, and how you turned to God from idols, to serve a living and true God . . .

letter (see esp. p. 67); Bickmann, *Kommunikation gegen den Tod*, 9ff.; P.-G. Müller, *Der erste und zweite Brief*, 44–45, 47; Schreiber, "Der erste Thessalonicherbrief," 384–85; E. D. Schmidt, *Heilig ins Eschaton*, 110–19 (cp. 2.1, n. 2 above).

219. "No matter how generously one interprets these words, both the one and the other is so unimaginable at the beginning of Paul's first stay in Corinth that Paul's words cannot be explained even as 'strong exaggeration'" (Schmithals, "Die historische Situation," 133–34, on 1:8–9). Cp. first F. C. Baur, *Paul the Apostle* 2, 88 (see 4.1 below), and most recently Richard, who therefore proposes a new variant on the letter in his commentary: Letter 1 = 2:13–4:2, and Letter 2 = 1:1–2:12; 4:3–5:28 (*First and Second Thessalonians*, esp. 11–17).

Practically speaking, according to this all of Greece and, beyond it, "the whole world," that is, all the congregations outside Greece (which would mean in the land of Israel, in Asia Minor, Syria, etc.) already know about the thus outstanding Thessalonian community, but certainly "Europe" at least: "Thus the example of the community in Thessalonica was instructive for Europe."[220] But if the apostles think it is really not necessary for them to say anything about this, how much less necessary would it have been to seek information about it through a messenger sent out of anxious concern? What can be learned "in every place" does not require a separate inquiry. After all this has been said, the purpose of Timothy's mission is superfluous.

Wolfgang Stegemann, for example, formulates the generally accepted description of Timothy's assignment this way: It appears from 2:17–19 "that Paul was in a state of deep concern about his just-founded community. He thought he had lost it (3:5). Because he could not stand it any longer he finally sent Timothy from Athens to Thessalonica to save what could still be saved. Meanwhile, Timothy had returned with excellent news: against all expectations, the community was standing fast in the Lord. A heavy weight fell from Paul's heart: now he could live again (3:8)."[221]

Supposedly a community that has already become a model to be imitated by a very broad circle of others has now at last overcome a precarious beginning stage and become certain of its identity. So it is not merely a matter of seeing a break between the situations of 2:17–3:5 and 3:6–10,[222] as we considered above, but also of a cleft between these parts and the situation presumed at the beginning of the letter. How does the brilliant reputation of a known community announced there fit with the supposed anxiety that a tempter is endangering their faith and may have made the arduous work of the apostles "empty" (εἰς κενόν), that is, in vain (3:5)? At the same time it was emphasized in 2:1 that their "coming" to Thessalonica was anything but "empty" (οὐ κενή), and besides, it is supposed to have led to great success. This second contradiction between the announcement that Paul is relieved by the news about the continuation of the community and the fact previously stated that people are "reporting" about it practically throughout the whole eastern

220. Knoch, *1. und 2. Thessalonicherbrief*, 29; cp. Bruce: "the faith of the Thessalonians had become a topic of general conversation" (*1 and 2 Thessalonians*, 17), to which he adds a narrative version of such an internationally disseminated report about a sensational conversion (p. 22). Schimanowski, "'Abgrenzung und Identitätsfindung'" (1994), 298, speaks of the "bridgehead effect" of the Thessalonian community "for the beginnings of the Pauline mission in Europe as a whole"; see also Malherbe, *The Letters to the Thessalonians*, 68: "This rapid expansion may have contributed to Paul's custom of speaking of provinces rather than cities."

221. Wolfgang Stegemann, "Anlass und Hintergrund der Abfassung von 1 Th 2,1–12" (1985), 412; similarly Riesner: "Through Timothy's return, Paul had only just learned that the church even still existed" (*Paul's Early Period*, 365–66), and many others similarly.

222. See 3.2.4.b above on the fragmentation hypotheses. Laub, *1. und 2. Thessalonicherbriefe*, 10–11, also offers a brief and concise description of these contradictions about the situation of the letter.

Mediterranean weighs heavily, for Corinth, where, according to the general view, Paul is staying when he writes 1 Thessalonians,[223] is part of the province of Achaia and thus the realm within which the faith of the Thessalonians is supposed to be most talked about. It is said that the delayed news and the high praise in 1:7–9 are "hyperbolically daring" eulogy[224] and not to be taken literally, but this raises the question why, then, the concerned situation depicted in 3:1–5 is supposed to be real and not a kind of exaggeration. The fact that the description of the community in 1 Thessalonians 1 fits better with a later stage of its history, together with other observations, caused Wilhelm Hadorn, for example, to date the letter many years later than is usually done, placing it during the so-called "third missionary journey": "Wherever Paul arrives, he has no need to tell about the Thessalonians. The success of the Pauline mission in Thessalonica is now thoroughly familiar everywhere. The people begin spontaneously to talk of it and praise it. . . . And the apostle is supposed to have written all that at the beginning of his stay in Corinth, shortly after the founding of the community?"[225]

The assertion first appearing in this section, that it is really unnecessary to say or write anything (1:8), strengthens the contradictory nature of the situation: it makes it nearly impossible to give a clear account of why this letter was written at all, also because it alludes again and again to an already existing knowledge of its content on the part of those addressed.

3.3.1 "There is no need to speak . . ." (1:8): The community "knows" everything

Karl Schrader and Ferdinand Christian Baur had already noticed the constant reminiscences about the supposed existence of prior knowledge on the part of those addressed.[226] The letter is peppered with statements that relativize or deny the newness of its information. In my opinion their location and the type of methodical use reveal the real goal, or at least one essential purpose of this writing.

223. This is the *communis opinio* of practically all commentators and works on 1 Thessalonians. Cp. only Schnelle, *Einleitung*, 62–63; Holtz, *Der erste Brief*, 19; Malherbe, *The Letters to the Thessalonians*, 71ff.; P.-G. Müller, *Der erste und zweite Brief*, 38; Schreiber, "Der erste Thessalonicherbrief," 390.

224. Holtz, *Der erste Brief*, 53. Holtz adduces (ibid., n. 142) the missionary activities of "the synagogue" and its "coworkers" as possible sources of the information in 1:7–10, affirmed, among other places, from 1 Corinthians and Philippians. It is significant that he neither notices that active reciprocal relationships, apart from the now-completed work of Timothy, are absent from 1 Thessalonians nor that this makes the reason given for Timothy's journey, the "devouring concern for the community's existence" (p. 116) implausible, since it presents a central contradiction.

225. Hadorn, *Die Abfassung der Thessalonicherbriefe*, 23ff., at 24.

226. Schrader, *Der Apostel Paulus*, 24; Baur, *Paul the Apostle* 2, 86. For more on Schrader and Baur and their role in the history of research as the first significant challengers of the authenticity of 1 Thessalonians, see below at 4.1.

*A. "You know" (*οἴδατε*)*

- 1:5: "... as you know (καθὼς οἴδατε) what kind of persons we proved to be among you for your sake";
- 2:1: "You yourselves know ..." (Αὐτοὶ γὰρ οἴδατε): the manner and success of the apostolic founding visit are known, and yet they are extensively recapitulated in 2:2–12. The section is full of other "you know" formulae referring to the individual descriptions of the attitudes of the missionaries;
- 2:2: despite the known (καθὼς οἴδατε) mistreatments they experienced in Philippi they have acted courageously and
- 2:5: they used no words of flattery, as the community knows (καθὼς οἴδατε);
- 2:11: and they knew (καθάπερ οἴδατε) that the apostles behaved in fatherly fashion;
- 3:3: the community themselves know (αὐτοὶ γὰρ οἴδατε) of the persecutions predicted beforehand
- 3:4: and that they happened (καθὼς ... οἴδατε);
- 4:2: "for you know (οἴδατε γὰρ) what instructions we gave you"—nevertheless, these are stated (4:3–12);
- 5:2: "For you yourselves know very well" (αὐτοὶ γὰρ ἀκριβῶς οἴδατε) that the day of the Lord is coming like a thief in the night; this is given more content in 5:3–11. The reference to the community's knowledge is associated here, in 5:1, with the formula about there being no "necessity" for writing.

*B. "Unnecessary (*μὴ / οὐ χρείαν ἔχειν *with infinitive) to say/write anything"*

- 1:8: the fame of the community is so widespread that the senders would have had no need to say anything about it (μὴ χρείαν ἔχειν ἡμᾶς λαλεῖν τι); but they do anyway;
- 4:9: the addressees have no need for the authors to write to them about love for the brothers and sisters (οὐ χρείαν ἔχετε γράφειν ὑμῖν), because they share it with all the members of God's family throughout Macedonia;
- 5:1: it is unnecessary to write to the community about the time of the day of the Lord (οὐ χρείαν ἔχετε ὑμῖν γράφεσθαι) because they know (οἴδατε, 5:2) ... that what they already "knew" will follow (vv. 3–11).

C. "You remember"

- 2:9: The community remembers the apostles' labor and toil (Μνημονεύετε γὰρ); those efforts are then immediately described (vv. 9–12)

Thus the section in 1 Thess 2:1–12 is especially saturated with formulae appealing to the knowledge and memory of the community. At the same time, however, these formulae are scattered throughout the whole letter. The extended description in chapters 1–3 of the encounter and relationship between the apostles and the members of the community in Thessalonica, their respective characteristics and behaviors, seems unable to dispense with that vocabulary, because these are reports of events that are supposed to be altogether familiar to the community. So why are they being told? The paraenetic sections of the last two chapters contain instructions that, as such, are not supposed to be new but are already known and have been learned, and yet here they are unfolded again. It seems as if this letter has practically nothing new to communicate in any area it touches on, even including the description of the parousia in 4:13–17. How can we explain this unique style,[227] something whose type and frequency are nowhere to be found in the other Pauline letters? The significant οἴδατε is used analogously to 1 Thessalonians only in Gal 4:13 and Phil 4:15, as an allusion to something known that is nevertheless about to be spoken of, but in each case it appears only in this one passage and accompanies a relatively brief reminiscence of some common experience. Interestingly, in both cases it is about recalling the founding visit. In Gal 4:13–14 Paul speaks of his physical weakness at that time and recalls the Galatians' kind response. In Phil 4:15–17 Paul reminds the community of their first times together in Philippi, when he received support in Macedonia only from them. He thus emphasizes the uniqueness of his relationship to that community—in contrast, of all things, to Thessalonica—to which they sent goods more than once. In contrast to these scattered instances, the "you know" language in 1 Thessalonians appears to be a style that is indispensable and constantly employed.

It is astonishing that exegesis has taken so little notice of 1 Thessalonians' constant references to the community's prior knowledge, much less offered any interpretation of it. The only place in which the thorough structuring of the text by means of references to the existing prior knowledge of those addressed could be noted and interpreted would be the commentaries, but at present they still largely ignore it.[228] If the frequency of the concept is recognized at all, it is characterized as "paraenetic commonplace" without further question or critique. At best some of the incidences are addressed and commented within the most immediate textual context as specially-motivated remarks by Paul.[229] Very rare is a reflection like that in Martin Dibelius's commentary regarding the thoroughly "rhetorical character"

227. Μνημονεύετε appears nowhere else in Paul, and χρείαν ἔχειν with the infinitive is equally rare. In 1 Corinthians οἴδατε is similarly frequent, but almost always with the particle οὐκ as "do you not know?" (1 Cor 3:16; 5:6; 6:2, 3, 9, 15, 16, 19; 9:13–24; cp. Rom 6:16; 11:2). It is found in an apparently heated discussion as a partial argument, citing something that is known (or should be known) to the discussion partner. In 1 Thessalonians, on the contrary, there is neither any discussion, much less controversy, nor the argumentative style of the Corinthian correspondence, for example. The only comparable passage would be 1 Cor 12:2, but there the purpose of the οἴδατε ὅτι phrase is to introduce matters (12:3) that are new to the community.

228. Differently, e.g., Dibelius on 1:2–2:16 (*An die Thessalonicher* [3d ed. 1937], 13). More recently even the extensive lists of vocabulary and style elements, for example that by Rigaux (*Thessaloniciens*, 80–94), tend more to obscure the striking employment of this stylistic means and are incomplete, for example, regarding οἴδατε, καθώς, and especially the use of the two together (ibid., 87, 93, 399). In commenting on 2:1, Rigaux at least remarks on

of 1 Thessalonians 1–2, where "known things are described at length" and "frequent references" are found "to the readers' knowledge." This is said to show a "retreat of the epistolary situation" together with a solemn, plerophoric manner of expression.[230]

Nevertheless, Elizabeth Struthers Malbon, in her structuralist work interpreting the construction of 1 Thessalonians in the context of mythical textual structures as proposed by Claude Lévi-Strauss, clearly recognizes the uniform character of the distribution of the "knowledge" conceptuality within the text as a whole. She definitively illustrates the ongoing repetition of the terms and the deep structure of the text shaped by that repetition.[231] But since Malbon, as she makes clear, is not posing historical questions, her overall results remain essentially within the "mythical" sphere in which "for Paul" the writing of letters is seen to be relevant as

the different use of οἴδατε elsewhere in the Corpus Paulinum (p. 399); see similarly Holtz, who sees 2:1–12 as "saturated" with it (*Der erste Brief*, 92). Malherbe, *The Letters to the Thessalonians*, 157, has a brief remark that in 1:5; 2:1, 2, 5, 11; 3:3, 4; 4:2; 5:2 Paul is using a paraenetic formula, referring to "the stereotyped nature of the phrase and his frequent use of it throughout the letter," but without further investigation.

229. Symptomatic are Rigaux, *Thessaloniciens* (one of the more extensive commentaries), who at 4:9, and only there, comments on χρείαν ἔχειν, otherwise referring to 1:8 (p. 517), though nothing is said about it there (p. 387). At 5:1 he again refers without comment to 4:9 (p. 555). Cp. also Holtz, *Der erste Brief*, 53, 173, 211–12, where particularly striking keywords in individual verses are considered more in depth; above all, works on textual linguistics are in a position to recognize the local abundance of the terms, especially in 2:1–12, as a rhetorical figure (e.g., Johanson, *To All the Brethren*, 89); others see it as "unusual" (e.g., Wolfgang Stegemann, "Anlass und Hintergrund," 397) but neglect to pose critical questions to 1 Thessalonians for that reason. Traditionally, 2:1–12 is evaluated as Paul's apology against "opponents," and with it the vocabulary of the community's "knowledge" as referring to its witness in that regard (thus, e.g., von Dobschütz, *Die Thessalonicherbriefe*, 83, 106–107), although then the appearance of the concept outside that section is ignored, completely so even by one opponent of the apology thesis (Schoon-Janssen, *Umstrittene 'Apologien' in den Paulusbriefen* [1991], 39–65).

230. Dibelius, *An die Thessalonicher*, 13.

231. Elizabeth Struthers Malbon, "'No Need to Have Any One Write'" (1983), esp. 58–63. Similarly also Daniel Patte, "Method for a Structural Exegesis of Didactic Discourses" (1983), 98ff. Previously, Davis ("Remembering and Acting" [1971]) described οἴδατε as an element shaping the motif of memory in 1 Thessalonians (see Collins, "Recent Scholarship on Paul's Letters to the Thessalonians" [1984], 26); cp. also Donfried, "The Cults of Thessalonica" (1985), 348, who speaks, with reference to Nils Dahl, of "superfluous rehearsals and reminders," and Walton, *Leadership and Lifestyle* (2000), 157–58, who emphasizes the striking frequency of οἴδατε and reference to the memory of the addressees in 1 Thessalonians in contrast to the other Pauline letters; see also the structural and grammatical analyses of Coulot, "Paul à Thessalonique" (2006), 397–80, 388, and Lambrecht, "Lack of Logic?" (2008), 328–33.

such, and to be regarded primarily as a necessary subject action, whereas the "facts" conveyed are to be considered altogether secondary.[232] Jutta Bickmann also, in her study based on communications theory, acknowledges the prominent role of the "knowledge formulae" in the structuring of 1 Thessalonians.[233] The analysis of the speech-acts shows that these expressions serve repeatedly and quite clearly as meta-communicative illocutionary marks, as address indicating a shift to a different level of communication. By following them we can discover the macrostructure of the divisions of the text as a whole. But what does such a structure show, beyond the purpose of consolation[234] pursued by Bickmann, about those who conduct such a conversation? Is it possible, without further evidence, to see such a thing as part of an authentic continuing dialogue?

To my knowledge Christoph Demke is the only recent exegete to give adequate attention to this striking finding, the constant reference to the knowledge possessed by the addressees, attending to its content, interpreting its function, and offering some further important observations on the unique character of 1 Thessalonians for discussion. These have received little attention thus far, in part because of his hypothesis of interpolations, which is so extensive and apparently arbitrary that it is difficult to comprehend[235] and is "practically equivalent to a declaration of spuriousness,"[236] and thus also in part because it broadly questions the authenticity of 1 Thessalonians. For Demke,[237] οἴδατε/"you know" is often and strikingly combined with the likewise stereotypical expression ἐγενήθημεν/"we were" or "it happened" (1:5; 2:5, 7, 10), culminating in the combined repetition in 3:4: καθὼς καὶ ἐγένετο καὶ οἴδατε ("so it turned out, as you know"). This stereotyped appeal to the community's knowledge betrays a lack of epistolary style and a word

232. Malbon, "'No Need to Have Anyone Write,'" 71. She also sees a parallel between 2:17–3:7 and 4:13–17 in that Paul's absence and that of the dead are related to one another.

233. Bickmann, *Kommunikation gegen den Tod*, 103–46, esp. 121ff.; cp. the brief remarks on "references to knowledge" as indicator of apologetic, on the one hand, in Gerber, *Paulus und seine 'Kinder,'* 271, and on the other hand her classification of 1 Thess 2:1–12, following Bickmann, as "relation-building pragmatics" (p. 313).

234. See the summary "1 Thessalonians as a Letter of Consolation" in Bickmann, *Kommunikation gegen den Tod*, 266–321, and also Wick, "Ist I Thess 2,13–16 antijüdisch?" (1994), who affirms that "the whole letter [appears to be] an unnecessary letter with unnecessary themes" (p. 16), but apparently for him this is adequately explained by the proposed rhetorical function of 1 Thessalonians as consolation (pp. 17ff.).

235. Demke, "Theology and Literary Criticism in 1 Thessalonians" (1996). Only 2:17–3:2a, 5b–11; 4:9, 10, 13–17; 5:1–22 are to be regarded as Pauline. A post-apostolic author is supposed to have composed 1:2–2:16; 3:12–4:8; 5:23–27 and combined them with the genuine parts (Part 4, Conclusion, and *passim*). The text of the essay can be found (without pagination) at https://depts.drew.edu/jhc/demke.html (accessed June 2017).

236. Holtz, *Der erste Brief*, 25.

237. Cp. Demke, "Theology and Literary Criticism," 3.3.

usage peculiar to the author. The community is appealed to as witness for unknown third parties, leading up to the statement that they, together with God, can attest to "Paul's" blameless behavior: "You are witnesses, and God also" (2:10). This only makes sense, according to Demke, if the really "intended addressees of this self-presentation are not those spoken to, but some third party.... The formulation only becomes understandable when what is said is directed outward, and with an appeal to the community and *so also* God, Paul is held up as an ideal model for holiness, righteousness, and blamelessness."[238] But Demke himself overlooks the fact that the significant οἴδατε also appears in 5:2, which he declares "genuine," and he does not pay attention to the analogously-employed expressions about "unnecessary" communication in 1:8; 4:9; 5:1, which he also places, in part, within the sections he declares authentic.[239] In reality, he should extend his suspicion of inauthenticity to more of 1 Thessalonians.

If we ask which texts are characterized by this style of constant reference to the knowledge and memory of the addressees we find a parallel in epistolary novels, especially in antiquity, in which the action is depicted through fictional letters. Timo Glaser has described this indispensable motif for the imaginative projection of a letter exchange in his work on the narratological approach to the interpretation of pseudepigraphical epistolary books, using ancient epistolary fiction: a pseudonymous letter differs from an authentic one in its relation to reality. "Whereas the genuine letter is meant to directly affect the communicative situation between sender and recipient, the fictional letter cannot do so. By choosing a pseudonym the author may indeed take on its authority and thereby affect the recipient but cannot influence the reciprocal relationship between the author and the recipient. To that extent the letter with a fictive indication of authorship reflects a communicative event that it cannot construct."[240] Consequently it is necessary to establish a kind of apparatus for verifying the genuine character of the epistolary communication on the level of the real readership of the epistolary novel: "A related necessity is the distinction between the external and the internal reader, each with a different pre-knowledge that the author must presume. Because the letter is normally the continuation of an ongoing 'conversation,' that is, a segment of a communicative action between persons known to one another, the two communication partners share a common knowledge to which they can refer in the letter communications but that need not necessarily be stated explicitly. *The external, real reader, on the contrary, does not have that knowledge, so that the demand on the author of a fictional correspondence is to convey that knowledge without undermining the fiction of a real correspondence.*"[241] There are possibilities for over-determination and under-determination in conveying this necessary knowledge to the "external real reader." In my opinion the first of the notes on the

238. Ibid.
239. Ibid., 3.4.
240. Glaser, "Erzählung im Fragment" (2009), 272.
241. Ibid., 273. Emphasis supplied.

pre-knowledge of the community that are scattered throughout 1 Thessalonians, each of which is nevertheless followed by the narration of what is said to be known, corresponds to over-determination: "absolutely necessary knowledge already available to the internal reader that the external reader must receive because otherwise the correspondence, or some statements within it, will remain incomprehensible.... At the same time the balancing between over- and under-determination provides *a possibility for uncovering the fiction by looking for the places where we find information superfluous for the internal reader but necessary for the external reader*. Such over-determined statements are often *given additional justification by the author* in order to maintain the fiction of a genuine exchange of letters despite the offense against plausibility."[242] Since the constant reference to knowledge and memory in 1 Thessalonians clearly corresponds to this stylistic mode of epistolary pseudepigraphy, and appears in significant quantity in proportion to the length of the writing, we have here another clear indication of its pseudepigraphical composition.

An apparently authentic epistolary communication[243] that, however, in truth is "directed outward," as Demke puts it in the passage quoted above—that is how the whole of 1 Thessalonians appears to me, in both form and content, in light of the thickly-strewn appeals to the pre-knowledge and memory of the addressees. For as we have seen, not only is the recitation of the successful first appearance of the missionaries (2:1–12) shaped by it, but so also, for example, is the introduction to the eschatological instruction in 5:1–2. The community "knows" practically everything that is communicated here at such length. An epistolary conversation "directed outward" is a planned, apparently spontaneous exchange between two or more persons that, however, is not conducted primarily for the speakers themselves but is aimed at third parties who, we might say, are listening outside the "open window" of an exchange of letters. In this way the latter receive information specifically directed at them, while those acting, in the nature of the thing, communicate things to one another that are not particularly new and possibly not entirely in accord with reality. We could say that a kind of theatre is being presented or a section from an epistolary novel is being written, with a moment of the drama being excised and displayed. In such a presentation, too-brief allusions to the content of the common knowledge and experience of the speakers would be awkward if the experiences themselves are the subject of the information being

242. Ibid., 274. Emphasis supplied. Glaser includes examples from ancient epistolary novels to show "how an author transmits information superfluous for the internal reader to the external reader," namely, through remarks that something being narrated is already known, or by an appeal to the memory of the fictional readers (pp. 274–75).

243. For ancient letters as communication form and the consequent similarity to a conversational situation see also Bickmann, *Kommunikation gegen den Tod*, 66–88; E.-M. Becker, *Schreiben und Verstehen*, 103–39; the "letter is shaped as a conversation between friends" (Glaser, "Erzählung im Fragment," 273 n. 27, with reference to Pseudo-Libanius, *De forma epistulari* 2).

offered to the listeners or readers. Therefore they are narrated. But since the appearance of genuine communication needs to be maintained, one remarks from time to time that the letter-partner of course already knows what one is talking about and really has no need to have it repeated. At the same time the matter *is* repeated in relatively full fashion, as we see especially in the section in 2:1–12, which requires four reminders of the community's prior knowledge regarding what is narrated about the apostle's arrival.

It is significant for 1 Thessalonians that the epistolary conversation it presents is depicted as coming from a single party, namely, the supposed senders Paul, Silvanus, and Timothy. They virtually usurp the role of the conversation partners by the insertions of "you know," etc., without that phrase serving to *abbreviate* a strand of information, something we frequently experience in live communication. On the contrary, they function to *introduce* the more or less redundant recitation of what is apparently known by everyone. This reveals the essential goal of this communication: if we consider the content of what is said in 1 Thessalonians 1–3, it is apparently about a written summary of the history of the community and their apostles in the shape of this particular depiction.[244] Thus the impression occasionally articulated, that in 1 Thessalonians, in contrast to the other Pauline correspondence, we are dealing with a writing that "really lacks a theme"[245] is correct, and yet it is not. As far as a veritable theme for epistolary communication is concerned, it appears deficient.[246] But as the documentation and confirmation of the fact that Thessalonica has an apostolic history, it is not. First Thessalonians pursues its own special agenda.

It was really "not necessary to write to you." But since it is being done, apparently it is, in fact, urgently necessary. Why? So that there may be something written, *so that it may exist at all.* As regards what is communicated as unnecessary or already known, it could therefore be about the really-intended content: it is about telling of this community and its apostles in order that such a history may exist, that is, in order that the story thus told may come to exist in this form. A letter is written to the community in Thessalonica so that a letter to the community in Thessalonica may exist and be published, so that in this way the community may have a letter from the apostle. The "command" at the end of the writing (5:27) then serves the purpose of this envisaged publication and handing on of the letter's text: "I command (ἐνορκίζω) you by the Lord that this letter be read to all of [the brothers

244. For the fact that 1 Thessalonians 4–5 makes space for some actual problems of the (later) community, see chap. 5 below.

245. Schnider and Stenger, *Studien zum neutestamentlichen Briefformular*, 53; epistolary self-commendation and repeated thanksgivings shape a letter that, alone among the others, appears to get along without any epistolary theme or thematic discussion (ibid., 53–54 n. 12).

246. Dibelius writes regarding 1 Thess 1:1–2:16: In the Pauline letters "we seldom find a section that contains so little 'correspondence,' that is, questions, answers, associations, and allusions to things unknown to us, and that presents itself so much as the rhetorical development of a single thought, that is, really the thanksgiving" (*An die Thessalonicher*, 13).

and sisters]!"[247] But a "letter" understood in that way is evidently written also as a sign that the community itself has existed or is to be regarded as still existing. After all, the text begins with over-the-top praise and is permeated by it. Honoring the character of the community is a focal point of the writing. The remarks that follow on this subject should be regarded as further solidifying the hypothesis that 1 Thessalonians is a pseudepigraphical writing: namely, I will attempt to give exegetical grounds for why such a fictive letter would have been written. This will also involve presenting some other odd features and problems in 1 Thessalonians.

3.3.2 *The ideal community (1:7–10; 4:9–12)*

The further exegesis of 1 Thess 1:2–2:16 and 2:17–3:13 as a complex web of speech-acts by a "community of communication" in the major section of Jutta Bickmann's work offers valuable points of reference for the thesis I want to pursue: the inauthenticity of 1 Thessalonians. She characterizes 1:2–2:16 as the "reconstruction of a relationship," and 2:17–3:10 as the "construction of death" against the background of the narrated endangerment of the community of communication, with 3:11–13 as "elimination of the separation" and "fulfillment of community." In particular, her analysis of the "reconstruction of a relationship"[248] is a persuasive description of the sense of 1 Thessalonians 1–2, aiming at a "reconstruction of the ideal community of communication" as its plot.[249] This result can also be applied outside the previous historical framing that dates 1 Thessalonians to Paul's early period. The hypothesis of later composition is not about *reconstructions* but about

247. Klauck, *Briefliteratur*, 281, calls this verse a "command to read." For the function of consolation as the intention of pseudepigraphical letters, or letters as literary testaments according to the example of pseudepigraphical SyrBar, see ibid., 209–15. In SyrBar 86,1–3, much as in 1 Thess 5:27, there is an injunction to read the letter aloud and meditate on it in the assembly in order to ritualize a mutual remembering (ibid., 214). Cp. Oestreich, "Leseanweisungen in Briefen" (2004) on other previous interpretations (pp. 228–35) of 1 Thess 5:27, this "singular and unusually sharp order from Paul" (p. 228). Oestreich himself sees this as a means to bring all the members of the community to the same degree of knowledge as the leadership has and, in addition to passages from a papyrus letter, he evaluates, among others, Col 4:16, the prayer for the reading of community letters in Colossae and Laodicea as well as exchange of letters, as parallels to this measure (pp. 235–40). But since Colossians is probably a pseudepigraphical writing (cp., e.g., Standhartinger, *Studien zur Entstehungsgeschichte*; on Col 4:16 at 15, 287), such an order for publication, which above all other things emphasizes the weight and validity, relevance and authority of a writing, can also shed light on the nature of 1 Thess 5:27, because something of the sort seems to be necessary in order to prepare the way to public notice for a writing that does not come from the historical apostle.

248. Bickmann, *Kommunikation gegen den Tod*, 156–265, esp. §7 on the "reconstruction of a relationship" (pp. 156–214).

249. Ibid., 240ff.

constructions, both the *construction of a relationship* and the *construction* of its participants, namely, *the community and its apostles* as ideal figures.

The community in Thessalonica is unsurpassable in its greatness, practice, and effectiveness—thus the secret message of 1 Thessalonians.[250]

There are scattered indications of this throughout the letter, beginning with a concentration in the first chapter, and indeed in the very first verse. The prescript deviates significantly from all other Pauline letter openings, especially as regards the naming of the senders and addressees. Alongside the equal naming of Paul, Silvanus, and Timothy as authors without other qualifiers,[251] there is the striking fact that the community is not addressed, as in other letters, as existing "in" (ἐν) a city,[252] but with the *nomen gentilicium*: τῇ ἐκκλησίᾳ Θεσσαλονικέων (1:1). That refers to all the citizens in a city, that is, properly the representative political assembly of all (male) citizens: "The citizens' assembly of the polis of Thessalonica could also have been addressed in this way."[253] This finding has not often been addressed or emphasized in research to date.[254] Apart from the political significance of such a choice of words[255] for the overall interpretation of 1 Thessalonians, for the present we must say that it expresses a certain degree of immoderation. While the added "in God our Father and the Lord Jesus Christ" makes it clear that this is really the "Christian" community, the fact that in the same breath they are

250. These reflections fill a gap that has existed since the beginnings of the debate about 1 Thessalonians' inauthenticity, with Karl Schrader and Ferdinand Christian Baur (see chap. 4 below), because heretofore no real purpose could be discovered (cp. 4.3 below) for the composition of such a fabricated apostolic letter to the Thessalonian community. The indicators mentioned below derive from other singular features of 1 Thessalonians that make it stand out within the Corpus Paulinum, including especially the strange presentation of the imitation motif (see 3.3.4 below).

251. Cp. 3.1.1 above.

252. Romans 1:6–7: κλητοὶ Ἰησοῦ Χριστοῦ, πᾶσιν τοῖς οὖσιν ἐν Ῥώμῃ; 1 Cor 1:2: τῇ ἐκκλησίᾳ τοῦ θεοῦ τῇ οὔσῃ ἐν Κορίνθῳ . . .; 2 Cor 1:1: τῇ ἐκκλησίᾳ τοῦ θεοῦ τῇ οὔσῃ ἐν Κορίνθῳ . . .; Phil 1:1: τοῖς ἁγίοις ἐν Χριστῷ Ἰησοῦ τοῖς οὖσιν ἐν Φιλίπποις. The letter to Galatia apparently goes to communities in more than one city: ταῖς ἐκκλησίαις τῆς Γαλατίας, Gal 1:2.

253. Stegemann and Stegemann, *The Jesus Movement: A Social History of Its First Century* (1999), 264; see also their remarks on the pragmatic social understanding of ἐκκλησία outside the land of Israel as an "analogy to the political common assembly." That understanding is presupposed in 1 Thessalonians and is further emphasized by the equal positioning of the two (namely, ἐκκλησία as community of faith and as political assembly).

254. Among older interpreters, von Söden, *Der erste Thessalonicherbrief*, 274, finds this to bespeak "assurance on the part of the apostle . . . who under the fresh impression of his success already thinks of the inhabitants of Thessalonica as a whole in relation to the community." He later recognized "that the communities only had a modest place in the great pagan cities, but were completely separate from them."

255. On this see esp. Donfried, "The Assembly of the Thessalonians" (1996), 390ff., and the remarks below at 5.5.

apostrophized as existing "among [the] Thessalonians" could suggest the idea that nearly the whole city might belong to the Christian community. So are we again dealing with one of the exaggerations in 1 Thessalonians, not intentional as to content but demanded by rhetoric? It is more probable that the idea was to give the impression of a numerous, strong community.

Interest in the geographical placement of the community continues as its significance is described in relation to its broader surroundings. Through the way they received the proclamation, in persecution, but also in their joy in the Holy Spirit (1:6) they have become a constructive model for all believers in the Roman provinces of Macedonia and Achaia (1:7). And it is not only into Macedonia and Achaia that "the word of the Lord" has gone forth from them; their reputation for faith in God has spread to "every place" (ἐν παντὶ τόπῳ), so that there is no need to speak of it (1:8). If we take that literally, the Thessalonian community has become a model at least for the Macedonian communities in Philippi and Beroea, for Athens and Corinth in Achaia, but beyond them for those in Asia, Syria, or Judea. The real lives and activities of other communities and their members receive no positive mention anywhere in the letter, apart from the generalized suffering of those in Judea (2:14). There was some unspecified mistreatment in Philippi (2:2), and those in Athens are concerned about Thessalonica (3:1). Thessalonica outshines them all and has a superlative reputation especially in Greece. It seems that the apostles' evangelization there had been like hurling a heavy stone into the wide sea, sending forth waves everywhere.

Add to this the perfect praxis of this community, which is constantly mentioned. In the context of the paraenetic instruction in 4:1–12 we find the repeated assertion that the community has long been doing what is being urged here: καθὼς καὶ περιπατεῖτε ("as, in fact, you are [already] doing"), 4:1; καὶ γὰρ ποιεῖτε ("and indeed you do"), 4:10. The instruction is only intended to encourage the further growth of this practice of mutual love, "more and more" (περισσεύητε μᾶλλον, 4:1; περισσεύειν μᾶλλον, 4:10), just as in 3:12 the existing practice of love in the community is elevated and, with a similar expression, hope is only expressed for further growth of what already exists, so that their love for one another and for all may increase and abound (περισσεύσαι τῇ ἀγάπῃ εἰς ἀλλήλους καὶ εἰς πάντας). Thus, besides the community's reputation for faith, its practical effects also shine far beyond the immediate environment of the city, and again the whole province of Macedonia is said to be influenced by it, namely, "all the brothers and sisters throughout Macedonia" (πάντας τοὺς ἀδελφοὺς (τοὺς) ἐν ὅλῃ τῇ Μακεδονίᾳ), 4:10.

According to Beverly Roberts Gaventa this section in 4:9–12 somewhat resembles an airplane that never really gets off the runway.[256] The beginning in vv. 9–10 seems unspecific but assured and tautological, mixing the motif of unnecessary writing, the already-existing knowledge of God on the part of the addressees, the affirmation of a far-reaching practice, and the urging to be still better. There would have been no need to write such pedestrian statements as letter communication and information, but in their own way they underscore the

256. Gaventa, *First and Second Thessalonians* (1998), 56.

exclusive status accorded this community. In particular the assertion that they have long since been instructed by God (θεοδίδακτοι, v. 9) in fraternal/sororal love (φιλαδελφία) constitutes the highest praise. The question of the context from which θεοδίδακτος, a *hapax legomenon* in the New Testament,[257] is taken, or what traditions might have inspired the authors to use that construction[258] is less important for the moment than its function for the overall picture of the lauded Thessalonian community. The peculiar predicate of being taught by God is not something the apostles claim for themselves; it appears in the context of the repeated exaltation of the Thessalonians above all the local communities throughout Macedonia (4:10). We could get the impression that the important *polis* of Thessalonica, as the capital of Macedonia,[259] is accorded an equally important congregation belonging to Christ, more or less as the capital community and hence the leading congregation at least of this Roman province in Greece, if not even beyond there.

257. Otherwise only in Barn 21:6: γίνεσθε δὲ θεοδίδακτοι; in John 6:45 it appears in a citation from Isa 54:13 (LXX): καὶ ἔσονται πάντες διδακτοὶ θεοῦ.

258. Suggestions include, e.g., (a) Isa 54:13, where Jerusalem's children are said to be "taught by YHWH" (LXX; so, *inter alia*, Holtz, *Der erste Brief*, 174; Witmer, "θεοδίδακτοι in 1 Thessalonians 4:9" [2006], 245–50); (b) Philo, who calls many figures in Israel's history "autodidacts" who received their knowledge from God (Roetzel, "Theodidaktoi and Handwork in Philo and 1 Thessalonians" [1986]), 327ff.; similarly Pax, "Beobachtungen zur Konvertitensprache" (1971), 233ff., and Koester, "1 Thessalonians—Experiment in Christian Writing" (1977), 39; (c) an allusion to the Epicureans' doctrine of friendship, from which Paul distances himself (Malherbe, "Exhortation in First Thessalonians" [1983/1989], 63–64); (d) the adoption of slogans from the context of Thessalonica's city cults, namely, the propaganda associated with the Dioscuri; this is the thesis of Kloppenborg (Φιλαδελφία, Θεοδίδακτος and the Dioscuri" [1993]). This last is not wholly improbable, although we would scarcely expect a positive reference to pagan cultic elements in a document of Christian resistance (1 Thess 1:9!). For dialogue with Kloppenborg see esp. Witmer, "θεοδίδακτοι," 240–45; for 1 Thessalonians as the expression of local Christian resistance to Rome see below, chap. 5.5.

259. For the city and its history see esp. Touratsoglou, *Die Münzstätte von Thessaloniki* (1988), 5–20: Thessalonica remained "the administrative and mercantile center throughout the imperial period, as it had already been in Hellenism and during the Roman republic" (p. 5). Cp. vom Brocke, *Thessaloniki* (2001), 12–20. Around the middle of the second century C.E. Thessalonica was the most populous city of the province (thus, ca. 150 years earlier, Strabo, VII, 7,4: ἣ νῦν μάλιστα τῶν ἄλλων εὐανδρεῖ), and the poet Antipatros of Thessalonica praises his city as "the mother of all Macedonia" (μήτερ ἡ πάσης <Μακεδονίας>, *Anthol. Palat.* IX, 428). For ancient witnesses to Thessalonica see Bornemann, *Die Thessalonicherbriefe*, 10–11; cp. also Evans, "Eschatology and Ethics" (1968), 1–63; Elliger, *Paulus in Griechenland* (1987), 78–90, at 89; Riesner, *Paul's Early Period*, 337–41; vom Brocke, *Thessaloniki*, 12–101, *passim*, esp. 107ff.; see also below at 5.5.

Finally, the exalted position of those in Thessalonica is emphasized in that the motifs of imitation and modeling are used differently than in the Pauline letters (1 Cor 4:16; 11:1; Phil 3:17), where they are in the imperative; here, in contrast, they are formulated in the indicative (1 Thess 1:6, 7; 2:14).[260] So it appears that the Thessalonian community has from the beginning advanced much more rapidly than the others we know of in Greece; it has already become their model and guide.

This multidimensional praise of the perfected community, however, lies crossways to the sequence of concern, sending of a messenger, and final sigh of relief at his return (2:17–3:6). There would really be no need to worry about the status of a well-known community that is the object of general admiration and from which news is received by way of many others (1:7–9). But it seems that praise of an outstanding community is more important than eliminating a contradiction arising out of the portrayal of a simultaneous "active" exchange between the concerned apostles and a community whose existence is precarious. The contradiction could exist and could even be accepted if there is no "real" early-community situation any longer and the intention is only to pretend that there is. The authors were successful in that, and to the present their effort is still successful in relation to nearly all readers who are accustomed to deal more or less uncritically with 1 Thessalonians.

3.3.3 *The ideal apostles (1:5; 2:1–12)*

The image of an outstanding ideal community is matched by the picture of its ideal apostles in 2:1–12. This is not so much in order to present an apology in the face of attacks by opponents, as exegetes first thought,[261] but, on the basis of the material used and its function in the context, it is a kind of instruction about the way in which apostles, and thus with them the communities as a whole, can best missionize, and how they should comport themselves in a difficult and even hostile environment.

The model chosen for describing the exemplary way of life adopted by the apostles during their stay in Thessalonica is anything but original. It only slightly resembles the image of the Paul who worked with his own hands, known to us from 1 Cor 4:12 and Acts 18:3 and taken up in 1 Thess 2:9,[262] elaborated in 2 Thess

260. For more on the idea of imitation, see below at 3.3.4.

261. Thus, e.g., von Dobschütz, *Die Thessalonicherbriefe*, 106–7; Willi Marxsen opts for an "apology" for the Pauline "gospel" (*Der erste Brief an die Thessalonicher*, 25, 43).

262. From the perspective of the Greco-Roman upper classes, work "with one's own hands" signaled despised and dirty jobs; see esp. Cicero (*De off.* I, 42, 150–51, and frequently; on this see Ivoni Richter Reimer, *Women in the Acts of the Apostles* (1995), 105–9). Because the greater part of early Christianity, together with the Pauline tradition about handicrafts, aligned itself with "dirty" work and thus with the lower classes, it retained the identification of gospel for the poor and social order for a long time; cp. Luise Schottroff, *Lydia's Impatient Sisters* (1994), 132–51. The craft of tentmaking is associated with Paul (as well as Prisca and

3:7–13. By far the majority of the remarks in 1 Thess 2:1–12, especially in vv. 1–8, agree with the sources of Greco-Roman popular philosophy. The question is: how did such material get into an early Christian letter, that is, how could and can anyone think it conceivable that Paul would cite popular philosophical commonplaces at length and in a central place in his very first apostolic community letter, and make it obligatory for his community?

Following Martin Dibelius, who in his commentary on 2:1–12 had already pointed out a great many echoes of descriptions of the ideal philosopher drawn from many philosophical schools and writings,[263] Abraham J. Malherbe has persuasively shown the close relationship between the text of 2:1–8 and passages from the speeches of the rhetor and itinerant Cynic philosopher Dion of Prusa (Dio Chrysostom). There are literal and formal parallels between "Paul" and Dion that every interpretation of 1 Thessalonians 2 must take into account.[264] The correspondences are arresting and, if one supposes pseudepigraphical authorship, could come close to answering the question of a written model for 1 Thess 2:1–8, for Dio Chrysostom, born in the province of Bithynia in Asia Minor, was a whole generation younger than Paul (40–ca. 120 C.E.) and developed his thinking in the wake of his banishment by Domitian (81–96 C.E.), becoming a Stoic-Cynic philosopher.[265] Those who favor a Pauline origin for 1 Thessalonians, which is to say nearly all its interpreters, and especially those many who essentially affirm the

Aquila); on this see esp. Richter Reimer, *Women*, 199–208, as well as Peter Lampe, "Paulus—Zeltmacher" (1987) and Hock, "Paul's Tentmaking" (1978); idem, "The Workshop as a Social Setting" (1979); idem, *The Social Context of Paul's Ministry* (1980); Hengel, "Der vorchristliche Paulus" (1991), 208ff. Hock also emphasizes how much the teaching of the Cynic philosophers was likewise associated with the sphere of the marketplace and craftspeople's shops (cp., *inter alia*, idem, "Workshop as Social Setting," 445ff.), something that should be attended to with regard to 1 Thessalonians. It does not seem as if the Cynics fundamentally linked their teaching with their own crafts, though that is attested for a minority; cp. Collins, *The Birth of the New Testament* (1993), 13–14. Ascough, "Paul's Macedonian Associations" (2003), 169–76, describes Paul's work, probably in leather, as a common activity carried on in cooperation with the Thessalonian community.

263. Dibelius, *An die Thessalonicher*, 7ff.

264. Malherbe, "'Gentle as a Nurse'" (1970/1989), with summary on p. 48. Cp. idem, "Exhortation in First Thessalonians"; idem, "Paul: Hellenistic Philosopher" (1986/1989); idem, *Paul and the Thessalonians* (1987), 2ff., 21–33, 46ff., and frequently; idem, *The Letters to the Thessalonians*, 133–63. Broad sections of Malherbe's work demonstrate the possible relationship between 1 Thessalonians in particular (among all the Pauline letters) and contemporary philosophical material and philosophical ethics.

265. See the remarks on Dio's life in the German text edition of his *Orationes* by Elliger (1967), xi–xvii. Now see also the Encyclopedia Britannica article at https://www.britannica.com/biography/Dio-Chrysostom, and the more extensive Wikipedia entry, https://en.wikipedia.org/wiki/Dio_Chrysostom.

results of Malherbe's investigations[266] (as well as Malherbe himself, of course) might have seen larger conundrums and broader questions in these parallels. The fact that this has not happened can be attributed to the common acceptance, until the very recent past, of placing Paul generally or primarily in the context of non-Jewish traditions. The recently increasing tendency to try to understand Paul positively, and primarily on the basis of possible Jewish parallels,[267] is certainly welcome in Pauline exegesis because it is producing more probable and more fruitful results. But precisely at 1 Thess 2:1–8 it necessarily fails in light of the real material available for comparison.

Malherbe, first of all, produces a passage from Dio's oration "To the Alexandrians," *Or.* 32,9–12, to establish the agreements with 1 Thess 2:1–8. According to Malherbe, the parallel Greek concepts are evident in the translation of the New Testament text:[268]

> (2:1) You yourselves know, brothers and sisters, that our coming to you was not in vain [κενή, "empty"], (2) but though we had already suffered and been shamefully mistreated (ὑβρισθέντες) at Philippi, as you know, we had courage [ἐπαρρησιασάμεθα] in our God to declare to you the gospel of God in spite of great opposition [ἐν πολλῷ ἀγῶνι]. (3) For our appeal does not spring from deceit (ἐκ πλάνης] or impure motives [ἐξ ἀκαρθασίας] or trickery [ἐν δόλῳ], (4) but just as we have been approved by God to be entrusted with the message of

266. E.g., Best, *Thessalonians*, 94–95; Koester, "1 Thessalonians—Experiment," 40ff.; Holtz, "Traditionen im 1. Thessalonicherbrief" (1983/1991), 57ff.; Marshall, *1 and 2 Thessalonians* (1983), 60ff.; Collins, "Paul, as seen through his own eyes" (1980), 185–86; Lyons, *Pauline Autobiography* (1985), 196ff.; Holtz, *Der erste Brief*, 69–77; idem, "On the Background of 1 Thessalonians 2:1–12" (2000), 72–76; Schoon-Janssen, *Umstrittene Apologien*, 54, 57–61; Perkins, "1 Thessalonians and Hellenistic Religious Practices" (1989), 329ff.; Gaventa, "Apostles as Babes and Nurses" (1991); eadem, *First and Second Thessalonians*, 22–39; Roberts, *Images of Paul*, 124–48; Winter, "The Entries and Ethics of Orators and Paul" (1993); Riesner, *Paul's Early Period*, 363–64; Smith, *Comfort One Another* (1995), esp. 78ff.; Richard, *First and Second Thessalonians*, 77–111, esp. 86–88; Haufe, *Der erste Brief*, 31–42; Still, *Conflict at Thessalonica* (1999), 139ff.; Seyoon Kim, "Paul's Entry," 524ff. and *passim*; Schreiber, "Der erste Thessalonicherbrief," 392–93, and many others.

267. For 1 Thessalonians cp., e.g., Bickmann, who considers this at length in her discussion of 1 Thess 2:7 (*Kommunikation gegen den Tod*, 171ff.), and Reinmuth, "Der erste Brief," 122ff. Cp. also the initiative of Pax, "Beobachtungen," who, it is true, remarks on the "uncommon and unusual words, many of them *hapax legomena*, that appear with relative frequency in this letter," and indeed in "centers of concentration," one of them 2:7–12 with the concepts of ἤπιος, τροφός, ὁμείρομαι, ὁσίως, ἀμέμπτως, as well as "the striking use of the reflexive pronoun," τὰ ἑαυτῆς τέκνα (2:7), τὰς ἑαυτῶν ψυχάς (2:8), and τέκνα ἑαυτοῦ (2:11) (pp. 257–58).

268. Cp. Malherbe, "'Gentle as a Nurse,'" 36, and the extensive adaptation by Richard, *First and Second Thessalonians*, 90–99.

> the gospel, even so we speak, not to please mortals, but to please God who tests our hearts. (5) As you know and as God is our witness, we never came with words of flattery [ἐν λόγῳ κολακείας] or with a pretext for greed [πλεονεξίας]; (6) nor did we seek praise [δόξαν] from mortals, whether from you or from others, (7) though we might have made demands as apostles of Christ [δυνάμενοι ἐν βάρει εἶναι].[269] But we were gentle [ἤπιοι][270] among you, like a nurse [τροφός] tenderly caring for her own children. (8) So deeply do we care for you[271] that we are determined to share with you not only the gospel of God but also our own selves, because you have become very dear to us.

An initial conclusion is that the antithetical structure of nearly every phrase, expressed by οὐ/οὐκ, οὔτε/-ἀλλὰ ("not . . . but" or "neither . . . not," vv. 1 / 2, 3 / 4, 5, 6, 7, 8) corresponds formally to the antithetical descriptions of the ideal Cynic philosopher in Dio Chrysostom's work (*Or.* 32, 11–12). There are even verbal correspondences (*Or.* 32, 11):[272] It is not easy to find a man "who in plain terms and without guile speaks his mind with frankness, (καθαρῶς καὶ ἀδόλως παρρησιαζόμενοι), and neither for the sake of reputation (μήτε δόξης χάριν) nor for gain (μήτ' ἐπ' ἀργυρίῳ)." Rare are noble, independent people, but "toadies (κολάκων), mountebanks, and sophists" are common. He himself did not choose his role of his own free will but through divine intent, for the gods provide not only

269. The expression ἐν βάρει εἶναι in the sense of "be a burden to" refers to the possible financial demands on the community if the apostles claimed the right to be housed and fed. Cp. Wolfgang Stegemann, "Anlass und Hintergrund," 407–8: "βάρος [is] in profane Greek almost a *terminus technicus* for the weight of taxation or other financial burdens. . . . In this sense also, for example, 1 Tim 5:16 uses the verb βαρέομαι for burdening the communities." The composite ἐπι-βαρέομαι appears with the same meaning very shortly thereafter in 1 Thess 2:9.

270. Reading ἤπιοι against Nestle-Aland[27] νήπιοι; see more on this below.

271. The nearly untranslatable concept of ὁμειρόμενοι "is a colloquialism characterizing a tender and personal, loving relationship" (Koester, "Apostel und Gemeinde" [1980], 291 n. 12). It appears neither in the NT nor elsewhere in Greek except in a tomb inscription from the fourth century C.E. (*CIG* 3.4000.7). In Job 3:21 LXX we seem to have a miswriting of ἱμείρονται, "have longing for"; cp. Koester, "1 Thessalonians—Experiment," 42 n. 20; Holtz, *Der erste Brief*, 83; John Gillman, "Paul's Εισοδος" (1990), 64 n. 8. To the contrary, Baumert, "Ὁμειρόμενοι in 1 Thess 2,8" (1988), 554, writes: "The doubtful word is constructed from the basic μείρεσθαι with a prophetic ο (unaspirated), and lies semantically along the line of 'divide, separate' with a passive meaning; at the place in question it means 'be separated from someone or something (by fate),' and indeed from someone to whom one belongs." Consequently he translates 1 Thess 2:8: "So, while we are kept separated from you, we have decided to share with you not only the gospel of God but also our own life, because you have become very dear to us" (p. 561).

272. Cp. Malherbe, "'Gentle as a Nurse,'" 45ff.; idem, *The Letters to the Thessalonians*, 154, and the translation by Elliger, *Dion Chrysostomos. Sämtliche Reden* (1967), 423.

good counselors who need no urging, but also words that are appropriate and useful to the listeners (*Or.* 32, 11–12).[273]

Thus we see that six of the motifs of the reliable behavior of the preachers in 1 Thess 2:1–8 are concentrated almost word for word in Dio Chrysostom's *Oration* 32, 11–12 as a description of the true Cynic philosopher: (1) frankness (ἐπαρρησιασάμεθα / παρρησιαζόμενον); (2) no impurity, that is, integrity or purity of motive (ἀκαρθασία / καθαρῶς); (3) refusal to deceive (ἐν δόλῳ / ἀδόλως); (4) they employ no flattery and are not toadies (κολακείας / κολάκων); (5) greed and monetary gain are refused (πλεονεξία / μήτ' ἐπ' ἀργυρίῳ); (6) this is not about fame or reputation (ἐξ ἀνθρώπων δόξαν / μήτε δόξης χάριν). The motif of deceit (ἐκ πλάνης, 1 Thess 2:3) appears in the immediate context in Dio (ἀπατῶσι[ν], *Or.* 32, 9). The conviction of having been divinely commissioned, in both cases in this context, is a further parallel and one that is found frequently in Dio Chrysostom.[274]

The remaining motifs marked above in the translation are adduced by Malherbe from more distant connections in Dio's extensive and verbose speeches and other Cynic literature; this is less persuasive than the parallels in *Or.* 32, 11–12, with their concentration of concepts in agreement with 1 Thess 2:1–8. Still, it is helpful to view the relevant provenance of the *topoi*. Thus there is an ἀγών motif that describes the philosophers' involvement in risk-laden public life in terms of fighting in the arena.[275] We also find the image of the activity of the nurse (τροφός) applied to the nourishing provision of wisdom and knowledge through deities and teachers (Dio Chrysostom, *Or.* 4, 41, 74).[276] In particular, the concept of παρρησία, "frankness, openness," so important and frequently used in Hellenistic popular philosophy and rhetoric, appears in many texts, and especially Dio's, as the opposite of "deception" and "flattery,"[277] which seems to shed light on the final position of παρρησιάζομαι in 1 Thess 2:2. Occasionally we find the motif of the friendly or gentle (ἤπιοι) behavior of teachers and philosophers characterizing their way of speaking,[278] so also in 1 Thess 2:7 as a kind condescension from what would ordinarily be a more exalted expression.

273. For translation see Dio Chrysostom, *Discourses*, from the LCL edition, at http://penelope.uchicago.edu/Thayer/E/Roman/Texts/Dio_Chrysostom/Discourses/32*.html.

274. Dio Chrysostom *Or.* 33,4; 34,4; cp. Holtz, *Der erste Brief*, 71–72 and n. 267; idem, "On the Background of 1 Thessalonians 2:1–12," 74–75.

275. Cp. Malherbe, "'Gentle as a Nurse,'" 38, 45; Roberts, *Images of Paul*, 131ff.

276. Malherbe, "'Gentle as a Nurse,'" 44ff.; Roberts, *Images of Paul*, 140–44 sees a usage of the nurse-motif in 1 Thess 2:7 that should be distinguished from that in Cynic literature.

277. Holtz, *Der erste Brief*, 68ff. n. 252; cp. Malherbe, "'Gentle as a Nurse,'" 39ff., 45ff.; Roberts, *Images of Paul*, 128–31.

278. Malherbe, "'Gentle as a Nurse,'" 42–43; Haufe, *Der erste Brief*, 38: the motif "as a synonym for φιλάνθρωπος" describes "the necessary qualities of the ideal philosopher"; thus also Reinmuth, "Der erste Brief," 126.

> Here we join many interpreters in reading ἤπιοι, "gentle, kind" rather than νήπιοι, "little children,"[279] against Nestle-Aland[26, 27]. The arguments against the latter as "lectio impossibilis" have been persuasively laid out by Joël Delobel.[280] Thus, for example, the better manuscript attestation as well as the context, with its parent-child metaphor, could favor the reading νήπιοι, but the result is nonsense: "we were little children among you like a nurse who cares for her own children." On the other hand, the manuscript frequency of νήπιοι can easily be explained, when taken together with the preceding word ἐγενήθημεν, as dittography in the copying of the less common and usual ἤπιοι, a mistake that could very easily happen in ancient writing in capital letters without space between the individual words and would not have been noticed by the copyists.[281] The numbers of those favoring νήπιοι have recently increased; they see here a "mixed metaphor" with the nurse-motif in the same verse 7,[282] or else νήπιοι is understood as a vocative.[283] But the less-common ἤπιοι fits well with the Hellenistic popular philosophical usage in the surrounding context[284] and is the *lectio difficilior* inasmuch as the word is much less common in ordinary Greek than the more frequent νήπιοι; for example, it is not used in the Septuagint at all.[285]

Otherwise in Greek ἤπιος expresses a kind, patronizing attitude of superior personages toward socially or situationally subordinate people. It is the mildness that fathers may show to sons, judges to the accused, rulers to their

279. Νήπιοι is advocated by, among others, Crawford, "Tiny Problem" (1973); he contends that νήπιοι should be read as a vocative. Also Fowl, "A Metaphor in Distress" (1990); Gaventa, "Apostles as Babes and Nurses"; Bickmann, *Kommunikation gegen den Tod*, 164 n. 40, 172ff. For Fee, *The First and Second Letters to the Thessalonians*, 65–72 (with bibliography) the argument of the better manuscript attestation of νήπιοι is decisive; besides, it is the *lectio difficilior*. Gerber, *Paulus und seine 'Kinder,'* 288–91, is more or less undecided but tends to agree with Crawford.

280. Delobel, "One Letter too Many" (1995); the quotation is on p. 131. Cp. previously Metzger, *Textual Commentary* (1971), 629–30.

281. Cp. Delobel, "One Letter too Many," 131ff.

282. Thus, e.g., Bickmann, *Kommunikation gegen den Tod*, 172ff.; Weima, "But We Became Infants" (2000); Sailors, "Wedding Textual and Rhetorical Criticism" (2000); Gaventa, *Our Mother Saint Paul* (2007), 17–28; Ulrich Schmidt, "1 Thess 2,7b, c" (2009); Fee, *The First and Second Letters to the Thessalonians*, 65–72.

283. Crawford, "Tiny Problem"; Gerber, *Paulus und seine 'Kinder,'* 288–91.

284. Haufe, *Der erste Brief*, 37–38; Still, *Conflict at Thessalonica*, 138–39; Hoppe, "Metaphorik im ersten Thessalonicherbrief" (1998), 274–75; Holtz, "On the Background of 1 Thessalonians 2:1–12," 73.

285. Reinmuth, "Der erste Brief," 126. Apart from 1 Thess 2:7 it appears in the NT otherwise only in 2 Tim 2:24.

subjects.[286] So we have in 1 Thess 2:7 the use of a political-patriarchal concept designating an unusual attitude on the part of the more highly placed; they really have no need to be especially friendly. That they nevertheless do so underscores the quality of their character or indicates a special relationship that, however, the choice of words shows not to be a genuine mutuality between people equally in need.

There is something princely about the apostle's self-presentation. Besides the emphasis on patriarchal kindness, there is the striking formulation whereby the apostles would be prepared to give the community a share not only in the "gospel of God" but also in "their own selves" or "their own souls" (τὰς ἑαυτῶν ψυχάς, 2:8), because those addressed have become beloved. The expression implies that the proclamation of the gospel and the missionaries' "selves" or "lives" are two different things, so that the contours of private and public are also applicable to the apostles' existence. Their preference for this community is accordingly expressed in the degree to which they are admitted into the private lives of the teachers. This is directly connected to the often-emphasized intimacy of the mother metaphor,[287] though the contrast between the two-level participation in the gospel on the one hand and in the lives of the apostles on the other hand also lends this a hierarchical note.

The grave aura of the missionaries in Thessalonica is underscored by the striking contrast between their appearance here (1 Thess 1:5) and the contrasting "weak" presence of Paul in Corinth (1 Cor 2:1–5). The noun ἀσθένεια, "weakness,"[288] the verb ἀσθενέω, "be weak,"[289] and the adjective ἀσθενής, "weak"[290] are generally Paul's own words in the New Testament. He frequently emphasizes the weakness of his own constitution and person during his visits to his communities and beyond: 1 Cor 2:3; 4:10; 9:22; 2 Cor 10:10; 11:21, 29, 30; 12:5, 10; 13:4, 9; Gal 4:13.

286. See the examples in Liddell-Scott, 776; Holtz, *Der erste Brief*, 82; cp. Wolfgang Stegemann, "Anlass und Hintergrund," 408; Hoppe, "Metaphorik im ersten Thessalonicherbrief," 275: "In Philo it is then the ἠπιότης who removes inequality in the hierarchical social structure" (with reference to, *inter alia*, Pseudo-Phocylides, at p. 207). it is precisely this understanding of ἤπιος, as serving for the moment to level the social structure while still presuming it and thus expressing an attribute of the higher-status person, that gives the image of the apostle in 1 Thess 2:7 a patronizing tone.

287. On this see esp. Gaventa, "Apostles as Babes and Nurses"; eadem, *First and Second Thessalonians*, 26ff. and 31–34, "Maternal Imagery in the Letters of Paul"; eadem, *Our Mother Saint Paul*, 17–28; similarly also Gerber, *Paulus und seine 'Kinder,'* 270–343, "Wie Mutter und Vater" [Like Mother and Father]."

288. Romans 6:19; 8:26; 1 Cor 2:3; 15:43; 2 Cor 11:30; 12:5, 9, 10; 13:4; Gal 4:13; eight other instances in the NT.

289. Romans 4:19; 8:3; 14:1, 2, 21; 1 Cor 8:11, 12; 2 Cor 11:21, 29; 12:10; 13:3, 4, 9; Phil 2:26, 27, and twenty-one other instances in the NT.

290. Rom 5:6; 1 Cor 1:25, 27; 4:10; 8:7, 9, 10; 9:22; 11:30; 12:22; 2 Cor 10:10; Gal 4:9; also in 1 Thess 5:14, and ten other instances in the NT.

In particular the recollections of his founding visits in 1 Cor 2:3–5 and Gal 4:13, as well as 2 Cor 10:10, say exactly the opposite of what 1 Thess 1:5 states; there we find no talk of personal weakness. Where 1 Cor 2:3 says that Paul had come "in weakness (ἐν ἀσθένειᾳ), in fear (ἐν φόβῳ), and in much trembling (ἐν τρόμῳ πολλῷ)," the message of 1 Thess 1:5 is to the contrary: "our message of the gospel came to you not in word only, but also in power (ἐν δυνάμει) and in the Holy Spirit (ἐν πνεύματι ἁγίῳ) and with full conviction (ἐν πληροσοφία πολλῇ)." Here we have a decisive difference from the dialectic between Paul's personal weakness and the power of God that is expressed elsewhere; the weaker the missionaries are, the more God's might appears, as is seen in 1 Cor 2:3–5; 2 Cor 12:9–10; 2 Cor 13:3–5 with reference to the fate of Jesus. There is not a trace of such a dialectic in 1 Thessalonians.[291] The key word δύναμις, "power," refers in 1 Thess 1:5 both to the quality of the gospel and also to the personal *habitus* of the missionaries that conforms to it. The added remark that the addressees know "what kind of persons we proved to be among you for your sake" (οἷοι ἐγενήθημεν ἐν ὑμῖν δι᾽ ὑμᾶς) applies the triad of power, Holy Spirit, and full conviction from the first clause to the personal characteristics of the proclaimers as well. Corresponding to this is the emphasis on frankness and openness in 2:2 (ἐπαρρησιασάμεθα), which represents a crass contrast to the combination of "weakness, fear, and trembling" in 1 Cor 2:3.[292] There was no drama of fearful, weak apostolic appearance accompanied by physical collapse in Thessalonica as there was in Corinth and Galatia; instead, the apostolic presence is said to have been convincing, dynamic, and powerful. These apostles appear as dominant personalities with a strong positive aura, as we would say today.

The "power" and first-class quality of the missionaries is thus underscored in any number of ways, and it is marked throughout by its embeddedness in the ideal image of itinerant Cynic philosophers. Malherbe's development of Dibelius's observations, described above, has been much cited and well received because it is so persuasive and can scarcely be disputed. But no one asks why "Paul" expresses himself like Dio, why nothing else occurs to him other than to swim within the broad current of the stream of popular philosophy—and beyond that, why he uses

291. Krug, *Kraft des Schwachen* (2001), 145, finds here a significant difference from 2 Cor 12:9–10 (explained as an "early phase of Pauline theology"): in 1 Thessalonians, he says, there is "no indication that feelings of weakness are linked to the claim of authority in the sense of a logical paradox.... There is no trace in 1 Thessalonians of the idea that his suffering is the mode in which his claim to authority appears. There is also nothing to indicate any kind of mutual refraction of the two dimensions."

292. That Paul's personal appearance seems basically and repeatedly to have given the impression of neediness and aroused sympathy is hinted at in 2 Cor 10:10, where he himself addresses the discrepancy between his weak oral expression and the strong impression made by his letters—evidently a phenomenon familiar to all those involved. On this cp., e.g., Heckel, *Kraft in Schwachheit* (1993), esp. 215–300; Krug, *Kraft des Schwachen*, 258–91; Ehrensperger, *Paul and the Dynamics of Power*, 106–16; Marlene Crüsemann, "Trost, *charis*," 126–34.

the framework of the imitation model[293] to make this, as it were, the content of apostolic teaching, and so of the gospel. In this "Paul" does not distinguish himself from the milieu of the itinerant philosophers, as authors so often insist,[294] but shows himself to be part of it. The apostles behave like "good" itinerant philosophers, to the letter. Like the model sketched by Dio Chrysostom, they differ, word for word, only from their "bad" colleagues and not from the milieu itself.[295] This in turn is the measure of apostles of Christ. Therefore in 1 Thessalonians Paul, Silvanus, and Timothy give the impression of being ideal apostles because their appearance coincides with that of the ideal popular itinerant philosophers. They thus produce the prototype and equivalent of the ideal community, for through the motif of imitation the behavior of the ideal apostles is linked both structurally and in its content to the image of the community described as an ideal.[296]

3.3.4 The imitation model (1:6, 7; 2:14)

The motif of imitation, so functionally important for 1 Thessalonians 1–2, appears on the surface to correspond to the terminology of other Pauline letters. But 1 Thessalonians shows a highly noticeable grammatical deviation from it and reveals a singular use of the terminology. While in other letters Paul admonishes the Greek Christian communities in the imperative to become his followers (μιμηταί μου γίνεσθε, 1 Cor 4:16; 11:1; συμμιμηταί μου γίνεσθε, Phil 3:17), it appears that the people of Thessalonica are already far beyond that stage. The authors can state in the indicative that the community has already followed them: ὑμεῖς μιμηταὶ ἡμῶν ἐγενήθητε (1 Thess 1:6), and the communities in Judea: ὑμεῖς γὰρ μιμηταὶ ἐγενήθητε (2:14), and have in turn become a model for others: γενέσθαι ὑμᾶς τύπον (1:7). What for other communities lies in the future, since they still have to be admonished to imitate the apostles, has therefore long since occurred in the Thessalonian community, and in such an impressive manner that others can already imitate them.

This odd and utterly clear grammatical finding is only occasionally addressed by individual exegetes.[297] There is no interpretation that does justice to the

293. See further below at 3.3.4.

294. E.g., Laub, *1. und 2. Thessalonicherbriefe*, 18ff.; Holtz, *Der erste Brief*, 92ff.; Roberts, *Images of Paul*, 173ff.; Winter, "Entries and Ethics," summary on p. 55.

295. On this, cp. the commentary by Richard, *First and Second Thessalonians*, 90–99, esp. 93–94, 98–102: "Paul claims that he and his colleagues approached their mission in a manner similar to that of certain Cynics, who employed gentle persuasion and admonition to present their demanding message" (p. 100).

296. On this see Schnelle, "Der erste Thessalonicherbrief," 211–12.

297. First by F. C. Baur, *Die beiden Briefe*, 343; thereafter by, e.g., Willis P. de Boer, *The Imitation of Paul: An Exegetical Study* (1962), 100, 123ff.; Hans Dieter Betz, *Nachfolge und Nachahmung Jesu Christi im Neuen Testament* (1962/63), 143ff., 169ff.; Laub, *Eschatologische Verkündigung und Lebensgestaltung nach Paulus* (1973), 80; Marxsen, *Der erste Brief an die Thessalonicher*, 39; Schade, *Apokalyptische Christologie*, 123ff.; Broer, "'Antisemitismus,'"

significant deviation from Paul's other usage, especially with regard to verb tense. It is indeed remarkable that, especially in a letter that is supposed to be the first and oldest document addressed to a community, there is repeated reference to imitation that has already happened, while in the later letters they must be admonished in the imperative to do it, which means that imitation is still not happening.

The fairly rare words μιμέομαι, "to imitate,"[298] and μιμητής, "imitator,"[299] occur in the New Testament only in the epistolary literature, not in the gospels; there the concept of "discipleship/following" (ἀκολουθεῖν, κτλ.) is used with great frequency in reference to Jesus.[300] We may suppose that Paul's choice of words was influenced more by the idea of *mimesis* in Hellenistic philosophy, more precisely Jewish-Hellenistic diaspora Judaism as exemplified by Philo;[301] but in fact Paul does not speak in 1 Cor 4:17 and Phil 3:17 about discipleship of Jesus. Rather, he asks the

68–69; Lüdemann, *Paulus und das Judentum* (1983), 25–26; Wolfgang Stegemann, "Anlass und Hintegrund," 413; Simpson, "Problems," 52; Castelli, *Imitating Paul* (1991), 92, 94; Gaventa, *First and Second Thessalonians*, 16; Krug, *Kraft des Schwachen*, 134 n. 410; Gerber, *Paulus und seine 'Kinder,'* 312, 415–16. Merk, "Nachahmung Christi" (1989, with bibliography) mentions this finding only very indirectly, and does not offer further interpretation (cp. pp. 193ff., 197, 203–204), while the otherwise thorough article by Michaelis in *TDNT* 4 does not remark on it at all, nor does Larsson in *EWNT* (1981). Similarly deficient are, e.g., the specialized works by Stanley, "'Become Imitators of Me'" (1959) and Getty, "The Imitation of Paul in the Letters to the Thessalonians" (1990). Schulz, *Nachfolgen und Nachahmen* (1962), 186ff., 314ff. does see a "special meaning of μιμητής" in 1 Thessalonians but refers it to the "assertion of an actual community of fate" without considering the grammatical finding in detail. Reinhartz, "On the Meaning of the Pauline Exhortation" (1987) avoids dealing with the special position of 1 Thessalonians in that she regards 2:14–16 as a gloss and therefore omits it from her study (pp. 395–96 n. 14). Brant, "The place of mimēsis in Paul's thought" (1993), 285, first speaks deceptively of 1 Thess 1:6–7, naming it with the instances in 1 Corinthians and Philippians as "Paul's … exhortation to imitate him," but later also gives it its correct tense (pp. 290, 293, 295); Malherbe, *The Letters to the Thessalonians*, 114, 130–31, and P.-G. Müller, *Der erste und zweite Brief*, 108ff., like many others, fail to note this serious difference from the other Pauline letters. Occasionally the tense is completely misrepresented: "Several times in the Thessalonian correspondence (1 Thess 1:6; 2:14; 2 Thess 3:7, 9) Paul called on the readers to imitate himself or others using the verb *mimeomai* …" (Michael Martin, "'Example' and 'Imitation' in the Thessalonian Correspondence" [1999], 40).

298. Μιμέομαι only in 2 Thess 3:7, 9 (with τύπος); Heb 13:7; 3 John 11.

299. Μιμητής: 1 Cor 4:16; 11:1; Phil 3:17 (συμμιμηταί, here with τύπος; cp. 2 Thess 3:9); 1 Thess 1:6; 2:14; Eph 5:1; Heb 6:12; 1 Pet 3:13.

300. On this see esp. the works of Schulz, *Nachfolgen und Nachahmen*, and Betz, *Nachfolge und Nachahmung Jesu Christi*.

301. Thus Betz, ibid., 138ff., 186ff. For discussion of the OT and Jewish background see ibid., 84ff. (with bibliography). To the contrary, Gerber, *Paulus und seine 'Kinder,'* 416, referring to Michaelis, art. μιμέομαι, identifies the *mimesis* concept as "Greco-Hellenistic."

addressees to imitate him, the apostle. This is also the principal idea in 1 Cor 11:1, to which is appended a reference to the apostle's own imitation of Christ (καθὼς κἀγὼ Χριστοῦ). According to these passages it thus appears characteristic of Paul to reference imitation of himself, Christ, and others (Phil 3:17) in the imperative. Likewise, statements not formulated by Paul that appeal for imitation of various figures are written in the imperative or as questions: Eph 5:1 calls for imitation of God; in Heb 6:12 the addressees are asked to imitate Old Testament models in faith; 1 Pet 3:13 asks who could do harm to the addressees if they imitate what is good. But an assertion using the μίμησις concept in the indicative, stating that a community is already an imitator of the apostle and even of other communities, appears in the New Testament only in 1 Thess 1:6; 2:14. Even in 2 Thess 3:9, in contrast, the verb is used only to urge imitation: the apostles want "to give you an example to imitate" (εἰς τὸ μιμεῖσθαι ἡμᾶς).[302] Thus as regards the idea of imitation, the language of 1 Thessalonians assumes a strikingly exceptional position within the New Testament.

Correspondingly, nowhere except in 1 Thess 1:7 is it said of any community, in so many words, that they have already become an "example"/τύπος for others. Paul uses the concept of "type" or "example"/τύπος in the sense of an already existing model for figures in the primitive history and history of Israel (Adam in Rom 5:14; "our ancestors"/πατέρες in 1 Cor 10:6, 11), or for a model or "form" of teaching (Rom 6:17). In Phil 3:17 there is reference to the example of the apostles: "according to the example you have in us" (καθὼς ἔχετε τὺπον ἡμᾶς). According to 2 Thess 3:9 the apostles want to offer themselves as an example to imitate (ἵνα ἑαυτοὺς τύπον δῶμεν ὑμῖν). In the Pastorals Timothy and Titus themselves are to be examples or models (1 Tim 4:12; Titus 2:7). First Peter 5:3 uses the imperative in speaking of the elders, in an expression dependent on v. 2, as examples for the "flock" (τύποι γινόμενοι).[303] The statement about a community as an existing type for others in 1 Thess 1:7 accordingly correlates with the idea of *mimesis*, which also appears there, as a present activity of the community, but without any other such use of the type-motif in the New Testament epistolary literature,[304] and especially not the Pauline epistles.

How can we describe the structure and content of the idea of imitation in 1 Thessalonians? The special character of 1 Thessalonians lies in an approach to a systematizing of imitation that cannot be placed on the same level with Paul's appeals to imitation of himself in 1 Cor 4:16; 11:1; Phil 3:17. What is presented

302. Even in 2 Thess 3:7 μιμέομαι is formulated as an admonition, an urging; in Heb 13:7 and 3 John 11 it is again in the imperative. For the social-historical background of the motif of imitation in 2 Thessalonians see Marlene Crüsemann, "'Wer nicht arbeiten will'" (2009), esp. 215ff.

303. Hebrews 8:5 adds a quotation from Exod 25:40 regarding a "pattern" for the tabernacle.

304. It appears otherwise only in John 20:25; Acts 7:43–44; 23:25.

here is a veritable *chain of imitation*[305] that is shown as both factually existent and as characterizing the relationship of the apostles to the community and that of each community with the others: a chain of successful imitation of models. In 1:6 the example of the apostles and that of the "Kyrios" are named as the beginning of the chain. The Thessalonian community, through its already successful imitation of the apostles and Jesus, constitutes the third link in the chain; the fourth (the third level of imitation) is represented by the Greek communities in Macedonia and Achaia, which in the mean time are supposed, in turn, to have imitated the "type/example" (1:7) of the Christian community in Thessalonica. Imitation by whole communities with the aid of the concepts of *mimesis* and example, a unique idea proper to 1 Thessalonians, is then taken up again in 2:14, where the community in Thessalonica functions as the imitator of the communities in Christ in Judea (τῶν ἐκκλησιῶν τοῦ θεοῦ τῶν οὐσῶν ἐν τῇ Ἰουδαίᾳ ἐν Χριστῷ Ἰησοῦ). The Thessalonian community thus stands on the same level within the schema of imitation as the first communities in Judea. In contrast, the lower rank of the other believers in Greece is doubly obvious since Thessalonica has already been acclaimed as a direct follower of the apostles. It is to be regarded on the one hand as the first copy of an original and on the other hand as itself constituting the model for others.

Thus the demonstrated structure of imitation in 1 Thessalonians assigns a foremost place in early Christian and apostolic history to the community in Thessalonica. According to Elizabeth Castelli, the Greco-Roman idea of imitation, which Paul adopts, always expresses a hierarchical relationship in which the copy can never attain the status of the original; its subjection beneath the authority of the primal model plays a fundamental role in the mimetic relationship.[306] Therefore the special place accorded the Thessalonian community within the chain of imitation, whereby it acquires its own function as a model for others, implies the exercise of authority over the communities in Greece.[307] If we then speak, as does Edvin Larsson, of a tendency "to expand *imitatio* into a 'hierarchical' system (God—Christ—Paul—this community—other communities," this does not, as he thinks, describe the sum total of "Pauline statements"[308] on the subject; rather, such a broad tendency to hierarchizing is reflected only in the imitation model in 1 Thessalonians, which begins with asserted facts[309] and does not operate in imperatives. It remains for us to ask: to what early Christian historical period should such a system of time-proven imitation be assigned?

In its content, the idea of imitation is powerfully connected to the motif of suffering: 1 Thess 1:6 speaks of severe persecution (ἐν θλίψει πολλῇ), which is related to imitation as regards the manner in which the Thessalonian community

305. Cp. Marxsen, *Der erste Brief an die Thessalonicher*, 38–39.

306. Castelli, *Imitating Paul*, 16, 86–87; cp. Gerber, *Paulus und seine 'Kinder*,' 418–19.

307. Castelli herself does not draw this likely conclusion in her exegesis of the *mimesis* passages in 1 Thessalonians (*Imitating Paul*, 90–95).

308. Larsson, art. μιμέομαι (1981), 1054.

309. Cp. Castelli, *Imitating Paul*, 92.

has "received the word" (δεξάμενοι τὸν λόγον).[310] Likewise, their imitation of the Judean communities is defined primarily through the experience of suffering (τὰ αὐτὰ ἐπάθετε, 2:14). Beyond the sufferings and mistreatment of the apostles in Philippi that are alluded to (προπαθόντες καὶ ὑβρισθέντες), and the motif of struggle (ἐν πολλῷ ἀγῶνι), the content of their *habitus* is associated with suffering and, together with their other efforts on behalf of the community, is described as exemplary. The overall conduct of the apostles is also recommended as obligatory for the community, as it has been in the past. This emerges from the clause in 1:5 that immediately precedes the statement about imitation in 1:6: "what kind of persons [i.e., preachers] we proved to be among you for your sake" (οἷοι ἐγενήθημεν <ἐν> ὑμῖν δι᾽ ὑμᾶς). Thus the whole conduct of the missionaries is said from the beginning to have possessed a pedagogical sense, that is, one that inspires imitation; after all, a behavior that strives to imitate its model cannot be referred simply to reception of the message (1:6), for the apostles, and even Jesus, could not be models in a totally receptive sense, namely, as those evangelized, but rather as proclaimers.

The next link in the chain of imitation clips on here: the community in Thessalonica itself has already exercised mission; the word of the Lord (λόγος τοῦ κυρίου) has sounded forth (ἐξήχηται) from then throughout Macedonia and Achaia and even beyond (1:8).[311] This is also to be regarded as an allusion to a successful and active mission because the keywords in the context, taken together with the model of imitation, point in that direction.[312] Once it has been said that the word of the *Kyrios* has sounded forth from Thessalonica, it follows that the faith of that place has become known, together with their "welcome" (εἴσοδος) of the apostles' first visit and their turning away from idols (1:9–10). The keyword "welcome"/εἴσοδος links to and introduces the extended retelling of the apostles' actions in the missionary situation (2:1). Now, by means of the idea of imitation, as described above, this conduct on the part of the apostles is attributed to the

310. Δέχεσθαι τὸν λόγον appears for the reception of the proclamation only here and in 2:13; otherwise it is not found in any Pauline letter, though it does appear in the Lukan writings at Luke 8:13; Acts 8:14; 11:1; 17:11. Otherwise Paul speaks, in 2 Cor 11:4, of receiving a gospel (cp. Demke, "Theology and Literary Criticism," n. 25). However, Acts 17:11 is directly related to the mission in Thessalonica, which is here denigrated in comparison to Beroea: the Jewish community in Beroea is said to have been more friendly than that in Thessalonica and to have received the word gladly, whereas according to Acts 17:1–9 the missionaries' success in Thessalonica seems to have been very modest, at best, and to have met with severe opposition. According to Acts 17:4 there were no Gentiles among those who believed in the Messiah; even the women mentioned were already God-fearers (cp. Jervell, *Apostelgeschichte* [1998], 433ff.). First Thessalonians 1:9 states the absolute opposite; here the congregation addressed is exclusively Gentile-Christian.

311. Ἐξηχέω, "let sound," is a *hapax legomenon* in the NT.

312. Cp. Knoch, *1. und 2. Thessalonicherbrief* (1987), 29; Schade, *Apokalyptische Christologie*, 133; Bruce, *1 & 2 Thessalonians*, 16; Ware, "The Thessalonians as a Missionary Congregation" (1992).

community as well, since it was done in the first place for their sake and, as a model, it has already been imitated by the community, as the apostles have learned (1:5–6).

The content of the Gospel, the actual proclamation "of the word" appears most unusual in 1 Thessalonians 1 and 2. It is again the achievement of Christoph Demke to have worked out and clearly described this remarkable understanding of the gospel in 1 Thessalonians. The fact that, according to 1:5,

> the gospel took place not *only* with word but *also* with power etc. shows that power is not intrinsic to the gospel *as word*.... The formulation here is only possible because the word of the gospel itself is not understood as the active and powerful word of God *by virtue of what is says*, as is the case in Rom 1:16f.; 1 Cor 1:18f. (cf. 2 Cor 2:16; 4:3f.). The power of the gospel is not activated in the content it communicates, but, as the continuation shows, in the manner and mode of the appearance and conduct of the apostle, which is then elaborated in detail in 2:1–12. This is confirmed by the continuation. In the manner of the word's reception, v. 6 sees the appearance and conduct of the apostle as an exemplar. [There is no reference to the power of what the gospel itself says.] One must now ask how the content of the gospel can be conceived in this context. The answer can only be that the content of the gospel is understood primarily as the *conduct* of the apostle and the faithful. That this interpretation is valid is shown by the sequence of vv. 7 and 8. For their part, the Thessalonians become an example for the faithful in Macedonia and Achaia, for the word of the Lord (with this meaning unique for Paul!) has gone out from them, and this word is nothing else than the faith of the Thessalonians. What needs to be said (v. 8c) consists of nothing else than the manner and mode of the appearance of the apostle, and the manner and mode of the conversion, the service, and the expectation of the Thessalonians (1:9f.)[313]

Thus the real content of the gospel, according to 1 Thessalonians 1–2, is the conduct of the missionaries and those missionized.[314] As imitators, the Thessalonians preach and practice it. That is, its content is based on the example of the apostles as recited in 2:1–12, and that example consists almost entirely of the ideal description

313. Demke, "Theology and Literary Criticism," 3.1. [Translation of a missing sentence from the German original supplied in brackets.] Emphases in the original. Cp. also Marxsen on 1 Thess 1:5: "Thus at this point Paul names no other content of the gospel other than his life among the Thessalonians" (*Der erste Brief an die Thessalonicher*, 37).

314. This corresponds also to the peculiar statement in 3:6 whereby the news from Timothy about their faithfulness, that is, the conduct of those in Thessalonica, is characterized as "good news," that is, verbally, as *evangelium*: "But Timothy has just now come to us from you, and has brought us the good news (εὐαγγελισαμένου) of your faith and love." The connotation of ἀπαγγέλλω in 1:9 is similar: the word-usage also shows that this is not about the "good news" of Jesus Christ; rather, the *conduct* of community and apostle is thus the explicit "*evangelium*" in 1 Thessalonians.

of model Cynic itinerant philosophers. In this way, however, the content of Hellenistic moral philosophy as regards the proper behavior of philosophers is declared to be the content of the Christian gospel[315]—to state the convoluted recitals in 1 Thess 1:4–2:12 in the most pointed terms. Likewise, the content of 1:9–10, often seen as a model for missionary preaching in a Gentile context,[316] is presented, through the overall construction of the context, as primarily a praiseworthy trait of the community: it is told of this community how it turned to the living and true God and expects his Son, Jesus, whom God raised from the dead, to come from heaven as their rescuer from or against the wrath to come. What is here cited as the possible content of apostolic preaching is part of the faith and thus the conduct of the model community. This way of behaving, characteristic of the converted, constitutes, together with the εἴσοδος of the apostles (1:9), the object of public proclamation and communication.[317]

3.3.5 *Temporal Order and Feminist Evaluation of the Imitation Model*

The way in which 1 Thessalonians was shaped in structure and content by the model of apostolic imitation, as shown above, points to a more advanced stage of the idea, beyond the related admonitions in 1 Cor 4:16; 11:1, and Phil 3:17. The indicative grammatical form of the statements about imitation in 1 Thessalonians, and their systematic application to the conduct of all the groups of persons

315. Εὐαγγέλιον (τοῦ θεοῦ) appears otherwise only in 1 Thess 2:2, 8, 9. This strengthens the impression that the concept is very closely linked to the conduct of the apostles, because those passages do not say anything about a particular and cited content of the gospel either.

316. Thus, e.g., Bussmann, "Themen der paulinischen Missionspredigt" (1971), 38–56, and Laub, *Eschatologische Verkündigung*, 26–40, who describe the passage in terms of its origins as traditional Hellenistic-Jewish or -Jewish-Christian missionary preaching. Cp. the previous discussion of this point in Munck, "1 Thess i.9–10 and the Missionary Preaching of Paul" (1963), 100ff., and similar exegetical opinions in Holtz, "'Euer Glaube an Gott'" (1977), 459ff. Holtz himself argues to the contrary, opting for a Pauline influence: see the summary on pp. 483ff. (where he unnecessarily adopts a splitting of God into a "pre-Christian Jewish" one identical with the "Christian" and a "post-Christian Jewish" one who is no longer the true one, giving this as Paul's opinion [ibid., 483–84]. But in my opinion it cannot be denied even of 1 Thessalonians that it holds fast to the unity of the "living and true God" for all). For 1 Thess 1:9–10 as "missionary kerygma for the Gentile mission" (p. 196) and a tradition of Jewish-Christian origin employed by Paul, see also Nebe, "Die Kritik am εἰδωλα-Kult in 1 Thessalonicher 1,9–10" (2006), with overview of the individual traditional motifs (p. 197). For another solution see, e.g., Hooker, "1 Thess 1.9–10: a Nutshell—but What Kind of a Nut?" (1996), who sees here a concentration of the themes that will be developed in the letter; similarly before her Munck, "1 Thess i.9–10," and after her Konradt, *Gericht und Gemeinde* (2003), 39–73; Woyke, *Götter, 'Götzen,' Götterbilder* (2005), 104–57. For more on 1 Thess 1:9–10 see below at 5.2.4 n. 112.

317. That this theme alone is the subject of the first three chapters of 1 Thessalonians has been developed esp. by Seyoon Kim, "Paul's Entry," 519–28.

addressed, constituting a chain of imitation, shapes the talk of imitation and the *typos* of this letter as no other within the Corpus Paulinum. A hierarchy of models appears: Jesus—apostles—community in Thessalonica—other Greek communities, augmented by the other sequence: communities in Judea—Thessalonica. The hierarchical aspect is, as we have seen, inherent in the idea of *mimesis*, and emerges also from the historical representation of the sequence of models, each of which shapes the next-lower stage.

There are no other New Testament texts comparable to this structuring; the nearest equivalent is found in the letters of Ignatius of Antioch, which should be dated to the beginning of the second century C.E., between 110 and 117.[318] The motifs of *mimesis* and *typos* are applied there fairly often and present some similarities to what is found in 1 Thessalonians as well as to the usage in 1 Corinthians and Philippians, so that we may detect a certain virtuosity in Ignatius's imitation.[319] Thus on the one hand he appeals in the imperative for imitation of Jesus (μιμηταί γίνεσθε Ἰησοῦ Χριστοῦ), as he imitated his Father (*Ign. Phld.* 7.2). But he can also assert an existing imitation in the indicative: the communities at Ephesus and Tralles are addressed as "imitators of God" (μιμηταὶ ὄντες θεοῦ, *Ign. Eph.* 1.1; εὑρὼν ὑμᾶς ... μιμητὰς ὄντας θεοὺ, *Ign. Trall.* 1.2).[320] Here, then, we see imitation envisaged as practiced by the collectivity of the communities, or asserted as in 1 Thessalonians, but this is about the imitation of God or Christ, at this point without a derived hierarchizing on the congregational level.

That, however, is achieved instead by use of the concept of the *typos* for the relatively developed Ignatian church order, led by its monarchical episcopate. The letter to the community in Tralles contains a hierarchical ideal[321] that introduces a

318. Paulsen, *Die Briefe des Ignatius von Antiochia und der Brief des Polykarp von Smyrna* (1985), 4; Merz, *Die fiktive Selbstauslegung des Paulus* (2004), 188: "shortly after the turn of the century"; see ibid., 72–73. Annette Merz, in her engagement with newer theories of a late dating of the letters of Ignatius, directs attention there (p. 73 n. 9) to the extensive appendix in the microfiche version of her book (which was her 2000 Heidelberg dissertation), 349–82: "The intertextual and historical location of the Pastoral Letters." Cp. also Skarsaune, "Evidence for Jewish Believers" (2007), 505–6 n. 1.

319. Cp. Michaelis, art. μιμέομαι, 677. For imitation in Ignatius see esp. Preiss, "La mystique de L'imitation du Christ et de L'unité chez Ignace d'Antioche" (1938), and Swartley, "The Imitatio Christi in the Ignatian Letters" (1973).

320. Μιμητής / μιμέομαι also in *Ign. Eph.* 10.3; *Ign. Magn.* 10.1; *Ign. Rom.* 5.3; *Ign. Smyrn.* 12.1. Mimesis also includes the concept of ἐξεμπλάριον / (exemplar; example), "image," in *Ign. Eph.* 2.1; *Ign. Trall.* 3.1; *Ign. Smyrn.* 12.1. The "disciple" terminology should also be noted; cp. the description of the conceptual "cluster" in Swartley, "Imitatio Christi," 91–95, 98ff.

321. Cp. the description of these relations by Preiss: "la hiérarchie terrestre soit une imitation, une réplique de la hiérarchie divine [the terrestrial hierarchy is said to be an imitation, a replica of the divine hierarchy]"—and vice versa ("La mystique," 230). The same hierarchies are introduced analogously, e.g., in *Ign. Magn.* 7.1; 13.2; cp. Rathke, *Ignatius von Antiochien und die Paulusbriefe* (1967), 78ff.

partial chain of authoritarian models for the individual leadership groups: "Likewise let all respect the deacons as Jesus Christ, even as the bishop is also a type of the Father, and the presbyters as the council of God and the college of Apostles. Without these the name of 'Church' is not given" (*Ign. Trall.* 3.1).[322] Thus the bishop alone is the "type" of God, while the deacons typologically represent Jesus Christ and the presbyters the divine Council and the apostles. Hence we have two implicit chains of models: God—Christ—apostles on the one hand and bishop—deacons—presbyters on the other. There is a typological correspondence between the individual links or levels in the chain, resulting in a kind of twofold subordination on the second and third levels. This refined model of lordship is repeated with variation in the letter to the community at Smyrna, using the term "follow" / ἀκολουθεῖν: "See that you all follow (ἀκολουθεῖτε) the bishop, as Jesus Christ follows the Father, and the presbytery as if it were the Apostles. And reverence the deacons as the command of God" (*Ign. Smyrn.* 8.1).[323] Here we can again recognize a direct chain, this time God—Christ—bishop, and also the partial correspondence of the individual levels of authority, as in *Ign. Trall.* 3.1.

In contrast to 1 Thessalonians, it appears that Ignatius uses the *typos* model primarily at the intra-community level in order to establish an apparently elaborate system of leadership, something we do not find in 1 Thessalonians. Nevertheless, the two models are similar in that collective entities, whole congregations in 1 Thessalonians and groups within the community in Ignatius, take one another as models. Both show us chains of models that also include groups. If we add to this the formula "you have become imitators," which appears in both, and the fact that Ignatius, like 1 Thessalonians, associates the motif of suffering closely with that of imitation,[324] it means that the text of 1 Thessalonians has more in common with the letters of Ignatius in its conception and use of the *mimesis* motif than it has with those of Paul. It follows that the *mimesis* idea in 1 Thessalonians reveals a greater or more established level of development than in 1 Corinthians and Philippians; in terms of church history it should be placed closer to the Apostolic Fathers, especially Ignatius, than to the early Pauline communities of the first half of the first century C.E.

A feminist assessment of the idea of imitation cannot avoid regarding it as an important instrument for ongoing patriarchalization in the development of hierarchical community organization. In that *mimesis* of male teachers and apostles is advocated, as in the case of Paul, or in that Timothy and Titus are meant to function as models of faith and practice for all (1 Tim 4:12; Titus 2:7), male-defined exemplars and leaders become the community standard. The letters to Thessalonica, with their systematic use of the motif of imitation, present such a

322. *The Apostolic Fathers*, trans. Kirsopp Lake, 2 vols. LCL 24 (Cambridge: Harvard University Press; London: Heinemann, 1985), 1:215.

323. Ibid., 261.

324. Swartley, "Imitatio Christi," 100.

model in the form of a group of men working in an exemplary manner.[325] Their conduct in the community was intended from the outset to have a pedagogical function; they wanted to serve as examples to transform and inspire imitation (1 Thess 1:5; 2 Thess 3:9). Here 1 Thessalonians is oriented primarily to the example of itinerant Cynic rhetors and philosophers and their disciples, male groups familiar in the public sphere of Greco-Roman cities. Thessalonica, in particular, was a hub through which many speakers and skilled orators passed; Lucian, who spoke there in the mid-second century C.E., praised his audience, "whose taste had been refined by the offerings of a multitude of rhetoricians passing through the place."[326] Second Thessalonians, in contrast, is more interested in emphasizing the exemplary Pauline tradition of working with one's own hands; this is also present in 1 Thessalonians, but in the second letter it is the exclusive determiner of the *typos* of the apostles (2 Thess 3:6–12). As the whole community strives to imitate the way the male collective works, the model is democratized downward, but at the same time it is associated with the names of those male leaders, is androcentrically fixated in its further tradition, and suggests that only men hold the top positions in the communities.

As the use of the ideas of *mimesis* and *typos* in the letters of Ignatius shows, this ultimately led to the absolutizing and theological justification of the solitary male leader in the form of the bishop. This paved the way for the marginalization of women, especially women in leadership roles. Elisabeth Schüssler Fiorenza, in her description of the church leadership structures in Ignatius, also emphasizes the asserted "archetypal relationship between the one God in heaven and God's representative or *typos* on earth," which ultimately means that "the patriarchal order is theologically justified by Ignatius."[327] This appears to have been an ultimately unavoidable and inherent goal of the imitation terminology, which operates exclusively with male or quasi-male figures. It easily led to a further masculinization of the idea of God, since only men functioned as earthly types of God, and they alone represented links in the chain of imitation extending into heaven. The countermovement perceived by Schüssler Fiorenza in the gospel traditions as they came to be written can propose a counter-image of female leadership, at least at the congregational level. The discipleship of women is asserted against the patriarchalization of church and office. The female figures in the gospels,[328] as "paradigms of true discipleship," show us alternative models in whose names a male-defined hierarchy could and can be defied. On the lexical

325. Marlene Crüsemann, "2 Thessalonians: Hope in God's Just Judgment," trans. Everett R. Kalin, in Luise Schottroff and Marie-Theres Wacker, eds., *Feminist Biblical Interpretation* (Grand Rapids: Eerdmans, 2012), 823–29, at 822–23.

326. Touratsoglou, *Münzstätte*, 8, with reference to Lucian, *Herodotus and Aëtion*, 7–8; *The Scythian*, 9–11.

327. Elisabeth Schüssler Fiorenza, *In Memory of Her*, 293–94.

328. Cp. ibid., 315–34.

level this is reflected in the fact that the *mimesis* terminology plays no part in the gospels and is replaced by that of discipleship/ἀκολουθεῖν.

3.4 *The Results Thus Far: 1 Thessalonians as a Pseudepigraphical Writing: an Apostolic Foundation Document*

The two previous chapters have attempted to point out some serious deviations from the other, authentic letters in the Corpus Paulinum:

- The unparalleled condemnation of the Jewish people, intended as a consolation for the communities represented as "Gentile Christian";
- the character of a collective writing by three apostles;
- the offense against the "rule for messengers," so that apparently at the Pauline level, despite the "sending" vocabulary, no person is designated for the actual transport of the letter, and no active communicative situation in the present or near future is indicated. Also contrary to an active exchange of letter communications is
- the structuring of the entire text by means of a constant recollection of the prior knowledge of the addressees, together with an extended listing and narration of facts that must actually be known to the community. This is a style and marker of non-genuine letter correspondence, as used especially in epistolary novels.

The hypothesis of an artfully arranged dialogue can then be further pursued in terms of exegesis and described, in terms of its content, as an idealized recitation of the history of the apostolic founding visit, with the image of audience and sender also presented in idealized form. The community in Thessalonica outstrips all other congregations, especially those in Macedonia but also throughout Greece, in faith and practice. Likewise, the apostles are supposed to have acted on behalf of the community in an outstanding manner, according to the model of the ideal Cynic itinerant philosophers, and with great success, thus showing themselves to be powerful and courageous personalities. The real content of the gospel preached is identified, in the course of the narrative in 1 Thessalonians 1–3, with the conduct of all the actors. That content is given a structural underpinning by means of an advanced idea of imitation, significantly different from all such ideas in Paul's letters and even in the Deutero-Pauline writings and the corresponding usage throughout the New Testament.

On the whole it has therefore become clearer where 1 Thessalonians, read as a pseudepigraphical text, originated, and who could have been responsible for writing it. The question about the letter's location, that is, its probable origins, is connected with the other question of who might have been interested in preparing such a broad depiction of stylized apostolic figures and an equally stylized community, along with their common relationship. Given the multiple and clear regional and geographical emphasis on Thessalonica (1:7, 8; 4:10), that city seems to be the most likely place of origin.[329] What we have before us is a construction shaped as a reconstruction of this one, unique, ideal Macedonian community (representing, indeed, all Greek territory), together with an ideal picture of its apostles. The chosen form, an extended listing of already-known facts about the foundation and the exuberant flourishing of that community as already achieved, permits us to draw some inferences about the motivation for the writing of 1 Thessalonians: with this writing in hand, the community had documentation of its highly successful apostolic founding that placed the other Pauline communities in Greece in Thessalonica's shadow, as mere imitators. It thus appears that the model of this unique community's conduct against the background of the depiction of its foundational history is more important than any possible emphasis on the singular apostolic authority of a Paul. The community and its history occupy the foreground. Declining to write a Pauline letter in clear first-person singular form and expressing the apostle's correspondent as a collective "we" seemed more advantageous. The reasons for this will be explained below in chapter 5.

The hypothesis thus advanced, namely, that we cannot be looking at an authentic, very early Christian letter to a community but instead are dealing with a later composition with a clear purpose will now be embedded in the lively discussions introduced above regarding the authenticity of 1 Thessalonians. This is appropriate because again and again in the course of the history of research individual voices have been raised, saying something like: "the fact that the authenticity of the entire letter, or its individual parts, and the question of its literary unity [have] been raised again and again by very different scholars on very different grounds must be regarded as an indication that the investigation of this letter is faced with a series of still unsatisfactorily resolved problems."[330]

329. For the possibility that 1 Thessalonians was written in the city of Thessalonica itself, see below at 5.5.

330. Demke, "Theology and Literary Criticism," Introduction, p. 194.

Chapter 4

SKETCH OF THE HISTORY OF RESEARCH AND DISCUSSION CONCERNING THE AUTHENTICITY OF 1 THESSALONIANS

The thesis of a pseudepigraphical composition of 1 Thessalonians is nothing new. The nineteenth century saw extended controversies on that subject that have left trails into today's theories of interpolations, compilation, and development. In what follows we will offer an overview[1] of that discussion in order to indicate the methods of argumentation that have made it possible to question every single part of 1 Thessalonians. In the course of this overview of research we will give pride of place to some individual observations by various exegetes touching the questionable nature of 1 Thessalonians that still deserve our attention.

4.1 The Assertion of the Non-Genuine Character of 1 Thessalonians by Karl Schrader and Ferdinand Christian Baur

The first and most representative scholars to dispute the authenticity of 1 Thessalonians as a whole,[2] Karl Schrader and Ferdinand Christian Baur,

1. Cp. the extended recapitulations of the discussions of the authenticity of 1 Thessalonians up to a particular point in time in Lünemann, *Die Briefe an die Thessalonicher* (1850/1867), 10–15; Bornemann, *Die Thessalonicherbriefe* (1894), 300–17; Askwith, *An Introduction to the Thessalonian Epistles* (1902), 53–75; Zahn, *Introduction* (1909), 247–55; von Dobschütz, *Die Thessalonicherbriefe* (1909), 31–49; see also Rigaux, *Saint Paul: Les Épitres aux Thessaloniciens* (1956), 112ff., 120–24; Best, *A Commentary on the First and Second Epistles to the Thessalonians* (1972), 22–29; Collins, "A propos the Integrity of 1 Thess" (1979/1984), 67ff. / 114; Trilling, "Die beiden Briefe des Apostels Paulus an die Thessalonicher. Eine Forschungsübersicht" (1987), 3370–74; Jurgensen, "Saint Paul et la Parousie" (1992), 277–92; Verhoef, *De Brieven aan de Tessalonicenzen* (1998), 28ff.; Porter, "Developments in German and French Thessalonians Research" (1999), 312–15; Trevor Thompson, "As If 'Genuine.' Interpreting the Pseudepigraphic Second Thessalonians" (2009), 473ff.

2. Previously Johann Friedrich Köhler, *Versuch über die Abfassungszeit* (1830), had perceived many of the suspicious points listed by Schrader and Baur as evidence supporting his extremely late dating of 1 Thessalonians, in the period after 66 C.E. (see his pp. 71, 112–20).

developed their theses independently of one another in the first half of the nineteenth century. Schrader was probably the first, something that Baur either did not know or did not care to acknowledge. Schrader's brief commentary is unique. First of all, he consistently translates the first person plural in 1 Thessalonians 1–3 as first person singular[3] and then begins his commentary with a paraphrase, emphatically placing himself within the psyche and personality of Paul. This tenderly sensitive and romanticizing interpretation comes to an abrupt end at 1 Thess 3:13 when it encounters the question of the "saints" mentioned there, who will suddenly appear at Jesus' parousia (μετὰ πάντων τῶν ἁγίων αὐτοῦ); this raises doubts in the commentator:

> It is quite striking that here the angels are simply given the name that Paul otherwise only applies to Christians. It is Christians whom Paul everywhere calls holy, except in the letters to the Thessalonians where it is the angels who are so called, and it is likewise only here that they, together with the archangels, are again active. *It is always possible that the two letters do not come from Paul*, and that they were only written after the destruction of Jerusalem and the punishment of the Jews, which would also explain why it is said that in the end wrath has fallen upon the Jews. It would also explain the language, different from that in the other letters, somewhat prolix, not so powerful and most certainly not, as elsewhere in Paul, trenchant in every word and always hitting its mark, and, moreover, some points of view we find here and there that do not appear anywhere in Paul. These differences have been noted by others, but they have attempted to explain them by saying that these letters must be regarded as the apostle's first productions; however, that position is not compatible with the content of the letters. It is also striking that the letter contains almost nothing but reminiscences, similarly to the letters to Timothy and Titus.[4]

Now Schrader's critical mind has conquered, and the rest of the commentary concentrates primarily on other suspicious instances. Regarding 1 Thess 4:1 he first remarks on the peculiar allusion to the community's prior knowledge: "The recollection of very familiar things, with ὄιδατε, καθάπερ ὄιδατε, καθὼς οἴδ, αὐτοὶ γὰρ οἴδ, is quite frequent in these letters; there is no similar recollection in the other letters, and these seem really in place only on the presupposition that the letter is not from Paul but from a later author who seeks entrée by means of constant appeal to things known, and whose intention is to bring together what tradition has retained."[5] Schrader is offended by the description of the Thessalonian community as superior to all others and of its practices as outstanding (4:10–11): "It is said that the Thessalonians, by their actions, have given a sign of their genuine brotherly love to all Christians in Macedonia. That could not be the case in the first weeks after their conversion; likewise, the Christians in Philippi and Beroea could

3. Karl Schrader, *Der Apostel Paulus* (1836), 3–8.

4. Ibid., 23–24. Emphasis supplied.

5. Ibid., 24.

scarcely be called all the brothers throughout Macedonia. Such expressions belong to a very late period when Christianity had put down roots everywhere."[6] Then Schrader argues again for a very late composition in view of the subsequent admonition to work with "your own hands" and to "live quietly" (4:11): "The admonition that follows is nothing special, as we find it also in Eph. IV, 28 A.G. XX, 35 1. Tim. II,2; it seems to come from a later time when it was no longer regarded as a good thing for many to remain unmarried in order to spread the Gospel throughout the world, or when many evangelists who had traveled far away found they had nothing more to do there and were now burdening their homelands with their idle way of life."[7] He finds that the apocalyptic parts in 4:13–5:11 are essentially a reworking of traditional material not especially associated with Paul: "Above all, it is extremely off-putting that, in the letters to the Thessalonians, the apostle's own particular views on the death of Christ, God's grace, laws, customs, and freedom do not appear at all; everything here runs along the usual lines."[8] In summary: "It seems that the letter is merely a collection of whatever one might suppose sounded like Paul, so that people might think the letter was Pauline even if Paul himself did not write it."[9]

It seems strange that Schrader evidently did not consider it necessary to revise his commentary so as to include the first chapters within his fundamental critique. Thus the work falls into two parts; its special charm is that it documents a process of discovery *in statu nascendi*.

For Ferdinand Christian Baur, who regarded only the four principal letters (Romans, 1 and 2 Corinthians, and Galatians) as genuine, 1 Thessalonians falls victim to the complete revision of all the Pauline letters: "In the whole collection of the Pauline Epistles there is none so deficient in the character and substance of its materials as 1st Thessalonians."[10] The specific form of Baur's argumentation arises out of his *a priori* skepticism; methodologically this places the burden of proof of authenticity on the writing itself. This explains why arguments that at first seem to be judgments of taste become bases for doubt. Later, such criteria were also of significant service to those who attacked the authenticity of the letter, together with their various shades of Pauline psychology, as underpinnings for their positions. The discussion of authenticity makes it altogether clear what hampers

6. Ibid., 26–27.

7. Ibid., 27.

8. Ibid., 31.

9. Ibid., 34.

10. Baur, *Paul the Apostle of Jesus Christ* (1873; 2003), 85. The following quotations are from this edition. The two-volume second edition of the German original was published by Eduard Zeller after Baur's death, retaining the original wording. A new printing of that edition appeared in 1968 from Otto Zeller, Osnabrück. An appendix to vol. II (on pp. 314–40) contains Zeller's edition of Baur's 1855 essay ("The two Epistles to the Thessalonians"), which, in Zeller's opinion, led Baur himself to a fundamental revision of the Thessalonians chapter in the second edition of *Paulus*. On this see also Trilling, "Die beiden Briefe des Apostels Paulus an die Thessalonicher," 3370–71 n. 16.

every interpretation of Paul: such interpretation inevitably becomes an apology for the image of Paul adopted by the particular interpreter.[11] Baur proposed the following grounds for doubting the letter's authenticity; they touch the most questionable points in 1 Thessalonians:

- With the exception of 4:13–18 "no dogmatic idea whatever is brought into prominence," unlike in, e.g., Ephesians, Colossians, Philippians, and even Philemon;[12]
- The whole letter "is made up of general instructions, exhortations, wishes"; what "is accessory in the other [letters] is here the preponderating and essential element.... The very insignificance of the contents ... the want of any special aim and of any intelligible occasion of purpose" also create suspicion.[13]
- In addition, we find here a "dependence and ... want of originality" not to be seen in any genuine letter of Paul;[14]
- The main content of chaps. 1–3 is said to be nothing but a "lengthy version" of the history of the conversion of the Thessalonians, which, however, must be in the immediate past (material is drawn from Acts and other sources); it contains "nothing that the Thessalonians would not know already," as indicated by the "perpetually recurring εἰδότες" as well as μνημονεύετε and οἴδατε in 1:4; 2:1, 2, 9, 11; 3:3, 4; 4:2;[15]
- The formulations in 1:5 and 1:6 are said to be reminiscent of 1 Cor 2:4 and 11:1, as 1:8 recalls Rom 1:8; there are also numerous echoes of 1 Corinthians;[16]
- 2:14–16 "has a thoroughly un-Pauline stamp."[17] The comparison with the Jews "is certainly far-fetched"; Paul could not report on the only persecution in Judea to which the passage can refer without mentioning himself as "the person principally concerned"; a general polemic against the Jews such as appears in v. 15, adopting the pagan accusation of *odium generis humani* to describe opposition to the Gentile mission, is foreign to the apostle; the source of the missionary vocabulary is the Acts of the Apostles, and as for ἔφθασεν δὲ ἡ ὀργὴ εἰς τέλος (v. 16c), "what does this suggest to us more naturally than the

11. For the methodological problem of exegetes' identification with the apostle see the above excursus at 3.1.2.

12. Baur, *Paul the Apostle*, 85.

13. Ibid.

14. Ibid. The comparison is only with the four "principal letters" (Romans, 1 and 2 Corinthians, Galatians).

15. Ibid., 85–86.

16. Ibid., 86. In 1:4 the text reads "we know," and the list of "you know" passages is incomplete: οἴδατε appears also in 2:5 and 5:2. The repeated assertion that it is not necessary to say or write something (χρείαν ἔχειν with infinitive) in 1:8; 4:9; 5:1 should also be taken into account; see 3.3.1 above.

17. Ibid., 87.

punishment that came upon them [i.e., the Jews] in the destruction of Jerusalem?";[18]

- On the basis of the historical situation in Acts 18:5 and the information in 1 Thess 3:1–5 it is generally accepted that the letter was written only shortly after the foundational encounter, "a few months after that visit." Under that supposition it is very hard to understand why Paul is writing to the community about things that "must have been fresh in their memory." At the same time it appears that the community must have been in existence for a much longer time: "How can it be said of Christians belonging to a Church only lately founded, that they were patterns to all the believers in Macedonia and Achaia, that the fame of their reception of the word of the Lord has not only gone abroad in Macedonia and Achaia, but that their faith ἐν παντὶ τόπῳ ἐξελήλυθεν, that people of every place were speaking of them. . .?";[19]
- "Were admonitions to a quiet and industrious life, such as are given in iv. 11, 12, necessary even at that early period?"[20]
- The passage in 4:13–17, "and the view it contains of the resurrection of the dead, and the relation of the departed and the living to the second coming of Christ" would seem to follow very logically after 1 Cor 15:52, but at the same time it goes far beyond it and offers "such a concrete representation of those transcendent matters as we never find in the apostle." At the same time Baur admits that the individual suspicions against this passage are not so strong that, taken by themselves, they could sustain the thesis of inauthenticity. That, however, is the conclusion to be drawn from an examination of the letter as a whole.[21]
- There follows a rather lengthy discussion of the relationship between 1 and 2 Thessalonians, underscoring not only the dependence of the second letter on the first and their individual attitudes toward the parousia but also their relative closeness in time. Finally, the conclusions of the two letters play an important part in Baur's argumentation. He says that 2 Thess 3:17, the manuscript signal of authenticity, belongs in an era "when spurious apostolic writings were known to be in circulation, and there was cause for inquiry into the genuineness of each production."[22] The repeated talk of letters in 1 Thess 5:27; 2 Thess 2:2, 15; 3:17 lends an importance to letter-writing that was not yet present for Paul but was certainly true for later authors to whom Paul was known only from his letters.
- 1 Thessalonians 5:27, the injunction to read the letter aloud to "all the brothers and sisters," comes from a time "which regarded the apostle's letters no longer as the natural channels of spiritual intercourse, but as sacred objects to which the proper reverence was to be shown by forming as minute as possible an acquaintance with their contents, especially through public reading of them.

18. Ibid., 87–88.
19. Ibid., 88–89.
20. Ibid., 89.
21. Ibid.
22. Ibid., 95.

> In this way the custom arose of reading those Epistles, and others deemed important, before the congregation. But how could the apostle himself have thought it necessary formally to adjure the Church to which his Epistles were addressed, not to leave them unread?"[23] This could only be said by an author who was placing himself or herself in a fictitious situation. The intention, says Baur, was that this letter should also receive the honor that was later accorded, as a matter of course, to certain Pauline texts.

In his 1855 essay, "The two Epistles to the Thessalonians: Their Genuineness and their Bearing on the Doctrine of the Parousia of Christ," Baur proposes a still later dating for 1 Thessalonians. Here he gives 2 Thessalonians priority over 1 Thessalonians by asserting that the "Antichrist" in 2 Thessalonians refers to Nero.[24] Arguing against his student R. A. Lipsius, who had attacked Baur's initial questioning of 1 Thessalonians,[25] Baur introduces further instances said to arouse suspicion against 1 Thessalonians. His findings are even more solidly grounded than previously because he now suggests that passages from the Corinthian letters served as sources for the forger, in contrast with which the themes and words of 1 Thessalonians are a kind of pale imitation. Baur introduces a long list of similarities and points out the differences that can be identified, all to the disadvantage of 1 Thessalonians. In terms of method, a critical observation is in order: this kind of proceeding arbitrarily assumes that forgery is the explanation, even though thematic similarities with other Pauline letters can, of course, in large part be explained in other ways, as Baur's critique in fact does afterward. Nevertheless, Baur succeeds in producing important observations on the peculiarities of 1 Thessalonians, including the matter of imitation: namely, that in 1 Thess 1:6, contrary to 1 Cor 11:1, "this imitation is spoken of and praised as a thing the Thessalonians had already practised."[26]

Baur believes that he finds the real reason for a posterior ordering of 1 Thessalonians after 2 Thessalonians in the differing approaches to "the parousia of Christ." According to his theory the parousia passage in 1 Thess 4:13–17 does not belong to the sphere of an immediate expectation of Christ's return, which has been otherwise seen as something early, but, on the contrary, to a very advanced era with its own specific existential themes. In my opinion, Baur again presents thoughts worth considering about the supposed situation in which the theme of resurrection in the version we find in 1 Thess 4:13–17 is relevant. When, exactly, did "Christians [begin] to regard the case of those who had fallen asleep as a matter of such anxiety"?[27] This seems rather improbable in the first few months after the founding of the community, as must be supposed if the letter is to be regarded as authentic. "The question of the prospects of their fellow-Christians who had died

23. Ibid., 96.
24. Ibid., 324–36; for 2 Thessalonians see esp. 328–36.
25. See 4.2.2 below.
26. Ibid., 316.
27. Ibid., 338.

would naturally rise into prominence with the church when there came to be a considerable number who had died without seeing what all hoped that they would live to see, when a whole generation perhaps had departed from the midst of the Christian community." Only then would it have been possible, and in fact necessary, to get used to the idea "that the Christian community consisted of the dead as well as of the living.... The apostle had indicated a belief that he himself would live to see the Parousia, and an author writing after his death would still make him express that belief, iv. 15, 17. Though the apostle had been mistaken, yet what he had said was true of those who did live to see the Parousia." This "marks a wide departure from the faith of the first Christians" that they would live to see the Parousia, "when instead of that expectation we find it urged that it did not make the least difference whether one became partaker of the blessings of that event in the ranks of the dead or of the living."[28]

Overall, the defect in Baur's thesis is his sole focus on the suspicious elements in 1 Thessalonians and his corresponding suggestions about the written model or source of each. A systematic demonstration of a written source can only be secondary in methodological terms. What is lacking is a proper exegesis of the whole text that is proposed as pseudepigraphical, including a plausible explanation of the motives, occasion, and purpose of such a post-apostolic writing.[29] Later authors who adopted Baur's theses also failed to pursue these necessary questions.

4.2 *The nineteenth-century discussion of authenticity: reactions to Baur's theses*

4.2.1 *Positive reception and extension*

Immediately following and extending Baur's theses came the comprehensive critique by Bruno Bauer, who apparently did not regard any of the Pauline letters as having been transmitted in authentic form, accepting only compilations making up the principal letters; he regarded the Thessalonian letters in their entirety as later productions.[30] Starting from the description of the constantly recurring statements that the community already knows everything, Bauer defines what those statements quote or introduce as phrases and snippets taken from other Pauline letters, e.g., the hope for another meeting, personal reasons why that is impossible, lack of faith on the part of the community, etc. None of it, however, represents a very successful attempt on the part of the author: "The writer is an unskillful copyist."[31] Paul's "unnatural anxiety over a community he had just left, the fear that supposedly moved him to send Timothy to Thessalonica again right

28. Ibid., 338–39.

29. See above at 3.3.1 and 3.4, and below at 5.5.

30. Bruno Bauer, *Kritik der paulinischen Briefe* (1852; repr. 1972), 89–100.

31. Ibid., 90.

away, imitates 2 Corinthians, from which letter he also takes the consolation his emissary brings back to him."[32] In this way Bauer names a great many possible sources for individual expressions and motifs in the letter, in the same problematic fashion as had F. C. Baur. Still, he shows the questionable nature of the constant reference to the community's prior knowledge, "the long-winded recollections of things and situations that must have been present to the eyes of the Thessalonians even without these laborious reminders,"[33] though he does not explain the possible intention of the usage. The letter's eschatology is said to be derived from 1 Corinthians, and the author was also familiar with Acts.

Ludwig Noack, a follower of F. C. Baur regarding the authenticity only of the "four principal letters,"[34] likewise offers only a brief reasoning for his version of the composition of 1 Thessalonians after 70 C.E.[35] According to Noack, 1 Thess 3:1–5 is incompatible with the information in Acts 17:15, 18:5; 1 Thess 1:8 presupposes that in the meantime Paul has left both Macedonia and Achaia, while 2:14–16 belongs to the initial period of the Jewish War. Noack finds other grounds in a brief rehearsal of Baur's theses on 1 Thessalonians. On the whole, adherents of Baur's position offer no deeper probings designed to secure his view of 1 Thessalonians and underpin it with new arguments.

That task was undertaken by what was practically the only major treatment of the pseudonymity thesis, Abraham Balthasar van der Vies's monograph on the two Thessalonian letters.[36] This, and the work by Willem C. van Manen on the authenticity of 1 Thessalonians discussed below, were written as contributions to a scholarly exchange instituted by the theological faculty of the University of Leiden in 1863, on the topic "Inquiratur in authentiam utriusque PAULI ad Thessalonicenses epistolae." In response to this assignment Van der Vies produced his fundamental reflection on an appropriate method. He begins with the assumption that the names of the authors in a letter's prescript, and particularly in the Pauline letters, can prove everything or nothing; if that is the decisive criterion for the authenticity of a writing, one can refrain from any further investigation.[37] Van der Vies's main starting point, then, lies in the presumption that it is not merely the possible inauthenticity of 1 Thessalonians that needs to be proved but and especially also its authenticity, which is generally assumed uncritically at the outset. Likewise, Pauline authorship is merely a hypothesis that needs to be proved.[38] Hence his task, as he saw it, was first of all to go through the letter critically, under the assumption that

32. Ibid., 91–92.

33. Ibid., 94.

34. Ludwig Noack, *Biblische Theologie* (1853), 191ff.

35. Ibid., 225–29.

36. Abraham Balthasar van der Vies, *De beiden brieven* (1865); on 1 Thessalonians see pp. 1–127. Van der Vies regarded only Romans, 1 and 2 Corinthians, and Galatians as genuine Pauline letters.

37. Ibid., 2, 14.

38. Ibid., 14ff.

it is genuine, and then to attempt an interpretation based on the assumption that it is inauthentic. The thesis that offers the best resolution to and explanation of the problems in 1 Thessalonians should then be preferred.

Besides any number of individual observations on every verse in 1 Thessalonians, which cannot be reproduced here, Van der Vies evidently regarded the following points as constituting the principal problems in 1 Thessalonians: (1) The depiction of the Thessalonian community as a model in 1:4–10 is incomprehensible in a first letter from Paul; a lengthier period of time must have elapsed;[39] (2) there is no perceptible motive for the passage on the arrival of the apostles in 2:1–12, especially since their departure must have been in the very recent past;[40] (3) the greatest *crux* is posed by 2:13–17, climaxing with the judgment on the Jews already taking place; if we suppose the authenticity of the letter, then 2:16c is the major puzzle, something no exegete has been able to explain satisfactorily on that supposition, much less link it to a historical event.[41] With regard also, for example, to the sending of Timothy, Van der Vies points in the first place to dissonances in the time sequence,[42] so that for him the *puzzling temporal contexts* in 1 Thessalonians on the whole present the key pivotal point for critique.

Given such a definition of the problems, it is no surprise that Van der Vies's exegesis of the text as pseudepigraphical yields a better understanding of it: (1) the community that has become a model for others reflects the later conditions at the time of Pseudo-Paul, as does (2) the picture of the apostle in 2:1–12;[43] (3) finally, 2:14–16, and especially v. 16c, can readily be understood in a letter written after 70 C.E., and on the basis of the similar statements and concepts in Matt 23:31–39 should be dated to the time shortly after the destruction of the Temple.[44] Hence for Van der Vies the hypothesis that Paul is not the author, but someone later, is better founded than the reverse. In the course of his review of the letter he offers little tables for many passages, showing what the forger probably used as written sources. In conclusion Van der Vies emphasizes that previous arguments against F. C. Baur have not represented positive proof *for* the authenticity of 1 Thessalonians. Such proof could only be given through a conclusive new overall interpretation after Baur had been refuted.[45] This was subsequently undertaken especially by Wilhelm Bornemann in his commentary (described below). In spite of his quite thorough

39. Ibid., 51ff.

40. Ibid., 53–61.

41. Ibid., 61–71.

42. Ibid., 71–74.

43. Cp. Van der Vies, *De beiden brieven*, 103–6; he sees 2:1–12 as the expression of a later time because it is no longer based on Paul's quarrel with Jewish Christians, since Christianity has separated from them and from the Jews. The supposed author has sought material from other Pauline letters to construct a picture of how such a foundational visit must have looked.

44. Ibid., 106–10, 119–20.

45. Ibid., 125–26; cp. the summary of the results on pp. 96–97, 123–27.

treatment of the theme, Van der Vies was also unable to reflect on and describe the meaning and purpose of 1 Thessalonians as a pseudepigraphical writing.

The next fairly extensive treatment[46] declaring the inauthenticity of 1 Thessalonians was Rudolf Steck's study on "Das Herrenwort" in 4:15. The reason for his doubt was precisely the passage that for others was the decisive proof of the letter's authenticity: namely, Steck identified the expression λόγος κυρίου, otherwise nonexistent in New Testament tradition, with 4 Esdras 5:41–42 ("I shall liken my judgment to a circle [or: crown]; just as for those who are last there is no slowness, so for those who are first there is no haste") because here, as in 1 Thess 4:15–17, there is the same main idea: that at the parousia there is no difference in time between the living and the dead. That question occupies a major portion of 4 Esdras and is associated with frequent mention of those left behind (*qui relicti sunt*), which corresponds to the New Testament *hapax legomenon* περιλειπόμενοι in 1 Thess 4:15. This shows that 1 Thessalonians depends on 4 Esdras and was composed only at the end of the first century.[47] After this, Steck addresses Baur's thesis, which by that time was far in the past, saying that in his opinion it deserves more attention than it has heretofore received. He then recapitulates the essence of its individual components without presenting any real supporting arguments.[48] It is said to be not at all impossible that a later author should write of Paul that he hoped to arrive at the parousia while still living, "but by its nature such an expectation is no more certain than such things can be, given the uncertainty of human life, and a later author could easily speak thus in Paul's name, but only if ἡμεῖς had not yet lost its meaning for him as the ideal subject, the community experiencing the parousia."[49] The letter's purpose is said to have been to enhance Pauline eschatology with corresponding current questions involving the relationship of the living to the dead at the second coming of Christ. This would have been the case around the turn of the first to the second century, "after the first Christian generation had gone down to the grave" and there was need of a new apostolic consolation concerning the dead.[50]

Let me mention the representatives of the so-called "Dutch radical critique" only for the sake of completeness; this group, among other things, regarded all the Pauline letters as products of the second century. However, Abraham Dirk Loman and Allard Pierson, together with Samuel A. Naber, contributed very few details regarding 1 Thessalonians and nothing at all that went beyond Baur's theses; hence

46. Previously Volkmar (*Mose Prophetie* [1867], 114–15), in his dating of the *Assumption of Moses*, agreed with Baur's location for 1 Thessalonians, on the basis of 2:16, in the period after 70 C.E.; Holsten ("Zur Unächtheit des ersten Briefes" [1877]) therefore uses almost a whole page in declaring 1 Thessalonians "inauthentic" because "faith, love, and hope" in 3:1 must be dependent on Rev 2:2.

47. Steck, "Das Herrenwort 1 Thess 4,15" (1883), 512–19.

48. Ibid., 519–24.

49. Ibid., 522–23.

50. Ibid., 524.

there is no point in giving a more detailed description of their work here.[51] Likewise, according to Eduard Verhoef's account, in about 1889 Willem Christiaan van Manen rejected the authenticity of all the Pauline letters and therefore his own work (mentioned below)[52] on the authenticity of 1 Thessalonians, written twenty years previously, but without preparing a second detailed writing on the pseudepigraphical 1 Thessalonians.[53] The latest adherent of the Dutch radical critique to appear is Hermann Detering.[54]

Daniel Völter, a Swiss exegete then teaching in Amsterdam, was close in his thinking to the Dutch school. In his book on the Pauline letters he however detected remnants of Pauline texts in some of the letters and thought that "sober critique could distinguish the authentic from the inauthentic and could pick out of the canonical letters to the Corinthians, Romans, and Philippians the original versions of the letters written by the apostle Paul to those communities."[55] He devoted a short section at the end of his volume to the Thessalonian letters, which he regarded as completely spurious.[56] His argumentation, like Baur's theses, suffered from the fact that he thought he had demonstrated the inauthenticity of 1 Thessalonians merely by indicating its supposed written sources. He mentioned as arguments against it: (1) the contradiction between the short time between the apostles' departure from the city and the asserted expansive development of the community (1 Thess 3:1–2); (2) the sending of Timothy (3:1–5), said to be modeled on that of Titus in 2 Cor 7:5–7; (3) an extensive listing of passages in Pauline letters that have been copied; (4) 1 Thess 2:16 can only be understood after the destruction of Jerusalem and the author intended that Paul should point to it prophetically; (5) the community leadership addressed in 5:12–13 reveals not an early but a late period. Völter finds his principal argument (6) in the eschatological passage in 4:13–17, said to be dependent on 4 Esdr 6:23–26, from which it takes the motifs of

51. A. D. Loman, "Quaestiones paulinae" (1882–1886); Pierson and Naber, *Verisimilia* (1886). In order to enable the reception of this Dutch school in Germany, a lack of which they deplored, Willem C. Van Manen ("Zur Literaturgeschichte" [1883]) and G. A. Van den Bergh van Eysinga (*Die holländische radikale Kritik* [1912], esp. 13ff., 60ff.), who also belonged to the movement, wrote reviews of the literature in German, though these scarcely point out exegetical connections but simply present sweeping historical theses and appear to have been intended primarily to honor individual scholars. Cp. esp. Hermann Detering, *Paulusbriefe ohne Paulus?* (1992); Verhoef, "Die holländische radikale Kritik" (1996); see also Wolfgang Trilling, "Die beiden Briefe" (1987), 3372ff.; Hubert Jurgensen, "Saint Paul et la Parousie" (1992), 289ff.

52. See 4.2.2.

53. For van Manen's change of heart, documented in his work on Paul (1890–1896), see Verhoef, "Die holländische radikale Kritik," 427ff.

54. Detering, *Paulusbriefe ohne Paulus?*; idem, *Der gefälschte Paulus* (1995); cp. Verhoef, "Die holländische radikale Kritik,"427ff.; idem, *Tessalonicenzen*, 28.

55. Völter, *Paulus und seine Briefe* (1905), vi.

56. Ibid., 327–31.

trumpets, those left behind, and being raptured into the air. The letter is said not to have been written before the beginning of the second century.

The critical view of the Pauline letters offered by Robert Scott of Bombay is not simply a late dating of individual writings, and thus of 1 Thessalonians, but an original definition of pseudepigraphy that, strictly speaking, and despite the assertion of non-Pauline authorship, cannot really be called pseudepigraphy. He separates the fifteen letters and other writings attributed to Paul into four groups said to have been written independently at intervals within a "period of time" together with and after Paul by some of his friends and companions.[57] In this theory the major part of 1 and 2 Corinthians, Romans, Galatians, and Philippians were attributed to Paul himself; at least half of 1 and 2 Thessalonians, together with other texts that need not be discussed here, derived from the co-authors Silvanus and Timothy, who are named in the prescript; 1 Thessalonians 4–5 and 2 Thessalonians 1–2, because of their more doctrinaire bent, are by Silvanus, while 1 Thessalonians 1–3 and 2 Thessalonians 3 are by Timothy, who put new questions and ideas on paper, using a Pauline style.[58] This is not a variant of the secretarial hypothesis; the different parts of the letters are said to be authentic texts by these two persons. Scott's evaluation and description of Paul's personality plays a role in his reasoning; this is said not to be reflected in 1 Thessalonians. Today this argument from the "personality of the apostles" seems one of the weakest; at that time it served both sides, attackers and apologists, as support for their own views.

Scott's actual exegetical observations in support of his thesis, besides the image of Paul's personality, are as follows:[59] The two Thessalonian letters are said to differ from all the others by their vague and trivial epistolary elements. They contain no burning questions about how to live; there are neither persons named nor plans discussed; no vivid picture of a community or a time is presented to us, as is the case, for example, with 1 Corinthians. Not only are the Pauline themes of reconciliation, law, justification, divine righteousness, the Pauline teaching on sin, the cross of Christ, living and becoming like Christ, life in the Spirit, divine love and grace all absent, but so is the characteristic antithetical Pauline style. The concepts of death, resurrection, and judgment can be called commonplace in contrast with Paul's. Speaking against the common opinion that 1 Thessalonians was written early, in Corinth in the first year of the "European" mission, are the following objections, among others, all of which suggest a different dating: (1) According to 4:10 the Christian family has already spread throughout Macedonia, animated by a general knowledge of the Thessalonians' love; (2) the existence of a regular church organization is implied by the fact that a formal church (1:1) is distinguished from outsiders (4:12), and that established offices of church

57. Scott, *Pauline Epistles* (1909), 5: "But all four writers belonged to one age, and were (as we suppose) personal friends, leading members of a circle of ardent associates of whom Paul was the centre or chief."

58. Ibid., 23–24.

59. Ibid., 215–33.

leadership, teaching, and admonition have been instituted (5:12–13); (3) there is anxiety about the dead, the number of whom must have been significant.[60]

The letters call for a considered interpretation because they themselves did not claim to be the work of Paul and Paul alone; after all, they are written in the names of Paul, Silvanus, and Timothy together. Thus it may very well be that the second and third of these are the principal authors, while Paul is mentioned only by courtesy in the sense of his being the head of a school. Or one could suppose that this is a genuine common product. But since both letters reveal a complete break in the middle (1 Thess 3:11–13; 2 Thess 2:16–17), with accompanying variations in style, Scott arrives at his thesis of particular, individual composition.[61] Given the reception of Matthew 24 both in 1 Thess 5:2–6 and in 2 Thess 2:1–11, both letters to Thessalonica belong to the same period, between 70 and 80 C.E.; 1 Thess 2:15–16 also favors this thesis. Philippians and, to a lesser degree, 2 Corinthians are to be regarded as literary models for 1 Thessalonians 1–3; those letters were known to Timothy.[62]

Apart from the fact of his scarcely provable overall thesis, especially regarding the origins of the whole Corpus Paulinum and other parts of the New Testament, and despite the unorthodox and ingenuous style of his thought process, which appears not to take any scholarly discussion into account, we should emphasize that Scott's work contains some important exegetical observations on the unique character of the Thessalonian correspondence. As an outsider he received, to my knowledge, neither reception nor thorough critique. But independently of Scott, the thesis that Silvanus was the primary author of the Thessalonian correspondence, or a co-author with Paul, was adopted some time later by F. C. Burkitt and, most recently, by Hermann Binder and François Vouga.[63]

4.2.2 Arguments and Positions Countering F. C. Baur

It is a striking fact that the publications of the opponents of the inauthenticity thesis from the very beginning appear for the most part to be more extensive than those of its proponents, so that on that basis alone the scale of official doctrinal opinion had to carry more weight on the side of the opponents. First Thessalonians, rather inconspicuous before and burdened with the "accusation of insignificance and lack of plan"[64] in contrast to the other Pauline letters, acquired more marked contours and weight as a result of these works. But that new evaluation, resulting from elaborations on its content and its probable occasion, cannot simply be

60. Ibid., 218.

61. Ibid., 220–21.

62. Cp. ibid., 225–33.

63. Francis C. Burkitt, *Christian Beginnings* (1924), 128ff.; Hermann Binder, "Paulus und die Thessalonicherbriefe" (1990); François Vouga, *Geschichte des frühen Christentums* (1994), 7.

64. Lipsius, "Über Zweck und Veranlassung" (1854), 906.

equated with a "proof of authenticity." At first it was merely a matter of a more or less persuasive reply to F. C. Baur and his followers, in which the primary interest was in defending the received status quo.

The first attempt to refute F. C. Baur, redundant in the extreme, was an essay by Wilibald Grimm that must have been written in a spirit of true zeal to defend Paul. When Grimm accuses Baur of having "made the proof of the letter's inauthenticity his goal at any price"[65] we may well suppose that Grimm himself, to the contrary, advocated the authenticity of 1 Thessalonians at all costs. The price, for example, was the denial of any problems at all in the interpretation of the text, 2:14–16 in particular:[66] every statement, including the idea of a judgment having fallen upon the Jewish people (for which numerous possible contemporary identifications from before the destruction of the Temple are adduced) can be understood easily and naturally from Paul's distress in the situation of omnipresent persecutions driven by the "unbelieving Jews"; these are an adequate means for expressing Paul's personality. "A special rhetorical point, highly appropriate to Paul's ingenious artistry, lies in the idea that the Jews envy the Gentiles their blessings because of their misanthropy."[67] The fact that in this connection F. C. Baur expects that a genuine Pauline letter would speak of Paul's own persecutory actions in Palestine is said to be the attitude of a "bullying criminal inquisitor"[68] and completely unfounded. This counterargument by Grimm would be far more persuasive if he himself did not pretend to know too fully and as a matter of course which statements are compatible with Paul's various impulses—namely, all of them.

Nevertheless, this essay also contains some important objections to Baur's method, mainly his postulating of possible sources for 1 Thessalonians. It is said that one cannot take agreement with information in Acts as a criterion for forgery because known historical situations are adduced; in addition, the individual differences from the account in Acts are simply overlooked in the process. In the same way, similarities with the Corinthian letters can be regarded as parallel passages from the same author, and not necessarily as indicating a written source for a later writer.[69] Finally, Grimm finds the principal proof of the authenticity of the text, in fact the only proof, in the treatment of the question of the resurrection of the dead in 4:13–18. The relationship of those who have just died to those still living is said to have been most unsettling to the communities of the very earliest period, and it is completely out of the question that "a forger could have placed this expectation on the lips of Paul, even in the first days after his death," since it shows Paul as expecting to be among those still alive at the parousia.[70] This states what

65. Grimm, "Die Echtheit der Briefe" (1850), 771.

66. Ibid., 770–75.

67. Ibid., 771.

68. Ibid., 772.

69. Cp. ibid., 761–68.

70. Cp. ibid., 777ff.; the quotation is on p. 779. "We thus are justified in using the passage in 1 Thess 4:15 as a positive proof of the Pauline authorship of the passage" (p. 816).

would subsequently be the most consistent and weighty argument for Pauline authorship of 1 Thessalonians.

R. A. Lipsius, Baur's student, offers no real refutation of Baur's arguments, either in general or in particular, in his plea for the authenticity of 1 Thessalonians. He says it is unnecessary because, in his opinion, his narrative interpretation took care of them simply by its re-telling of the contents of the letter.[71] He constructed a historical situation for 1 Thessalonians that was quite in tune with the contemporary Tübingen School, assuming omnipresent Jewish and Judaizing opponents of Paul and narrating the content of 1 Thessalonians under that presupposition, finding in nearly every verse a reference to the Jewish opponents. Only occasionally is there an explicit argument against one of Baur's observations, for example, the frequency with which 1 Thessalonians alludes to the knowledge and pre-knowledge of the community.[72] These, says Lipsius, are precisely the explicit indications that we are dealing with an apology and self-defense on the part of the apostle before the forum of the community; he presents it because the Judaizers are disputing his office as missionary to the Gentiles. There are situational parallels similar to those seen in passages in the Corinthian letters: "But the first letter to the Thessalonians is of such great interest precisely because here the opposition to the apostle does not yet have the clear profile found in the letters to Corinth."[73]

A second argument Lipsius presents against Baur is the opinion, which he also expresses, that in 1 Thess 4:15, 17 Paul counts those still alive as among those present at Christ's parousia.[74] It seems, then, that Baur "did not seriously doubt" that "the teaching in 4:14–18, 5:1–11 is Pauline."[75] Baur responded in 1855 by attempting to propose a plausible later situation for the writing.[76] Ultimately, the closing remarks "about leaders in the community" in 1 Thess 5:12–13 constitute evidence for the "original, not yet fully developed conditions of the community's organization."[77]

This refutation in the form of an explanation based on the premises of a nineteenth-century historical school cannot measure up to the paradigmatic models of the present. It was only with the works of Adolf Hilgenfeld and, later, Wilhelm Bornemann, with its sprawling, self-identifying Pauline psychology, that proposals approaching current exegetical discussions appeared on the scene.

Gottlieb Lünemann's commentary was the first to offer a brief summary of and confrontation with Baur's theses;[78] however, he really does not take them, or the

71. Lipsius, "Über Zweck und Veranlassung," 932.

72. Cp. ibid., 905ff.

73. Ibid., 917.

74. Ibid., 924–25.

75. Ibid., 928.

76. Baur, *Die beiden Briefe an die Thessalonicher* (1855/67); cp. 4.1 above.

77. Lipsius, "Über Zweck und Veranlassung," 929.

78. Lünemann, *Die Briefe an die Thessalonicher* (1850/1867), 10–15. There are further engagements with Baur throughout the commentary, for example at 2:14ff., where he is accused of a "grammatically false exegesis" and "interpretation contrary to the context" (pp. 72–73). However, Lünemann does not agree with Lipsius either (pp. 5ff.).

problems with 1 Thessalonians they indicate, seriously. It should be emphasized that he meets the argument of redundancy and lack of Pauline teaching with an objection that remains significant today: this in itself is said to be a sign of the lively conditions in the community that are reflected in the letter. One cannot engage a pastoral letter arising out of "apostolic love and concern for the community" with dogmatic expectations. This is no "product of Christian bookishness"; rather, its real importance lies in its supposed defects: "if, however, the letter, as seems clear to every unprejudiced person, reflects the conditions and needs of the community, its content acquires its weight and particular interest *by that very fact*, something Baur did not see."[79]

Adolf Hilgenfeld's treatment, countering Baur and Van der Vies,[80] assumes that the occasion for the writing of 1 Thessalonians can be very easily explained by the historical situation that can be perceived in it. This is a respectable argument for the authenticity of the text, one that is also effective today. Paul writes in response to the very good news brought by Timothy, who had previously been sent because of Paul's concern. On the one hand the community he had recently left had already become widely recognized; on the other hand there were still deficiencies in its faith, especially questions about the return of Christ. The purpose of the letter is said to be an overall strengthening of the community's faith. Within this framework Hilgenfeld presents an affirmative, sensitive review of the content of the letter, which presents itself more or less as the *vox Pauli* and analyst of his feelings in the assumed situation. This, too, is something we find till today in many interpretations, together with the sense of having to counter all critical questions and not having any of one's own.

Here we may mention some of the arguments adduced against F. C. Baur as to content: (1) The fact that the community has already become a familiar model has nothing to do with a necessarily long history; Paul says this out of "politeness, which attributes as much good as possible to the Christian communities." It is as pointless to lay such things "in the scales" as to do so with the praise in Rom 1:8.[81]

79. Ibid., 12–13. I have explained above, in terms of the unresolved question of the letter-carrier and thus the lack of discussion of further contacts between apostle and community, that 1 Thessalonians cannot really be about "lively conditions in the community" (3.2).

80. Hilgenfeld, "Die beiden Briefe an die Thessalonicher" (1862), 225–64 (225–42 on 1 Thess). A shorter reply to Schrader and Baur had previously been published by August Neander, *Geschichte der Pflanzung und Leitung der christlichen Kirche durch die Apostel* (1862), 259ff. He accurately describes Baur's inadequate methodology: "If there are expressions similar to those in other Pauline letters, they must be borrowed from those. But if phrases appear that do not recur in other Pauline letters, that, too, is a mark of non-Pauline origins." But it is precisely the non-Pauline expressions that point to authenticity, since a "dependent imitator" would certainly have used only Pauline words (ibid., 262 n. 1).

81. Hilgenfeld, "Die beiden Briefe," 232–33; he does not mention that this praise of the Roman community, whose faith is spoken of throughout the world, is directed to a community that, unlike that in Thessalonica, has existed for a long time and is not a fresh foundation.

(2) The "outpourings about the hostile Jews" are completely understandable, as is their motivation, and they are not dependent on any prior destruction of Jerusalem. "The *odium generis humani*, here attributed to the Jews, in part corresponded to the real attitude of Jews toward all non-Jews, and in part is ... more particularly determined by the immediately preceding obstruction of the conversion of Gentiles." Difficulties with this passage would completely disappear "if we simply suppose that Paul regards the future destruction of the Jews as already happening because of the certainty that it will occur."[82] (3) The discussion in 4:13–18 is said to agree in essence with 1 Cor 15:23–24, 51. It was only in the beginnings of Christianity that the fate of those who died before the parousia could have disturbed the communities so deeply. (4) The distinction between "spirit" and "soul" in 5:23 is not un-Pauline, and the injunction to public reading in 5:27 is similar to the admonition to keep the writings holy found in the apocalypticist John. Thus one must "recognize" 1 Thessalonians as "a genuine writing by Paul that, while it cannot compare in wealth of ideas and significance with the four principal letters, is by no means unworthy of the apostle." He appears "not yet at the summit of his dialectic and his apostolic consciousness ... but in the full graciousness of his tender concern for a young Christian community in need of fatherly affirmation in its trials."[83]

Willem Christiaan van Manen's dissertation on 1 Thessalonians was intended as a confrontation with and refutation of F. C. Baur's and Karl Schrader's positions and a solid contribution to the discussion of authenticity. He accords great significance to the external attestation of the letter he documents since Justinian.[84] After this author determines that Baur's assertion that the forger of 1 Thessalonians used the Acts of the Apostles cannot be true because of the differences between the two writings,[85] he also adduces the prescript of 1 Thessalonians and its difference from all other Pauline letters as evidence for its authenticity. A forger would have adhered more closely to the other prescripts, according to Van Manen.[86] He argues similarly against the parallels Baur sees with the Corinthian letters, repeatedly holding that all the expressions in 1 Thessalonians are completely Pauline. Here, as with all the defenders of 1 Thessalonians, a great respect for the person of Paul holds the field, and beyond that, 1 Thessalonians receives an extra *a priori* bonus for authenticity. Disputing the genuine character of this letter is regarded somewhat indignantly as an affront to the great apostle.[87] This is expressed, for example, when 1 Thess 2:14–16 is justified by saying that it is no wonder that Paul criticizes the

82. Ibid., 236–37.

83. Ibid., 242.

84. Van Manen, *De echtheid van Paulus' brieven aan de Thessalonicensen* I (1865), 5–21; none of this withstands examination except for the fixed point of the Marcionite canon of the mid-second century; on this cp., e.g., Van der Vies, *De beiden brieven*, 6ff.

85. Van Manen, *De echtheid* I, 22–43.

86. Ibid., 43ff.

87. Cp., e.g., ibid., 48ff.

Jews so harshly because he has suffered so much from them.[88] The comparison to other Pauline letters in historical perspective reaches the conclusion that 1 Thessalonians contains no presentation of the apostle's person, of the Thessalonian community, or of the relationship of the two to one another that differs from those in the other letters of Paul.[89]

Likewise, the investigation of the eschatological passages, which the author understands as dogmatic, concludes to Pauline origin;[90] similar-sounding parallels in other texts serve as an argument for authenticity, including Paul's expectation, stated in 4:15, that he will experience the parousia.[91] This clearly reveals the weakness of Baur's method of pointing rather sweepingly to parallel passages as written bases for 1 Thessalonians. Each, taken by itself, can just as easily be seen as typically Pauline and therefore authentic. The apostle sometimes repeats himself, with minor variations. Thus there is no great difficulty for defenders of authenticity who only have to engage with Baur's arguments, especially since they have the weight of tradition on their side. Van Manen's solid work suffers somewhat from the fact that he later mutated into an advocate of Dutch radical criticism, which regarded no Pauline letter as authentic; in that sense he withdrew his contribution to the defense of 1 Thessalonians.[92]

Hans von Soden gratefully continued Van Manen's work in similar style, devoting himself first to a stylistic investigation of the concepts and expressions in 1 Thessalonians; his conclusion was that this is a free usage of Paul's language and concepts "hard to explain in the case of an imitator, but natural for their original creator."[93] In such an investigation no expression has a chance of arousing any radical suspicion. Even the non-Hebraic anthropology expressed in 5:23 in the formula "spirit, soul, and body" cannot change this: "this [i.e., the psychological trichotomy] is as impossible for the Paulines as for Paul, because it is unheard-of in a Hebraic context, and therefore is no more to be sought in 5:23 than in Luke 1:46–47."[94] The formula thus has no "psychological" significance; it is probably an expression of rhetorical expansiveness and therefore not contrary to Pauline usage. In the same style all the possible suspicious moments are defanged, from the form of the letter to its "dogmatic content."

Nevertheless, von Soden also investigates the question whether the actual historical references and presuppositions of the letter might not place it at a later time.[95] Here, as regards the anti-Jewish passage in 2:14–16, he notes the differences from Acts 17 and says that the latter passage speaks of local pagan persecutors and

88. Ibid., 65–66.

89. Ibid., 93.

90. Ibid., 116.

91. Ibid., 98.

92. See above at 4.2.1 and n. 53.

93. Von Soden, "Der erste Thessalonicherbrief" (1885), 263–310, at 268.

94. Ibid., 269.

95. Ibid., 287–310.

the former of Jewish. He thinks it improbable that a later author would "contrary to history, remove the reproach of hostile attitudes from the Jews and just as anti-historically load it onto the Gentiles" in 1 Thess 2:14–16. A later forger would instead "have relieved the Gentile conscience of such memories of enmity and also charged the hardened, hostile Jews with all the enmity that had previously fallen upon the Christians."[96] In other words: from the pen of a forger the passage would be much too mild and toothless toward the Jews; a later author would have written much more harshly. Since persecution of the people in Thessalonica is also lamented here, the words must be those of Paul. It is, however, remarkable that von Soden recognizes the instrumentalizing of the Jews in 2:14–16.

Others of Baur's objections are addressed one after another and a refutation of them is attempted, including the question of how a just-founded community could already be a model for others, spoken of throughout the world (1:7–8): "But had not Paul himself and his companions traveled from Thessalonica through Macedonia and Achaia? Would he have been silent about his successes in Thessalonica?"[97] There is gossip everywhere, and Thessalonica is said to have been a city prominent in international commerce, with a great deal of traffic, so that sailors or messengers by land could have spread the word about the community there. In this way every remarkable feature of the text can be declared normal. Only contrary opinions are subjected to a critical view. The text itself is regarded from the outset as nearly sacrosanct. Von Soden finds that 1 Thessalonians can be explained without difficulty only if one accepts its Pauline origins, and hereafter must be given much more attention in Pauline research. It is more enjoyable than the great letters and offers "a more benign effusion of Pauline spirit."[98]

Paul Schmidt's shorter commentary was intentionally written against those who dispute the authenticity of the letter; he grants that among them Van der Vies has the best argumentation,[99] and occasionally he conducts brief discussions against Baur. On 1:7–8 he writes that the reputation of this model community outside Greece is no exaggeration, since the subject is only the spread of news of the first conversion; besides, Paul also praises the Roman community for being known throughout the world (Rom 1:8). News traveled fast and needed only a couple of ships' voyages.[100] Regarding 2:14–16: the statements about the Jews are those of the author; 2:16 does not refer to the fall of Jerusalem but to the Edict of Claudius.[101] In his conclusion Schmidt particularly attacks Baur's statistics on the Corinthian parallels and says that suspicion based on their relationship is simply incomprehensible, since that is what certifies the identity of their authors.[102] He

96. Ibid., 288.

97. Ibid., 293.

98. Ibid., 310.

99. Paul Schmidt, *Der erste Thessalonicherbrief, neu erklärt* (1885), 4–9 (Introduction), 86–110 (time of origin and historical situation).

100. Ibid., 21–22.

101. Ibid., 34ff., 86ff.

102. Ibid., 105–6.

thus shows himself a fairly coherent critic of Baur's weak points and not so much a burning admirer of 1 Thessalonians: "Even if Baur's thorough disputing of the authenticity of our letter, understandable in terms of the whole of his New Testament achievements, had succeeded, the sacrifice of the Thessalonian letters would have been ... relatively easy to endure."[103]

The monumentally conceived, often highly redundant commentary on the Thessalonian letters by Wilhelm Bornemann, couched in florid prose, begins with the methodological decision to interpret 1 Thessalonians under the presumption of its authenticity, since the few voices disputing it seem relatively tame in contrast to the great general acknowledgment of this first letter.[104] Counterarguments are addressed in each passage, and at the end there is a fairly long review of the question of authenticity.[105] The scattered disputes with opponents of authenticity appear, as a rule, somewhat like the following one on the phenomenon of the all-too-rapid imitation of the apostle asserted in 1 Thess 1:6–7, and the model function of the Thessalonian community so soon—about six months—after its foundation:

> Certainly these are phrases that betray a high degree of Christian self-awareness on the part of the apostle, but their being accompanied by expressions of his profound modesty and self-abasement should not be forgotten or weakened today if we want to obtain a correct idea of primitive Christian faith and a genuine picture of Paul's character. Where there is a Christian life like that of the apostle such expressions are neither unjustified nor immodest; they combine truth with humility. Still, Paul would probably have had trouble using them were they not the simplest and most understandable way to say much to his communities in a few words. . . .[106]

Bornemann's unreserved readiness to identify with the supposed personal profile of the apostle is clearly evident and in this case, as in what follows, constantly leads him to declare with utter sympathy that every linguistic and stylistic peculiarity is a matter of course and appropriate to Paul's personality. In that light any critical consideration of the text appears from the outset to be psychologically uncomprehending and impertinent. Over long stretches the commentary is more of a novelistic, sentimental, sprawling re-telling of this short letter than a critical or even a sober scholarly explanation, despite its abundance of information on the letter's grammar and the history of its interpretation. Certainly Bornemann comes, on the whole, very close to current interpretations and evaluations of 1 Thessalonians when, with imagination and impressive repetitions, he presents a picture of the historically early composition, produced from a motive of strengthening a young community just previously left behind and therefore still especially in need of assurance and admonition.

103. Ibid., 6.

104. Bornemann, *Die Thessalonicherbriefe*, 19.

105. Ibid., 300–17.

106. Ibid., 60–61.

Regarding the passage in 2:14–16, Bornemann admits that for modern readers it seems in a sense to interrupt the context and may contain problematic statements. It all depends on a different attitude: "It may be asked whether, if we undertake a vivid and appropriate return to the events and situations of Paul and the Thessalonians at that time, even what today at first seems to us odd and labored may appear altogether simple, appropriate, and sensible in the context of the letter."[107] Against Baur's citation of this passage as his principal argument for a late dating of 1 Thessalonians, Bornemann brings his most important hermeneutical principle to bear: "But the suspicions raised by Baur indeed lose their force when we explain the peculiarities attached to our passage positively from the context and clarify the whole situation. But for that purpose we need not only a critical astuteness but, even more, an imagination that can accustom us to a way of thinking that is strange to us, that can make present these odd, distant circumstances, something that few commentators seem to have."[108]

From today's point of view, as well as from the equally fundamental hermeneutical interest in obtaining a social-historical appreciation of what is strange to us, these statements strike home and underscore that a sympathetic exegesis without deliberate, critically-reflective, and appropriately stated standards tends to run the risk of making us want to and be able to accept anti-Semitic expressions. Thus Bornemann sympathizes with Paul, who is supposed to have been hunted out of Thessalonica by a Jewish mob after having successfully missionized the place; for this picture he draws on Acts 17 and equates it with 1 Thess 2:14 in that by now the Gentile neighbors are also threatening the young community. In what follows, then, all kinds of anti-Jewish labels are sympathetically explained in terms of the supposedly basic hostile attitude of "the Jews," which in turn is supposed to be a result of the successful Gentile mission: "For the preaching of salvation that was given to the Gentiles destroyed the prerogative of the Jewish people with means derived from Judaism itself, and consequently aroused among them an inextinguishable rage and impregnable opposition, a stronger rejection than the gospel preaching had encountered as long as it remained on Jewish soil."[109] God's rage at this is said to be justified, and εἰς τέλος (2:16) should be translated "to the last" and interpreted in the sense of a sudden fit of anger, a historical divine judgment.[110] In light of the misdeeds of the Jews listed by Paul it is simply appropriate to close with this statement in v. 16; a reference to the destruction of Jerusalem would be superfluous.

In a review of his own exegesis Bornemann again approved his overall procedure, which, in his view, had produced a convincing proof of the genuineness of 1 Thessalonians: "Perhaps never again—unless in Paul's letter to the Philippians—did Christian love find such an immediate, genuine, tender expression in a Christian letter to a Christian community. . . . And could this language of tender love, which

107. Ibid., 102.
108. Ibid., 105.
109. Ibid., 113.
110. Ibid., 114–19.

is healthy and natural because it is true and has labor, sweat, blood, experience, deeds, and power on its side, come from the refined evaluation of a man who, under the name of Paul, pursued his own purposes, be they ever so well-intended and pious?!" etc.[111] Here we may be allowed to ask: why would it not be possible for anyone to write such an epistle if she or he were familiar with the Corinthian correspondence, as Baur supposed, as well as that with Philippi? The end of the commentary is taken up with an extended review of Baur's theses and those of his followers, each of them answered with reference to the commentary at that point.

E. H. Askwith's *Introduction* then again offered an extended discussion of Schrader and Baur, with equally long-winded presentations[112] and concluding to the authenticity of 1 Thessalonians, primarily because of its personal note. Askwith formulated a veritable objection from that very point: "No writer who was concerned with establishing a doctrine and giving to it apostolic authority would have been capable at that time of writing the first three and a half chapters of the epistle."[113] But what if the motive for a forgery were something other than introducing a new doctrine with apostolic authority? Theodor Zahn's introduction also refers to and discusses the two Thessalonian letters in a treatment of the authenticity issue[114] and expresses one of the oft-introduced objections to a forgery: "for no one ascribing a letter to Paul after his death could have made him say—more definitely here than in any passage in the unquestioned letters of Paul—that he himself expected to experience the parousia. Moreover, the particular kind of grief for the dead which appears in iv. 13 ff. is inconceivable in a Church which for decades had been losing its members by death one after the other."[115]

4.3 Conclusion, Effects, and Implicit Endurance of the Authenticity Discussion

The defenders of authenticity, on the one hand, put their stress on Paul; their interpretation may not be subjected to any critical objection because it identifies

111. Ibid., 260–61. Anyone who has tasted the next pages of Bornemann's outpouring on the fervent, moral, mature, tender, holy, Spirit-anointed, etc. character of 1 Thessalonians, as well as the imaginative paintings of the community's reaction after receipt of this letter, may well for quite a while lose her or his taste for the sympathetic exegesis of Thessalonians that is still common today.

112. Askwith, *An Introduction to the Thessalonian Epistles* (1902), 53–75.

113. Ibid., 75.

114. Zahn, *Introduction*, 247–55; cp. von Dobschütz, *Thessalonicherbriefe*, 31–32, with the tenor: "Baur's objections only show an inability to understand the rich personality of the great apostle.... There is no feeling here for the tenderness of his relationship to the community, for the power of his own devotion, with all its anxieties and hopes.... First Thessalonians in particular is as vivid, as individually concrete as one might wish a genuine letter to be" (p. 31).

115. Zahn, *Introduction*, 249.

completely with the text and its presumed author, Paul. This elevates 1 Thessalonians above the efforts of earlier exegesis, and any number of emotional signals are detected in the text, with its rather weak theology; those would be called "degrees of relationship" today. This was something new in contrast with the customary dogmatizing interpretation of Paul; it led to the emergence of 1 Thessalonians from its theretofore shadowy existence. A more precise analysis of the communicative processes was not possible at the time, so that the scenario of the possible staging of a letter situation remained obscure in contrast to the communicative sections of the other Pauline letters. Those who, less emotionally susceptible, attacked the genuine character of the letter were confronted with a question they thought unanswerable: why would anyone have made the effort to forge such an insignificant letter? Supposing that there must always and primarily be a doctrine to be promulgated, 1 Thessalonians does not appear to be a forged writing. As we have come to see, that does not mean that there could be no other reason for an apostolic letter. The probability that there was a Pauline community that did not possess an old and authentic letter of its own, as other communities did, and that had need of one because, among other reasons, it wanted written proof of its apostolic origins, was something that simply could not occur to anyone at the time. The fact that those who argued for the letter's inauthenticity began with such a weak methodology, and the fact that after the work of Van der Vies (1865) practically no other important writing, no new arguments, and no more penetrating discussion of the old ones appeared made the work of the apologists for authenticity very easy. For decades all they needed to do was to cite one another, until the discussion simply ceased. I do not believe that the apparently settled status of the question regarding the authenticity of 1 Thessalonians rests on its persuasive power and the absence of any problems; it is the result of a long-established consensus in scholarship that no one dared disturb without placing oneself immediately in the position of a complete outsider. But occasional theses positing interpolations in parts of 1 Thessalonians, as well as the idea of development in Paul, point, as in the past, to existing problems.

The omissions of those who dispute the authenticity of 1 Thessalonians since F. C. Baur have already been mentioned repeatedly. It is questionable whether similar passages from other Pauline letters can be explained, as a first step, as written models, without first laying a foundation in the exegesis of 1 Thessalonians itself. There is also a general absence of any detailed discussion of these points of comparison, which certainly could have yielded further doubtful instances: for example, 1 Thessalonians' neglect to depict the apostles in their weakness as well, to allow them to criticize the community, or to build in a small fault in the relationship between the two parts of the letter, etc. Nevertheless, we should grant the usefulness of the total rejection of the authenticity of 1 Thessalonians at that time. In the first place, a historical critique of the text was more intensively pursued thereafter. The problems in 1 Thessalonians began to be discussed, along with the methodological demand that Pauline authorship be treated as just as much a hypothesis as its contrary. In my opinion it was the strength of F. C. Baur that he instinctively detected false notes in an apparently genuine communication, and that he sensed the lack of original content and of stylistic power on the part of the author behind 1 Thessalonians. He established that it had little to say to the community in the Pauline sense, but he did not see what it really wanted to convey. Thus the principal weakness of all previous challenges to 1 Thessalonians lies in their silence about the question of its purpose, if it is a forged letter.

The dominant affirmative overall interpretation of 1 Thessalonians today cannot, however, conceal the fact that the problems remain. References to them, and critical consideration of them, have not vanished from scholarship; they have survived, in a sense, under the guise of second-level hypotheses, insofar as individual parts of 1 Thessalonians still call for challenges. Thus the repeatedly-noted questionable nature of the anti-Jewish passage in 2:14–16 has evoked corresponding theses about interpolations,[116] but such theses could also apply to 1:2–10[117] and 5:1–11.[118] The discrepancies in the stated lengths of time in 1:7–9 and the supposedly early composition, together with other questions, have led to a relatively late dating within the Pauline chronology[119] and, even recently, to hypotheses of separate parts of the letter.[120] Thus for Earl Richard the difference in time and the associated tension between chapters 1–2, 4–5, and 2:17–3:13 are a compelling reason for presupposing, in his commentary, that this is a compilation of two letters to Thessalonica: according to 2:17, Paul is writing shortly after his departure from the community, while 1:6–7 suggests a longer period of time since the foundation, because in the meantime the community has acquired a notable degree of recognition.[121]

The differences, and the distance from the other Pauline letters, are then pursued farther in terms of a theory of *development* in the theology and personality of Paul, with 4:13–18 functioning as the basic text. Recent works show that by this means the particular contours of 1 Thessalonians can be described with a special clarity not to be found elsewhere. This method reveals the fundamental content-theological uniqueness of 1 Thessalonians among the Pauline letters, as summarized by Thomas Söding: "The theology of 1 Thessalonians is clearly different from that of the principal letters." Lacking are the keywords and themes of

> God's *dikaiosyne* and justification, the Law, works, and the freedom of a Christian, reconciliation and the initiative to reconcile, the cross of Christ, preexistence

116. See 2.2.3 above.

117. Ernst Fuchs, "1. Thessalonicher 1,2–10, 14" (1963/64); he here expands his critique of 1 Thessalonians 1–3 as "post-Pauline" overall (pp. 300ff.).

118. Thus Gerhard Friedrich, "1 Thessalonicher 5,1–11" (1973).

119. Thus, e.g., Wilhelm Hadorn, *Die Abfassung der Thessalonicherbriefe* (1919), and Wilhelm Michaelis, *Einleitung* (3d ed. 1961), 221–25, 231–32; see also the listing of comparable previous positions in Bornemann, *Die Thessalonicherbriefe*, 26.

120. See above, 3.2.4 (b).

121. Richard, *Thessalonians* (1995), 11–19, 29–32: The first letter, a brief missive in the style of ancient papyrus correspondence, contains 2:13–4:2; the later one, more in the style of other Pauline community letters, is in 1:1–2:12; 4:3–5:28 (with 2:14–16 an interpolation).

> and exaltation, the rule of the evil powers of sin and death, the temptation to false self-praise and the fleshly nature of human beings. Scripture is nowhere mentioned or cited. There is no explicit ecclesiology.... But beyond that, 1 Thessalonians contains important ideas and motifs that are also found in the principal letters, but interpreted differently.... Present eschatology is much overshadowed by future. Present salvation is only loosely connected with the works of the Risen Jesus Christ. The *pneuma* is indeed seen in its close relationship to God, but not in its dynamic working unity with Jesus Christ (cp. 1 Cor 15:45; 2 Cor 3:17). Σὺν Χριστῷ (1 Thess 4:14, 17; 5:10) refers solely to future perfection and not (yet) to the present community of Christ, including suffering with him (Rom 8:17), being buried with him (Rom 6:4), and being crucified with him (Gal 2:19).

Add to this the "sharp polemic against the Jews in 2:15–16," etc.[122]

No matter with what certainty one might otherwise describe or give different weight to one or another point, this overall view of the theological profile of 1 Thessalonians is all the more convincing as soon as one compares it with the theologoumena of the other letters. Of special importance is that 1 Thessalonians deviates in its content from all the other Pauline letters: as far as the "problem of the Law" is concerned, "not only is a central group of themes in later Pauline letters [absent], but the oldest letter of Paul differs in its Christology, its eschatology, its anthropology, its soteriology, and its ethics from the letters that follow. The multiplicity of remarkable features in itself justifies us in supposing that

122. Thomas Söding, "Der erste Thessalonicherbrief" (1991), 184–85. There is a similar listing of the peculiarities of 1 Thessalonians in Edgar Krentz, "Evangelism and Spirit: 1 Thessalonians 1" (1987), 23–24: "It is a striking letter that never once cites the Old Testament.... Little use is made of Old Testament cultic or sacrificial language.... The language of the letter is strongly hellenistic in character. The great themes of the later Pauline letters are absent or, at best, minimally present. 1 Thessalonians has no developed doctrine of Christ's death (though 5:9–10 mentions it in a framework given by earlier Christian tradition).... The great Pauline antitheses, law/promise, faith/works, flesh/spirit, are totally absent, and terms such as 'justification,' 'law,' and 'grace' do not appear ('Grace' does appear as part of a formula in the letter opening 1:1).... In short, this letter shows us an unusual Paul.... Its early date and lack of controversy make 1 Thessalonians a precious document for the student of primitive Christianity." Although Krentz writes that Paul is not newly called but has already been preaching the gospel for about twenty years (p. 23), this finding points him to the idea of a further development ("later Pauline letters," 24). But the time-frame of Pauline chronology sets narrow limits for such a development: "Since all the surviving Pauline letters come from a brief period (probably 50–56) the possibility of demonstrating a theological development is in any case very limited" (Schreiber, "Früher Paulus mit Spätfolgen" [2007], 280); cp. the skeptical remarks of Reinhard von Bendemann, "'Frühpaulinisch' und/oder 'spätpaulinisch'?" (2000), 223ff., on the development hypotheses, against which speaks, among other things, the temporal frame of the Pauline chronology (p. 226).

1 Thessalonians holds a special place within the Corpus Paulinum!"[123] This leads us to the question whether a development theory can fundamentally do justice to these findings. After all, it implies a continuing process whose stages should be discoverable between the other writings as well. Here we may dare to predict that such a thing can scarcely be demonstrated for all the specifics of 1 Thessalonians; instead, we will find a consistency in most theological themes and concepts among the other letters.[124]

Accordingly, the development theory really consists of a leap from the level of 1 Thessalonians to the nearest Pauline letter, probably 1 Corinthians. Among the consequences of supposing such a qualitative leap is that an interval of two to three years seems scarcely adequate to accomplish it, and a longer period of up to ten years is occasionally suggested.[125] But if we suppose a development that in fact must involve a number of different things, and yet only one of those things, in contrast to all the others—so only 1 Thessalonians among all the Pauline letters—gives us clear reason to postulate such a process, the question arises whether that theory can give a right description of the phenomenon. An alternative would be not to suppose changes in *one* author, but to suspect a shift in authorship. Since, as Thomas Söding's remarks quoted above suggest, 1 Thessalonians betrays a kind of theological thinking that differs from all other Pauline letters, for that reason also it is not far-fetched to suppose that a mind other than Paul's could be associated with it.

123. Udo Schnelle, "Die Ethik des 1. Thessalonicherbriefes" (1990), 304–5; cp. idem, "Der erste Thessalonicherbrief und die Entstehung der paulinischen Anthropologie" (1986); Hans-Heinrich Schade, *Apokalyptische Christologie bei Paulus* (1981), 22ff.; Donfried, "1 Thessalonians, Acts and the Early Paul" (1990). It is true that Schnelle's thesis that Pauline anthropology begins with 1 Thessalonians ("Anthropologie," esp. 214ff.) rests on a problematic exegesis of 4:13–17 according to which Paul is more or less the first to invent the idea of a general resurrection of the Christian dead, for contemporary reasons; up to this point in his life (and thus in early Christianity!) there had supposedly been nothing said about it (thus also, first, Marxsen, "Auslegung von 1 Thess 4,13–18" [1969], 32; Gerd Lüdemann, *Paulus, der Heidenapostel* I [1983], 229ff., and Schade, *Apokalyptische Christologie*, 163ff.)—a historically questionable idea; see further below at 5.1.1.

124. Schnelle's study, "Wandlungen im paulinischen Denken" (1989), also again shows, ultimately, how much 1 Thessalonians deviates from all the other Pauline letters; see only pp. 88ff.

125. See, e.g., Donfried, "1 Thessalonians, Acts, and the Early Paul" (1990), 4ff., 16ff. (with Lüdemann, *Paulus, der Heidenapostel*, 207ff., 272–73), who at the same time, like Söding, "Der erste Thessalonicherbrief," esp. 198ff., is at pains to show how the themes that are absent from 1 Thessalonians, or are treated differently there, are nevertheless present, and to almost the same degree. On the other hand, Donfried notes what a great quantity of extra-Pauline tradition from the sphere of the "Hellenistic Church's missionary movement" is contained in 1 Thessalonians, so that he, too, has to ask what there is in it that is genuinely Pauline (pp. 9–10). In addition, he finds conceptual and content agreements with the image of Paul in Acts (pp. 19ff.).

Chapter 5

THE FUTURE OF THE GREEK GENTILE CHRISTIAN COMMUNITY: 1 THESSALONIANS 4:13–5:11

This chapter will revisit the social-historical question that follows on a conclusion drawn above in chap. 2, on 1 Thess 2:14–16: 1 Thessalonians seems to present a particular idea about judgment that presumes a separation in time and place between God's judgments on different groups and nations. Since, on the basis of that text, it appears that God's judgment on the Jewish people has already happened, we need to ask what fate the rest of humanity should expect in terms of this idea about judgment. We will now undertake an exegesis of 1 Thess 4:13–18 and 5:1–11 in search of an answer to that question.

But a review of previous scholarship examining the issue of the authenticity of 1 Thessalonians, described in chap. 4, has shown that at times 1 Thess 4:15 has been taken as a proof of the letter's genuine Pauline character. Therefore we should first address that particular issue and test the plausibility of non-Pauline authorship by examining the verse itself. In the process the weight of all the observations we have previously noted becomes debatable once again, as Wilhelm Hadorn so succinctly writes: "And how can anyone imagine that after Paul's death a forger could put the words of 1 Thess 4:15 on his lips: ἡμεῖς οἱ ζῶντες οἱ περιλειπόμενοι εἰς τὴν παρουσίαν? That statement alone suffices to lay low every doubt about the authenticity of the letter."[1] I hope it will be possible to show that the statements in 4:13–18 are precisely those that not only place no obstacle to an overall impression of a later dating of 1 Thessalonians but instead point toward it. Therefore this chapter will serve especially to lend support to the heuristic value of a hypothesis of pseudepigraphical authorship for 1 Thessalonians in the post-apostolic period.

1. Wilhelm Hadorn, *Die Abfassung der Thessalonicherbriefe* (1919), 14. This is the principal argument for Pauline authorship of 1 Thessalonians that is emphasized also by Wilibald Grimm, "Die Echtheit der Briefe" (1850), 779, 816; E. H. Askwith, *An Introduction to the Thessalonian Epistles* (1902), 74, and others.

5.1 "We who are alive, who are left" (4:15, 17): A flexible quantity

[4:13] But we do not want you to be uninformed, brothers and sisters, about those who have died (κοιμωμένων), so that you may not grieve as others (οἱ λοιποί) do who have no hope. [14] For since we believe that Jesus died and rose again (ἀνέστη), even so, through Jesus, God will bring (ἄξει) [together] with him those who have died (κοιμηθέντας). [15] For this we declare to you by the word of the Lord (ἐν λόγῳ κυρίου), that we who are alive, who are left (ἡμεῖς οἱ ζῶντες οἱ περιλειπόμενοι) until the coming (εἰς τὴν παρουσίαν) of the Lord, will by no means precede (οὐ μὴ φθάσομεν) those who have died.[2] [16] For the Lord himself, with a cry of command (ἐν κελεύσματι), with the archangel's call (ἐν φωνῇ ἀρχαγγέλου) and with the sound of God's trumpet (σάλπιγγι θεοῦ), will descend (καταβήσεται) from heaven, and the dead (οἱ νεκροί) in Christ[3] will rise first (ἀναστήσονται πρῶτον). [17] Then we who are alive, who are left (ἡμεῖς οἱ ζῶντες οἱ περιλειπόμενοι), will be caught up (ἁρπαγησόμεθα) in the clouds together (ἅμα) with them to meet (εἰς ἀπάντησιν) the Lord in the air (εἰς ἀέρα); and so we will be with the Lord (σὺν κυρίῳ ἐσόμεθα) forever.

[18] Therefore encourage one another with these words.

5.1.1 According to 1 Thess 4:13–17, does Paul count himself among those who will live to see Christ's parousia?

The question whether, according to 1 Thess 4:13–17, Paul counts himself among those who will be alive at Christ's parousia is almost universally answered with "yes" in current exegetical literature. This means that Paul must have been mistaken about the date of the parousia and his own expectations about his lifespan. That opinion matches current descriptions of the eschatology of 1 Thessalonians, which is said to be marked by an "immediate" or "fervent expectation"[4] according to which there is no thought of a great number of deaths before Christ's return, and so Paul and the community he addresses feel secure in

2. Here φθάνω is used in its original meaning in the sense of preceding (with acc.), something that is accordingly known to the authors; cp. the discussion of 1 Thess 2:16c in 2.5.2 above, as well as 2.1 n. 5.

3. For the question whether ἐν Χριστῷ refers to the dead or to the resurrection, see the grammatical study by David Konstan and Ilaria Ramelli, "The Syntax of ἐν Χριστῷ in 1 Thessalonians 4:16" (2007), which concludes that it cannot be answered on the basis of syntax alone, though early church exegesis more strongly supports the verbal reference (p. 593).

4. Thus, e.g., Gerd Lüdemann, "Ein Fälscher am Werk" (1996), 33, along with other formulations of this fixed *topos*: a "positively unreflective expectation" (Günter Klein, "Apokalyptische Naherwartung bei Paulus" [1973], 247); "this climate of fervent expectation" (Joseph Plevnik, "The Parousia as Implication of Christ's Resurrection" [1975], 203).

counting themselves among those who will still be alive.[5] Thus we can summarize the assumptions of exegetes regarding this pericope compactly and see it as an ongoing consensus:

> An important premise for an adequate explanation of our passage is the insight that 1 Thessalonians is marked by a burning expectation of the imminent end. So in 1 Thess 4:13ff., following tradition, Paul proposes this picture of the future: The Lord comes from heaven and, after the resurrection of the few Christians who have died in the meantime, the majority of believers who will still be alive at the parousia, including Paul himself, will be drawn up into the air together with the resurrected Christians to meet the Lord and to be forever with the Kyrios.[6]

The degree to which this kind of interpretation of 1 Thess 4:13–17 has become the overwhelmingly dominant doctrinal interpretation is indicated by a remark of Joël Delobel in which he brands a reading that deviates from it and speaks against such a definite expectation a "rather unusual theory" and a "highly hypothetical interpretation.[7] Central to the definition of the identity or number of the living is always the expression "we who are alive, who are left" (ἡμεῖς οἱ ζῶντες οἱ περιλειπόμενοι), which appears twice, in vv. 15 and 17. Can we really derive from that a definite idea of Paul's personal expectations, a particular stage in his biography, and thereby an early point in Pauline theology? Can we get from it any kind of clear picture of the assumed numbers of dead and living at Jesus' parousia, and thus a date for the text before us? Can we really take it as absolutely certain that only a few members of the community have already died? The question, then, is about the information and ideas about this theme that are present in the text itself, and not about problems associated with the generally accepted early or earliest dating as the supposed framing limitations given by the text, which consequently determine its interpretation. Finally, here we will need also to bring

5. Cp. only Lüdemann, *Paulus, der Heidenapostel* 1 (1980), 216: "The expectation in early Christianity can be specified: the first generation after Jesus' death as a rule thought that they would not have to die because the arrival of the Son of Man/reign of God would happen in the immediate future." This idea is said also to be expressed in 1 Thess 4:13–18 as Paul's own stated opinion (esp. pp. 256ff.). Thus also Traugott Holtz, *Der erste Brief an die Thessalonicher* (1986), 182–208, esp. 187, 197; Matthias Konradt, *Gericht und Gemeinde* (2003), 128–29: "In the relatively short time between Paul's founding visit to Thessalonica and Timothy's visit there had apparently been a number of deaths of Christians; these represented a serious problem for the community in terms of its expectations of the end"; or Claude Coulot, "À la venue du Seigneur" (2006), 505ff., and many others.

6. Lüdemann, *Paulus und das Judentum* (1983), 23–24.

7. Joël Delobel, "The Fate of the Dead" (1990), 342 n. 9, on Heinz Giesen, "Naherwartung des Paulus in 1 Thess 4,13–18?" (1985); see further below.

into the picture the considerations presented above about the use of the first person plural in 1 Thessalonians.[8]

First we must be clear that central to this text is the relationship between two groups at the parousia: those "who have fallen asleep" and the group that includes "we/us."[9] The question is whether "we" come before "those who have fallen asleep" and might have a temporal or other advantage (4:15). Since "we" are juxtaposed to "those who have fallen asleep," it seems probable that "we" are not among them and therefore are still alive. This simple juxtaposition is thus sufficient to express, and to admit the conclusion, that "we" will experience the parousia while still alive, as is clear, in passing, in 1 Cor 15:52 in the contrast of "the dead" and a group called "we," and that "we" (for the present) are not among the dead but belong to the living. Thus, besides the "we" in 1 Thess 4:15, 17, who are not to be reckoned among those "fallen asleep," there would have been nothing else necessary to convey the implicit statement that the author or authors of the text define themselves, together with their addressees, as living. And yet there is a striking double addition by means of two participles: "we who are alive, who are left." Accordingly it seems that "we" find it necessary to be particularly and emphatically designated as "living," and beyond that to be fully defined by means of the rather rare concept of those "who are left"/περιλειπόμενοι.[10] This finding in itself would allow us to conclude that the association of "we" with the living does not appear to be a matter of course. And yet the *syntagma* is repeated again, word for word, in v. 17,[11] this time to say that the dead will achieve a temporal and qualitative equality with the living, that they will have overtaken them, so to speak: "We who are alive, who are left" will be taken up at the same time as they, into the air, as it were. Verse 17 then closes with the result, that "we" will "be with the Lord forever." Since at this point that status is supposed to be the case for all, living and dead, we may conclude that through it the previous juxtaposition of the two groups has been dissolved, and that in the end "we" applies to both the living and the dead. Ultimately, "we" are both the previously "who are left" and the formerly "fallen asleep." Hence the usage in v. 17b apparently abrogates the previous use of "we" and demonstrates that in this section "we" are not limited to the living. The striking double expression "we who are alive, who are left" / ἡμεῖς οἱ ζῶντες οἱ περιλειπόμενοι has a particular function of its own, to the same purpose, as will now be explained.

The interpretation now almost universally accepted sees the two participles as both referring to a group contrasted with the dead, in apposition to "we," with the

8. See 3.1 above.

9. Cp. Stefan Schreiber, "Eine neue Jenseitshoffnung in Thessaloniki" (2007), 331, on the "juxtaposition of two groups."

10. The verb περιλείπομαι / περιλείπεσθαι appears in the NT only in 1 Thess 4:15, 17; in the Greek middle and passive forms it means "be left over" or "survive"; cp. Liddell/Scott 1378 and below at 5.1.2b.

11. Only a few mss. omit περιλειπόμενοι at this point.

sense of "it is we who are alive, who are left."[12] This understanding automatically means, as far as Paul is concerned, that "he belongs to the living and expects that he will continue to belong to the living."[13] "In exceptional cases, at most, will death still claim anyone before the parousia."[14] Because of the general agreement on this understanding there is no longer much discussion of the construction as such,[15] although occasionally someone expresses wonderment at the expression, which seems so superfluous and apparently without function: "'We' are already well enough defined by 'the living.' In the present context οἱ περιλειπόμενοι has no proper function and even appears inappropriate."[16] But can it be that such a double definition of the "living," which, moreover, reappears in the same words in v. 17,

12. Béda Rigaux, *Thessaloniciens* (1956), 539: "nous, qui sommes vivants, qui sommes laissés" [we, who are alive, who are left]; cp. Peter Siber, *Mit Christus leben* (1971), 50, who regards this wording as "unambiguous," and many others.

13. Ernst von Dobschütz, *Die Thessalonicherbriefe* (1909), 192.

14. Holtz, *Der erste Brief*, 195. Klein, "Apokalyptische Naherwartung," 245: for Paul the parousia is "apparently not so imminent that experiencing it represents a normal event for him."

15. For one of the few commentaries to do so see, for example, Ernest Best, *A Commentary on the First and Second Epistles to the Thessalonians* (1972), 194ff.

16. Holtz, *Der erste Brief*, 196. As a rule περιλειπόμενοι is seen as part of the tradition that is supposedly quoted here as a "word of the Lord" (ἐν λόγῳ κυρίου) in 4:15. The principal questions still remain: the supposed scope, the origins of the tradition, and the author's way of dealing with it. On this see the discussions in the commentaries *ad loc* and in Poul Nepper-Christensen, "Das verborgene Herrenwort" (1965); Paul Hoffmann, *Die Toten in Christus* (1966), 218ff.; Ulrich Luz, *Das Geschichtsverständnis des Paulus* (1968), 326–31; Siber, *Mit Christus leben*, 35–59; Wolfgang Harnisch, *Eschatologische Existenz* (1972), 39–51; Plevnik, "The Parousia as Implication," 229ff.; idem, *Paul and the Parousia*, 78–98; Jürgen Becker, *Auferstehung der Toten im Urchristentum* (1976), 51ff.; Gerhard Löhr, "1 Thess 4,15–17: Das Herrenwort" (1980); Lüdemann, *Paulus, der Heidenapostel* 1, 242–63; Dietfried Gewalt, "1 Thess 4,15–17" (1982); John P. Mason, *The Resurrection According to Paul* (1993), 90–100; David Luckensmeyer, *The Eschatology of First Thessalonians* (2009), 225–73, and many others, as well as the reviews of the literature and pointers by Hubert Jurgensen, "Saint Paul et la Parousie" (1992), 483–98; Otto Merk, "1. Thessalonicher 4,13–18," 227ff.; Sebastian Schneider, *Vollendung des Auferstehens* (2000), 231ff.; Konradt, *Gericht und Gemeinde*, 129–30 n. 591; Michael Pahl, *Discerning the 'Word of the Lord'* (2009), 6–34, and the tabular overview by Luckensmeyer, *Eschatology*, 192–211. There is speculation on possible sources: a saying of the earthly Jesus (e.g., Holtz, *Der erste Brief*, 183ff.; Colin R. Nicholl, *From Hope to Despair in Thessalonica* [2004], 38–41; Schreiber, "Eine neue Jenseitshoffnung," 328–29; Pieter H. van Houwelingen, "The Great Reunion" [2007], 316–17 thinks of Jesus' eschatological discourse in Mark 13:16–17 *par.*, as before him Seyoon Kim, "The Jesus Tradition in 1 Thess 4.13–5.11" [2002], 233–37), even though there is no literal corresponding matter in the gospels. Or perhaps it is a word of the Risen One in the form of a personal prophetic revelation to Paul (thus, e.g., von Dobschütz, *Die Thessalonicherbriefe*, 194; Helmut Merklein, "Der Theologe als Prophet" [1992]; Plevnik, *Paul and the Parousia* (1997), 90–98; Schneider, *Vollendung des Auferstehens*,

really has no function? We should instead suppose at the outset that such a striking phrase, and its remarkable repetition, are indispensable and of special significance for the context as well as for the whole statement.

There is, however, a fairly broad basis in older, and indeed the oldest interpretations for an alternative reading; the expression was discussed repeatedly and in detail in those sources. Hubert Jurgensen's report of research on 1 Thess 4:13–5:11 is informative regarding this branch of exegetical discussion. His comprehensive dissertation is extremely helpful because it devotes careful attention especially to the interpretation of the περιλειπόμενοι in both "traditional Protestant" and "traditional Catholic" exegesis.[17] The key point in all these interpretations was assigning a function to the participles that restricted the "we." The result is an interpretation contrary to the assumption of Paul's certainty of living until the parousia of Jesus. For example, Johann Friedrich von Flatt wrote that "there is no conclusive reason to suppose that with these words Paul wanted to indicate that he himself and the Christians living at that time will survive until the Return."[18] He assigns more of a future sense to the participles, thus limiting the number of those included in the "we," whereas εἰς τὴν παρουσίαν is understood to mean "*until* the parousia." "The ἡμεῖς οἱ ζῶντες can now be translated: we (Christians), i.e., some of us or of those belonging to us, some of the Christians who (namely, those who) are alive (who are not among the dead at the time of Christ's return), who remain (or will remain)."[19] Adrianus van Veldhuizen's

233–40), or common early Christian prophecy (thus, e.g., Luz, *Geschichtsverständnis*, 327–28), or an origin in Jewish-Christian apocalyptic (thus, e.g., Günter Haufe, *Der erste Brief des Paulus an die Thessalonicher* [1999], 78–79). However, it is highly probable that nothing is being quoted here, but that what we have is a general reference to the Christian message, or the Gospel, since 1 Thess 1:8 also mentions a λόγος τοῦ κυρίου in that sense. Arguing in favor of this kind of solution are, e.g., Giesen, "Naherwartung des Paulus," 132ff.; Delobel, "The Fate of the Dead," 341–42 and n. 7; Coulot, "À la venue du Seigneur," 505, who sees a primitive Christian creed being introduced here; also, most recently, Pahl, *Discerning the 'Word of the Lord'*, who defines the λόγος as a message "about" Jesus, that is, about the Lord's death and resurrection, and correspondingly translates the beginning of 4:15 "Therefore we say this to you in accordance with the message about the Lord" (p. 154; see also the context, pp. 156–71).

17. Hubert Jurgensen, "Saint Paul et la Parousie," *passim*; for this question see esp. pp. 17–179. Cp. also Rigaux, *Thessaloniciens*, 540–41. There are other reviews of the literature on 1 Thess 4:13–18 and/or 5:1–11, etc., in ibid., xxiii–xxix; Collins, *Studies on the First Letter to the Thessalonians* (1984), 385–401; Merk, "1. Thessalonicher 4,13–18"; Schneider, *Vollendung des Auferstehens*, 275–79.

18. Johann Friedrich von Flatt, *Vorlesungen über die Briefe Pauli an die Philipper, Kolosser, Thessalonicher und an Philemon* (1829), 353–59, at 353.

19. Ibid., 357. Cp. Frederic Godet, *Einleitung in das Neue Testament* (1894), 87: Paul reckons himself only in a limited way to the living, "i.e., if we are left," because he does not believe that not a single Christian will die before the parousia. The meaning would thus be "*those among us Christians* who will be alive at that moment."

study, on the grammatical and lexicographical level, comes to the conclusion that Paul is by no means assuring his readers that they will experience the parousia; quite the contrary. His review of instances in the older Greek classical literature shows that περιλειπόμενοι always means "be left" in the sense of a remnant, more or less a group or quantity that is melded together. Its occasional use in the Septuagint also confirms this with regard to remnants and remnant situations (2 Chr 34:31; 2 Macc 1:31; 8:14, etc.).[20] Van Veldhuizen concludes from this that the addition does not strengthen the first participle, οἱ ζῶντες, but restricts and attenuates it: those who are left are "we," at least for the moment, as long as "we" can be counted in that category. That does *not* mean that all those who are left behind will be alive at the parousia. This is underscored by the use not of the aorist (περιλείφθεντες), analogous to "those who have fallen asleep" (κοιμηθέντες) but of the present tense, which instead means: now we are still alive, but it "would have been too glorious if all believers could have come together, living, to the parousia, yet the ground of life is crumbling under their feet . . . in short, περιλείπεσθαι points not to the open heaven but to the open grave."[21]

This line of interpretation began already in the time of the church fathers and stems from an interest in saving Paul from a major eschatological error. Thus John Chrysostom asserts that Paul certainly was not among the "we," which instead refers to believers in general.[22] Traditional Catholic exegesis in particular rests on this; that exegesis was intended to be preserved against the "erroneous path" of advancing historical criticism by the Papal Biblical Commission in a decree issued in 1915. The scholarly sensation of incipient historical critique then derived from an attempt to charge Paul with an error in this passage regarding his expectations for Christ's imminent return and his own life, an idea first introduced by Hugo Grotius that, thanks to nineteenth-century historical-critical exegesis, has become the dominant interpretation up to the present time.[23] The decree of the Papal Biblical Commission under Pope Benedict XV, *De parousia seu secundo adventu*

20. Adrianus van Veldhuizen, "I Thessal. 4:15, 17" (1911), 103ff. Louis Billot, *La Parousie* (1920), 253–62, also emphasizes the meaning "remnant" or remnant situation for 1 Thess 4:15–17; see esp. his pp. 261–62.

21. Van Veldhuizen, "I. Thessal. 4:15–17," 105–6 (in Dutch; translation M.C./L.M.M.).

22. Johannes Chrystomos, *Hom. in 1 Thess* 7.2, on 4:15 (PG 62, 436). Cp. von Dobschütz, *Die Thessalonicherbriefe*, 200, and Rigaux, *Thessaloniciens*, 540; also Gerhard Friedrich, "1 Thess 5,1–11" (1973), 310–11 for other patristic and later interpreters. Von Dobschütz mentions at that point the 18th-century *terminus technicus* for a restrictive-concessive interpretation of the p. c.: the "*ennallage personae* or *anakoinosis*, which says something about a collective that is true of only one part." On this see also Urban Holzmeister, "Zum Dekret der Bibelkommission über die Parusieerwartung in den paulinischen Briefen" (1916), 175–76; Schneider, *Vollendung des Auferstehens*, 271–72, 275–79.

23. Hugo Grotius, *Annotationes in Novum Testamentum* (1757), 706–10; cp. Jurgensen, "Saint Paul et la Parousie," 182, and 180–276 *passim*.

Domini Nostri Iesu Christi in epistolis sancti Pauli, devotes its third paragraph explicitly to 1 Thess 4:15–17 and dictates as the required interpretation that the solid foundation given the interpretation of this passage by the Fathers (especially John Chrysostom) cannot be questioned. It gives no indication of a "parousia so proximate that the Apostle numbers himself and his readers among those faithful who are to go to meet Christ as survivors."[24] Certainly councils and biblical commissions can err, but they can also be exegetically correct, as seems to be the case here. This is said without any intent to make light of the authoritarian pressure intended to be laid on obedient interpreters. In the wake of the decree some works appeared within the sphere of Roman Catholic exegesis that built on the foundation of the church fathers referred to. In particular Urban Holzmeister took it upon himself to construct a broader foundation for the papal decision regarding 1 Thess 4:15–17.[25] First he offered a general discussion of the difference between hope and expectation in Paul, and from that he proposed that it would be better to speak of the hope of a parousia that would admit a number of possibilities for how it would occur. In terms of grammar, Holzmeister pointed to other New Testament examples in which participles were also used in a restrictive sense, and sometimes with definite articles (Luke 9:25 *parr.*; Heb 2:3; 4:3; 12:25; Rev 2:7 *parr.*, etc.).[26] The grammatical possibility of an idea of a conditional survival becomes a probability when one includes 1 Thess 5:10, according to which the apostle explicitly leaves both living until and dying before the parousia open for himself and his readers. Hence he could not assert the contrary in 4:15–17.[27] Subsequently any number of Roman Catholic exegetes followed this line in justifying the decree; they included Konstantin Rösch, Antoninus Romeo, and Alois Wimmer,[28] and independently of that background there were occasional individual opinions like that of Arthur L. Moore,[29] who also, referring to patristic interpretation, said that Paul did not expect to experience the parousia but only supposed it might happen to some Christians. He also adduces 1 Thess 5:10 as an argument from which we may

24. Denzinger and Hünermann, et al., *Compendium of Creeds* (1978), 2179–81; on 1 Thess 4:15–17 at 2181. Cp. Siber, *Mit Christus leben*, 50–51 n. 33; Jurgensen, "Saint Paul et la Parousie," 126–27; for continuing influence on Roman Catholic exegesis see ibid., 128–79.

25. Holzmeister, "Zum Dekret," 174–82.

26. Ibid., 177ff.

27. Ibid., 180.

28. Konstantin Rösch, "'Wir Lebenden, wir Übrigbleibenden'" (1918); Antoninus Romeo, "*Nos qui vivimus, qui residui sumus*" (1929); Anselm Wimmer, "Trostworte des Apostels Paulus an Hinterbliebene" (1955). For discussion of this exegetical direction see esp. Schneider, *Vollendung des Auferstehens*, 269–79, and previously Friedrich, "1 Thess 5,1–11," 310–14, who ultimately decides in favor of the present majority solution to περιλειπόμενοι: Paul counts himself and his community among the living. He speaks against orthodox Roman Catholic exegesis primarily because of its dogmatic-apologetic character, something that in fact does counsel an initial caution with regard to its theses.

29. Arthur L. Moore, *The Parousia in the New Testament* (1966), 108ff.

conclude that the "we" refers to both the dead and the living simultaneously. The double participle in 4:15, 17 indicates that the actual number of the living in each instance should remain open.

An essay by Heinz Giesen then offered a penetrating philological discussion of "those who are left," without entering into the history of exegesis sketched above, though in my opinion his accurate interpretation goes in the same direction. Giesen proposes to test the thesis of an intense imminent expectation, supposedly expressed in 1 Thess 4:13–17, and again raises the question of error: "Is Paul really convinced that he will certainly live to see the parousia? If so, then he was certainly mistaken."[30]

That question points particularly to the sub-thesis occasionally associated with it, namely, that on the basis of 1 Thess 4:15–17 the apostle really expects there will be no more deaths, perhaps with a few exceptions, a position advocated by Willi Marxsen and others.[31] This thesis combines an absolute early dating of 1 Thessalonians with the exegetical finding that the passage is by no means primarily about explaining the resurrection of the dead; that functions as a sort of aid to a hoped-for rapture into an eventual communion with Christ.[32] What is remarkable in such conclusions is that historically experienced researchers could believe that in the year 50 C.E. the apostle Paul, who was relatively knowledgeable, experienced, and often (in fact, "daily" and "hourly") placed in dangerous situations (1 Cor 15:30–31), could quite seriously think that there would be no further deaths among believers until the return of the Lord. In the roughly twenty years that had passed since Jesus' crucifixion a great many people must have died already.[33] In that case the apparent idea (in some ways still more divorced from real life) that no one in Thessalonica had yet heard about a resurrection of the dead, or that Paul is

30. Heinz Giesen, "Naherwartung des Paulus," 124.

31. Marxsen, "Auslegung von 1 Thess 4,13–18" (1969), 26–27; idem, *Der erste Brief an die Thessalonicher* (1979), 65; Franz Laub, *Eschatologische Verkündigung und Lebensgestaltung nach Paulus* (1973), 131; Lüdemann, *Paulus, der Heidenapostel* 1, 226, 266ff.; Niels Hyldahl, "Auferstehung Christi, Auferstehung der Toten (1 Thess 4,13–18)" (1980), 122, 134–35; Hans-Heinrich Schade, *Apokalyptische Christologie bei Paulus* (1981), 162ff.; Haufe, *Der erste Brief des Paulus an die Thessalonicher*, 80ff. An earlier advocate of this and the following thesis (see n. 34 below) was Friedrich Guntermann, *Die Eschatologie des hl. Paulus* (1932), 36–49 (cp. Siber, *Mit Christus leben*, 16–17). Andreas Lindemann votes against this supposition, which "is offered by exegetes with an astonishing matter-of-factness," referring to the fact that the text reveals nothing of the sort ("Paulus und die korinthische Eschatologie" [1991], 337, and quotation in n. 16; similarly Konradt, *Gericht und Gemeinde*, 131–32; Schreiber, "Eine neue Jenseitshoffnung," 335).

32. See further below at 5.1.2.

33. As Paul himself, for example, admits (1 Cor 15:6): some of the more than five hundred witnesses to the resurrection have already fallen asleep; cp. also Luz, *Geschichtsverständnis*, 320.

here speaking about it to a congregation for the first time,[34] and is proposing it independently and *ad hoc* because of the situation and the creed, seems highly improbable.[35] But in light of the belief in a resurrection that had been alive in Israel for centuries, is it realistic that the message of Jesus' resurrection could ever have been preached without the hope of a general resurrection? The tenor of 1 Corinthians 15 in particular speaks for knowledge and spread of the hope of resurrection in all the communities, because "Paul saw the denial of the resurrection of the dead as a total attack on the faith itself."[36] The subordination of talk of the resurrection of the dead in 1 Thess 4:13–17 must certainly be subject to a different explanation.

Let us return to Heinz Giesen's argument, in which the syntagma "we who are alive, who are left" / ἡμεῖς οἱ ζῶντες οἱ περιλειπόμενοι plays a primary role.[37] He engages with the appositional correlation of the two participles with "we," dominant in exegesis at that time, and defines their relationship differently, noting that their mere use is striking. The first by itself would have been sufficient to define the living, and so the second must add a further differentiation consisting not in a determinative but in a specifying function: "Accordingly, our sentence must be translated: 'we who are alive, to the extent that we remain behind until the parousia of the Lord, will have no advantage over those who have fallen asleep.'"[38] In this statement, he says, the theme of the whole section, that there is no difference between the survivors and those who have died, is given its definitive expression. The repetition in v. 17a strengthens the impression that it is meant to refer not to those who are alive at the time of the letter's writing but only to those who remain alive until the parousia. "The thesis that Paul was convinced that no member of the

34. "I therefore consider it out of the question that the resurrection of the dead had been a 'subject of Paul's teaching' in Thessalonica" (Marxsen, "1 Thess 4,13–18," 32); so also Lüdemann, *Paulus, der Heidenapostel* 1, 229ff.; see also (at n. 58) the listing of previous advocates of this idea, beginning with Ernst Teichmann, *Die paulinischen Vorstellungen von Auferstehung und Gericht* (1896); on this see also Konradt, *Gericht und Gemeinde*, 131–32.

35. Udo Schnelle, "Der erste Thessalonicherbrief und die Entstehung der paulinischen Anthropologie" (1986), 210: In the expectation of the rapidly approaching parousia Paul not only did not preach about it but could have "abstained" from doing so on purpose. The death of some Christians and the resulting problem of the delay of the parousia ultimately "force him to introduce the idea of the resurrection of dead believers." Cp. also Schade, *Apokalyptische Christologie*, 163ff.

36. Siber, *Mit Christus leben*, 21. For the OT witness to belief in the resurrection as a precondition for the corresponding statements in the NT see Reinhard von Bendemann, "Die Auferstehung Jesu von den Toten als 'basic story'" (2000), 149ff.; Frank Crüsemann, "Rhetorische Fragen?" (2003); idem, *Das Alte Testament als Wahrheitsraum des Neuen* (2011), chap. 8, "Auferstehung als Schriftauslegung."

37. Giesen, "Naherwartung des Paulus," esp. 136–40.

38. Ibid., 137.

community would die henceforth, until the parousia, is thus refuted."[39] Giesen calls the "we" in this section an "ecclesial we," expressing the common faith and leaving a good deal undetermined: present and future Christians can belong to it. "Whoever is still among the living at the parousia will have no advantage over the dead." There is nothing here about imminent expectation in the sense that large numbers of the community members, and Paul himself, will certainly experience the parousia while still living: "Those still alive at this point *can* thus be among those who are living at the parousia, but they *need* not be. The question of the time of the parousia is thus not at issue."[40]

Sebastian Schneider argues similarly under the heading "Imminent Expectation in v. 15b?"[41] in favor of a restrictive connotation of περιλειπόμενοι, referring to the older interpretation described above according to which "Paul obviously does not use 'we' to refer to himself and his generation, but only to those who will, in fact, ultimately experience the end of the world during their lifetimes."[42] Referring to John Chrysostom and others, Schneider emphasizes that the reference to the περιλειπόμενοι only makes sense "as a restriction of the subject field," which in plain language means "we, *to the extent that* we remain until he comes."[43] This interpretation is also favored by the Greek grammar, according to which we should not see a second attributive participle as describing "a second characteristic" of all the persons included in "we," "but rather a restriction, so that only the statement in the predicate applies to the subject," insofar as a "*specifying* attributive participle" is present.[44] The same grammatical possibility can be claimed for 1 Thess 4:13, in that οἱ μὴ ἔχοντες ἐλπίδα can also be read restrictively as a specifying attributive participle, because "Paul would scarcely have wanted to equate all the Thessalonians with the Gentiles, but only to compare them in regard to hopelessness with those 'others': 'like others *to the extent that* or *considering that* they have no hope," and something similar applies also to the translation of 1 Thess 4:4.[45] This makes it clear that the double use of περιλειπόμενοι in 1 Thess 4:15, 17 represents anything but a superfluous construction; when used together with and in contrast to οἱ ζῶντες it facilitates a statement that makes sense as a "restriction of the subject field."[46]

On the whole, then, we may say that the use of the specifying double expression about those who are "left," which is to be understood as a restriction and conditioning of the we-saying, speaks against both the thesis of a supposedly

39. Ibid., 138.

40. Ibid., 139; see also Richard, *First and Second Thessalonians* (1995), 241–42: οἱ περιλειπόμενοι could indicate that those who survive till the end will be more the exception than the rule.

41. Schneider, *Vollendung des Auferstehens*, 269–79.

42. Ibid., 271.

43. Ibid., 272. Emphasis in original.

44. Ibid., 276. Emphasis in original.

45. Ibid., 277. Emphasis in original.

46. Ibid., 278.

"burning" imminent expectation in 1 Thess 4:13–17 and the supposition that Paul reckoned himself with certainty among those who would be alive at the parousia. But add to this the question that is the subject of this study, namely, whether in this letter it is Paul himself who is speaking, for the above analysis eliminates a principal objection by those who see 1 Thess 4:15, 17 as positive proof of the authenticity of 1 Thessalonians. These statements are no obstacle to a later composition of the letter. In what follows we will also reflect on the extent to which, on the contrary, their peculiar form makes them particularly useful for the purposes of the supposed real author. These reflections link with the remarks above (in 3.1) about the plurality of authorship.

5.1.2 Function and purpose of the "we" statements about "those who are left" in describing the parousia

The conclusions of Heinz Giesen and Sebastian Schneider, as well as the previous discussion about those "left," touched only the supposed number of the dead in the community addressed, as well as the probability that Paul leaves open the question of his own fate before the parousia. But the nearly consistent first person plural in statements by the author in 1 Thessalonians involves the methodological consequence that there appears to be a genuine plural intended: exegesis must always reckon with the three authors Paul, Silvanus, and Timothy. That this is also and especially the case if the writing is of post-apostolic origin is shown by the way it speaks of "us" as the living and those who are left, for the "we" in 1 Thess 4:15, 17 includes not only the community addressed, together with the authors, but in the first instance the group of the authors themselves. That group is contrasted with the other group, the community. Thus if a distinction is to be drawn between the dead and those who are left within the group that is the community, the same is true for the group of authors. The distinguishing function of the phrase "we who are alive, who are left" must be applied to the authorial group as well. The distinction applies to them, too: "we, insofar as we are alive, insofar we remain until Christ's parousia." *And that means that the distinction between the dead and those still alive applies just as much to this community of apostles, that is, the statement remains open to the death of one, two, or all three of them.* Hence the authorial plural particularly suggests at this point that it is not necessarily Paul who will be the survivor among those who are left. In this way the letter acquires an openness to addressing a flexible life-expectancy for its several authors just as it addresses the same regarding the community, and it makes it possible to refer obliquely to the death of Paul as having already happened. At the same time, we should not accuse the authors of presenting an erroneous idea from Paul's perspective, no matter when the text was conceived, for death does not deprive the living Paul himself of the chance to see and encounter the Lord at his coming. None of the people who have to that point survived Paul have any advantage over him: that is the logical consequence of 1 Thess 4:15.

Still, the nearly consistent use of the first person plural in the overall text signals that by no means should Paul, as an individual, be the focus; the fate of the two named co-authors is of equal importance. The achievement of the plural formulation is that Paul can disappear within the plural of co-authors named in the prescript; he can in a sense vanish, so that no singular Pauline, personal statement can be found in what is said about expectations of the parousia. Since the relationship between the dead and the living at the coming of the Lord is the main subject of that section,[47] and since it is thereby assured that the different statuses of being dead or living ultimately play no decisive part, the person of Paul also disappears into a still greater "we," the sum total of the living and the dead. The statement in v. 17b, that "we will be with the Lord forever," ultimately includes everyone, living and dead, within a single "we," no matter which of those categories includes the addressees and the authors in the end. Thus this "we" describes a community of living and dead within which, no matter what may have happened beforehand, there is no more separation due to the arrival of death, and thus also no separation caused by the death of Paul beforehand. On this level the "we" in v. 17b can refer to the dead and the living on the same level, therefore signaling that Paul, as the wording suggests, can just as easily count himself among the dead.

a. Imminent expectation?

This speaks against the traditional idea of a "burning expectation of the end" out of which it is supposed that the text is written. In fact, on close inspection the style and form of the argumentation corresponds more to an idea of the "delay of the parousia," if anyone wants to use that kind of categorization.

In essence we need to get beyond the ruts in which the special discussion of 1 Thess 4:13–17 has run and recall here the increasing and penetrating doubt among exegetes concerning the long-accepted pattern of ideas about imminent expectation. The paradigmatic idea of "imminent expectation," in the sense of a return of Christ in the immediate future, with its correlative of the "delay of the parousia," the thwarting of that expectation, should be regarded as the expression of a one-sided, linear idea of time that can also be associated with schemas of development, one that should not simply be imposed on biblical and extra-biblical apocalyptic texts. Luise Schottroff emphasized that in terms of her feminist-social-historical exegesis of the eschatological passages in the Synoptic Gospels. The latter, on the contrary, reveal completely different ideas about time that can be defined as an "eschatology of presence" or "permanent preparedness": "the time for growing and ripening, of being roused from the slumber of patriarchy's confidence in its structures of alleged security; it is the time of the ominous strain of watching slaves and the time of festive rejoicing."[48] That means that so-called statements

47. See 5.2 below.

48. Luise Schottroff, "Impenitent Patriarchy and the Nearness of God (Matt. 24:37–39; Luke 17:26–27, 30; and Mark 13:28–33): The Eschatology of Early Christianity," in eadem, *Lydia's Impatient Sisters* (1995), 152–71, at 171, 161. See also "Delayed Parousia or Hope in the Nearness of God?" in eadem, Silvia Schroer, and Marie-Theres Wacker, *Feminist Interpretation: The Bible in Women's Perspective* (1998), 215–17, at 216.

about delay or others that speak of a fulfillment of eschatological hopes that is close at hand should be interpreted as expressions of one and the same present, a phenomenon that should be kept in mind also in the interpretation of 2 Thessalonians.[49] Here again, structural anti-Judaism plays a fundamental role; it is genuinely inherent in the model of imminent expectation and delay as well as the idea of development, because these "always went hand in hand with contrasting New Testament eschatology and Jewish apocalyptic, with the latter being judged negatively in an anti-Judaistic fashion. Jewish apocalyptic, it has often been said, was intent on determining the span of time left until the end."[50] Kurt Erlemann's review of a large number of Jewish and early Christian texts on the end-time has shown that statements about delay and nearness express concurrent and competing hopes for imminence, and that these simultaneous and varying perspectives are to be found scattered equally throughout Jewish and early Christian texts. This means that Jewish and early Christian eschatologies or apocalyptics were by no means shaped by disparate, to say nothing of qualitatively different or even contrary ideas about time. "As a parameter for the history of early Christianity the alternatives of imminent expectation and delay of the parousia prove useless; no one-way development in the common sense can be discerned."[51]

For the interpretation of 1 Thess 4:13–17 this means one must abandon attempts at dating based on the character of the eschatological statements. A "burning expectation" does not mean an absolutely or relatively early time of composition, just as the idea of a delay need not point to a late date. The common assumption that there had been a few deaths in Thessalonica and that this had caused unrest in the community, leading to Paul's taking a position on the matter, rests not on information in the text but on the presumption that this is the first of Paul's letters, written only a few weeks or months after the founding of the community. If those presuppositions are eliminated there remains little to indicate a fixed time or historical point based on imminent expectation other than the equation of the living author with those who are "left." Once that usual reading is shaken, as I have attempted above, there is no need for the idea of an anticipation of the parousia in the near future because not

49. See 6.3.2 below.

50. Schottroff, *Lydia's Impatient Sisters*, 169, with reference to Günther Klein, art. "Eschatologie IV. Neues Testament, *TRE* 10 (1982): 270–99.

51. Kurt Erlemann, *Naherwartung und Parusieverzögerung* (1995), 417. In addition to the summary theses on pp. 417ff., see the overall systematic consideration of "understanding of time" and "functionality of nearness" (pp. 367–97), with the determination of the simultaneity of different quantities of time in biblical thinking as well as a tentative alternative description of early Christianity with regard to its messianic conceptions of time (pp. 398–417). For the problem of the concept of imminent expectation vs. delay of the parousia in light of biblical statements about time see also Claudia Janssen, *Anders ist die Schönheit der Körper* (2005), 281–306, and Frank and Marlene Crüsemann, art. "Zeitvorstellungen" (2009), 627ff. ("Gott und Zeit—theologische Zeitansagen" = God and time—theological statements about time).

many further deaths are expected before it comes. Rather, precisely the repeated talk of those who are "left" may advance the contrary thesis: that it reflects a situation of remaining behind, of successively being left alone, even an existential remnant situation such as must have been experienced in the wake of the deaths of the first generation of members of the Christian communities. That could be associated with a relatively late dating, as was also seen in the wake of the discussion of authenticity by those who dispute the genuine nature of 1 Thessalonians.[52] But such a dating can only be undertaken within the framework of a completely new conception of how 1 Thessalonians is to be interpreted, and not because of this or that difference in eschatological ideas. A social-historical definition of the problem being addressed here could certainly yield some points of reference for the supposed period in which the text was composed.

b. "We will by no means precede those who have died . . .": The situation of the real addressees

What, exactly, is the theme or underlying problem in the teaching in 1 Thess 4:13–17? According to v. 13 the community is uninformed about those who have died (περὶ τῶν κοιμωμένων),[53] and the result is a lack of hope. The fact that what is not demanded first of all is the clarification of the reality of a hoped-for resurrection—in which case the opening question might have been "will the dead also rise?"—is evident from the first reply in v. 14: "For since we believe that Jesus died and rose again (ἀνέστη), even so, through Jesus, God will bring with him (ἄξει) those who have died (κοιμηθέντας)." It has been repeatedly remarked that the faith formula about Jesus' death and resurrection[54] does not lead directly to a conclusion about the resurrection of the other dead.[55] Rather, the goal of the hope here conveyed is

52. Thus, e.g., Ferdinand Christian Baur, "The two Epistles to the Thessalonians" (1866/67), 338–39; see 4.1 above.

53. For the widely-used metaphors κοιμᾶσθαι or καθεύδω as euphemisms for the sleep of death in Greek philosophy and poetry and in Greek-speaking Judaism see the comprehensive surveys in Hoffmann, *Die Toten in Christus*, 186–206, and Schneider, *Vollendung des Auferstehens*, 129–44 (with references to biblical usage); see also Howard, "Literary Unity" (1988), 167 n. 13; Lautenschlager, "Εἴτε γρηγορῶμεν" (1990), 43ff., who argues vehemently against the (sleep of) death as a meaning for καθεύδω in general and especially in 1 Thess 5:10 (pp. 42–50); on this, see below in 5.4. In the Pauline letters, κοιμᾶσθαι appears only in 1 Thessalonians and 1 Corinthians: in the indicative in 1 Cor 7:39; 11:30; 15:6 and as a participle in 1 Cor 15:18, 20 as well as in 1 Thess 4:13, 14, 15; the synonym καθεύδω appears only in 1 Thess 5:6, 7(2x), 10.

54. For the "traditional *pistis* formula" see, e.g., Siber, *Mit Christus leben*, 23–35; Wengst, *Christologische Formeln und Lieder des Urchristentums* (1972), 45–46.

55. It is sometimes remarked as surprising that the statement about Jesus' death and resurrection is not followed by a fully parallel statement about dead believers: e.g., Hoffmann, *Die Toten in Christus*, 216ff.; Harnisch, *Eschatologische Existenz*, 35 n. 33; Jürgen Becker, *Auferstehung der Toten*, 49–50; Holtz, *Der erste Brief*, 192–93; Haufe, *Der erste Brief des Paulus an die Thessalonicher*, 83.

an action that leads to union[56] with Jesus. We can also see in v. 14 the intended summary of the whole pericope, which aims at the idea that "we" will be forever with the "Kyrios" (v. 17b).[57] Central to the concern of the community we can deduce from this is thus the danger that the dead might be excluded from community or union with the returning Christ. This is about a possible temporary disadvantage of the dead.[58]

That is why the fear is immediately addressed, in v. 15 as well, and deprived of its power through the assurance that the authors, together with those they address, insofar as they live and remain until the parousia, will have no position of advantage: "We will by no means precede (οὐ μὴ φθάσομεν) those who have died." Only in the course of giving reasons for this assurance do the authors finally mention the resurrection of the dead (v. 16), within the framework of a little apocalyptic scene; however, it only serves as a precondition for the common rapture, together with the living (v. 17), which again is governed by the principal theme of the relationship between the living and the dead at the parousia. The consolation to be exchanged (v. 18) thus consists of the certainty that no serious loss of position is associated with death. Ultimately it is of no consequence whether one must die without having seen the Lord. And it is also unimportant who will have died before that time. The resurrection of the dead appears within the overall composition only as an aid. It makes possible the future union of the dead also with Jesus, and that is all that is important in the text. This accomplishes a general broadening of perspective: basically, it does not matter how great the number of those who die in the meantime may be, and whether in the interim the survivors in the community are a minority compared to those known to have died. This vision guarantees the end-time community of them all.

If we inquire about a possible social-historical background for such a problem complex, characterized by a verbal emphasis on "being left," the language suggests a remnant situation marked by hopelessness. In the case of a pseudepigraphical

56. Ἄξει (4:14), future of ἄγω; Liddell/Scott, 17: "lead, carry, fetch, bring, of living creatures." The word is mainly translated "lead, bring" (e.g., Holtz, *Der erste Brief*, 192–93: "lead up"; Reinmuth, "Der erste Brief an die Thessalonicher" (1998), 145: "bring [together]"). This matches the possible interpretation that at the parousia the dead will be brought along, brought back again (Best, *Thessalonians*, 188–89: "bring with him"). But in the context a different "direction of transportation" is possible: analogously to Acts 5:26; 11:26; 17:19; 21:16 the word here could also connote "bring, take along" [to another place] (cp. BAGD 16), as shown by the continuation of the pericope in v. 17, where a rapture takes place. (On this, see the discussion in Hoffmann, *Die Toten in Christus*, 216ff.) See also below at 5.2.3.

57. For the correspondence of vv. 14 and 17 see, *inter alia*, Siber, *Mit Christus leben*, 29ff.

58. Cp. esp. Merklein, "Der Theologe als Prophet," 403–9, on this problem, which is answered by the section in 4:13–18: "So this is not about the resurrection as such but about a specific scenario: the community of the dead with Jesus at the parousia, or the participation of the dead in the parousia movement" (p. 405); similarly van Houwelingen, "The Great Reunion," 311ff.

writing it is necessary to distinguish at least two time-levels the text must express: the fictive situation of the supposed author(s) and, alongside it, the actual time when the work was written and with regard to which particular existing themes must be treated and problems resolved with the aid of apostolic authority. Angela Standhartinger, in her study of Colossians, introduced into exegetical discussion of epistolary pseudepigraphy the description of this phenomenon as involving "implicit addressees," drawing on a category from modern literary studies.[59] Thus well-considered and devised pseudepigraphical letters sensitively make the two compositional situations evident to the recipients: "The genre of pseudepigraphical letters makes it possible to give an insight into the character of a historical personality at turning points in her or his life and to introduce their actions and thoughts, or to give an empathetic imitation of them. Through the depiction of the (fictional) addressees of the letter . . . it also creates the precondition for obtaining insights into the relationships between the fictional sender and the fictional addressees at important turning points. The fiction of addressees also prepares a basis for identification within which readers can recognize themselves and apply what is said to their own particular situation."[60] What is purported to have been written on the level of the early apostolic period in which the first letter to the Thessalonians is supposed to have been composed appears as a possibility—that not everyone identified as "we" will remain alive—that may be the dominant sense of the really intended readers on the second level of time about their own lives: the community sees itself as a group of survivors, of those left behind, who are attacked by an increasing sense of hopelessness because they have nothing in their previous knowledge and faith to set against the dying off of the first generations of community members from the apostolic period. What about those who go on dying; are they lost or at least very disadvantaged at the return of Christ? This may well have become quite a personal question for many, concerning their own future fate, as years went by and they themselves aged. Add to this the external threat

59. Angela Standhartinger, *Studien zur Entstehungsgeschichte & Intention des Kolosserbriefs* (1999), 153 and *passim*. Eckart Reinmuth, "Der zweite Brief an die Thessalonicher" (1998), 193–94, had previously proposed a similar distinction. Thus it is necessary to distinguish "between real, intended, and fictive readers." Cp. also Annette Merz, *Die fiktive Selbstauslegung des Paulus* (2004), who usually chooses the term "intended readers" for the level of the actual contemporary addressees of the forged letter (e.g., pp. 223–24), since a distinction must be drawn between the supra-historical category "implicit readers" and that of the "intended readers" as the historically and sociologically perceptible first addressees (p. 224 n. 82). Other terms used in research on epistolary pseudepigraphy include "internal" readers on the level of fiction, as distinct from the "external," real first readers of the forgery: thus, e.g., Timo Glaser, "Erzählung im Fragment" (2009), 273–74 and *passim*. A unified nomenclature for this phenomenon of multiple communicative time-levels in pseudepigraphy would be highly desirable for the purpose of preventing misunderstandings.

60. Standhartinger, *Studien zur Entstehungsgeschichte*, 153.

from political-social repression, repeatedly mentioned in this letter, that, in the form of real present threats, may be forcing the "survivors" into a remnant situation. Especially at the beginning of the anti-Jewish sermon in 2:14 the initial description of the problem gives a clear pointer to a repression brought about by communal forces, "your own compatriots."[61] The two time-levels are now combined as the authors present themselves as prophets of "persecutions" that have since come to pass: "In fact, when we were with you, we told you beforehand (προελέγομεν)[62] that we were to suffer persecution (ὅτι μέλλομεν θλίβεσθαι); so it turned out, as you know" (3:4). In the preceding v. 3 it is definitively stated that "we" are fated to endure these persecutions, as the community knows through the prophesying apostles. The prophetic way of speaking, here transposed to the past, thus opens ongoing prophecy of persecutions, in principle, for an implicit later readership.

One indication of existence in a dangerous remnant situation is, in particular, the double use of the verb περιλείπεσθαι, "remain, be left," the passive of περιλείπω, "leave behind." We cannot locate a direct conceptual reference to the "remnant" of Israel in Old Testament texts, because "For the nouns שְׁאָר and . . . שְׁאֵרִית, which are most important theologically, the LXX usually has verbal forms of καταλείπειν or ὑπολείπειν."[63] By contrast, "περιλείπομαι is very uncommon, only uncertainly attested in the translated parts (i.e., of the LXX), and not very incisive,"[64] thus revealing no significant lexical link to the theological content of the idea of the remnant in Israel. The verb, found in the New Testament only here in 1 Thess 4:15, 17, is to be interpreted more in a social-historical sense than as a general expression for a remnant situation, a state of remaining behind after experiences of the decimation of a group,[65] such as we find primarily in apocalyptic circles. There is an analogous situation especially in 4 Ezra, which is repeatedly adduced as an aid to clarifying what is meant here.[66] The problem of belonging to a disadvantaged group at the last judgment because of an earlier or later lifetime is resolved thus in 4 Ezra 5:42: "He said unto me: I shall liken my judgment to a circle; just as for those who are last there is no slowness, so for those who are first there is no

61. See 2.4.3 and 2.5.1 above. Donfried, "The Cults of Thessalonica" (1985), 349–50, for example, sees "those who have died in Christ" in 4:16 as Christian martyrs slain by public persecution.

62. Here we see the use of an iterative imperfect that "places a repeated or customary action . . . in the past" (BDR, §325); cp. Holtz, *Der erste Brief*, 126 and n. 625. The authors of 1 Thessalonians thus appear as genuine and steady prophets in the past whose reliability, especially in case of situations of persecution of the addressees, acquires additional dignity.

63. Volkmar Herntrich, art. λεῖμμα B, *TDNT* IV, 196–209, at 196.

64. Holtz, *Der erste Brief*, 195 n. 264. But Holtz does think (ibid.) that the expression is part of the terminology of the Old Testament idea of the remnant.

65. According to Richard, *Thessalonians*, 241–42, this usage may signal that survival to the end should be regarded as more the exception than the rule.

66. Thus, e.g., Walter Radl, *Die Ankunft des Herrn* (1981), 120–21; Holtz, *Der erste Brief*, 195ff.; Haufe, *Der erste Brief des Paulus an die Thessalonicher*, 84 n. 104.

haste."[67] In addition, the problem of remaining to the last days is treated explicitly and at length in 4 Ezra; underlying this seems to be the same idea or apprehension reflected in 1 Thess 4:13–17, namely, that those who remain to the end may have an advantage. Differently from 1 Thess 4:13–17, according to which the living will not "have an advantage" over the dead, 4 Ezra affirms the disadvantaging of those who do not remain and have died in the meantime:

> . . . alas for those who will be left in those days! And still more, alas for those who are not left! For those who are not left will be sad[18] because they understand the things that are reserved for the last days, but cannot attain them.[19] But alas for those also who are left, and for that very reason![24] Understand therefore that those who are left are more blessed than those who have died.
>
> 4 Ezra 13:16–19, 24[68]

Independent of the question of literary relationships, in case 1 Thessalonians belongs to a later time[69] the similarity of the social-historical situations of the groups behind each text is interesting. It can be described as a despairing remnant situation marked by increasing numbers of deaths among the members of the group. There are ideas in circulation that suggest it might be better to die before the end that God will bring about, in order to avoid further afflictions. On the other hand it is feared that in that case one would be completely excluded from the experience of eschatological salvation. The texts give different answers to the question of the fate of the dead, but they betray a similar set of problems in a life-situation in which people are threatened with decimation.

On the whole, the achievement of the use of the first person plural, "we," in this section, in case this is a post-apostolic composition, can be described as follows: "We" is completely open in every respect, including the fate of the three named authors, however it may have developed, and an increasing number of dead. The additional appeal to the authority of the "Kyrios" introduces a greater, higher instance that guarantees the plausibility of the vision. The chief statement of the pericope is that those still living will have no advantage over the dead; on the

67. NRSV, 2 Esdras 5:42.

68. Ibid. "Survive" in each case represents *derelicti sunt*, corresponding to the Greek περιλειπόμενοι. On this see A. F. Klijn, *Die Esra-Apokalypse* (*IV. Esra*) [1992], 35 on 4 Ezra 6:25; cp. 4 Ezra 13:24: *Scito ergo, quoniam magis beatificati sunt qui derelicti sunt super eos qui mortui sunt* (from Klijn's Latin edition, *Der lateinische Text der Apokalypse des Esra* [1983], 83; cp. 4 Ezra 6:25; 7:28).

69. On this see Rudolf Steck, "Das Herrenwort 1 Thess 4,15" (1883), 512–19; cp. 4.2.1 above. The *Apocalypse of Ezra* (= *4 Ezra*) was probably created ca. 100 C.E. (Josef Schreiner, "Das 4. Buch Esra" [1981], 301). Klijn, "1 Thessalonians 4.13–18 and Its Background in Apocalyptic Literature" (1982), 70ff., and Seth Turner, "The Interim, Earthly Messianic Kingdom in Paul" (2003), 331–32, emphasize that the same idea of an eschatological disadvantage for the dead at the judgment or the coming of the Messiah underlies both 4 Ezra 13:16–24 and 1 Thess 4:13–17.

contrary. The time of one's death makes no difference. This is an extraordinarily sweeping statement. The transparency of "we" to many stages in time, in the case of pseudepigraphy, represents the special achievement of the actual later author: all the dead, those presently living, and future Christians who die are addressed at their own place in time, that is, in whatever status they find themselves. "We" proves especially productive and important because it has a flexibility that Paul's own "I" alone does not express and that cannot be replaced by the special function of the two participles describing those who are "left." Thus by the use of this plural number and the specifying participles the authors of a pseudepigraphical writing would have been able to speak both for the fictive historical situation and for their own time of writing, at least a generation later. In addition, the scale of consolation is open upward: it makes no difference at all how many people will yet die in the course of time, because those surviving are in any case and at every time no better off than they, as patristic interpretation already emphasized. Communion with the Kyrios belongs to both groups, independently of their relative numbers and also independently of the death of the authors of the letter, in particular the death of Paul. The community of Thessalonica at the second stage, in the time when the letter was really written, probably finding itself in a stressful remnant situation, thus receives an effective consolation that reaches beyond the supposed apostolic period to touch their own afflictions, and that promises to lead Christians of all generations into the eschatological community of all who will then live again with Jesus.

5.2 The Parousia of the Kyrios in 1 Thessalonians 4:13–17 and the Future Fate of the Community

We turn now to the scene in which the future fate of the community in Thessalonica and its apostles is painted, the detailed description of the parousia. We should first note that everything in 1 Thessalonians is aimed toward the future thus defined. There is no other kind of statement about the future in the letter, especially not about the concrete near future of the relationships between the authors and their audience. Plans for visits, even by those sent in one direction or another, are not mentioned, nor is the organization of the collection for Jerusalem.[70] The future of

70. See 3.2.5 above. It should again be emphasized that, as far as any perceptible network of relationships among the early Pauline communities is concerned, 1 Thessalonians reveals a vast gap. By contrast, in the other "Greek" letters we find discussion of the existence and planning for further contacts among the respective community, its messengers, and the apostles: organization of the collection (1 Cor 16:1–4; 2 Cor 8–9), vocabulary describing current and future emissaries (1 Cor 4:17; 16:10–11; 2 Cor 8:16–19; 9:3–5; Phil 2:19–30), Paul's concrete plans for visits (1 Cor 16:5–9; 2 Cor 12:14–18; 13:1–3), greetings from other people at the place from which the letter is sent (1 Cor 16:19–20; 2 Cor 13:12; Phil 4:22)—epistolary references to moments within an ongoing, lively, and open relationship between apostles and communities as well as communities with one another by means of people who link them together and who are accordingly mentioned and greeted—all these are absent from 1 Thessalonians.

relationships yet to be realized, the reunion of the letter-partners: these are only manifest in the course of the establishment of the eschatological communion of all believers with one another after the resurrection of those who have died, together with the Kyrios coming from heaven.[71] This alone appears to guarantee the coming together of all participants.

This fact finds its unmistakable expression in 1 Thessalonians' special use of the word παρουσία, "arrival," "presence." The fact that there are none of the signs of a network of relationships in this letter corresponds to the absence of the usual concept of the παρουσία, which is elsewhere used for the arrival of Paul and other apostles or messengers. In 1 Cor 16:17 it speaks of the arrival of the community's emissaries, Stephanas, Fortunatus, and Achaicus. In 2 Cor 7:6–7 Titus has arrived, while in 10:10 the subject is the presence of Paul. In Phil 1:26 Paul speaks of his future coming, and in 2:12 he contrasts his presence in and absence from Philippi. In contrast, 1 Thessalonians lacks both the mention of an apostolic visitation planned for the future and, above all, the *terminus technicus* itself, the παρουσία as applied to earthly messengers, the "apostolic parousia."[72] It is not the parousia of Paul or other travelers that appears against the future horizon of the writing; it is only the eschatological parousia of Christ. Of the five instances mentioning the coming of the Messiah in the Pauline letters, four are in 1 Thessalonians: 2:19; 3:13; 4:15; 5:23; elsewhere it is only in 1 Cor 15:23 that Christ's arrival is called a παρουσία: that is, we can observe a "curious distribution within the Corpus Paulinum."[73] The blanket use of the term "parousia" of Christ in New Testament scholarship, in the sense of his eschatological coming, often conceals the astonishing fact that the term itself, within the compass of the Pauline letters, dominates and is nearly exclusively[74] connected with 1 Thessalonians.[75] We are justified in speaking of the "technical use"[76] of the parousia-concept in describing the "'coming' of Christ in Messanic glory" because, differently from the arrival of community

71. Communion with Christ appears in 1 Thessalonians exclusively in a future-eschatological context: 4:14, 17; 5:10. (On this cp. Jürgen Becker, *Auferstehung der Toten*, 49 n. 5, who interprets this situation as a not-yet-fully-developed idea of baptism on Paul's part.) That is, such communion does not exist "now."

72. See above, 3.2.3, for an argument against Funk, "Apostolic Parousia" (1967).

73. Holtz, *Der erste Brief*, 120.

74. In 1 Cor 1:8 D, F, and G have παρουσία in place of ἡμέρα.

75. Παρουσία (of Jesus) does not appear in the Deutero-Pauline texts either, with the exception of 2 Thess 2:1, 8. It is found elsewhere in Jas 5:7, 8; 2 Pet 1:16; 3:4, 12; 1 John 2:28. We should emphasize the usage in the Matthean apocalypse in Matt 24:3, 27, 37, 39, concerning the coming of the υἱός τοῦ ἀνθρώπου. Second Thessalonians 2:9 speaks of the parousia of the "lawless one"; for this, see below at 6.3.2.

76. Albrecht Oepke, art. παρουσία, 865; cp. Luz, *Geschichtsverständnis*, 310; Holtz, *Der erste Brief*, 119–20; see also Luckensmeyer, *Eschatology*, 190ff., who calls the concept "quasi-technical" on p. 191.

emissaries, this is about a political concept from the realm of the Hellenistic cult of the ruler, now associated with Jesus as the Lord.

5.2.1 The Parousia of the Ruler

Albrecht Oepke's instructive article very clearly depicts the Hellenistic-pagan origins of the idea of the parousia, for which there is no Hebrew equivalent since in the Old Testament the coming of God in particular is always expressed verbally. Hence παρουσία first appears within Jewish writings in texts written in Greek.[77] Otherwise it is used in Greek not only to describe the appearance of gods but as a *terminus technicus* for visits by Hellenistic rulers to the cities of their realms,[78] especially upon entry into office, and its *Sitz im Leben* is the arrangements to be made by individual communes in the form of expensive celebrations and expensive gifts to greet the new ruler. The papyri in particular speak of cleaning and repairing streets, provision of mounts, golden wreaths and enormous sums of money, all to be presented "voluntarily" by the local population or demanded of them by repressive means.[79] In the Roman imperial period the parousia of the ruler was often connected additionally with the opening of a new era that received its material expression also through the construction of monuments and the minting of "advent coins,"[80] for example under Nero and Hadrian. These monuments, such as Hadrian's buildings in Athens and Eleusis, or the witnesses to an era following the appearance on the island of Cos of C. Caesar (that is, probably Caligula), designated by the related term "epiphany," represent the watershed moments in the history of individual cities as marked by "parousia eras."[81] An inscription from Tegea shows how the local reckoning of time was associated with the number of visits from a god: "in the year 69 of the first parusia of the god Hadrian in Greece (ἔτους ξθ' ἀπὸ τῆς θεοῖ Ἀδριανοῦ τὸ πρῶτον ἰς τὴν Ἑλλάδα παρουσίας)."[82]

77. Cp. Oepke, παρουσία, 863–65.

78. This is pointed out by George Milligan, *St. Paul's Epistles to the Thessalonians* (1908; 1953), 145ff.; Adolf Deissmann, *Light from the Ancient East* (1927; 1978), 372–78, and Martin Dibelius, *An die Thessalonicher* (^{3}1937), 13ff., and more recently especially by Robert Gundry, "The Hellenization of Dominical Tradition" (1987), 161–69; Mason, *The Resurrection According to Paul*, 105–9; Donfried, "The Cults of Thessalonica," 434; idem, "The Assembly of the Thessalonians" (1996), 394; Mikael Tellbe, *Paul between Synagogue and State* (2001), 127ff.

79. Examples in Milligan, *St. Paul's Epistles*, 145; Deissmann, *Light from the Ancient East*, 372–73, especially as regards the "expenses" of the parousia; Oepke, παρουσία, 859–60.

80. For Latin *adventus* as a synonym for παρουσία see Deissmann, *Light from the Ancient East*, 375, relating it also (p. 378) to the closely related cultic word ἐπιφάνεια (epiphany; appearance).

81. Ibid., 375 and n. 3, 376–77, with examples; cp. Oepke, παρουσία, 859–60.

82. *Bulletin de Correspondence Hellénique* 25 (1901), 275, quoted in Deissmann, *Light from the Ancient East*, 377.

Against this background the parousia terminology in 1 Thessalonians cannot be accidental. The fact that it undoubtedly represents a technical use of the word, the parousia of a ruler, is evident from the analogous use of the Kyrios title in 1 Thessalonians. In 2:19; 3:13; 4:15; 5:23—that is, in the passages that speak of the parousia, Jesus is also given the Kyrios title, or he is referred to by it. He is the real ruler whose coming the community awaits. This is underscored by the fact that every one of these passages except 4:15 speaks pointedly of "our Lord Jesus" in the sense of an exclusive relationship. As such he is a competitor with the Hellenistic-Roman ruler figures, their festal arrivals and political claims. That is the consequence of the use of the Kyrios title itself; it was the common address to rulers in the Hellenistic East, and beginning with Nero it also adorned the Roman emperor.[83] Thus whoever read the letter in the Hellenistic-Roman period could not avoid comparing the coming of Jesus with the visit of an imperial ruler or high official, given the self-reference and the combination of terms.[84] This was all the more true when a third notable concept was added (4:17) with the ἀπάντησις, the "welcoming," or "meeting"[85] that links the scene still more powerfully with such imperial inaugural visitations and the corresponding festivities.

5.2.2 *The welcoming of the Kyrios*

The parousia of a Hellenistic-Roman emperor in a *polis* included a special program of greeting; usually the population met him outside the city, before the gate, forming an entry procession. The ordinary concept of ἀπάντησις, "welcoming," acquired a festive technical meaning in this context. The work of Erik Peterson has shown the probability that this greeting of a ruler as "welcoming" forms the

83. Cp. Foerster, art. κύριος, *TDNT* 3 (1965), 1039–58, at 1054–58; also Deissmann, *Light from the Ancient East*, 355–59, with numerous inscriptional examples, esp. from ostraca.

84. This has been emphasized especially by Gundry, "The Hellenization of Dominical Tradition," 162ff., as also by Mason, *The Resurrection According to Paul*, 108–9; Helmut Koester, "Imperial Ideology and Paul's Eschatology in 1 Thessalonians" (1997), 158ff.

85. Donfried in particular has repeatedly pointed to the political background and connections of the concepts as used here: "The Cults of Thessalonica," 344; "The Theology of 1 Thessalonians as a Reflection of its Purpose" (1989), 16–17; "The Assembly of the Thessalonians," (394); see also Gundry, "The Hellenization of Dominical Tradition," 162–63, 165–69; idem, "A Brief Note on Hellenistic Formal Receptions and Paul's Use of ΑΠΑΝΤΗΣΙΣ in 1 Thessalonians 4,17" (1996); Koester, "From Paul's Eschatology to the Apocalyptic Schemata of 2 Thessalonians" (1990), 445–48; idem, "Imperial Ideology and Paul's Eschatology," 158–60; Yeo Khiok-Khng, "A Political Reading of Paul's Eschatology in I and II Thessalonians" (1998), 81ff.; Tellbe, *Paul Between Synagogue and State*, 126–30; J. R. Harrison, "Paul and the Imperial Gospel at Thessaloniki" (2002), esp. 82–86; Schreiber, "Eine neue Jenseitshoffnung," 331–34; Marga J. Ströher, "Cuidado com os que proclamam paz e segurança" (2007), 62ff.; van Houwelingen, "The Great Reunion," 321ff.; cp. the discussion in Luckensmeyer, *Eschatology*, 260–68; on this see further below.

background for ἀπάντησις in 1 Thess 4:17 (otherwise unknown in Paul). He writes that it is about "a tech. term for a civic custom of antiquity whereby a public welcome was accorded by a city to important visitors. Similarly, when Christians leave the gates of the world, they will welcome Christ in the ἀήρ, acclaiming Him κύριος."[86] Peterson's choice of epigraphical, literary, and papyrus texts from the time of the Seleucid rulers to that of the Christian-Roman emperors[87] shows the relatively homogeneous sequence in such public welcomes and the accompanying arrangements, which are regularly designated with ἀπάντησις and its synonym, ὑπάντησις, or with the corresponding verbs, and also used together with the word παρουσία.[88] Translating it as "welcoming" seems sensible because some of the people of the city often traveled considerable distances, apparently in order to be seen by the exalted guest in as early an encounter as possible, which must have made the subsequent triumphal march into the city all the more imposing and tumultuous.[89] The festal procession reflected the political organization of the city: for example, women and girls were placed at the very end—with the exception of priestesses, whose office was the most prominent and most frequently attested for women in the ancient *polis*:[90] a decree for Attalos III of Pergamum gives an

86. Peterson, art. ἀπάντησις, *TDNT* 1 (1964), 380–81; the examples are discussed in idem, "Die Einholung des Kyrios" (1930); this interpretation had previously been mentioned by James E. Frame, *A Critical and Exegetical Commentary on the Epistles of St. Paul to the Thessalonians* (1912), 177. For controversial discussion and the probability of this thesis see Luckensmeyer, *Eschatology*, 260–68, 272.

87. Peterson, "Die Einholung des Kyrios," 683–92; cp. Michael R. Cosby, "Hellenistic Formula Receptions and Paul's Use of ΑΠΑΝΤΗΣΙΣ in 1 Thessalonians" (1994), 20–28, and the critical description of Peterson's position in Plevnik, "1 Thessalonians 4,17: The Bringing in of the Lord or the Bringing in of the Faithful?" (1999), 537–41. Some of the epigraphical and papyrus texts adduced by Peterson can be found in English translation in Cosby's article, pp. 23ff.

88. E.g., Polybius XVI, 25,3 on the reception of King Attalus by the people of Athens: ὁ δὲ τῶν Ἀθηναίων δῆμος γνοὺς τὴν παρουσίαν αὐτοῦ μεγαλομερῶς ἐψηφίσατο περὶ τῆς ἀπαντήσεως καὶ τῆς ὅλης ἀποδοχῆς τοῦ βασιλέως (Peterson, "Die Einholung des Kyrios," 686). Cp. the extended descriptions of the *apantesis* at the reception of Vespasian in Rome after his triumph over the Jewish people (Josephus, *Bell.* VII, 68–71) and of Titus in Antioch for the same reason (Josephus, *Bell.* VII, 100–3; Peterson, "Die Einholung des Kyrios," 687–88).

89. On this see esp. the two passages in Josephus cited in the previous note; in each instance the greeting must have taken place a considerable distance outside the city (*Bell.* VII, 68, 110–11).

90. Cp. Winfried Elliger, *Paulus in Griechenland* (1987), 90–91; she considers this the only office held by women, whereas Ross Kraemer, *Her Share of the Blessings* (1992), 80–92 ("Women's Religious Offices in Greco-Roman Paganism") points out that within the framework of the Roman benefaction system it occasionally happened that civic offices of leadership and governance were accorded to women (see esp. pp. 87–88).

impressive picture of the political significance of the ranks of groups entering the city: priests and priestesses, the upper military, leading officers of the city, crowned victors in the sports competitions, the *gymnasiarch* with his young men, the teacher with his students, citizens, women, all the virgins, and the rest of the city-dwellers—in the last case probably for the most part foreigners.[91] According to Peterson, analysis of the sources reveals the following recurring elements in festal processions: "It was required that for the entrance procession all were to wear white garments . . . and wreaths. . . . Besides the wreaths worn by all participants there was special emphasis on those of the *agons* . . . and the golden crowns. . . . We also learn that the city itself was crowned . . . that incense was burned . . . or scented oil (μύρον) was poured out . . . the temple was opened . . . and sacrifices were made to the gods . . . with the one being celebrated of course participating. . . . One feature repeatedly reported is that cultic objects were carried in the procession."[92] Add to all this the jubilant shouts, loud acclamations, and ovations for the ruler as he slowly moved into the decorated city.

In view of the political language in 1 Thess 4:15–17, which speaks in a short space of parousia, the Kyrios, and ἀπάντησις, there really can be no doubt that this is an allusion to the festal reception of a ruler approaching for a visitation, and thus to a familiar civic action. "The combination of παρουσία and ἀπάντησις together with the emphatic use of the title κύριος in 1 Thess 4:15–17 carries strong connotations of imperial ideology, and in particular of the coming of imperial visitors to a provincial city."[93]

91. The decree for Attalos III of Pergamum lists, e.g., ἀπαντῆσαι δὲ (α)ὐτ(ῶιτ)ούς τε προγεγραμμένους ἱερεῖς καὶ τὰς ἱερείας καὶ τοὺς στρατηγοὺς καὶ τοὺς ἄρχοντας καὶ τοὺς ἱερονίκας ἔχοντας τοὺς ἀπὸ (τῶ)ν ἀ(γώνω)ν (στεφάν)ους καὶ (τ)ὸν (γυ)μνασίαρχον μετὰ τῶν ἐφήβων καὶ τῶν ν(έων καὶ τ)ὸν (π)αι(δ)ο(ν)ό(μ)ον μετ(ὰ τω)μ [sic!] παίδων καὶ τοὺς πολίτας καὶ τὰς (γυναῖκας καὶ παρθένους πάν)τας καὶ τοὺς ἐνοικοῦντας ἐν ἐσθ(ῆ)σιν λ(αμπραῖς ἐστεφανωμένους): OGIS 332, ll. 33ff.; text and commentary in Peterson, "Die Einholung des Kyrios," 684–85, 694; cp. Cosby, "Hellenistic Formal Receptions," 23 and n. 25; he points to problems of reconstruction, especially of the women participants at the end of the list: the article τάς "indicates a missing feminine noun, but the masculine form πάντας does not match παρθένους, and the lack of an article prior to 'virgins' represents a definite break in the pattern followed throughout."

92. Peterson, "Einholung des Kyrios," 695–96.

93. Tellbe, *Paul between Synagogue and State*, 129 (italicized in the original); see also the argumentation on pp. 125–30. This position is also maintained very emphatically by Gundry, "The Hellenization of Dominical Tradition," 161–69; Koester, "From Paul's Eschatology," 445ff.; idem, "Imperial Ideology"; Khiok-Khng, "Political Reading," 81ff., who also stresses εὐαγγέλιον as a political term (p. 82); Harrison, "Paul and the Imperial Gospel"; Peter Oakes, "Re-mapping the Universe" (2005), 315ff.; Schreiber, "Eine neue Jenseitshoffnung," 331ff.; see also, e.g., Best, *Thessalonians*, 199; Heinrich Schlier, *Der Apostel und seine Gemeinde* (1972), 82–83; F. F. Bruce, *1 & 2 Thessalonians* (1962), 102–3; Merklein, "Der Theologe als Prophet," 412; J. P. Mason, *The Resurrection According to Paul*, 105–9.

Nevertheless, there seems to be no explicit depiction here of the usual circumstances, which caused Michael R. Cosby, for example, to question this concrete background for the interpretation of 1 Thess 4:13–17.[94] This leads to the proposal that we may have here a critical use of the relevant language, as an attempt to formulate a fundamental alternative to an imperial or royal visitation. "The political overtones carried in the combination of the terms παρουσία, κύριος and ἀπάντησις provide a powerful and positive statement against imperial ideology."[95] Indeed, in my opinion this is more than a mere rejection of the imperial ideology of state and *polis*; we have here an alternative image of a ruler, an alternative depiction of his longed-for arrival: by an unmistakable play on the well-known language of the ruler's parousia, which would bring before the eyes of every member of the letter's ancient readership the role played by the population and the costs and efforts ordinarily expected of them, the parousia of Jesus Christ is presented as a counterimage. This ruler is different from the others. In the end his arrival is different from the well-known jubilant city processions in which a new victor and emperor shows himself to his subjects, who have to make both material and ideological display of their obedience. To the contrary, 1 Thess 4:13–17, in combination with 5:1–11, shows, as we will discuss further below, that Kyrios Jesus comes in a way that will finally and effectively abolish every other political claim to power and the oppressions associated with it for those believers in him who are still left, and for the re-awakened who believed in him before their deaths.

5.2.3 Salvation as "Divine Theft"

A closer look at all the parousia sayings in 1 Thessalonians, however, reveals that perhaps at least one[96] of the familiar elements of ancient parousia- and encounter-celebrations has found its way into the letter: namely, the wreaths or crowning. At

94. Cosby, "Hellenistic Formal Receptions," 28–33; likewise Plevnik, "1 Thessalonians 4,17," 542–46; Konradt, *Gericht und Gemeinde*, 68, and previously others such as Dupont, "Σὺν Χριστῷ" (1952), 64–73; to the contrary Gundry, "A Brief Note on Hellenistic Formal Receptions"; cp. the discussion in Luckensmeyer, *Eschatology*, 263ff.

95. Luckensmeyer, *Eschatology*, 265.

96. See also 1 Thess 3:13, where Jesus appears at his parousia accompanied by "all his saints" (μετὰ πάντων τῶν ἁγίων αὐτοῦ). That is an extremely un-Pauline formulation, since for Paul "saints," that is, holy people, are always earthly siblings in the individual communities, or as a whole (e.g., Rom 1:7; 15:25; 16:15; 1 Cor 1:2; 2 Cor 1:1; 8:4; 13:12; Phil 1:1; 4:21–22; but never in this sense in 1 Thessalonians: see above at 2.5.2). This passage led Karl Schrader to his overall suspicion of the authenticity of 1 Thessalonians (*Der Apostel Paulus* [1836], 23; cp. 4.1 above). Whom the authors meant, exactly, by this entourage is a question that must remain open (cp. the discussion in Rigaux, *Thessaloniciens*, 491–92; Holtz, *Der erste Brief*, 146–47; E. D. Schmidt, *Heilig ins Eschaton* [2010], 334ff.). In any case it appears to be a kind of escort, a ruler's entourage, which fits with a royal procession and thus also a ruler's parousia.

2:19–20 we read the enthusiastic "For what is our hope or joy or crown of boasting (στέφανος καυχήσεως) before our Lord Jesus at his coming (παρουσία)? Is it not you? Yes, you are our glory and joy!" Here we do not find (as elsewhere in Paul) the context of athletic competition when "boasting" and "crowns" are mentioned. In 1 Cor 9:25 the text speaks only of an imperishable "wreath" to be presented after a race, and Phil 2:16 solely of "boasting" on the "day of Christ" because of the virtue embodied in the community, showing that Paul has not run in vain. Philippians 4:1 reads: "my brothers and sisters, whom I love and long for, my joy and crown (στέφανος)." The image is thus one of a kind of (eschatological) prize that is won,[97] so that the community represents a victory wreath that adorns the apostle. The image-context is different in 1 Thess 2:19: the keywords "wreath"/στέφανος, "Lord"/κύριος, and "coming"/παρουσία combine to present a compact allusion to the ceremonies surrounding a ruler's parousia. The community is imagined as a wreath or crown that the apostles will have at hand for adornment at the encounter with the Kyrios, or that they will give to him as a precious gift by which they can do him honor and proclaim their joy. Adolf Deissmann described this connection with reference to a papyrus that mentions a golden crown to be made for the king, to be given to him at his parousia, and for which contributions are needed.[98] By means of such an allusion to crowns or wreaths bestowed at a parousia and *apantēsis*, which the population had to provide for the ruler's reception, the text of 1 Thessalonians lets its readers see that for the ruler named Jesus no kind of material expenditure on the part of the community must be provided. The community itself is the adornment or gift its own lord will receive from the apostles, or that the latter "wear" as an honor. No other precious items or wealth are necessary for an appropriate ceremony of welcome.

The process of encounter in 1 Thess 4:16–17 reveals still more critical differences from the usual reception of emperors. The community made up of those still living and the reawakened dead is summoned to a particular ἀπάντησις. First, the Kyrios descends from heaven to his parousia, accompanied by apocalyptic sound effects, whereupon the dead will arise (4:16). But before the Kyrios reaches his presumed goal, the earth, there is a multiply sensational *apantēsis*: the community does not go out to meet him but instead is carried aloft to a greeting in the air; no action on their part is needed (4:17). The verb used here, ἁρπάζω, is commonly used for the

97. See also the "crown of righteousness" in 2 Tim 4:8.

98. 𝔭 *Flinders Petrie* II 39e (3d c. b.c.e.) in Deissmann, *Light from the Ancient East*, 373. A reference to the presentation of a wreath at a ruler's parousia or *apantēsis* is seen here also by Gundry, "Hellenization," 162–63; idem, "A Brief Note on Hellenistic Formal Receptions," 40; and J. P. Mason, *Resurrection*, 108 n. 52, who emphasizes that in 1 Thess 2:19–20 there is definitely no reference to sporting events in the arena. The wreaths could represent a bridge from Paul's competitive metaphor to the ruler's parousia, as victorious athletes sometimes wore them at the *apantēsis*; see n. 91 above.

phenomenon of snatching away;[99] it thus underscores the complete passivity of the community in this encounter. Nothing more need be undertaken on their part; rather, they will be snatched out of their earthly conditions and thus also out of the *polis* of Thessalonica. Altogether singular here is the rapturing of a large group of people, because otherwise there is reference only to the apocalyptic snatching away of individuals.[100]

The verb ἁρπάζω, with its connotation of "stealing," "take away suddenly and/or by force," or "abduct, seize, place under arrest" expresses the violent aspect of this removal from the earth.[101] Attention is thus drawn to the accompanying procession in honor of the heavenly ruler and it "happens through a 'theft' by God, who snatches them (i.e., believers) out of the world to the triumphant Kyrios."[102] When the believers appear in this section in connection with the political terminology that dominates it as "God's booty," it means that they are taken away from the other concrete and presently active rulers and the earthly circumstances brought about by them. In the process the city of Thessalonica is also robbed of part of its population; that is how one must describe the political consequences of this vision, so it seems. In any case, it is a striking feature of this apocalypse that its worldwide and universal effects are missing, differently, for example, from 1 Cor 15:24–28, 54–57; those passages are about the destruction of all violence, lordship, and death itself. In comparison with other apocalypses, 1 Thess 4:13–17 offers a kind of one-act play that appears to be tailored strictly to the special needs of this community.

It is, in fact, inherent in the concept of ἀπάντησις, the "welcoming of the Kyrios," that one would return to the city or, as seems to be the consequence of 1 Thess 4:17, to the earth.[103] But if, on the one hand, 4:17 suggests the reception of the alternative ruler, Jesus, with full honors and, on the other hand, the return is in fact omitted and instead a new perspective is opened by the verb "steal, be snatched away," then we are faced with a significant transformation of the usual civic scenario: people remove themselves, together, from both the city and the earth simultaneously.[104]

99. Thus, e.g., in 2 Cor 12:2 to Paradise; for interpretation and the early Jewish context to which this Pauline account belongs see Frank Crüsemann and Marlene Crüsemann, "Gegenwart des Verlorenen" (2007), 54–62. The term ἁρπάζω, frequently used in Greek literature, "is the oldest Greek term for 'carry off'" and "quite frequently also describes rapturings within the earthly realm (being snatched away to other countries, to the Isles of the Blessed, to the Elysian Fields) and expresses especially the suddenness and unexpected nature of the event" (Gerhard Lohfink, *Die Himmelfahrt Jesu* [1971], 42).

100. Lohfink, *Die Himmelfahrt Jesu*, 55–74.

101. Ἁρπαγησόμεθα, future 2d passive of ἁρπάζω. Cp. Matt 12:29; John 6:15; 10:12; Acts 23:10, 25 (ἁρπαγή is the "theft" or "booty"; see Matt 23:25; Heb 10:34). This aspect is emphasized especially by Schlier, *Der Apostel und seine Gemeinde*, 81ff.

102. Ibid., 83.

103. Cp. Dibelius, *An die Thessalonicher*, 28; Best, *Thessalonians*, 200; Holtz, *Der erste Brief*, 203; Richard, *Thessalonians*, 247.

104. This is also Best's opinion (*Thessalonians*, 199).

Coherent with this is also the conclusion, "so we will be with the Lord forever" (4:17), which does *not* say "the Kyrios is with us," but "we are with the Kyrios," who does not touch the earth and the city at all.[105] The welcoming, the "bringing in" of the Kyrios thus becomes the "bringing out" of believers. On the other hand, the kings and other worthies so festively received are always only visitors to the Greco-Roman cities, with the exception of the capital, and as a rule they will depart again after a time. To that extent the text's presentation corresponds to that practice of the ruler's parousia as a visitation for a particular and limited time.

The crucial difference between the New Testament text and the familiar political custom consists, overall, in the passivity of the crowd waiting to welcome the Lord, who have no need to do or pay anything, and who in reality are deprived of their own motive power toward the encounter by a snatching-away; moreover, this Lord desires an enduring community with them and removes those who belong to him from their earthly existence forever in order to keep them with him in a utopian, spherical space.[106] Ultimately this greeting of a ruler, now transformed into the

105. On this see Holtz, *Der erste Brief*, 201. According to Peterson the encounter thesis can thus be connected with the idea that, according to the text, a final rapture takes place in which the Kyrios is by no means led down to earth by the crowd that greets him (see n. 94 above). For discussion of the believers' remaining, see the next note.

106. No other place for the community to remain with Christ is indicated beyond this scene of encounter in the air, εἰς ἀέρα (4:17). This has led exegetes to a great many ideas about where the participants abide. On this see, e.g., the standpoints in earlier research discussed by von Dobschütz, *Die Thessalonicherbriefe*, 198–99: (1) The ἀπάντησις requires a return to the earth; (2) because of the subsequent καὶ οὕτως "the realm of the air is itself considered the place of enduring union"; (3) Christians, together with the Lord, belong in heaven. Since the text itself has no interest in clarifying this question and offers no relevant information, we must conclude that its sole point is the removal from the earth it describes. For an extended discussion of 1 Thess 4:17a see Schneider, *Vollendung des Auferstehens*, 244–54, who answers the "question about the place where the unending communion with God is to be sought" (p. 244) with an interpretation of εἰς ἀέρα based on parallels with ancient church writers and Greco-Roman authors: "in the open air, in the vastness of space" (p. 253). This avoids the idea of a precisely defined place, because such a meaning "is much less descriptive than the more representational and comprehensible 'in the air.'" Accordingly, "the righteous" arrive "in the end at a new reality entirely shaped by God" (pp. 253–54; cp. Plevnik, "The Taking Up of the Faithful" [1984], 280–83; idem, "The Destination of the Apostle and of the Faithful" [2000], 86ff., 94–95). At any rate, with this choice of words 1 Thessalonians makes it clear that there will be a movement away from earthly conditions. Some interpret differently: e.g., Turner, "The Interim, Earthly Messianic Kingdom in Paul," 331 ("1 Thess 4,17 speaks of all Christians dwelling on earth with Christ"); van Houwelingen, "The Great Reunion," 322 ("They were caught up to meet him in order to accompany him on the last stage of his journey to the earth"); and Jürgen Becker, *Der Auferstehung Jesu Christi nach dem Neuen Testament* (2007), 160: "One should think of the earth, not heaven, as the place of salvation," a statement founded primarily on statements in other New Testament writings and not so much on 1 Thessalonians alone (see his pp. 160–61 and n. 24).

abduction of the inhabitants of a city, signifies hope for a collective "removal" effected by this true Kyrios, so that the expression first used in v. 14, ἄξει σὺν αὐτῷ, acquires a further nuance by means of the overall interpretation of the passage.

5.2.4 Salvation without Judgment? On 1 Thess 4:6 and 1:10

The impression that this vision of the "last things" in the form of a removal of the collective community of living and dead is an "apocalypse light," a kind of one-act play instead of the great final drama, is evoked by the fact that 1 Thess 4:13–18 makes no mention of apocalyptic battles, cosmic divisions, or a judgment scene.[107] The community awaiting Christ and abducted by him, so to speak, is to experience an exception *sui generis*; the unquestioned belonging to those thus saved that is incidentally communicated is mentioned in passing after the problem of a possible disadvantaging of the dead has been eliminated. Is it possible that 1 Thessalonians sees believers taken up to Christ in eternity without an eschatological judgment?

One important indicator of this is that the concept of ὀργή, God's wrathful judgment, is not mentioned in this passage. It thus appears at first that the community is to have nothing to do with that, and in particular that it remains exempt from a judgment according to "works," the judgment of the deeds of all people, including those who belong to Christ, thus here differing from Rom 2:15–16; 1 Cor 4:4–5; 2 Cor 5:10, even though the eschatological future is the focus of a large part of the letter.

However, it was previously said in 1 Thess 4:6 that ἔκδικος κύριος περὶ πάντων τούτων, "the Lord is an avenger/judge in all these things,"[108] namely, the ethical

107. Von Dobschütz, *Die Thessalonicherbriefe*, 200: "This is a grand reduction of the multiform Jewish eschatology to two principal ideas: union of all Christians with the Lord, with no disadvantage to any believers." In contrast, we hear "nothing about the fate of the non-Christians, nothing about the preliminary signs of the parousia, nothing about the gathering of those who are scattered, nothing about judgment." Cp. also the observations about the lack of a judgment in 1 Thess 4:13–18 in Lindemann, "Paulus und die korinthische Eschatologie," 380 n. 29; Hanna Roose, "2 Thessalonians as Pseudepigraphic Reading Instruction for 1 Thessalonians" (2006), 145, and in general Konradt, *Gericht und Gemeinde*, 128–82, 187–96, who arrives at conclusions about the structure of the statements about judgment in 1 Thessalonians similar to those previously drawn by Marlene Crüsemann in "Die Briefe nach Thessaloniki und das gerechte Gericht" (1999), 187–244 and *passim*; for the connection to 1 Thess 5:1–11 see 5.3 below. The apocalyptic presentations in 2 Thessalonians are contrary to these; see chap. 6 below.

108. The powerful influence of such meanings as vengeance, reprisal, and punishment is emphasized by BAGD, 720–21, and the examples in Liddell/Scott, 504. The idea of vengeance and reprisal also appears clearly in the quasi-parallel Rom 12:19, with its citation of Deut 32:35 and the use of ἐκδίκος; cp. Konradt, *Gericht und Gemeinde*, 116–17, 124, who also emphasizes the strong affinity in language and content between 1 Thess 4:3–6 and the ethics of the deutero-Pauline Col 3:5–11 and Eph 5:3–7, as well as 1 Pet 1:14–17 (pp. 119–26).

matters previously discussed. To what extent does that refer to the eschatological judgment? The only other passage in the New Testament that mentions an ἔκδικος is Rom 13:4, which is about earthly punitive justice. In that verse the ἔκδικος is the ἐξουσία (Rom 13:3), the "governing authorities,"[109] who serve God by their judging. There Paul writes in such a way that the ἐξουσία functions as the present earthly agent of God's punishing judgment: ἔκδικος εἰς ὀργήν. The eschatological judgment of wrath[110] accordingly also stands behind secular-earthly punishments. If we do not choose to import this subject from Rom 13:4 into 1 Thess 4:6, we must maintain that "wrath" is certainly *not* mentioned at this point in 1 Thessalonians. It is a different matter with the retributory deed of the "Kyrios,"[111] so that it remains unclear whether this is to be understood as a retribution and judgment within history or as an eschatological judging.[112] The dialectics of Rom 13:1–7 is able to

109. For the social-historical *Sitz im Leben* of Rom 13:1–7 as that of a declaration of loyalty to Rome by members of conquered peoples see Luise Schottroff, "'Gebt dem Kaiser, was dem Kaiser gehört, und Gott, was Gott gehört,'" in eadem, *Befreiungserfahrungen* (1990), 185–92.

110. Ὀργή as God's wrath appears frequently in Paul and, apart from 1 Thessalonians, only in the letter to the community in Rome: Rom 1:18; 2:5, 8; 3:5; 4:15; 5:9; 9:22; 12:19, as well as 13:4–5. We can clearly see from Rom 2:5–16 that Paul's idea of judgment includes a general judgment by God "through Christ"; on "the day," the deeds of each individual will be judged without regard for persons and according to the measure of Torah. Cp., e.g., Klaus Wengst, *"Freut euch, ihr Völker, mit Gottes Volk!"* (2008), 155–75; for the scope of ὀργή in Romans see esp. von Bendemann, "'Zorn' und 'Zorn Gottes' im Römerbrief" (2006), 182–91. This corresponds, within the four types of judgment defined by Egon Brandenburger (*Gerichtskonzeptionen im Urchristentum und ihre Voraussetzungen* [1993], 30) to the category of "universal world judgment." On this cp. Konradt, *Gericht und Gemeinde*, 496–515.

111. The question of who the κύριος is here has been variously answered: for example, Rigaux, *Thessaloniciens*, 511, argues for Jesus, as does Collins, "Paul's Early Christology" (1984), 270–71 (with other voices in agreement); for God, with reference to OT texts, are, e.g., Holtz, *Der erste Brief*, 164; Richard, *Thessalonians*, 204; Eduard Verhoef, *De brieven aan de Tessalonicenzen* (1998), 175.

112. For example, Holtz, *Der erste Brief*, 164, presumes an eschatological judgment. Ekkehard Stegemann emphasizes in his interpretation of 1 Thess 2:16, together with other Pauline letters, that Paul alludes to "chastising judgments within history" in order to link with the hope for preservation from the eschatological final judgment. He wants to understand the ὀργή on "the Jews" also as a "chastising judgment within history" ("1 Thess 2,16" [1990], 58–59; see 2.5.2 above). But in any consideration only of the language and content of the statements in 1 Thessalonians, ὀργή is each time associated with the eschatological perspective (see below), while 1 Thess 4:6 is to be seen rather as a punishment within history, as Stegemann also suggests (ibid., p. 58). On this, see the arguments of Konradt, *Gericht und Gemeinde*, 116–28, who does place 4:6 within an eschatological horizon of judgment but remarks that, by contrast, the ὀργή-sayings in 2:16 and 5:9 are not associated with any threat, especially not toward the community (p. 192).

relate the two, but that kind of subtle argumentation is not a concern of 1 Thessalonians. Since the horizon of "wrath" does not appear in 1 Thess 4:6, we have to look at the broader context of the text in order to establish the underlying idea about the eschatological fate of the community and all those who believe in Christ.

Controlling here is, first of all, 1 Thess 1:10, which reads "... to wait for his Son from heaven, whom he raised from the dead—Jesus, who rescues (lit: "our rescuer," ῥυόμενον) us from the wrath that is coming (ἐκ τῆς ὀργῆς τῆς ἐρχομένης)." We may suppose that 1 Thess 9:10 is drawn from the field of Jewish or Jewish-Christian missional language and preaching.[113] Independently of its origins, which if the letter is by Paul must always be regarded either as pre-Pauline or as Paul's creation, but in case of pseudepigraphy should be seen as extra-Pauline—the introduction

113. Cp. the corresponding conceptual studies by Ulrich Wilckens, *Die Missionsreden der Apostelgeschichte* (1961), 81–86; Friedrich, "Ein Tauflied hellenistischer Judenchristen" (1965), 502–16; Bussmann, *Themen der paulinischen Missionspredigt* (1971), 39–56; Laub, *Eschatologische Verkündigung*, 26–49, esp. 29ff. (with older literature); Nebe, "Die Kritik am εἴδωλα-Kult" (2006), 191–221, where ἐπιστρέφειν, "convert"; εἴδωλον, "idol"; and θεός ζῶν καὶ ἀληθινός, "living and true God," as well as rescue from wrath are the crucial words, some of them also part of the special language in Acts. For the "amazing parallels between v. 9b and Acts 14:15" see Johannes Woyke, *Götter, 'Götzen,' Götterbilder* (2005), 106–7, 128–32, 153–54, 156–57, at 106. Woyke says that in this work he cannot further pursue the "reasons for the unusual semantics of 1 Thessalonians in contrast to the later Pauline letters, namely, on the one hand many similarities to formulations in Acts" etc. (p. 131). For the use of ἐπιστρέφειν, unusual for Paul, see Luckensmeyer, *Eschatology*, 86–89. Holtz, "'Euer Glaube an Gott'" (1977; cp. idem, *Der erste Brief*, 54–62), sees 1 Thess 1:9–10 as a passage originally formulated by Paul (cp. above at 3.3.4 n. 98 and the literature indicated there; similarly Konradt, *Gericht und Gemeinde*, 39–73, who works out the close thematic and also linguistic relationships as far as ὀργή is concerned between 1:9–10 and the whole of 1 Thessalonians: "the most important themes of the letter are brought together here," p. 55); Konradt also speaks of Pauline creation using Jewish traditions: "The proposal that 1 Thess 1:9–10 represents a formulaic compilation of the missionary preaching cannot be sustained ... v. 9b.c reveals a high degree of affinity with Jewish ways of speaking that have also left their mark elsewhere in early Christian texts, but this by itself demonstrates the rootedness of Paul, and of Christianity in Judaism in general" (p. 56; for the anchoring of 1:9–10 in the context of 1 Thessalonians see also Woyke, *Götter, 'Götzen,' Götterbilder*, 104–57). In my opinion only the premise that 1 Thessalonians was written by Paul yields the conclusion that the language of 1:9–10 shows a direct rootedness in Judaism. The close linguistic parallels with Acts 14:15 or Heb 6:1–2, on the contrary, attest to the spread of this early Christian tradition and in themselves say nothing about the origins of the writings' authors or a definitely determined place in the chain of tradition. (Cp. the arguments on the adoption of Jewish-Christian traditions at the end of 2.5.2 above.) For the most striking parallels between 1 Thessalonians and the "Miletus speech" in Acts 20:18–35, see Steve Walton, *Leadership and Lifestyle* (2000), 157–85, and the critical evaluation and substantiation of this work by Paul Elbert, "Paul of the Miletus Speech" (2004).

of an independent Jewish-Christian tradition or the combination of various traditional elements by the presumed later author[114]—the question arises: what does this text contribute to the content of the idea of judgment in 1 Thessalonians, and how does it fit with its contours as already indicated? That is, does the choice or formulation of this passage, with its definition of "wrath," serve to create a coherent concept of judgment in 1 Thessalonians?[115] Thus 1:9–10 is closely connected with 4:13–5:11,[116] which must now be described in more detail with regard to the expectation of judgment proclaimed to the community. The principal statement of 1:10 is the assurance that Jesus "rescues us from the wrath that is coming." This, then, is about a future action of Jesus for the community, because divine wrath is yet to come; in the present time of the letter's statement it has not yet happened. Accordingly, the rescue consists of a preservation, not otherwise specified, within the wrath-event or ahead of it.

> If instead of the preposition ἐκ ("out of") we should here read ἀπό ("from"), the rescue would consist of a still more extensive keeping of the "we" of community and apostles apart from the sphere of divine wrath. This text-critical choice is advocated by Daniel Wallace,[117] who relativizes the external grounds (better manuscript attestation) for ἐκ in terms of internal arguments for ἀπό. He writes that, because of the two other occurrences of this preposition within 1:10, ἐκ should be regarded as a scribal error or a stylistic correction; the contrary case, a change of ἀπό to ἐκ, is improbable. Add to this the incorrect listing of the Latin manuscripts for the ἐκ version in Nestle-Aland since the 26th edition. Finally, the exegesis of 4:13–5:11 may speak for ἀπό as the original reading, since it offers a fuller clarification of 1:10.[118]

If 1:10 is read together with 4:13–18,[119] it quickly becomes evident how the rescue "from" or "out of" the wrath is to be defined: first of all, it simply takes place in the form of a rapture (4:17) by which believers are removed to a higher sphere where

114. Analogous to the collection and special application of judgments on the "Jews" in 2:14–16; cp. chap. 2 above.

115. With Laub, *Eschatologische Verkündigung*, 40, who inquires about the thought process within which the statements are included, and that should primarily be defined as an announcement of judgment (pp. 41ff.).

116. Ibid., 33, 43, and frequently; Konradt, *Gericht und Gemeinde*, 39–73; cp. n. 113 above.

117. Daniel Wallace, "A Textual Problem in 1 Thessalonians 1:10" (1990).

118. Ibid., 479. English translations consistently write "from" (= ἀπό). The Authorized Version has the verb in the past tense, "delivered," but NRSV and other modern translations use the present tense, i.e., Jesus is "the one who" delivers/rescues "us."

119. Cp. also the positions that see in 1 Thess 1:9–10 an extract of the themes that will be developed in the course of the letter: e.g., Hooker, "1 Thess 1.9–10: a Nutshell" (1996).

there is not even a hint of a wrathful judgment. This can rightly be called a removal or snatching away from the end-time distress.[120] In light of such a consequence of viewing 1:10 and 4:13–18 together, the action in 4:13–18 has been described, in preliminary fashion, as an event of salvation or rescue. The absence of any kind of judgment or battle terminology in the parousia vision can thus be explained as an adequate expression of the hoped-for matter-of-fact and battle-free future in the presence of the Kyrios. The bare statement that "we will be with the Lord forever" (4:17) is the ultimate goal of Jesus' saving action on behalf of his own. The escape of the One from earthly distresses and the resurrection of the Other immediately links a conflict-free existence without any battle against principalities and powers; this appears among other things to mean that any further crisis, namely, God's judgment, will no longer be of any existential importance. "Jesus [is] in this eschatological scenario not given the function of entering into a judicial process on behalf of the Christians, but is rather to lead them into the heavenly sphere where they will be with him forever, and in this way to snatch them away from the judgment of destruction that is to come."[121]

A study of 1 Thess 5:1–11 focused on this question also shows that the rescue is equivalent for the Christian community and its apostles to its preservation from the end-time judgment of wrath. Now it is clear why the alternative removal of Jesus, as the ruler who is the measure of all rulers, should involve a distancing from the earth: it, and thus also the realm of the *polis* of Thessalonica, is the stage for the events on the "day of the Lord" (5:2) from which believers are delivered in a special sense. The political terminology, both subliminal and explicit, continues here, and with it a pointed statement of intent.

120. "Pretribulation rapture" (Wallace, "Textual Problem," 479). For American evangelical discussions of a rapture before, during, or after the apocalyptic woes ("pre-, mid-, or post-tribulational"), cp. Howard, "Literary Unity," 164, 178ff.; 1 Thess 4:13–17 in particular, in relation to 5:1–10, is seen as a preservation from the final judgment. That 4:13–17 is about rescue from the wrath announced in 1:10 is emphasized especially by Daniel Völter, *Paulus und seine Briefe* (1905), 330, and more recently Richard, *Thessalonians*, 247; cp. also the remarks by Laub on the motif of judgment (*Eschatologische Verkündigung*, 63–66), according to whom statements about judgment in the overall context of 1 Thessalonians "assure the Thessalonians of rescue from judgment" (p. 64, with reference to 1:10; 5:4, 9), and especially Konradt, *Gericht und Gemeinde*, 39–73: "If we think of 1:10 and 4:14–17 together we have a unified, coherent idea: Christians will be rescued from the judgment of wrath/destruction by the fact that they will be (previously) carried up to the heavenly world at the parousia; there they will be πάντοτε σὺν κυρίῳ. We should understand 5:9 in the same sense: Christians do not fall under God's wrathful judgment; they are destined to achieve salvation through Jesus (at his parousia)" (pp. 68–69).

121. Konradt, *Gericht und Gemeinde*, 188–89.

5.3 Judgment and Salvation in 1 Thessalonians 5:1–11

> [5:1] Now concerning the times (χρόνων) and the seasons (καιρῶν), brothers and sisters, you do not need to have anything written to you. [2] For you yourselves know very well that the day of the Lord (ἡμέρα κυρίου) will come like a thief (κλέπτης) in the night (ἐν νυκτί). [3] When they say, "There is peace and security" (εἰρήνη καὶ ἀσφάλεια), then sudden (αἰφνίδιος) destruction (ὄλεθρος) will come upon them, as labor pains (ἡ ὠδίν) come upon a pregnant woman (τῇ ἐν γαστρὶ ἐχούσῃ), and there will be no escape (ἐκφύγωσιν)! [4] But you, beloved, are not in darkness (σκότει), for that day (ἡμέρα) to surprise you like a thief (κλέπτης); [5] for you are all children of light (υἱοὶ φωτός) and children of the day (υἱοὶ ἡμέρας); we are not of the night (νύκτος) or of darkness (σκότους). [6] So then let us not fall asleep (καθεύδωμεν) as others (οἱ λοιποί) do, but let us keep awake (γρηγορῶμεν) and be sober (νήφωμεν); [7] for those who sleep sleep at night (καθεύδοντες νυκτὸς καθεύδουσιν), and those who are drunk get drunk at night (νύκτος). [8] But since we belong to the day (ἡμέρας ὄντες), let us be sober (νήφωμεν), and put on the breastplate of faith and love (θώρακα πίστεως καὶ ἀγάπης), and for a helmet the hope of salvation (περικεφαλείαν ἐλπίδα σωτηρίας). [9] For God has destined us not for wrath (εἰς ὀργήν) but for obtaining salvation (εἰς περιποίησιν σωτηρίας) through our Lord Jesus Christ, [10] who died for us, so that whether we are awake (γρηγορῶμεν) or asleep (καθεύδωμεν) we may live with him (ἅμα σὺν αὐτῷ ζήσωμεν). [11] Therefore encourage one another and build up each other, as indeed you are doing.

What does this passage contribute to a clarification of 1 Thessalonians' concepts of the future and the judgment? To what extent is the tendency of the overall text maintained (namely, that the community in Thessalonica will be preserved from an end-time wrathful judgment), and what about the fate of the "others" or the "rest" (οἱ λοιποί)? And who are those others? The passage in 1 Thess 5:1–11 needs to be read under those aspects if we are to perceive the outline of its political-social location and the associated worldview regarding its present and hoped-for future. When, at the beginning, 5:1 speaks of the era and point in time when "the day" (v. 2) will come, this suggests an intention to link the content of the previous passage with what follows. The events described in 4:13–17 are thus also among the elements that make up the "day." Now—so we may understand the introductory statement—there is an intention to go deeper into the time when this "day" will appear, which indicates an intention also to announce other events in what follows. That connection, in and of itself, strengthens the supposition that a special, or even a separate eschatological fate of this community is associated with the ἀπάντησις and rapture (4:17).

If, as initially above with regard to 4:13–17, we first attempt to define the relationship of the groups named in this passage, the first thing we notice is that on the whole it is the same entities that appear, at least as regards their critical relationship. But the accents are very different. In 4:13–17 it is first the groups of "we" and "you" and "those who have fallen asleep" who are contrasted; however, this is not to be understood as a confrontation but as a (still preliminary) separation. In the course of the apocalyptic narrative it ultimately comes about that all these partial groups are melded into an all-of-us. That is the goal: "we will be with the Lord forever" (v. 17).

But from beginning to end of the passage one group remained apart, namely, the "others" (οἱ λοιποί), who sorrow and have no hope (4:13). Nothing more is said about them in 4:13–18. That changes sharply in 5:1–11 in that the "others" are suddenly mentioned again in 5:6, making it clear that there will be an extended discussion of the behavior and fate of the group that is diametrically opposed to the unified group of "we" and "you." These are and remain "they," because they are not integrated into the we-group, even at the end. A strict dualism separates the groups "we/you" and "they." "You are" children of light and of the day; "they" belong to darkness and the night (5:5). "They," the others, sleep at night, while "we" desire to stay awake and be sober (5:6). From 5:8 onward it is again only about "us," though the contrast with "them" is maintained by the adversative δέ, "but."

Thus the analysis thus sketched of the two apocalyptic passages, 1 Thess 4:13–18 and 5:1–11, shows that the active groups in them are related to one another; it is only the particular focus that is different. While 4:13–18 is primarily about the fate and salvation of the inner group and all its members, the focus in 5:1–11 is a negatively-characterized outsider group that was only briefly mentioned in the previous passage (at 4:13), whereas 5:1–11 is not sparing in further positive statements about the we-group. This difference in perspective does not separate the passages in 4:13–18 and 5:1–11, but rather binds them together.[122]

5.3.1 The destruction of the "others": 1 Thessalonians 5:1–3

In 1 Thess 5:1–3 the other side of the parousia, the destructive power of the "day of the Kyrios" that unfolds against opponents of the community, is given fuller description. The phrase "day of the Kyrios" (ἡμέρα κυρίου) in 5:2 echoes the tradition of the "day of Yhwh" in the Old Testament,[123] and thus was also familiar

122. Cp. Howard, "Literary Unity," 178: "Instead of presenting two different events, it is suggested that Paul is presenting a *single* eschatological event from two perspectives. In 1 Thessalonians 4:13–18 Paul describes this event as a time of blessing for Christians and hence he uses the term παρουσία whereas in 5:1–3 he describes the judgment this event brings and thus he uses the term ἡμέρα κυριου." For the literary context see also Nicola Wendebourg, *Der Tag des Herrn* (2003), 158.

123. Cp. Isa 13:6, 9; Ezek 7:10, 12; 13:5; Joel 2:1; 3:4; Amos 5:18, 20; Zephaniah 1, and elsewhere.

to Paul. On the other hand, it appears here in a form Paul does not otherwise use.[124] The expression reveals a close kinship to 2 Pet 3:10, a literal parallel, which also simultaneously adds the parable of the thief alongside it: Ἥξει δὲ ἡμέρα κυρίου ὡς κλέπτης ("The day of the Lord will come like a thief").[125]

Thus the coming of the "day of the Kyrios" in 1 Thess 5:1–10 is about an event simultaneous with parousia and rapture, since time, "the times and the seasons" (5:1), as traditionally considered in exegesis, refers to both happenings. And yet there is a certain separation between the events thus announced, since the rescue of the community is the primary subject and the first to be dealt with, in some sense to create a free space for the eschatological destruction of the "others." Now we can see the practical sense of an alternative reception of the ruler, a removal from the earth and the *polis*: in that way the community is sheltered apart from the catastrophic future, in a higher world. Thus the earth and the city are laid open to an unimpeded vengeance on the enemies, with no need for the community to fear being involved and affected by those struggles. As regards the separation of the rescued and the lost, the eschatological plan in 1 Thessalonians reveals a spatial solution on behalf of its own group prior to the final battle. Now the catastrophic and future fate of the opponents can be unmistakably proclaimed within this geographical and chronological frame.

First of all, the other group must be identified as unmistakably as possible. Who are the decidedly "not-you" in 5:3, so clearly surrounded by statements about the you-group in 5:2 and 5:4–5, to which after 5:5 the still larger we-group, the sum of authors and addressees, is added? Rhetorically there is a coherence between those

124. Namely, without the article in association with κύριος. The article is added by A Ψ 0226 μ. Holtz, *Der erste Brief*, 212, concludes from this that we therefore have here a "precise translation of the Hebrew יוֹם יהוה." Elsewhere in Paul there is always the added ἡμῶν with the name of Jesus (1 Cor 1:8; 2 Cor 1:14; Phil 1:6, 10) or ἡμέρα Χριστοῦ (without the article) in Phil 2:16; otherwise frequently ἡμέρα without further additions (Rom 2:16; 8:36; 10:21; 1 Cor 3:13, and elsewhere). In Rom 2:5 it is ἡμέρα ὀργῆς; cp. Holtz, *Der erste Brief*, 212 n. 344; P.-G. Müller, *Der Erste und Zweite Brief an die Thessalonicher* (2001), 190.

125. In 2 Pet 3:4–13 the sudden arrival of the "day," with the image of a thief's attack, serves as a consolation in light of unfulfilled promises and long waiting, a social-historical situation that may be similar to that in 1 Thessalonians; for discussion of this close parallel see, e.g., Harnisch, *Eschatologische Existenz*, 98–113; he sees a literary dependence between the two passages (pp. 110–11) and yet thinks there are fundamental differences. For the parallel between 2 Pet 3:10 and the traditional motif of the thief in Luke 12:29 // Matt 24:43; Rev 3:3; 16:15; *GThom* 21, see also Konradt, *Gericht und Gemeinde* (2003), 139–43 (the motif is said to have "some early Christian parallels, but only distant links to Old Testament-Jewish tradition," p. 139); Christopher D. Stanley, "Who's Afraid of a Thief in the Night?" (2002), 482–83 on 1 Thess 5:3, with social-historical information on thieves and thievery in the ancient world (pp. 472–78) and a gender-critical view of the thief metaphor (pp. 478ff.); and see, e.g., the overview in Luckensmeyer, *Eschatology*, 285.

who talk of "peace and security" (5:3), the "rest" (5:6), and "those who sleep" (5:7),[126] all contrasted absolutely with the insider group. We are thus justified in regarding them as the crucial opposing group whom the language itself locates outside the community.[127] But their special political character is evident as well. The ὅταν λέγωσιν in 5:3, apparently lacking a subject, can, of course, mean "if anyone says," "they say," and seem vague,[128] but the announcement of the destruction that immediately follows, a destruction that will fall upon "them" (αὐτοῖς), is clearly tied to the group to be destroyed. Hence the community's opponents talk of "peace and security." That is, so to speak, the label and distinctive mark by which "you" and "we" can agree on the identity of those who are meant by it.

a. "Peace and Security" (1 Thess 5:3)

What the "others" stand for, the cry of "peace and security," makes them propagandists for the *Pax Romana*, because when they say εἰρήνη καὶ ἀσφάλεια (5:3) they are quoting a slogan of Roman state ideology, common since the early Principate: *pax et securitas*. Though until the 1980s this was scarcely noted in the exegetical literature,[129] it has since been more frequently pointed out, though it is taken as a matter of course that we have here an expression of the apostle's state-critical stance.[130] Independently of the acceptance of Pauline authorship, the

126. Bruce C. Johanson, *To All the Brethren* (1987), 131; cp. Harnisch, *Eschatologische Existenz*, 77–78.

127. Cp. Wengst, *Pax Romana* (1987), 98.

128. Thus, e.g., Marxsen, *Der erste Brief an die Thessalonicher* (1979), 62; Holtz, *Der erste Brief*, 215.

129. See Wengst, *Pax Romana*, 216–17 n. 50. Until then it was usual to seek a location for the expression in the Old Testament prophetic tradition: thus, e.g., Rigaux, *Thessaloniciens*, 558; Harnisch, *Eschatologische Existenz*, 79ff.; Holtz, *Der erste Brief*, 215ff.

130. Cp. Bammel, "Ein Beitrag zur paulinischen Staatsanschauung" (1960), 837: "But *pax et securitas* is the program of the early Principate"; Lindemann, "Christliche Gemeinden und das Römische Reich im ersten und zweiten Jahrhundert" (1985), 115–16: "Words used by the Roman Empire to ideologically glorify its own political mission"; Donfried, "The Cults of Thessalonica," 344: "in 5.3 there is a frontal attack on the *Pax et Securitas* programme of the early Principate"; Wengst, *Pax Romana*, 97–112, at 98: one of "its [the *Pax Romana*'s] most important theses"; Johanson, *To All the Brethren*, 131–32; Koester, "From Paul's Eschatology," 449–50: "political term ... best ascribed to the realm of imperial Roman propaganda"; Faust, *Pax Christi et Pax Caesaris* (1993), 444: εἰρήνη καὶ ἀσφάλεια reflects "the equivalent *pax et securitas* program of the Roman Principate"; cp. Rainer Riesner, *Paul's Early Period* (1998), 357; Koester, "Imperial Ideology and Paul's Eschatology," 161–62; Khiok-Khng, "Political Reading," 81ff., 86; Still, *Conflict at Thessalonica* (1999), 261–66; Harrison, "Paul and the Imperial Gospel," 86–87; then on the whole problem esp. vom Brocke, *Thessaloniki—Stadt des Kassander und Gemeinde des Paulus* (2001), 167–85; Oakes, "Re-mapping the Universe," 317–18; Ströher, "Cuidado com os que proclamam," 62ff.; see also Luckensmeyer, *Eschatology*, 290ff., and Konradt, *Gericht und Gemeinde*, 144ff., who distances himself somewhat from this interpretation.

analysis of this citation permits both conclusions about the political stance of the authors of 1 Thessalonians and their placement within that part of the population that was prepared to resist Rome. The slogan had been known outside Rome since the campaigns of Pompey in the East (66–63 B.C.E.)—the earliest attestation is *PsSol* 8:18[131]—but it was particularly associated with the imperial ideology of Augustus (31 B.C.E.–14 C.E.), which subsequently underlay the Roman ideal of the state. That notion of peace rested fundamentally on military conquest and the forced integration of peoples; Rome's installed military dominance was intended to prevent local conflicts and thus secure "peace." Associated with it was the imperial political, economic, legal, religious, and cultural influence and the corresponding idea of a "pacified" world from the Roman point of view, which developed into an ideally-conceived imperial ideology, as attested by the numerous testimonies of the Roman intellectual elite.[132] The *Pax Romana* "in its expanded breadth, conceptually viewed," corresponded "to each one of the pax-conditions created by victorious battle, secured by the imposition of *ius* and *leges*, and whose effects were regarded as *securitas*, just as, on the other hand, from a historical point of view all battles, victories, and reasons for dominance … were subsumed in it."[133]

The concept of *securitas* is also a fixed element of the *pax* ideology and accordingly is often found on coins, together with the related *concordia*.[134] It is the "deification of the security of public and private life"[135] and thus an expression of the need for security on the part of those who profit from this "peace" and their demand that the maintenance of such an order be understood as a requirement for "inner security," to their own advantage. Thus, for example, Seneca praises "the security of the State" as "the benefits of this peace" that should be made use of (Seneca, *Ep*. 73.2, 5). When 1 Thess 5:3 prophesies the destruction of those who cling to security thus understood, based on Roman peace, that means in the first place the "destruction of the Roman Empire" as a whole,[136] and in relation to the

131. There it is said of Pompey's entrance: εἰσῆλθεν ὡς πατὴρ εἰς οἶκον υἱῶν αὐτοῦ μετ' εἰρήνης, ἔστησεν τοὺς πόδας αὐτοῦ μετὰ ἀσφάλειας πολλῆς; see Faust, *Pax Christi et Pax Caesaris*, 444 n. 42, with further references.

132. Cp. Wengst, *Pax Romana*, 23–68; Schwier, *Tempel und Tempelzerstörung* (1989), 202–50; Faust, *Pax Christi et Pax Caesaris*, 280–314.

133. Harald Fuchs, *Augustin und der antike Friedensgedanke* (1926; 1973), 202, quoted by Schwier, *Tempel und Tempelzerstörung*, 213.

134. Cp. Schwier, *Tempel und Tempelzerstörung*, 202–3; Lindemann, "Christliche Gemeinden und das römische Reich," 116 n. 36; cp. the epigraphical and literary sources in Wengst, *Pax Romana*, 32ff., and vom Brocke, *Thessaloniki*, 176ff., 181ff. for corresponding coin mintings, and 171–76 on *pax et securitas* in Roman literary and historical works, with numerous examples.

135. Abel, art. "Securitas" (1975), 60.

136. Lindemann, "Christliche Gemeinden," 116.

polis of Thessalonica[137] it is practically a declaration of war on the whole of the city and state officialdom as the organs of a Rome-friendly commune, with its representatives and protagonists. In light of the history of the city, which owed its rise and its economic and political status to an early adherence to Octavian Augustus's faction during the civil war, and which enjoyed a thick network of Greco-Roman systems of privilege and patronage,[138] such a critique could only be expressed by critics of or defectors from such a system. That is because the "peace" propagated and executed by civic offices was probably experienced only as "affliction" by those who had to put up with the means employed to "pacify" local conflicts.

We can thus establish a connection between the text's repeated statements about affliction and suffering (1 Thess 1:6; 2:14; 3:3–4) and the hoped-for destruction of those who produced and approved "peace and security" in the Roman sense. The latter's means to that end fell primarily on smaller and larger local groups such as Jewish and Christian communities that roused suspicions of endangering public order in some fashion or that revealed loyalties to other masters, another κύριος.[139] Hence the partisans of the *Pax Romana* condemned to destruction in 1 Thess 5:3 would be none other than the locals (NRSV: "compatriots") who, according to 2:14–17, were putting pressure on the community.[140] The catastrophe prophesied directly or indirectly for the local pagan persecutors in the anti-Jewish passage[141] is thus explicitly described in 5:3.

137. In the first century C.E. Thessalonica was the seat of the Roman proconsul and hence of numerous administrative officials; as a military base it lodged shifting groups of army personnel (Touratsoglou, *Die Münzstätte von Thessaloniki in der römischen Kaiserzeit* [1988], 16); see further vom Brocke, *Thessaloniki*, 83ff. Judith L. Hill, "Establishing the Church of Thessalonica" (1990), 18–70 also offers a good historical and geographical introduction to Thessalonica.

138. For Thessalonica as *civitas libera*, see, e.g., Touratsoglou, *Münzstätte*, 6ff.; Regina Börschel, *Die Konstruktion einer christlichen Identität* (2001), 65ff.; vom Brocke, *Thessaloniki*, 12–20; for the political-religious development of the city and the Battle of Actium as the turning point for an extremely Rome-friendly politics in Thessalonica, see Christopher Steimle, *Religion im römischen Thessaloniki* (2008), 28–56, 201–5: "All these witnesses—building of temples, erection of monuments, games, dating, coinage—taken together show that in the period after the Battle of Actium the city positively outdid itself in greeting the victor" (p. 56). For an overview of the previous participation of the city in Roman privileges and the reverence for Roman benefactors see Hendrix, "Thessalonicans Honor Romans" (1984); idem, "Benefactor/Patron Networks in the Urban Environment" (1992); Steimle, *Religion im römischen Thessaloniki*, 132–40. For more on the history of the city of Thessalonica and the relation of that history to the exegesis of 1 Thessalonians, see 5.5 below.

139. For 1 Thessalonians as a local Christian resistance document see further below at 5.5.2.

140. For the connection of 5:3 to 2:14–17 and the identification of the "compatriots" with the propagandists of the *Pax Romana*, see also Johanson, *To All the Brethren*, 132.

141. See above at 2.5.1 and 2.5.2.

b. The death of the "pregnant" (1 Thess 5:3)

"When they say, 'There is peace and security,' then sudden (αἰφνίδιος) destruction (ὄλεθρος) will come upon them, as labor pains (ἡ ὠδίν) come upon a pregnant woman (τῇ ἐν γαστρὶ ἐχούσῃ), and there will be no escape (ἐκφύγωσιν)!" The suddenness of the destruction corresponds to the unexpected attack in the night associated with the thief metaphor.[142] The coming of the "day" like a thief can also apply to the previously pictured rapture of the believers (4:17). They are unexpectedly and violently snatched out of the earthly-social sphere, "stolen" in the truest sense of the word. An inescapable catastrophe will fall on those who triumph in their reliance on the blessings of the *Pax Romana* and think themselves secure. The picture is of a concrete event to be experienced physically, not a merely metaphysical-spiritual experience of judgment, which places the community's hope within a historical horizon.

The image of childbirth used here is, of course, a common and widely-used motif in apocalyptic texts.[143] In this verse, however, it appears in a purely negative sense.[144] The birth-event is equated solely with a destruction (ὄλεθρος),[145] "eschatological destruction."[146] The pains as necessary and ultimately productive overpowering force, the work of the pregnant woman in giving birth to a new life, and thus the view of childbearing as a transitional stage to a new existence, as

142. Harnisch, *Eschatologische Existenz*, 84–116, presents a broad-based investigation of the thief metaphor in the New Testament literature, designating Luke 12:39–40 // Matt 24:43–44; 2 Pet 3:10; Rev 3:3; 16:15; *GThom* 21b as "substantive parallels" (p. 84); see also the collection in Stanley, "Who's Afraid of a Thief in the Night?" 469–72, which critically illuminates the negative side of the thief metaphor in 1 Thess 5:3 for women's reception of the text (pp. 482–83, 485).

143. Cp. Harnisch, *Eschatologische Existenz*, 62–74, on the birth-motif in OT and Jewish apocalyptic texts; for a feminist exegesis of the motif in the NT and in Jewish apocalypses see Luzia Sutter Rehmann, *Geh, frage die Gebärerin* (1995).

144. Jutta Bickmann, "1 Thessalonians: Opposing Death by Building Community" (2012), 818; cp. also Holtz, *Der erste Brief*, 216ff.; see n. 146 below.

145. In the NT ὄλεθρος always means deadly destruction ("of the flesh" of the man who has committed incest in 1 Cor 5:5; in 1 Tim 6:9 on the same level as ἀπώλεια, "damnation"). It appears again in 2 Thess 1:9, where it is understood as eternal punishment; see 6.2 below.

146. Thus Holtz, *Der erste Brief*, 216ff., who emphasizes the peculiar way in which "the image of birthpangs" is used here. In view of the "terminological and material relationship to Luke 21:24ff." (p. 216), he attempts a tradition-critical explanation, with a focus on a false translation: ὠδίν, "birthpangs" and παγίς, "trap" in Luke 21:35 are supposed to rest on nearly identical Hebrew words that have been confused: חֵבֶל "birthpangs" and חֶבֶל "snare" (ibid., n. 371; cp. Koehler/Baumgartner 271–72). That can remain entirely open here: the derivation of the negative usage of the birth-metaphor is secondary in relation to the intended statement and effect. For the relationship of 1 Thess 5:2–3 and Luke 21:34–36 see further below at 5.3.2.

formulated in Rom 8:22[147] (even though from a male perspective)—none of that is in view in the use of the image in 1 Thess 5:3. Added to this is a largely external perspective on childbearing. The image is used in the sense of an inescapable punishment for the enemies, which implicitly allows for no sort of sympathy for the metaphorical-sounding distress of the woman in pain, but rather the contrary. Since childbearing is equated with destruction there is no room for the additional idea of recovery, which is normally part of birth-imagery. The metaphor is used in such a way that the readers, who desire the punishment of their opponents, must not only reckon with the death—the inevitable death—of the pregnant woman but long for it. This effects a dehumanization of the experience of birth and also of the apocalyptic birth-image, which was again and again capable of depicting the productive dimension of childbearing and, in the case of a loss, the lamentation over it.[148] The position of those who speak here, and of those who are supposed to receive the text affirmatively, is like that of war criminals who treat pregnant women viciously. The birthpang /ἡ ὠδίν is like the soldier's sword that kills. The striking singular form of the noun here is unique in the New Testament.[149] Thus what the "inner eye" sees is not the long and painful process of childbearing and the rhythm of many contractions, but isolated and total destruction by a single blow, expressing a certain alienation from the situations of childbearing and midwifery, altogether different from the background experience Paul expresses in Rom 8:22–23. There is little to indicate that 1 Thess 5:3 is speaking to anyone who has either active or passive experience of childbirth or is accustomed to associate an existential sympathy with it. If that were the case it would not be possible to make use of this image so bluntly, without regard for its social context in experience, solely for prophesying an unconditional and desired destruction of opponents.

The emphasis lies on the unavoidability of the pangs, which resemble an attack that brings those affected to their knees so that flight, avoidance, and escape are

147. In Rom 8:22 Paul uses the verb συνωδίνω, "give birth together (experience birthpangs)." The collective subject is "we" together with all creation; on this see Luise Schottroff, "Befreite Eva" (1988), 110ff.; Sutter Rehmann, *Geh, frage die Gebärerin*, 69–119. For the "profound difference" between Rom 8:22 and 1 Thess 5:3 see Holtz, *Der erste Brief*, 217: here "the birthpangs of the end-time are already universally determinative for the present; according to 1 Thess 5:3 the birthpangs will begin suddenly and destructively on the day of the Lord." In my opinion the very fact of the fundamentally different use of the image of birth in 1 Thess 5:3 and Rom 8:22–23 says definitively that these texts cannot come from the same person.

148. See only 4 Ezra 4:40ff.; 5:46–55; 10:12ff.; on this see Sutter Rehmann, *Geh, frage die Gebärerin*, 160–213; eadem, "4 Ezra: On the Struggle for New Life" (2012), 573–76.

149. Ὠδίν plural in Matt 24:8; Mark 13:8; Acts 2:24. Acts 2:24 equates the "pangs of [Jesus'] death" (τὰς ἡ ὠδίνας τοῦ θανάτου) [which NRSV simply renders "death"] with an ultimately fatal birth whose painful course is, however, "annulled" or "resolved" by God's action and turned into life. In this image God acts as a rescuing midwife. The narrative perspective reflects thanksgiving for a happy outcome.

impossible: *there will be no escape* (ἐκφύγωσιν)! Here again there seems to be an echo of a motif from apocalyptic texts: the distress of pregnant women in flight from the end-time tribulations. In Mark 13:17–18, Matt 24:19–20, and Luke 21:23 we find the same conceptual echoes combined: the "pregnant women" (ταῖς ἐν γαστρὶ ἐχούσαις) and the context of "fleeing" (φευγέτωσαν, Mark 13:14 *parr.*). But in those passages a sympathy with the experience and lament about the fate of pregnant women who have to flee in times of war[150] is in the foreground: "Woe to those who are pregnant and who are nursing infants. . . ." Here the Markan and Matthean versions add a prayer that this not happen in winter or on the Sabbath, so that their flight may ultimately succeed. The perspective is thus that of those who are fleeing and those who are fearful for them and pray for them,[151] whereas in 1 Thess 5:3 the pregnant are surrendered to the view of their pursuers and destroyers, whose whole desire is to violently speed their flight, as well as the onlookers who profit from the event.

Hence in 1 Thess 5:3 the motif of childbearing is used in an unusual and altogether negative manner; it is envisioned as divine vengeance on hostile people in the form of unavoidable death during childbirth. It must be said that this metaphorical fusion and the distress of childbearing women in general, as well as the sufferings of the helpless victims of all wars, pregnant women and those giving birth, together with the children in their wombs, are exploited to illustrate a catastrophic destruction of enemies. A greater distancing from this elementary female and human experience is scarcely possible. The androcentric imagery has acquired additional sexist and sadistic facets, evoked by an unhappy choice of images for the hoped-for destruction of third parties. Within the broader context this prophesied deadly destruction of opposing forces is to be understood as ὀργή, God's judgmental wrath because, differently from these "others," according to 1 Thess 5:9 "we," the authors and the community, are already saved; "we" are not subjected to the "wrath."

5.3.2 "We," the rescued "sons and daughters of light" (1 Thess 5:4–10)

It is no problem at all to separate the perspective of the we-group from the fate of destruction destined for the "others," the fellow-Macedonians oppressing the

150. For the social-historical context of these texts, the only ones in the New Testament to express women's experiences of suffering in the "birthpangs of the end-time" amid the catastrophes of the Jewish War, see Luise Schottroff, *Lydia's Impatient Sisters*, 162–67. She emphasizes that pregnant and nursing women are always the "first casualties of flight" (p. 163) because if they are alone they cannot manage to flee; hence the primary thought is not of the gruesome deeds that may be perpetrated by pursuing soldiers. This is different from the metaphors in 1 Thess 5:3.

151. "Mark 13:17 and par. give visibility to this fundamental patriarchal injustice. . . . In spite of their androcentrism, these apocalyptic texts are sensitive to victims of catastrophes made by human beings. They are in the tradition of Jewish prophecy, which looks first to the victims" (ibid., 167).

community. We find an opposition between night and day; there is a fixed separation of all persons into the realms of darkness and light, and that separation is elaborated more and more in circling repetitions. The *Pax Romana* and those who speak its slogan of "peace and security" belong to the zone of night and darkness.[152] The counter-position in every respect, but especially the political, belongs to the "you-and-we" group, which claims for itself all the contrasting attributes: not-night and not-darkness, that is, day and light, children of light, children of the day, not sleeping and therefore watching, sober people. These concepts are multiply and meanderingly combined in 1 Thess 5:4–8 in order again to separate the day-people from the night-people, to clarify the opposing fronts. All that is added in 5:8 is the picture of taking up weapons, an image into which the "triad of faith, love, and hope . . . has been violently forced."[153] Finally, beginning at 5:9, we can read the sum total of all that it means to belong to the day and the light: God's intention for this group is that it will possess salvation[154] and not divine wrath (οὐκ ἔθετο[155] ἡμᾶς ὁ θεός εἰς ὀργήν). Thus the summary retrospectively classifies the nature of the destruction of the "others" announced in 5:3: it is the divine judgment of wrath. And so the shining fate of the "sons and daughters of light" also appears in monotonous clarity. The wrathful judgment is definitely not for them; they will be set apart from God's judging act. Their position on the side of the saved and preserved seems fully established.[156]

The attempt to combine ethical instruction and admonition with this division and prospect seems awkward and not especially compelling. The choice of such a dominating dualism of light and darkness has its pitfalls, because the one metaphor distorts the other: what is special about being awake in the daytime if one belongs to "the day," after all? It is keeping awake at night that is difficult. Ethical injunction and ontic qualification stand alongside one another here without connection, that is, the ethic is steadily relativized. The metaphors seem especially overloaded in 5:4: "you" are not in darkness, so that the "day" would surprise you like a thief. The *cantus firmus* of the whole passage is: "we" belong in any case to the "day" (5:5), so that when the actual "day of the Kyrios" arrives our group will always be on the day-side, no matter what. Every decision is thus already made. The conceptual tautology matches that of the content.

152. Cp. Wengst, *Pax Romana*, 99–100, 105–6.

153. Friedrich, "1 Thess 5,1–11," 295.

154. Περιποίησις σωτηρίας is more properly "possession" of rescue or salvation than "earning" it; thus, e.g., Rigaux, *Thessaloniciens*, 570–71; Holtz, *Der erste Brief*, 228–29; Lautenschlager, "Εἴτε γρηγορῶμεν," 54 n. 85. The concept, not otherwise present in Paul, appears repeatedly in the late epistolary writings of the NT: 2 Thess 2:14; Eph 1:14; 1 Pet 2:9; Heb 10:39, where we find a dualism and a set of concepts similar to those in 1 Thess 5:9.

155. For τίθεσθαι τινά εἰς τι, "destine someone for something," cp. Holtz, *Der erste Brief*, 228 n. 461. The expression, like many of those in this passage, does not (otherwise) appear in Paul. (See the text above and below.)

156. For this "privileged status of the Christians" based on 1 Thess 5:4–10, see esp. Konradt, *Gericht und Gemeinde*, 156–82.

The text again skates around the resulting consequences of a weakening of the ethical argumentation: since, according to this, it has long since become clear who is on either the "dark" or the "light" side, in essence it is secondary whether one is awake and sober, clothed in the appropriate armor of faith, love, and hope (5:8). Since one belongs to the "day," it is, after all, easy to remain awake and sober, while those belonging to the night-side naturally sleep and are drunk, since it is night and they remain exclusively in that zone (5:7). Hence the matter has long since been decided, the verdict pronounced (5:9).

Hence it is only consequent when 5:10 suddenly speaks of "Jesus Christ, who died for us, so that whether we are awake or asleep (εἴτε γρηγορῶμεν εἴτε καθεύδωμεν) we may live with him." In the context of the imagery this means that it really does not matter whether one can remain awake or sober. If one were to fall asleep, would one not still be on the light side? On the basis of the contextual statement in 5:10, the answer must surely be "yes," because the verbs repeated here point clearly in that direction: γρηγορέω, "stay awake," and καθεύδω, "sleep" are the ethical keywords in the preceding passage and tend to re-emphasize the previous injunctions. Accordingly, the community could even afford to act like the night-side, that is, to "sleep,"[157] without losing its place in the salvific proximity to Jesus.

At the end as at the beginning of the passage in 1 Thess 5:1–11 it is the authors' primary concern to assure the in-group of their own salvation, their rescue. The metaphorical expenditure for that purpose makes the images designating the "good" and the "bad" and the circumlocutions about their respective actions tumble into and over one another. It seems as if the authors were more interested in an ornamental and thus impressive presentation of the underlying material than in a theologically sound and coherent thought process. That, together with the contradictory consequence of ethical indifference in 5:10, raises doubts about whether these phrasings are really among "the most characteristic and most important [products] of the Pauline genius."[158] Gerhard Friedrich is more probably correct in saying that the pericope "is very generalized, contains a great many formulaic expressions, and offers almost nothing but traditional material."[159]

157. Accordingly, the conclusion of Lautenschlager's study ("Εἴτε γρηγορῶμεν") is that "waking" and "sleeping" in 5:10 must be interpreted only within the context, since it cannot be shown that καθεύδω is an image for "sleep of death," as exegetes suppose: God remains "faithful to his saving decision about the Christians even … if they were to fail ethically (καθεύδειν)" (pp. 57–58).

158. Rigaux, "Tradition et Rédaction" (1975), 340 ("un des aspects les plus caractéristiques et les plus importants du génie paulinien").

159. Friedrich, "1 Thess 5,1–11," 292. Friedrich's essay comes to the conclusion that 1 Thess 5:1–11 must be read as an insertion "by a man from the Lukan circle" (p. 309) into the genuine Pauline letter. Besides his (in my opinion accurate) observations on the traditional and theological content of this text, a supposed temporal contradiction to 4:13–17 (pp. 298ff., 309ff.) plays the principal role in his interpolation thesis: there "imminent expectation," here "delay of the parousia."

Friedrich's analysis reveals a patchwork quilt of various traditional phrases and images in 1 Thess 5:1–11. Thus talk of χρόνοι καὶ καιροί in this plural form is common in classical Greek literature and especially in Luke's work (Acts 1:7; 3:20–21), where both terms also appear singly in the plural as well; in Paul this is almost never the case.[160] Besides the traditional images of the birthpangs of the pregnant woman and the thief-motif, which appear especially in the later New Testament writings, the contrast of light and darkness is particularly widespread, not only in Qumran but also in Luke 16:8; John 12:36, and especially in Eph 5:8–14. Equally common and formulaic are the injunction to wakefulness and sobriety in contrast to drunkenness (1 Pet 5:8).[161] The armament is connected to Isa 59:17 and Eph 6:14–17, though 1 Thess 5:8 combines the Pauline pattern of three (faith, love, and hope) quite unorganically and artificially.[162] "If we glance over the few verses in this passage we are astonished to see how many well-worn formulations and time-honored images are used, and how little that is original, concrete, and typically Pauline they contain. What we find here is the common material of Christian *paraclesis*."[163] Add to this the piling up of non-Pauline expressions such as ἀκριβῶς, κλέπτης (as a metaphor; it is used literally only in 1 Cor 6:10), ἀσφάλεια, αἰφνίδιος, ἐφίστημι, ὠδίν, γαστήρ, καθεύδω, μεθύσκομαι, νήφω, θώραξ, περικεφαλεία, περιποίησις, and the frequent deviation from expressions found in Pauline usage.[164]

Still, among the most striking features is the conceptual synchronicity with the apocalyptic passage in Luke 21:34–36:[165] "Be on guard so that . . . that day does not catch you unexpectedly, like a trap (καὶ ἐπιστῇ ἐφ' ὑμᾶς αἰφνίδιος ἡ ἡμέρα . . . ὡς παγίς). . . . Be alert at all times, praying (ἀγρυπνεῖτε δὲ ἐν παντί καιρῷ) that you may have the strength to escape all these things (ἐκφυγεῖν ταῦτα πάντα). . . ." Here we find crowded together the words αἰφνίδιος, ἐφίστημι, ἡμέρα, ἐκφυγεῖν, all literal agreements with 1 Thess 5:2–3; add "keeping awake" with a different word in the broader context.[166] The remarkable similarity of the vocabulary combines with an

160. Ibid., 292–93, 307.

161. For these metaphors, popular "in early Christianity as also in the 'world,'" see also the numerous examples in Dibelius, *An die Thessalonicher*, 29.

162. Friedrich, "1 Thess 5,1–11," 293ff.

163. Ibid., 295.

164. Ibid., 295ff.

165. In addition, we can also see in 1 Thessalonians 4–5 an agreement with numerous motifs and concepts from Synoptic material in the form found in Matthew 24–25. Cp. only the tables and discussion in Howard, "Literary Unity," 180–86; previously esp. Orchard, "Thessalonians and the Synoptic Gospels" (1983), 23–30, which also points to the piling up of synonymous concepts in 1 Thess 2:14–16 and Matt 23:29–38; 24:2b (pp. 20ff.)

166. Cp. Friedrich, "1 Thess 1,1–11," 308; the parallels are emphasized also by, e.g., Frame, *Critical and Exegetical Commentary*, 183; Rigaux, *Thessaloniciens*, 559; idem, "Tradition et Rédaction," 325; Harnisch, *Eschatologische Existenz*, 76 n. 83; Holtz, *Der erste Brief*, 216 (see n. 146 above), where the question of tradition-critical relationships is raised. Lars

equal degree of deviation in both passages. Luke 21:34–35 describes an open apocalyptic situation: the catastrophe will break upon all, but the in-group can escape it by behaving as they are instructed. The result is thus dependent on their own praxis. The question of who may escape thus remains open. In 1 Thess 5:1–11 the catastrophe is meant only for the "others," and nothing is said about flight except in connection with them, although in such a way that flight will be of no avail. The status of the in-group and its ultimate rescue is, in contrast, long settled. The apocalyptic situation is no longer open; everything seems to be determined ahead of time. In short, the static character of 1 Thess 5:1–11 lies in the fact that everything revolves around and is ordered to the certainty of salvation on the part of the in-group in contrast to the destruction of others. There is no trace here of a kind of eschatological thinking that considers the idea of a comprehensive and universal process like that in Rom 8:18–25; 13:11–14,[167] and Luke 21:34–36.

A concluding look at 1 Thess 5:10 must not ignore the connections within the larger context, especially to the preceding passage, 4:13–18. The *opinio communis* in exegesis[168] is that "sleeping" and "waking" are not to be taken literally or, in the immediate context, as attitudes within an eschatological ethic, but again, deviating from that, as metaphors for "living" and "dying," connected to the theme of 4:13–18. Accordingly, "sleeping" / καθεύδω in 5:10 refers to the previous question about the fate of the dead (τοῖς κοιμωμένοις, κοιμηθέντοις, 4:13, 15). Despite the objection that καθεύδω is not used as an image for the sleep of death in Greek literature elsewhere,[169] the repetition in 4:17 of the rare expression ἅμα σύν, "together with" (them, or him, i.e., Jesus)[170] points to a thematic association of these two keywords. Thus the day-night metaphors in 5:1–11 are abandoned and it is once again indicated that it is not crucial for community with Jesus and the

Aejmelaeus, *Wachen vor dem Ende* (1985), in his work on this subject attempts to answer the question by presenting 1 Thess 5:1–11, with its various received traditions, as largely the source for Luke 21:34–36; the gospel gives an "abbreviated paraphrase" of it (see his summary on pp. 131–37). Cp. the discussion in Konradt, *Gericht und Gemeinde*, 154–55 n. 702, who tends, with Richard, *Thessalonians*, 250–52, and others to a dependence of both texts on a common tradition.

167. The passage in Rom 13:11–14 at first seems to contain a metaphoric and thematic content like that of 1 Thess 5:1–9, although at the same time with a very different worldview (cp. Friedrich, "1 Thess 5,1–11," 305ff.). The "night" in the Romans text is not simply attached to one group of people; it is the ambience and space-time also of believers, out of which they begin to move into the new eon. For this difference between Rom 13:11–14 and 1 Thess 5:1–9 see also Konradt, *Gericht und Gemeinde*, 161–62.

168. See only Siber, *Mit Christus leben*, 59–67, who also works out the content-links to 1 Thess 4:13–18.

169. Lautenschlager, "εἴτε γρηγορῶμεν," esp. 40–50 (see n. 157 above).

170. Ἅμα σύν is not found elsewhere in the NT; cp., e.g., Holtz, *Der erste Brief*, 232 (and n. 493), who argues for a "deliberate adoption" of 4:17 (with simultaneous shift in meaning), and also Konradt, *Gericht und Gemeinde*, 179.

associated communion with all who belong to Christ whether one is alive or has already died.

For that reason I believe that the intent of 1 Thess 5:10, similarly to 4:17, is to say a great many things "simultaneously," despite all the contradictions that arise from the immediate context in 5:1–11. In this verse "we" achieves a comprehensiveness that encompasses and relativizes all existing differences: those in ethical behavior, and in the addressees as well as the senders being dead or alive. This once again achieves something that was already attained by the distinguishing "we" in 4:13–17:[171] for the communion of believers with one another, and for the community of the addressees and senders, it is ultimately unimportant which of them are still living and which have died; it is unimportant whether "Paul, Silvanus, and Timothy" are still alive or whether they are all already dead. If this is a pseudepigraphical writing that would be a way of achieving a transparency and combination of all time-levels and fates of the people concerned, who all are counted on the "we" side. That is the decisive consolation, pointing to parallel formulations about mutual consolation in 4:18 and 5:11 that conclude their respective passages.

5.4 The Three-Part Depiction of Judgment in 1 Thessalonians

Following the analysis of the political aspects of 1 Thess 2:14–17 in chapter 2 and the corresponding discussion of 1 Thess 4:13–5:11 in this fifth chapter, we are now in a position to describe the specific vision of judgment in the first letter to the Thessalonians. This involves both the underlying views of the authors about the fate of individual groups and peoples and the associated hopes for their own group.

The concept of eschatological judgment in the first letter to the community in Thessalonica is indicated by the use and context of the concept of ὀργή, "wrath" or "wrathful judgment." It conveys a clear threefold idea of God's eschatological act of judgment. According to this,

- "the Jews" are already handed over to divine wrath and have also experienced judgment, an idea unmistakably conveyed by the statement in 2:16 in the aorist;[172]

171. See 5.1.2 and 5.1.2b above, as well as 6.3.2 below for the different life-levels in a pseudepigraphical letter. We can discover another passage in which the time-levels of the fictional and real situations of writing are transparent, namely, in 1 Thess 3:8: "For we now live (again), if you continue to stand firm in the Lord." On the level of the early community letter to Thessalonica that would mean a momentary upward swing in the mood of the letter-writers (which is also the common interpretation, though focused on Paul alone); on the level of later recipients of the pseudepigraphical writing it would indicate a revival of the memory and legacy of their apostles.

172. See 2.5.2 above.

- "the others," namely, the non-Jewish persecutors and compatriots of the community, will undergo God's judgment in the future, as the implicit prophecy based on 2:14–17 says.[173] Added to this is the succinct portrayal of the sudden and unavoidable "destruction" of the opponents in 5:3, which, in connection with 5:9, is to be understood as an expression of God's ὀργή;[174]
- as for the "you/we" group made up of community and apostles, they will miraculously escape the ὀργή and so are exempt from the wrathful judgment. This appears from a combined view of the statements about rescue from the "wrath that is coming" in 1:10,[175] the rapture of the community according to 4:17, which will remove them from the place where the opponents are being destroyed,[176] and the summary in 5:9 that absolves the in-group from experiencing the wrath: it is not meant for "us."[177] The community enjoys the privilege of an exclusive rapturing away from all struggles. The overall impression of a predetermined end-time rescue of the community cannot be seriously dampened by the allusion to God's avenging act in 4:6.[178] Likewise, the formulae about an ultimate irreproachable and worthy appearance of the community before God, or at Christ's parousia, in 2:12, 19; 3:13; 5:23, which are occasionally read as references to a judgment that will affect the community,[179] ultimately express nothing but the firm expectation that God has no objection to raise against the community. According to the overall picture in 1 Thessalonians it will be protected in time, and above all in space, beyond or between the zones in which the wrath of God has already been unloaded on the Jews and in future will rush upon non-Jewish people who are hostile to the community and oppress it.[180]

173. Cp. 2.5.2 above.

174. Cp. 5.3.1 and 5.3.2 above.

175. Cp. 5.2.4 above.

176. Cp. 5.2.3 above.

177. Cp. 5.3.2 above.

178. Cp. 5.2.4 above.

179. Thus, e.g., Brandenburger, art. "Gericht Gottes," 475: "the brief keyword 'before' (ἔμπροσθεν) God or Kyrios Jesus (1 Thess 2,19; 3,13) signals such a judicial proceeding before the (heavenly) throne"; cp. Synofzik, *Die Gerichts- und Vergeltungsaussagen bei Paulus* (1977), 16–30. To the contrary, Konradt asserts: "1 Thess 2:19–20 and 3:13 have nothing to do with a judgment scenario" (*Gericht und Gemeinde*, 182–87, 193, at 186).

180. Cp. what von Dobschütz writes (*Die Thessalonicherbriefe*, 212) about 1 Thess 5:9: "The non-Christian world falls victim to the wrathful judgment . . . but the Christians (ἡμᾶς . . .) are certain that they are destined to achieve salvation." Likewise Konradt, *Gericht und Gemeinde*, 181–82: "The judgment of the non-Christians and the designation of believers for salvation are pointedly contrasted in 5:1–11 (see esp. 5:9). . . . The direction of the judgment statement thus links organically to 2:14–16."

This reveals the specific concept of God's end-time judgment in 1 Thessalonians as a production in several acts.[181] What takes place in it is a corresponding separation in time and space between the peoples and groups.

5.5 The Place of 1 Thessalonians as a Pseudepigraphical Letter: The Resistance of the Christian Community of Thessalonica

First let us look back briefly at the results thus far gained, pointing to a new view of the first letter to the Thessalonians. As a pseudepigraphical writing by the three apostles Paul, Silvanus, and Timothy, who, shortly after the founding of this local community, cast a lengthy glance back at the successful foundation, the text serves in outstanding fashion to provide a written proof of the apostolic foundation and importance of the community and thus its present existence, as well as being an ideal foundation for its endurance to the time of writing (chaps. 1–3). What remains questionable is the future (chaps. 4–5). That is not (i.e., no longer) marked by the possibility of an apostolic visitation, as the above analysis of the mission vocabulary and the absence of concrete plans for further contact has shown.[182] It is no longer a subject for discussion because it lies outside the reality of 1 Thessalonians as a pseudepigraphical letter, which, in addition to the purpose just indicated, must and will deal also with problems existing at the time of writing. These problems are connected to the death of members of the community, a question that is becoming more and more urgent as time goes on, so that those still living are being gradually forced into the position of a "remnant," "those who are left," in relation to the dead of the first generation. This, together with the sufferings alluded to, raises questions about a hope for all of them. That hope is the future of the coming of Christ and communion with him, which will only be accomplished at that time. An idea like the one Paul expresses, of the community as the body of Christ (Rom 12:4–7; 1 Cor 12:12–30), according to which communion with one another and simultaneously with Kyrios Jesus is being lived *now*, is foreign to 1 Thessalonians.

181. See the results of Konradt's study (*Gericht und Gemeinde*, 23–196, summarized on 181–96): "On the contrary, in none of the passages named is the idea of a wrathful judgment directed as a threat at Christians. The references to God's punishment in 1:10; 2:16; 5:3, 9 have, instead, a stabilizing function. Those affected by it are the opponents of the community (2:16; 5:3), while the Christians are assured that they will be rescued by Jesus (1:10; 5:9–10)" (p. 191). See also the compositional placement and linkage of two statements about judgment in 1 Thessalonians (indicated by Bornemann, *Die Thessalonicherbriefe* [1894], 119), which thus indirectly point to the separate concepts of judgment: "We should also note that while the first section in the letter about the outlook for Christians concluded that they are rescued by Jesus from the coming wrath's falling upon them (1:10), the second, about the history of the Jews, judges that divine wrath has come upon them to the very end (2:16). This divine justice, too, is a consolation for the believers in Thessalonica."

182. Cp. 3.2.3 and 3.2.5 above.

The time of bodily experience of Christ lies solely in the future. Only that future will reveal a being-with-Christ, and besides, it will happen not on earth but in the airy realms. The destruction of the opponents, on the other hand, will take place on earth as a wrathful judgment, just as prior to that the judgment on the Jewish people must take place on earth and in earthly time; indeed, it is supposed to have happened already.

If it is possible that the intended statement of a pseudepigraphical 1 Thessalonians consists primarily in affirming apostolic foundation, confirming the history and existence of this ideal community, and the achievement of current hope by means of a specific depiction of the parousia and the associated theory of judgment, we should ask about the place where it may have originated. An interest in an ideal narrative about the apostolic community in Thessalonica, of course, lies there, in the city and the remaining community itself. Richard Bauckham and Mario Frenschkowski, in the context of pseudepigraphy research concentrated mainly on the Pastorals, have proposed the thesis that one can sometimes deduce the actual author of the text from the addressee of a pseudepigraphical letter—in their case, Timothy.[183] Likewise in the case of the Thessalonian correspondence this could provide a key for discovering the origin(s) of the author(s): "The fictive addressee then coincides with the real author."[184] Thus Regina Börschel suspects that the pseudepigraphical 2 Thessalonians comes from Thessalonica itself: we should assume "that 2 Thessalonians stems from the context of the community in Thessalonica and is addressed to that community as well."[185] I think we should also suspect that 1 Thessalonians was composed in the same place, above all because of the local color in it, as I will discuss below. The political features of the writing could thus be interpreted in terms of the local circumstances. Previous attempts to interpret the individual features of the text against the background of the history and archaeology of the city of Thessalonica[186] must be regarded as methodologically problematic because of their starting point; hence Helmut Koester's critique of too-hasty linkings of individual words and phrases in the letter to the local

183. Bauckham, "Pseudo-Apostolic Letters" (1988), 494; Frenschkowski, "Pseudepigraphie und Paulusschule" (2001), 263–70; cp. Zimmermann, "Unecht—und doch wahr?" (2003), 34.

184. Zimmermann, "Unecht—und doch wahr?" 34.

185. Börschel, *Die Konstruktion einer christlichen Identität*, 62–63; quotation on p. 368; so also Taesong Roh, *Der zweite Thessalonicherbrief als Erneuerung apokalyptische Zeitdeutung* (2007), 22–27 and *passim*.

186. E.g., Jewett, *Thessalonian Correspondence* (1986), who links the enthusiastic movement in Thessalonica he posits with the local Cabirus cult; Kloppenborg, "ΦΙΛΑΔΕΛΦΙΑ" (1993; see 3.3.2 n. 41 above); see also the works of Donfried, "The Cults of Thessalonica" and "The Assembly of the Thessalonians" (1996), and that of Oakes, "Re-mapping the Universe," who sees 1 Thessalonians and Philippians as conflicting with Roman imperial ideology; see further below in this section.

situation.[187] This is especially true if one has to assume, in terms of the usual historical location, that the letter was written after the founding visitation, which had been hurriedly interrupted—that is, after Paul's first and thus far only contact with the Thessalonians (1 Thess 2:18). In that case Paul could scarcely have been intimately acquainted with local traditions, cults, and politics. The chances for that kind of interpretive starting point, of course, look very different if, as in this study, one supposes that 1 Thessalonians is more a product of the community in Thessalonica than of Paul. The very possibility that it originated in that place makes it more justified to connect the history of the city of Thessalonica and its organizations with the significant political vocabulary of the text.

Such a methodology is related to that of Gerd Theissen, who has used social-historical methods for the interpretation of the Synoptic Gospels in his *The Gospels in Context*, positing a possible connection between the origins of the texts and the local and contemporary conditions in the land of Israel in the Roman period. "I understand the investigation of cultural context to mean the effort to evaluate biblical texts in terms of localizable data, in such a way that text and land, including the archeological remains found there, shed light on one another."[188] Unlike the questions of place of origin of the gospels and the traditions they record, not easily determined in this way, in the case of 1 Thessalonians its rootedness in this particular Macedonian city on the Gulf of Thermae presents a much more secure basis for interpretation. Above all, we may assume that the people at the origins of this text consciously or unconsciously stood, when writing of current topics and conflicts, on the ground of a known history of the city and region, and that they also stood within the struggle over an existential confession of their Kyrios Jesus and holding fast to him in conflict with the deities and political authorities who dominated their city. Starting there, in what follows we will look again at certain concepts in 1 Thessalonians, by way of an initial sketch of the political resistance of a Gentile Christian community that can be discerned in it. It is significant that nearly all the concepts in 1 Thessalonians that allude to the political sphere are different from the Pauline vocabulary and usage in the other letters attributed to him:

First, we come back to the address to the community with the *nomen gentilicum* in the prescript at 1 Thess 1:1, unique within the Corpus Paulinum: τῇ ἐκκλησίᾳ

187. Koester, "Archäologie und Paulus in Thessalonike" (1994), 396: "They try to make use of facts determined by archaeology to anchor New Testament texts in a particular historical situation and a limited locality; this is nothing more than a continuation of 'biblical archaeology'"; cp. idem, "From Paul's Eschatology," 441ff.

188. Gerd Theissen, *The Gospels in Context* (1991), 9; for method in general see the Introduction, pp. 1–23; for the nuances in dealing with the factors of "cultural context," "local tradition," "cultural milieu," "time factor," and "local archaeological remains," see ibid., 9–12.

Θεσσαλονικέων, "the community of the Thessalonians."[189] By the fact that here, differently from all other Pauline prescripts, there is no prepositional qualification such as "the community *in* (ἐν)" Thessalonica (or Rome, Rom 1:7; Corinth, 1 Cor 1:1, 2 Cor 1:1; Philippi, Phil 1:1), the Christian community, as "the community of the Thessalonians," is nominally equated with the political community, the citizen assembly of the *polis*. What could be the backgrounds[190] for such a linguistic identification? First of all, the phrase is well-designed to signal, as we have noted above (3.3.2), that the Christian community in this city is to be portrayed as impressively numerous, since apparently it consists of practically all the inhabitants. Such an entity would be without peer in Macedonia or anywhere in Greece, for the port city of Thessalonica apparently contained something on the order of 100,000 inhabitants within and outside its walls in the first century C.E.[191] An important city contains an important community; that would be one of the implicit messages of the unusual formula. Another could be: the Christian congregation represents the unique, true, and legitimate citizen assembly; it stands against the claim of the pagan inhabitants and their administrative organs to represent the city. Associated with this would be the arbitrary claim both to refer to their own Kyrios by name as the true Kyrios of this commune and to proclaim his lordship over it, which was equivalent to a crime against the state. That is exactly what happens in the first verse of the letter, 1 Thess 1:1: the community, which apparently consists of all the inhabitants of Thessalonica, exists "in God the Father and the Kyrios Jesus

189. Cp. 3.3.2 above. For the social-historical background of the concept of ἐκκλησία see Ekkehard and Wolfgang Stegemann, *The Jesus Movement* (1999), 262–64: the term "gained its usefulness in early Christianity because it designated an assembly both in Jewish and Greek culture" (p. 263). See also, *ad loc*, the references to the usage in Acts, where both political (Acts 19:32, 39, 41) and Christ-believing (Acts 11:26; 14:27) assemblies are described with the same word.

190. Donfried, "The Assembly of the Thessalonians," 390ff., poses this question in regard to the ecclesiology of 1 Thessalonians. He links it to a deliberate intention on the part of Paul to make a political statement, against the background of Thessalonian archaeology, although he does not speak of resistance or anything like it (see below).

191. Riesner, *Paul's Early Period*, 340–41, for the archaeologically indicated extent of the Greco-Roman city: Thessalonica "because of this total population doubtless was counted among the preeminent larger cities in the Roman empire" (p. 341); similarly Hill, "Establishing the Church of Thessalonica," 45–49: "an approximate population figure of 75,000 to 100,000 for first-century Thessalonica" (p. 48). Vom Brocke, *Thessaloniki*, 71ff., is critical of Riesner; he reckons with at most 40,000 inhabitants in the first century C.E.; Steimle, *Religion im römischen Thessaloniki*, 202–5, tends to the same opinion, though emphasizing the remarkable growth of the city in the Roman imperial period. For the topography of the city in the later Roman period see Vickers, "Towards Reconstruction of the Town Planning of Roman Thessaloniki" (1970).

Christ."[192] Their Kyrios is the Kyrios of all Thessalonica; that is the meaning of the statement on one level. A sharper affront to the Rome-oriented leadership, government, and associated cultic-religious structure of the city is scarcely imaginable.[193]

The people of the city were in daily contact with the inscription "ΘΕΣΣΑΛΟΝΙΚΕΩΝ" stamped on all the bronze coins in circulation, which Thessalonica, as an autonomous city with its own coinage, had been allowed to mint, with permission of the Roman overlords, since 32/31 B.C.E.[194] There were, throughout, two genres of issues: (1) "those with a portrait of the current emperor or a member of the imperial family on the obverse of the coins" and (2) those that "in place of a ruler's portrait showed the bust of the Tyche of the city, a Cabirus or a Nike, or very general motifs that could be regarded as expressions of the 'autonomy' of a city." The latter are called "pseudo-autonomous coins" in professional literature.[195] These pseudo-autonomous coins bear symbols of the city and Greek tradition and are thus an expression of regional independence; the numbers in circulation were only half as great as those of the imperial coins. In addition, both kinds were always on the market simultaneously, and the stamping of the imperial coins reveals a close dependency of the city on the minting city of Rome, since the portraits of the rulers are copies of those on the imperial coinage.[196] Hence it is not really justifiable to interpret the existence of pseudo-autonomous coins as the city's "normative coinage" and thus as an expression of its weak participation in the imperial cult in the first two post-Christian centuries.[197] In Thessalonica, too, imperial propaganda in the form of the coins produced there,

192. This ἐν θεῷ πατρί, the existence of the community "in" God the Father, appears in no other prescript of a Pauline letter; elsewhere the blessing of peace "from God our Father" is formulated with the preposition ἀπό: Rom 1:7; 1 Cor 1:3; 2 Cor 1:2; Gal 1:3; Phil 1:2; Phlm 3. On this see also Donfried, "The Assembly of the Thessalonians," 393–94: "This is in striking contrast to the coinage of ancient Thessalonica! Because these Thessalonians are 'in God' and 'in the Lord Jesus Christ' they are not like pagans 'who do not know God' (4:5)."

193. See Deissmann, *Light from the Ancient East*, for the "polemical parallelism between the cult of Christ and the cult of Caesar in the application of the term κύριος, 'lord'" (p. 353). "And then we cannot escape the conjecture that the Christians of the East who heard St. Paul preach in the style of Phil. ii. 9, 11 and 1 Cor. viii. 5,6 must have found in the solemn confession that Jesus Christ is 'the Lord' a silent protest against other 'lords,' and against 'the lord,' as people were beginning to call the Roman Caesar" (p. 359).

194. For what follows cp. Touratsoglou, *Münzstätte*, 20–24. For the different ways of writing the *ethnikon* in the genitive plural on the coin inscriptions see ibid., 115–16. According to this, during individual reigns coins appeared simultaneously and alternatingly with the legends ΘΕΣΣΑΛΟΝΙΚΕΩΝ, ΘΕΣΣΑΛΟΝΙΚΕΙΩΝ, ΘΕΣΣΑΛΟΝΕΙΚΑΙΩΝ, and/or ΘΕCCΑΛΟΝΙΚΕΩΝ, etc.

195. Touratsoglou, *Münzstätte*, 20.

196. Cp. ibid., 20–23.

197. Thus Koester, "Archäologie und Paulus," 399.

apparently out of loyalty, was massively present. "Coins are the oldest means of mass communication—in antiquity the only medium through which powerful political figures could reach almost all their subjects. The images on coins reflect political programs."[198]

To take one of the many imperial-portrait coins from Thessalonica into one's hand is literally to grasp the official relationship to the ruling power under which the citizens stood. In particular, the early minting of a Julius Caesar coin under Augustus (ca. 28–27 B.C.E.) impresses because of the divinized image of the emperor: on the obverse is the laurel-crowned head of Julius Caesar with the legend ΘΕΟΣ / "GOD," and on the reverse the head of Octavian/Augustus with the legend ΘΕΣΣΑΛΟΝΙΚΕΩΝ.[199] Since this is the first coin struck at Thessalonica under the regime of Augustus after the Battle of Actium, which made him the sole ruler, the city thus venerates the Emperor's political program by adopting the divinization of Julius Caesar in propagandistic form. This means that Thessalonica also proclaims Caesar as its own god. By this means the political community of the Θεσσαλονικέων is united, by the two sides of a coin, with the worship of the divine emperor. Hence we can read rejection and resistance in the prescript to 1 Thessalonians when the community of the Θεσσαλονικέων is oriented to another θεός than the divine emperor, namely, "God the Father and the Kyrios Jesus Christ."

It is true that subsequent mintings with other imperial portraits on the coins of the first century C.E. did not at first replicate the title ΘΕΟΣ; other titles dominated, such as ΣΕΒΑΣΤΟΣ for Augustus and his successors.[200] But that does not mean that the deification of the Roman emperor in that city receded into the background. It was constantly present in the cityscape and in public life. Toward the end of the first century, under Domitian, there was a new issue of the Julius-Caesar-god coin, this time in greater numbers. This was a memorial- and jubilee-coin for the divine emperor on the occasion of the 125th anniversary of his death (81 C.E.), or the dedication of his temple in Rome (96 C.E.).[201] Thessalonica had had a temple for Caesar since the early part of Augustus's reign, and hence an official cult with its own priests, and a temple for the goddess Roma with a corresponding cult for the Roman benefactors of the city. The inscriptions attest that, among his other titles, Augustus was called "god" and "son of god." Sporting contests and games were

198. Theissen, *The Gospels in Context*, 29.

199. Touratsoglou, *Münzstätte*, 24ff. (with bibliography), catalogue nos. 140–144. Cp. Hendrix, "Thessalonicans honor Romans," 170ff.; Helmut Koester and Holland L. Hendrix, eds., *Archaeological Resources for New Testament Studies* I (1987), Thessaloniki 21; Harrison, "Paul and the Imperial Gospel," 81–82; Oakes, "Re-mapping the Universe," 308. Considering the Julius-Caesar-Theos coin alongside the prescript in 1 Thess 1:1 inspired Donfried in particular ("The Assembly of the Thessalonians," 391ff.) to a political interpretation.

200. Cp. Touratsoglou, *Münzstätte*, Catalog nos. 14ff. However, Livia appears as a goddess on Thessalonian coins, with the inscription ΘΕΑ ΛΙΒΙΑ or ΘΕΟΥ ΛΙΒΙΑ (ibid., 28, Catalog no. 147).

201. Ibid., 42–43, Catalog nos. 182–185.

staged in his honor, and to celebrate the victory at Actium, until the second third of the first century C.E.[202] Attesting also to the eager willingness of the magistrates of Thessalonica to develop ever-new forms of divine worship of the Roman emperor over time is the veneration of the peculiar god Fulvus, who seems to have been a son of Marcus Aurelius who was divinized after his death at the age of four (165 C.E.). This god, too, had young men (ephebes) as his priests, and festal games in Thessalonica; it appears that the cult flourished for sixty years after Fulvus's death.[203] Overall, the official representatives of the *polis* of Thessalonica seem to have been characterized, from the beginnings of Roman rule and for a long time afterward, by an impressive enthusiasm for spending remarkable sums of money on the worship of rulers.

Against the background of these politico-religious structures, the political allusions in 1 Thessalonians look like the program of an anti-community that drew boundaries between itself and the strong traditional and omnipresent worship of the imperial potentates, their local officialdom and priesthoods—in short, all "outsiders" (4:12). It is prepared for repression on this account from the other side (2:14). It confesses a different God, a different Son of God, and it is preparing for a ruler's parousia of its own particular Kyrios. Its program for his visitation differs from that of the emperors and their followers. At his ἀπάντησις, the welcoming of the noble guest before the city, something remarkable will occur: the citizens will be snatched away from the city and its devotion to the Roman ruler-deities, with its officials, priests, soldiers, and the threat they pose (4:17). Finally, the formula *pax et securitas* / εἰρήνη καὶ ἀσφάλεια (5:3) is used to point to the local culture of Thessalonica, because its profound devotion to and early partisanship for Octavian/Augustus had placed it to a special degree under the influence of his imperial *pax* ideology, used as propaganda to shore up his support during the period of his Principate in all parts of the Empire: Augustus had himself celebrated as the bringer of peace; that was the real foundation of the imperial cult

202. IG X/2, nos. 31, 32, 131–33, thoroughly described and discussed in Edson, *Macedonica* (1940), 130–35, and in Hendrix, "Thessalonicans Honor Romans," 106ff., 116–39; cp. Evans, *Eschatology and Ethics* (1968), 65ff.; Donfried, "The Cults of Thessalonica," 344ff.; Touratsoglou, *Münzstätte*, 8ff. (with bibliography); Harrison, "Paul and the Imperial Gospel," 81–82, 88–95 (on the cult of Augustus in the East), as well as Elliger, *Paulus in Griechenland*, 96ff., who emphasizes the special place of the imperial cult in Thessalonica. For the imperial temple to Augustus, which must have been relocated into the city from outside it at the beginning of the Augustan era, and for the imperial shrines in the forum, with corresponding inscriptions, see also Vom Brocke, *Thessaloniki*, 138ff.

203. Touratsoglou, *Münzstätte*, 14–15; Edson, *Macedonica*, 135–36; Hendrix, "Thessalonicans Honor Romans," 323ff., and esp. Steimle, *Religion im römischen Thessalonica*, 142–56, with an image of the corresponding inscriptions; from the evidence this ephebe-cult existed only in Thessalonica.

of his person and his successors.[204] Against this background it is again very clear to what degree the text of 1 Thessalonians opposes the concrete representatives of the worship of the Roman "benefactor" that distinguished Thessalonica from the days of Augustus (but even as early as the second century B.C.E.),[205] and how much it desires their ruin and destruction.

The conclusion must be that the first letter to the community in Thessalonica can be read as a local resistance document against Rome, assuring it of the founders' approving support of the community's existential struggle. The fictional letter speaks to an actual situation, aiming to console the community and prepare it for the coming rescue by Kyrios Jesus of those who in the meantime have died, together with those still alive, and encouraging it to persevere. The expressions about resistance and hope for the destruction of the local oppressors are provided at the expense of self-protective denunciations directed against the Jewish people. The "Jews" function in the writing as an alien group. The letter asserts that God's wrath has already fallen on them and draws from that an assured consolation that current, non-Jewish persecutors will be destroyed in the end. Jewish people, associated solely with the province of Judea, serve the "Gentile Christian" community in a sense as "straw men." The addressees are invited to join with current Greco-Roman propaganda, on the one hand to denounce Jews as genuine enemies of the state (a group that also includes the community's own enemies), and on the other hand to draw attention away from their own role as outsiders. Against the background of the dangerous practices of denunciation in the first-century Roman Empire, the passage in 1 Thess 2:14–17 reads like a polished bill of indictment that, based on the seriousness of the accusations of misanthropy and godlessness raised against Judaism, can really only lead to juridical condemnation and ultimately to the penalty of death.[206]

The text of 1 Thessalonians as a whole, on the other hand, reveals no hint of a common life and fate shared with Jewish people.[207] That is, it has no interest in reflecting a common life joining people of Jewish and non-Jewish background in the communities; instead, it distances itself from that nation and its members. When a Jewish catastrophe is taken as a sign of hope for a pagan Christian

204. Cp. Schwier, *Tempel und Tempelzerstörung*, 202–18, esp. 210ff. Vom Brocke, *Thessaloniki*, 178–84, emphasizes that a majority in the *polis* of Thessalonica, because of its history with Rome, adopted the *pax et securitas* slogan in positive fashion; he also indicates the contrary claims of 1 Thess 5:3 (pp. 184–85).

205. On this see Hendrix, "Thessalonicans Honor Romans," 189–255.

206. Cp. Luise Schottroff, "Die Gegenwart in der Apokalyptik der synoptischen Evangelien," (1983/1990), 84, and above at 2.4.1 *passim*.

207. What Wolfgang Trilling regards as an indication of the non-Pauline authorship of 2 Thessalonians applies completely to 1 Thessalonians as well: there is "in the whole letter not even a weak indication ... that the communities are made up of Jews and Gentiles, and that the church has grown together as a community of Jews and Gentiles" (*Untersuchungen zum 2. Thessalonicherbrief* [1972], 112).

community, the obvious impression conveyed is one of de-solidarization and complete detachment from the fate of Israel. Within Jewish-Christian history this writing represents the extreme of the utmost alienation and distance between "Gentile Christian" and Jewish people. Moreover, there are no signs of existential ties with the Jewish-Christian communities in Judea mentioned in 1 Thess 2:14 such as those initially constructed by Paul's great work of creating solidarity through the collection for the Jewish-Christian community in Jerusalem, and the authors give no indication whatsoever that they themselves possess a Jewish identity. The local "Christian" resistance movement in Thessalonica does not see Rome as an enemy it shares with broad parts of Judaism, including the local Jewish synagogue communities.[208] Judaism, as a beaten group, is essentially equated with the imperial state and its structures now being combatted, in the hope that the latter will soon be cut down like the former, the Jewish people, who in the opinion of the authors have been judged by God.

Does 1 Thess 2:16 allude to a concrete historical catastrophe that has befallen Judaism, and in that case, which one? If we suppose a pseudepigraphical post-apostolic composition, there is scarcely any way not to see this as a reference to the conquest and destruction of Jerusalem by Vespasian and Titus in 70 C.E. and its consequences. In any case, however, that Jewish catastrophe had happened close in time to the post-apostolic 2 Thessalonians and within its political perspective. We will now turn our attention to that letter and its alternative eschatological proposal.

208. See, e.g., 4 Ezra 3:27–36; 5:3; 10:21–24.

Chapter 6

Judgment in Second Thessalonians: The Relationship of the Two Letters

The relationship of 2 Thessalonians to 1 Thessalonians is that of the most unusual pair of writings and their connections within the New Testament. It is unique in the sense that, if we think through the pair consistently, we come to the conclusion that the second letter (especially 2 Thess 2:2; 3:17) pronounces the pseudepigraphical character of the first.[1] This would make 2 Thessalonians the first and oldest challenger to the authenticity of 1 Thessalonians, and the one closest to it in terms of its origins. Accordingly, the discussion of the genuineness of 1 Thessalonians began in the last years of the first century C.E.

6.1 *The Purpose of 2 Thessalonians as a Pseudepigraphical Writing*

Since the influential study by William Wrede, the nearly indisputable principal argument for the pseudepigraphical character of 2 Thessalonians has existed in the form of a persuasive examination: the authors of 2 Thessalonians used 1 Thessalonians as a literary model;[2] it must practically have lain "on the

1. Thus esp. Lindemann, "Zum Abfassungszweck des Zweiten Thessalonicherbriefes" (1977); see further below.

2. See the listing and pairing of the parallels in Wrede, *Die Echtheit des zweiten Thessalonicherbriefs untersucht* (1903), 4–12, 19, 24–27. The authenticity of 2 Thessalonians was previously questioned (besides F. C. Baur and his school, for which see 4.1 above as well as Trevor Thompson, "As If Genuine'" [2009], 473–81) by, among others, J. E. Chr. Schmidt, "Vermuthungen über die beiden Briefe an die Thessalonicher" (1801); F. H. Kern, "Ueber 2 Thess. 2,1–12" (1839); Adolf Hilgenfeld, "Die beiden Briefe an die Thessalonicher" (1862); Christian Rauch, "Zum zweiten Thessalonicherbrief" (1895); Heinrich J. Holtzmann, "Zum zweiten Thessalonicherbrief" (1901); cp. the remarks on the history of research on the topic by Ernst von Dobschütz, *Die Thessalonicherbriefe* (1909), 32ff.; Béda Rigaux, *Saint Paul: Les Épîtres aux Thessaloniciens* (1956), 124–52); Ernest Best, *A Commentary on the First and Second Epistles to the Thessalonians* (1972), 50ff.; Wolfgang Trilling, *Untersuchungen zum. 2. Thessalonicherbrief* (1972), 11–45; idem, *Der zweite Brief an die Thessalonicher* (1980), 22ff.; idem, "Die beiden Briefe des Apostels Paulus an die Thessalonicher. Eine Forschungsübersicht" (1987); Paul-Gerhard Müller, *Der Erste und Zweite Brief an die Thessalonicher* (2001), 227ff.; Edgar Krentz, "A Stone that Will not Fit" (2009), 438ff.

desk."[3] This procedure makes it seem improbable—or, better, impossible—that the document goes back to the historical Paul. "The two letters agree not only in individual expressions but also in the outline of the letters as a whole and the sequence of many textual segments."[4] With regard to the letter form we should emphasize the striking double thanksgiving in 1 Thess 1:2; 2:13 and in 2 Thess 1:3; 2:13. Two parallels are, surprisingly, almost word-for-word, something not found in that form in any Pauline letter. Besides 1 Thess 2:9, which is copied in 2 Thess 3:8, especially striking are the repetition of the unusual prescript in 1 Thess 1:1, containing the names of the three authors and nothing else, and the address to the community in the form of the *nomen gentilicium* (2 Thess 1:1).[5]

Besides this, from the authorial side 2 Thessalonians is couched almost entirely in the first person plural; singular forms appear only in 2:5 and 3:17.[6] This conspicuous feature, contrasting as it does with the other Pauline letters,[7] is simply copied by the authors of 2 Thessalonians, so that the secondary character of the letter can be demonstrated from that fact alone. The fact that we have in 2 Thessalonians a pseudepigraphical Pauline letter written almost entirely in we-form also shows that not all imitators of Paul felt it necessary to emphasize the authority of the individual person of the apostle along with teachings presented in doctrinaire fashion. Thus the plural character of the authorship of 1 Thessalonians is likewise not an objection against post-apostolic origins. It appears that the community in Thessalonica wanted to uplift all three of its founders, with a certain emphasis on Paul as the first to be named, but also on Timothy, the "co-worker of [NRSV: for] God" (1 Thess 3:2).

3. Maarten J. J. Menken, *2 Thessalonians* (1994), 39: "He had the other letter, so to say, on his desk" (following Wrede); cp., *inter alia*, Willi Marxsen, *Der zweite Brief an die Thessalonicher* (1982), 34; Hans-Josef Klauck, *Die antike Briefliteratur und das Neue Testament* (1998), 299–300; for an intensive literary appropriation of 1 Thessalonians in the pseudonymous 2 Thessalonians cp. esp. the tables and evaluations in J. Michael Gilchrist, "Intertextuality and the Pseudonymity of 2 Thessalonians" (2006).

4. Rainer Reuter, *Synopse zu den Briefen des Neuen Testaments. Teil I* (1997), 621. See also Fred O. Francis and J. Paul Sampley, eds., *Pauline Parallels*, 2d ed. (Philadelphia: Fortress Press, 1984), 325–59, which takes no stance on authorship.

5. Wrede, *Echtheit*, 27–28; cp. also the corresponding lists in Earl Richard, *Thessalonians* (1995), 20ff.; P.-G. Müller, *Der Erste und Zweite Brief*, 235–38; Outi Leppä, "A Pseudonymous Writer" (2006), 183ff., 194ff.; David J. Clark, "Structural Similarities in 1 and 2 Thessalonians" (2006), 198ff.; Krentz, "A Stone that Will not Fit," 456–63, concluding: "Wrede's argument still stands. It has been reinforced by subsequent detailed investigation, not overturned. It is a powerful argument for the non-Pauline origin of Second Thessalonians" (p. 463).

6. Wrede, *Echtheit*, 82–83; Marlene Crüsemann, "2 Thessalonians" (2012), 821–22.

7. See 3.1.1 above. As was already remarked in the case of 1 Thessalonians, nearly all exegetical scholarship on 2 Thessalonians is marked by the fact that no significance is granted to the authorial plural in the text: scholars constantly speak only of an "author," and that independently of the particular scholar's decision regarding authenticity.

Thus the form of 1 Thessalonians and its epistolary expressions were used as a framework for 2 Thessalonians,[8] which was used to transport an alternative content regarding a particular theme of the first letter. The second letter presents the theme in two parts, characteristic of that writing, 1:5–10 and 2:1–12,[9] on the events of the end-time. The principal focus in what follows will be on a new interpretation of the alternative eschatological passages in 2 Thessalonians that deviate from the corresponding thematic sections of 1 Thessalonians, and thus to attempt a more extended answer to the question of the purpose of 2 Thessalonians. But first we need to examine in detail the verdict of 2 Thessalonians on its model. How do we come to the conclusion that 2 Thessalonians declares the first letter a forgery?

The authors of 2 Thessalonians use the word "letter" a number of times; it is striking that it is always the singular ἐπιστολή,[10] which seems to suggest that the pronounced warnings against another letter addressed to the same community must mean 1 Thessalonians: the attack on another letter "as though from us"

8. The literary dependence of the second letter on the first is accepted, discussed, and in part further strengthened by, *inter alia*, Trilling, *Untersuchungen*; idem, *Der zweite Brief*, 21–32; Gerhard Krodel, "2 Thessalonians" (1978), 77–83; Janice K. Fraser, "A Theological Study of Second Thessalonians" (1979); Marxsen, *Der zweite Brief*, 15–41; Franz Laub, *1. und 2. Thessalonicherbrief* (1985), 37–38; idem, "Paulinische Autorität in nachpaulinischer Zeit" (1990); Michael Ernst, "Distanzierte Unpersönlichkeit" (1998); Peter Müller, *Anfänge der Paulusschule* (1988), 5ff.; Glenn S. Holland, *The Tradition That You Received From Us* (1988), 6–90; Menken, *2 Thessalonians*, 36–40; Paul Metzger, *Katechon* (2005), 53–80. Cp. also, e.g., Frank W. Hughes, *Early Christian Rhetoric and 2 Thessalonians* (1989), 84ff., 91ff.; Krentz, "Through a Lens" (1994); Udo Schnelle, *Einleitung in das Neue Testament* (1994), 371–72; Richard, *Thessalonians*, 19ff.; Eckart Reinmuth, "Der zweite Brief an die Thessalonicher" (1998), 159–66; Gerhard Hotze, "Die Christologie des 2. Thessalonicherbriefs" (2000), 135–36; Regina Börschel, *Die Konstruktion einer christlichen Identität* (2001), 35–63; P.-G. Müller, *Der Erste und Zweite Brief*, 227–45; Hanna Roose, "Polyvalenz durch Intertextualität im Spiegel der aktuellen Forschung zu den Thessalonicherbriefen" (2005); eadem, "2 Thessalonians as Pseudepigraphic Reading Instruction for 1 Thessalonians" (2006); eadem, '"A Letter as by Us"' (2006); Gilchrist, "Intertextuality"; Leppä, "A Pseudonymous Writer"; Clark, "Structural Similarities"; Taesong Roh, *Der zweite Thessalonicherbrief* (2007), 18–21; Stefan Schreiber, "Der zweite Thessalonicherbrief" (2008), 441–45; Krentz, "A Stone that Will not Fit"; E.-M. Becker, "Ὡς δι΄ἡμῶν" (2009), 55–61.

9. In addition, we should name as interests of this writing the parts on the theme of "work," expanded in 2 Thess 3:6–15 beyond what is found in 1 Thessalonians. These, however, are also outwardly oriented to the theme of the parousia (cp. above at 3.3.5; Marlene Crüsemann, "2 Thessalonians," 822–23; eadem, '"Wer nicht arbeiten will"' [2010]; Otto Merk, "Arbeiten" [2007]).

10. Reinmuth, "Der zweite Brief an die Thessalonicher," 162–63; Angela Standhartinger, *Studien zur Entstehungsgeschichte & Intention des Kolosserbriefs* (1999), 53.

(ἐπιστολῆς ὡς δι᾽ ἡμῶν)[11] begins in 2 Thess 2:2 and ends in 3:17, where the letter ends with a personal greeting as a kind of "proof of authenticity" from the hand of "Paul": "This is the mark in every letter" (ὅ ἐστιν σημεῖον ἐν πάσῃ ἐπιστολῇ). Since such a mark is lacking in precisely the model used by 2 Thessalonians (namely, 1 Thessalonians), the latter is thus explicitly declared here to be inauthentic. Rather, the readers are called to adhere to the right tradition and instruction, "either by word of mouth or by our letter" (εἴτε δι᾽ ἐπιστολῆς ἡμῶν, 2:15). Since, lacking a mark of authenticity, 1 Thessalonians can only be "supposedly our letter," that is, a non-letter, 2:15 must be understood as committing the recipients to 2 Thessalonians as the only real letter to Thessalonica. According to 3:14, unconditional obedience is to be given to the present 2 Thessalonians as the only letter: "Take note of those who do not obey what we say in this letter (τῷ λόγῳ ἡμῶν διὰ τῆς ἐπιστολῆς) . . . ." This logical conclusion from what is said in 2 Thessalonians, namely, that it is intended to suppress the first letter by declaring it a forgery, has in my opinion been convincingly demonstrated by Andreas Lindemann: (the author of) 2 Thessalonians "asserts directly in 2:2 and indirectly in 3:17 that 1 Thessalonians is a forgery, and that assertion is his primary means for demonstrating that his own letter is genuine."[12] One consequence of the thesis maintained in this book is that

11. The literal meaning of the expression ὡς δι᾽ ἡμῶν, "as if from us" could also contain a broader accusation against 1 Thessalonians, namely, that it in turn has tried to imitate "our letter," that is, 2 Thessalonians. For more on ὡς δι᾽ ἡμῶν in 2:2, see 6.3.1 below.

12. Lindemann, "Zum Abfassungszweck des Zweiten Thessalonicherbriefs" (1977), esp. 36–40, at 40. This thesis was previously defended, with different arguments, e.g., by Hilgenfeld, "Die beiden Briefe," 249ff.; Holtzmann, "Zum zweiten Thessalonicherbrief"; Martin Rist, "Pseudepigraphy and the Early Christians" (1972), 82–83 (cp., e.g., Trilling, *Der zweite Brief*, 24), and was positively received, e.g., by Krodel, "2 Thessalonians" (1978), 85; idem, "2 Thessalonians" (1993), 56–57; Marxsen, *Der zweite Brief*, 33ff.; Laub, *1. und 2. Thessalonicherbrief*, 39–40; idem, "Paulinische Autorität," 404–9; Helmut Koester, "From Paul's Eschatology to the Apocalyptic Schemata of 2 Thessalonians" (1990), 455; Gerd Lüdemann, "Ein Fälscher am Werk" (1996), 34ff.; Lambertus J. Lietaert Peerbolte, *The Antecedents of Antichrist* (1996), 67–68; Reuter, *Synopse*, 621. For critical discussion see, e.g., Roose, "Polyvalenz," 258–61; eadem, "2 Thessalonians as Pseudepigraphic," 133ff.; eadem, "'A Letter as by Us,'" 111–15, esp. n. 21; E.-M. Becker, "Ὡς δι᾽ ἡμῶν," 62ff. Hanna Roose develops the thesis that the author of 2 Thessalonians, by means of the statements in 2:2 and 3:17, attempted to make his letter appear authentic and the first letter to Thessalonica, since he uses the literary schema of 1 Thessalonians, but without quoting it; however, 1 Thessalonians is not declared to be false ("'A Letter by Us,'" 107, 115–19): "The underlying argument is simple: If 2 Thessalonians precedes 1 Thessalonians, it must be genuine. (Alleged) chronological priority is indirectly presented as a guarantee for (alleged) authenticity" (p. 116). In my opinion this thesis fits well with Lindemann's analysis ("Abfassungszweck"), though Roose distances herself from it (see above), because the "mark of authenticity" in 3:17 does seem to say that only the letter that bears such a supposed manual signature is actually apostolic, and that means 2 Thessalonians, because it is absent from 1 Thessalonians (cp. Lindemann,

the authors of 2 Thessalonians were fully aware that 1 Thessalonians was certainly not an authentic Paul-Silvanus-Timothy letter, and that they must have had fairly certain knowledge about the circumstances of its origin. The fact that in that period there were circles in which faked apostolic letters were written and circulated is sufficiently attested by the existence of 2 Thessalonians itself. So if 2 Thessalonians only attacks one letter, 1 Thessalonians, as being similarly false, this may soften the moral indignation sometimes expressed[13] at the impertinence of simply declaring the oldest letter of Paul to be a forgery.

That the main reason for the writing of 2 Thessalonians was to present a theory about the parousia that differed from the teaching about it in 1 Thessalonians can be regarded as the *opinio communis* of those exegetes who consider 2 Thessalonians to be deutero-Pauline.[14] The same is true for positions that see here only a correction of certain opinions derived from 1 Thessalonians. It is true that the deviation is often regarded stereotypically as a correction or erasure of the immediate expectation supposedly propagated by 1 Thess 4:13–5:11,[15] by means of

"Abfassungszweck," 39–40). For that reason 2 Thessalonians must at the same time and as a matter of course always claim its own priority as the supposed sole genuine letter.

13. Thus Lüdemann, "Ein Fälscher am Werk." Of course, in that case the accusation of unscrupulous action falls all the more strongly on the authors of 1 Thessalonians.

14. The majority of German-speaking exegetes at present regard 2 Thessalonians as inauthentic (cp. Hotze, "Christologie," 125ff.), but its Pauline authorship is still often asserted, especially among English-speaking scholars: e.g., Roger D. Aus, "II Thessalonians" (1984), who wrote this short commentary under the premise of Pauline authorship despite his own opinion that it is inauthentic (pp. 196–97); Robert Jewett, *Thessalonian Correspondence* (1986); idem, "A Matrix of Grace" (1991); John M. G. Barclay, "Conflict in Thessalonica" (1993); Todd D. Still, *Conflict at Thessalonica* (1999), 46–60; Abraham J. Malherbe, *The Letters to the Thessalonians* (2000); Gregory K. Beale, *1–2 Thessalonians* (2010); Colin R. Nicholl, *From Hope to Despair in Thessalonica* (2004); Ivor H. Jones, *The Epistles to the Thessalonians* (2005); Ben Witherington III, *1 and 2 Thessalonians* (2006); Gordon D. Fee, *The First and Second Letters to the Thessalonians* (2009)—probably because, in the first place, too little attention is paid to the argument of the demonstrable literary dependency of 2 Thessalonians on 1 Thessalonians; cp. Schreiber, "Früher Paulus mit Spätfolgen" (2007), 280–81; Trevor Thompson, "A Stone that Still Won't Fit" (2009). Most recently see Florence M. Gillman, Mary Ann Beavis, and HyeRan Kim-Cragg, *1 and 2 Thessalonians*, Wisdom Commentary 52 (Collegeville, MN: Liturgical Press, 2017), with a review of the state of the question prior to publication of the present book, and opting for pseudonymous authorship of 2 Thessalonians.

15. On this see only Lindemann, "Abfassungszweck" (1977), 38–39, 40ff., and, e.g., Paul Metzger, "Der Fall des Imperiums" (2008), 102ff. ("Die Zurückweisung der Naherwartung" [The Rebuttal of Imminent Expectation]), or Lüdemann, "Ein Fälscher am Werk": "1 Thessalonians, as a 'letter of fire,' is filled with a glowing imminent expectation" (p. 33), "that literally simmers with excitement in anticipation of Jesus' coming from heaven in the immediate future" (p. 35). Here it is supposed (as is frequently the case) that 2 Thess 2:2 is

a kind of "apocalyptic schedule" in 2 Thess 2:1–12,[16] subjecting the idea of the timing to a kind of "delay."[17] But since the conclusions reached in chap. 5 regarding 1 Thess 4:13–5:11 show that it does not explicitly or even implicitly speak of a "burning imminent expectation," the intended statement of 2 Thessalonians must be sought somewhere else than in the focus on an apocalyptic time-scheme that dominates scholarship. Here a social-historical perspective on the relationship among Jewish, Jewish-Christian, Gentile-Christian, and Gentile-pagan groups provides the key. The second letter to the community in Thessalonica stems, with a probability that borders on certainty, from Jewish-Christian circles, or at least from a group whose stylistic expression[18] and way of using Old Testament traditions and Jewish materials, as well as its positioning in the vicinity of a Judaism faithful to the Temple,[19] points to the conclusion that the authors were Jewish persons who confessed Jesus as Messiah.

In general there is an overall advocacy for this origin of 2 Thessalonians in the branch of scholarship that regards the letter as post-Pauline; the Jewish background of the writing is not a matter of controversy. Still, it is surprising how little emphasis is placed on this fact in individual exegeses and overall evaluations of the text. As a rule, scholars content themselves with remarks such as that the author was "marked by certain features of Old Testament thought"[20] or that "the whole concept" betrays "… a return to the ideas about time and the world in Old Testament-Jewish apocalyptic."[21] Less frequently there is a clear statement like that of Christian Rauch: "The aim of the second Thessalonian letter is the correction

intended to oppose a group that appeals to 1 Thess 4:13–18 in order to maintain such a "burning" expectation: "The letter is composed to combat this apocalyptic fervor" (Richard, *Thessalonians*, 28). The fact that needs to be kept in mind, namely, that 1 Thessalonians must have been more than a generation old and consequently was scarcely apt for an announcement of the "day" that had not happened after such a long time is scarcely noted (but see Lindemann, "Abfassungszweck," 41–42).

16. See only Marxsen, *Der zweite Brief*, 76–89; Koester, "From Paul's Eschatology," esp. 454ff.; Laub, "Paulinische Autorität," 406: "… with the intention to shift the date into as undefined and indefinable distance as possible"; Nicola Wendebourg, *Der Tag des Herrn* (2003), 327: "The letter fends off the overdrawn expectation cited in v. 2 by means of a listing of the events that must precede the 'day of the Lord.'"

17. Trilling, *Der zweite Brief*, 26–27 and frequently elsewhere; there are also theories of a complementary reading of the two eschatological proposals: for the hermeneutical model of 2 Thessalonians as "directions for reading" 1 Thessalonians, cp. Roose, "Polyvalenz," 261–65 and *passim*; eadem, "2 Thessalonians as Pseudepigraphic," esp. 147–51.

18. On this see esp. Trilling, *Untersuchungen*, 46–66; numerous parallelisms, Hebraisms, and a multitude of expressions related to Old Testament prayer language should be emphasized.

19. See 6.2 and 6.3 below.

20. Trilling, *Der zweite Brief*, 27.

21. Laub, *1. und 2. Thessalonicherbrief*, 47, on 2 Thess 1:5–10.

of Pauline eschatology in the sense and spirit of Jewish Christianity."[22] Such a derivation is nowhere denied, so far as I can see. The differing character of the two Thessalonian letters in this regard was most clearly emphasized by Adolf von Harnack, who held the opinion that the two letters were written by Paul to different groups within the community, the Gentile-Christian majority and the Jewish-Christian faction. Independently of that solution, his emphasis on the different profiles of the two letters is persuasive: "The first letter presumes that the community at Thessalonica is entirely Gentile-Christian and testifies to it that it has incurred the same kind of suffering from its own people as the communities in Judea has from theirs.... The first letter shows almost no references to the OT or any Old Testament features.... The second letter nowhere describes the addressees as Gentile Christians" but has "a very strong Old Testament coloring and suggests that we should infer Jewish presuppositions among the addressees."[23] And for 2 Thessalonians as a post-Pauline writing it seems especially appropriate to seek Jewish presuppositions on the part of the *author(s)*.

The fact that 2 Thessalonians very probably comes from Jewish-Christian authors is of the greatest significance for the new view of the relationship between the two Thessalonian letters to be developed here. If 2 Thessalonians declares the first letter—whose clearly "Gentile-Christian" features are best explained, according to the view I am presenting here, by the fact that it not Pauline—to be a forgery and intends to replace it, then it is ultimately about correcting pagan tendencies from a Jewish point of view as held within a group that confesses Christ. Here Jewish Christians present an eschatology as an alternative to that held by Christians from among the Gentiles,[24] and with it an alternative view of history, as will be described

22. Rauch, "Zum zweiten Thessalonicherbrief," 46; or, e.g., Aus, "Comfort in Judgment" (1971), 358: "The author of II [Thess] is clearly a Jewish Christian"; P.-G. Müller, *Der Erste und Zweite Brief*, 240: "2 Thessalonians has much more recourse than 1 Thessalonians to the OT and contemporary Judaism; it is precisely by that means that the unknown author shows himself to be a Jewish Christian, familiar with the body of apocalyptic thought and previous Jewish literature"; Metzger, *Katechon*, 85: the knowledge of apocalyptic thought points to the conclusion that the author "probably had Jewish-Christian roots"; above all Martin Karrer, "Der zweite Thessalonicherbrief und Gottes Widersacher" (2007), 110: "We here find ourselves far removed from the sharp criticism of Israel in 1 Thess 2:14–16. The counter-society that 2 Thessalonians builds requires an intensive orientation to the holiness of Israel, without the break found there." This social positioning of 2 Thessalonians as a "counter-society" to the world proposed in 1 Thess 2:14–16, which in my opinion is very accurately expressed, will be further described below.

23. Adolf von Harnack, "Das Problem des zweiten Thessalonicherbriefs" (1910), 562–63.

24. In my opinion both writings, as pseudepigraphical products, are more probably to be traced to male than female authors, though neither the one nor the other can be positively demonstrated or excluded. Indicators of male authorship—besides the strictly androcentric perspective—are the three authorial names, the only names mentioned at all in the two letters (!), the stylization of the three as a representative and model group of men, and the

in what follows. The means employed by the authors of 2 Thessalonians, namely, declaring an already existing writing to be both wrong in its content and a falsification besides—while at the same time making use of the same method of pseudepigraphy to promote their own point of view—has to be seen as a sign of extremely acute conflict between the different early Christian groups. Second Thessalonians 2:3 contains an intense warning against the previously-mentioned other, forged letter, said to be an attempt to deceive in order to confuse minds and spread fear (2:2): "let no one deceive you in any way!"—not by means of the names of apostolic authors or community letters supposedly from their pens that evoke trust! So we might paraphrase this direct reference. This existential strife is taking place simultaneously with the threats and persecutions from without that are lamented in both texts (1 Thess 2:14; 3:3–4; 2 Thess 1:4–7).

So what, exactly, does 2 Thessalonians mean to say and to achieve by its rejection of 1 Thessalonians and its content? If the eschatological passages in 2 Thessalonians contain their own message, directed against what they regard as the false idea of the parousia in the forged 1 Thessalonians, we first need to pay attention to those differences in any detailed exegesis. In what follows we will focus solely on them. That procedure will very quickly reveal a completely different idea of history in each of the two letters, with grave consequences for an alternative view of the relationship among Jewish, Jewish-Christian, and Gentile-Christian and Gentile-pagan groups.

6.2 Second Thessalonians 1:5–10: What Characterizes God's Just Judgment?

> [1:3] We must always give thanks to God for you, brothers and sisters, as is right, because your faith is growing abundantly, and the love of everyone of you for one another is increasing. [4] Therefore we ourselves boast of you among the churches of God for your perseverance (τῆς ὑπομονῆς)[25] and faith during all your persecutions (τοῖς διωγμοῖς) and the afflictions that you are enduring. [5] [This is] evidence of the righteous judgment of God (ἔνδειγμα τῆς δικαίας κρίσεως τοῦ θεοῦ), and is intended to make you worthy of the kingdom of God, for which you are also suffering (πάσχετε). [6] For it is indeed just (δίκαιον) of God to repay with affliction (θλῖψιν) those who afflict you (τοῖς θλίβουσιν), [7] and [to give] relief to [you,] the afflicted (τοῖς θλιβομένοις) as well as to us,

lack of (almost) any explicit reference to the existence of female members of the community. Cf. Lone Fatum, "1 Thessalonians" (1994), 250–52, 256–61; Mary Ann Beavis, "2 Thessalonians" (1994), 263–65; Jutta Bickmann, "1 Thessalonians" (2012), 810–11, 815; Marlene Crüsemann, "2 Thessalonians," 821–23; Christine Gerber, *Paulus und seine 'Kinder'* (2005), 251–52 n. 3.

25. NIV. For this translation of ὑπομονή, which better expresses the active aspect of this attitude on the part of threatened Jewish and early Christian apocalypticists than do previous translations ("patience" [AV; LB]; "steadfastness" [NRSV]); see Luise Schottroff, "Befreite Eva" (1988), 103ff.

> when the Lord Jesus is revealed (ἐν τῇ ἀποκαλύψει) from heaven with his mighty angels [8] in flaming fire (ἐν πυρὶ φλογός), inflicting [just] vengeance (ἐκδίκησιν) on those who do not know God (τοῖς μὴ εἰδόσιν θεόν), and on those who do not obey the gospel (τοῖς μὴ ὑπακούουσιν τῷ εὐαγγελίῳ) of our Lord Jesus. [9] These will suffer the punishment (δίκην) of eternal destruction (ὄλεθρον αἰώνιον), separated from the presence of the Lord and from the glory/majesty (τῆς δόξης) of his might, [10] when he comes to be glorified (ἐνδοξασθῆναι) by [or: among] his saints and to be marveled at on that day (ἐν τῇ ἡμέρᾳ ἐκείνῃ) among all who have believed, because our testimony (μαρτύριον) to you was believed.

Together with 2 Thess 2:1–12, but even by itself, this first apocalyptic (ἀποκάλυψις, v. 7)[26] section has great weight[27] and already contains some essential features of the second letter's changed view of history in contrast to 1 Thessalonians. The continual reminiscences and reconnections, clear and easily perceived, show how precisely these verses of 2 Thessalonians 1 are conceived as an answer to the concepts and theme of 1 Thessalonians. But first we need to emphasize the overall scene, clad as it is in the robes of a grand Old Testament theophany of judgment. Jesus appears from heaven as the powerful eschatological Messiah who comes for judgment; he is feared by the opponents, admired by his own; he imposes God's eternally valid judgment (1:5). Behind it all is primarily the scene in Isa 66:5–6, 15–24, in which YHWH judges the whole earth with fire and sword from Zion, and the כבוד, the δόξα of the God of Israel will be revealed to all peoples, as is attested by the conceptual agreements with the LXX.[28] By themselves the echoes of this

26. The original meaning of the word "apocalypse" "is *not* the destruction of the world, *not* catastrophe, but first and foremost: *unveiling, uncovering!*" Thus Jürgen Ebach, "Apokalypse" (1985), 11; consequently, "apocalyptic literature is resistance literature" because it "claims to *unveil* the secret course of history, to *uncover* the real forces behind historical and political powers, to *unmask* the superficially-existing situations of power and violence and to *reveal* the true power of God" (ibid., 12; emphasis in original). In this sense 2 Thessalonians is genuine apocalyptic literature, as will be shown below. For the book of Revelation, see the corresponding initiative by Klaus Wengst, *"Wie lange noch?"* (2010), 11–26 ("Apokalypse: Enthüllung der Macht" [Apocalypse: Unveiling Power]). For 2 Thessalonians' belonging within the "milieu" of Jewish apocalyptic see Menken, *2 Thessalonians*, 44–66; cp. Krentz, "Through a Lens," 52ff.

27. For an evaluation of 2 Thessalonians 1 together with 2:1–12, see Aus, "Comfort in Judgment," 36–39; for the social-historical connection of the two chapters see also Roh, *Der zweite Thessalonicherbrief*, 126–27.

28. Cp. Aus, "The Relevance of Isaiah 66:7 to Revelation 12 and 2 Thessalonians 1" (1976), 263–68, esp. 266–68: ἀνταποδιδόντος ἀνταπόδοσιν, Isa 66:6 / ἀνταποδοῦναι, 2 Thess 1:6; ἐν φλογὶ πυρός, Isa 66:15 / ἐν πυρὶ φλογός, 2 Thess 1:8; τὸ ὄνομα κυρίου δοξασθῇ, Isa 66:5 / ἐνδοξασθῇ τὸ ὄνομα, 2 Thess 1:12. See Klaus Berger, *Theologiegeschichte des Urchristentums* (1994), 345: 2 Thess 1:4–12 is "to be read primarily as a midrash on Isa 66:4–19." But also expressions from, e.g., Isa 2:10–21; Obadiah 13–15; Ps 78:6–7 LXX may have entered into the text; cp. the tables in Aus, "Comfort in Judgment," 113–14; Trilling, *Der zweite Brief*, 55ff.,

scene in Isaiah 66 uncover the more demanding function of the returning Kyrios in contrast to the "one-act play" in 1 Thessalonians' depiction of the parousia: here we read of an end-time process of struggle and judgment, with Jesus at its center, while in 1 Thess 4:13–17 there is an uncontested reunion with him, undramatic in contrast to 2 Thess 1:5–10. The second letter broadens the apocalyptic event to the cosmic stage, stretching from heaven to the profound depths of eternal destruction, and Kyrios Jesus is the universal agent. The general eschatological judgment, omitted from the parousia as depicted in 1 Thess 4:13–17, appears to be the major interest of 2 Thessalonians.[29]

Let us now take a look at the expressions from the first letter that are used in 2 Thessalonians, indicators of the social-historical relationship of the two letters in the matter of eschatological hopes. The sufferings (πάσχετε, 2 Thess 1:5) for the reign of God correspond to those caused by the fellow Macedonians in 1 Thess 2:14 (ἐπάθετε). Then the emphasis on the threatening current situation is also adopted; the persecution [better: affliction] (1 Thess 3:3 + 4: ταῖς θλίψεσιν ταύτας; μέλλομεν θλίβεσθαι) is presented somewhat redundantly in 2 Thess 1: 6 + 7: "to repay with affliction (θλῖψιν) those who afflict you (τοὶς θλίβουσιν), and to give relief to [you], the afflicted (τοῖς θλιβομένοις) . . . ." Alongside the afflictions already mentioned in 2 Thess 1:4, there are some sort of generalized "persecutions" (τοῖς διωγμοῖς) the community has to endure, whereas according to 1 Thess 2:15 the apostles had been "driven out" (NRSV; or "persecuted severely," ἐκδιωξάντων) by "the Jews." The "revelation" (ἐν τῇ ἀποκαλύψει) of Kyrios Jesus from heaven "with his mighty angels" (2 Thess 1:7) takes up the theme of 1 Thess 3:13; 4:15 + 16, there associated with the concept of παρουσία: the coming of Jesus from heaven with the saints, and his descent from there. The anonymous imposition of "destruction" (ὄλεθρος) in 1 Thess 5:3 becomes in 2 Thess 1:9 "eternal destruction" (ὄλεθρον αἰώνιον), rushing upon the damned before the eyes of the Kyrios. Likewise the motif of the "day" from 1 Thess 5:2 (ἡμέρα κυρίου) is adopted by 2 Thess 1:10: "on that day" (ἡμέρᾳ ἐκείνῃ). The emphatic placement of the "day" in 1:10 at the end of the long Greek sentence, which makes up the whole unit starting at 1:3,[30] shows

58ff., and, for example, Stephen G. Brown, "The Intertextuality of Jes 66.17 and 2 Thessalonians 2.7" (1993), 267–68; Hotze, "Christologie," 139ff., and the tables on reception of Scripture in 2 Thess 1:8–10 in Karrer, "Der zweite Thessalonicherbrief und Gottes Widersacher," 108–9. For the reception of Isaiah 2 see also Nicola Wendebourg, *Der Tag des Herrn*, 325–26. On the method of prophetic and apocalyptic groups of assembling collections of quotations from Scripture to use as subversive messages of political resistance see Ebach, "Apokalypse," 12–20, esp. 17ff.; idem, "Apokalypse und Apokalyptik" (1998), 225–29.

29. Marlene Crüsemann, "2 Thessalonians," 824–25; cp. Roose, "2 Thessalonians as Pseudepigraphic Reading Instruction," 145–46.

30. For a grammatical and structural analysis of the unit cp., e.g., Trilling, *Der zweite Brief*, 39–40; Richard, *Thessalonians*, 312–13; P.-G. Müller, *Der Erste und Zweite Brief*, 249, and with an emphasis on translation questions, D. A. Dunham, "2 Thessalonians 1:3–10: A Study in Sentence Structure" (1981).

that for these authors the "day" in any case involves such a previously described event of judgment. In other words: they cannot imagine a ἡμέρα κυρίου without such a comprehensive judgment; it is a given. This fact is of great importance for the interpretation of 2 Thess 2:2,[31] where the announcement of such a "day" as having already occurred is denied.

What emerges, then, from this collection of motifs and expressions that 2 Thessalonians 1 has derived in such concentrated fashion from 1 Thessalonians? It circles around the themes of threats to the community, retribution for those who are giving them pain, and the revelation of the Kyrios from heaven on his day. This demonstrates that 2 Thessalonians is concerned above all to describe the events of that decisive "day" in context, to tie them all together with the action of Kyrios Jesus. It is Messiah Jesus[32] himself who will accomplish the end-time retribution, and it will happen only on that "day," accompanied by mighty and marvelous surrounding events in the form of a just judgment. Before this there is no real relief or rest in the face of the hostile people, but neither is there a definitive eschatological decision! The emphasis on judgment on "the day" shows, of itself, that all possible eschatological judgments spoken beforehand necessarily represent an illegitimate anticipation of the last judgment day. This constitutes the first attack on the concept of judgment in 1 Thessalonians, which (in 1 Thess 2:16) announces the wrathful judgment as having already fallen on the Jewish people.

The second attack consists of an unmistakable declaration that *all*, non-Jewish and, very particularly, Jewish as well, will encounter judgment for the first and only time on the day of the Messiah. He will inflict "vengeance" (ἐκδίκησιν) on those who do not know God (τοῖς μὴ εἰδόσιν θεόν) and who are not obedient to the Gospel of our Kyrios Jesus (τοῖς μὴ ὑπακούουσιν τῷ εὐαγγελίῳ) (2 Thess 1:8). It seems that the discussion in the exegetical literature about whether these predicates are supposed to apply to a single group (of persecutors) or to two groups—namely, those who do not know God, members of the pagan peoples, and Jewish people who do not follow the Christian gospel[33]—must be decided in this

31. On this see further below at 6.3.

32. The title Χριστός is applied to κύριος Jesus in 2 Thess 1:2 + 12 and so in a sense frames the judgment scene, in which Jesus alone is given the κύριος-title (in 1:7, 8; v. 9 has the absolute κύριος).

33. See the discussion in Trilling, *Der zweite Brief*, 56, who discerns three solutions proposed by scholars: (a) the first part of the statement in 2 Thess 1:8 is about Gentiles, the second about Jews; (b) both parts are "in the same sense" about enemies of the community; (c) the author "is faced by an undifferentiated group of nonbelievers." Trilling agrees with the last solution; similarly Malherbe, *Thessalonians*, 400–1, or P.-G. Müller, *Der Erste und Zweite Brief*, 254. Arguing in favor of solution (b) are, e.g., Reinmuth, "Der zweite Brief an die Thessalonicher," 171–72: "Gentiles and Jews, to the extent that they agree in rejecting the Gospel"; hence it is about those "who persecute and afflict the community." Cp. also, e.g., Rigaux, *Thessaloniciens*, 629; Krodel, "2 Thessalonians," 44; Menken, *2 Thessalonians*, 89; Nicola Wendebourg, *Der Tag des Herrn*, 324 n. 25. Martin Karrer, "Der zweite

sense: the repeated article with καὶ indicates that the text refers to two groups of people, but in such a way that both Jewish and non-Jewish people may be included in both predicates. "The expression 'who do not know God' is often used to characterize Gentiles (Jer 10:25; Ps 79:6; Gal 4:8; 1 Thess 4:5). It is frequently said of the Jews, in a variety of ways, that they are disobedient (Rom 10:3, 16–21; 11:30ff.). . . . Occasionally it is also said of Jews that they do not know God (Jer 9:6; John 8:55)."[34] But since the characteristics of deficient knowledge of God and faulty obedience to the Gospel are so emphatically set alongside one another, we must suppose that this is an attempt at the most universal statement possible, one that may apply in different ways to each and every person who has been repressive toward this group belonging to Christ. The first group, "who do not know God," could essentially refer to people from the non-Jewish nations; this is favored by the same formulation appearing in 1 Thess 4:5. But a lack of Christian obedience may apply to them as well. From the perspective of 2 Thessalonians that same reproach equally touches Jews who do not believe in the Messiah Jesus and who also oppress the community. But ultimately the second category, more than the first, could also include people from community circles who have latterly changed sides and become enemies. In short: whoever threatens and persecutes the community, whether his or her background be pagan or Jewish, will be judged on "the day." In reference to 1 Thessalonians, then, it is clear that this applies to the Greek, non-Jewish persecutors named in 1 Thess 2:14, and their destruction according to 1 Thess 5:3 is also addressed.

What is critical, however, is that the statement in 2 Thess 1:8 intends an explicit retraction of the stinging anti-Jewish diatribe in 1 Thess 2:14–17, in particular v. 16, which resolves the problem of Jewish persecutors by seeing God's destroying judgment as having already happened. The judgment vision in 2 Thessalonians 1 counters that prejudgment by pointing out that ultimately nothing but the verdict pronounced before Jesus at his revelation will be the valid and just one. Thus 2 Thessalonians also contradicts 1 Thessalonians' view of history in fundamental

Thessalonicherbrief und Gottes Widersacher," 109–10, sees only the "people among the Gentiles who tend their sacred groves against the one God, and through their eating practices make a common life impossible" and "make offerings to false gods" as affected by the divine declaration of guilt. At the same time, 2 Thessalonians combines "the community members from among the Gentiles with the saints in Israel. They live in common, awaiting the amazing glorification of the Lord at the judgment" (p. 110).

34. Gerhard Friedrich, "Der zweite Brief an die Thessalonicher" (1985), 260. Friedrich is also inclined to the opinion that the reference is simply to all nonbelievers as a group: "Anyone who does not believe, no matter whether Jew or Gentile, does not know God and is not obedient to the Gospel" (pp. 260–61). The Jewish perspective from which the two groups are so pointedly set alongside one another is emphasized by Pheme Perkins, "2 Thessalonians" (1988), 1235. It must be maintained that, in any specification of partitioning in the expression the overall statement remains: *all* people who are questionable from God's point of view and that of Jesus will be equally affected by the judgment.

fashion: the Jewish people have not yet been judged; the decision will come later. The Kyrios will hold a day of judgment in the future, and only on that day will there be a general judgment of all possible persecutors of the community, and of the community itself. The reverse side of the destructive judgment on those who oppress the community will be a compensatory judgment that the oppressed will experience as recompense for their persecutions,[35] namely, the relief accorded the faithful here addressed in the face of their enemies (1:6–7).

This relief (ἄνεσις, 1:7) in face of hostile people is not yet attainable in the present time of the writing, but certain hope for it can be read in signs already received. While there is no preliminary judgment before Christ's judgment day, there are signs of how it may result. The community is, in fact, in possession of such a sign for itself as regards the judgment of God that is approaching. The strange phrase "evidence of the righteous judgment of God" (ἔνδειγμα τῆς δικαίας κρίσεως τοῦ θεοῦ) in 2 Thess 1:5 refers to the persecutions and oppressions named in 1:4. These are the infallible signs of ultimate justice. Here it is said with special clarity that there is and thus far has been no divine judgment! There is only a sign or indicator of the coming judgment, and that sign is oppression and the suffering resulting from it. With this theological idea, which at first glance seems so surprising, the picture of judgment in 2 Thessalonians aligns itself with the so-called *Jewish theology of suffering*.

Wolfgang Wichmann's work is especially helpful in giving a systematic view of this doctrine of Jewish practical theology, with a focus on the first two centuries C.E. Its core is the "complete reversal of the previous understanding of suffering"[36] in Israel, which until that time, because of the suffering of the righteous, had led to the broadest kind of questioning of the justice of God, as the struggle over the theodicy question in the book of Job shows. Now there came an alternative interpretation, according to which suffering could be seen as a sign of acceptance by God, "whose occasion is to be sought in the hardships of practical life." "In the present eon the pious—the 'righteous'—suffer in order that the few sins that even they must have committed, deliberately or unknowingly, can be atoned for already on earth, and in the world beyond they have only the reward for their overwhelmingly good deeds awaiting them. The godless, on the contrary, live happily so that they receive already in this life the reward for the few fulfillings of the Law that they also surely have to present, and so that for them the coming eon will contain only punishment and damnation."[37]

35. Cp. Marxsen, *Der zweite Brief*, 69–70.

36. Wolfgang Wichmann, *Die Leidenstheologie* (1930), 9; cp. ibid., 15ff. for previous work on the topic; especially worthy of mention is Paul Volz, *Die jüdische Eschatologie von Daniel bis Akiba* (1903), 97–98, 110–11, 155–ff. (The second edition of Volz's work appeared in 1934 under the title *Die Eschatologie der jüdischen Gemeinde im neutestamentlichen Zeitalter*.)

37. Wichmann, *Leidenstheologie*, 10–11.

> This is the most common form of Jewish theology of suffering, beginning with 2 Macc 6:12–17 as its earliest witness,[38] and attested especially throughout the Syrian Apocalypse of Baruch, which, "under the impression of the national catastrophe," sought "to engage religiously with the newly-kindled problem of evil."[39] For early rabbinic theology, the recorded words of Rabbi Akiba (d. 135 C.E.) and his school should be emphasized: "He deals strictly with both, even to the great deep. He deals strictly with the righteous, calling them to account for the few wrongs which they commit in this world, in order to lavish bliss upon and give them a goodly reward in the world to come; He grants ease to the wicked and rewards them for the few good deeds which they have performed in this world in order to punish them in the future world" (*Ber.R.* on Gen 8:1).[40]

We can find clear traces of this Jewish theology of suffering in 2 Thess 1:4–12. The pericope can "only be rightly understood in terms of the theology of suffering" and thus can be interpreted as follows: The "persecutions and sufferings you are enduring are a proof that God judges justly.... That is, they are happening to the end that you may see the reign of God as of value ... for otherwise it would not be just of God to repay with rest (ἄνεσιν) those who oppress you and you who are oppressed in the eschatological future (εἴπερ δίκαιον παρὰ θεῷ ἀνταποδοῦναι), to inaugurate a reversal of all relationships of suffering, as is his plan.... In particular it must be stressed that it is *God*'s avenging action that is the driving force behind this whole understanding of suffering."[41] When, in this way, suffering under

38. Cp. ibid., 18ff.

39. Ibid., 33; cp. *SyrBar* 13:1–12; 14:1–9; 15:1–15, and frequently (Wichmann, *Leidenstheologie*, 32–42).

40. Available at https://archive.org/details/RabbaGenesis. The many witnesses to this "theology of suffering" reveal their value for everyday Jewish practice and for overcoming catastrophes and suffering. Wichmann emphasized that at a time when any number of other New Testament scholars in Germany were using the same sources to project anti-Jewish images such as "Jewish wage morality" or "ideas of entitlement." Wichmann's work was rediscovered, evaluated, and made available for the exegesis of 2 Thessalonians through its pioneering reception by Roger Aus, "Comfort in Judgment," and Jouette Bassler, "The Enigmatic Sign" (1984); see the next footnote.

41. Wichmann, *Leidenstheologie*, 27–28. The connection of 2 Thess 1:4–12 to Jewish theology of suffering was taken up by Aus, "Comfort in Judgment," 69–75, 358–59, and Bassler, "The Enigmatic Sign," 501–6, 509–10; see also Charles A. Wanamaker, *The Epistles to the Thessalonians* (1990), 222–23; Krodel, "2 Thessalonians," 43; Menken, *2 Thessalonians*, 85ff.; Richard, *Thessalonians*, 316–17; Beverly R. Gaventa, *First and Second Thessalonians* (1998), 102–3; Marlene Crüsemann, "2 Thessalonians," 824–25; Roose, "2 Thessalonians as Pseudepigraphic Reading Instruction," 146–47; cp. the remarks on the adoption of OT-early Jewish ideas about the eschatological reversal of the fate of the suffering community in Nicola Wendebourg, *Der Tag des Herrn*, 325.

persecution is the unmistakable criterion by which a group can recognize that it is on the way to God's equalizing and saving judgment, it is possible that there can be a certain existential openness to the suffering of other groups under the same aggressor, since it is never certain how broad the influence of that aggressor may be and how far it may extend in the future. Suffering as the principal criterion for God's eschatological judgment is well suited for establishing a degree of solidarity among various communities that are marginalized and persecuted. Thus 2 Thess 1:4–12 leads us to the thesis that the authors have a clear view of the comparably threatening situation of Jewish communities and groups that are not made up of Christ-believers, and that they do not approve of a definitive separation from them before the all-deciding final judgment. The question becomes still more profound in the next passage. The probability that 2 Thessalonians makes use of Jewish theology of suffering announces its proximity to the Jewish-apocalyptic circles that had been affected by the catastrophe of 70 C.E.[42]

We maintain: In its very first verses, 2 Thessalonians offers a correction of the concept of judgment in 1 Thessalonians. No one has been judged thus far, certainly not the Jewish people. There is only one judgment for every group of people and nations. It will take place on the "day" of the Kyrios Jesus when he comes from heaven. God's act of judgment is associated with the person of Jesus, and him alone. It is the primary function of his coming, something that is as much absent from 1 Thess 4:13–17 as is any eschatological drama. On the one hand, 2 Thessalonians brings the idea of an end-time day of judgment in the Pauline sense into the Thessalonian correspondence, thus associating itself with the statements about each one's being judged according to her or his deeds, without regard for persons, that we find in Rom 2:5–16;[43] 1 Cor 3:12–15;[44] 2 Cor 5:10. In

42. Thus esp. Krodel, "2 Thessalonians," 86ff.; see further below at 6.3.1.

43. The formula in Rom 2:5–6, "when God's righteous judgment will be revealed" / ἀποκαλύψεως δικαιοκρισίας τοῦ θεοῦ (lit.: of the revelation of God's righteous judgment), when all deeds will be "repaid" / ἀποδώσει, seems especially close to 2 Thess 1:5–6, where the sign of "the righteous judgment of God" / δικαίας κρίσεως τοῦ θεοῦ points to the final "repayment" / ἀνταποδοῦναι: "It is God who is the judge, not some human being; God has the last word. God's judgment is characterized as righteous—contrary to multitudes of experience of the corruptibility of human judges.... God repays each one according to her or his deeds. That is, God is the eschatological representative of the connection between deeds and consequences. The hope that lies in him, that those who do good will receive good in return and 'that the murderer may not triumph over the innocent victim,' will be fulfilled. Because God has the last word, it will be so" (Wengst, *"Freut euch, ihr Völker, mit Gottes Volk!"* [2008], 161–62, quoting Max Horkheimer, *Die Sehnsucht nach dem ganz Anderen* [1970], 62). For the link to motifs in Paul's sayings about judgment and their alteration in 2 Thessalonians cp. Popkes, "Die Bedeutung des zweiten Thessalonicherbriefs" (2004), 53–61.

44. Cp. David W. Kuck, *Judgment and Community Conflict* (1992), 150–239 on 1 Cor 3:5–4:5; Kuck considers 2 Thess 1:5–6, viewed against the background of other judgment texts in Paul, to be Pauline because of its comprehensive vision of judgment for Christians and outsiders.

that, among other things, a prejudgment of Judaism is rejected, 2 Thessalonians thus achieves a certain *rapprochment* with the Jewish people as a whole. That tendency continues in 2 Thess 2:1–12, for if the experience of suffering is a sign pointing to God's righteous future judgment, then the question of suffering and its causes is the focal point in separating the righteous from the unrighteous, and not so much the fact of belonging to a faith-community.

6.3 The Present as the Time of the "Enemy of the Law" and the Coming Apocalyptic Struggle: 2 Thessalonians 2:1–12

[2:1] As to the coming (τῆς παρουσίας) of our Lord Jesus Christ and our being gathered together (ἐπισυναγωγῆς) to him, we beg you, brothers and sisters, [2] not to be quickly shaken (σαλευθῆναι) in mind or alarmed (θροεῖσθαι), either by spirit[-revelation] (πνεύματος) or by word (διὰ λόγου) or by letter, as though from us (δὶ ἐπιστολῆς ὡς δι' ἡμῶν), to the effect that the day of the Lord is already here. [3] Let no one deceive you in any way (ἐξαπατήσῃ); for [that day will not come][45] unless the rebellion (ἀποστασία) comes first and the lawless one (ἄνθρωπος τῆς ἀνομίας) is revealed (ἀποκαλυφθῇ), the [son of] destruction (υἱὸς τῆς ἀπωλείας), [4] [the enemy (ἀντικείμενος) who] opposes and exalts himself above every so-called god (πάντα λεγόμενον θεὸν) or object of worship (σέβασμα), so that he takes his seat in the temple of God (ναὸν τοῦ θεοῦ), declaring himself to be God (ἀποδεικνύντα ἑαυτὸν ὅτι ἔστιν θεός).

[5] Do you not remember that I told you these things when I was still with you? [6] [But now] you know what is restraining him (τὸ καέχον), so that he may be revealed (ἀποκαλυφθῆναι) when his time comes (ἑαυτοῦ καιρῷ). [7] For the mystery (μυστήριον) of lawlessness (τῆς ἀνομίας) is already at work, but only until the one who now restrains it (ὁ κατέχων) is removed [from the center] (ἐκ μέσου γένηται).[46]

[8] And then the lawless (ὁ ἄνομος) one will be revealed (ἀποκαλυφθήσεται), whom the Lord Jesus will destroy (ἀνελεῖ) with the breath of his mouth (πνεύματι τοῦ στόματος αὐτοῦ), annihilating him by the manifestation of his coming (ἐπιφανείᾳ τῆς παρουσίας αὐτοῦ). [9] The coming (παρουσία) of the lawless one is apparent in the working of Satan, who uses all power (δυνάμει), signs, lying wonders, [10] and every kind of wicked (ἀδικίας) deception (ἀπάτῃ) for those who are perishing, because they refused to love the truth and so be saved. [11]

45. Vv. 3b–4 are an anacoluthon. "'The day of the Lord will not come' [fut.] must be supplied prior or supplementary to ἐὰν" (von Dobschütz, *Die Thessalonicherbriefe*, 268).

46. This clause is an ellipsis. Many translations (though not NRSV) add a verb, e.g., "it only lasts until..." (thus NIV: "[the one who now holds it back] will continue to do so"; cp., e.g., Rigaux, *Thessaloniciens*, 670–71; Trilling, *Der zweite Brief*, 94). For a grammatical analysis of this *crux* in 2 Thess 2:6–7 see esp. Barnouin, "Problèmes de traduction" (1977), 489–90; also, e.g., Menken, *2 Thessalonians*, 108–9; Röcker, *Belial und Katechon* (2009), 410.

For this reason God sends them a powerful delusion, leading them to believe what is false, [12] so that all who have not believed the truth but took pleasure in unrighteousness (ἀδικίᾳ) will be condemned.

6.3.1 Second Thessalonians 2:2: What does it mean to say "the day of the Kyrios is already here"?

At the center of the argumentation in opposition to 1 Thessalonians we find 2 Thess 2:2, the verse that calls the possible means of deceiving the community by name: a spiritual revelation, an apostle's or preacher's word, or even a letter bearing the names of the three apostles. Apart from 2 Thessalonians, it is only 1 Thessalonians that bears the names of those three senders. This means that only 1 Thessalonians can be meant, and it is thus branded as false—that is the only letter that is said to come from "us," that is, from Paul, Silvanus, and Timothy. Attention to the authorial plural in both writings[47] thus produces a clear answer to the question about the letter or letters referred to in 2 Thess 2:2. The authors of 2 Thessalonians are thus speaking of this 1 Thessalonians; they copy its form and intend to replace it with their own writing. Among other things, that letter,[48] so they say, announces that the day of the Kyrios is already here. That message, which evokes alarm and uncertainty, is a deception, leading the community astray (2:2–3). Now we must examine what statements and content in 1 Thessalonians could evoke and support such a supposition. Who are these people who think that 1 Thessalonians announces that the "day" has already arrived? But is this a correct presentation of the slogan in the first place? Frequently in exegetical literature one finds support for the opinion that the expression ἐνέστηκεν ἡ ἡμέρα τοῦ κυρίου

47. In exegetical literature—as also in the case of 1 Thessalonians—scarcely any attention is paid to the stated threefold authorship in interpreting the letter, resulting again and again in less-than-concrete statements such as "2 Thess presents itself as a Pauline letter" (Schreiber, "Der zweite Thessalonicherbrief," 443). But the fact that a supposed Paul-Silvanus-Timothy letter attacks another letter supposedly "from us" can, in fact, only mean that it is aiming at 1 Thessalonians, the sole letter yet known to have come supposedly from Paul, Silvanus, and Timothy. Hence attention to the authorial plural makes a crucial contribution to the interpretation of 2 Thessalonians also; in the case of 2:2 it produces a better-grounded clarification of the reference to an ἐπιστολή as pointing to 1 Thessalonians.

48. For the question whether ὡς δι᾽ ἡμῶν, "as though from us" refers only to "letter," to "word and letter," or to "spirit, word and letter" cp. Trilling, *Der zweite Brief*, 77: "All that is certain is that it refers to 'letter.'" For suggested interpretations in exegetical discussion see E.-M. Becker, "Ὡς δι᾽ ἡμῶν," 62ff. Her own suggestion is that the reference is to a no-longer-surviving Pauline or pseudo-Pauline letter and its interpretation of 1 Thessalonians, which is deemed false (pp. 64–69). Becker also speaks of 2 Thessalonians alone as an intended "Pauline letter" and does not discuss the authorial plural. See below for a possible answer to the question of the reference of ὡς δι᾽ ἡμῶν, that is to say, which statements of 1 Thessalonians are contradicted by 2 Thessalonians.

must be translated "the day of the Lord is coming in the immediate future."[49] But in light of the perfect tense of the verb ἐνίστημι, emphatically placed before it and meaning "be present," it is grammatically certain[50] that the text is speaking of a "being present," a day of the Kyrios that has supposedly already arrived at the present time of the text. In 2 Thess 1:5–9 the authors have already introduced the definition of the "day" (1:10) as a comprehensive and universal event of judgment in order to contradict that idea; the added remarks in 2:3–12 are intended to give their position additional support.

What is the information in 1 Thessalonians to which this announcement of the "day" having come could refer? First of all, it is clear that the key words of the statement that begins in 2 Thess 2:1, "parousia, coming" (παρουσία) and "being gathered together, joining" (ἐπισυναγωγή), must represent a reference to the description of the parousia in 1 Thess 4:13–17 (4:15 + 17). But nothing is said there about the hoped-for event having already occurred. The keyword ἡμέρα, "day," then points to 1 Thess 5:2 and the following text about the destruction of the opponents, who embody "night." Here we could somehow read something like the presence of the "day," because the repeated and emphatic assurance that "we" are already of the "day" (5:5, 8) could have been taken by some recipients to mean that that "day" was already present.[51] But that kind of interpretation is too vague; it gives no compelling ground for the conviction that the Last Day has already dawned. These are the grounds that cause some exegetes to translate the saying about the coming of the "day" in 2 Thess 2:2 as referring to something imminently expected. That is, they rightly assume that the element of judgment is always associated with the motif of the "day" in the Old Testament and in Judaism,[52]

49. Cp. the multiple shifts in common translations of the expression as reported by Allen M. Stephenson, "On the meaning of ἐνέστηκεν ἡ ἡμέρα τοῦ κυρίοῦ in 2 Thessalonians 2,2" (1968); see further, e.g., Lietaert Peerbolte, *The Antecedents of Antichrist*, 73–74, who argues for the translation "is about to come."

50. Cp. Trilling, *Untersuchungen*, 124; idem, *Der zweite Brief*, 78; Bruce, *1 & 2 Thessalonians* (1982), 165; Marxsen, *Der zweite Brief*, 43; Menken, *2 Thessalonians*, 98–99; Gaventa, *First and Second Thessalonians*, 109; Reinmuth, "Der zweite Brief an die Thessalonicher," 177; Nicholl, *From Hope to Despair*, 115–25. The translation "the day is immediately at hand" then does not rest on grammatical arguments but on an otherwise undiscoverable meaning of the sentence, because supposedly it does not fit the situation of the readers; thus von Dobschütz, *Die Thessalonicherbriefe*, 267–68, and esp. Stephenson, "On the meaning," 451; cp. the review of research and discussion in Röcker, *Belial und Katechon*, 346–61, who himself argues for the future solution, referring, *inter alia*, to parallels in Hippolytus, *Comm. in Dan.* IV, 19, 3ff. (pp. 357–58). It is important that in any case the present time, whichever it is, is already filled and shaped by the event of the "day," whether one thinks it has already arrived or is imminent, so that the difference in readings is relative.

51. On this see, e.g., Marxsen, *Der zweite Brief*, 46–47.

52. Thus, e.g., Lietaert Peerbolte, *The Antecedents of Antichrist*, 73, who therefore cannot see any "already present day" in 1 Thessalonians.

YHWH's last judgment, which belongs especially also to the vision from Isaiah 66 in 2 Thessalonians 1, previously cited, and that is declared explicitly in 1:10 to be the major event of the "day."

However, there is a statement in 1 Thessalonians that can refer to this "has come" in the sense of stating an eschatological date and fact as having happened, and that also contains an unmistakable allusion to a judgment that has already occurred. In 1 Thess 2:16 we find the only remark in the letter about an eschatological event that has definitively happened; at the same time, it consists of an elementary statement of judgment: God's wrath has already fallen upon "the Jews." Thus 2 Thess 2:2 can be primarily connected only to 1 Thess 2:16; the concepts of "parousia" and "day of the Kyrios" that also appear in the course of 1 Thessalonians must, in the mind of the authors of 2 Thessalonians, be connected with an event of judgment. Thus 2 Thess 2:2 implicitly holds the position, as previously in 1:5–10 with regard to the concept of separate judgments in 1 Thessalonians, that all the elements of the "day" belong together as parts of a universal and unified event. To put it more precisely, the letter speaks to people, or at least is written from the perspective of people, who also hold for a unified eschatological idea of judgment, to a readership of 1 Thessalonians that is also Jewish-Christian.[53] Consequently, according to 2 Thess 2:1–2, one must suppose that these people have been shaken and terrified by an event of great significance that could also be interpreted as a judgment on the Jewish people, so that they believe the "day" has come. A reading of 1 Thess 2:14–17 and engagement with that text that coincided with a catastrophe that could be interpreted as a judgment on the Jewish people would then be the moment that evoked great unrest, and for which 2 Thess 2:2 wants to offer a corrective. It makes no essential difference whether one regards 1 Thessalonians as authentic or not. The simple existence of the passage in 1 Thess 2:14–17 was sufficient, at the time of the composition of pseudepigraphical 2 Thessalonians—generally supposed to have been in the second half of the first century C.E.[54]—to connect the

53. For the origins of the supposed authors of both letters and their readership see further below at 6.5.

54. See, e.g., Trilling, *Der zweite Brief*, 28: "from ca. 80 C.E. to the early second century"; Marxsen, *Der zweite Brief*, 112: "soon after 70 C.E. or around the turn of the first century"; Laub, *1. und 2. Thessalonicherbrief*, 40: "some time in the last two decades of the first century"; Menken, *2 Thessalonians*, 66: "some time between the year 80 and the early second century CE"; Simon Légasse, *Les épîtres aux Thessaloniciens* (1999), 356: "a particular time at the end of the first century or beginning of the second"; Börschel, *Die Konstruktion einer christlichen Identität*, 62: "within the last decades of the first century"; P.-G. Müller, *Der Erste und Zweite Brief*, 233–34: "the late apostolic era, the time from 100 to 120 C.E." (234); Paul Metzger, *Katechon*, 90: "toward the end of the first century C.E."; Schreiber, "Der zweite Thessalonicherbrief," 444–45: "probably . . . in one of the generations after Paul, that is, in the late first century." Martin Karrer, following Otto Merk, differs and votes for a dating in the 60s of the first century, not long after Paul's death ("Der zweite Thessalonicherbrief und

events during the Roman-Jewish war and in the time thereafter with the event of judgment announced there.

To my knowledge the only exegete who has thus far pointed out and interpreted this possible relationship between the two letters is Gerhard Krodel in his short commentary on 2 Thessalonians.[55] Krodel, together with Pearson, regards 1 Thess 2:13–16 as an interpolation and thinks that the authors of 2 Thessalonians are reacting to the people responsible for it. They are supposed to have declared, in light of the destruction of Jerusalem, that the day of the Lord had come: "Jerusalem's fate of A.D. 70 was viewed by them as the inbreaking of God's ultimate judgment (1 Thess. 2:16). If the wrath of God has already come upon the Jews (*eis telos*) and the Christians already experience the messianic woes in their suffering (2 Thess. 1:4), then the conclusion could be drawn that 'the Day of the Lord is present' (2:2a). Against this background our letter was written in order to give directions to Christians 'shaken in mind and excited' (2:2a)."[56] This reading as about an event that has taken place in the presence of the authors is also favored by the fact that the use of the verb φθάνω in 1 Thess 2:16 indicates the presence of a qualified point in time in apocalyptic texts such as Dan 4:11, 20, 22, 24, 28; 7:13; 8:7; 12:1 (LXX), and in particular the messianic one.[57] This underscores the way in which especially Jewish and Jewish-Christian readers, and thus also the authors of 2 Thessalonians, could have understood 1 Thess 2:16: it announces the coming of the messianic judgment, but only as a destroying catastrophe for (nearly) all Jews, the people Israel. The point of the correction in 2 Thess 2:2 is thus an alternative

Gottes Widersacher," 105, following, *inter alia*, Merk, "Nachahmung Christi" [1989], 326). The *terminus ad quem* for the dating of 2 Thessalonians is the first definite external attestation, in the Marcionite canon at the middle of the second century; the proposal occasionally made, that it is cited in *PolPhil* 2,11,3, is not well-founded; on this see Lindemann, "Abfassungszweck," 42ff. (He dates 2 Thessalonians to "the end of the first century," p. 44.) For 1 Thessalonians as well, the first certain external witness is the Marcionite canon. Even so, a listing of possible allusions to 1–2 Thessalonians in early texts of the church fathers in P.-G. Müller, *Der Erste und Zweite Brief*, 55, assumes a relatively early attestation, without any discussion.

55. Krodel, "2 Thessalonians" (1978), 85ff.; idem, "2 Thessalonians" (1993), 45–46; cp. idem, "The 'religious power of lawlessness' (katéchon)" (1990), 444. Cp. also Best, *Thessalonians*, 276, 279, who considers such a relationship, among others, as does Marxsen, *Der zweite Brief*, 45, although without this interpretation in terms of contemporary events.

56. Krodel, "2 Thessalonians" (1978), 87. The same historical location of 2 Thess 2:2, though without reference to 1 Thess 2:16 and without really entering into the question of Jewish or Jewish-Christian relationships and perspectives, is proposed by Roh, *Der zweite Thessalonicherbrief*, 121–26: it is said to be about the arrival, the "day," and the proclamation of Vespasian as the new world ruler in the year 69 C.E., which is the focus of 2 Thess 2:2. For this interpretation, in my opinion tendentially accurate in connection with 2 Thess 2:1–12, see further below at 6.3.3.

57. Fitzer, art. φθάνω, *TDNT* 9 (1974), 89–92; see 2.1 n. 5 above.

interpretation of the present and the then-present defeats of Judaism, from the point of view of Jewish Christians: the day of the Kyrios has not yet come! Because the events of the present are not to be equated with the general and sole judgment it has not yet arrived and so neither has the parousia of Christ. The one who has come is someone else.

6.3.2 Time and Chronology in 2 Thessalonians 2:3–12

The continuation in 2 Thess 2:3–12 brings a further development of the great apocalyptic mural in 1:5–10, now moving to a depiction of the end-time battle that will precede the divine judgment. It is dominated by mysteriously-announced eschatological figures, including the powerful and all-determining action of Jesus. The exegete should attend primarily to the chronology. If, according to 2 Thess 2:2, the actual judgment event on the day of the Kyrios has not yet begun, at what point in time are "we," the senders and recipients of the letter, now living? What are the marks of this time, and what events are before us, either immediately or later? Because of the fact that a saying like "the day of the Kyrios is already here!" is denied and instead, in what follows, among other things a "restraining figure" is introduced (2:6, 7), it has become a habit among exegetes to see here an "apocalyptic schedule"[58] in the sense of a "delay" of the end-time events; this becomes a means for dismissing, for example, Gnostics, visionaries, and all types of enthusiasts[59] as preachers of an "immediate return."[60]

But the real significance of the supposed theoretical chronologies adopted by apocalyptic groups lies in the problem of what to say about the present time, and what kinds of behavior and attitudes are appropriate for those chronologies. Luise Schottroff has emphasized this function of apocalyptic statements about time in the context of her social-historical analysis of the Synoptic apocalypses: "The terms 'immediate expectation,' 'enthusiasm,' and 'delay of the parousia' are not particularly useful for describing the content of the apocalyptic expectations in the Synoptic tradition because they are too one-sided; they shift attention to the idea of time periods. Crucial, rather, are the behaviors tied to the different forms of imminent expectation: does one react to present suffering with agitation or watchfulness—*that* is what is decisive. The longing for the end and the agitation that Mark opposes should not be regarded as the position of 'opponents' or 'false

58. See above, 6.1 n. 16.

59. Cp., e.g., Lütgert, *Die Vollkommenen im Philipperbrief und die Enthusiasten in Thessalonich* (1909), 82–102 ("visionaries")"; Schmithals, *Paulus und die Gnostiker* (1965), 123–218 ("gnostics"); Jewett, *Thessalonian Correspondence*, 161–78 ("millenarians").

60. Trilling, *Der zweite Brief*, 78: "immediate expectation"; Marxsen, *Der zweite Brief*, 54–55: "apocalypticists" in "enthusiastic excitement"; Börschel, *Die Konstruktion einer christlichen Identität*, 409: "The problem of acute expectation," and many others; for further expressions of this sort see the list in Nicholl, *From Hope to Despair*, 125 n. 55.

teaching,' but as the expressions of the lives of suffering people."[61] If, then, this is about an "eschatological dating of the present,"[62] in a pastoral sense as well, then "apocalyptic prophecies [are] ... a theological confrontation with a present experienced as oppressive. They are the expression of a *present* that is taken altogether seriously."[63] This means that a right description of the present time of the apocalyptic text and the people it is meant to influence is central; the so-called calculation of the future and lengths of time is subordinated to it. This is about a genuine insight into the present, so that the attitudes and behaviors that are appropriate to and demanded by it may be encouraged. It is always—and this is true for today also—about judging the current political situation through an interpretation of the signs of the times that does justice to the reality, in order not to fall into a panic or cultivate harmful illusions. Within the lives of messianic communities this also coincides with the question of the truth of their confession of their own Lord in the current political context and the question of how fidelity to him can be maintained.

We can also perceive in the passage at 2 Thess 2:1–12, whose resemblance to the Synoptic Gospels is often and rightly emphasized,[64] the kind of pastoral attitude

61. Luise Schottroff, "Die Gegenwart in der Apokalyptik der synoptischen Evangelien" (1983/1990), 77; emphasis in the original. See also in the same place n. 10 on "apocalyptic fever," which should not be seen as the *topos* of a doctrine but as "expression of a situation of suffering."

62. Ibid., 74.

63. Ibid., 87.

64. Orchard, "Thessalonians and the Synoptic Gospels" (1938), 31–42; he shows that the Matthean apocalypse is particular reveals numerous parallels to both the Thessalonian letters; see also, *inter alia*, Cothenet, "La deuxième Épître aux Thessaloniciens et l'Apocalypse synoptique" (1954); Rigaux, *Thessaloniciens*, 95–105; Holland, *The Tradition That You Received From Us*, 134–42; Hartman, "The Eschatology of 2 Thessalonians" (1990), 480ff.; Menken, *2 Thessalonians*, 100–1; Karrer, "Der zweite Thessalonicherbrief und Gottes Widersacher," 112–13; most recently esp. Röcker, *Belial und Katechon*, 365–69, 411–14, 416–17, 485ff., 505–6, 513–14, 520ff. (with bibliography). The comparison with the Synoptic apocalypses also demonstrates that the suddenness-motif of the "thief" in 1 Thess 5:2–3 and the "schedule" in 2 Thess 2:1–12 does not force us to separate the two letters. In Matthew 24 we find the signs of the end (vv. 3–28, 32), which can be regarded as a kind of "schedule," and the sudden arrival of the "day" in the form of the thief-parable (vv. 42–44) are placed side by side as the expression of *one* time at the redactional level. This shows that the eschatology of 1 and 2 Thessalonians, too, need not be separated by a hiatus in time: see esp. the advocates of the authenticity of 2 Thessalonians such as Schmid, "Der Antichrist und die hemmende Macht" (1949), 343, Barclay, "Conflict in Thessalonica," 525; Still, *Conflict at Thessalonica*, 46–60 (esp. 53ff.); idem, "Eschatology in the Thessalonian Letters" (1999); Nicholl, *From Hope to Despair*, 115–32; or Fee, *The First and Second Letters*, 268–97, none of whom proposes a significant distance in time between 2 Thess 2:1–12 and the content of 1 Thessalonians 4–5.

intended to soothe minds seized by panic and horror[65] to the point of a destabilized state of awareness (νοῦς, v. 2). The minds of those addressed have been exposed to deception through a false interpretation of the present. The source of that deception is, among other things, a supposed apostolic letter (v. 3). But lies, deception, and leading astray are the signs of the time of the "lawless one" (2:9–12). Does that mean that his time and the present, in which a false letter has been received, are not far apart? The time levels to which the end-time figures belong must be distinguished before their content can be interpreted.[66]

The statement to be refuted is clear: ὡς ὅτι ἐνέστηκεν ἡ ἡμέρα τοῦ κυρίου: "the day of the Lord is already here" (2:2). That "day," apart from the previously described events of judgment that, according to 1:10, are part of it, is defined here in 2:1 first of all by the keywords "parousia" (παρουσία) of Jesus Christ and "being gathered together" (ἐπισυναγωγή) with him, which are to take place simultaneously. These events have not yet happened: no return of Jesus, no opportunity to join with him,[67] and hence not the "day." With 2:3 begins the authors' own view of the course of time, to which the text aims to bind its readers and recipients; in contrast to it, the assertion of a present "day" is said to be a deception. It is clear that this is a kind of alternative view of time because of the adverbial πρῶτον ("first," 2:3) and the subsequent sequence of different apocalyptic circumstances and figures, accompanied by further linguistic signals about timing: first the "rebellion" /ἡ ἀποστασία[68] and the "lawless one" (or: enemy of the law) /ὁ ἄνθρωπος τῆς ἀνομίας,[69] the "one destined for destruction" (lit.: son of destruction) /ὁ υἱός τῆς ἀπωλείας, the "opponent" /ὁ ἀντικείμενος and his deeds (2:3). Then the text speaks twice of something or someone that delays or restrains, τὸ κατέχον ("what is now restraining," 2:6) and ὁ κατέχων ("the one who now restrains," 2:7)[70] whom or

65. Θροεῖσθαι (v. 2), to be moved to terror and/or alarm, is also a keyword in the Markan apocalypse (Mark 13:7); on this see Luise Schottroff, "Gegenwart," 76 n. 8.

66. Cp. Marlene Crüsemann, "2 Thessalonians," 826–27.

67. This purely future idea of communion with Jesus Christ is something 2 Thessalonians shares with 1 Thessalonians; cp. the exegesis of 1 Thess 4:13–17; 5:1–11 above in chap. 5.1–5.4.

68. For this concept see 6.3.3 below.

69. For the concept, its usual translation in exegetical literature, and its political implications see below, 6.3.3. For the question of the original character of the reading ὁ ἄνθρωπος τῆς ἀνομίας, especially on the basis of the OT parallels, against the majority of the mss., which read ὁ ἄνθρωπος τῆ ἁμαρτίας, see Börschel, *Die Konstruktion einer christlichen Identität*, 417–18.

70. Substantivized neuter participle and substantivized masculine participle of κατέχειν, which "here undoubtedly means 'hold back,' 'hinder,' not 'hold fast' or (mythologically) 'hold bound,' 'bind'" (Trilling, *Der zweite Brief*, 89 n. 341, with reference to Liddell/Scott 926, et al.). He himself translates Katechon here as "restraining force"; for the semantic determination of the concept see, e.g., Rigaux, *L'Antéchrist et l'Opposition au Royaume Messianique* (1932), 296ff.; Paul Metzger, *Katechon*, 3–10.

which the readers should "now" recognize / νῦν ... οἴδατε. This is apparently at work until the "lawless one" is revealed at its own time / ἐν τῷ ἑαυτοῦ καιρῷ (2:6). But the "mystery of lawlessness" / μυστήριον ... τῆς ἀνομίας is "already" / ἤδη at work in some way; it only remains for the delaying force to be removed (2:7).[71] "Then" / τότε will come the revelation of the lawless one previously named, now in Greek the "enemy of the law" /ὁ ἄνομος, whom Kyrios Jesus at his return will destroy with the breath of his mouth (2:8). From vv. 9–10 onward there is a further description of the evil "parousia" / παρουσία of the "enemy of the law" until the judgment of all who do not believe the truth (2:12). The use here of the key word "parousia," and hence the same concept as that used for the coming and presence of Jesus, is an important textual signal that requires evaluation. It is thus about distinguishing two different parousias.[72]

The result is the understanding of the course of time in 2 Thessalonians 2 that is common in scholarship today. It can be summarized,[73] *pars pro toto*, in Klaus Berger's depiction of it as "the extension of time until the end":

> The idea of time can be reconstructed as follows: 1. Near future: (a) the "mystery of iniquity" is effective, but still veiled ... (b) he/it that restrains (v. 6); 2. Middle future: (a) destruction of the one who restrains (v. 7), (b) revelation of the "son of corruption" (vv. 3, 6b, 8) ...; 3. The day of the Lord: (a) Jesus destroys the "adversary" ... (b) Judgment on all who do not believe the truth.

This example of an overview shows clearly that as a rule it is presumed that 2 Thess 2:1–12 depicts a stepwise extension over time of ever-new, essentially future entities in a far-distant future time. The ultimate point is the "day of the Lord," which will be preceded by a mediate and, before that, a proximate future. What remains completely absent from this model is the actual present. At most, a certain kind of present activity is accorded the "mystery of lawlessness."[74] An otherwise

71. Literally "removed from the center" / ἐκ μέσου γένηται. This takes up the LXX's Hebraizing expression for the removal of whatever is evil from the midst of Israel (Gen 35:2; Exod 31:14; Num 16:33, 19:20; Deut 2:15–16, and frequently elsewhere). Cp., e.g., Reinmuth, "Der zweite Brief an die Thessalonicher," 179. In light of that it is a dubious matter to see the Katechon as fundamentally positive; cp. the opinions in n. 81.

72. See further below at 6.3.3.

73. Klaus Berger, *Theologiegeschichte des Urchristentums*, 345; see also Menken, *2 Thessalonians*, 375ff.; Trilling, *Untersuchungen*, 78ff. ("... since all the events named there lie in the future," 79); Krodel, "2 Thessalonians" (1978), 90ff.; idem, "2 Thessalonians" (1993), 46–47, 49, and many others.

74. Berger, *Theologiegeschichte des Urchristentums*, also sets that "mystery" in a future sphere. Regarding the idea of time that underlies many interpretations, see the presentation in Trilling, *Der zweite Brief*, 113–17, which projects the imagined sequence of time into the future of the text and sees its present shaped only by the "mystery of iniquity" and the "knowledge" of the might of the Katechon (ibid., 88–89). Cp. the overview in Donfried,

event-free textual present is seen as being extended almost to infinity through the "restrainer" or the "delay" (κατέχον / -ων); something that in terms of the history of the text's effects has also made possible a speculative reception of this phenomenon.[75] Then the main message of the text is that nothing special is really happening "now"; the events that can be called the "day" do not belong to the present. This means that the authors of the text are contrasting a proclamation of the "day of the Kyrios" that is determinative of the present and the associated excitement against the stepladder of a receding futurity. The present would in effect be emptied; instead of the exciting "day," nothing at all is happening "now."

But in a writing that is to be conceived as pseudepigraphical and therefore from a fictive or real person or persons in the past—in the case of 1 and 2 Thessalonians these are supposed to be the apostles Paul, Silvanus, and Timothy—such a determination of the future and thus also of the present must be seen as utterly improbable. This is because in cases of pseudepigraphy one must reckon with multiple presents, pasts, and futures, in various mixtures, in every writing. We need to attend to that first in this special text, because the common description of the stages of time in 2 Thessalonians 2 stems essentially from the epoch when people generally assumed Pauline authorship of 2 Thessalonians.[76] It is odd that there has been practically no revision of the traditional analysis of the "time scheme" in 2 Thessalonians 2 since people began to accept the idea of pseudepigraphical authorship,[77] something that in my opinion this text truly demands.

"2 Thessalonians and the Church of Thessalonica" (1993), 93 (in agreement with Holland, *The Tradition That You Received From Us*, 112); Lietaert Peerbolte, "The KATEXON / KATEXΩN of 2 Thess 2:6–7" (1997), 140; P.-G. Müller, *Der Erste und Zweite Brief*, 269, etc. For the translation of ἀνομία and ἄνομος see 6.3.3 below. Börschel, *Die Konstruktion einer christlichen Identität*, 409–30, arrives at a somewhat different analysis that orders the present to the "mystery" and also to the Katechon, and the future to the "lawless one"; similarly before her Barnouin, "Problèmes de traduction," 483–84; Donfried, "The Theology of 2 Thessalonians" (1993), 93–94; idem, "2 Thessalonians and the Church of Thessalonica," 137; Richard, *Thessalonians*, 346; Reinmuth, "Der zweite Brief an die Thessalonicher," 176, 180, 182.

75. For the interpretation and special history of reception of the "Katechon," see n. 81 below.

76. And, in case one still or again begins with that assumption (see 6.1 n. 14 above), one can still legitimately go on doing so. On the contrary, Lietaert Peerbolte, *KATEXON*, 139, 145ff., is one of the few authors who explicitly declares the pseudepigraphic authorship of 2 Thessalonians to be the hermeneutical starting point for an investigation of the apocalyptic figures. The pseudepigraphical letter is deliberately vague in speaking of the Katechon; no historical identification was intended. (See the next footnote.)

77. My conclusions on this point are essentially confirmed by Roh, *Der zweite Thessalonicherbrief*, 85–88 (esp. 88 n. 208). Cp. Marlene Crüsemann, "2 Thessalonians," 826–27; eadem, "Die Briefe nach Thessaloniki und das gerechte Gericht" (1999), 257–74; cp. also the indications in Popkes, "Die Bedeutung des zweiten Thessalonicherbriefs," 62–63.

Eckart Reinmuth, within an excursus on New Testament Pauline pseudepigraphy in his commentary on 2 Thessalonians, has very helpfully formulated some conclusions regarding the communication of time-levels in a pseudepigraphical text;[78] I will cite him here at length:

> The fictive and—in the thought-world of the addressees—inconsistent datings in this example of early Jewish writings prove sensible at the moment when we *understand them in terms of their intended effect, that is, as speaking to the historical "now" of the addressees*, their actual situation and experience of history against the background of the presumed situation. But that would only be possible if the corresponding *references* were understandable for the recipients, that is, if they could be *appropriately decoded*. This *actual evidence of cultural-historical allusions, mainly clothed in the form of prophecies about the future*, is also a decisive moment and criterion for the modern identification of pseudepigraphical writings. Critical scholarship *recognizes prophetic statements of events that have already happened (vaticinia ex eventu) by their concreteness.* That concreteness is relative within the text itself, inasmuch as for the most part the *vaticinia ex eventu are embedded in depictions of the future that do not adhere to the present they project*. Hence within the text the transition from the concrete to the general is key, for it is in that changeover that we can recognize the *point of intersection with the present* in which the recipients can recognize themselves. The book of Daniel offers a revealing example: the prophecies in chaps. 10–12 become more concrete, the closer they approach to the "now" of the author .... In 11:3–39 the history since Alexander the Great is narrated as prophecy; beginning with v. 21 the text relates the events since the appearance of Antiochus IV. Epiphanes in the year 175. *Here the degree of detail increases*, without any apparent narrative necessity for it. But after 11:40 that degree of detail disappears; we find here a prophetic style that actually speaks of the future from the perspective of the time between 167 and 164. *Consequently, the unlocking of the historical present of the addressees is an important function of the vaticinium ex eventu for the application of the text. It is about the existence of the predictions of the future in the present of the recipients*—and not in the present time in which it is supposed to have been written.

The stages in 2 Thess 2:1–12 that, in previous opinion, are described as future thus present their purely future image in a pseudepigraphical writing solely on the fictional time-level of the apostolic past. Seen from the time of the historical

78. Reinmuth, "Der zweite Brief an die Thessalonicher," 195–96 (emphasis supplied; the excursus is on pp. 190–200). It is a shame that the author of these observations did not apply them consistently in his own preceding interpretation of 2 Thess 2:1–12 (pp. 174–83; see n. 74 above). For the analogous time-structure of the political "prophecy" in the book of Daniel, see also Jürgen Ebach, "Apokalypse," 33–42; idem, "Apokalypse und Apokalyptik," 219–23, 238ff.

apostles, all the events and figures from the "lawless one" to the returning Messiah appear as arriving only in the future. That is important also within the imagined and pretended time of writing. But since the authors want to convey crucial information to their real contemporaries in a later era, we need to pay attention to signals in the text that indicate a leap in time. The possibilities for the "trick" of *vaticinia ex eventu*, after all, consist primarily in "predicting" the real present of the authors with the aid of an apparent prophecy, and with the aid of such a "prediction," as detailed as possible, to support the believability of a statement about something that, at the authorial level, really has not yet happened, that is, a genuine prediction of the future.

Thus the questions that need to be asked if we are to discover the real time of the later authors, and connected with that, their idea of their times, are:

1. Where is something called "prophecy"?
2. What era is described in particular detail, so that it allows us to conclude that this is a description of the actual present?

Beginning at 2:3, the text answers these questions quite clearly: (1) In v. 5, between the first mention of the "lawless one" and his deeds and the resumption of that theme in 2:7 + 8, we find an insertion that is clearly marked as "prophetic": "Do you not remember that I told you these things when I was still with you?" This explicitly states that the appearance of the "lawless one" has been prophesied, on the one hand, in the distant past of the historical community between apostle(s) and congregation. But on the other hand that element of a past prophecy also remains effective on the level of the fictive apostolic time of writing in which the letter is supposed to have been written; we thus are dealing with an apparently doubly-prophesied saying, perhaps going back to the time of the community's founding. So we should see v. 5 as a kind of time marker that assures the real later readers that their own present was prophetically foreseen. Since the authors have thus affirmed their role as prophets, in vv. 6 + 7 they remain a moment longer on the level of the fictive early period, since they have to go on acting as though they were speaking to the community of that apostolic time. Hence νῦν in v. 6 is to be read as a "now" of the past, because at the level of the historical apostles Paul, Silvanus, and Timothy the announced prophecy has not yet been fulfilled. There is a need to explain why nothing that was prophesied has yet happened. "You know" / οἴδατε (v. 6) is a means used in pseudepigraphical letters to introduce a new subject[79] by "referring" to supposed existing knowledge.

79. Trilling, *Der zweite Brief*, 88: "The frequent references to the 'knowledge' of the recipients and the appeals to their 'memory' by Paul (cp. only 1 Thess 2:9; 3:3b, 4; 4:2) are deployed as elements of pseudepigraphical style." Since, according to my analysis, 1 Thessalonians already used such elements, and so much more frequently, that we can recognize pseudepigraphical technique thereby (see above at 3.3.1), this means for 2 Thessalonians that it follows its model in its choice of methods.

The vague figure of the "one who restrains" fulfills precisely that function; this is the κατέχον, to be understood by the actual, later readers as a figure in the past. This can be readily seen simply from its placement immediately after the "prophetic" statement in 2:5. As if it had suddenly become clear to the authors that they had to play their role as real apostles as believably as possible, they now mention a reason why the predicted revelation of the "lawless one" cannot happen "now," because that "now" is still at a fictive point in time, that is, from the perspective of the later pseudepigraphical letter-writers it lies in a long-ago past. There is a need to bridge a period of several decades before the "prophecy" can become reality. The numinous "Katechon" is ideal for that purpose: an undefined entity about whom or which the Thessalonians are supposed at some level and "somehow" to know already (v. 6).[80] Since the Katechon, according to the later, actual situation of the letter, belongs to the apostolic past and is simply there to bridge the "wide gulf" between the two, further explanations are unnecessary; he or it has (in the mean time) been removed "from their midst" (2:7). Independent of the powerful history of the effects of "katechonism" and the multiple interpretations of this entity throughout history,[81]

80. Cp. the interpretation by Lietaert Peerbolte, *KATEXON*, 147ff., who evaluates 2:5 as a deliberately ambiguous statement of the pseudo-Paul who is attempting to lead the real readers to believe he is presenting a Pauline teaching that at the same time will inform their later time about the "*anomos*" and his delay (p. 149). And yet the "*anomos*" still remains a figure in the future. Trilling, *Der zweite Brief*, 92, also emphasizes this functionality, though as a future entity on the second level of reading as well: "The Katechon is primarily a formal concept whose function is to embody the extension of time until the end"; cp. to the contrary the accurate temporal analysis by Roh, *Der zweite Thessalonicherbrief*, 86ff. (cp. previously Marlene Crüsemann, "2 Thessalonians," 826–27; eadem, "Die Briefe nach Thessaloniki und das gerechte Gericht," 257–74); see also Popkes, "Die Bedeutung des zweiten Thessalonicherbriefs," 62–63: the Katechon is the product of the "post-Pauline author," and hence the "apostasy" belongs to the time of the later readers.

81. For extensive discussion of the identity of the Katechon, and hence the history of its influence, see, e.g., the overview in Rigaux, *L'Antéchrist et l'Opposition*, 296–308; Best, *Thessalonians*, 295–301; Fraser, "A Theological Study," 142–301 (with bibliography); Trilling, *Der zweite Brief*, 95–105 (with bibliography); Richard, *Thessalonians*, 337–40; P.-G. Müller, *Der erste und zweite Brief*, 268–72; Paul Metzger, *Katechon*, 15–47 (with bibliography); and esp. Röcker, *Belial und Katechon*, 422–58, in which especially the positive identification of the Katechon with the Roman Empire as a positive force since the time of the ancient church is worth noting; on this see also Lietaert Peerbolte, *KATEXON*, 141–44. The history of influence also includes "katechonism," e.g., in Bonhoeffer; on this see not only Röcker, *Belial und Katechon*, 425ff., but also Martin Berger, "Die Katechon-Vorstellung 2 Thess 2,6f." (1996) (there see also 35–42 on the tradition of interpretation), and its role in Carl Schmitt's interpretation of the state, on which see Richard Faber, *Die Verkündigung Vergils* (1975), 159–77; Wolfgang Schuller, "Dennoch die Schwerter halten" (1996); Jürgen Ebach, "Apokalypse und Apokalyptik," 236ff. (with further bibliography). The following different solutions to the identification of the restraining power, among others, have been advocated in recent exegesis: Friedrich Freese, "Τὸ κατέχον und ὁ κατέχων" (1920/21), 77:

the parousia is restrained by "something impersonal" as well as by "sinful" people as Katechon; Rigaux, *L'Antéchrist et l'Opposition*, 307–8: an obstacle to the coming of the Antichrist, prophesied by Paul but not definitely identified; Oscar Cullmann, "Der eschatologische Charakter des Missionsauftrages" (1936/1966), 327–36: the Katechon in 2 Thessalonians, as a Pauline letter, is a clear allusion to the still incomplete mission to the Gentiles; the Katechon is Paul himself; Schmid, "Der Antichrist und die hemmende Macht," 339: the "figure of the Katechon [is] shrouded in darkness that we can no longer remove"; Léas Sirard, "La parousie de l'Antéchrist" (1961): The Katechon and the Anomos are identical and are an "evil" power; August Strobel, *Untersuchungen zum eschatologischen Verzögerungsproblem* (1961), 98–116: God is the Katechon, and the Katechon is God's plan of salvation; Otto Betz, "Der Katechon" (1962/63), 284ff.: the Katechon is the Roman emperor; D. W. B. Robinson, "II Thess 2,6: 'That which restrains' or 'That which holds away'?" (1963): Katechon and Anomos are identical; Charles H. Giblin, *The Threat to Faith* (1967), 167–242: a pseudo-prophet or a false prophetic power; Roger D. Aus, "God's Plan and God's Power" (1977): the Katechon (neuter) is God's plan; the Katechon (masculine) is God himself; Josef Ernst, *Die eschatologischen Gegenspieler* (1967), 48–57: it is the delay of the parousia; Jeffrey A. Weima, "'The man of lawlessness'" (1987), 42ff.: a "good" figure who fulfills the will of God; Douglas Farrow, "Showdown. The Message of Second Thessalonians 2:1–12 and the Riddle of the 'Restrainer'" (1989): the Katechon restrains both the Anomos and the judgment; Gerhard Krodel, "The 'religious power of lawlessness' (katéchon) as precursor of the 'lawless one' (ánomos)" (1990): a negative power in the present; Paul S. Dixon, "The Evil Restraint" (1990): the "evil" Katechon (neuter) is the "mystery of lawlessness," the Katechon (masculine) is Satan; Brown, "Intertextuality," 267ff.: the Katechon is an entity to be removed from the Temple; van Aarde, "The Second Letter to the Thessalonians Reread as Pseudepigraph" (2000), 265: the Roman regime is the Katechon; Lietaert Peerbolte, *KATEXON*: a deliberately indefinable entity; Charles E. Powell, "The Identity of the 'Restrainer'" (1997), 328ff.: the Katechon (neuter) is the Gospel; the Katechon (masculine) is God or the Holy Spirit; this is about the worldwide mission yet to be fulfilled; Nicholl, "Michael, the Restrainer removed" (2000): the archangel Michael; so also Weima, "The Slaying of Satan's Superman" (2006), 81–82; Franz Mussner, "Die 'aufhaltende' Macht von 2 Thess 2,6f" (2006), 230–31: the Katechon is the "great Western-Jewish-Christian tradition" through which God restrains the Antichrist; Sigve K. Tonstadt, "The Restrainer Removed: A Truly Alarming Thought" (2007),142–45: God is the restrainer; Karrer, "Der zweite Thessalonicherbrief und Gottes Widersacher," 127–28: an indeterminate figure who "delays," whether the Pauline preaching or the "oppressive Imperium Romanum"; Paul Metzger, *Katechon*, 283–95: the Katechon (whether neuter or masculine) is the Roman Empire and/or the Roman emperor; differently from the ancient church's evaluation, however, it is to be regarded negatively; *Roh*, *Der zweite Thessalonicherbrief*, 53–85, 99–100: a prophetic motif mentioned by Paul during his visits to Thessalonica as a reference to God, but that the later author of 2 Thessalonians refers to the political events and the Roman emperors before the appearance of Vespasian; Röcker, *Belial und Katechon*, 458–73, 487–88, follows Cullman's interpretation and supports it by comparisons to Matthew 24: the Katechon (neuter) is the proclamation of the Gospel; the Katechon (masculine) "is the one who preaches the Gospel by God's command 'to the ends of the earth'" (p. 488).

what is important for unlocking the apocalyptic ideas in the text is primarily its bridge-function. Only the delaying function is important, and those dubbed κατέχον are vividly presented. Since they serve to bridge the gap to a time that lies in the past—between the fictive prophecy and its realization in the actual present—it cannot and need not be defined as to content. Its time has passed. The Katechon is a functionally refined invention for the purpose of placing the pseudo-prophecy of a *vaticinium ex eventu* in the present scene.

Thus we already have an implicit answer to the subsequent question of how the second, actual present is to be defined, how it is supposed to influence the text and be described in particular detail in a pseudepigraphical text. The structure of the text suggests that first and especially 2 Thess 2:3–4 on the one hand is formulated as prophecy and on the other hand as a relatively concrete description of the intended present toward which the text is written: there are "apostasy/rebellion" and an "enemy of the law/lawless one"[82] of unbounded infamy and blasphemous activity who exalts himself above every divinity and exercise of religion, sits in the Temple of God and claims to be God. Supposing a coded message like those common in apocalyptic writings, the initiated addressees will get a relatively clear picture of an absolute enemy here. The time of the ἄνομος, the "lawless one" or "enemy of the law" would thus be the actual present time of the text, something that is then continued with further depictions of the time in 2:9–12. The allusion in v. 7, according to which the μυστήριον τῆς ἀνομίας is "already" (ἤδη) at work (that is, perhaps for a long time already on the pseudepigraphical level), also points to this. It shows how important it is for the authors that their readers in any case reckon with "lawlessness" and hence the "lawless one" in their own time.

The only real statement about the future on the actual time-level of the pseudepigraphical writing is the coming of the Messiah, who will put an end to the "lawless one" (2:8) while bringing the actual "day of the Kyrios." Only that event has yet to arrive. Thus this initial, purely formal analysis of the levels in time points especially to a precise characterization of the actual present: any announcement that the "day" is already here (2:2) is denied, and there is a coded announcement about who, instead, has really come, the one whose "days" accordingly make up the present: it is the "lawless one." The introduction of two "parousias" side by side in vv. 8 + 9 then points to an elementary conflict over the interpretation of the times: the two "parousias," that of the ἄνομος and that of Jesus, must be distinguished. Jesus, and therefore the "day," will only come when they have removed the "lawless one." This perspective will be further investigated below through an exegetical discussion of the "apocalyptic battle," and will be combined with an interpretation in terms of the history of the times.

In summary, let me refer again to the new time-scheme that appears when we consider the pseudepigraphical nature of the text. On the level of the actual addressees in a post-Pauline period, the sequence of time conveyed in 2 Thess 2:3–12 looks like this:

82. For the description of the content and contemporary cultural significance of these figures, see 6.3.3 below.

Time-Levels in 2 Thessalonians 2:3–12 (as Pseudepigraphy)

1. Past:
   - The fiction of the restraining power, the κατέχον (vv. 6–7), is *past*. On the level of the supposed first addressees and "apostles" it is present and immediate future. The Katechon serves to bridge the period between the actual and the supposed writing, depicted as the "now."
2. Present:
   - The ἄνομος, the "lawless one," and his deeds, the violation of the Temple and its consequences: lawlessness, deception, false and lying signs and wonders (vv. 3–4, 7a, 8a, 9–11) shape the *present* of the actual communication on the time-level of the pseudepigraphical writing. These are presented as prophecies by the supposedly apostolic authors;
3. Future:
   - Jesus' coming will occur in the (near?) *future*; he will destroy the "lawless one" (v. 8) and bring about God's righteous judgment on everyone (v. 12). This second part of the prophetic proclamation by the "apostles" is an event that actually has not yet happened on the pseudepigraphical level.

With this actual statement about the future the text answers the question why the words "the day of the Kyrios has come" in 2:2 are not yet true. That will only come to be when the "lawless one" has been slain and so God's day of judgment has arrived. Thus 2 Thess 2:3–12 is not about an extension and lengthening of time in contrast to an acute sense of imminent expectation but in the first place an alternative depiction of the *quality* of the different times and thus of what both call the "parousia" (vv. 8–9). It is about interpreting *present* events.

6.3.3 *Distinguishing Parousias: The "Lawless One" and the Messiah in 2 Thessalonians 2:3–12*

The analysis of the time-levels in 2 Thess 2:1–12 thus strongly suggests that this text is essentially describing its immediate present. The "day" has neither appeared nor has Jesus himself arrived; instead, another has come. The present is shaped by the working of the ἄνομος, the "lawless one." The horrible events of the present are not to be interpreted as expression of God's judgmental wrath but the wicked deeds of the opponent. Certainly there are signs of God's approaching judgment (2 Thess 1:5), but they are to be found in the sufferings of those who have to bear the persecutions of this enemy. Those sufferings are to be seen as a down-payment on the future rest and recuperation from these dangers, not as God's punishment in the sense of an ultimate condemnation, certainly not of eschatological destruction. Punishment awaits those who have to answer for the suffering. The future belongs to the coming Christ and his victory over that enemy.

Accordingly, there are two opposing interpretations of the signs of the times in view. They are characterized by different understandings of Jesus' parousia and the eschatological judgment. The idea of the parousia opposed by 2 Thessalonians does not involve a general judgment on a "day." From the perspective of 1 Thessalonians, the Jewish people have already been judged, independent of Jesus' parousia. Second Thessalonians evaluates the event that caused the authors of 1 Thessalonians to write the passage in 1 Thess 2:14–17 differently. It was not an expression of God's judgment but the activity of God's enemy. Hence all that must be looked for is his parousia, his coming in power. That, in the view of 2 Thessalonians, is what shapes the present. Thus an interpretation of the actual situation pits parousia against parousia. That dissension is directly expressed in the association of both parousias in 2 Thess 2:8 and 2:9,[83] the parousia of the lawless one (to which the "parousia of Satan," τῇ παρουσία κατ' ἐνέργειαν τοῦ σατανᾶ, v. 9, refers), and the parousia of Jesus, doubly and multiply referred to as "the manifestation of his parousia" (τῇ ἐπιφανείᾳ τῆς παρουσιας αὐτοῦ, v. 8). This description of the two parousias makes it abundantly clear what characterizes Jesus' parousia and why everyone can know that the "day of the Kyrios" has most certainly not come (2:2). Jesus' parousia is characterized by the fact that it brings an end for the satanic figure; that is the essence of his messianic manifestation. As long as that has not happened there can be no talk of a messianic parousia. The real deception is a confusion of the two parousias (v. 3).

Both on the level of contemporary interpretation of the times and also of the hoped-for end-time struggles, the issue is one of competition between parousias and the corresponding persons who appear in them, as well as what these figures and events are to be called. In order to avoid a confusion in which "now already" the coming of the Kyrios is to be proclaimed, the authors write that "first" (πρῶτον, v. 3), that is, before Jesus' parousia, the effects of the opponent's parousia will be manifest. That alone can be experienced already. This is also represented by the reference to the "mystery of lawlessness" that is "already" at work (v. 7), an indication of how important it is for the authors that their readers understand their present time as an era of ἀνομία, of lawlessness and hostility to the law. It accordingly reveals itself as a time of rebelliousness / ἀποστασία (v. 3), an era that causes many to "fall away" from the God of Israel.[84] In numerous Jewish-apocalyptic texts that "falling away" is one of the signs of the end of the world (Dan 11:32; *Jub* 23:14–21; *4 Esdr* 5:1–12), as also in early Christian traditions (Matt 24:10; 1 Tim 4:1; *Did.* 16:3–4). The word is also found in Acts 21:21 for rejection of the Torah, the Jewish way of life.[85] In the context of

83. In the broader context, besides, there is a competition between two "apocalypses," that of Jesus in 1:7 and that of the "lawless one" in 2:3, pointing to the same conditions in two differently-interpreted realities.

84. For what follows see Reinmuth, "Der zweite Brief an die Thessalonicher," 178; Röcker, *Belial und Katechon*, 373–79.

85. Paul is accused in Jerusalem of seducing Jewish people away from the Torah, a charge he weakens by, among other things, visiting the Temple as a deeply-believing Jew (Acts 21:26).

2 Thessalonians and its reference to "sitting in the temple" (2:4), it is in any case important that "apostasy" [also translated "rebellion" and "faithlessness"] includes especially the violation and desecration of the Jerusalem Temple: according to 2 Chron 29:19 (LXX), King Ahaz "when he was faithless" had the vessels of the Temple thrown away; 2 Chron 33:19 speaks of the sins and faithlessness of King Manasseh, who, among other things, erected altars for foreign gods and a great idol in the Jerusalem Temple; the apostasy in 1 Macc 2:15 is in the context of the desecration of the Temple by Antiochus IV (1 Macc 1:49, 57; 2:12; cp. 2 Macc 5:8).[86] In 2 Thess 2:3–4 the theme of peril to the Temple from a pagan ruler is likewise addressed.

Now it is time to give a more precise description of the figure of a great eschatological opponent with whom, according to 2 Thess 2:1–12, the real contest will be conducted. The writing is veiled—though it is by no means altogether cryptic—so as to describe the person in question unmistakably, not for just anyone but in any case for the initiates. His names are "the one of lawlessness" or "the one hostile to the law" (ὁ ἄνθρωπος τῆς ἀνομίας), the "son of destruction" (NRSV "one destined for destruction," ὁ υἱός τῆς ἀπωλείας, v. 3),[87] the "lawless one" or "enemy of the law" (ὁ ἄνομος, v. 8). While English-language exegesis has almost consistently and unquestioningly translated this as "man of lawlessness" or "lawless one," keeping close to the text,[88] until recently German-language writers chose another word in order to avoid that text-appropriate translation (and thus the sin of lawlessness or hostility to the law on the part of Christ's opponent?). In older exegesis the rather deceptive word "Antichrist" dominated,[89] though this figure is known to appear only in 1 John 2:18, 22; 4:3; 2 John 7. Newer relevant works and translations undertake paraphrases of the concept, e.g., "person of wickedness"[90] or

86. On this see Légasse, *Les épîtres aux Thessaloniciens*, 386–87.

87. Cp. Isa 57:4.

88. Exceptions are, e.g., Best, who writes "man of rebellion" (*Thessalonians*, 283ff.), and Lietaert Peerbolte, who speaks of a "man of ungodliness" (*The Antecedents of Antichrist*, 63 and *passim*.). French-language writers veil the figure as, e.g., "l'homme du péché" ["the man of sin"], so Rigaux, *L'Antéchrist et l'Opposition*, 250–398, and often in the running text as "l'Antéchrist"), or "l'homme de impiété," or "l'impie" ["the man of impiety" or "the impious one"], so Rigaux in his commentary (*Thessaloniciens*, 247–80, 655, 659, 771), or Légasse, *Les épîtres aux Thessaloniciens*, 379 and passim.

89. Cp. only the classic work of Wilhelm Bousset, *Der Antichrist in der Überlieferung des Judentums* (1895; 1999), in which all opponents of God in the NT, the ancient church, and above all, paradoxically, in Judaism are given that title, including the "lawless one [Mensch der Gesetzlosigkeit]" in 2 Thess 2:2 (pp. 12–13), to whom the "name of the Antichrist" is repeatedly given (pp. 86, 99). Von Dobschütz, *Die Thessalonicherbriefe*, 272, remarks: "the familiar name of Antichrist is absent from our letter!" Cp. also the critique by Reinmuth, "Der zweite Brief an die Thessalonicher," 176, concerning this usage.

90. Trilling, *Der zweite Brief*, 69, who speaks analogously of the "mystery of wickedness" (2:7) and "the evil one" (2:8); cp. Strobel, *Untersuchungen zum eschatologischen Verzögerungsproblem*, 103: "mystery of wickedness," "appearance/revelation of the Antichrist," *passim*.

"the wicked/evil one."[91] Still, recently correct descriptions such as "one hostile to the law [Mensch der Gesetzesfeindschaft],"[92] "unlawful one [Mensch der Ungesetzlichkeit],"[93] "lawless one [Mensch der Gesetzlosigkeit],"[94] or "opponent of the law" [Mensch der Gesetzwidrigkeit],"[95] have generally come to dominate. This is about enmity toward the Old Testament Law, the Torah, which is why the opponent can also be called the "enemy of the Torah."[96] After all, the keywords ἀνομία (Gen 19:15; Exod 34:7; Lev 16:21; 19:29; 20:14; 22:16; 26:43, and frequently) and ἄνομος were used in the LXX translation for sins or people who hold attitudes hostile to or act against things corresponding to the commands of the Torah. "According to the Jewish view" ἀνομία "is what is contrary to life according to the Law of Moses, the removal of the normal conditions of Jewish life, in the first place damage to the holiness of the Temple cult and the purity laws."[97] That corresponds to the usage of the New Testament,[98] in which on the one hand people and deeds are called "lawless" when they do not know the Torah, that is, people who from a Jewish perspective are not Jewish (Acts 2:23; Rom 2:12; 1 Cor 9:21). But there is also "opposition to the Law," violations of the Law by those who know and accept the Torah (Matt 7:23; 23:28; 24:12; Luke 22:37; Rom 4:7; 6:19).

91. Luther revision 1984. Analogously, in German Bible translations the ἀνομία in Matt 24:12 is not always rendered "lawlessness [Gesetzlosigkeit]" or something similar; the Luther revision of 1956 even chose "unbelief [Unglauben]." "Text-critically speaking, that is clearly a dogmatic correction" (Frank Crüsemann, "Tora und christliche Ethik" [1980], 162). The 1975 Luther revision, in contrast, translates with fidelity to the text "rebellion against the law [Auflehnung gegen das Gesetz]," but that was again revised in 1984 with "unrighteousness [Ungerechtigkeit]."

92. Cullmann, "Der eschatologische Charakter des Missionsaftrages," 335, in apposition to "Antichrist."

93. Marxsen, *Der zweite Brief*, 76–77, as well as "enemy of the law [Gesetzesfeind]" in 2:8. The *Zürcher Bibel* (2007) translates "enemy of the law [Feind des Gesetzes]" (2:3) and "enemy of the law [Gesetzesfeind]," similarly to the earlier edition of the *Zürcher Bibel* of 1931.

94. Friedrich, "Der zweite Brief an die Thessalonicher," 50–51; 2:8 "the lawless one [der Gesetzlose]"; Börschel, *Die Konstruktion einer christlichen Identität*, 417 and frequently; P.-G. Müller, *Der Erste und Zweite Brief*, 259–60, who nevertheless speaks in his commentary also of the "Antichrist idea" or "expectation of the Antichrist" (p. 267; we also find here the word "Anti-Yahweh," p. 260). So also Hotze, "Christologie," 145ff. in distinguishing Christology from "Antichrist"ology.

95. Thus, e.g., Laub, *1. und 2. Thessalonicherbrief*, 50–51, with the *Einheitsübersetzung*: "the one opposed to the law"; unique is Popkes, "Die Bedeutung des zweiten Thessalonicherbriefs," 44: "man of unrighteousness [Mann der Ungerechtigkeit]."

96. *Die Bibel in gerechter Sprache* (2006): "the person who is an enemy of the Law [Mensch, der Feind der Tora ist]" (2:3) and "enemy of the Torah [Feind der Tora]" (2:8).

97. Von Dobschütz, *Die Thessalonicherbriefe*, 272.

98. Cp. Meinrad Limbeck, art. "ἀνομία, ἄνομος, ἀνόμως," *EWNT* I (1980), 254–55; Gutbrod, art. "ἀνομία," *TDNT* IV (1967), 1085–86.

When now, in 2 Thess 2:3, 8, the figure of the opponent is apostrophized and given the substantive name of the "lawless one" or "enemy of the law," this means he has revealed himself as a radical enemy of the Torah, the Law of Israel; his purpose is "simply the destruction of the all-encompassing order revealed in the νόμος,"[99] the order and principles of the Torah that YHWH has given to Israel. Jesus' antagonist is thus not simply the "Antichrist" but literally the "One Who Is Against the Torah." In that in the end Jesus will destroy that person, he thus fights for the Torah and its restoration in the Land and everywhere: that must be the conclusion from the coded naming. So the Jewish-Christian authors of 2 Thessalonians are concerned with fidelity to Torah, the opportunity to live in conformity with the Law, as also vv. 10–12 at the close of the section show; there what is at stake is the "truth" / ἀλήθεια against "unrighteousness" / ἀδικία, and thus right human living, זדכה They thus share the standard of the Torah that Matthew's gospel represents, and so they attack lawlessness (Matt 7:23; 13:41; 23:28; 24:12), as does Paul (Rom 4:7; 6:19; 2 Cor 6:14).[100] In this way the authors of 2 Thessalonians introduce the conceptuality of Torah and righteousness, so important to Paul, into the Thessalonian correspondence,[101] after 1 Thessalonians had been silent about the νόμος and δίκαιος / δικαιοσύνη.[102]

99. Limbeck, "ἀνομία," 255. Against Trilling, who thinks that in 2 Thessalonians the "originally Old Testament-Jewish content (the Law of Moses)... has been cast off; the word is a summary term for an overall attitude that is now opposed to the claims of the *Christian* way of life" (*Der zweite Brief*, 84). Such a view rests on the assumption that Jewish-Christian members of the community "cast off" what is Jewish. In my opinion, the terminology of 2 Thessalonians demonstrates the contrary.

100. For the Torah as standard for Matthew's gospel see esp. Martin Vahrenhorst, *"Ihr sollt überhaupt nicht schwören"* (2002), esp. 234–48; Peter Fiedler, *Das Matthäusevangelium* (2006), esp. 122–29, pointing out that ἀνομία appears nowhere in the Gospels apart from Matthew and is to be understood as "acting contrary to Torah" (p. 126); cp. also Matthias Konradt, "Die vollkommene Erfüllung der Tora" (2006); for the Torah in Romans see, e.g., Luise Schottroff, "Die Schreckensherrschaft der Sünde und die Befreiung durch Christus nach dem Römerbrief des Paulus (1979/1990); eadem, "'Wir richten die Tora auf'" (2003); Peter von der Osten-Sacken, "Das Verständnis des Gesetzes im Römerbrief" (1989); Gerbern S. Oegema, "Versöhnung ohne Vollendung? Röm 10,4 und die Tora der messianischen Zeit" (1996); Klaus Haacker, *Der Brief des Paulus an die Römer* (1999), 206–13; Klaus Wengst, *"Freut euch, ihr Völker, mit Gottes Volk!"* 330ff., 400ff.; Marlene Crüsemann, "'Heisst das, dass wir die Tora durch das Vertrauen ausser Kraft setzen?" (2010); for the Torah in 2 Cor 6:14–18, see Marlene Crüsemann, "Das weite Herz und die Gemeinschaft der Heiligen" (2004).

101. Differently, e.g., Paul Metzger, "Eine apokalyptische Paulusschule?" (2006), who denies the reception of any kind of Pauline thought in 2 Thessalonians (see esp. pp. 156–57). But that downplays the Pauline faith in a righteous judgment of God for all, as attested, for example, in Romans 2 (on which see Konradt, *Gericht und Gemeinde* [2003], 501–15) or 2 Cor 5:10 (cp. Konradt, *Gericht und Gemeinde*, 473–86).

102. On this see, e.g., Thomas Söding, "Der erste Thessalonicherbrief" (1991), 187; Reinhard von Bendemann, "'Frühpaulinisch' und/oder 'spätpaulinisch'?" (2000), 223ff., and 4.3 above. In 1 Thess 2:10 δικαίως as irreproachable behavior can scarcely be understood in the sense of Torah-righteousness.

The deeds of the lawless one indicated thereafter in 2 Thess 2:4, we must conclude, show him to be the common enemy of the exercise of both Jewish and Christian religion: he is "the enemy (ἀντικείμενος) who [NRSV: He opposes and] exalts himself (ὑπεραιρόμενος) above everything called [NRSV: every so-called] god (πάντα λεγόμενον θεόν) or holy [NRSV: object of worship] (σέβασμα), so that he takes his seat in the Temple of God (ναὸν τοῦ θεοῦ), declaring himself to be God (ἀποδεικνύντα ἑαυτὸν ὅτι ἐστὶν θεός)." The dangerous primary activity of the lawless one consists in his usurpation of all worship of God; this is said from a Jewish-Christian perspective, which understands that to mean the sole worship of the God of Israel. The summary description of that threat is the self-exaltation "above everything called God or holy," a quasi-citation of Dan 11:36 (LXX), which says of Antiochus IV Epiphanes: "He shall exalt himself and consider himself greater than any god (ὑψωθήσεται καὶ μεγαλυνθήσεται ἐπὶ πάντα θεόν). Also, "he shall speak horrendous things against the God of gods (καὶ ἐπὶ τὸν θεὸν τῶν θεῶν ἔξαλλα λαλήσει). He shall prosper until the period of wrath is completed."[103] It is also worth noting here that the keyword "wrath" / ὀργή is used in connection with the appearance of the imperial usurper, a combination used by the authors of 2 Thessalonians, in thus citing Daniel, to indicate how the ὀργή in 1 Thess 2:16c can be interpreted: The Jewish people are again existentially threatened by a period of wrath under a pagan ruler. Hence the "*anomos*" appears in the first of the series of allusions in 2 Thessalonians as a copy of the Temple-desecrating Antiochus IV (2 Macc 5:15–21), and then explicitly in 2 Thess 2:4b as appointing himself God; that is to be seen as the summit of his misdeeds. But the initial characterization brings a central concern of 2 Thessalonians to the fore. The insolence of the pagan ruler,[104] accused as such by 2 Thess 2:3–4, is directed against all worship of the one God, as a certain redundancy in the formulation indicates: it extends to all places where God is worshiped, all sanctuaries and holy things.[105]

So we are dealing with an enemy who permits no worship or religion other than that devoted to himself. If that means in the broadest sense that in essence every cult is threatened by this ruler, in any case it means in the narrower sense that all

103. Cp. von Dobschütz, *Die Thessalonicherbriefe*, 274; Rigaux, *L'Antéchrist et l'Opposition*, 260–63; Trilling, *Der zweite Brief*, 85; Hans K. Larondelle, "Paul's Prophetic Outline in 2 Thessalonians 2" (1983); Friedrich, "Der zweite Brief," 264; Lietaert Peerbolte, *The Antecedents of Antichrist*, 76–77; P.-G. Müller, *Der erste und zweite Brief*, 267; Roh, *Der zweite Thessalonicherbrief*, 38, 40–41 (Roh, like Larondelle, cites Ezek 28:2 and Isa 14:13–14 as other possible parallels; ibid., pp. 38–39); and esp. Röcker, *Belial und Katechon*, 387–410, with further OT and Synoptic parallels as lines of tradition for the motif of the desecration of the Temple and esp. association with Antiochus IV. Epiphanes (pp. 391ff.).

104. Cp. Holland, *The Tradition That You Received From Us*, 107.

105. For σέβασμα as "objects of veneration, holy things, sanctuaries, temples, altars, offerings" see Trilling, *Der zweite Brief*, 85–86. There could also be a play on Σεβάστος, the title given to Roman emperors since Augustus (so Holland, *The Tradition That You Received From Us*, 108). But the "holy" also includes sacred actions and every kind of worship activity.

forms of worship of the God of Israel are opposed by him. These include not only the Jewish communities in Temple and synagogues, but also the Jewish-Christian communities and Christians from among the nations equally, those who meet in house-churches to celebrate baptism and eucharist. The threat falls upon the various and common places of worship and liturgical celebrations of the different worshipers of the one God of Israel and the churches among the Gentiles. By their global statement that the lawless one destroys all other worship and adoration of God, the authors put a spotlight on the possible cause of their current persecutions of their own group, which can be defined as Jewish-Christian or Jewish-messianic. But equally in view are the Jews who do not believe in Messiah Jesus and the repressions that they may have to endure. In the third place there is an address to all Gentile Christian groups who are likewise under pressure from the ruling power. The text of 2 Thess 2:4 describes an all-encompassing threat to the Jewish-Christian way of life from the pagan state authorities. In this way 2 Thessalonians, contrary to the efforts at separation in 1 Thessalonians, which distances itself especially and explicitly from the Jewish people, produces an alternative view of the situation of persecution that honors the fact that all religious groups are suffering from the same enemy. But above all a summary condemnation of Judaism is impossible for the authors of 2 Thessalonians because they continue to cling to the Temple in Jerusalem.

That is clear from the culminating statement about the wicked deeds of the "lawless one," that he "takes his seat in the temple of God, declaring himself to be God" (2:4b). This links to previous Jewish traditions and sayings about the figure of the pagan and godless tyrant, for example, Isa 14:13–14, according to which the king of Babylon intends to make himself superior over all gods.[106] The series of pretenders to divine status continued with the Hellenistic king Antiochus IV and his invasion of the Jerusalem Temple, as depicted in Dan 11:36–37. He forbids services in the Temple, plunders it, and probably makes it a sanctuary for Olympian Zeus (2 Macc 6:2).[107]

Then came the Roman general Pompey, who conquered Jerusalem in 63 B.C.E. and entered the Holy of Holies, as *PsSol* 17:11–15 laments. Pompey is also called a "lawless one," ἄνομος, in that passage (v. 11).[108] *Psalms of Solomon* 17 and 2 Thess

106. On this see esp. Best, *Thessalonians*, 287ff.; Menken, *2 Thessalonians*, 104–7; Roh, *Der zweite Thessalonicherbrief*, 38–39; see n. 103 above.

107. See above at n. 103.

108. Because of these clear historical references the first century B.C.E. is taken to be the time of origin of the *Psalms of Solomon*; their "Sitz im Leben" was "the synagogues" and their attitude one of "hostility to the Maccabees and the Romans," according to Stefan H. Brandenburger, "Der 'Gesalbte des Herrn' in Psalm Salomo 17" (1998), 217; cp. Svend Holm-Nielsen, *Die Psalmen Salomos* (1977), 51–61 (pp. 97–107 on *PsSol* 17); Joachim Schüpphaus, *Die Psalmen Salomos* (1977), 1–20 (pp. 64–73 on *PsSol* 17); Mikael Winninge, *Sinners and the Righteous* (1995), 9–21 (89–109 on *PsSol* 17); Robert B. Wright, *The Psalms of Solomon* (2007), 3–5 (176–201 on *PsSol* 17); Eberhard Bons and Patrick Pouchelle, eds., *The Psalms of Solomon* (2015).

2:3–8 contain a number of parallel concepts, indicating that the authors of 2 Thessalonians are using a code that would be clearly legible to Jewish or Jewish-Christian readers to point to the Roman state power as the enemy of the Jerusalem Temple: a Roman ruler called ἄνομος (*PsSol* 17:11, plural in v. 18; 2 Thess 2:8; 2:3 ἄνθρωπος τῆς ἀνομίας) and his deeds (devastation of the Land, desecration of Jerusalem: *PsSol* 17:11, 22; occupation of the Temple and all religious exercises, lies and injustice: 2 Thess 2:4, 9–10) threaten the Land and the communities. Against him arises a messianic savior who fights successfully, not with military means but through words, who smites/destroys (*PsSol* 17:35: ἀπειλῇ; 2 Thess 2:8: ἀνελεῖ; cp. also *PsSol* 17:36) the enemy or enemies with the "words of his mouth" (*PsSol* 17:24: ἐν λόγῳ στόματος αὐτοῦ) or the "breath of his mouth" (2 Thess 2:8: τῷ πνεύματι τοῦ στόματος αὐτοῦ). Both texts, together with 2 Thessalonians 1, likewise contain the motif of just judgment (2 Thess 1:5–9; *PsSol* 17:19, 23, 26–27, etc.), the keyword "destruction" of Israel (ἀπωλεία, *PsSol* 17:22) or "son of destruction/one destined for destruction" (υἱός τῆς ἀπωλείας, 2 Thess 2:3), as well as the δόξα that accompanies the Messiah (*PsSol* 17:31; 2 Thess 1:9–10, 12). These parallels with *PsSol* 17 above all place 2 Thessalonians 1–2 in the sequence of resistance by devout Jews to the "lawless one," the "cover" in each case for the Roman occupying power. Inasmuch as *PsSol* 17 actually constitutes the background for 2 Thessalonians 1–2, it also offers the key to the political-eschatological statements of the pseudepigraphical community letter, and it is possible that it was available to the recipients.

The next attempt to desecrate the Temple, after the Roman conquest of Jerusalem under Pompey, was Caligula's plan, in about 39 C.E., to have Petronius set up statues of himself in the Holy of Holies in order to have himself worshiped there as God; the plan was thwarted by the Emperor's death (Josephus, *Bell.* II, 184–203).[109] That event also was attacked from the Jewish side, with motifs strikingly similar to those in 2 Thess 2:3–4, as an expression of the greatest possible blasphemy by Caesar. Martin Karrer[110] points to a contemporary parallel from the first half of the first century C.E. in Philo, *Legatio ad Gaium*, on the Jewish embassy to Caligula: "Gaius . . . amid his lawless acts (ἀνομίαι) [30] "went even beyond the demigods . . . and invaded the veneration and worship (σεβασμοί) paid to . . . the supreme deities" [93]; he "ordered a colossal statue of himself to be erected in . . . their temple" [188, 265, 337]; he, "[though but] a man (ἄνθρωπος)" [118, 347], "[sought] to take to [himself] the air of heaven" [347] and insisted "that I [Caligula]

109. For the events surrounding Caligula and the relation to 2 Thess 2:4 see Roh, *Der zweite Thessalonicherbrief*, 41–47, who regards v. 4 as a contemporary historical statement by Paul (p. 53) inserted in 2 Thessalonians by the later author of the letter. In my opinion such a literary-critical operation is unnecessary for the purpose of connecting the obvious allusions in 2 Thess 2:4 to numerous desecrations of the Temple in the history of Israel with the very current ones in its own time, the seizure of Jerusalem by Vespasian and Titus (see further below).

110. Karrer, "Der zweite Thessalonicherbrief und Gottes Widersacher," 120–25.

am a god (θεὸν εἶναι με)" [353].[111] "The parallels are so dense that we cannot disprove an influence exercised by the memory of Caligula on the sketch in 2 Thessalonians."[112]

Second Thessalonians 2:3–4 fits seamlessly within these traditions of lament and outrage over the desecration of the Jerusalem Temple by pagan ruler figures.[113] It thus demonstrates that solidarity with the people suffering from that catastrophe had not been terminated by confession of Jesus; indeed, that the Jewish-Christian authors themselves mourn over the Jerusalem Temple.[114] At the time when 2 Thessalonians was written the most consequential conquest of the sanctuary and its destruction by the troops of the Flavians, Vespasian and Titus,[115] was already a historical fact. The most recent intruder into the Temple's Holy of Holies (Josephus, *Bell.* VI, 260) was Titus, who had followed his father as Roman emperor. It is probable that in the last years of the first century no one from Jewish or Jewish-Christian circles could have read the text of 2 Thess 2:3–4 without thinking of the conquest of Jerusalem and the destruction of the Temple, as well as the form the "sitting" of the Roman rulers in it had assumed.[116] Therefore it was easy, and a

111. Ibid., Table on 122.

112. Ibid., 123. Since Karrer regards 2 Thessalonians as a deutero-Pauline writing from shortly after the death of Paul, that is, the 60s of the first century (pp. 103–6), he does not propose any historical reference of this significant motif-field to the destruction of Jerusalem in 70 C.E., and yet for any dating of 2 Thessalonians to the second half of the 1st century, as accepted here and by the majority who think it is a pseudepigraphical writing, such a reference is unavoidable: the authors make use of familiar OT-Jewish allusions and cover-names for the "lawless one" in order to denounce the Roman emperor and his seizure of the Jewish sanctuary. See further below.

113. Cp. also the "desolating sacrilege," βδέλυγμα τῆς ἐρημώσεως in Mark 13:14, in connection with Dan 11:31, in which a quotation is used to allude to the Roman occupation of the Temple in 70 C.E. On this see, e.g., Peter Dschulnigg, *Das Markusevangelium* (2007), 342–45, with an early dating of Mark before the catastrophe (pp. 55–56); Röcker, *Belial und Katechon*, 392ff.

114. "There is no longer any doubt that the 'temple of God' refers to the Jerusalem Temple" (Trilling, *Der zweite Brief*, 86). See also Nicholl, *From Hope to Despair*, 122; Röcker, *Belial und Katechon*, 402ff.

115. Josephus, *Bell.* VI, 149–322; see, e.g., Helmut Schwier, *Tempel und Tempelzerstörung* (1989), 35–40. At the time 2 Thessalonians was written, usually supposed to be in the second half of the 1st century (see 6.3.1 n. 54 above), the fall of Jerusalem had lately occurred and was *the* Jewish catastrophe. For the echo and the interpretation of that catastrophe in Jewish and Christian texts of the first three centuries see Heinz-Martin Döpp, *Die Deutung der Zerstörung Jerusalems* (1998).

116. The way in which Vespasian and Titus had settled themselves in the Jerusalem Temple since the year 70 is, I believe, symbolized by the *fiscus Judaicus*, the fund that had rededicated the Jewish temple tax, a double drachma. Now that the Temple had gone up in flames the tax was devoted to, of all things, the building of a temple for Jupiter Capitolinus in Rome; it was a

matter of course, to identify the "lawless one" who seats himself in the Temple with the Roman emperors who were now responsible for just that. This is a further indication that 2 Thessalonians must have regarded its present era as that of the "lawless one."

This contemporary interpretation of the deeds of the ἄνομος in 2 Thess 2:1–12 as a disguised denunciation of the rule of the Flavians and its catastrophic effects on the Jewish people has recently been profiled again by Taesong Roh, who relates historical testimonies to the military campaigns and triumphal processions of Vespasian and Titus, with their corresponding propaganda, in the course of the Roman-Jewish war to the statements in 2 Thess 2:1–12.[117] "Therefore when

poll tax to be paid by all Jews throughout the world, beginning at the age of 3; see Josephus, *Bell.* VII, 218; Dio Cassius 65,7; *CPJ* II, 160–229, 421; *CPJ* III, 460, and the literature listed above in 2.4.1 n. 135. The annual payment of that tax probably evoked a constant and provocative memory of the shame associated with the destruction of the Temple in all Jewish people, probably including the authors of 2 Thessalonians; it was a material expression of the victory of a pagan god over the one God. (On this, cp. esp. Werner Stenger, *"Gebt dem Kaiser, was des Kaisers ist . . . !"* (1988), 87: "because in order to remain a Jew one had to pay a tax that in fact no Jew who wanted to remain a Jew could pay"). The question is: what attitude toward this did a text like 2 Thessalonians want to convey to its community when it denounced the "sitting" in the temple of God (2:4)? Should Jewish Christians continue to pay the tax, which furnished proof of their Judaism, or should they abandon Judaism and be relieved of this additional payment? And what about the non-Jewish members of the community? The temptation to prove oneself to the authorities from now on as not belonging to the Jewish people, to remove oneself from it or even denounce it—as we can read in 1 Thess 2:14–16—certainly existed, if only for financial reasons. The question probably became of signal importance for partial separations between "Jews" and "Christians." (On this subject see now Marius Heemstra, *The* Fiscus Judaicus *and the Parting of the Ways* [2010].) Since 2 Thessalonians expects the eschatological victory of Christ over the desecrators of the Temple we may suppose there was hope that the dilemma would be resolved in the very near future.

117. Roh, *Der zweite Thessalonicherbrief*, 85–127 ("History of the Present Time in the Eschatological Tradition in 2 Thess 2:1–12"). For the identification of the "lawless one" in 2 Thess 2:3, 8 with the Roman emperor, and for the relation of the text to the present time of 2 Thessalonians, see previously Marlene Crüsemann, "2 Thessalonians," 827–28; eadem, "Die Briefe nach Thessaloniki," 257–74. Witherington, *1 and 2 Thessalonians*, sees an allusion here—by Paul, who might still have been alive in 70 C.E.—to the Roman emperor: "It would have been the destruction of the right temple by a pagan emperor claiming divine honors . . . . Since, however, this is an apocalyptic scenario Paul is dealing with, he may well have added, had he lived to the end of the first century A.D., that Titus was but one manifestation, one incarnation of the Lawless One, perhaps only the foreshadowing of the final one" (p. 212). In the exegetical literature we find other identifications of the "lawless ones" such as the Sadducees (van Aarde, "The Second Letter to the Thessalonians," 259–66) or Belial (Röcker, *Belial und Katechon*, 380–87). Overall it is striking how little inquiry there has thus far been in scholarship about the possible identity of the ἄνομος in 2 Thessalonians 2, in sharp contrast to the surplus of identifications of the κατέχον (see n. 81 above).

2 Thessalonians speaks of the day of the Lord as having already come, it seems likely that this is about the arrival of a real world ruler. But in the opinion of 2 Thessalonians that real world ruler was a false one."[118]

In contrast, the event indicated by 2 Thess 2:1–12 as actually approaching, the one the community hopes for, is the true parousia, namely, that of Jesus (1:7–10; 2:8).[119] It is characterized by the fact that it puts an end to the ἄνομος and his parousia, which consists in the usurpation of the Temple (2:8). It is only that action, together with the eschatological judgment of all, that points to his coming. Only then could it truly be said: "The day of the Kyrios has come!" This quality of Jesus' action is what especially characterizes the inbreaking of that last day, and not so much any speculations about temporal stages to be expected. The authors' pastoral intention is to name a clear criterion for Jesus' parousia, contrary to all deceptions about the nature of the end-time events and their interpretation: He will strike the pagan emperor and liberate the Temple from his grasp. This victory by Jesus will happen without the use of military force, because Kyrios Jesus will destroy (ἀνελεῖ, v. 8) the enemy by "the breath of his mouth" (πνεύματι τοῦ στόματος αὐτοῦ). This is a citation of Isa 11:4,[120] and with it, indirectly, of the beginning of the verse, which embodies the purpose of the vision of judgment in 2 Thess 1:5–10: the Messiah from the stump of Jesse "shall judge the poor with righteousness and decide with equity for the meek of the earth." Jesus is thus revealed as the Jewish Messiah who will create justice for the Christians from Israel and the nations, they who live under oppression and suffering, but also establish a sign for the non-Christian Jews affected by the destruction of the Temple. The fact that a common enemy is struck down is significant not only for pagan adherents to Christ like those responsible for 1 Thessalonians who are in the act of turning away from the Jewish people, but also for Jewish people who do not believe in Jesus as Messiah. Second Thessalonians 1:10–12 describes the appearance of Jesus on the last "day" as a miracle of the δόξα, the glory, the brilliance and the dignity of

118. Roh, *Der zweite Thessalonicherbrief*, 123.

119. Cp. ibid., 121ff.

120. Isaiah 11:4 LXX: πατάξει γῆν τῷ λόγῳ τοῦ στόματος αὐτοῦ καὶ ἐν πνεύματι διὰ χειλέων ἀνελεῖ ἀσεβῆ. For the tradition history of the motif cp. Röcker, *Belial und Katechon*, 490–97: "We have been able to show as regards 2 Thess 2:8 that the idea of the killing of the enemies by the breath of the Messiah's mouth was certainly shaped by Isa 11:4" (p. 497). In particular the parallel in *PsSol* 17:24b, with the statement that the Messiah would kill "lawless nations" in that fashion, an allusion to the Roman occupying force at the time of the conquest of Jerusalem by General Pompey (the "figure of the Anointed and his rule is . . . a counter to the rule of the Hasmoneans and Romans," Brandenburger, "Der 'Gesalbte des Herrn,'" 235; for the adoption of Isa 11:4 in *PsSol* 17:24b see ibid., 223–24, and for the "nearly word-for-word quotation of Isa 11:4 LXX" in *PsSol* 17:35 see ibid., 231; see the text above at n. 108) demonstrates that the authors of 2 Thessalonians are to be located in the direct line of resistance to the *Imperium Romanum*—in their own time after the destruction of the Temple by the Flavians—and share the hopes of the Messiah expressed in *PsSol* 17.

Messiah Jesus, which likewise means the honor, dignity, and glorification of the community (1:12). This is to be understood as hope for a final justification of those who believe in Christ, an affirmation of their holding fast to Jesus as Messiah, in face of the manifestations of weakness in their own group but also of the whole Jewish people. That justification consists of the quality and power of this Messiah, which will then be visible to all, he who also functions as the liberator of the Jewish Temple and thus demonstrates that ultimately the common liberation of all, including Israel, from the current "lawless one," the Roman emperor, is bound up with this Name.

6.4 The Composition of 2 Thessalonians: Correction of the View of History, Judgment, and Resistance in 1 Thessalonians

Second Thessalonians asserts that 1 Thessalonians is a forgery, and presents itself as the real and only apostolic letter to the community in Thessalonica. The teaching about eschatology in 1 Thessalonians is to be regarded as deceptive and designed to lead astray. The dissent consists not so much in the reckoning of "times and seasons," but in the different interpretations of the present and, on the part of 2 Thessalonians, a more comprehensive expectation about Christ and his messianic action. One could appeal to the first letter and say "the day of the Kyrios is here!"—but the second defines its own time as one of lawlessness and hostility to the Torah. This is also to say that in this view the "day" is not characterized by distance from the "law," but quite the contrary. The essential deed of Christ appearing from heaven will consist in battling against the enemy of the Torah and thus, in a sense, establishing it.

In this way the authors of 2 Thessalonians express their enduring closeness to Judaism, which holds fast to Temple and Torah. In 1 Thessalonians, by contrast, we can find no traces of any special nearness to Judaism or even a local closeness to Jewish Christianity. The judgment on the Jewish people announced in 1 Thess 2:16 is interesting only insofar as it is useful for demonstrating how things will go with the local enemies of the community. They will ultimately be handed over to destruction (by an anonymous entity? 5:3), after the community addressed by 1 Thessalonians has been elevated from the place of the action, the *polis* and the earth, and carried up into the air. Jesus' eschatological action is, according to 1 Thessalonians, explicitly restricted to this rescue of the community, which had begun as the welcoming of Jesus as the true Kyrios (4:17). According to 1 Thessalonians, then, judgment is an extended action that will be accomplished at different times and in different places.

Thus above all the first letter lacks the universal and cosmic quality of God's judging action and that of his Messiah, Jesus. In contrast, the authors of 2 Thessalonians give it pride of place at the beginning of the writing (1:7–10) in the grand vision of the general judgment of all groups and nations on the "day." This is followed by their view of the eschatological battle between Jesus and the "lawless one" (2:8). In this way the figure of Jesus and its function for the universal salvation of the community is significantly evaluated and enhanced, as is his role as principal actor in the universal eschatological events of judgment and struggle. The alternative projection in 2 Thessalonians challenges the separated concept of judgment in 1 Thessalonians, asserting that a definitive decision is still awaited, in every sense, and in particular the events of the present are not to be understood as the effects of Jesus' parousia but as those of his opponent, the "lawless one."

At the time when the counter-forgery of 2 Thessalonians originated, on the one hand the complete 1 Thessalonians already existed, and on the other hand the capture of the Jerusalem Temple by a pagan ruler, as addressed in 2 Thess 2:8, had very recently occurred as a result of Roman victory in the Jewish War. Anyone at that time who read 1 Thessalonians, whether Jewish, Jewish-Christian, non-Jewish Christian, or pagan, could scarcely avoid applying the saying about the "wrath [that] has overtaken them [the Jews] at last" (1 Thess 2:16) to the fall of Jerusalem. At this point it does not matter whether 1 Thessalonians is a forgery, though from the point of view offered here it is probable. From the perspective of the authors of 2 Thessalonians, 1 Thess 2:14–17 has to be associated with the events of 69/70 C.E. and the consequences for Judaism thereafter. They interpret the catastrophe not as a judgment in the sense of the eschatological and definitive action of God and Jesus but as the act of the "enemy of the Torah." With that they revise the view of history in 1 Thessalonians and its possible interpretation, especially as regards Jewish history.

Thus 2 Thessalonians denies that God's judgment has already fallen on "the Jews," and raises objections: the "day of the Kyrios" is in the future and is characterized especially by the common, simultaneous judgment of all groups of people, with an unmistakably cosmic quality whereby the common enemy of all, Jewish, Jewish-Christian, and Gentile-Christian people. In this view of the hostile power that threatens every other form of worship of God and every sacred action lies the alternative to the concept of resistance in 1 Thessalonians. The latter has only its own group in the Greek city in view, along with those who are oppressing them. The "Jews" appear as an altogether foreign group who can be denounced as the real enemies of the state in order, possibly, thereby to shift official pressure away from one's own group. In contrast, the experiences of suffering on the part of the authors of 2 Thessalonians and their readers become an opportunity to identify a common enemy of their own and other communities and groups, and to offer resistance. That does not mean abandoning critical distance from people "who do not know God" or "do not obey the gospel of our Lord Jesus" (2 Thess 1:8). But the final eschatological verdict on them is left to God and his Messiah; it is by no means declared to have been accomplished. In that 2 Thess 2:1–12 denounces lawlessness, injustice, and the occupation of the Temple by an enemy of the Torah who has himself worshiped as a god, the enemy of Jesus, the "Antichrist" is at the same time represented as an extreme enemy of the Jewish people. In this way the door of this Christian community is opened to the experiences and sufferings of the whole Jewish people. Jesus will also be the liberator of the Jewish people and its sanctuary.

6.5 Prospect: The Place of the Two Letters to the Community in Thessalonica in a Jewish-Christian Social History

The existence of the two letters to the community in Thessalonica is a multifaceted curiosity. Not only the fact that the second declares the first to be a falsification, pretends to be the only one, and then both stand alongside one another in the later canon reveals the tangled paths of early Christian history. It is above all the correction of content that 2 Thessalonians undertakes by its attempt to replace the first letter that enables us to question previous assumptions about the linear progress of that history. This has a pivotal application to the discussion about the "parting of the ways between Christianity and Judaism" or the "separation of Jews and Christians." The text that proclaims a general separation from Jewish people, both within and outside the sphere of the Christian communities, and already in the time of the mixed and combined groupings established in the time of Paul, is, of all things, the first writing. In contrast, the theological and political line of 2 Thessalonians must be regarded as a re-Judaizing, or simply a Judaizing, of the Thessalonian correspondence. Thus against a widespread theory of separation that assumes something like an ongoing, compartmentalizing pulling-apart of "Judaism" and "Christianity" as monolithic entities, we here document a nuanced process, and especially one that worked in the reverse direction. Second Thessalonians withdraws an announced condemnation of the Jewish people and thereby declares a final separation from them at the time of its writing to be misguided or, with respect to Jesus' judgment, at least premature.

The conflicts within and among these groups, which are by definition linked to the community in Thessalonica, are accompanied by accusations of lying and deception; they express a certain mutual rigidity and intolerance that is underscored by the assertion of pretended authorship. Even so, 2 Thessalonians is directed to the same community as was 1 Thessalonians and so is possibly intended to affect the same people. The question whether the authors and readers are uniformly non-Jewish or Jewish-Christian cannot be completely answered. It seems certain that there is a Jewish-Christian group behind 2 Thessalonians and that they consider it scandalous to speak of the Jewish people as 1 Thess 2:14–17 does. They lament the destruction of Jerusalem and the Second Temple and do not consider it a definitive judgment of God on God's people. They continue to hold to God's Torah and the right way of life it demands. With whom do they share their views? Since they have chosen the same address as 1 Thessalonians we may surmise that the intention is again to speak especially to Christians from among the non-Jewish peoples. They are to see in Rome the common enemy of all those who pray Jesus' "Our Father" to the God of Israel.

The community from which 1 Thessalonians originated represents a congregation that knows of Jewish people only by hearsay. Judaism appears foreign to them and is not supposed to play any further role as a present reality. Nor is there any depiction of an existing or intended contact with the Christian communities in Judea, for there is not the least hint in 1 Thessalonians of the great collection project that Paul had instituted precisely among the communities in Macedonia and Achaia (1 Cor

16:1–4; 2 Cor 8–9; Gal 2:10; Rom 15:25–28; see also Acts 11:29–30). Not even Paul himself is called a Jew.[121] The group sees its life as relatively isolated within the great Greek port city; it has no living or positive contact to Jews, or it does not (any longer) desire to have any, either to believers in Christ or others living in the Diaspora. Its concern is to survive, as inconspicuously as possible, in the city environment it experiences as hostile. It also seeks to avoid the social consequences that might follow from being considered Jewish. There is assurance that they are not Jewish or hostile to the state, like those others, who are enemies not only of the state but also of their own group. At the same time, the message of resistance to Rome is upheld. Did the group hope to avoid losses due to friction with the Greco-Roman officials, or to gain advantages by denouncing "the Jews"? The revisions by the authors of 2 Thessalonians work against that; these authors address the same community and/or are Jewish-Christian members of it, seeking a re-solidarization with the fate of the Jews, which is also their own. We may assume this was associated with maintaining a broader community of life with non-messianic Jews, the intensity of which cannot be described in detail since the intent is to maintain confession of Jesus Christ as the first criterion in the judgment and to see other options as certainly condemned. But we can clearly see in the emphasis on Temple, Torah, and righteousness an interest in common resistance, together with other Jewish people.

Among the most interesting features are the different ideas about the role to be played by non-Jewish Christians toward Israel as a whole. First Thessalonians expresses, at least as an intention, the greatest possible distancing of Christians of Gentile background from the Jewish people, who are no longer regarded as relevant to salvation-history. That distancing is combined with a movement of social degradation to the point of denunciation. The goal of 2 Thessalonians is that the Christian community in Thessalonica should, instead, take a persuasive stance toward Israel and stand up for the truth of Jesus, the Jewish Messiah. They are told that they are suffering under a hostile power, together with Israel. This will continue until the "day of the Kyrios": then Jesus will reveal himself in his δόξα, his כבוד, his significance and his beauty, his dignity, glory, and majesty, and the Christians in Thessalonica have a share in that δόξα. That means that their own truth and their confession will be affirmed before all eyes, and especially the eyes of Israel.

Inasmuch as people of pagan origin among the Christians in Thessalonica are to be moved, from a Jewish-Christian perspective, to a *rapprochement* with the whole Jewish people, there is also a special destiny and role to be played by Christians from among the nations in their relationship with the people of Israel. The type of scriptural interpretation in 2 Thessalonians may be an indication of it.

121. To mention only a few of the otherwise explicit expressions of or allusions to Paul's belonging to the Jewish people that are found in his authentic letters: Rom 9:3–5; 16:7; 1 Cor 10:1; 2 Cor 11:22; Gal 1:13–24; Phil 3:5–6. Moreover, there is not a single citation of Scripture in 1 Thessalonians.

The intensive use of Isaiah 66 in 2 Thessalonians 1–2[122] shows that, in addition to its reception of other Old Testament texts in a kind of collage, 2 Thessalonians intends to present a kind of midrash[123] on Isaiah 66. The end of that chapter describes a vision of God who comes "to gather all nations and tongues; and they shall come and shall see my glory" (v. 18). According to v. 19, people from all nations will come to Zion, people "that have not heard of my fame or seen my glory; and they shall declare my glory among the nations."[124] There is a keyword link here to 2 Thess 1:10–12, where Jesus' δόξα, his glory and magnificence, also causes his name to be glorified by the addressees themselves, the Greek community in Thessalonica. The LXX-version of Isa 66:19 replaces "the coastlands far away" (MT: הָאִיִּים הָרְחֹקִים) from which, among other places, the peoples from among the nations will come to Zion, with a different word, namely, "Greece," Ἑλλάδα! According to that, Greek people are among those who will bring the Israelites scattered throughout the worldwide Diaspora back to Jerusalem (Isa 66:20). Considering that the authors of 2 Thessalonians refer especially to this chapter, Isaiah 66, it would seem that they intend to imply a possible role for Christians from among the nations, and so also from Greece, in the history of salvation. This may be given explicit expression in the address to them as the "first fruits" / ἀπαρχή in 2 Thess 2:13.[125] The Christians of Thessalonica are invited by this address to learn to understand themselves as the first fruits from among the nations to have been converted to Israel's God through his Messiah, Jesus, whose δόξα they will themselves preach widely among the Gentiles (Isa 66:19).

In conclusion: the purportedly apostolic correspondence with a Christian community in Thessalonica yields a surprising answer to the question of Jewish-Christian separation. It shows that at the end of the first century C.E. there were a number of possible ways, differing according to place, even in the Diaspora outside the Land of Israel, and some of those ways were pursued: these included remaining

122. On this see esp. Roger D. Aus, "The Relevance of Isaiah 66:7 to Revelation 12 and 2 Thessalonians 1" (1976), 263ff.; idem, "God's Plan and God's Power" (1977); Brown, "Intertextuality," 267ff.; Menken, *2 Thessalonians*, 88–89; cp. 6.2 above.

123. For the method in NT texts of producing a midrash on OT motifs and texts, cp. the interpretation of Luke 1–2 on "resistant older women" by Claudia Janssen, *Elisabet und Hanna* (1998), 80–115.

124. The motif of the pilgrimage of nations in Isa 66:18–23 is also present in *PsSol* 17:31 (see 6.3.3 above): "so that nations will come from the ends of the earth to see his glory, bringing as gifts her children who had become quite weak, and to see the glory of the Lord with which God has glorified her" (cp. Brandenburger, "Der 'Gesalbte des Herrn,'" 228; Holm-Nielsen, *Die Psalmen Salomos*, 103–4).

125. This is to be preferred to the alternative reading ἀπ' ἀρχῆς / "from the beginning" (α D Ψ μ it sy^{p} sa; Ambst); cp. P.-G. Müller, *Der Erste und Zweite Brief*, 282–83; differently, e.g., Trilling, *Der zweite Brief*, 120–21. Harnack, "Das Problem des zweiten Thessalonicherbriefs," 575ff., concludes from this word that 2 Thessalonians was written for the Jewish first converts in Thessalonica.

together, separation, and attempted *rapprochement*. First Thessalonians advocates separation, employing an absolute condemnation of Judaism as something belonging to the past and opposing God. Second Thessalonians retracts and contradicts that condemnation by declaring 1 Thessalonians' solution a forgery and asserting that the general judgment is yet to come; only then will it become fully clear who belongs on the side of the condemned, the damned, the unrighteous, and who can withstand Jesus' judgment. Second Thessalonians shows that there must have been people in the communities that consisted in large part of Christians from among the Gentiles who resisted the temptation to denounce Judaism and opposed a broad distancing from its historical destiny. They did this by insisting on a common interpretation of events in the world, a common place within it, and the acceptance of the mutual social consequences. The sufferings that resulted were seen as a sign and a down-payment, one of the criteria for experiencing Jesus as Savior when he comes to judge the enemies of God and the Torah.

Chapter 7

SUMMARY: THESES

1. The anti-Jewish passage in 1 Thessalonians 2:14–16 is a genuine element of the letter and not an interpolation. It declares that divine judgment has already fallen upon the Jewish people. The function of the text is to denounce Jewish people as the true enemies of the Roman state. The divine wrath they are experiencing, according to this text, serves as a sign of hope for a community defined as non-Jewish Christians, telling them that in the end they will triumph over their pagan persecutors.
2. The question of who wrote 1 Thessalonians remains. It is a letter from Paul, Silvanus, and Timothy. The nearly consistent authorial plural announces that the text is not to be taken as a letter written by Paul alone. The plural form must be considered methodologically and consistently reflected in the language of the interpretation.
3. It appears that the letter was not sent, because there is no mention of any real bearer of the letter. That is unusual for a Pauline letter, which ordinarily contains information about the envoy and details of that person's journey. A thorough analysis of this information shows that 1 Thessalonians appears merely to try to present itself as a communication by letter, but it contains no logical sequence of a material exchange of letters, as do the other Pauline letters that are addressed to a local congregation or house church.
4. The numerous references to the community's prior knowledge belong to the method of pseudepigraphy. They lead to the conclusion that someone is imitating an apostolic epistolary contact, because what the congregation in fact has long known is nevertheless recited at length: it has the appearance of "talking out the window" to a different audience, a third party.
5. First Thessalonians purports to be the letter of ideal apostles who are sketched according to the model of good Cynic philosophers. They maintain an ideal relationship to a model community with major regional influence that is supposed already to have become a model in turn for many other communities.
6. Hence 1 Thessalonians, as a pseudepigraphical letter, is in the first place a piece of evidence for the importance of apostolic origins; it is conceived as the foundational document for the congregation in Thessalonica (1 Thessalonians 1–3), and it must have originated there.

7. The discussion of the authenticity of 1 Thessalonians in the nineteenth century attests to knowledge of the problematic aspects of the text among scholars, and the necessity to seek solutions for them. It has proceeded without dealing decisively with the observations of Karl Schrader and Ferdinand Christian Baur and without attempting, thus far, to describe the purpose of 1 Thessalonians as a pseudepigraphical writing. The problems in the text led exegetes to hypotheses involving interpolation, partial letters, or compilations, or to positing a development of Pauline theology.
8. "We who are alive, who are left" in 1 Thess 4:15, 17 does not mean that, for example, Paul supposes he will be alive at Jesus' parousia. The older interpretation that saw "those who are left," and the like as a restriction of the numbers of the living should be restored to its rightful place.
9. The "we" in 1 Thess 4:13–17; 5:10 is a special contribution of the pseudepigraphical authors whose purpose is to address Christians of all times and assure them that the steadily increasing numbers of those among them who have died in the course of time will by no means be disadvantaged at Jesus' parousia. This speaks clearly to the contemporary problems of the later community that is actually addressed.
10. The union with Jesus is described as an alternative kind of reception like those accorded ancient rulers, without any end-time judgment for the community itself. It is made up of the "children of the day" (5:4–8), who are already saved.
11. The judgment yet to come will fall only on their opponents, the supporters of the *Pax Romana*.
12. First Thessalonians documents a three-part idea about the final judgment, as shown by the placement of the concept of ὀργή, "wrath": "The Jews" are already judged; the community will avoid judgment; their opponents will be destroyed in the future.
13. The local anti-Roman Christian resistance in Thessalonica is anti-Jewish and consists of denunciation, at the expense of Jewish groups.
14. Second Thessalonians, which stems from Jewish-Christian authors, asserts that 1 Thessalonians is a forgery and that it is itself the real letter to Thessalonica. Thus the eschatology of 1 Thessalonians is replaced by something different.
15. Second Thessalonians withdraws the three-part concept of judgment in 1 Thessalonians and replaces it with the vision of an expected single judgment by God on the "day" of the Kyrios in the future, at which all peoples and groups will be judged by Messiah Jesus at the same time.
16. The spatial and temporal unity of 2 Thessalonians' concept of judgment says that the Jewish people have not yet been judged. With this the pseudepigraphical 2 Thessalonians interprets the historical catastrophe of the Jewish people, the destruction of Jerusalem and the Temple in 70 C.E., which had already happened, as the work of the "enemy of the Law," the pagan world power of Rome.
17. The time-levels in pseudepigraphical 2 Thessalonians are: the past as time of

the "*katechon*," the restraining power; the present as time of the "enemy of the Law"; the future as the parousia of Jesus, who, as Messiah, will destroy the "enemy of the Law." The coming parousia of Jesus is thus distinguished from the present parousia of the enemy of the Torah.

18. In this way Jewish-Christian 2 Thessalonians documents an alternative historical scenario over against that in the pagan-Christian-oriented 1 Thessalonians, which had already abandoned the whole Jewish people, both historically and in the history of salvation.
19. First Thessalonians must necessarily be read, at the time when 2 Thessalonians was written, as an abandonment of the Jewish people, based on its integral component in 2:14–16, apart from the question of the pseudepigraphical character of that first letter.
20. Second Thessalonians must be regarded as a Judaizing of the Thessalonian correspondence. Its authors call for a right way of life in accordance with the Torah, and they see in Jesus, among other things, the end-time liberator of the Temple in Jerusalem. They thus call for a common stance of resistance by Jewish, Jewish-Christian, and pagan-Christian groups.
21. The Thessalonian correspondence shows that in the late first century there were Christian—that is, non-Jewish and Jewish-Christian—groups who were struggling over their nearness to or distance from the whole Jewish people. Here an attempted definitive local separation from Judaism is withdrawn and approval is given to an existential *rapprochement*.
22. The historical and exegetical paradigm of the "parting of the ways" between Christians and Jews in early Christian times requires revision. It demands a thorough restructuring and refinement through the application of social-historical discoveries.

BIBLIOGRAPHY

Abbreviations from *The SBL Handbook of Style for Biblical Studies and Related Disciplines*, 2d ed. (Atlanta: SBL Press, 2014).

Citations in the Notes are initially with full title and thereafter with short title, with the year of publication as an aid to identification. Titles by a single author are in alphabetical order in this bibliography. Works by several authors are given in full at the first author's name and as short titles elsewhere.

1. *Source Works, Text Editions, and Translations of Ancient Works*

Anthologia Graeca = *The Greek Anthology in Five Volumes*. LCL 85. London: Heinemann; Cambridge, MA: Harvard University Press, 1991.

Apostolic Fathers, The. 2 vols. Edited and translated by Bart D. Ehrmann. LCL 24, 25. London: Heinemann; Cambridge, MA: Harvard University Press, 2003.

BGU = *Ägyptische Urkunden aus den Staatlichen Museen Berlin. Griechische Urkunden*. 15 vols. Berlin: Staatliche Museen Preussischer Kulturbesitz, 1895–. English: *Financial and Administrative Documents from Roman Egypt*. Edited by Clyde A. Nelson. Berlin: Staatliche Museen Preussischer Kulturbesitz, 1983.

Bibel in Gerechter Sprache. Edited by Ulrike Bail, Frank Crüsemann, Marlene Crüsemann, Erhard Domay, Jürgen Ebach, Claudia Janssen, Hanne Köhler, Helga Kuhlmann, Martin Leutzsch, and Luise Schottroff. Gütersloh: Gütersloher Verlagshaus, 2006, 3d ed. 2007.

Biblia Hebraica Stuttgartensia. Edited by Karl Elliger and Wilhelm Rudolph. Stuttgart: Deutsche Bibelgesellschaft, 3d ed. 1987.

Assumption of Moses

Johannes Tromp. *The Assumption of Moses: A Critical Edition with Commentary*. Leiden and New York: Brill, 1993.

Cicero

Letters to Atticus. 4 vols. Edited and Translated by D. R. Shackleton Bailey. LCL 7–8, 97, 141. Cambridge, MA: Harvard University Press, 1999.

On Obligations: De Officiis. Translated by P. G. Walsh. Oxford World's Classics. Oxford: Oxford University Press, 2001.

Scripta quae mansuerunt omnia. BSGRT. Leipzig: Teubner, 1984.

The Letters to his Friends, with an English translation by W. Glynn Williams. 3 vols. LCL 205, 216, 230. Cambridge, MA: Harvard University Press, 1972–1979.

CIG = *Corpus Inscriptionum Graecarum*. Reprint. Edited by August Boeckh, et al. Hildesheim and New York: G. Olms, 1977.

CPJ = *Corpus Papyrorum Judaicarum*. 3 vols. Edited by Victor A. Tcherikover, Alexander Fuks, and Menachem Stern, with a contribution by David M. Lewis.

Cambridge, MA: Harvard University Press for Magnes Press, Hebrew University, 1957–1964.

Demetrius of Phaleron

Demetrius on Style: The Greek Text of Demetrius De elocutione. Edited by W. Rhys Roberts. Hildesheim: G. Olms, 1969.

Didache

Kurt Niederwimmer. *The Didache: A Commentary.* Translated by Linda M. Maloney. Edited by Harold W. Attridge. Hermeneia. Minneapolis: Fortress Press, 1998.

Dio Cassius

Dio's Roman History, with an English Translation by Earnest Cary, on the basis of the version by Herbert Baldwin Foster. 9 vols. LCL 32, 37, 53, 66, 82–83, 175–77. London: Heinemann; Cambridge, MA: Harvard University Press, 1970–1987.

Dion Chrysostomos (Dion of Prusa)

Discourses. 5 vols. Translated by J. W. Cohoon and H. Lamar Crosby. LCL 257, 339, 358, 376, 385. Cambridge, MA: Harvard University Press, 1932.

Dion von Prusa, Olympische Rede oder über die erste Erkenntnis Gottes. Eingeleitet, übersetzt und interpretiert von Hans-Joachim Klauck, mit einem archäologischen Beitrag von Balbina Bäbler. Sapere 2. Darmstadt: Wissenschaftliche Buchgesellschaft, 2000.

Diodorus Siculus

Diodorus Siculus. 11 vols. Translated by Charles Henry Oldfather, et al. LCL 279, 303, 340, 375, 377, 384, 389–390, 399, 409, 422-423. London: Heinemann; Cambridge, MA: Harvard University Press, 1961–1983.

Griechische Papyri aus Ägypten, als Zeugnisse des öffentlichen und privaten Lebens. Edited by Joachim Hengstl with Gunther Häge and Hanno Kühnert. Greek and German. Munich: 1978.

Flavius Josephus

Josephus. 10 vols. Translated by Henry St. John Thackeray, Ralph Marcus, and Louis H. Feldman. LCL. London: Heinemann; Cambridge, MA: Harvard University Press, 1926–1956.

Flavius Josephus. Translation and Commentary. Edited by Steve Mason. Vol. 3: *Judean Antiquities* 1–4. Translation and Commentary by Louis H. Feldman. Leiden and Boston: Brill, 2000.

IV Ezra

Der lateinische Text der Apokalypse des Esra. Edited by Albertus Frederik Johannes Klijn, with an *Index Grammaticus* by Gerard Mussies. TU 131. Berlin: Akademie Verlag, 1983.

Die Esra-Apokalypse (IV Esra): Nach dem lateinischen Text unter Benutzung der anderen Versionen übersetzt. Edited by Albertus Frederik Johannes Klijn. Berlin: de Gruyter, 1992.

Josef Schreiner, *Das 4. Buch Esra.* JSHRZ V/4. Gütersloh: Gütersloher Verlagshaus Mohn, 1981, 291–412.

Michael E. Stone and Matthias Henze. *4 Ezra and 2 Baruch. Translations, Introductions, and Notes.* Minneapolis: Fortress Press, 2013.

IG = *Inscriptiones Graecae X/2: Inscriptiones Graecae Epiri, Macedoniae, Thraciae, Sythiae, Fasc. 1: Inscriptiones Thessalonicae et viciniae.* Edited by Charles Edson. Berlin: de Gruyter, 1972.

John Chrysostom

Eight Homilies Against the Jews. n.p.: Lulu Com, 2011.

In epistulam primam ad Thessalonicenses commentarius. In J. P. Migne, *PG* 62: 391–468.

S. P. N. Joannis Chrysostom, Opera omnia quae exstant. Edited by J. P. Migne, *PG* 47–64 (1862–).

Justin Martyr

Saint Justin Martyr. The First Apology, The Second Apology, Dialogue with Trypho, Exhortation to the Greeks, Discourse to the Greeks, The Monarchy or The Rule of God. Translated by Thomas B. Falls. Fathers of the Church 6. Washington, DC: Catholic University of America Press, repr. 2008.

Lucian

Lucian. 8 vols. Translated by A. M. Harmon, K. Kilburn, M. D. MacLeod. LCL 14, 54, 130, 162, 302, 430, 431, 432. London: Heinemann; Cambridge, MA: Harvard University Press, 1913–1969.

Martin Luther

D. Martin Luther, *Die gantze Heilige Schrifft Deutsch.* Wittenberg, 1545. Last ed. in Luther's lifetime. 2 vols. Edited by Hans Volz, with Heinz Blanke; text editing by Friedrich Kur. Munich: 1972.

Die Bibel oder die ganze Heilige Schrift des Alten und Neuen Testaments nach der deutschen Übersetzung D. Martin Luthers. Revised text 1964 (OT) and 1956 (NT). Cansteinsche Bibelanstalt Witten, 1968.

Die Bibel oder die ganze Heilige Schrift des Alten und Neuen Testaments nach der Übersetzung Martin Luthers. Revised text 1975. Grosse Lutherbibel. Stuttgart: Deutsche Bibelstiftung, 1979.

Die Bibel nach der Übersetzung Martin Luthers, mit Apokryphen. Bible text in the revised version of 1984. Stuttgart: Deutsche Bibelgesellschaft, 1999.

Nestle, Eberhard, and Erwin Nestle. *Novum Testamentum Graece.* Edited by Kurt Aland and Barbara Aland, et al. Stuttgart: Deutsche Bibelgesellschaft, 27th ed. 1995.

Philo

Philo. 10 vols. Translation by F. H. Colson. LCL 226, 227, 247, 261, 275, 289, 320, 341, 363, 379, 380, 401. London: Heinemann; Cambridge, MA: Harvard University Press, 1929–1962.

P. Mich. = *Michigan Papyri*

VIII: Papyri and Ostraca from Karanis. 2d series. 2 vols. Edited by Herbert C. Youtie and John G. Winter. University of Michigan Studies, Humanistic Series 50. Ann Arbor: University of Michigan Press, 1944–1951. Papyri nos. 464–521; Ostraca nos. 972–1111.

Polybius

The Histories. 6 vols. Translated by W. R. Paton, et al. LCL 128, 137, 138, 159, 160, 161. London: Heinemann; Cambridge, MA: Harvard University Press, 2d ed. 2010–2012.

P. Oxy.

The Oxyrhynchus Papyri. Memoirs/Egypt Exploration Fund, Graeco-Roman Branch, 1–2, 5–6, 8–16; Graeco-Roman Memoirs, v. 17–20, 26–27, 29–31, 34–36, 38–41, 44–46, 48–51, 53–58, 60, 62–63, 65–67, 69–92, 94–101, 103. London: Egypt Exploration Society, 1898–2016.

Part II, edited by Bernard P. Greenfell and Arthur S. Hunt (1899), Nos. 208–400.

Part IV, edited by Bernard P. Greenfell and Arthur S. Hunt (1904), Nos. 654–839.

Psalms of Solomon

The Psalms of Solomon: A Critical Edition of the Greek Text. Translated and edited by Robert B. Wright. New York: T & T Clark, 2007.

The Odes and Psalms of Solomon. Translated by by J. Rendel Harris. Cambridge: Cambridge University Press, 1909.

OGIS = Wilhelm Dittenberger, ed. *Orientis Graeci Inscriptiones Selectae. Supplementum Sylloges Inscriptionum Graecarum*. 2 vols. Leipzig: S. Hirzel, 1903, 1905. Third reprint ed. Hildesheim and New York: G. Olms, 1986.

Seneca

Lucius Annaeus Seneca. *Seneca* in 10 volumes. Edited by John W. Basore, Richard M. Gummere, Thomas H. Corcoran, and Frank Justus Miller. LCL 62, 75–78, 214, 254, 310, 450, 457. London: Heinemann; Cambridge, MA: Harvard University Press, 1968–1979.

Septuagint

Septuaginta. Id est vetus testamentum graece iuxta LXX interpretes. 2 vols. in 1. Edited by Alfred Rahlfs. Stuttgart: Deutsche Bibelgesellschaft, many editions.

Stern

Greek and Latin Authors on Jews and Judaism. Vol. 1: *From Herodotus to Plutarch*. Vol. 2: *From Tacitus to Simplicius*. Vol. 3: *Appendixes and Indexes*. Edited with introduction and commentary by Menachem Stern. Jerusalem: Israel Academy of Sciences and Humanities, 1974–1984.

Suetonius

Gaius Suetonius Tranquillus. *Suetonius I–II*. English translation by John C. Rolfe. LCL 31, 38. London: Heinemann; Cambridge, MA: Harvard University Press, 1913–1914.

Strabo

The Geography of Strabo. 8 vols. Translated by Horace Leonard Jones and J. R. Sitlington Sterrett. LCL 49–50, 182, 196, 211, 223, 241, 267. London: Heinemann; Cambridge, MA: Harvard University Press, 1982–1989.

Syr. Baruch

Second Baruch: A Critical Edition of the Syriac Text; with Greek and Latin fragments. English translation, introduction, and concordances by Daniel M. Gurtner. New York: T & T Clark, 2009.

Tacitus

Tacitus. 5 vols. Translated by Maurice Hutton, et al. Revised by R. M. Ogilvie, et al. LCL 35, 111, 249, 312, 322. London: Heinemann; Cambridge, MA: Harvard University Press, 1914–1937.

Talmud

The Babylonian Talmud. 7 vols. in 18. Edited by Isidor Epstein. London: Soncino Press, 1935–1959.

Testaments of the Twelve Patriarchs

Jürgen Becker, *Die Testamente der zwölf Patriarchen.* JSHRZ III/1. Gütersloh: 1974.

The Apocryphal Old Testament. Edited by H. F. D. Sparks. *The Testaments of the Twelve Patriarchs.* Translated by M. de Jonge. Oxford: Oxford University Press, 1985, 505–600.

Vulgate

Biblia sacra iuxta Vulgatam versionem. Edited by Robert Weber. Stuttgart: Deutsche Bibelgesellschaft, 1983.

Zürcher Bibel

Die Heilige Schrift des Alten und Neuen Testaments (1931). Zürich: Kirchenrat der Evangelisch-Reformierten Kirche des Kantons Zürich, Verlag der Zürcher Bibel, 2003.

Zürcher Bibel 2007. Zürich: Kirchenrat der Evangelisch-reformierten Landeskirche des Kantons Zürich, Genossenschaft Verlag der Zürcher Bibel beim Theologischen Verlag Zürich, 2007.

2. *Reference Works*

Aland, Kurt, ed. *Concordance to the Novum Testamentum Graece of Nestle-Aland, 26th edition, and to the Greek New Testament, 3rd edition/ Konkordanz zum Novum Testamentum Graece von Nestle-Aland, 26. Auflage, und zum Greek New Testament, 3rd edition.* Berlin and New York: de Gruyter, 1983.

BDAG = *A Greek-English Lexicon of the New Testament and other Early Christian Literature*, revised and edited by Frederick William Danker, based on Walter Bauer's *Griechisch-deutsches Wörterbuch zu den Schriften des Neuen Testaments und der frühchristlichen Literatur.* Chicago and London: University of Chicago Press, 2000.

BDB = Francis Brown, S. R. Driver, and Charles A. Briggs. *A Hebrew and English Lexicon of the Old Testament with an Appendix containing the Biblical Aramaic. Based on the Lexicon of William Gesenius.* Translated by Edward Robinson. Oxford: Clarendon Press, [198–?].

Blass, Friedrich, Albert Debrunner, and Friedrich Rehkopf. *Grammatik des neutestamentlichen Griechisch.* Göttingen: Vandenhoeck & Ruprecht, 17th ed. 1990.

Clavis Patrum Apostolicorum. Catalogum vocum in libris patrum qui dicuntur apostolici non raro occurentium, adiuvante Ursula Früchtel congessit contulit Henricus Kraft. Darmstadt: Wissenschaftliche Buchgesellschaft, 1998. = Edgar J. Goodspeed, *Index patristicus; sive, Clavis Patrum Apostolicorum Operum*. Naperville, IL: A. R. Allenson, 1960.
Exegetical Dictionary of the New Testament. Edited by Horst R. Balz and Gerhard Schneider. 3 vols. Grand Rapids: Eerdmans, 1990–1993.
Hatch, Edwin, and Henry A. Redpath. *A Concordance to the Septuagint and other Greek Versions of the Old Testament (Including the Apocryphal Books)*. 2 vols. Oxford: Clarendon Press, 1906.
Haubeck, Wilfrid, and Heinrich von Siebenthal. *Neuer sprachlicher Schlüssel zum griechischen Neuen Testament*. 2 vols. Giessen: Brunnen, 1994, 1997.
Kohlenberger, John R. III, and James A. Swanson. *The Hebrew English Concordance to the Old Testament: with the New International Version*. Grand Rapids: Zondervan, 1998.
Liddell, Henry George, Robert Scott, Henry Stuart Jones, and Roderick McKenzie. *A Greek-English Lexicon*. Oxford and New York: Oxford University Press, 1996.
Lisowsky, Gerhard, and Leonard Rost. *Konkordanz zum Hebräischen Alten Testament*. Stuttgart: Württembergische Bibelanstalt, 1958.
Pauly, August Friedrich von, Wilhelm Kroll, and Georg Wissowa, eds. *Paulys Real-encyclopädie der classischen Altertumswissenschaft*. Stuttgart: Metzler, 1894–1963. (Numerous editions.)
Theological Dictionary of the New Testament. Edited by Gerhard Kittel and Gerhard Friedrich. 10 vols. Translated and edited by Geoffrey W. Bromiley. Grand Rapids: Eerdmans, 1972.

3. *Secondary Literature*

Aarde, Andries G. van. "The Second Letter to the Thessalonians Reread as Pseudepigraph," *Hervormde teologiese studies* 56 (March 2000), 105–36.
———. "The Struggle against Heresy in the Thessalonian Correspondence and the Origin of the Apostolic Tradition," in: *The Thessalonian Correspondence* (1990), 418–25.
Abel, Karlhans. art. "Securitas," in: *Der Kleine Pauly* 5 (1979), 60–61.
Aejmelaeus, Lars. *Wachen vor dem Ende. Die traditionsgeschichtlichen Wurzeln von 1. Thess 5:1-11 und Luk 21:34-36*. SFEG 44. Helsinki: Kirjapaino Raamattutalo, 1985.
Aland, Kurt. "Das Problem der Anonymität und Pseudonymität in der christlichen Literatur der ersten beiden Jahrhunderte," pages 23–34 in idem, *Studien zur Überlieferung des Neuen Testaments und seines Textes*. ANTF 2. Berlin: de Gruyter, 1967.
———. "Noch einmal: Das Problem der Anonymität und Pseudonymität in der christlichen Literatur der ersten beiden Jahrhunderte," pages 121–30 in *Pietas. Festschrift für Bernhard Kötting*. Edited by Ernst Dassmann and Karl Suso Frank. JAC Ergänzungsband 8. Münster: Aschendorff, 1980.
Alexander, Philip S. "'The Parting of the Ways' from the Perspective of Rabbinic Judaism," pages 1–25 in *Jews and Christians: The Parting of the Ways, A.D. 70 to 135: The Second Durham Tübingen Research Symposium on Earliest Christianity and Judaism, Durham, September, 1989*. Edited by James D. G. Dunn. Tübingen: Mohr (Siebeck), 1992.
Alexander, Phoebe S. "Epistolary Literature," pages 579–96 in *Jewish Writings of the Second Temple Period*. Edited by Michael E. Stone. CRINT II.2. Assen: Van Gorcum; Philadelphia: Fortress Press, 1984.

Alkier, Stefan. "Der 1. Thessalonicherbrief als kulturelles Gedächtnis," pages 175–94 in *Logos und Buchstabe. Mündlichkeit und Schriftlichkeit im Judentum und Christentum der Antike*. Edited by Gerhard Sellin and François Vouga. Texte und Arbeiten zum neutestamentlichen Zeitalter 20. Tübingen: Francke, 1997.

Alvarez Cineira, David. *Die Religionspolitik des Kaisers Claudius und die paulinische Mission*. Herders biblische Studien 19. Freiburg and New York: Herder, 1999.

Amir, Yehoshua. "Das jüdische Paradox auf dem Hintergrund der hellenistischen Judenfeindschaft," pages 114–23 in idem, *Studien zum Antiken Judentum*. BEATAJ 2. Frankfurt and New York: Peter Lang, 1985.

———. "Die Stellungnahme der hellenistischen Welt zum Judentum," *Frankfurter Rundschau* 27 (1975), 167–72.

Amphoux, Christian B. "1 Th 2,14–16: Quels Juifs sont-ils mis en cause par Paul?" *Filologia neotestamentaria* 16 (2003), 85–101.

Andresen, Carl. "Zum Formular frühchristlicher Gemeindebriefe," *ZNW* 56 (1965), 233–59.

Annen, Franz. "Saulus, der Christenverfolger—Paulus, der Kritiker des Judentums," pages 37–63 in *Kritik und Gegenkritik in Christentum und Judentum*. Edited by Simon Lauer. JudChr 3. Bern, Frankfurt, and Las Vegas: Peter Lang, 1981.

Arzt, Peter. "Ägyptische Papyri und das Neue Testament. Zur Frage der Vergleichbarkeit von Texten," *PzB* 6 (1997), 21–29.

———. "Analyse der Paulusbriefe vor dem Hintergrund dokumentarischer Papyri," *PzB* 3 (1994), 99–114.

Arzt-Grabner, Peter. *Philemon*. Papyrologische Kommentare zum Neuen Testament 1. Göttingen: Vandenhoeck & Ruprecht, 2003.

Ascough, Richard S. "A Question of Death: Paul's Community-Building Language in 1 Thessalonians 4:13–18," *JBL* 123 (2004), 509–30.

———. *Paul's Macedonian Associations: The Social Context of Philippians and 1 Thessalonians*. WUNT 2d ser. 161. (Tübingen: Mohr Siebeck, 2003).

Askwith, E. H. *An Introduction to the Thessalonian Epistles. Containing a vindication of the Pauline Authorship of both Epistles and an interpretation of the Eschatological section of 2 Thess. ii*. London and New York: Macmillan, 1902.

———. "'I' and 'We' in the Thessalonian Epistles," *Expositor* Series 11, 1 (1911), 149–59.

Aus, Roger D. "Comfort in Judgment: The Use of the Day of the Lord and Theophany Traditions in Second Thessalonians 1," Diss. Yale, 1971 (Microfilm).

———. "God's Plan and God's Power: Isaiah 66 and the restraining Factors of 2 Thess 2:6–7," *JBL* 66 (1977), 537–53.

———. "The Liturgical Background of the Necessity and Propriety of Giving Thanks According to 2 Thess 1:6," *JBL* 92 (1973), 432–38.

———. "The Relevance of Isaiah 66:7 to Revelation 12 and 2 Thessalonians 1," *ZNW* 67 (1976), 252–68.

———. "II Thessalonians," pages 191–223 in *I–II Timothy, Titus, II Thessalonians*. Edited by Arnold J. Hultgren and Roger D. Aus. Minneapolis: Augsburg, 1984.

Avotri, Salomon K. "Possessing One's Vessel in 1 Thess 4:4: Marital or Martial Metaphor?" Diss. University of Denver, 1991. Microfiche.

Bacon, B. W. "Wrath 'unto the Uttermost,'" *Expositor* Series 8, 24 (1922), 356–76.

Bahr, Gordon J. "Paul and Letter Writing in the First Century," *CBQ* 28 (1966), 465–77.

Bailey, J. A. "Who Wrote II Thessalonians?" *NTS* 25 (1979), 131–45.

Baltensweiler, Hans. "Erwägungen zu I. Thess. 4,3–8," *TZ* 19 (1963), 1–13.

Balz, Horst R. "Anonymität und Pseudepigraphie im Urchristentum. Überlegungen zum literarischen und theologischen Problem der urchristlichen und gemeinantiken Pseudepigraphie," *ZTK* 66 (1969), 403–36.

Bammel, Ernst. "Ein Beitrag zur paulinischen Staatsanschauung," *TLZ* 85 (1960), 837–40.

———. "Judenverfolgung und Naherwartung. Zur Eschatologie des Ersten Thessalonicherbriefs," *ZTK* 56 (1959), 294–315.

Bammer, Andreas. "Erwählung inmitten einer multikulturellen Gemeindesituation. Zum papyrologischen Befund von ἐκλογή in 1 Thess 1,4," *PzB* 16 (2007), 103–18.

Barclay, John M. G. "Conflict in Thessalonica," *CBQ* 55 (1993), 512–30.

———. *Jews in the Mediterranean Diaspora. From Alexander to Trajan (323 BCE–117 CE).* Edinburgh: T & T Clark, 1996.

Barnouin, M. "Problèmes de traduction concernant 2 Thess 2,6–7," *NTS* 23 (1977), 482–98.

Bassler, Jouette M. "I and II Thessalonians," pages 311–18 in *The Books of the Bible*. Vol. 2, *The New Testament*. Edited by Bernhard W. Anderson. New York: Scribner's, 1989.

———. "The Enigmatic Sign: 2 Thessalonians 1:5," *CBQ* 46 (1984), 496–510.

Bauckham, Richard. "James and the Jerusalem Community," pages 55–95 in *Jewish Believers in Jesus: The Early Centuries*. Edited by Oskar Skarsaune and Reidar Hvalvik. Peabody, MA: Hendrickson, 2007.

———. "Pseudo-Apostolic Letters," *JBL* 107 (1988), 469–94.

Bauer, Bruno. *Kritik der paulinischen Briefe*. Berlin, 1850–52; reprint Aalen: Scientia, 1972).

Baum, Armin Daniel. *Pseudepigraphie und literarische Fälschung im frühen Christentum.* WUNT, 2d ser. 138. Tübingen: Mohr (Siebeck), 2001.

Baumbach, Günther. art. "Antisemitismus II. Die jüdische Reaktion auf den antiken Anti-semitismus," *TRE* 3 (1978), 119–22.

Baumert, Norbert. "Brautwerbung. Das einheitliche Thema von 1 Thess 4,3–8," pages 316–39 in *The Thessalonian Correspondence* (1990).

———. "Ὀμειρόμενοι in 1 Thess 2,8," *Bib* 68 (1988), 553–63.

Baumgarten, Jörg. *Paulus und die Apokalyptik. Die Auslegung apokalyptischer Überlieferungen in den echten Paulusbriefen*. WMANT 44. Neukirchen-Vluyn: Neukirchener Verlag, 1975.

Baur, Ferdinand Christian. "Die beiden Briefe an die Thessalonicher, ihre Aechtheit und Bedeutung für die Lehre von der Parusie Christi," pages 141–68 in *Theologisches Jahrbuch* 14 (1855) = idem, *Paulus, der Apostel Jesu Christi* 2 (1866–67), 341–69 (Appendix). (See reference to English translation below.)

———. *Die sogenannten Pastoralbriefe des Apostels Paulus, aufs neue kritisch untersucht.* Stuttgart and Tübingen: Gotta, 1835.

———. *Paulus, der Apostel Jesu Christi. Sein Leben und Wirken, seine Briefe und seine Lehre.* 2 vols. Original pub. 1845–67. New ed. by Eduard Zeller. Osnabrück: Zeller, 1968. English: *Paul the Apostle of Jesus Christ: His Life and Works, His Epistles and Teachings.* 2 vols. in 1. London: Williams and Norgate, 1873; repr. Peabody, MA: Hendrickson, 2003.

Beale, Gregory K. *1–2 Thessalonians*. IVP New Testament Commentary 12. Downers Grove and Leicester: InterVarsity Press, 2010.

Beavis, Mary Ann. "2 Thessalonians," pages 263–71 in *Searching the Scriptures*. Vol. 2: *A Feminist Commentary*. Edited by Elisabeth Schüssler Fiorenza. New York: Crossroad, 1994.

Becker, Adam H., and Annette Y. Reed, eds. *The Ways that Never Parted. Jews and Christians in Late Antiquity and the Early Middle Ages*. Minneapolis: Fortress Press, 2007.

Becker, Eve-Marie. "Ὡς δι' ἡμῶν in 2 Thess 2.2 als Hinweis auf einen verlorenen Brief," *NTS* 55 (2009), 55–72.

———. *Schreiben und Verstehen. Paulinische Briefhermeneutik im Zweiten Korintherbrief.* Neutestamentliche Entwürfe zur Theologie 4. Tübingen: Francke, 2002.

———. "Von Paulus zu 'Paulus.' Paulinische Pseudepigraphie-Forschung als literaturgeschichtliche Aufgabe," pages 363–86 in *Pseudepigraphie und Verfasserfiktion in frühchristlichen Briefen*. Edited by Jörg Frey, et al., with Michaela Engelmann. WUNT 246. Tübingen: Mohr Siebeck, 2009.

Becker, Jürgen. *Auferstehung der Toten im Urchristentum*. SBS 82. Stuttgart: Katholisches Bibelwerk, 1976.

———. *Die Auferstehung Jesu Christi nach dem Neuen Testament. Ostererfahrung und Osterverständnis im Urchristentum*. Tübingen: Mohr Siebeck, 2007.

———. "Die Erwählung der Völker durch das Evangelium. Theologiegeschichtliche Erwägungen zum 1. Thessalonicherbrief," pages 82–101 in *Studien zu Text und Ethik des Neuen Testaments. Festschrift zum 80. Geburtstag von Heinrich Greeven*. Edited by Wolfgang Schrage. BZNW 47. Berlin: de Gruyter, 1986.

Beilner, Wolfgang. "Weltgericht und Weltvollendung bei Paulus," pages 85–105 in *Weltgericht und Weltvollendung. Zukunftsbilder im Neuen Testament*. Edited by Hans-Josef Klauck. QD 150. Freiburg, et al.: Herder, 1994.

Ben-Chorin, Schalom. "Antijüdische Elemente im Neuen Testament," *EvT* 40 (1980), 203–14.

Bendemann, Reinhard von. "Die Auferstehung Jesu von den Toten als 'basic story,'" *Glaube und Lernen* 15 (2000), 148–62.

———. "'Frühpaulinisch' und/oder 'spätpaulinisch?' Erwägungen zu der These einer Entwicklung der paulinischen Theologie am Beispiel des Gesetzesverständnisses," *EvT* 60 (2000), 210–29.

———. "'Zorn' und 'Zorn Gottes' im Römerbrief," pages 179–215 in *Paulus und Johannes. Exegetische Studien zur paulinischen und johanneischen Theologie und Literatur*. Edited by Dieter Sänger and Ulrich Mell. WUNT 198. Tübingen: Mohr Siebeck, 2006.

Bengel, Johann Albrecht. *Gnomon of the New Testament*. 5 vols. Edited by Andrew R. Fausset, Ernest Bengel, and J. C. F. Steudel. Translated by Andrew Robert Fausset, James Bryce, and William Fletcher. Eugene, OR: Wipf & Stock, 2004 (orig. pub. 1877).

Berger, Klaus. *Theologiegeschichte des Urchristentums. Theologie des Neuen Testaments*. UTB. Tübingen: Francke, 1994.

———. "Apostelbrief und apostolische Rede. Zum Formular frühchristlicher Briefe," *ZNW* 65 (1974), 190–231.

Berger, Martin. "Die Katechon-Vorstellung 2 Thess 2,6f. Dietrich Bonhoeffers Interpretation im Kontext der Rezeptionsgeschichte," *PzB* 5 (1996), 33–56.

Best, Ernest. *A Commentary on the First and Second Epistles to the Thessalonians*. BNTC 13, 14. New York: Harper & Row, 1972.

Betz, Hans Dieter. *2 Corinthians 8 and 9. A Commentary on Two Administrative Letters of the Apostle Paul*. Hermeneia. Philadelphia: Fortress Press, 1985.

———. *Galatians: A Commentary on Paul's Letter to the Churches in Galatia*. Hermeneia. Philadelphia: Fortress Press, 1979.

———. *Nachfolge und Nachahmung Jesu Christi im Neuen Testament*. BHT 37. Tübingen: Mohr, 1967.

Betz, Otto. "Der Katechon," *NTS* 9 (1962/63), 276–91.

Bickerman(n), Elias J. *Der Gott der Makkabäer: Untersuchungen über Sinn und Ursprung der makkabäischen Erhebung*. Berlin: Schocken, 1937.

———. *The Jews in the Greek Age*. Cambridge, MA: Harvard University Press, 1988.
———. "The Name of the Christians" (1949). Pages 139–51 in idem, *Studies in Jewish and Christian History*. AGJU IX/3. Leiden: Brill, 1986; new ed. 2007.
Bickhoff-Böttcher, Nicole. "Das Judentum in der griechisch-römischen Welt. Gesellschaftliche und politische Beziehungen und Konflikte von der Mitte des 1. Jahrhunderts v. Chr. bis zum Ende des 2. Jahrhunderts n. Chr," Dissertation Osnabrück, 1984.
Bickmann, Jutta. *Kommunikation gegen den Tod. Studien zur paulinischen Briefpragmatik am Beispiel des Ersten Thessalonicherbriefs*. FB 86. Würzburg: Echter Verlag, 1998.
———. "1 Thessalonians: Opposing Death by Building Community," Translated by Everett R. Kalin. Pages 810–20 in *Feminist Biblical Interpretation: A Compendium of Critical Commentary on the Books of the Bible and Related Literature*. Edited by Luise Schottroff, Marie-Theres Wacker, and Martin Rumscheidt. Grand Rapids and Cambridge: Eerdmans, 2012.
Bieringer, Reimund. "Plädoyer für die Einheitlichkeit des 2. Korintherbriefes," pages 131–79 in *Studies on 2 Corinthians*. Edited by Reimund Bieringer and Jan Lambrecht. BETL 125. Leuven: Leuven University Press/Peeters, 1994.
———. "Teilungshypothesen zum 2. Korintherbrief. Ein Forschungsüberblick," pages 67–105 in *Studies on 2 Corinthians* (1994).
Billerbeck, Paul (Hermann L. Strack). *Kommentar zum Neuen Testament aus Talmud und Midrasch*. Munich: Beck, 1974–1975 (© 1924–1961).
Binder, Hermann. "Paulus und die Thessalonicherbriefe," pages 87–93 in *The Thessalonian Correspondence* (1990).
Bockmuehl, Markus. "1 Thessalonians 2:14–16 and the Church in Jerusalem," *TynBul* 52 (2001), 1–31.
Boer, Willis P. *The Imitation of Paul: An Exegetical Study*. Kampen: Kok Pharos, 1962; repr. [Eugene, OR]: Wipf & Stock, 2016.
Boers, Hendrikus. "The Form Critical Study of Paul's Letters. I Thessalonians as a Case Study," *NTS* 22 (1976), 140–58.
Börschel, Regina. *Die Konstruktion einer christlichen Identität. Paulus und die Gemeinde von Thessalonich in ihrer hellenistisch-jüdischen Umwelt*. BBB 129. Berlin: Philo, 2001.
Bonsack, Bernhard. "Literarkritische Kapricen zu den Thessalonicherbriefen," pages 180–90 in *Theologische Kaprizen. Festschrift für Hans Friedrich Geisser*. Edited by Hans Friedrich Geisser, Markus Baumgartner, and Hans Jürgen Luibl. Zürich: M. Baumgartner and H. J. Luibl, 1988.
Bonz, M. P. "The Jewish Donor Inscriptions from Aphrodisias: Are They Both Third-Century?" and "Who Are the *theosebeis*?" *HSCP* 96 (1994), 281–99.
Bornemann, Wilhelm. *Die Thessalonicherbriefe*. KEK 10. Göttingen, 5th & 6th eds. 1894.
Bosenius, Bärbel. *Die Abwesenheit des Apostels als theologisches Programm. Der zweite Korintherbrief als Beispiel für die Brieflichkeit der paulinischen Theologie*. Texte und Arbeiten zum neutestanemtlichen Zeitalter 11. Tübingen: Francke, 1994.
Botermann, Helga. *Das Judenedikt des Kaisers Claudius. Römischer Staat und* Christiani *im 1. Jahrhundert*. Hermes Einzelschriften 71. Stuttgart: Steiner, 1996.
———. "Der Heidenapostel und sein Historiker. Zur historischen Kritik der Apostelgeschichte," *TBei* 24 (1993), 62–84.
———. "Griechisch-Jüdische Epigraphik. Zur Datierung der Aphrodisias-Inschrift," *ZPE* 98 (1993), 184–94.

Bousset, Wilhelm. *Der Antichrist in der Überlieferung des Judentums, des neuen Testaments und der alten Kirche. Ein Beitrag zur Auslegung der Apocalypse*. Göttingen: Vandenhoeck & Ruprecht, 1895. English: *The Antichrist Legend: A Chapter in Christian and Jewish Folklore*. Translated by A. H. Keane. AAR Texts and Translations 24. Atlanta: Scholars Press, 1999.

Boyarin, Daniel. *Border Lines: The Partition of Judaeo-Christianity*. Philadelphia: University of Pennsylvania Press, 2004.

———. "Semantic Differences; or 'Judaism'/'Christianity,'" Pages 65–85 in *The Ways That Never Parted* (2007).

Brandenburger, Egon. "Gerichtskonzeptionen im Urchristentum und ihre Voraussetzungen. Eine Problemstudie," pages 289–338 in idem, ed., *Studien zur Geschichte und Theologie des Urchristentums*. Stuttgart: Katholisches Bibelwerk, 1993.

Brandenburger, Stefan H. "Der 'Gesalbte des Herrn' in Psalm Salomo 17," pages 217–36 in *Wenn drei das Gleiche sagen: Studien zu den ersten drei Evangelien*. Edited by Stefan H. Brandenburger and Thomas Hieke. Münster: Aschendorff, 1998.

Brandon, Samuel G. F. *The Fall of Jerusalem and the Christian Church. A Study of the Effects of the Jewish Overthrow of A. D. 70 on Christianity*. London: S.P.C.K., 1951.

Brant, Jo-Ann A. "The place of *mimēsis* in Paul's Thought," *SR* 22 (1993), 285–300.

Braun, Herbert. "Zur nachapostolischen Herkunft des zweiten Thessalonicherbriefes," *ZNW* 44 (1952/53), 152–56.

Breytenbach, Cilliers, with Ingrid Behrmann, eds. *Frühchristliches Thessaloniki*. Studien und Texte zu Antike und Christentum 44. Tübingen: Mohr Siebeck, 2007.

Brocke, Christoph vom. *Thessaloniki: Stadt des Kassander und Gemeinde des Paulus. Eine frühe christliche Gemeinde in ihrer heidnischen Umwelt*. WUNT 2d ser. 125. Tübingen: Mohr Siebeck, 2001.

Broer, Ingo. "Antijudaismus im Neuen Testament? Versuch einer Annäherung anhand von zwei Texten (1 Thess 2,14–16 und Mt 27,24)," pages 321–55 in *Salz der Erde, Licht der Welt: Exegetische Studien zum Matthäusevangelium. Festschrift für Anton Vögtle*. Edited by Lorenz Oberlinner and Peter Fiedler. Stuttgart: Katholisches Bibelwerk, 1961.

———. "'Antisemitismus' und Judenpolemik im Neuen Testament: Ein Beitrag zum besseren Verständnis von 1 Thess 2,14–16," *BN* 20 (1983), 59–91.

———. "'Der ganze Zorn ist schon über sie gekommen.' Bemerkungen zur Interpolationshypothese und zur Interpretation von 1 Thess 2,14–16," pages 137–59 in *The Thessalonian Correspondence* (1990).

———. "Die Juden im Urteil der Autoren des Neuen Testaments. Anmerkungen zum Problem historischer Gerechtigkeit im Angesicht einer verheerenden Wirkungsgeschichte," *TGl* 82 (1992), 2–33.

Brooten, Bernadette J. "Frühchristliche Frauen und ihr kultureller Kontext. Überlegungen zur Methode historischer Rekonstruktion," pages 62–93 in *Einwürfe 2*. Edited by Jürgen Ebach and Friedrich-Wilhelm Marquardt. Munich: Kaiser, 1985.

———. "The Gender of Ιαηλ in the Jewish Inscription from Aphrodisias," pages 163–73 in *Of Scribes and Scrolls. Studies on the Hebrew Bible, intertestamental Judaism, and Christian origins, presented to John Strugnell*. Edited by Harold W. Attridge, et al. Lanham, MD: University Press of America, 1990.

———. "Jael προστάτης in the Jewish Donative Inscription from Aphrodisias," pages 149–62 in *The Future of Early Christianity. Essays in Honor of Helmut Koester*. Edited by Birger A. Pearson. Minneapolis: Fortress Press, 1991.

Brown, Stephen G. "The Intertextuality of Jes 66.17 and 2 Thessalonians 2.7: A Solution to the 'Restrainer' Problem," pages 254–75 in *Paul and the Scriptures of*

Israel. Edited by Craig A. Evans and James A. Sanders. JSNTSup 83. Sheffield: JSOT Press, 1993.

Brox, Norbert. *Falsche Verfasserangaben. Zur Erklärung der frühchristlichen Pseudepigraphie*. SBS 79. Stuttgart: Katholisches Bibelwerk, 1975.

———, ed. *Pseudepigraphie in der heidnischen und jüdisch-christlichen Antike*. Wege der Forschung 484. Darmstadt: Wissenschaftliche Buchgesellschaft, 1977.

Bruce, Frederick F. *1 & 2 Thessalonians*. WBC 45. Waco, TX: Word Books, 1962.

———. art. "Travel and Communication (NT World)," *ABD* 6 (1992), 648–53.

Buchhold, Jacques. "1 Thessaloniciens 2.13–16," *Théologie Évangelique* 6 (2007), 229–40.

Buck, Charles Henry, and Greer Taylor. *Saint Paul: A Study of the Development of His Thought*. New York: Scribner, 1969.

Burke, Trevor J. *Family Matters. A Socio-Historical Study of Kinship Metaphors in 1 Thessalonians*. London and New York: T & T Clark International, 2003.

Burkitt, F. Crawford. *Christian Beginnings: Three Lectures*. London: University of London Press, 1924; repr. Eugene, OR: Wipf & Stock, 2005.

Bussmann, Claus. *Themen der paulinischen Missionspredigt auf dem Hintergrund der spätjüdisch-hellenistischen Missionsliteratur*. Europäische Hochschulschriften 3. Bern, et al.: Lang, 1971.

Byrskog, Samuel. "Co-Senders, Co-Authors and Paul's Use of the First Plural," *ZNW* 87 (1996), 230–50.

Calov, Abraham. *Biblia novi testamenti illustrata*. 4 vols. Dresden and Leipzig: Zimmermann, 1719.

Carras, George P. "Jewish Ethics and Gentile Converts: Remarks on 1 Thess 4,3–8," pages 306–15 in *The Thessalonian Correspondence* (1990).

Casson, Lionel. *Travel in the Ancient World*. Baltimore: Johns Hopkins University Press, 1994.

Castelli, Elizabeth. *Imitating Paul. A Discourse of Power*. Louisville: Westminster John Knox, 1991.

Chapa, Juan. "Consolatory Patterns? 1 Thess 4,13.18; 5,11," pages 220–28 in *The Thesssalonian Correspondence* (1990).

———. "Is First Thessalonians a Letter of Consolation?" *NTS* 40 (1994), 150–60.

Chester, Andrew. "The Parting of the Ways. Eschatology and Messianic Hope," pages 239–313 in James D. G. Dunn, ed., *Jews and Christians* (1992).

Clark, David J. "Structural Similarities in 1 and 2 Thessalonians: Comparative Discourse Anatomy," pages 196–207 in *The Intertextuality of the Epistles. Explorations of Theory and Practice*. Edited by Thomas L. Brodie, Dennis R. MacDonald, and Stanley E. Porter. Sheffield: Sheffield Phoenix Press, 2006.

Clemen, Carl. *Die Einheitlichkeit der paulinischen Briefe an der Hand der bisher mit bezug auf sie aufgestellten Interpolations- und Compilationshypothesen*. Göttingen: Vandenhoeck & Ruprecht, 1894.

Cohen, Shaye J. D. "Crossing the Boundary and Becoming a Jew," *HTR* 82 (1989), 13–33.

———. "The Rabbinic Conversion Ceremony," *JJS* 41 (1990), 177–203.

Collins, Raymond F. "A propos the Integrity of 1 Thess" (1979), in idem, *Studies* (1984), 96–135.

———. "Paul, as seen through his own eyes" (1980), in idem, *Studies* (1984), 175–208.

———. "Paul's Early Christology," in idem, *Studies* (1984), 253–84.

———. "Recent Scholarship on Paul's Letters to the Thessalonians," in idem, *Studies* (1984), 3–75.

———. "'I Command That This Letter Be Read': Writing as a Manner of Speaking," pages 319–39 in *The Thessalonians Debate*. Edited by Karl P. Donfried and Johannes Beutler. Grand Rapids and Cambridge: Eerdmans, 2000.
———. *Studies on the First Letter to the Thessalonians*. BETL 66. Leuven: University Press, 1984.
———. *The Birth of the New Testament. The Origin and Development of the First Christian Generation*. New York: Crossroad, 1993.
———. "The Church of the Thessalonians" (1974/75), in idem, *Studies* (1984), 336–49.
———. "The Faith of the Thessalonians" (1978/79), in idem, *Studies* (1984), 209–29.
———. "'The Gospel of Our Lord Jesus' (2 Thess 1,8): A Symbolic Shift of Paradigm," pages 426–40 in idem, ed., *The Thessalonian Correspondence* (1990).
———. "Tradition, Redaction and Exhortation in 1 Thess 4,13–5,11" (1980), in idem, *Studies* (1984), 154–72.
———, ed. *The Thessalonian Correspondence*. BETL 87. Leuven: Leuven University Press; Peeters, 1990.
Colpe, Carsten. "Das deutsche Wort 'Judenchristen' und ihm entsprechende historische Sachverhalte. Pages 50–68 in *Gilgul. Essays on Transformation, Revolution and Permanence in the History of Religions, dedicated to R. J. Zwi Werblowski*. Edited by Shaul Shaked, David Dean Shulman, and Guy G. Stroumsa. SHR 50. Leiden: Brill, 1978. (Expanded version: Carsten Colpe, *Das Siegel der Propheten. Historische Beziehungen zwischen Judentum, Judenchristentum, Heidentum und frühem Islam* ANTZ 3. Berlin: Institut Kirche und Judentum, 1990, 35–58.)
Conzelmann, Hans. *Der erste Brief an die Korinther*. KEK 11th ed. Göttingen: Vandenhoeck & Ruprecht, 1969. English: *1 Corinthians: A Commentary on the First Epistle to the Corinthians*. Translated by James Leitch. Hermeneia. Philadelphia: Fortress Press, 1975.
———. *Heiden, Juden, Christen. Auseinandersetzungen in der Literatur der hellenistisch-römischen Zeit*. BHT 62. Tübingen: Mohr, 1981. English: *Gentiles, Jews, Christians. Polemics and Apologetics in the Greco-Roman Era*. Translated by M. Eugene Boring. Minneapolis: Fortress Press, 1992.
Conzelmann, Hans, and Andreas Lindemann. *Arbeitsbuch zum Neuen Testament*. UTB 52. Tübingen: Mohr Siebeck, 2014. English: *Interpreting the New Testament: An Introduction to the Principles and Methods of N. T. Exegesis*. Translated by Siegfried S. Schatzmann from the 8th rev. German ed. Peabody, MA: Hendrickson, 1988.
Cook, John Granger. "Pagan Philosophers and 1 Thessalonians," *NTS* 52 (2006), 514–32.
Coppens, Josef C. "Une Diatribe antijuive dans 1 Thess 2:13–16," *ETL* 51 (1975), 90–95.
Cosby, Michael R. "Hellenistic Formula Receptions and Paul's Use of ΑΠΑΝΤΗΣΙΣ in 1 Thessalonians," *BBR* 4 (1994), 15–34.
Cothenet, Édouard. "La deuxième Épitre aux Thessaloniciens et l'Apocalypse synoptique," *RSR* 42 (1954), 5–39.
Coulot, Claude. "À la venue du Seigneur (1 Th 4,13–18)," *RSR* 80 (2006), 499–509.
———. "Paul à Thessalonique (1 Th 2.1–12)," *NTS* 52 (2006), 377–93.
Cranfield, Charles E. B. "Changes of Person and Number in Paul's Epistles," pages 280–89 in *Paul and Paulinism. Essays in Honor of C. K. Barrett*. Edited by Morna D. Hooker and Stephen G. Wilson. London: S.P.C.K., 1982.
Crawford, Charles. "The Tiny Problem of 1 Thessalonians 2,7: The Case of the Curious Vocative," *Bib* 54 (1973), 69–72.
Crüsemann, Frank. *Das Alte Testament als Wahrheitsraum des Neuen*. Gütersloh: Gütersloher Verlagshaus, 2015.

———. *Die Tora. Theologie und Sozialgeschichte des alttestamentlichen Gesetzes*. Gütersloh: Gütersloher Verlagshaus, 3d ed. 2005. English: *The Torah: Theology and Social History of Old Testament Law*. Translated by Allen W. Mahnke. Minneapolis: Fortress Press, 1996.

———. *Maßstab: Tora. Israels Weisung für christliche Ethik*. Gütersloh: Kaiser; Gütersloher Verlagshaus, 2003; 2d ed. 2004.

———. "Rhetorische Fragen!? Eine Aufkündigung des Konsenses über Psalm 88,11–13 und seine Bedeutung für das alttestamentliche Reden von Gott und Tod," *BibInt* 11 (2003), 345–60.

———. "Tora und christliche Ethik," pages 159–77 in *Auschwitz - Krise der christlichen Theologie*. Edited by Rolf Rendtorff and Ekkehard W. Stegemann. Abhandlungen zum christlich-jüdischen Dialog 10. Munich: Kaiser, 1980.

———, and Marlene Crüsemann. art. "Zeitvorstellungen," in *Sozialgeschichtliches Wörterbuch zur Bibel*. Edited by Frank Crüsemann, Kristian Hungar, Claudia Janssen, Rainer Kessler, and Luise Schottroff. Gütersloh: Gütersloher Verlagshaus, 2009, 669–75.

———. "Die Gegenwart des Verlorenen. Zur Interpretation der biblischen Vorstellung vom 'Paradies.'" Pages 25–68 in *"Schau an der schönen Gärten Zier ...," Über irdische und himmlische Paradiese*. Edited by Jürgen Ebach, Hans-Martin Gutmann, Magdalene L. Frettlöh, and Michael Weinrich. *Jabboq* 7. Gütersloh: Gütersloher Verlagshaus, 2007. (NT section by Marlene Crüsemann reprinted in eadem, *Gott ist Beziehung* [2014], 228–49.)

Crüsemann, Marlene. art. "Paulus," in *Wörterbuch der Feministischen Theologie*. Edited by Elisabeth Gössmann, et al. Rev. and expanded ed. Gütersloh: Gütersloher Verlagshaus, 2002, 444–48 (= eadem, *Gott ist Beziehung* [2014], 132–38).

———. "'Das weite Herz und die Gemeinschaft der Heiligen. 2 Kor 6,11–7,4 im sozialgeschichtlichen Kontext," pages 351–75 in *Dem Tod nicht glauben. Sozialgeschichte der Bibel. Festschrift für Luise Schottroff zum 70. Geburtstag*. Edited by Frank Crüsemann, Marlene Crüsemann, Claudia Janssen, Rainer Kessler, and Beate Wehn. Gütersloh: Gütersloher Verlagshaus, 2004 (= eadem, *Gott ist Beziehung* [2014], 206–227.

———, "Der Gottesname im Neuen Testament (zu 2 Kor 3,16)," *Junge Kirche* 68 (2007), 16–18 (= eadem, *Gott ist Beziehung* [2014], 123–26).

———. "2 Thessalonians: Hope in God's Just Judgement," Translated by Everett R. Kalin. Pages 821–29 in *Feminist Biblical Interpretation* (2012).

———. "Die Briefe nach Thessaloniki und das gerechte Gericht. Studien zu ihrer Abfassung und zur jüdisch-christlichen Sozialgeschichte," Dissertation Kassel, 1999 (Microfiche).

———. "Gefässe der Ehre. Sozialgeschichtliche Bibelauslegung zu 1 Thess 4,1–8," *Junge Kirche* 59 (1998), 518–20 (= pages 80–83 in *Wie Freiheit entsteht. Sozialgeschichtliche Bibelauslegungen*. Edited by Claudia Janssen and Beate Wehn. Gütersloh: Gütersloher Verlagshaus, 1999; also in Marlene Crüsemann, *Gott ist Beziehung* [2014], 74–77).

———. *Gott ist Beziehung. Beiträge zur biblischen Rede von Gott*. Edited by Claudia Janssen and Luise Schottroff. Gütersloh: Gütersloher Verlagshaus, 2014.

———. "'Heißt das, dass wir die Tora durch das Vertrauen ausser Kraft setzen?' Röm 3,28–31 und die Bibel in gerechter Sprache," pages 482–96 in *Fragen wider die Antworten*. Edited by Kerstin Schiffner, et al. Gütersloh: Gütersloher Verlagshaus, 2010 (= eadem, *Gott ist Beziehung*, [2014], 53–66).

———. "Trost, *charis* und Kraft der Schwachen. Eine Christologie der Beziehung nach dem zweiten Brief an die Gemeinde in Korinth," pages 111–37 in *Christus und seine Geschwister. Christologie im Umfeld der Bibel in gerechter Sprache*. Edited by Marlene Crüsemann and C. Jochum-Bortfeld. Gütersloh: Gütersloher Verlagshaus, 2009 (= eadem, *Gott ist Beziehung* [2014], 184–205).

———. "Unrettbar frauenfeindlich. Der Kampf um das Wort von Frauen in 1 Kor 14,(33b)34–35 im Spiegel antijudaistischer Elemente der Auslegung," pages 199–223 in *Von der Wurzel getragen: Christlich-feministische Exegese in Auseinandersetzung mit Antijudaismus*. Edited by Luise Schottroff and Marie-Theres Wacker. Leiden and New York: Brill, 1996 (= eadem, *Gott ist Beziehung* [2014], 144–62). Edited English translation by Brian McNeil: "Irredeemably Hostile to Women: Anti-Jewish Elements in the Exegesis of the Dispute about Women's Right to Speak (1 Cor. 14.34–35)," *JSNT* 79 (2000), 19–36.

———. "'Wer nicht arbeiten will, soll auch nicht essen.' Sozialgeschichtliche Beobachtungen zu 2 Thess 3,6–12," pages 212–23 in *Essen und Trinken in der Bibel: ein literarisches Festmahl für Rainer Kessler zum 65. Geburtstag*. Edited by Michaela Geiger, Christl M. Maier, and Uta Schmidt. Gütersloh: Gütersloher Verlagshaus, 2009 (= eadem, *Gott ist Beziehung* [2014], 78–88).

Crüsemann, Marlene, and Frank Crüsemann. "Das Jahr, das Gott gefällt. Die biblischen Traditionen von Erlass- und Jobeljahr in Tora und Propheten, Altem und Neuem Testament (Dtn 15; Lev 25; Jes 61; Lk 4)," *BK* 55 (2000), 19–25 (= in Marlene Crüsemann, *Gott ist Beziehung* [2014], 40–47.

Cullmann, Oscar. "Der eschatologische Charakter des Missionsauftrages und des apostolischen Selbstbewusstseins bei Paulus. Untersuchung zum Begriff des κατέχων in 2 Thess 2,6–7" (1936). Pages 305–36 in idem, *Vorträge und Aufsätze 1925–1962*, edited by Karlfried Fröhlich. Tübingen: Mohr (Siebeck); Zürich: Zwingli Verlag, 1966.

Danker, Frederick, and Robert Jewett. "Jesus as the Apocalyptic Benefactor in Second Thessalonians," pages 486–98 in *The Thessalonian Correspondence* (1990).

Dautzenberg, Gerhard. "Mt 5,43c und die antike Tradition von der jüdischen Misanthropie," pages 47–77 in *Studien zum Matthäusevangelium. Festschrift für Wilhelm Pesch*. Edited by Ludger Schenke. SBS 132. Stuttgart: Katholisches Bibelwerk, 1988.

Davis, Richard H. "Remembering and Acting. A Study of the Moral Life in Light of 1 Thessalonians," Dissertation Yale University, 1971.

Davies, William D. "Paul and the People of Israel," *NTS* 24 (1978), 4–39.

De Vos, Craig Steven. *Church and Community Conflicts. The Relationship of Thessalonian, Corinthian, and Philippian Churches with Their Wider Civic Communities*. SBLDS 168. Atlanta: Scholars Press, 1999.

Deeleman, C. F. M. "2 Thess. 2:1–12," *ThSt* 23 (1905), 252–76.

Deissmann, Adolf. *Light from the Ancient East: The New Testament Illustrated by Recently Discovered Texts of the Graeco-Roman World*. Translated by Lionel R. M. Strachan. London: Hodder & Stoughton, 1927; repr. Grand Rapids: Baker Book House, 1978.

De Jonge, Henk J. "The Original Setting of the Χριστός ἀπέθανεν ὑπέρ Formula," pages 229–35 in *The Thessalonian Correspondence* (1990).

Delobel, Joël. "One Letter Too Many in Paul's First Letter? A Study of νήπιοι in 1 Thess 2:7. *LS* 20 (1995), 126–33.

———. "The Fate of the Dead according to 1 Thess 4 and 1 Cor 15," pages 340–47 in *The Thessalonian Correspondence* (1990).

Demke, Christoph. "Theology and Literary Criticism in 1 Thessalonians," *Journal of Higher Criticism* 3 (1996), 194–214).

Denzinger, Heinrich, Peter Hünermann, Helmut Hoping, Robert L. Fastiggi, and Anne Englund Nash. *Compendium of Creeds, Definitions, and Declarations on Matters of Faith and Morals*. San Francisco: Ignatius Press, 2012.

Detering, Hermann. *Der gefälschte Paulus*. Düsseldorf: Patmos, 1995.

———. *Paulusbriefe ohne Paulus? Die Paulusbriefe in der holländischen Radikalkritik*. Frankfurt and New York: Peter Lang, 1992.

Dibelius, Martin. *An die Thessalonicher I. II. An die Philipper*. HNT 11. Rev. ed. Tübingen: J. C. B. Mohr (P. Siebeck), [2]1925; [3]1937.

Dick, Karl. *Der schriftstellerische Plural bei Paulus*. Halle: E. Karras, 1899.

Dietzfelbinger, Christian. *Die Berufung des Paulus als Ursprung seiner Theologie*. WMANT 58. Neukirchen-Vluyn: Neukirchener Verlag, 1985.

Dixon, Paul S. "The Evil Restraint in 2 Thess 2:6," *JETS* 33 (1990), 445–49.

Dobschütz, Ernst von. *Die Thessalonicherbriefe*. KEK [7]10. Göttingen: Vandenhoeck & Ruprecht, 1909; repr. 1974.

———. "Wir und ich bei Paulus," *ZST* 10 (1932), 252–77.

Donfried, Karl P. "1 Thessalonians, Acts and the Early Paul," pages 3–26 in *The Thessalonian Correspondence* (1990).

———. "2 Thessalonians and the Church of Thessalonica," pages 128–44 in *Origins and Method: Towards a New Understanding of Judaism and Christianity. Essays in Honour of John C. Hurd*. Edited by Bradley H. McLean. JSNTS 86. Sheffield: JSOT Press, 1993.

———. "Paul and Judaism: I Thessalonians 2:13-16 as a Test Case," *Int* 38 (1984), 242–53.

———. "The Assembly of the Thessalonians. Reflections on the Ecclesiology of the Earliest Christian Letter," pages 390–408 in *Ekklesiologie des Neuen Testaments: für Karl Kertelge*. Edited by Rainer Kampling and Thomas Söding. Freiburg: Herder, 1996.

———. "The Cults of Thessalonica and the Thessalonian Correspondence," *NTS* 31 (1985), 336–56.

———. "The Epistolary and Rhetorical Context of 1 Thessalonians 2:1-12," pages 31–60 in *The Thessalonians Debate* (2000).

———. "The Theology of 1 Thessalonians as a Reflection of Its Purpose," pages 243–60 in *To Touch the Text. Biblical and Related Studies in Honor of Joseph A. Fitzmyer, S.J.* Edited by Maurya P. Horgan and Paul J. Kobelski. New York: Crossroad, 1989.

———. "The Theology of 2 Thessalonians," pages 81–113 in *The Theology of the Shorter Pauline Letters*. Edited by Karl P. Donfried and I. Howard Marshall. Cambridge and New York: Cambridge University Press, 1993.

———. "War Timotheus in Athen? Exegetische Überlegungen zu 1 Thess 3,1-3," pages 189–96 in *Die Freude an Gott, unsere Kraft. Festschrift für Otto Bernhard Knoch*. Edited by Johannes Joachim Degenhardt, Eleonore Beck, and Eugen Sitarz. Stuttgart: Katholisches Bibelwerk, 1991.

Donfried, Karl P., and Johannes Beutler, eds. *The Thessalonians Debate. Methodological Discord or Methodological Synthesis?* Grand Rapids and Cambridge: Eerdmans, 2000.

Döpp, Heinz-Martin. *Die Deutung der Zerstörung Jerusalems und des Zweiten Tempels im Jahre 70 in den ersten drei Jahrhunderten n. Chr.* Texte und Arbeiten zum neutestamentlichen Zeitalter 24. Tübingen and Basel: Franke, 1998.

Doty, William. *Letters in Primitive Christianity*. Philadelphia: Fortress Press, 1973.

Dschulnigg, Peter. *Das Markusevangelium* THKNT 2. Stuttgart Kohlhammer, 2007.

Dunham, Duane A. "2 Thessalonians 1:3-10: A Study in Sentence Structure," *JETS* 24 (1981), 39–64.

Dunn, James D. G. *The Partings of the Ways: between Christianity and Judaism and their Significance for the Character of Christianity*. London: SCM Press, 2006.

———. "The Question of Anti-Semitism in the New Testament Writings of the Period," pages 177–211 in idem, ed., *Jews and Christians* (1992).

———, ed. *Jews and Christians. The Parting of the Ways, A.D. 70 to 135: The Second Durham-Tübingen Research Symposium on Earliest Christianity and Judaism*. Grand Rapids: Eerdmans, 1999.

Dupont, Jacques. Σὺν Χριστῷ. *L'úníon avec le Christ suivant Saint Paul*. Bruges: Saint-André, 1952.

Ebach, Jürgen. "Apokalypse. Zum Ursprung einer Stimmung," pages 5–61 in *Einwürfe 2* (1985).

———. "Apokalypse und Apokalyptik," pages 213–73 in *Zeichen der Zeit: Erkennen und Handeln*. Salzburger Hochschulwochen 1998. Edited by Heinrich Schmidinger. Innsbruck and Vienna: Tyrolia, 1998.

———. art. "Antisemitismus," *Handbuch Religionswissenschaftlicher Grundbegriffe* I (1988), 495–504.

———. "Das Zitat als Kommunikationsform. Beobachtungen, Anmerkungen und Fragestellungen am Beispiel biblischen und rabbinischen Zitierens," pages 27–84 in idem, ed., *Gott im Wort. Drei Studien zur biblischen Exegese und Hermeneutik*. Neukirchen-Vluyn: Neukirchener Verlag, 1997.

Eckart, Karl G. "Der zweite echte Brief des Apostels Paulus an die Thessalonicher," *ZTK* 58 (1961), 30–44.

Edson, Charles. "Cults of Thessalonica," *HTR* 41 (1948), 153–204.

———. "Macedonia," *HSCP* 51 (1940), 125–36.

Ehrensperger, Kathy. *Paul and the Dynamics of Power. Communication and Interaction in the Early Christ-Movement*. London and New York: T & T Clark, 2007.

Elbert, Paul. "Paul of the Miletus Speech and 1 Thessalonians: Critique and Considerations," *ZNW* 95 (2004), 258–68.

Elliger, Winfried. *Paulus in Griechenland. Philippi, Thessaloniki, Athen, Korinth*, Stuttgart: Katholisches Bibelwerk, 1987.

Ellis, E. Earle. "Paul and his Co-Workers," *NTS* 17 (1971), 437–52.

Ellis, J. Edward. *Paul and Ancient Views of Sexual Desire. Paul's Sexual Ethics in 1 Thessalonians 4, 1 Corinthians 7 and Romans 1*. London and New York: T & T Clark, 2007.

Epp, Eldon J. "New Testament Papyrus Manuscripts and Letter Carrying in Greco-Roman Times," pages 35–56 in *The Future of Early Christianity: Essays in Honor of Helmut Koester*. Edited by Birger A. Pearson, A. Thomas Kraabel, George W. E. Nickelsburg, and Norman R. Petersen. Minneapolis: Fortress Press, 1991.

Erlemann, Kurt. *Naherwartung und Parusieverzögerung*. Texte und Arbeiten zum neutestamentlichen Zeitalter 17. Tübingen and Basel: Francke, 1995.

Ernst, Josef. *Die eschatologischen Gegenspieler in den Schriften des Neuen Testaments*. Biblische Untersuchungen 3. Regensburg: Pustet, 1967.

Ernst, Michael. *Distanzierte. Unpersönlichkeit. Der Stil des 2 Thess: eine Analyse der Sprache eines pseudepigraphischen Autors im Vergleich mit paulinischen Texten*. Salzburg: Institut für Neutestamentliche Bibelwissenschaft, 1998.

———, ed. *Die Wüste spricht. Papyri beleuchten Literatur und Alltagsleben der Antike*. Salzburg: Institut für Neutestamentliche Bibelwissenschaft, 1996.

Esler, Philip F. "'Keeping It in the Family.' Culture, Kinship, and Identity in 1 Thessalonians and Galatians," pages 145–84 in *Families and Family Relations as Represented in Early*

Judaisms and Early Christianities. Studies in Theology and Religion 2. Edited by Jan Willem van Henten and Athalya Brenner. Leiderdorp: Deo, 2000.

Evans, Robert M. *Eschatology and Ethics. A Study of Thessalonica and Paul's Letters to the Thessalonians*. Dissertation Basel 1967. Princeton, NJ: McMahon Printing, 1968.

Ewald, Heinrich. *Die Sendschreiben des Apostels Paulus übersetzt und erklärt*. Göttingen: Dieterich, 1857.

Exler, Francis Xavier J. *The Form of the Ancient Greek Letter. A Study in Greek Epistolography*. Washington: Catholic University, 1923.

Faber, Richard. *Die Verkündigung Vergils. Reich, Kirche, Staat. Zur Kritik der "Politischen Theologie,"* Hildesheim and New York: Olms, 1975.

Farrow, Douglas. "Showdown. The Message of Second Thessalonians 2:1-12 and the Riddle of the 'Restrainer,'" *Crux* 25 (1989), 23–26.

Fascher, Erich. "Der Vorwurf der Gottlosigkeit in der Auseinandersetzung bei Juden, Griechen und Christen," pages 78–105 in *Abraham unser Vater: Juden und Christen im Gespräch über die Bibel. Festschrift für Otto Michel*. Edited by Hans-Dieter Betz, Martin Hengel, and Peter Schmidt, AGSU 5. Leiden: Briill, 1963.

Fatum, Lone. "1 Thessalonians," pages 250–62 in *Searching the Scriptures 2: A Feminist Commentary*. Edited by Elisabeth Schüssler Fiorenza. New York: Crossroad, 1994.

Faust, Eberhard. *Pax Christi et Pax Caesaris. Religionsgeschichtliche, traditionsgeschichtliche und sozialgeschichtliche Studien zum Epheserbrief*. NTOA 24. Fribourg: Universitätsverlag; Göttingen: Vandenhoeck & Ruprecht, 1993.

Faw, Chalmer E. "On the Writing of First Thessalonians," *JBL* 71 (1952), 217–25.

Fee, Gordon D. "Pneuma and Eschatology in 2 Thess 2:1-12: A Proposal about 'Testing the Prophets' and the Purpose of 2 Thessalonians," pages 196–215 in *To Tell the Mystery: Essays on New Testament Eschatology in Honor of Robert H. Gundry*. Edited by Thomas E. Schmidt and Moisés Silva. JSNTS 100. Sheffield: JSOT Press, 1994.

———. *The First and Second Letters to the Thessalonians*. NICNT. Grand Rapids and Cambridge: Eerdmans, 2009.

Feldmeier, Reinhard, and Ulrich Heckel, eds. *Die Heiden: Juden, Christen und das Problem der Fremden*. Tübingen: Mohr, 1994.

Ferreira, Joel Antônio. *Primeira epístola aos Tessalonicenses. A Igreja surge como esperança dos oprimidos*. Comentário Bíblico. Petrópolis: Vozes, 1991.

Festiguère, A. M. "La trichotomie de 1 Thess 5,23 et la philosophie grecque," *RSR* 20 (1930), 385–415.

Fiedler, Peter. *Das Matthäusevangelium*. THKNT 1. Stuttgart: Kohlhammer, 2006.

Findlay, George G. "Recent Criticism of the Epistles to the Thessalonians," *Expositor* Series 9, 24 (October 1900), 251–61.

Finsterbusch, Karin. *Die Thora als Lebensweisung für Heidenchristen. Studien zur Bedeutung der Thora für die paulinische Ethik*. SUNT 20. Göttingen: Vandenhoeck & Ruprecht, 1996.

Fitzer, Gottfried. art. φθάνω κτλ. *TDNT* 9, 88–92.

Flatt, Johann Friedrich von. *Vorlesungen über die Briefe Pauli an die Philipper, Kolosser, Thessalonicher und an Philemon*. Tübingen: L. F. Fues, 1829.

Flusser, David. "Thesen zur Entstehung des Christentums aus dem Judentum" (1975). Pages 94–102 in idem, *Bemerkungen eines Juden zur christlichen Theologie*. Abhandlungen zum christlich-jüdischen Dialog 16. Munich: Kaiser, 1984.

Focant, Camille. "Les fils du Jour (1 Thes 5,5)," pages 348–55 in *The Thessalonian Correspondence* (1990).

Foerster, Werner. art. κύριος A.B. *TDNT* 3, 1039–1058.

Fowl, Stephen E. "A Metaphor in Distress. A Reading of ΝΗΠΙΟΙ in 1 Thessalonians," *NTS* 36 (1990), 469–73.

Frame, James E. *A Critical and Exegetical Commentary on the Epistles of St. Paul to the Thessalonians*. ICC. Edinburgh: T & T Clark, 1912; 6th ed. 1960.

Frankemölle, Hubert. "Die Entstehung des Christentums aus dem Judentum. Historische, theologische und hermeneutische Aspekte. Pages 11–43 in idem, *Jüdische Wurzeln christlicher Theologie. Studien zum biblischen Kontext neutestamentlicher Texte*. BBB 116. Bodenheim: PHILO, 1998.

———. "Die Tora Gottes für Israel, die Jünger und die Völker nach dem Matthäusevangelium. Pages 261–93 in idem, *Jüdische Wurzeln christlicher Theologie* (1998).

———. *Frühjudentum und Urchristentum. Vorgeschichte, Verlauf, Auswirkungen (4. Jahrhundert v.Chr. bis 4. Jahrhundert n. Chr.)*. Kohlhammer Studienbücher Theologie 5. Stuttgart: Kohlhammer, 2006.

Frankfurter, David. "Beyond 'Jewish Christianity': Continuing Religious Subcultures of the Second and Third Centuries and Their Documents," pages 131–43 in *The Ways That Never Parted* (2007).

Fraser, Janice K. "A Theological Study of Second Thessalonians. A Comprehensive Study of the Thought of the Epistle and Its Sources," Dissertation Durham 1979.

Fredriksen, Paula. "What 'Parting of the Ways'? Jews, Gentiles, and the Ancient Mediterranean City," pages 35–63 in *The Ways That Never Parted* (2007).

Freese, Friedrich. "Τὸ κατέχον und ὁ κατέχων, (2 Thess. 2,6 und 7)," *TSK* 93 (1920/21), 73–77.

Frenschkowski, Marco. "Erkannte Pseudepigraphie? Ein Essay über Fiktionalität, Antike und Christentum," pages 181–232 in *Pseudepigraphie und Verfasserfiktion in frühchristlichen Briefen*. Edited by Jörg Frey, et al., with Michaela Engelmann. WUNT 246. Tübingen: Mohr Siebeck, 2009.

———. "Pseudepigraphie und Paulusschule. Gedanken zur Verfasserschaft der Deuteropaulinen, insbesondere der Pastoralbriefe," pages 239–72 in *Das Ende des Paulus. Historische, theologische und literaturgeschichtliche Aspekte*. Edited by Friedrich Wilhelm Horn. BZNW 106. Berlin and New York: de Gruyter, 2001.

Frettlöh, Magdalene L., "Der Charme der gerechten Gabe. Motive einer Theologie und Ethik der Gabe am Beispiel der paulinischen Kollekte für Jerusalem," pages 105–61 in *"Leget Anmut in das Geben," Zum Verhältnis von Ökonomie und Theologie*. Edited by Jürgen Ebach, Hans-Martin Gutmann, Magdalene L. Frettlöh, and Michael Weinrich. *Jabboq* 1. Gütersloh: Kaiser, 2001.

Frey, Jörg, Jens Herzer, Martina Janssen, and Clare K. Rothschild, eds., *Pseudepigraphie und Verfasserfiktion in frühchristlichen Briefen*. WUNT 246. Tübingen: Mohr Siebeck, 2009.

Friedrich, Gerhard. "1. Thessalonicher 5,1-11, der apokalyptische Einschub eines Späteren," *ZTK* 70 (1973), 288–315 (= idem, *Auf das Wort kommt es an*. Göttingen: Vandenhoeck & Ruprecht, 1978, 251–78).

———. "Der erste Brief an die Thessalonicher," pages 203–51 in *Die Briefe an die Galater, Philipper, Kolosser, Thessalonicher und Philemon*. Edited by Jürgen Becker, Hans Conzelmann, and Gerhard Friedrich. NTD 8. Göttingen: Vandenhoeck & Ruprecht, [16]1985.

———. "Der zweite Brief an die Thessalonicher," pages 252–76 in *Die Briefe an die Galater, Philipper, Kolosser, Thessalonicher und Philemon*. Edited by Jürgen Becker, Hans Conzelmann, and Gerhard Friedrich. NTD 8. Göttingen: Vandenhoeck & Ruprecht, [16]1985.

———, "Ein Tauflied hellenistischer Judenchristen. 1 Thess 1,9f," *TZ* 21 (1965), 502–16.
Frohnhofen, Herbert, ed. *Christlicher Antijudaismus und jüdischer Antipaganismus. Ihre Motive und Hintergründe in den ersten drei Jahrhunderten*. Hamburger Theologische Studien 3. Hamburg: Steinmann & Steinmann, 1990.
Fuchs, Ernst. "1. Thessalonicher 1,2-10. 14. Sonntag nach Trinitatis," *Göttinger Predigtmeditationen* 18 (1963/64), 299–303.
———. "Die Zukunft des Glaubens nach 1. Thess 5,1-11," pages 334–63 in idem, *Glaube und Erfahrung. Zum christologischen Problem im Neuen Testament*. Gesammelte Aufsätze III. Tübingen: Mohr, 1965.
———. "Hermeneutik?" (*Theologia Viatorum* 40). Pages 116–35 in idem, *Glaube und Erfahrung* (1965).
Fuchs, Harald. *Augustin und der antike Friedensgedanke. Untersuchungen zum neunzehnten Buch der Civitas Dei*. Neue Philologische Untersuchungen H.3. Berlin: Weidmann, 1926; repr. New York: Garland, 1973.
Funk, Robert W. "The Apostolic Parousia. Form and Significance," pages 249–68 in *Christian History and Interpretation: Studies Presented to John Knox*. Edited by William R. Farmer, C. F. D. Moule, and Richard R. Niebuhr. Cambridge: Cambridge University Press, 1967.
Furfey, Paul Hanley. "'The Mystery of Lawlessness,'" *CBQ* 8 (1946), 179–91.
Furnish, Victor Paul. "Faith, Love, and Hope: First Thessalonians as a Theological Document," pages 221–31 in *The Impartial God: Essays in Biblical Studies in Honor of Jouette M. Bassler*. Edited by Calvin J. Roetzel and R. L. Foster. Sheffield: Sheffield Academic Press, 2007.
———. "Development in Paul's Thought," *JAAR* 38 (1970), 289–303.
Gager, John G. "Did Jewish Christians See the Rise of Islam?" pages 361–72 in *The Ways That Never Parted* (2007).
———. *The Origins of Anti-Semitism: Attitudes Towards Judaism in Pagan and Christian Antiquity*. New York and Oxford: Oxford University Press, 1983.
Gaventa, Beverly Roberts. "Apostles As Babes and Nurses in 1 Thessalonians 2:7," Pages 193–207 in *Faith and History: Essays in Honor of Paul W. Meyer*. Edited by John T. Carroll, Charles H. Cosgrove, and E. Elizabeth Johnson. Atlanta: Scholars Press, 1991.
———. *First and Second Thessalonians*. IBC. Louisville: Westminster John Knox, 1998.
———. *Our Mother Saint Paul*. Louisville: Westminster John Knox, 2007.
Geiger, Georg. "1 Thess 2,13-16: Der Initiationstext des christlichen Antisemitismus?" *BL* 59 (1986), 154–60.
Geller-Nathanson, Barbara H. "Toward a Multicultural Ecumenical History of Women in the First Century(ies) C. E," pages 272–89 in *Searching the Scriptures. Vol. 1: A Feminist Introduction*. Edited by Elisabeth Schüssler Fiorenza. New York: Crossroad, 1993.
Georgi, Dieter. *Der Armen zu gedenken. Die Geschichte der Kollekte des Paulus für Jerusalem*. Revised and expanded. Neukirchen-Vluyn: Neukirchener Verlag, [2]1994.
Gerber, Christine. *Ein Bild des Judentums für Nichtjuden von Flavius Josephus. Untersuchungen zu seiner Schrift* Contra Apionem. AGJU 40. Leiden and New York: Brill, 1997.
———. *Paulus und seine "Kinder," Studien zur Beziehungsmetaphorik der paulinischen Briefe*. BZNW 136. Berlin and New York: de Gruyter, 2005.
Gese, Michael. *Das Vermächtnis des Apostels. Die Rezeption der paulinischen Theologie im Epheserbrief*. WUNT 2d ser. 99. Tübingen: Mohr Siebeck, 1997.

Getty, Mary Ann. "The Imitation of Paul in the Letters to the Thessalonians," pages 277–83 in *The Thessalonian Correspondence* (1990).
Gewalt, Dietfried. "1 Thess 4,15-17; 1 Kor 15,51 und Mk 9,1: Zur Abgrenzung eines 'Herrenwortes,'" *LB* 51 (1982), 105–13.
Giblin, Charles Homer. "2 Thessalonians 2 Re-read as Pseudepigraphical: A Revised Reaffirmation of 'The Threat to Faith,'" Pages 459–69 in *The Thessalonian Correspondence* (1990).
———. "The Second Letter to the Thessalonians," pages 871–75 in *The New Jerome Biblical Commentary*. Edited by Raymond E. Brown, Joseph A. Fitzmeyer, and Roland E. Murphy. Englewood Cliffs, NJ: Prentice Hall, 1968.
———. *The Threat to Faith. An Exegetical and Theological Re-examination of 2 Thessalonians 2*. AnBib 31 Rome: Pontifical Biblical Institute, 1967.
Gielen, Marlis. "Der erste Petrusbrief," pages 511–21 in *Einleitung in das Neue Testament*. Edited by Martin Ebner and Stefan Schreiber. Kohlhammer Studienbücher Theologie 6. Stuttgart: Kohlhammer, 2008.
———. "Der zweite Petrusbrief," pages 522–29 in *Einleitung in das Neue Testament* (2008).
———. *Tradition und Theologie neutestamentlicher Haustafelethik. Ein Beitrag zur Frage einer christlichen Auseinandersetzung mit gesellschaftlichen Normen*. BBB 75. Frankfurt: Hain, 1990.
Giesen, Heinz. "Naherwartung des Paulus in 1 Thess 4,13-18?" *SNTSU* 10 (1985), 123–49.
Gilchrist, J. Michael. "Intertextuality and the Pseudonymity of 2 Thessalonians," pages 152–75 in *The Intertextuality of the Epistles* (2006).
Gilliard, Frank D. "Paul and the Killing of the Prophets in 1 Thess 2:15," *NT* 36 (1994), 259–70.
———. "The Problem of the Antisemitic Comma Between 1 Thessalonians 2.14 and 15," *NTS* 35 (1989), 481–502.
Gillman, John. "Paul's Εἴσοδος: The Proclaimed and the Proclaimer (1 Thess 2,8)," pages 62–70 in *The Thessalonian Correspondence* (1990).
———. "Signals of Transformation in 1 Thessalonians 4,13-18," *CBQ* 47 (1985), 263–81.
Ginsburg, M. S. "Fiscus Judaicus," *JQR* 21 (1930/31), 281–91.
Glaser, Timo. "Erzählung im Fragment. Ein narratologischer Ansatz zur Auslegung pseudepigrapher Briefbücher," pages 267–94 in *Pseudepigraphie und Verfasserfiktion in frühchristlichen Briefen* (2009).
Gnadt, Martina. "Gospel of Matthew: Jewish-Christian Churches in Opposition to the Pax Romana," Translated by Everett R. Kalin. Pages 607–25 in *Feminist Biblical Interpretation* (2012).
Godet, Frederic. *Einleitung in das Neue Testament*. Vol. 1: *Die Briefe des Apostels Paulus*. Translated from the French by Ernst Reineck. Hannover: Meyer, 1894.
Goodman, Martin. "Diaspora Reactions to the Destruction of the Temple," pages 27–38 in *Jews and Christians* (1992).
———. "Jewish proselytizing in the first century," pages 53–78 in *The Jews among Pagans and Christians in the Roman Empire*. Edited by Judith Lieu, John A. North, and Tessa Rajak. London: Routledge, 1992.
———. *Mission and Conversion. Proselytizing in the Religious History of the Roman Empire*. Oxford and New York: Oxford University Press, 1994.
———. "Modeling the 'Parting of the Ways,'" pages 119–29 in *The Ways That Never Parted* (2007).
———. "Nerva, the 'fiscus Judaicus' and Jewish identity," *JRS* 79 (1989), 40–44.
Goulder, Michael D. "Silas in Thessalonica," *JSNT* 48 (1992), 87–106.

Grässer, Erich. "Bibelarbeit über 1 Thess 4,13-18, gehalten auf der Rheinischen Landessynode 1967 in Bad Godesberg, Mühlheim/Ruhr 1967," 10–20.
———. *Der zweite Brief an die Korinther*. 2 vols. ÖTK 8/1, 8/2. Gütersloh: Gütersloher Verlagshaus, 2002, 2005.
Granskou, David. "Anti-Judaism in the Passion Accounts of the Fourth Gospel," pages 201–16 in *Anti-Judaism in Early Christianity*. Vol. 1: *Paul and the Gospels*. Studies in Early Christianity and Judaism 2. Edited by Peter Richardson, et al. Waterloo, ON: Wilfrid Laurier University Press, 1986.
Gregson, R. "A Solution of the Problems of the Thessalonian Epistles," *EvQ* 38 (1966), 76–80.
Grimm, Wilibald. "Die Echtheit der Briefe an die Thessalonicher, gegen D. Baur's Angriff vertheidigt," *TSK* 23 (1850), 753–813.
Grotius, Hugo. *Annotationes in Novum Testamentum*. Editio Nova, Tom. II/1–2. Erlangen, et al.: Tetzschner, 1756/57.
Gülzow, Hennecke. "Soziale Gegebenheiten der Trennung von Kirche und Synagoge und die Anfänge des christlichen Antijudaismus," pages 95–120 in *Christlicher Antijudaismus und jüdischer Antipaganismus* (1990).
Gundry, Robert H. "A Brief Note on 'Hellenistic Formal Receptions and Paul's Use of ΑΠΑΝΤΗΣΙΣ in 1 Thessalonians 4,17," *BBR* 6 (1996), 39–41.
———. "The Hellenization of Dominical Tradition and Christianization of Jewish Tradition in the Eschatology of 1–2 Thessalonians," *NTS* 33 (1987), 161–78.
Gundry Volf, Judith M. *Paul and Perseverance*. WUNT 2d ser. 37. Tübingen: Mohr; Louisville: Westminster John Knox, 1990.
Guntermann, Friedrich. *Die Eschatologie des hl. Paulus*. NTAbh 13, 4–5. Münster: Aschendorff, 1932.
Gupta, Nijay K. "An Apocalyptic Reading of Psalm 78 in 2 Thess 3," *JSNT* 31 (2008), 179–94.
Gutbrod, Walter. art. ἀνομία, ἄνομος. *TDNT* 4, 1085–86.
Guyot, Peter, and Richard Klein, eds. *Das frühe Christentum bis zum Ende der Verfolgungen. Eine Dokumentation*. Vol. 1: *Die Christen im heidnischen Staat*. Texte zur Forschung 60. Darmstadt: Wissenschaftliche Buchgesellschaft, 1993.
———. *Das frühe Christentum bis zum Ende der Verfolgungen. Eine Dokumentation*. Vol. 2: *Die Christen in der heidnischen Gesellschaft*. Texte zur Forschung 62. Darmstadt: Wissenschaftliche Buchgesellschaft, 1994.
Haack, Ernst. "Eine exegetisch-dogmatische Studie zur Eschatologie über 1. Thess. 4,13-18," *ZST* 15 (1938), 544–69.
Haacker, Klaus. "Elemente des heidnischen Antijudaismus im Neuen Testament," *EvT* 48 (1988), 404–18.
Hadorn, Wilhelm. *Die Abfassung der Thessalonicherbriefe in der Zeit der dritten Missionsreise des Paulus*. BFCT 24, 3–4. Gütersloh: Bertelsmann, 1919.
Hafemann, Scott J. *Paul, Moses, and the History of Israel: The Letter/Spirit Contrast and the Argument from Scripture in 2 Corinthians 3*. Peabody, MA: Hendrickson, 1996.
Hagner, Donald A. "Paul as a Jewish Believer According to His Letters," pages 96–120 in *Jewish Believers in Jesus: The Early Centuries* (2007).
———. "Paul's Quarrel with Judaism," pages 128–50 in *Anti-semitism and Early Christianity: Issues of Polemic and Faith*. Edited by Craig A. Evans and Donald A. Hagner. Minneapolis: Fortress Press, 1993.
Hahn, Ferdinand. *Frühjüdische und urchristliche Apokalyptik. Eine Einführung*. Biblisch-theologische Studien 36. Neukirchen-Vluyn: Neukirchener Verlag, 1998.

Harnack, Adolf von. *Das Problem des zweiten Thessalonicherbriefs*. SPAW, Philosophisch-Historische Klasse XXXI. Berlin: Reimer, 1910.
———. *Der Vorwurf des Atheismus in den ersten drei Jahrhunderten*. TU n.s. 13, 4a. Leipzig: Hinrichs, 1905.
Harnisch, Wolfgang. *Eschatologische Existenz. Ein exegetischer Beitrag zum Sachanliegen von 1. Thess 4,13-5,11*. FRLANT 110. Göttingen: Vandenhoeck & Ruprecht, 1973.
Harrington, Daniel J. *Paul and the Mystery of Israel*. Collegeville, MN: Liturgical Press, 1992.
Harris, J. Rendel. "A Study in Letter-Writing," *Expositor* Series 5, 8 (1898), 161–80.
Harrison, J. R. "Paul and the Imperial Gospel at Thessaloniki," *JSNT* 25 (2002), 71–96.
Hartman, Lars. "The Eschatology of 2 Thessalonians as Included in a Communication," pages 470–85 in *The Thessalonian Correspondence* (1990).
Haufe, Günter. *Der erste Brief des Paulus an die Thessalonicher*. THKNT 12, 1. Leipzig: Evangelische Verlagsanstalt, 1999.
Heckel, Ulrich. *Kraft in Schwachheit. Untersuchungen zu 2. Kor. 10–13*. WUNT 2d series 56. Tübingen: Mohr (Siebeck), 1993.
Heemstra, Marius. *The* Fiscus Judaicus *and the Parting of the Ways*. WUNT 2d ser. 277. Tübingen: Mohr Siebeck, 2010.
Heid, Stefan. *Chiliasmus und Antichrist-Mythos. Eine frühchristliche Kontroverse um das Heilige Land*. Hereditas 6. Bonn: Borengässer, 1993.
Heinemann, Isaak. art. "Antisemitismus," In Pauly-Wissowa, *Real-enyclopädie der classischen Altertumswissenschaft*, Suppl. V (Stuttgart: Metzler, 1894–1963), 3–43.
Hendrix, Holland L. "Benefactor/Patronage Networks in the Urban Environment: Evidence from Thessalonica," *Semeia* 56 (1992), 39–58.
———. "Thessalonicans Honor Romans," Dissertation Harvard Divinity School, Cambridge, MA, 1984 (Microfilm Ann Arbor, 1993).
Hengel, Martin. "Anonymität, Pseudepigraphie und 'literarische Fälschung' in der jüdisch-hellenistischen Literatur," pages 229–308 in *Pseudepigrapha* I. Edited by Kurt von Fritz (1972), 229–308.
———. "Das früheste Christentum als jüdische messianische und universalistische Bewegung," *TBei* 28 (1997), 197–210.
———. "Der vorchristliche Paulus," pages 177–291 in idem and Ulrich Heckel, eds., *Paulus und das antike Judentum*. WUNT 58. Tübingen: Mohr, 1991.
———. "Messianische Hoffnung und politischer 'Radikalismus' in der 'jüdisch-hellenistischen Diaspora.' Zur Frage der Voraussetzungen des jüdischen Aufstandes unter Trajan 115–117 n. Chr," pages 655–86 in *Apocalypticism in the Mediterranean World and the Near East*. Edited by David Hellholm. Tübingen: Mohr, 1983.
Hengel, Martin, and Anna Maria Schwemer. *Paulus zwischen Damaskus und Antiochien. Die unbekannten Jahre des Apostels*. WUNT 108. Tübingen: Mohr Siebeck, 1998.
Herntrich, Volkmar. art. λεῖμμα κτλ B. *TDNT* 4, 196–209.
Hester, James D. "The Invention of 1 Thessalonians: A Proposal," pages 251–79 in *Rhetoric, Scripture and Theology*. JSNTS 131. Edited by Stanley E. Porter and Thomas H. Olbricht. Sheffield: Sheffield Academic Press, 1996.
Hiebert, D. Edmond. *1 & 2 Thessalonians*. Chicago: Moody Bible Institute, 1971; rev. ed. 1992.
Hilgenfeld, Adolf. "Die beiden Briefe an die Thessalonicher," *ZWT* 7 (1862), 225–64.
Hill, Judith L. "Establishing the Church of Thessalonica," Dissertation Duke University, 1990.

Hirschberg, Peter. "Jewish Believers in Asia Minor according to the Book of Revelation and the Gospel of John," pages 217–39 in *Jewish Believers in Jesus* (2007).

Hock, Ronald F. "Paul's Tentmaking and the Problem of his Social Class," *JBL* 97 (1978), 555–64.

———. *The Social Context of Paul's Ministry. Tentmaking and Apostleship*. Philadelphia: Fortress Press, 1980.

———. "The Workshop as a Social Setting for Paul's Missionary Preaching," *CBQ* 41 (1979), 438–50.

Hoffmann, Paul. *Die Toten in Christus. Eine religionsgeschichtliche und exegetische Untersuchung zur paulinischen Eschatologie*. NTAbh n.s. 2. Münster: Aschendorff, 1966.

Hofmann, Johann Christian Konrad von. "Der erste Brief Pauli an die Thessalonicher," In idem, *Die Heilige Schrift neuen Testaments zusammenhängend untersucht. 1. Die Aufgabe, Ausgangspunkt der Untersuchung, der erste und zweite Brief Pauli an die Thessalonicher*. Nördlingen: Beck, 1869, 141–284; 285–366.

Holland, Glenn S. "'A Letter Supposedly from Us': A Contribution to the Discussion about the Authorship of 2 Thessalonians," pages 394–402 in *The Thessalonian Correspondence* (1990).

———. *The Tradition That You Received from Us: 2 Thessalonians in the Pauline Tradition*. HUT 24. Tübingen: Mohr (Siebeck), 1988.

Hollmann, Georg. "Die Unechtheit des 2. Thessalonicherbriefes," *ZNW* 5 (1904), 28–38.

Holsten, Carl. "Zur Unächtheit des ersten Briefes an die Thessalonicher und zur Abfassungszeit der Apocalypse," *JPT* (1877), 731–32.

Holtz, Traugott. "The Judgement on the Jews and the Salvation of All Israel. 1 Thess 2,15-16 and Rom 11,25-26," pages 284–94 in *The Thessalonian Correspondence* (1990).

———. *Der erste Brief an die Thessalonicher*. EKK 13. Zürich: Benziger; Neukirchen-Vluyn: Neukirchener Verlag, 1986.

———. "'Euer Glaube an Gott.' Zu Form und Inhalt von 1 Thess 1,9f," pages 459–88 in *Die Kirche des Anfangs. Festschrift für Heinz Schürmann*. Edited by Rudolf Schnackenburg, Josef Ernst, and Joachim Wanke. Leipzig: St. Benno-Verlag, 1977 (= idem, *Geschichte und Theologie des Urchristentums* [1991], 297–312).

———. *Geschichte und Theologie des Urchristentums. Gesammelte Aufsätze*. Edited by Eckart Reinmuth and Christian Wolff. WUNT 57. Tübingen: Mohr, 1991.

———. "On the Background of 1 Thessalonians 2:1-12," pages 69–80 in *The Thessalonians Debate* (2000).

———. "Traditionen im 1. Thessalonicherbrief," pages 55–78 in *Die Mitte des Neuen Testaments: Einheit und Vielfalt neutestamentlicher Theology: Festschrift für Eduard Schweizer*. Edited by Ulrich Luz and Hans Weder. Göttingen: Vandenhoeck & Ruprecht, 1983 (= idem, *Geschichte und Theologie des Urchristentums* [1991], 246–69).

Holtzmann, Heinrich J. "Zum zweiten Thessalonicherbrief," *ZNW* 2 (1901), 97–108.

Holzmeister, Urban. "Zum Dekret der Bibelkommission über die Parusieerwartung in den paulinischen Briefen," *ZKT* 15 (1916), 167–82.

Hooker, Morna D. "1 Thessalonians 1.9-10: a Nutshell—but What Kind of a Nut?" pages 435–48 in *Geschichte, Tradition, Reflexion: Festschrift für Martin Hengel*. Vol. 3: *Frühes Christentum*. Edited by Hubert Cancik, Peter Schäfer, and Hermann Lichtenberger. Tübingen: Mohr, 1996.

Hoppe, Rudolf. "Der erste Thessalonicherbrief und die antike Rhetorik," *BZ* n.s. 41 (1997), 229–37.

———. "Der Topos der Prophetenverfolgung bei Paulus," *NTS* 50 (2004), 535–49.

———. "Metaphorik im ersten Thessalonicherbrief. Zur Rede von der 'Amme' und vom 'Vater' in 1 Thess 2,7.11," pages 269–81 in *An-Denken. Festgabe für Eugen Biser*. Edited by Erwin Möde, Felix Unger, and Karl Matthäus Woschitz. Europäische Akademie der Wissenschaften und Künste. Graz: Styria, 1998.

———. "The Epistolary and Rhetorical Context of 1 Thessalonians 2:1-12: A Response to Karl P. Donfried," pages 61–68 in *The Thessalonians Debate* (2000).

Houwelingen, Pieter H. van. "The Great Reunion: The Meaning and Significance of the 'Word of the Lord' in 1 Thessalonians 4:13-18," *CTJ* 42 (2007), 308–24.

Horbury, William. "I Thessalonians II 3 as Rebutting The Charge of False Prophecy," *JTS* n.s. 33 (1982), 492–508.

Horst, Pieter W. van der. "Einige Beobachtungen zum Thema Frauen im antiken Judentum," *BTZ* 10 (1993), 77–93.

Hotze, Gerhard. "Die Christologie des 2. Thessalonicherbriefs," pages 124–48 in *Christologie in der Paulus-Schule: zur Rezeptionsgeschichte des paulinischen Evangeliums*. Edited by Klaus Scholtissek. SBS 181. Stuttgart: Katholisches Bibelwerk, 2000.

Horkheimer, Max. *Die Sehnsucht nach dem ganz Anderen. Ein Interview mit Kommentar von Helmut Gumnior*. Hamburg: Furche, 1970.

Howard, Tracy L. "The literary unity of 1 Thessalonians 4:13-5:11," *Grace Theological Journal* 9 (1988), 163–90.

Hruby, Kurt. *Juden und Judentum bei den Kirchenvätern*. Schriften zur Judentumskunde 2. Zürich: Theologischer Verlag, 1971.

Hübner, Hans. *Gottes Ich und Israel*. FRLANT 136. Göttingen: Vandenhoeck & Ruprecht, 1986.

Hughes, Frank W. *Early Christian Rhetoric and 2 Thessalonians*. JSNTS 30. Sheffield: JSOT Press, 1989.

———. "The Rhetoric of 1 Thessalonians," pages 94–116 in *The Thessalonian Correspondence* (1990).

———. "The Rhetoric of Letters," pages 194–240 in *The Thessalonians Debate* (2000).

———. "The Social Situations Implied by Rhetoric," pages 241–54 in *The Thessalonians Debate* (2000).

Hunzinger, Claus-Hunno. "Die Hoffnung angesichts des Todes im Wandel der paulinischen Aussagen," pages 69–88 in *Leben angesichts des Todes. Beiträge zum theologischen Problem des Todes. Helmut Thielicke zum 60. Geburtstag*. Edited by Bernhard Lohise and Hans P. Schmidt. Tübingen: Mohr (Siebeck), 1968.

Hurd, John C. "1 Thessalonians 3:11-13: The Pivotal Importance of Prayer in the Structure of Paul's Letters," *ARC: The Journal of the Faculty of Religious Studies, McGill University* 33 (2005), 257–80.

———. "Paul Ahead of His Time: 1 Thess 2:13-16," pages 21–36 in *Anti-Judaism in Early Christianity*. Vol. 1: *Paul and the Gospels* (1986).

Hvalvik, Reidar. "Jewish Believers and Jewish Influence in the Roman Church until the Second Century," pages 279–216 in *Jewish Believers in Jesus* (2007).

———. "Named Jewish believers Connected with the Pauline Mission," pages 154–78 in *Jewish Believers in Jesus* (2007).

———. "Paul as a Jewish Believer According to the Book of Acts," pages 121–53 in *Jewish Believers in Jesus* (2007).

———. *The Struggle for Scripture and Covenant. The Purpose of the Epistle of Barnabas and Jewish-Christian Competition in the Second Century*. WUNT 2d ser. 82. Tübingen: Mohr (Siebeck), 1996.

Hyldahl, Niels. "Auferstehung Christi, Auferstehung der Toten (1 Thess 4,13-18)," pages 119–35 in *Die Paulinische Literatur und Theologie = The Pauline Literature and Theology*. Edited by Sigfred Pedersen. Aarhus: Forlaget Aros; Göttingen: Vandenhoeck & Ruprecht, 1980.

Jacobs, Andrew S. "The Lion and the Lamb: Reconsidering Jewish-Christian Relations in Antiquity," pages 95–118 in *The Ways That Never Parted* (2003).

Jankowski, Gerhard and Ton Veerkamp. "Was ist sexistisch: der Text oder die Auslegungsgeschichte? Notwendige Anmerkungen zur traditionellen Auslegung von 1 Thess 4,1-8," *Text & Kontexte* 56 (1992), 3–24.

Janssen, Claudia. art. "Heidenchristentum," pages 47–49 in *Antijudaismus im Neuen Testament? Grundlagen für die Arbeit mit biblischen Texten*. Edited by Dagmar Henze, Claudia Janssen, Stefanie Müller, and Beate Wehn. Gütersloh: Kaiser, 1997.

———. *Elisabet und Hanna. Zwei widerständige alte Frauen in neutestamentlicher Zeit. Eine sozialgeschichtliche Untersuchung*. Mainz: Matthias Grünewald, 1998.

———. "Paul. Walking the Line Between Traditions and Ages," pages 31–38 in *Transgressors: Toward a Feminist Biblical Theology*. Edited by Claudia Janssen, Ute Ochtendung, and Beate Wehn. Translated by Linda M. Maloney. Collegeville, MN: Liturgical Press, 2002.

———. *Anders ist die Schönheit der Körper. Paulus und die Auferstehung in 1 Kor 15*. Gütersloh: Gütersloher Verlagshaus, 2005.

Janssen, Martina. *Unter falschem Namen. Eine kritische Forschungsbilanz frühchristlicher Pseudepigraphie*. Arbeiten zur Religion und Geschichte des Urchristentums 14. Frankfurt and New York: Peter Lang, 2003.

Jervell, Jacob. *Die Apostelgeschichte*. KEK 3. 17th ed. and 1st of the revision. Göttingen: Vandenhoeck & Ruprecht, 1998.

———. *The Unknown Paul. Essays on Luke-Acts and Early Christian History*. Minneapolis: Augsburg, 1984.

Jewett, Robert. "A Matrix of Grace. The Theology of 2 Thessalonians," pages 63–70 in *Pauline Theology I*. Edited by Jouette M. Bassler. Minneapolis: Fortress Press, 1994.

———. *A Chronology of Paul's Life*. Philadelphia: Fortress Press, 1979.

———. "Tenement Churches and Communal Meals in the Early Church: The Implications of a Form-Critical Analysis of 2 Thess 3:10," *BR* 38 (1993), 23–43.

———. *The Thessalonian Correspondence. Pauline Rhetoric and Millenarian Piety*. Philadelphia: Fortress Press, 1986.

Johanson, Bruce C. "1 Thessalonians 2:15-16: Prophetic Woe-Oracle with ἔφθασεν as Proleptic Aorist," pages 519–34 in *Texts and Contexts: Biblical Texts in their Textual and Situational Contexts: Essays in Honor of Lars Hartman*. Edited by Tord Fornberg, David Hellholm, and Christer D. Hellholm. Oslo and Boston: Scandinavian University Press, 1995.

———. *To All the Brethren. A Text-Linguistic and Rhetorical Approach to 1 Thessalonians*. CBNT 16. Stockholm: Almqvist & Wiksell, 1987.

Johnson, E. Elizabeth. "2 Thessalonians," pages 351–52 in *The Women's Bible Commentary*. Edited by Carol A. Newsom and Sharon H. Ringe. Louisville: Westminster John Knox, 1992.

Jones, Ivor H. *The Epistles to the Thessalonians*. Epworth Commentaries. Peterborough: Epworth, 2005.

Jossa, Giorgio. *Jews or Christians? The Followers of Jesus in Search of their Own Identity*. WUNT 202. Tübingen: Mohr Siebeck, 2006.

Jowett, Benjamin. *The Epistles of St. Paul to the Thessalonians, Galatians, Romans*. 2 vols. London: J. Murray, 1859.

Judge, Edwin A. "The Decrees of Caesar at Thessalonica," *RTR* 30 (1971), 1–7.

Jurgensen, Hubert. "Saint Paul et la Parousie. 1 Thessaloniciens 4,13-5,11 dans l'exégèse moderne et contemporaire." Dissertation Strasbourg 1992 (microfiche).

Kabisch, Richard. *Die Eschatologie des Paulus in ihren Zusammenhängen mit dem Gesamtbegriff des Paulinismus*. Göttingen: Vandenhoeck & Ruprecht, 1893.

Kampling, Rainer. "Eine auslegungsgeschichtliche Skizze zu 1 Thess 2,14-16," pages 183–213 in *Begegnungen zwischen Christentum und Judentum in Antike und Mittelalter. Festschrift für Heinz Schreckenberg*. Edited by Dietrich-Alex Koch and Hermann Lichtenberger. Göttingen: Vandenhoeck & Ruprecht, 1993.

Karrer, Martin. "Der zweite Thessalonicherbrief und Gottes Widersacher," *HBT* 29 (2007), 101–31.

Katz, Steven T. "Issues in the Separation of Judaism and Christianity After 70 C. E.: A Reconsideration," *JBL* 103 (1984), 43–76.

Kaye, Bruce N. "Eschatology and Ethics in 1 and 2 Thessalonians," *NT* 17 (1975), 47–57.

Keck, Leander E. "Images of Paul in the New Testament," *Int* 43 (1989), 341–51.

Keresztes, Paul. "The Imperial Roman Government and the Christian Church, I. From Nero to the Severi," *ANRW* II, 23.1 (1979), 243–315.

———. "The Jews, the Christians, and the Emperor Domitian," *VC* 27 (1973), 1–28.

Kern, F. H. "Über 2 Thess. 2,1-12. Nebst Andeutungen über den Ursprung des zweiten Briefs an die Thessalonicher," *Tübinger Zeitschrift für Theologie* 10 (1839), 145–214.

Khiok-Khng, Yeo. "A Political Reading of Paul's Eschatology in I and II Thessalonians," *Asia Journal of Theology* 12 (1998), 77–88.

Kieffer, René. "L'eschatologie en 1 Thessaloniciens dans une perspective rhétorique," pages 206–19 in *The Thessalonian Correspondence* (1990).

Kim, Chan-Hie. *Form and Structure of the Familiar Greek Letter of Recommendation*. SBLDS 4. Missoula, MT: Scholars Press, 1972.

Kim, Seyoon. "Paul's Entry (εἴσοδος) and the Thessalonians' Faith (1 Thessalonians 1–3)," *NTS* 51 (2005), 519–42.

———. "The Jesus Tradition in 1 Thess 4.13-5.11," *NTS* 48 (2002), 225–42.

———. "The structure and function of 1 Thessalonians 1–3," pages 170–88 in *History and Exegesis: New Testament Essays in Honor of Dr. E. Earle Ellis*. Edited by Sang-Won Son. New York and London: T & T Clark, 2006.

Kirchhoff, Renate. *Die Sünde gegen den eigenen Leib. Studien zu pornē und porneia in 1 Kor 6,12-20 und dem kulturellen Kontext der paulinischen Adressaten*. SUNT 18. Göttingen: Vandenhoeck & Ruprecht, 1994.

Klappert, Bertold. "Traktat für Israel (Römer 9–11). Die paulinische Verhältnisbestimmung von Israel und Kirche als Kriterium neutestamentlicher Sachaussagen über die Juden," pages 58–137 in *Jüdische Existenz und die Erneuerung der christlichen Theologie*. Abhandlungen zum christlich-jüdischen Dialog 11. Edited by Martin Stöhr. Munich: Kaiser, 1981.

Klauck, Hans-Josef. "Compilation of Letters in Cicero's Correspondence," pages 317–37 in idem, *Religion und Gesellschaft im frühen Christentum. Neutestamentliche Studien* WUNT 152. Tübingen: Mohr Siebeck, 2003.

———. *Die antike Briefliteratur und das Neue Testament. Ein Lehr- und Arbeitsbuch*. UTB 2022. Paderborn: Schöningh, 1998.

———, and Rudolf Schnackenburg, eds. *Weltgericht und Weltvollendung. Zukunftsbilder im Neuen Testament*. QD 150. Freiburg, et al.: Herder, 1994.

Klein, Günter. "Apokalyptische Naherwartung bei Paulus," pages 241–62 in *Neues Testament und christliche Existenz: Festschrift für Herbert Braun*. Edited by Hans-Dieter Betz and Luise Schottroff. Tübingen: Mohr, 1973.

———. art. "Eschatologie IV. Neues Testament," *TRE* 10. Berlin: de Gruyter, 1982, 270–99.

Klijn, Albertus F. J. "I Thessalonians 4.13-18 and Its Background in Apocalyptic Literature," pages 67–73 in *Paul and Paulinism. Essays in Honour of C. K. Barrett*. Edited by Morna D. Hooker and Stephen G. Wilson. London: S.P.C.K., 1982.

Klinghardt, Matthias. *Gesetz und Volk Gottes. Das lukanische Verständnis des Gesetzes nach Herkunft, Funktion und seinem Ort in der Geschichte des Urchristentums*. WUNT 2d ser. 32. Tübingen: Mohr (Siebeck), 1988.

———. "Sünde und Gericht von Christen bei Paulus," *ZNW* 88 (1997), 56–80.

Klöpper, Albert. "Der zweite Brief an die Thessalonicher," pages 73–140 in *Theologische Studien und Skizzen aus Ostpreussen*, vol. 2. Edited by Friedrich Zimmer and Albert Klöpper. Königsberg: Hartung, 1889.

Kloppenborg, John S. "Φιλαδελφία, Θεοδίδακτος and the Dioscuri: Rhetorical Engagement in 1 Thessalonians 4.9-12," *NTS* 39 (1993), 265–89.

Knoch, Otto. *1. und 2. Thessalonicherbrief*. SKKNT 12. Stuttgart: Katholisches Bibelwerk, 1987.

Knopf, Rudolf. *Das nachapostolische Zeitalter. Geschichte der Christlichen Gemeinden vom Beginn der Flavierdynastie bis zum Ende Hadrians*. Tübingen: Mohr, 1905.

Köhler, Johann Friedrich. *Versuch über die Abfassungszeit: der epistolischen Schriften im Neuen Testament und der Apokalypse*. Leipzig: Barth, 1830.

Kolb, Anne. *Transport und Nachrichtentransfer im Römischen Reich*. Klio Beihefte n.s. 2. Berlin: Akademie-Verlag, 2000.

Konradt, Matthias. "Εἰδέναι ἕκαστον ὑμῶν τὸ ἑαυτοῦ σκεῦος κτᾶσθαι ... Zu Paulus' sexualethischer Weisung in 1 Thess 4,4f.," *ZNW* 92 (2001), 128–55.

———. "Die vollkommene Erfüllung der Tora und der Konflikt mit den Pharisäern im Matthäusevangelium," pages 129–52 in *Das Gesetz im frühen Judentum und im Neuen Testament. Festschrift für Christoph Burchardt*. Edited by Dieter Sänger and Matthias Konradt. NTOA 57. Fribourg: Universitätsverlag; Göttingen: Vandenhoeck & Ruprecht, 2006.

———. *Gericht und Gemeinde. Eine Studie zur Bedeutung und Funktion von Gerichtsaussagen im Rahmen der paulinischen Ekklesiologie und Ethik im 1 Thess und 1 Kor*. BZNW 117. Berlin and New York: de Gruyter, 2003.

Konstan, David, and Ilaria Ramelli. "The Syntax of ἐν Χριστῷ in 1 Thessalonians 4:16," *JBL* 126 (2007), 579–93.

Koskenniemi, Heikki. *Studien zur Idee und Phraseologie des griechischen Briefes bis 400 n. Chr*. AASF Series B, 102, 2. Helsinki: Suomalainen Tiedeakatemia, 1956.

Koester, Helmut. "I Thessalonians: Experiment in Christian Writing," pages 33–44 in *Continuity and Discontinuity in Church History: Essays Presented to George Huntston Williams*. Edited by F. Forrester Church and Timothy George. Leiden: Brill, 1979.

———. "Apostel und Gemeinde in den Briefen an die Thessalonicher," pages 287–98 in *Kirche. Festschrift für Günther Bornkamm*. Edited by Dieter Lührmann and Georg Strecker. Tübingen: Mohr, 1980.

———. "Archäologie und Paulus in Thessalonike," pages 393–404 in *Religious Propaganda and Missionary Competition in the New Testament World: Essays Honoring Dieter Georgi*. Edited by Lukas Bormann, Kelly Del Tredici, and Angela Standhartinger.

NovTSup 34. Leiden and New York: Brill, 1994. (repr. in *Frühchristliches Thessaloniki*, STAC 44. Edited by Cilliers Breytenbach, Ingrid Behrmann, and Helmut Koester. Tübingen: Mohr Siebeck, 2007, 1–9).

———. "From Paul's Eschatology to the Apocalyptic Schemata of 2 Thessalonians," pages 441–58 in *The Thessalonian Correspondence* (1990).

———. "Imperial Ideology and Paul's Eschatology in 1 Thessalonians," pages 158–66 in *Paul and Empire. Religion and Power in Roman Imperial Society*. Edited by Richard A. Horsley. Harrisburg, PA: Trinity Press International, 1997.

Koester, Helmut, and Holland Hendrix, eds. *Archaeological Resources for New Testament Studies*, Vol. 1: *Athens, Corinth, Olympia, Thessalonike, Philadelphia*. Cambridge, MA: Harvard University Press, 1987.

Kraemer, Ross S. *Her Share of the Blessings. Women's Religions among Pagans, Jews, and Christians in the Graeco-Roman World*. New York: Oxford University Press, 1992.

———. "On the meaning of the term 'Jew' in Graeco-Roman inscriptions," *HTR* 82 (1989), 35–53.

Kraft, Robert A. "The Pseudepigrapha in Christianity," pages 55–86 in *Tracing the Threads. Studies in the Vitality of Jewish Pseudepigrapha*. Edited by John C. Reeves. Early Judaism and its Literature 6. Atlanta: Scholars Press, 1994.

———. "The Weighing of the Parts: Pivots and Pitfalls in the Study of Early Judaisms and their Early Christian Offspring," pages 87–94 in *The Ways That Never Parted* (2003).

Kraus, Wolfgang. *Das Volk Gottes. Zur Grundlegung der Ekklesiologie bei Paulus*. WUNT 85. Tübingen: Mohr, 1996.

Krauss, Samuel. *The Jewish-Christian Controversy from the Earliest Times to 1789*. Vol. 1: *History*. Edited and revised by William Horbury. TSAJ 56. Tübingen: Mohr (Siebeck), 1995.

Krentz, Edgar. "1 Thessalonians: Rhetorical Flourishes and Formal Constraints," pages 287–318 in *The Thessalonians Debate* (2000).

———. "A Stone that Will not Fit. The Non-Pauline Authorship of Second Thessalonians," pages 439–70 in *Pseudepigraphie und Verfasserfiktion in frühchristlichen Briefen* (2009).

———. "Evangelism and Spirit: 1 Thessalonians 1," *CurTM* 14 (1987), 22–30.

———. "Through a lens: theology and fidelity in 2 Thessalonians," pages 53–62 in *Pauline Theology I* (1994).

———. "Tradition Held Fast: Theology and Fidelity in 2 Thessalonians," pages 505–15 in *The Thessalonian Correspondence* (1990).

Krodel, Gerhard. "2 Thessalonians," pages 73–96 in *Ephesians, Colossians, 2 Thessalonians, the Pastoral Epistles*. Edited by J. Paul Sampley, et al. Proclamation Commentaries. Philadelphia: Fortress Press, 1978.

———. "2 Thessalonians," pages 39–58 in idem, et al. *The Deutero-Pauline Letters: Ephesians, Colossians, 2 Thessalonians, 1–2 Timothy, Titus*. Minneapolis: Fortress Press, 1993.

———. "The 'religious power of lawlessness' (*katēchon*) as precursor of the 'lawless one' (*anomos*): 2 Thess 2:6-7," *CurTM* 17 (FS F. W. Danker) (1990), 440–46.

Krug, Johannes. *Die Kraft des Schwachen. Ein Beitrag zur paulinischen Apostolatstheologie*. Texte und Arbeiten zum neutestamentlichen Zeitalter 37. Tübingen and Basel: Franke, 2001.

Kuck, David W. *Judgment and Community Conflict. Paul's Use of Apocalyptic Judgment Language in 1 Corinthians 3:5-4:5*. NovTSup 66. Leiden and New York: Brill, 1992.

Kümmel, Werner Georg. "Das literarische und geschichtliche Problem des ersten Thessalonicherbriefes" (1962). Pages 406–16 in idem, *Heilsgeschehen und Geschichte*.

Gesammelte Aufsätze. Vol. 1. Edited by Erich Grässer, Otto Merk, and Adolf Fritz. Marburger Theologische Studien 3. Marburg: Elwert, 1965.
———, *The New Testament: The History of the Investigation of its Problems*. Nashville: Abingdon Press, 1972.
Kuhli, Horst. art.'Ἰουδαῖος. *EWNT* II (1981), 472–82.
Kuhn, Heinz-Wolfgang. "Die Bedeutung der Qumrantexte für das Verständnis des Ersten Thessalonicherbriefes. Vorstellung des Münchner Projekts Qumran und das Neue Testament," pages 339–54 in *The Madrid Qumran Congress 1991*. Edited by Julio C. Trebolle Barrera and Luis Vegas Montaner. STDJ IX/1, 2. Leiden and New York: Brill; Madrid: Complutense, 1992.
Lambrecht, Jan. "A Call to Witness by All: Evangelization in 1 Thessalonians" (1991). Pages 343–61 in idem, *Pauline Studies: Collected Essays*. BETL 115. Leuven: Leuven University Press; Peeters, 1994.
———. "A Structural Analysis of 1 Thessalonians 4–5," pages 163–78 in Karl P. Donfried and Johannes Beutler, eds., *The Thessalonians Debate* (2000).
———. "Lack of Logic? A Close Reading of 1 Thessalonians 2,1-12," pages 327–35 in *Nuovo Testamento: teologie in dialogo culturale: scritti in honore Romano Penna nel suo 70 cumpleano*. Bologna: EDB, 2008.
———. "Thanksgivings in 1 Thessalonians 1–3," pages 183–205 in *The Thessalonian Correspondence* (1990) (= idem, *Pauline Studies* [1994], 319–41; = *The Thessalonians Debate* [2000], 135–62).
Lamp, Jeffrey S. "Is Paul Anti-Jewish? *Testament of Levi* 6 in the Interpretation of 1 Thessalonians 2:13-16," *CBQ* 65 (2003), 408–27.
Lampe, Peter. "Paulus: Zeltmacher," *BZ* 31 (1987), 256–61.
———. "Rhetorische Analyse paulinischer Texte: *Quo vadit*? Methodologische Überlegungen," pages 170–90 in *Das Gesetz im frühen Judentum und im Neuen Testament* (2006).
Lang, Friedrich. *Die Briefe an die Korinther*. NTD 7. 16th ed., 1st of the new revision. Göttingen: Vandenhoeck & Ruprecht, 1986.
Larondelle, Hans K. "Paul's Prophetic Outline in 2 Thessalonians 2," *AUSS* 21 (1983), 61–69.
Larsson, Edvin. art. μιμέομαι, μιμητής. *EWNT* II (1981), 1053–57.
Laub, Franz. *1. und 2. Thessalonicherbrief*. Neue Echter Bibel, NT 13. Würzburg: Echter Verlag, 1985.
———. *Eschatologische Verkündigung und Lebensgestaltung nach Paulus. Eine Untersuchung zum Wirken des Apostels beim Aufbau der Gemeinde in Thessalonike*. Biblische Untersuchungen 10. Regensburg: Pustet, 1973.
———. "Paulinische Autorität in nachpaulinischer Zeit (2 Thess)," pages 403–17 in *The Thessalonian Correspondence* (1990).
Laurent, Johann Carl Mauriz. *Neutestamentliche Studien*. Gotha: Berthes, 1866.
Lautenschlager, Markus. "Εἴτε γρηγορῶμεν, εἴτε καθεύδωμεν. Zum Verhältnis von Heiligung und Heil in 1 Thess 5,10," *ZNW* 81 (1990), 39–59.
Légasse, Simon. *Les épîtres aux Thessaloniciens*. LD 7. Paris: Cerf, 1999.
———. "Paul et les Juifs d'après 1 Thessaloniciens 2,13-16," *RB* 104 (1997), 572–91.
Leipoldt, Johannes. *Antisemitismus in der alten Welt*. Leipzig: Dörffling & Franke, 1933.
Leppä, Outi. "A Pseudonymous Writer Warning about Pseudonymous Letters: Tracing the Literary Link Between 2 Thessalonians and other Pauline Epistles," pages 176–95 in *The Intertextuality of the Epistles* (2006).

Leutzsch, Martin. *Die Bewährung der Wahrheit. Der dritte Johannesbrief als Dokument urchristlichen Alltags*. Bochumer altertumswissenschaftliches Colloquium 16. Trier: Wissenschaftlicher Verlag Trier, 1994.

Lewy, Jochanan (Hans). "Die Epoche des Zweiten Tempels im Lichte der griechischen und römischen Literatur. Ursachen und Aspekte der Judenfeindschaft in der Antike" (in Hebrew: *Studies in Jewish Hellenism* [Jerusalem, 1960]); translated into German by M. Brocke, *Freiburger Rundbrief* 24 [1972], 20–26).

Lietaert Peerbolte, Lambertus J. *The Antecedents of Antichrist. A Traditio-Historical Study of the Earliest Christian Views on Eschatological Opponents*. JSJSup 49. Leiden and New York: Brill, 1996.

———. "The KATEXON / KATEXΩN of 2 Thess. 2:6-7," *NT* 39 (1997), 138–50.

Lichtenberger, Hermann. "Paulus und das Gesetz," pages 361–74 (discussion 375–78) in *Paulus und das antike Judentum* (1991).

Lieu, Judith M. *Christian Identity in the Jewish and Graeco-Roman World*. Oxford and New York: Oxford University Press, 2004.

———. "Circumcision, Women and Salvation," *NTS* 40 (1994), 348–70.

———. "History and theology in Christian views of Judaism," pages 79–96 in *The Jews* (1992).

Lieu, Judith M., John North, and Tessa Rajak, eds. *The Jews among Pagans and Christians in the Roman Empire*. London and New York: Routledge, 1992.

Lifshitz, Baruch, and J. Schiby. "Une Synagogue samaritaine à Thessalonique," *RB* 75 (1968), 368–78.

Limbeck, Meinrad. art. ἀνομία, ἄνομος, ἀνόμως. *EWNT* I (1980), 254–55.

Limor, Ora, and Guy G. Stroumsa, eds. *Contra Iudaeos. Ancient and Medieval Polemics between Christians and Jews*. Texts and Studies in Medieval Judaism 10. Tübingen: Mohr (Siebeck), 1996.

Lindemann, Andreas. "Christliche Gemeinden und das Römische Reich im ersten und zweiten Jahrhundert," *WD* n.s. 18 (1985), 105–33.

———. *Der Erste Korintherbrief*. HNT 9/1, Tübingen: Mohr Siebeck, 2000.

———. *Paulus im ältesten Christentum. Das Bild des Apostels und die Rezeption der paulinischen Theologie bis Marcion*. BHT 58. Tübingen: Mohr, 1979.

———. "Paulus und die korinthische Eschatologie. Zur Frage von einer 'Entwicklung' im paulinischen Denken," *NTS* 37 (1991), 373–99.

———. "Zum Abfassungszweck des Zweiten Thessalonicherbriefes," *ZNW* 68 (1977), 35–47.

Lipsius, R. A.. "Ueber Zweck und Veranlassung des ersten Thessalonicherbriefs," *TSK* 4 (1854), 905–34.

Llewelyn, Stephen R. "The Conveyance of Letters," pages 1–57 in idem, with R. A. Kearsley, *New Documents Illustrating Early Christianity*. Vol. 7, *A Review of the Greek Inscriptions and Papyri Published in 1982–83*. Sidney: The Ancient History Documentary Research Centre, Macquarie University, 1994.

Lofthouse, W. F. "'I' and 'We' in the Pauline Letters," *BT* 6 (1955), 72–80.

Lohfink, Gerhard. *Die Himmelfahrt Jesu. Untersuchungen zu den Himmelfahrts- und Erhöhungsvorstellungen bei Lukas*. SANT 26. Munich: Kösel, 1971.

Löhr, Gebhard. "1 Thess 4,15-17: Das Herrenwort," *ZNW* 71 (1980), 269–73.

Loisy, Alfred. *La naissance du Christianisme*. Paris: Nourry, 1933. English: *The Birth of the Christian Religion*. Translated by L. P. Jacks. Library of the Mystic Arts. New Hyde Park, NY: University Books, 1962.

———. *Les Livres du Nouveau Testament*. Paris: Nourry, 1922.

———. *Remarques sur la littérature épistolaire du Nouveau Testament*. Paris: Nourry, 1935.

Loman, Abraham Dierk. "*Quaestiones paulinae*," *Theologisch Tijdschrift* 16 (1882), 141–85; *Theologisch Tijdschrift* 17 (1883), 14–57; *Theologisch Tijdschrift* 20 (1886), 42–113.
———. "Paulus en de Kanon," *Theologisch Tijdschrift* 20 (1886), 387–406.
Longenecker, Richard L. "The Nature of Paul's Early Eschatology," *NTS* 31 (1985), 85–95.
———, ed. *The Road from Damascus. The Impact of Paul's Conversion on His Life, Thought, and Ministry*. Grand Rapids and Cambridge: Eerdmans, 1997.
Lowe, Malcom F. "Who were the Ἰουδαῖοι?" *NT* 18 (1976), 101–30.
Luckensmeyer, David. *The Eschatology of First Thessalonians*. NTOA 71. Göttingen: Vandenhoeck & Ruprecht, 2009.
Lüdemann, Gerd. "Ein Fälscher am Werk. Das Schicksal des Ersten Thessalonicherbriefs in seiner 'Interpretation' durch den Zweiten Thessalonicherbrief," pages 32–39 in *Theologisches geschenkt. Festschrift für Manfred Josuttis*. Edited by Christoph Bizer, Jochen Cornelius-Bundschuh, and Hans-Martin Gutmann. Bovenden: Foedus, 1996.
———. *Paulus, der Heidenapostel*. Vol. 1: *Studien zur Chronologie*. FRLANT 123. Göttingen: Vandenhoeck & Ruprecht, 1983.
———. *Paulus und das Judentum*. Theologische Existenz heute 215. Munich: Kaiser, 1983.
Lührmann, Dieter. "The beginnings of the Church at Thessalonica," pages 237–49 in *Greeks, Romans, and Christians: Essays in honor of Abraham J. Malherbe*. Edited by David L. Balch, Everett A. Ferguson, and Wayne A. Meeks. Minneapolis: Fortress Press, 1990.
Lünemann, Gottlieb. *Die Briefe an die Thessalonicher*. KEK 10 (1850); 4th ed. 1878.
Lütgert, Wilhelm E. *Die Vollkommenen im Philipperbrief und die Enthusiasten in Thessalonich*. BFCT 13. Gütersloh: Bertelsmann, 1909.
Luz, Ulrich. *Das Geschichtsverständnis des Paulus*. BEvT 49. Munich: Kaiser, 1968.
———. "Neutestamentliche Lichtblicke auf die dunklen Seiten Gottes. Überlegungen zu den Gerichtsaussagen der Paulustradition," pages 257–75 in *Gott wahr nehmen: Festschrift für Christian Link zum 65. Geburtstag*. Edited by Magdalene L. Frettlöh and Hans P. Lichtenberger. Neukirchen-Vluyn: Neukirchener Verlag, 2003.
Lyons, George. *Pauline Autobiography. Toward a New Understanding*. SBLDS 73. Atlanta: Scholars Press, 1985.
Mach, Michael. "Justin Martyr's *Dialogus cum Tryphone Judaeo* and the Development of Christian Anti-Judaism," pages 27–47 in *Contra Judaeos* (1996).
Malbon, Elizabeth Struthers. "'No Need to Have Any One Write': A Structural Exegesis of 1 Thessalonians," *Semeia* 26 (1983), 57–83.
Maleparampil, Joseph. "The 'Church of the Thessalonians' (1 Thess 1,1) and Paul's Early Insights into the Nature of a Local Church," *Ephrem's Theological Journal* 10 (2006), 6–16.
Malherbe, Abraham J. *Ancient Epistolary Theorists*. SBLSBS 19. Atlanta: Scholars Press, 1988.
———. "Did the Thessalonians Write to Paul?" pages 246–57 in *The Conversation Continues. Studies in Paul and John in honor of J. Louis Martyn*. Edited by Robert T. Fortna and Beverly R. Gaventa. Nashville: Abingdon Press, 1990.
———. "Exhortation in First Thessalonians," *NT* 25 (1983), 238–56 (= pages 49–66 in idem, *Paul and the Popular Philosophers*. Minneapolis: Fortress Press, 1989).
———. "'Gentle as a Nurse.' The Cynic Background to I Thess ii," *NT* 12 (1970), 203–17 (= pages 35–48 in idem, *Paul and the Popular Philosophers* [1989]).
———. "'Pastoral Care' in the Thessalonian History and Hypotheses," *NTS* 36 (1990), 375–91.
———. *Paul and the Thessalonians. The Philosophic Tradition of Pastoral Care*. Philadelphia: Fortress Press, 1987.

———. "Paul: Hellenistic Philosopher or Christian Pastor?" *AThR* 68 (1986), 3–13 (= pages 67–77 in idem, *Paul and the Popular Philosophers* [1989]).
———. *The Letters to the Thessalonians*. AncB 32B. New York: Doubleday, 2000.
Manson, Thomas W. "St. Paul in Greece. The Letters to the Thessalonians," *BJRL* 35 (1952/53), 428–47.
Manus, Chris Ukachukwu. "1 Thess 2:17-20. A Reflection on Paul's Use of the Plural Number and its Significance for Ministry in the African Churches," *Africa Theological Journal* 12 (1983), 76–87.
———. "Luke's Account of Paul in Thessalonica (Acts 17,1-9)," pages 27–38 in *The Thessalonian Correspondence* (1990).
Marguerat, Daniel, ed. *Le déchirement. Juifs et chrétiens au premier siècle*. MdB 32. Geneva: Labor et fides, 1996.
Marshall, I. Howard. *1 and 2 Thessalonians*. NCB. Grand Rapids and London: Eerdmans, 1983.
———. "Election and Calling to Salvation in 1 and 2 Thessalonians," pages 259–76 in *The Thessalonian Correspondence* (1990).
———. "Pauline Theology in the Thessalonian Correspondence," pages 173–83 in *Paul and Paulinism. Essays in Honor of C. K. Barrett* (1982).
Marshall, Peter. *Enmity in Corinth. Social Conventions in Paul's Relations with the Corinthians*. WUNT 2d ser. 23. Tübingen: Mohr, 1987.
Martin, Michael. "'Example' and 'Imitation' in the Thessalonian Correspondence," *SwJT* 42 (1999), 39–49.
Marxsen, Willi. "Auslegung von 1 Thess 4,13-18," *ZTK* 66 (1969), 22–37.
———. *Der erste Brief an die Thessalonicher*. ZBK NT 11/1. Zürich: Theologischer Verlag, 1979.
———. *Der zweite Brief an die Thessalonicher*. ZBK NT 11/2. Zürich: Theologischer Verlag, 1982.
Mason, John P. *The Resurrection According to Paul*. New York: Mellen Biblical Press, 1993.
Mason, Steve. "Jews, Judaeans, Judaizing, Judaism: Problems of Categorization in Ancient History," *JSJ* 38 (2007), 457–512.
Masson, Charles. *Les deux épitres de Saint Paul aux Thessaloniciens*. CNT 11a. Neuchâtel and Paris: Delachaux & Niestlé, 1957.
Mattern, Lieselotte. *Das Verständnis des Gerichtes bei Paulus*. ATANT 47. Zürich: Zwingli Verlag, 1966.
Maurer, Christian. art. σκεῦος. *TDNT* 7, 358–367.
McGehee, Michael. "A Rejoinder to Two Recent Studies Dealing with 1 Thess 4:4," *CBQ* 51 (1989), 82–89.
Meade, David G. *Pseudonymity and Canon: An Investigation into the Relationship of Authorship and Authority in Jewish and earliest Christian Tradition*. WUNT 39. Tübingen: Mohr, 1986; Grand Rapids: Eerdmans, 1987.
Mearns, Christopher L., "Early Eschatological Development in Paul: The Evidence of I and II Thessalonians," *NTS* 27 (1981), 137–57.
Meeks, Wayne A. *The First Urban Christians: The Social World of the Apostle Paul*. New Haven: Yale University Press, 2003.
Menken, Maarten J. J. *2 Thessalonians*. London and New York: Routledge, 1994.
———. "Paradise regained or still lost? Eschatology and disorderly behaviour in 2 Thessalonians," *NTS* 38 (1992), 271–89.
———. "The Structure of 2 Thessalonians," pages 373–82 in *The Thessalonian Correspondence* (1990).

Merk, Otto. "1 Thessalonians 2:1-12: An Exegetical-Theological Study," pages 89–113 in Karl P. Donfried and Johannes Beutler, eds., *The Thessalonians Debate* (2000).

———. "1. Thessalonicher 4,13-18 im Lichte des gegenwärtigen Forschungsstandes. Pages 213–30 in *Eschatologie und Schöpfung. Festschrift für Erich Grässer*. Edited by Martin Evang, Helmut Merklein, and Michael Wolter. BZNW 89. Berlin and New York: de Gruyter, 1997.

———. "Nachahmung Christi. Zu ethischen Perspektiven in der paulinischen Theologie," pages 172–206 in *Neues Testament und Ethik: für Rudolf Schnackenburg*. Edited by Helmut Merklein. Freiburg, et al.: Herder, 1989 (= pages 302–36 in idem, *Wissenschaft und Exegese. Gesammelte Aufsätze zum 65. Geburtstag*. BZNW 95. Berlin: de Gruyter, 1998).

———. "Arbeiten. Zu Begriff und Thematik von ἐργάζεσθαι in den beiden Thessalonicherbriefen," pages 19–25 in *Fragmentarisches Wörterbuch. Beiträge zur biblischen Exegese und christlichen Theologie; Horst Balz zum 70. Geburtstag*. Edited by Kerstin Schiffner, Klaus Wengst, and Werner Zager. Stuttgart: Kohlhammer, 2007.

Merklein, Helmut. "Der Theologe als Prophet. Zur Funktion prophetischen Redens im theologischen Diskurs des Paulus," *NTS* 38 (1992), 402–29.

Merz, Annette. *Die fiktive Selbstauslegung des Paulus. Intertextuelle Studien zur Intention und Rezeption der Pastoralbriefe*. NTOA 52. Fribourg: Universitätsverlag; Göttingen: Vandenhoeck & Ruprecht, 2004.

Metzger, Bruce M. *A Textual Commentary on the Greek New Testament*. London and New York: United Bible Societies, 1971.

Metzger, Paul. "Der Fall des Imperiums. Zur Frage der Parusieverzögerung im II. Thessalonicherbrief," *SNTSU* 33 (2008), 99–113.

———. "Eine apokalyptische Paulussschule? Zum Ort des Zweiten Thessalonicherbriefs," pages 145–66 in *Apokalyptik als Herausforderung neutestamentlicher Theologie*. Edited by Michael Becker and Markus Öhler. WUNT 2d ser. 214. Tübingen: Mohr Siebeck, 2006.

———. *Katechon. II Thess 2,1-12 im Horizont apokalyptischen Denkens*. BZNW 135. Berlin and New York: de Gruyter, 2005.

Meyer, Ben F. "Did Paul's View of the Resurrection of the Dead Undergo Development?" *TS* 47 (1986), 363–87.

Michaelis, Wilhelm. art. μιμέομαι κτλ. *TDNT* 4, 659–74.

———. *Einleitung in das Neue Testament*. Bern: Haller, 3d ed. 1961.

Michaels, J. Ramsey. "Everything that Rises Must Converge: Paul's Word from the Lord," pages 182–95 in *To Tell the Mystery* (1994).

Michel, Otto. "Fragen zu I Thessalonicher 2,14-16: Antijüdische Polemik bei Paulus," pages 50–59 in *Antijudaismus im Neuen Testament? Exegetische und systematische Beiträge*. Edited by Willehad Paul Eckert, Peter Levinson, and Martin Stöhr. Abhandlungen zum christlich-jüdischen Dialog 1. Munich: Kaiser, 1967.

Milligan, George. *St. Paul's Epistles to the Thessalonians. The Greek Text with Introduction and Notes*. London: Macmillan, 1908; repr. Grand Rapids: Eerdmans, 1953.

Mitchell, Margaret M. "Envoys in the Context of Greco-Roman Diplomatic and Epistolary Conventions. The Examples of Timothy and Titus," *JBL* 111 (1992), 641–62.

Moffatt, James. *An introduction to the literature of the New Testament*. Edinburgh: Clark, 3d ed. 1918.

———. *The First and Second Epistles of Paul the Apostle to the Thessalonians*. The Expositor's Greek Testament 4/1. Edited by W. Robinson Nicoll. London: Hodder & Stoughton, 1910.

Mommsen, Theodor. "Die Rechtsverhältnisse des Apostels Paulus," *ZNW* 2 (1901), 81–96.
———. *Römisches Strafrecht*. Leipzig: Duncker & Humblot, 1899; reprint Darmstadt: Wissenschaftliche Buchgesellschaft, 1955.
Moore, Arthur Lewis. *1 and 2 Thessalonians*. Century Bible, n.s. London: Nelson, 1969.
———. *The Parousia in the New Testament*. NovTSup 13. Leiden: Brill, 1966.
Morton, Andrew Q. *Christianity and the Computer*. London: Hodder and Stoughton, 1964.
Müller, Karlheinz. "Gott als Richter und die Erscheinungsweisen seiner Gerichte in den Schriften des Frühjudentums. Methodische und grundsätzliche Vorüberlegungen zu einer sachgemäßen Einschätzung," pages 23–53 in *Weltgericht und Weltvollendung* (1994).
Müller, Markus. *Vom Schluss zum Ganzen. Zur Bedeutung des paulinischen Briefabschlusses*. FRLANT 172. Göttingen: Vandenhoeck & Ruprecht, 1997.
Müller, Paul-Gerhard. *Der Erste und Zweite Brief an die Thessalonicher*. RNT. Regensburg: Pustet, 2001.
———. "Entschränkung des Judentums im 1. Thessalonicherbrief," pages 107–27 in *Wohin du auch gehst. Festschrift für Franz Josef Stendebach OMI*. Edited by Thomas Klosterkamp. Stuttgart: Katholisches Bibelwerk, 2005.
———. "Judenbeschimpfung und Selbstverfluchung bei Paulus," *BK* 44 (1989), 58–65.
Müller, Peter. *Anfänge der Paulusschule. Dargestellt am zweiten Thessalonicherbrief und am Kolosserbrief*. ATANT 74. Zürich: Theologischer Verlag, 1988.
Mullins, Terence Y. "Visit Talk in the New Testament Letters," *CBQ* 35 (1973), 350–58.
Munck, Johannes. "1 Thess i.9-10 and the Missionary Preaching of Paul. Textual Exegesis and Hermeneutic Reflexions," *NTS* 9 (1963), 95–110.
Munro, Winsome. *Authority in Peter and Paul: The Identification of a Pastoral Stratum in the Pauline Corpus and 1 Peter*. SNTSMS 54. Cambridge: Cambridge University Press, 1983.
Murphy-O'Connor, Jerome. *Paul. A Critical Life*. Oxford and New York: Oxford University Press, 1996.
———. *Paul the Letter-Writer. His World, His Options, His Skills*. GNS 41. Collegeville, MN: Liturgical Press, 1995.
Murrell, N. Samuel. "The Human Paul of the New Testament: Anti-Judaism in 1 Thess 2:14-16," *Proceedings (Eastern Great Lakes and Midwest Biblical Societies)* 14 (1994), 169–86.
Mussner, Franz. "Die 'aufhaltende' Macht von 2 Thess 2,6f," pages 226–34 in *Unterwegs mit Paulus. Otto Kuss zum 100. Geburtstag*. Edited by Josef Hainz. Regensburg: Pustet, 2006.
Neander, August. *Geschichte der Pflanzung und Leitung der christlichen Kirche durch die Apostel*. Gotha: Perthes, 5th ed. 1862.
Nebe, Gottfried. "Die Kritik am εἴδωλα-Kult in 1 Thessalonicher 1,9-10 im Rahmen der paulinischen Missionstätigkeit und Soteriologie. Zugleich ein Beitrag zum Verständnis von 'Tora-Gesetz' und 'Natur-Gesetz,'" pages 191–221 in *Das Gesetz im frühen Judentum* (2006).
Nepper-Christensen, Poul. "Das verborgene Herrenwort. Eine Untersuchung über 1. Thess 4, 13–18," *ST* 19 (1965), 136–54.
Neumann, Kenneth J. *The Authenticity of the Pauline Epistles in the Light of Stylostatistical Analysis*. SBLDS 120. Atlanta: Scholars Press, 1990.
Neusner, Jacob, William Scott Green, and Ernest S. Frerichs, eds. *Judaisms and their Messiahs at the Turn of the Christian Era*. Cambridge and New York: Cambridge University Press, 1987.

Nestle, Wilhelm. art. "Asebieprozesse." *RAC* I (1950), 735–40.
———. art. "Atheismus." *RAC* I (1950), 866–70.
———. "*Odium humani generis*," *Klio* 21 (1927), 91–93.
Nicholl, Colin R. *From Hope to Despair in Thessalonica: Situating 1 and 2 Thessalonians*. SNTSMS 126. Cambridge and New York: Cambridge University Press, 2004.
———. "Michael, the Restrainer removed (2 Thess 2:6-7)," *JTS* n.s. 51 (2000), 27–53.
Niebuhr, Karl-Wilhlem. *Heidenapostel aus Israel. Die jüdische Identität des Paulus nach ihrer Darstellung in seinen Briefen*. WUNT 62. Tübingen: Mohr, 1992.
———. "'Judentum' und 'Christentum' bei Paulus und Ignatius von Antiochien," *ZNW* 85 (1994), 218–33.
Noack, Bent. "Current and Backwater in the Epistle to the Romans," *ST* 19 (1965), 155–66.
Noack, Ludwig. *Die biblische Theologie. Einleitung in's Alte und Neue Testament und Darstellung des Lehrgehaltes der biblischen Bücher nach ihrer Entstehung und ihrem geschichtlichen Verhältnis. Ein Handbuch zum Selbstunterricht*. Halle: Pfeffer, 1853.
Noethlichs, Karl Leo. *Das Judentum und der römische Staat. Minderheitenpolitik im antiken Rom*. Darmstadt: Wissenschaftliche Buchgesellschaft, 1996.
Oakes, Peter. "Re-mapping the Universe: Paul and the Emperor in 1 Thessalonians and Philippians," *JSNT* 27 (2005), 301–22.
Oegema, Gerbern S. "Versöhnung ohne Vollendung? Röm 10,4 und die Tora der messianischen Zeit," pages 229–61 in *Bund und Tora. Beiträge zur theologischen Begriffsgeschichte in alttestamentlicher, frühjüdischer und urschristlicher Tradition*. Edited by Friedrich Avemarie and Hermann Lichtenberger. WUNT 92. Tübingen: Mohr, 1996.
Oepke, Albrecht. art. παρουσία, πάρειμι. *TDNT* 5, 858–71.
———. "Die Briefe an die Thessalonicher," pages 155–85 in *Die kleineren Briefe des Apostels Paulus*. NTD 8. Göttingen: Vandenhoeck & Ruprecht, 1962.
Oestreich, Bernhard. "Leseanweisungen in Briefen als Mittel der Gestaltung von Beziehungen (1 Thess 5.27)," *NTS* 50 (2004), 224–45.
Okeke, George E. "I Thessalonians 2.13-16. The Fate of the Unbelieving Jews," *NTS* 27 (1980/81), 127–36.
Okorie, Andrew M. "The Pauline Work Ethic in I and II Thessalonians," *Deltion Biblikon Meleton* 24 (1995), 55–64.
Olbricht, Thomas H. "An Aristotelian rhetorical analysis of 1 Thessalonians," pages 216–36 in *Greeks, Romans, and Christians* (1990).
Oldenhage, Tania. "Spiralen der Gewalt (Die bösen Winzer). Mk 12,1-12 (Mt 21,33-46 / Lk 20,9-19 / EvThom 65)," pages 352–66 in *Kompendium der Gleichnisse Jesu*. Edited by Ruben Zimmermann, with Detlef Dormeyer, Gabi Kern, Annette Merz, Christian Münch, and Enno Edzard Popkes. Gütersloh: Gütersloher Verlagshaus, 2007.
Ollrog, Wolf-Henning. *Paulus und seine Mitarbeiter*. WMANT 50. Neukirchen-Vluyn: Neukirchener Verlag, 1979.
Orchard, J. Bernard. "Thessalonians and the Synoptic Gospels," *Bib* 19 (1938), 19–42.
Osten-Sacken, Peter von der. "Das Verständnis des Gesetzes im Römerbrief," Pages 9–59 in idem, *Die Heiligkeit der Tora. Studien zum Gesetz bei Paulus*. Munich: Kaiser, 1989.
———. "Die Decke des Mose. Zur Exegese und Hermeneutik von Geist und Buchstabe in 2. Korinther 3," pages 87–115 in idem, *Die Heiligkeit der Tora* (1989).
———. "Paulus und die Wahrheit des Evangeliums. Zum Umgang des Apostels mit Evangelium, Gegnern und Geschichte in Galater 1–2" (1980). Pages 116–60 in idem, *Die Heiligkeit der Tora* (1989).

———. "Vom Saulus zum Paulus? Gestalt und Weg des Apostels," pages 9–26 in *Paulus der Jude. Seine Stellung im christlich-jüdischen Dialog heute*. Edited by Sung-Hee Lee-Linke. Frankfurt: Lembeck, 2005.

Pahl, Michael W. *Discerning the "Word of the Lord": The "Word of the Lord" in 1 Thessalonians 4:15*. LNTS 389. London and New York: T & T Clark, 2009.

Paget, James Carleton. "The Definition of the Terms *Jewish Christian* and *Jewish Christianity* in the History of Research," pages 22–52 in *Jewish Believers in Jesus* (2007).

Parkin, Vincent. "Some Comments on the Pauline Prescripts," *IBS* 8 (1986), 92–99.

Patte, Daniel. "Method for a Structural Exegesis of Didactic Discourses. Analysis of 1 Thessalonians," *Semeia* 26 (1983), 85–129.

Paulsen, Henning. art. "Pseudepigraphen II. Neues Testament," *EKL* 3 (1992), 1381–83.

———. *Die Briefe des Ignatius von Antiochia und der Brief des Polykarp von Smyrna*. 2d rev. ed. of the translation by Walter Bauer. HNT 18. Tübingen: Mohr, 1985.

Pax, Elpidius. "Beobachtungen zur Konvertitensprache des ersten Thessalonicherbriefes," *SBFLA* 21 (1971), 220–61.

Pearson, Birger A. "1 Thessalonians 2:13-16: A Deutero-Pauline Interpolation," *HTR* 64 (1971), 79–94.

Penna, Romano. "L'évolution de l'attitude de Paul envers les juifs," pages 390–421 in *L'apôtre Paul: Personnalité, style et conception du ministère*. Edited by Albert Vanhoye. Leuven: Leuven University Press; Peeters, 1986.

Perkins, Pheme. "1 Thessalonians and Hellenistic Religious Practices," pages 325–34 in *To Touch the Text* (1989).

———. "2 Thessalonians," *Harper's Bible Commentary*, edited by James L. Mays. San Francisco Harper & Row, 1988, 1234–36.

Pesch, Rudolf. *Die Apostelgeschichte I (Apg 1–12)*. EKK V/1. Zürich: Benziger; Neukirchen-Vluyn: Neukirchener Verlag, 1986.

———. *Die Entdeckung des ältesten Paulus-Briefes. Paulus: neu gesehen. Die Briefe an die Gemeinde der Thessalonicher*. Freiburg and Vienna: Herder, 1984.

Peterson, Erik. art. ἀπάντησις. *TDNT* 1, 380–81.

———. "Die Einholung des Kyrios," *ZST* 7 (1930), 682–702.

Pfleiderer, Otto. *Der Paulinismus. Ein Beitrag zur Geschichte der urchristlichen Theologie*. Leipzig: Reisland, 1873.

Pierson, Allard, and Samuel A. Naber. *Verisimilia. Laceram conditionem novi Testamenti exemplis illustrarunt et ab origine repetierunt*. Amsterdam: Van Kampen, 1886.

Plevnik, Joseph. "1 Thess 5,1-11: Its Authenticity, Intention and Message," *Bib* 60 (1979), 71–90.

———. "1 Thessalonians 4,17: The Bringing in of the Lord or the Bringing in of the Faithful?" *Bib* 80 (1999), 537–46.

———. *Paul and the Parousia: An Exegetical and Theological Investigation*. Peabody, MA: Hendrickson, 1997.

———. "Pauline Presuppositions," pages 50–61 in *The Thessalonian Correspondence* (1990).

———. "The Destination of the Apostle and of the Faithful: Second Corinthians 4:13b-14 and First Thessalonians 4:14," *CBQ* 62 (2000), 83–95.

———. "The Parousia as Implication of Christ's Resurrection: An Exegesis of 1 Thess 4:13-18," pages 199–277 in *Word and Spirit: Essays in Honor of David Michael Stanley, S.J.* Edited by Joseph Plevnik. Willowdale, ON: Regis College Press, 1975.

Pöhlmann, Wolfgang. *Die heidnische, jüdische und christliche Opposition gegen Domitian: Studien zur neutestamentlichen Zeitgeschichte*. Erlangen: by the author, 1966.

Pokorný, Petr. art. "Pseudepigraphie I. Altes und Neues Testament," *TRE* 27 (1997), 645–55.

———. "Das Problem der neutestamentlichen Pseudepigraphie," *EvT* 44 (1984), 486–96.

Popkes, Enno Edzard. "Die Bedeutung des zweiten Thessalonicherbriefs für das Verständnis paulinischer und deuteropaulinischer Eschatologie," *BZ* 48 (2004), 39–64.

Porter, Stanley E. "Developments in German and French Thessalonians Research: A Survey and Critique," *CurBS* 7 (1999), 309–34.

Powell, Charles E. "The Identity of the 'Restrainer' in 2 Thessalonians 2:6-7," *BSac* 154 (1997), 320–32.

Preiss, Theodor. "La mystique de l'imitation du Christ et de l'unité chez Ignace d'Antioche," *RHPR* 17 (1938), 197–241.

Probst, Hermann. *Paulus und der Brief. Die Rhetorik des antiken Briefes als Form der paulinischen Korintherkorrespondenz.* WUNT 2d ser. 45. Tübingen: Mohr (Siebeck), 1991.

Radl, Walter. *Ankunft des Herrn. Zur Bedeutung und Funktion der Parusieaussagen bei Paulus.* BBET 15. Frankfurt: Peter Lang, 1981.

Rajak, Tessa. "The Jewish Community and its Boundaries," pages 9–28 in Judith Lieu, John A. North, and Tessa Rajak, eds., *The Jews among Pagans and Christians in the Roman Empire* (1992).

Rathke, Heinrich. *Ignatius von Antiochien und die Paulusbriefe.* TU 99. Berlin: Akademie-Verlag, 1967.

Rau, Gerhard. "Die antijüdisch-antisemitische Predigt," pages 26–48 in *Auschwitz: Krise der christlichen Theologie* (1980).

Rauch, Christian. "Zum zweiten Thessalonicherbrief," *ZWT* 38 (1895), 451–65.

Reck, Reinhold. *Kommunikation und Gemeindeaufbau. Eine Studie zu Entstehung, Leben und Wachstum paulinischer Gemeinden in den Kommunikationsstrukturen der Antike.* SBB 22. Stuttgart: Katholisches Bibelwerk, 1991.

Reed, Annette Yoshiko. "'Jewish Christianity' after the 'Parting of the Ways.' Approaches to Historiography and Self-Definition in the Pseudo-Clementines," pages 189–232 in *The Ways That Never Parted* (2003).

Refshauge, Ebba. "Literærkritiske overvejelser til de to Thessalonikerbreve," *DTT* 34 (1971), 1–19.

Reinach, Théodore. *Textes d'auteurs grecs et romains relativs au Judaïsme.* Paris: Ernest Leroux, 1895; repr. Hildesheim: Olms, 1963.

Reinbold, Wolfgang. "Die 'Hellenisten.' Kritische Anmerkungen zu einem Fachbegriff der neutestamentlichen Wissenschaft," *BZ* n.s. 42 (1998), 96–102.

Reinhartz, Adele. "On the Meaning of the Pauline Exhortation: '*mimetai mou ginesthe*'—'Become Imitators of Me,'" *SR* 18 (1987), 393–403.

Reinmuth, Eckart. "Der erste Brief an die Thessalonicher," pages 103–56 in Nikolaus Walter, Eckart Reinmuth, and Peter Lampe, *Die Briefe an die Philipper, Thessalonicher und an Philemon.* NTD 8/2. Göttingen: Vandenhoeck & Ruprecht, 18th ed. 1998.

———. "Der zweite Brief an die Thessalonicher," pages 157–202 in Walter, Reinmuth, and Lampe, *Die Briefe an die Philipper, Thessalonicher und an Philemon* (1998).

Rese, Martin. "Der eine und einzige Gott Israels bei Paulus," pages 85–106 in *Und dennoch von Gott zu reden. Festschrift für Herbert Vorgrimler.* Edited by Matthias Lutz-Bachmann and Erich Zenger. Freiburg: Herder, 1994.

Reuter, Rainer. *Synopse zu den Briefen des Neuen Testaments. Teil I: Kolosser-, Epheser-, II. Thessalonicherbrief.* Arbeiten zur Religion und Geschichte des Urchristentums 5. Frankfurt, et al.: Peter Lang, 1997.

Reynier, Chantal. "Le thème de la colère: l'apport original de Paul en 1 Thessaloniciens," pages 281–95 in *Le jugement dans l'un et l'autre Testament*. Vol. 2. *Mélanges offerts à Jacques Schlosser*. Edited by Claude Coulot. LD 198. Paris: Cerf, 2004.

Reynolds, Joyce, and Robert Tannenbaum. *Jews and God-Fearers at Aphrodisias. Greek Inscriptions with Commentary, Texts from the Excavations at Aphrodisias conducted by Kenan T. Erim*. The Cambridge Philological Society Supplementary Volume 12. Cambridge: Cambridge Philological Society, 1987.

Richard, Earl J. "Contemporary Research on 1 (& 2) Thessalonians," *BTB* 20 (1990), 107–15.

———. *First and Second Thessalonians*. SP 11. Collegeville, MN: Liturgical Press, 1995.

Richards, E. Randolph. *The Secretary in the Letters of Paul*. WUNT 2d ser. 42. Tübingen: Mohr, 1991.

Richardson, Peter, ed. *Anti-Judaism in early Christianity*. Vol. 1: *Paul and the Gospels*. Studies in Christianity and Judaism 2. Waterloo, ON: Wilfrid Laurier University Press, 1986.

Richter Reimer, Ivoni. *Women in the Acts of the Apostles: A Feminist Liberation Perspective*. Translated by Linda M. Maloney. Minneapolis: Fortress Press, 1995.

Riepl, Wolfgang. *Das Nachrichtenwesen des Altertums mit besonderer Rücksicht auf die Römer*. Leipzig: Teubner, 1913; repr. Hildesheim and New York: Olms, 1972.

Riesner, Rainer. *Die Frühzeit des Apostels Paulus. Studien zur Chronologie, Missionsstrategie und Theologie*. WUNT 71. Tübingen: Mohr, 1994. English: *Paul's Early Period: Chronology, Mission Strategy, Theology*. Translated by Doug Stott. Grand Rapids: Eerdmans, 1998.

Rigaux, Béda. *L'Antéchrist et l'Opposition au Royaume Messianique dans l'Ancien et le Nouveau Testament*. Universitas Catholica Lovaniensis, Dissertationes ad gradum magistri in facultate theologica conequendum conscriptae, ser. 2, 24. Gembloux and Paris: Duculot, 1932.

———. *Saint Paul: Les Épîtres aux Thessaloniciens*. EBib, Paris: Gabalda; Gembloux: Duculot, 1956.

———. "Tradition et rédaction dans 1 Th. V. 1-10," *NTS* 21 (1975), 318–40.

Rist, Martin. "Pseudepigraphy and the Early Christians," pages 75–91 in *Studies in New Testament and Early Christian Literature: Essays in Honor of Allen P. Wikgren*. Edited by David E. Aune. NovTSup 33. Leiden: Brill, 1972.

Ritschl, Albrecht. (On 1 Thess 2,16c) *Halle'sche Allgemeine Literaturzeitung* I (1847), 1000.

———. *Die christliche Lehre von der Rechtfertigung und Versöhnung*. Vol. II. Bonn: A. Marcus, 1889; repr. Hildesheim: Olms, 1978.

Ritter, Adolf Martin. "Chrysostomos und die Juden, neu überlegt," *Kirche und Israel* 5 (1990), 109–22.

Roberts, Mark David. "Images of Paul and the Thessalonians," Dissertation Harvard 1992. (microfiche)

Robinson, D. W. B. "II Thess. 2,6: 'That which restrains' or 'That which holds away'?" *TU* 87 (1963), 635–38.

Röcker, Fritz W. *Belial und Katechon. Eine Untersuchung zu 2 Thess 2,1-12 und 1 Thess 4,13-5,11*. WUNT 2d ser. 262. Tübingen: Mohr Siebeck, 2009.

Rodrigues, Hippolyte. *Les seconds chrétiens: Saint Paul*. Paris: M Lévy Frères, 1876.

Rösch, Konstantin. "'Wir Lebenden, wir Übrigbleibenden' in 1. Thess. 4,15.17," *TGl* 10 (1918), 492–95.

Roetzel, Calvin J. "*Theodidaktoi* and Handwork in Philo and 1 Thessalonians," pages 324–31 in *L'Apôtre Paul* (1986).

Roh, Taesong. *Der zweite Thessalonicherbrief als Erneuerung apokalyptischer Zeitdeutung.* NTOA 62. Fribourg: Universitätsverlag; Göttingen: Vandenhoeck & Ruprecht, 2007.
Roller, Otto. *Das Formular der paulinischen Briefe.* BWANT 58. Stuttgart: Kohlhammer, 1933.
Romaniuk, Kazimierz. "Les Thessaloniciens étaient-ils des paresseux?" *ETL* 69 (1993), 142–45.
Romeo, Antoninus. "*Nos qui vivimus, qui residui sumus,*" *VD* 9 (1929), 307–12; 339–47; 360–64.
Roose, Hanna. "2 Thessalonians as Pseudepigraphic Reading Instruction for 1 Thessalonians: Methodological Implications and Exemplary Illustration of an Intertextual Concept," pages 133–51 in *The Intertextuality of the Epistles* (2006).
———. "'A Letter as by Us': Intentional Ambiguity in 2 Thessalonians 2.2," *JSNT* 29 (2006), 107–24.
———. "Polyvalenz durch Intertextualität im Spiegel der aktuellen Forschung zu den Thessalonicherbriefen," *NTS* 51 (2005), 250–69.
Russell, Ronald. "The idle in 2 Thess 3,6-12. An eschatological or a social problem?" *NTS* 34 (1988), 105–19.
Rydelnik, Michael A. "Was Paul Anti-Semitic? Revisiting 1 Thessalonians 2:14-16," *BS* 165 (2008), 58–67.
Safrai, Shmuel. "Relations between the Diaspora and the Land of Israel," pages 184–215 in idem and Menachem Stern, eds., *The Jewish People in the First Century*, Vol. I (1974).
Safrai, Shmuel, and Menachem Stern, eds. *The Jewish People in the First Century. Historical Geography, Political History, Social, Cultural and Religious Life.* 2 vols. CRINT I 1, 2. Assen: Van Gorcum 1974, 1976.
Sailors, Timothy B. "Wedding Textual and Rhetorical Criticism to Understand the Text of 1 Thessalonians 2.7," *JSNT* 80 (2000), 81–98.
Salvesen, Alison. "A Convergence of the Ways? The Judaizing of Christian Scripture by Origen and Jerome," pages 233–58 in *The Ways That Never Parted* (2003).
Sanchez Bosch, Jorge. "La chronologie de la première aux Thessaloniciens et les relations de Paul avec d'autres églises," *NTS* 37 (1991), 336–47.
Sanders, Edward P. *Judaism: Practice and Belief, 63 BCE–66 CE.* London: SCM; Philadelphia: Trinity Press International, 1992; repr. Minneapolis: Fortress Press, 2016.
———. *Paul, the Law, and the Jewish People.* Philadelphia: Fortress Press, 1983.
Schäfer, Peter. *Judeophobia. Attitudes toward the Jews in the Ancient World.* Cambridge, MA: Harvard University Press, 1997.
Schade, Hans-Heinrich. *Apokalyptische Christologie bei Paulus. Studien zum Zusammenhang von Christologie und Eschatologie in den Paulusbriefen.* GTA 18. Göttingen: Vandenhoeck & Ruprecht, 1981.
Schaller, Berndt. "Hekataios von Abdera über die Juden. Zur Frage der Echtheit und der Datierung," *ZNW* 54 (1963), 15–31.
Schenke, Hans-Martin. "Das Weiterwirken des Paulus und die Pflege seines Erbes durch die Paulus-Schule," *NTS* 21 (1975), 505–18.
———, and Karl Martin Fischer. *Einleitung in die Schriften des Neuen Testamentes.* I. *Die Briefe des Paulus und die Schriften des Paulinismus.* Gütersloh: Gütersloher Verlagshaus Mohn, 1978.
Schiffner, Kerstin. *Lukas liest Exodus. Eine Untersuchung zur Aufnahme ersttestamentlicher Befreiungsgeschichte im lukanischen Werk als Schrift-Lektüre.* BWANT 172. Stuttgart: Kohlhammer, 2008.

Schimanowski, Gottfried. "'Abgrenzung und Identitätsfindung.' Paulinische Paränese im 1. Thessalonicherbrief," pages 297–316 in *Die Heiden* (1994).
Schippers, Reinier. "The Pre-Synoptic Tradition in I Thessalonians II 13–16," *NT* 8 (1966), 223–34.
Schlier, Heinrich. *Der Apostel und seine Gemeinde. Auslegung des ersten Briefes an die Thessalonicher*. Freiburg: Herder, 1972.
Schlueter, Carol J. *"Filling up the measure": polemical hyperbole in 1 Thessalonians 2:14-16*. JSNTSup 98. Sheffield: Sheffield Academic Press, 1994.
Schmeller, Thomas. "Der zweite Korintherbrief," pages 326–46 in *Einleitung in das Neue Testament* (2008).
———. "Die Cicerobriefe und die Frage nach der Einheitlichkeit des 2. Korintherbriefes," *ZNW* 95 (2004), 181–208.
Schmid, Josef. "Der Antichrist und die hemmende Macht (2 Thess 2,112)," *TQ* 129 (1949), 323–43.
Schmiedel, Paul W. *Die Briefe an die Thessalonicher und an die Korinther*. Hand-Commentar zum NT. Freiburg: Mohr, 1892.
Schmidt, Daryl D. "1 Thess 2:13-16: Linguistic Evidence for an Interpolation," *JBL* 102 (1983), 269–79.
———. "The Authenticity of 2 Thessalonians: Lingustic Arguments," SBLSP 22 (1983), 289–96.
———. "The Syntactical Style of 2 Thessalonians: How Pauline is it?" pages 383–93 in *The Thessalonian Correspondence* (1990).
Schmidt, Eckart David. *Heilig ins Eschaton. Heiligung und Heiligkeit als eschatologische Konzeption im 1. Thessalonicherbrief*. BZNW 167. Berlin and New York: de Gruyter, 2010.
Schmidt, Johann Ernst Christian. "Vermuthungen über die beiden Briefe an die Thessalonicher," in idem, ed., *Bibliothek für Kritik und Exegese des Neuen Testamentes und älteste Christentumsgeschichte* II/3. Hadamar, 1801 (repr. in Wolfgang Trilling, *Untersuchungen zum 2. Thessalonicherbrief* [1972], 159–61).
Schmidt, Paul. *Der erste Thessalonicherbrief, neu erklärt, nebst einem Exkurs über den zweiten gleichnamigen Brief*. Berlin: Georg Reimer, 1885.
Schmidt, Ulrich. "1 Thess 2.7b, c: 'Kleinkinder, die wie eine Amme Kinder versorgen,'" *NTS* 55 (2009), 116–20.
Schmithals, Walter. "Die historische Situation der Thessalonicherbriefe," in idem, *Paulus und die Gnostiker* (1965), 89–157.
———. "Die Thessalonicherbriefe als Briefkompositionen," pages 295–315 in *Zeit und Geschichte. Dankesgabe an Rudolf Bultmann*. Edited by Erich Dinkler. Tübingen: Mohr, 1964.
———. "Eschatologie und Apokalyptik," *VF* 33 (1988), 64–82.
———. "Methodische Erwägungen zur Literarkritik der Paulusbriefe," *ZNW* 87 (1996), 51–82.
———. *Paulus und die Gnostiker. Untersuchungen zu den kleinen Paulusbriefen*. TF 35. Hamburg-Bergstedt: Reich, 1965. English: *Paul and the Gnostics*. Translated by John E. Steely. Nashville: Abingdon Press, 1972.
Schneider, Gerhard. art. Χριστιανός. *EWNT* III (1983), 1145–47.
Schneider, Sebastian. *Vollendung des Auferstehens. Eine exegetische Untersuchung von 1 Kor 15,51-52 und 1 Thess 4:13-18*. FB 97. Würzburg: Echter Verlag, 2000.
Schnelle, Udo. "Der erste Thessalonicherbrief und die Entstehung der paulinischen Anthropologie," *NTS* 32 (1986), 207–24.

———. "Die Ethik des 1. Thessalonicherbriefes," pages 295–305 in *The Thessalonian Correspondence* (1990).
———. *Einleitung in das Neue Testament*. UTB 1830. Göttingen: Vandenhoeck & Ruprecht, 1994. English: *The History and Theology of the New Testament Writings*. Translated by M. Eugene Boring. Minneapolis: Fortress Press, 1998.
———. *Wandlungen im paulinischen Denken*. SBS 137. Stuttgart: Katholisches Bibelwerk, 1989.
Schnider, Franz, and Werner Stenger. *Studien zum neutestamentlichen Briefformular*. NTTS 11. Leiden and Boston: Brill, 1987.
Schoon-Janßen, Johannes. "On the Use of Elements of Ancient Epistolography in 1 Thessalonians." pages 179–93 in *The Thessalonians Debate* (2000).
———. *Umstrittene "Apologien" in den Paulusbriefen. Studien zur rhetorischen Situation des 1. Thessalonicherbriefes, des Galaterbriefes, und des Philipperbriefes*. GTA 45. Göttingen: Vandenhoeck & Ruprecht, 1991.
Schottroff, Luise. "Antijudaismus im Neuen Testament" (1984). Pages 217–28 in eadem, *Befreiungserfahrungen* (1990).
———. "Auf dem Weg zu einer feministischen Rekonstruktion der Geschichte des frühen Christentums," pages 173–248 in Luise Schottroff, Silvia Schroer, and Marie-Theres Wacker, *Feministische Exegese* (1995). English: "Toward a Feminist Reconstruction of the History of Early Christianity," pages 178–253 in Schottroff, Schroer, and Wacker, *Feminist Interpretation* (1998).
———. "Befreite Eva. Schuld und Macht der Mächtigen und Ohnmächtigen nach dem Neuen Testament," pages 15–151 in Christina Schaumberger and Luise Schottroff, *Schuld und Macht. Studien zu einer feministischen Befreiungstheologie*. Munich: Kaiser, 1988.
———. *Befreiungserfahrungen. Studien zur Sozialgeschichte des Neuen Testaments*. TB 82. Munich: Kaiser, 1990. Partially translated as *Let the Oppressed Go Free: Feminist Perspectives on the New Testament*. Translated by Annemarie S. Kidder. Louisville: Westminster John Knox, 1993.
———. "Der erste Brief an die Gemeinde in Korinth. Wie Befreiung entsteht," pages 574–92 in eadem and Marie-Theres Wacker, eds., *Kompendium feministische Bibelauslegung* (2003). English: "1 Corinthians: How Freedom Comes to Be," pages 718–42 in *Feminist Biblical Interpretation* (2012).
———. "Der Sieg des Lebens. Auslegung von 2. Korinther 4,6-12," pages 46–62 in eadem, *Der Sieg des Lebens. Biblische Traditionen einer Friedenspraxis*. Kaiser Traktate 88. Munich: Kaiser, 1982.
———. "Die Gegenwart in der Apokalyptik der synoptischen Evangelien (1983)," pages 73–95 in eadem, *Befreiungserfahrungen* (1990).
———. *Die Gleichnisse Jesu*. Gütersloh: Gütersloher Verlagshaus, 2005. English: *The Parables of Jesus*. Translated by Linda M. Maloney. Minneapolis: Fortress Press, 2006.
———. "Die Schreckensherrschaft der Sünde und die Befreiung durch Christus nach dem Römerbrief des Paulus" (1979). Pages 57–72 in eadem, *Befreiungserfahrungen* (1990).
———. "Die Schuld 'der Juden' und die Entschuldung des Pilatus in der deutschen neutestamentlichen Wissenschaft seit 1945," pages 324–57 in eadem, *Befreiungserfahrungen* (1990).
———. "Die Theologie der Tora im ersten Brief des Paulus an die Gemeinde in Korinth," Paper given at the international meeting of New Testament scholars, "Neuestes vom Neuen Testament," at the Ev. Akademie Tutzing, 12–14 June 2009. In *Alte Texte in*

Neuen Kontexten. Wo steht die Sozialwissenschaftliche Bibelexegese? Edited by Wolfgang Stegemann. Stuttgart: Kohlhammer, 2010.

———. "A Feminist Hermeneutic of 1 Corinthians," pages 208–15 in *Escaping Eden. New Feminist Perspectives on the Bible*. Edited by Harold C. Washington, Susan Lochrie Graham, and Pamela Thimmes. Sheffield: Sheffield Academic Press; Washington Square, NY: New York University Press, 1999.

———. "Frauen und Geld im Neuen Testament. Feministisch-theologische Beobachtungen," pages 25–56 in *"Geld regiert die Welt," Reader der Projektgruppenbeiträge zur feministisch-befreiungstheologischen Sommeruniversität 1990*. Kassel: Gesamthochschule Kassel, 1991.

———. "'Gebt dem Kaiser, was dem Kaiser gehört, und Gott, was Gott gehört.' Die theologische Antwort der urchristlichen Gemeinde auf ihre gesellschaftliche und politische Situation" (1984). Pages 184–216 in eadem, *Befreiungserfahrungen* (1990).

———. "'Gesetzesfreies Heidenchristentum'—und die Frauen? Feministische Analysen und Alternativen. Pages 227–45 in *Von der Wurzel getragen: christlich-feministische Exegese in Auseinandersetzung mit Antijudaismus*. Edited by Luise Schottroff and Marie-Theres Wacker. Biblical Interpretation Series 17. Leiden and New York: Brill, 1996.

———. *Lydias ungeduldige Schwestern. Feministische Sozialgeschichte des frühen Christentums*. Gütersloh: Kaiser/Gütersloher Verlagshaus, 1994. English: *Lydia's Impatient Sisters. A Feminist Social History of Early Christianity*. Translated by Barbara and Martin Rumscheidt. Louisville: Westminster John Knox, 1995.

———. "'Nicht viele Mächtige.' Annäherungen an eine Soziologie des Urchristentums" (1985). Pages 247–56 in eadem, *Befreiungserfahrungen* (1990).

———. "Sozialgeschichtliche Bibelauslegung zu 1. Thessalonicher 4,18," *Junge Kirche* 53 (1992), 500–501.

———. "Verheißung und Erfüllung aus der Sicht einer Theologie nach Auschwitz" (1987). Pages 275–83 in eadem, *Befreiungserfahrungen* (1990).

———. "Wie berechtigt ist die feministische Kritik an Paulus? Paulus und die Frauen in den ersten christlichen Gemeinden im Römischen Reich" (1985). Pages 229–46 in eadem, *Befreiungserfahrungen* (1990). English: "How Justified is the Feminist Critique of Paul?" pages 35–59 in *Let the Oppressed Go Free* (1993).

———. "'Wir richten die Tora auf' (Röm 3,31 und 1 Kor 5,1-3). Freiheit und Recht bei Paulus," pages 429–50 in *Freiheit und Recht. Festschrift für Frank Crüsemann zum 65. Geburtstag*. Edited by Christof Hardmeier, et al. Gütersloh: Kaiser, 2003.

———. "Zur historischen Einordnung der neutestamentlichen Texte," pages 20–25 in *Antijudaismus im Neuen Testament? Grundlagen für die Arbeit mit neutestamentlichen Texten*. Edited by Dagmar Henze, Claudia Janssen, Stefanie Müller, and Beate Wehn. Kaiser Taschenbücher 149. Gütersloh: Kaiser, 1997.

Schottroff, Luise, Silvia Schroer, and Marie-Theres Wacker, eds. *Feministische Exegese. Forschungserträge zur Bibel aus der Perspektive von Frauen*. Darmstadt: Primus, 1995. English: *Feminist Interpretation: The Bible in Women's Perspective*. Translated by Martin and Barbara Rumscheidt. Minneapolis: Fortress Press, 1998.

Schottroff, Luise, and Marie-Theres Wacker, eds. *Kompendium Feministische Bibelauslegung*. Gütersloh: Gütersloher Verlagshaus, 3d ed. 2007. English: *Feminist Biblical Interpretation. A Compendium of Criticial Commentary on the Books of the Bible and Related Literature*. American edition Martin Rumscheidt. Translated by Lisa E. Dahill, Everett R. Kalin, Nancy Lukens, Linda M. Maloney, Barbara Rumscheidt, Martin Rumscheidt, and Tina Steiner. Grand Rapids: Eerdmans, 2012.

———. *Von der Wurzel getragen. Christlich-feministische Exegese in Auseinandersetzung mit Antijudaismus* (1996).

Schottroff, Willy. "Das Gleichnis von den bösen Weingärtnern (Mk 12,1-19 parr.). Ein Beitrag zur Geschichte der Bodenpacht in Palästina," *ZDPV* 112 (1996), 18–48 (= pages 165–204 in idem, *Gerechtigkeit lernen. Beiträge zur biblischen Sozialgeschichte*. Edited by Frank Crüsemann and Rainer Kessler. Gütersloh: Kaiser/Gütersloher Verlagshaus, 1999).

Schrader, Karl. *Der Apostel Paulus* 5. Leipzig: Kollmann, 1836.

Schrage, Wolfgang. *Der erste Brief an die Korinther. 1 Kor 1,1-6,11*. EKK VII/1. Neukirchen-Vluyn: Neukirchener Verlag; Zürich: Benziger, 1991.

Schreckenberg, Heinz. *Die christlichen Adversus-Judaeos-Texte und ihr literarisches und historisches Umfeld (1.–11. Jh.)*. Europäische Hochschulschriften XXIII, 172. Frankfurt and Bern: Peter Lang, 1982.

Schreiber, Stefan. "Briefliteratur im Neuen Testament," pages 250–64 in *Einleitung in das Neue Testament*. Edited by Martin Ebner and Stefan Schreiber. Kohlhammer Studienbücher Theologie 6. Stuttgart: Kohlhammer, 2008.

———. "Der erste Thessalonicherbrief," pages 384–96 in *Einleitung in das Neue Testament* (2008).

———. "Der zweite Thessalonicherbrief," pages 440–49 in *Einleitung in das Neue Testament* (2008).

———. "Eine neue Jenseitshoffnung in Thessaloniki und ihre Probleme (1 Thess 4,13-18)," *Bib* 88 (2007), 326–50.

———. "Früher Paulus mit Spätfolgen. Eine Bilanz der neuesten Thessalonicherbrief-Forschung," *TRu* 103 (2007), 267–84.

Schrenk, W. art. βάρος κτλ. *TDNT* 1. 553–61.

Schubert, Paul. *Form and Function of the Pauline Thanksgivings*. BZNW 20. Berlin: de Gruyter, 1939.

Schuller, Wolfgang. "Dennoch die Schwerter halten. Der κατέχον Carl Schmitts," pages 389–408 in *Glaube, Tradition, Reflexion. Festschrift für Martin Hengel*. Vol. 2. Edited by Hubert Cancik. Tübingen: Mohr, 1996.

Schulz, Anselm. *Nachfolgen und Nachahmen. Studien über das Verhältnis der neutestamentlichen Jüngerschaft zur urchristlichen Vorbildethik* SANT 6. Munich: Kösel, 1962.

Schüpphaus, Joachim. *Die Psalmen Salomos. Ein Zeugnis Jerusalemer Theologie und Frömmigkeit in der Mitte des vorchristlichen Jahrhunderts*. ALGHJ 7. Leiden: Brill, 1977.

Schürer, Emil. *Geschichte des jüdischen Volkes im Zeitalter Jesu Christi*. 4 vols. Leipzig: Hinrichs, 3d & 4th eds. 1901; repr. New York and Hildesheim: Olms, 1970. English: *The History of the Jewish People in the Age of Jesus Christ*. New English version rev. and ed. Geza Vermes, Fergus Millar, Matthew Black, and Martin Goodman, with Pamela Vermes. New York: Bloomsbury T & T Clark, 2014.

Schüssler Fiorenza, Elisabeth. *Bread Not Stone: The Challenge of Feminist Biblical Interpretation*. Boston: Beacon, 1984; rev. ed 1995.

———. *But She Said: Feminist Practices of Biblical Interpretation*. Boston: Beacon, 1992.

———. *In Memory of Her. A Feminist-Theological Reconstruction of Christian Origins*. New York: Crossroad, 1994.

———, ed. *Searching the Scriptures*. Vol. 1: *A Feminist Introduction*. New York: Crossroad, 1993; Vol. II: *A Feminist Commentary*. New York: Crossroad, 1994.

Schweitzer, Albert. *Geschichte der paulinischen Forschung von der Reformation bis auf die Gegenwart*. Tübingen: Mohr, 1911; repr. Hildesheim, Zürich, and New York: Olms, 2004. English: *Paul and His Interpreters, a Critical History*. Translated by W. Montgomery. New York: Schocken Books, 1964.

Schweizer, Eduard. *Der Brief an die Kolosser*. EKK XII. Zürich: Benziger; Neukirchen-Vluyn: Neukirchener Verlag, 1976.

Schwier, Helmut. *Tempel und Tempelzerstörung. Untersuchungen zu den theologischen und ideologischen Faktoren im ersten jüdisch-römischen Krieg (66–74 n. Chr.)*. NTOA 11. Fribourg: Universitätsverlag; Göttingen: Vandenhoeck & Ruprecht, 1989.

Scott, J. Julius. "Paul and Late-Jewish Eschatology. A Case Study, 1 Thessalonians 4:13-18 and II Thessalonians 2:1-12," *JETS* 15 (1972), 133–45.

Scott, Robert. *The Pauline Epistles. A Critical Study*. Edinburgh: T & T Clark, 1909.

Seeliger, Hans Reinhard. "Gemeinsamkeiten in der antijüdischen und antichristlichen Polemik in der Antike," pages 88–94 in *Christlicher Antijudaismus und jüdischer Antipaganismus* (1990).

Segal, Alan F. *Paul the Convert. The Apostolate and Apostasy of Paul the Pharisee*. New Haven: Yale University Press, 1990.

Selwyn, Edward G. *The First Epistle of St. Peter*. London: Macmillan, 1947.

Setzer, Claudia J. *Jewish Responses to Early Christians. History and Polemics 30–150 C. E.* Minneapolis: Fortress Press, 1994.

Sevenster, Jan N. *The Roots of Pagan Antisemitism in the Ancient World*. NovTSup 41. Leiden: Brill, 1975.

Siber, Peter. *Mit Christus leben. Eine Studie zur paulinischen Auferstehungshoffnung*. ATANT 61. Zürich: Theologischer Verlag, 1971.

Simon, Marcel. *Verus Israel. Étude sur les relations entre Chrétiens et Juifs dans l'empire romain (135–425)*. Bibliothèque des écoles françaises d'Athènes et de Rome 166. Paris: Boccard, 1948; 1964. English: *Verus Israel: A Study of the Relations between Christians and Jews in the Roman Empire, AD 135–425*. Translated by H. McKeating. Littman Library of Jewish Civilization. London and Portland, OR: Vallentine Mitchell & Co., 1996.

Simpson, John W. "The problems posed by 1 Thessalonians 2,14-15 and a solution," *HBT* 12 (1990), 42–73.

Sirard, Léas. "La parousie de l'Antéchrist. 2 Thess 2,3-9," pages 89–100 in *Studiorum Paulinorum Congressus Internationalis Catholicus 1961*. AnBib 17–18, Vol. II. Rome: Pontifical Biblical Institute, 1963.

Skarsaune, Oskar. "Evidence for Jewish Believers in Greek and Latin Patristic Literature," pages 505–67 in *Jewish Believers in Jesus* (2007).

———. "Fragments of Jewish Christian Literature Quoted in Some Greek and Latin Fathers," pages 325–78 in *Jewish Believers in Jesus* (2007).

———. "Jewish Christian Sources Used by Justin Martyr and Some Other Greek and Latin Fathers," pages 379–416 in *Jewish Believers in Jesus* (2007).

———. "The History of Jewish Believers in the Early Centuries: Perspectives and Framework," pages 745–81 in *Jewish Believers in Jesus* (2007).

Skarsaune, Oskar, and Reidar Hvalvik, eds. *Jewish Believers in Jesus: The Early Centuries*. Peabody, MA: Hendrickson, 2007.

Smallwood, E. Mary. "Domitian's Attitude towards Jews and Judaism," *Classical Philology* 51 (1956), 1–13.

———. *The Jews under Roman Rule. From Pompey to Diocletian. A Study in Political Relations*. Leiden: Brill, 1976; 2d ed. 1981.

Smith, Abraham. *Comfort One Another. Reconstructing the Rhetoric and Audience of 1 Thessalonians*. Louisville: Westminster John Knox, 1995.
———. "The social and ethical implications of the Pauline rhetoric in 1 Thessalonians," Dissertation Vanderbilt 1989.
Söding, Thomas. "Der Erste Thessalonicherbrief und die frühe paulinische Evangeliumsverkündigung. Zur Frage einer Entwicklung der paulinischen Theologie," *BZ* n.s. 35 (1991), 180–203.
———. *Die Trias Glaube, Hoffnung, Liebe bei Paulus. Eine exegetische Studie*. SBS 150. Stuttgart: Katholisches Bibelwerk, 1992.
———. "Zur Chronologie der paulinischen Briefe. Ein Diskussionsvorschlag," *BN* 56 (1991), 31–59.
Sordet, Jean-Michel. "La venue du Seigneur. Deux discours d'espérance à la lumière de deux hypothèses. 1 Thessaloniciens 4,13-18 et 2 Thessaloniciens 2,1-12," *Hok* 35 (1987), 35–57.
Speyer, Wolfgang. art. "Fälschung, literarische." *RAC* VII (1969), 236–77.
———. *Die literarische Fälschung im heidnischen und christlichen Altertum. Ein Versuch ihrer Deutung*. Handbuch der Altertumswissenschaft I, 2. Munich: Beck, 1971.
———. "Fälschung, pseudepigraphische freie Erfindung und 'echte religiöse Pseudepigraphie.'" Pages 331–66 in *Pseudepigrapha* I. Edited by Kurt von Fritz. Genève: Fondation Hardt, 1972.
———. "Religiöse Pseudepigraphie und literarische Fälschung im Altertum" (1965/66). Pages 195–263 in *Pseudepigraphie in der heidnischen und jüdisch-christlichen Antike* (1977).
Spitta, Friedrich. *Zur Geschichte und Literatur des Urchristentums*. Vol. 1. Göttingen: Vandenhoeck & Ruprecht, 1893.
Staab, Karl. "Die Briefe an die Thessalonicher," pages 9–49 in *Die Thessalonicherbriefe, die Gefangenschaftsbriefe und die Pastoralbriefe*. Edited by Karl Staab and Joseph Freundorfer. RNT 7/2. Regensburg: Pustet, 1950.
Stähli, Hans-Peter. "Judenfeindschaft. Zum Verhältnis zwischen Christen und Juden in der Vergangenheit," *WD* 19 (1987), 137–75.
Standhartinger, Angela. *Studien zur Entstehungsgeschichte & Intention des Kolosserbriefs*. NovTSup 94. Leiden and Boston: Brill, 1999.
Stanley, Christopher D. "Who's Afraid of a Thief in the Night?" *NTS* 48 (2002), 468–86.
Stanley, David M. "'Become imitators of me': The Pauline Conception of Apostolic Tradition," *Bib* 40 (1959), 859–77.
Starnitzke, Dierk. "Der Dienst des Paulus. Zur Interpretation von Ex 34 in 2 Kor 3," *WD* 25 (1999), 193–207.
Steck, Odil Hannes. *Israel und das gewaltsame Geschick der Propheten. Untersuchungen zur Überlieferung des deuteronomistischen Geschichtsbildes im Alten Testament, Spätjudentum und Urchristentum*. WMANT 23. Neukirchen-Vluyn: Neukirchener Verlag, 1967.
Steck, Rudolf. "Das Herrnwort I Thess 4,15," *JPTh* 13 (1883), 509–24.
Stegemann, Ekkehard W. "Zwischen Juden und Heiden, aber 'mehr' als Juden und Heiden? Neutestamentliche Anmerkungen zur Identitätsproblematik des frühen Christentums," *Kirche und Israel* 9 (1994), 53–69.
———. "Zur antijüdischen Polemik in 1 Thess 2,14-16," *Kirche und Israel* 5 (1990), 54–64.
Stegemann, Wolfgang. "Am Anfang war die Unterscheidung. Sozialgeschichtliche Beobachtungen zum Auseinandergehen der Wege von Christentum und Judentum," pages 76–90 in *Das christlich-jüdische Gespräch. Standortbestimmungen*. Edited by

Christina Kurth and Peter Schmid. Judentum und Christentum 3. Stuttgart: Kohlhammer, 2000.

———. "Anlaß und Hintergrund der Abfassung von 1 Th 2,1-12, pages 397–416 in *Theologische Brosamen für Lothar Steiger*. Edited by Gerhard Freund and Ekkehard Stegemann. Dielheimer Blätter zum Alten Testament Beiheft 5. Heidelberg: Wissenschaftliches-Theologisches Seminar, 1985.

———. *Zwischen Synagoge und Obrigkeit. Zur historischen Situation der lukanischen Christen*. FRLANT 152. Göttingen: Vandenhoeck & Ruprecht, 1991.

Stegemann, Ekkehard W., and Wolfgang Stegemann. *Urchristliche Sozialgeschichte. Die Anfänge im Judentum und die Christengemeinden in der mediterranen Welt*. Stuttgart: Kohlhammer, 1995. English: *The Jesus Movement: A Social History of its First Century*. Translated by O. C. Dean, Jr. Minneapolis: Fortress Press, 1999.

Steimle, Christopher. *Religion im römischen Thessaloniki. Sakraltopographie, Kult und Gesellschaft 168 v. Chr.–324 n. Chr*. Studien und Texte zu Antike und Christentum 47. Tübingen: Mohr Siebeck, 2008.

Stemberger, Günter. "Die Juden im Römischen Reich: Unterdrückung und Privilegierung einer Minderheit," pages 6–22 in *Christlicher Antijudaismus* (1990).

Stenger, Werner. *"'Gebt dem Kaiser, was des Kaisers ist . . .!" Eine sozialgeschichtliche Untersuchung zur Besteuerung Palästinas in neutestamentlicher Zeit*. BBB 68. Frankfurt: Athenäum, 1988.

Stephenson, Allen M. G.. "On the meaning of ἐνέστηκεν ἡ ἡμέρα τοῦ κυρίου in 2 Thessalonians 2,2," pages 442–51 in *The New Testament Message*. Edited by Frank Leslie Cross. *SE* 5 = *TU* 103. Berlin: Akademie-Verlag, 1968.

Stern, Menachem. *Greek and Latin Authors on Jews and Judaism*. 3 vols. Jerusalem: Israel Academy of Sciences and Humanities, 1974–1984.

———. "The Jews in Greek and Latin Literature," pages 1101–59 in *The Jewish People* (1976).

Still, Todd D. *Conflict at Thessalonica. A Pauline Church and its Neighbours*. JSNTS 183. Sheffield: Sheffield Academic Press, 1999.

———. "Eschatology in the Thessalonian Letters," *RevExp* 96 (1999), 195–210.

———. "Interpretive Ambiguities and Scholarly Proclivities in Pauline Studies: A Treatment of Three Texts from 1 Thessalonians 4 as a Test Case," *CurBR* 5 (2007), 207–19.

Stirewalt, M. Luther. "Paul's Evaluation of Letter-Writing," pages 179–96 in *Search the Scriptures: New Testament Studies in Honor of Raymond T. Stamm*. Edited by Jacob M. Myers, Otto Reimherr, and Howard N. Bream. Gettysburg Theological Studies 3. Leiden: Brill, 1969.

Stowers, Stanley K. *Letter Writing in Greco-Roman Antiquity*. LCC 5. Philadelphia: Westminster, 1986.

Strecker, Christian. art. "Judentum/Christentum," pages 279–83 in *Sozialgeschichtliches Wörterbuch zur Bibel* (2009).

Strobel, August. *Untersuchungen zum eschatologischen Verzögerungsproblem auf Grund der spätjüdisch-urchristlichen Geschichte von Habakuk 2,2ff*. NovTSup 2. Leiden: Brill, 1961.

Stroher (Ströher), Marga J. "Cuidado com os que proclamam *paz e segurança*—eis que virá destruição e dor. Uma escatologia da resistência em 1 Tessalonicenses," *EstBib* 93 (2007), 59–64.

Stroumsa, Guy G. "From Anti-Judaism to Antisemitism in Early Christianity?" pages 1–26 in *Contra Ioudaeos* (1996).

Stuhlmacher, Peter. *Der Brief an Philemon*. EKK. Zürich: Benziger; Neukirchen-Vluyn: Neukirchener Verlag, 1975.

Stuhlmann, Rainer. *Das eschatologische Mass im Neuen Testament*. FRLANT 132. Göttingen: Vandenhoeck & Ruprecht, 1983.
Suhl, Alfred. "Der Beginn der selbständigen Mission des Paulus. Ein Beitrag zur Geschichte des Urchristentums," *NTS* 38 (1992), 430–47.
———. *Paulus und seine Briefe. Ein Beitrag zur paulinischen Chronologie*. SNT 11. Gütersloh: Gütersloher Verlagshaus Mohn, 1975.
Sumney, Jerry L. "The Bearing of a Pauline Rhetorical Pattern on the Integrity of 2 Thessalonians," *ZNW* 81 (1990), 192–204.
Sutter Rehmann, Luzia. "4 Ezra: On the Struggle for New Life, the Time That is Being Fulfilled, and the Transformation of the Earth (2 Esdras 3–14)." Translated by Linda M. Maloney. Pages 566–77 in *Feminist Biblical Interpretation* (2012).
———. *Geh, frage die Gebärerin! Feministisch-befreiungstheologische Untersuchungen zum Gebärmotiv in der Apokalyptik*. Gütersloh: Kaiser/Gütersloher Verlagshaus, 1995.
Swartley, Willard M. "The Imitatio Christi in the Ignatian Letters," *VC* 27 (1973), 81–103.
Synofzik, Ernst. *Die Gerichts- und Vergeltungsaussagen bei Paulus. Eine traditionsgeschichtliche Untersuchung*. GTA 8. Göttingen: Vandenhoeck & Ruprecht, 1977.
Taatz, Irene. *Frühjüdische Briefe. Die paulinischen Briefe im Rahmen der offiziellen Briefe des Frühjudentums*. NTOA 16. Fribourg: Universitätsverlag; Göttingen: Vandenhoeck & Ruprecht, 1991.
Tamez, Elsa. *The Amnesty of Grace: Justification by Faith from a Latin American Perspective*. Translated by Sharon H. Ringe. Nashville: Abingdon Press, 1993.
———. "Romans: A Feminist Reading." Translated by Nancy Lukens. Pages 698–717 in *Feminist Biblical Interpretation* (2012).
Taylor, Nicholas H. "Who persecuted the Thessalonian Christians?" *HTS* 58 (2002), 784–801.
Teichmann, Ernst. *Die paulinischen Vorstellungen von Auferstehung und Gericht und ihre Beziehungen zur jüdischen Apokalyptik*. Freiburg and Leipzig: Mohr, 1896.
Tellbe, Mikael. *Paul between synagogue and state. Christians, Jews, and civic authorities in 1 Thessalonians, Romans, and Philippians*. ConBNT 34. Stockholm: Almqvist & Wiksell, 2001.
The Thessalonian Correspondence. Edited by Raymond F. Collins. BETL 87. Leuven: Leuven University Press; Peeters, 1990.
Theissen, Gerd. "Aporien im Umgang mit den Antijudaismen des Neuen Testaments," pages 535–53 in *Die hebräische Bibel und ihre zweifache Nachgeschichte: Festschrift für Rolf Rendtorff*. Edited by Erhard Blum, Christian Macholz, and Ekkehard W. Stegemann. Neukirchen-Vluyn: Neukirchener Verlag, 1990.
———. "Die Bekehrung des Paulus und seine Entwicklung vom Fundamentalisten zum Universalisten," *EvT* 70 (2010), 10–25.
———. *The New Testament: A Literary History*. Translated by Linda M. Maloney. Minneapolis: Fortress Press, 2012.
———. "Judentum und Christentum bei Paulus. Sozialgeschichtliche Überlegungen zu einem beginnenden Schisma," pages 331–56 in *Paulus und das antike Judentum* (1991).
———. *The Gospels in Context: Social and Political History in the Synoptic Tradition*. Translated by Linda M. Maloney. Minneapolis: Fortress Press, 1991.
———. "Zur Entstehung des Christentums aus dem Judentum. Bermerkungen zu David Flussers Thesen," *Kirche und Israel* 3 (1988), 179–89.
Theissen, Gerd, and Annette Merz. *The Historical Jesus: A Comprehensive Guide*. Translated by John Bowden. Minneapolis: Fortress Press, 1998.

Thieme, Karl. "Die Struktur des ersten Thessalonicherbriefes," pages 450–58 in *Abraham unser Vater* (1963).
Thoma, Clemens. "Verhängnis, Missverständnis und Schuld beim frühen Eindringen der Judenfeindschaft in die christliche Botschaft," pages 13–27 in *Gottesverächter und Menschenfeinde? Juden zwischen Jesus und frühchristlicher Kirche*. Edited by Horst Goldstein, et al. Düsseldorf: Patmos, 1979.
Thompson, Lloyd A. "Domitian and the Jewish Tax," *Historia* 31 (1982), 329–42.
Thompson, Trevor. "A Stone that *Still* Won't Fit. An Introductory and Editorial Note for Edgar Krentz's 'A Stone that Will Not Fit,'" pages 433–38 in *Pseudepigraphie und Verfasserfiktion in frühchristlichen Briefen* (2009).
———. "'As If Genuine.' Interpreting the Pseudepigraphic Second Thessalonians," pages 471–88 in *Pseudepigraphie und Verfasserfiktion in frühchristlichen Briefen* (2009).
Thraede, Klaus. *Grundzüge griechisch-römischer Brieftopik*. Munich: Beck, 1970.
Thrall, Margaret E. *The Second Epistle to the Corinthians*. 2 vols. ICC. Edinburgh: T & T Clark, 1994–2000.
Tillmann, Fritz. "Die Wiederkunft Chisti nach den paulinischen Briefen," *BibS* 14 (1909), 62–69.
Tomson, Peter J. *Paul and the Jewish Law: Halakha in the Letters of the Apostle to the Gentiles*. Assen: van Gorcum; Minneapolis: Fortress Press, 1990.
Tonstadt, Sigve K. "The Restrainer Removed: A Truly Alarming Thought (2 Thess 2:1-12)," *HBT* 29 (2007), 133–51.
Touratsoglou, Ioannis. *Die Münzstätte von Thessaloniki in der römischen Kaiserzeit (32/31 v.Chr. bis 268 n. Chr.)*. Deutsches Archäologisches Institut, Antike Münzen und geschnittene Steine, Vol. XII, Berlin and New York: de Gruyter, 1988.
Trilling, Wolfgang. *Der zweite Brief an die Thessalonicher*. EKK XIV. Zürich: Benziger; Neukirchen-Vluyn: Neukirchener Verlag, 1980.
———. "Die beiden Briefe des Apostels Paulus an die Thessalonicher. Eine Forschungsübersicht," *ANRW* II (1987), 3365–3403.
———. *Untersuchungen zum 2. Thessalonicherbrief*. ETS 27. Leipzig: St. Benno Verlag, 1972.
Trobisch, David. *Die Entstehung der Paulusbriefsammlung. Studien zu den Anfängen christlicher Publizistik*. NTOA 10. Fribourg: Universitätsverlag; Göttingen: Vandenhoeck & Ruprecht, 1989.
Trudinger, Paul. "The Priority of 2 Thessalonians Revisited: Some Fresh Evidence," *DRev* 113 (1995), 31–35.
Tuckett, Christopher M. "Synoptic Tradition in 1 Thessalonians?" pages 160–82 in *The Thessalonian Correspondence* (1990).
Turner, Seth. "The Interim, Earthly Messianic Kingdom in Paul," *JSNT* 25 (2003), 323–42.
Ulonska, Herbert. "Christen und Heiden. Die paulinische Paränese in 1 Thess 4,3-8," *TZ* 43 (Festschrift for Walter Neidhart) (1987), 210–18.
Umemoto, Naoto. "Juden, 'Heiden' und das Menschengeschlecht in der Sicht Philons von Alexandria," pages 22–51 in *Die Heiden* (1994).
Usteri, Leonhard. *Entwickelung des Paulinischen Lehrbegriffs mit Hinsicht auf die übrigen Schriften des Neuen Testamentes. Ein exegetisch-dogmatischer Versuch*. Zürich: 4th ed. 1832.
Van den Bergh van Eysinga, Gustaaf Adolf. *Die holländische radikale Kritik des Neuen Testaments. Ihre Geschichte und Bedeutung für die Erkenntnis der Entstehung des Christentums*. Jena: Diederichs, 1912.

Van der Vies, Abraham Balthasar. *De beiden Brieven aan de Thessalonicensen, historisch-kritisch onderzoek naar hunnen oorsprong*. Leiden: S. C. van Doesburgh, 1865.
Van Manen, Willem C. *De echtheid van Paulus' brieven aan de Thessalonicensen*. Vol. 1: *De eerste Brief*. Weesp: Brugman, 1865; Vol. 2: *De tweede Brief*. Utrecht: L. E. Bosch en Zoon, 1865.
———. *Paulus*. 3 vols. Leiden: Brill, 1890–1896.
———. "Zur Literaturgeschichte der Kritik und Exegese des Neuen Testaments," *Jahrbücher für protestantische Theologie* 9 (1883), 593–618.
Vander Stichele, Caroline. "The Concept of Tradition and 1 and 2 Thessalonians," pages 499–504 in *The Thessalonian Correspondence* (1990).
Vanhoye, Albert. "La composition de 1 Thessaloniciens," pages 73–86 in *The Thessalonian Correspondence* (1990).
Vahrenhorst, Martin. "*Ihr sollt überhaupt nicht schwören." Matthäus im halachischen Diskurs*. WMANT 95. Neukirchen-Vluyn: Neukirchener Verlag, 2002.
———. *Kultische Sprache in den Paulusbriefen*. WUNT 230. Tübingen: Mohr Siebeck, 2008.
Verhoef, Eduard. "1 Thessalonians 4:1-8: The Thessalonians should live a holy life," *HTS* 63 (2007), 347–63.
———. *De brieven aan de Tessalonicenzen*. Kampen: Kok, 1998.
———. "Die Bedeutung des Artikels τῶν in 1 Thess 2,15," *BN* 80 (1995), 41–46.
———. "Die holländische radikale Kritik," pages 427–32 in *The Corinthian Correspondence* (1996).
———. "Numerus, Sekretär und die Authentizität der paulinischen Briefe," *PzB* 4 (1995), 45–58.
———. "The Senders of the Letters to the Corinthians and the Use of 'I' and 'We,'" pages 417–25 in *The Corinthian Correspondence* (1996).
Vickers, Michael J. "Towards Reconstruction of the Town Planning of Roman Thessaloniki," pages 239–51 in *Ancient Macedonia*. Edited by Basileios Lourdas and C. I. Makaronas. Thessaloniki: Institut for Balkan Studies 1970.
Vielhauer, Philipp. *Geschichte der urchristlichen Literatur*. Berlin and New York: de Gruyter, 1975.
Volkmar, Gustav. *Mose Prophetie und Himmelfahrt. Eine Quelle für das Neue Testament, zum ersten Male deutsch herausgegeben im Zusammenhang der Apokrypha und der Christologie überhaupt*. Leipzig: Fues, 1867.
Volz, Paul. *Die Eschatologie der jüdischen Gemeinde im neutestamentlichen Zeitalter*. Tübingen: Mohr, 1934; repr. Hildesheim: Olms, 1966.
———. *Die jüdische Eschatologie von Daniel bis Akiba*. Tübingen: Mohr, 1903.
Völter, Daniel. *Paulus und seine Briefe. Kritische Untersuchungen zu einer neuen Grundlegung der paulinischen Briefliteratur und ihrer Theologie*. Strassburg: J. H. E. Heitz, 1905.
Von Fritz, Kurt, ed. *Pseudepigrapha I*. Entretiens sur l'Antiquité classique 18. Genève: Fondation Hardt, 1972.
Von Soden, Hans. "Der erste Thessalonicherbrief," *TSK* 58 (1885), 263–310.
Vos, Johan S. "On the Background of 1 Thessalonians 2:1-12: A Response to Traugott Holtz," pages 81–88 in *The Thessalonians Debate* (2000).
Vouga, François. *An die Galater*. HNT 10. Tübingen: Mohr Siebeck, 1998.
———. "Der Brief als Form der apostolischen Autorität," pages 7–58 in Klaus Berger, François Vouga, Michael Wolter, and Dieter Zeller, *Studien und Texte zur Formgeschichte*. Texte und Arbeiten zum Neutestamentlichen Zeitalter 7. Tübingen and Basel: Francke, 1992.

———. *Geschichte des frühen Christentums*. UTB 1733. Tübingen: Francke, 1994.
Wagener, Ulrike. *Die Ordnung des "Hauses Gottes," Der Ort von Frauen in der Ekklesiologie und Ethik der Pastoralbriefe*. WUNT 2d ser. 65. Tübingen: Mohr, 1994.
Walker, William O. "The Burden of Proof in Identifying Interpolations in the Pauline Letters," *NTS* 33 (1987), 610–18.
Wallace, Daniel B. "A textual problem in 1 Thessalonians 1:10, *ἐκ τῆς ὀργῆς vs. ἀπὸ τῆς ὀργῆς*," *BS* 147 (1990), 470–79.
Walter, Nikolaus. "Der Brief an die Philipper," pages 10–101 in *Die Briefe an die Philipper, Thessalonicher und an Philemon* (1998).
Walton, Steve. *Leadership and Lifestyle. The portrait of Paul in the Miletus speech and 1 Thessalonians*. SNTSMS 108. Cambridge: Cambridge University Press, 2000.
———. "What has Aristotle to do with Paul? Rhetorical Criticism and 1 Thessalonians," *TynBul* 46 (1995), 229–50.
Wanamaker, Charles A. "Apocalypticism at Thessalonica," *Neot* 21 (1987), 1–10.
———. "Epistolary vs. Rhetorical Analysis: Is a Synthesis Possible?" Pages 255–86 in *The Thessalonians Debate* (2000).
———. *The Epistles to the Thessalonians. A Commentary on the Greek Text*. NIGTC. Grand Rapids: Eerdmans, 1990.
Wander, Bernd. *Gottesfürchtige und Sympathisanten. Studien zum heidnischen Umfeld von Diasporasynagogen*. WUNT 104. Tübingen: Mohr Siebeck, 1998.
———. *Trennungsprozesse zwischen Frühem Christentum und Judentum im 1. Jh. n. Chr. Datierbare Abfolgen zwischen der Hinrichtung Jesu und der Zerstörung des Jerusalemer Tempels* TANZ 16. Tübingen: Francke, 1994.
Ware, James. "The Thessalonians as a Missionary Congregation: 1 Thessalonians 1,5-8," *ZNW* 83 (1992), 126–31.
Wasserberg, Günter. *Aus Israels Mitte: Heil für die Welt. Eine narrativ-exegetische Studie zur Theologie des Lukas*. BZNW 92. Berlin and New York: de Gruyter, 1998.
Waterman, G. Henry. "Sources of Paul's Teaching on the 2nd Coming of Christ in 1 and 2 Thessalonians," *JETS* 18 (1975), 105–13.
Watson, Francis. *Paul, Judaism and the Gentiles. A Sociological Approach*. SNTSMS 56. Cambridge: Cambridge University Press, 1986.
Weatherly, John A. "The authenticity of 1 Thessalonians 2.13-16. Additional evidence," *JSNT* 42 (1991), 79–98.
Wegner, Judith Romney. *Chattel or Person? The Status of Women in the Mishnah*. Oxford: Oxford University Press, 1988.
Wehnert, Jürgen. *Die Reinheit des "christlichen Gottesvolkes" aus Juden und Heiden. Studien zum historischen und theologischen Hintergrund des sogenannten Aposteldekrets*. FRLANT 173. Göttingen: Vandenhoeck & Ruprecht, 1997.
Weima, Jeffrey A. "An Apology for the Apologetic Function of 1 Thessalonians 2.1-2," *JSNT* 68 (1997) 73–99.
———. *Neglected Endings: The Significance of the Pauline Letter Closings*. JSNTSup 101. Sheffield: JSOT Press, 1994.
———. "The Function of 1 Thessalonians 2:1-12 and the Use of Rhetorical Criticism: A Response to Otto Merk," pages 114–31 in *The Thessalonians Debate* (2000).
———. "'The man of lawlessness': A Critical Examination of 2 Thessalonians 2:1-12. Dissertation Calvin Seminary, Grand Rapids, 1987.
———. "The Slaying of Satan's Superman and the Sure Salvation of the Saints: Paul's Apocalyptic Word of Comfort (2 Thessalonians 2:1-17)," *CTJ* 41 (2006), 67–88.

Weiss, Johannes. *Das Urchristentum*. Edited by Rudolf Knopf. Göttingen: Vandenhoeck & Ruprecht, 1914–1917. English: *Earliest Christianity: A History of the Period A.D. 30–150*. Translated and edited by Frederick C. Grant. Harper Torchbooks 53–54. New York: Harper & Row, 1959.
Weiss, Wolfgang. "Glaube, Liebe, Hoffnung. Zu der Trias bei Paulus," *ZNW* 84 (1993), 196–217.
Wendebourg, Nicola. *Der Tag des Herrn. Zur Gerichtserwartung im Neuen Testament auf ihrem alttestamentlichen und frühjüdischen Hintergrund*. WMANT 96. Neukirchen-Vluyn: Neukirchener Verlag, 2003.
Wengst, Klaus. *Bedrängte Gemeinde und verherrlichter Christus. Ein Versuch über das Johannesevangelium*. Munich: Kaiser, 1990.
———. "Christliche Identitätsbildung gegenüber dem Judentum zwischen 70–135 d.Zt.," *Kirche und Israel* 13 (1998), 99–105.
———. *Das Johannesevangelium*. 2 vols. TKNT 4.1, 2. Stuttgart: Kohlhammer, 2000–2001.
———. *Der Brief an Philemon*. TKNT 16. Stuttgart: Kohlhammer, 2005.
———. *Pax Romana: Anspruch und Wirklichkeit. Erfahrungen und Wahrnehmungen des Friedens bei Jesus und im Urchristentum*. Munich: Kaiser, 1986. English: *Pax Romana: and the Peace of Jesus Christ*. Philadelphia: Fortress Press, 1987.
———. *"Freut euch, ihr Völker, mit Gottes Volk!" Israel und die Völker als Thema des Paulus: ein Gang durch den Römerbrief*. Stuttgart: Kohlhammer, 2008.
———. *"Wie lange noch?" Schreien nach Recht und Gerechtigkeit: eine Deutung der Apokalypse des Johannes*. Stuttgart: Kohlhammer, 2010.
Wenham, David. "Paul and the Synoptic Apocalypse," pages 345–75 in *Gospel Perspectives II: Studies of History and Tradition in the Four Gospels*. Edited by R. T. France and David Wenham. Sheffield: JSOT Press, 1981.
West, J. C. "The Order of 1 and 2 Thessalonians," *JTS* 15 (1914), 66–74.
White, John L. "Ancient Greek Letters," pages 85–105 in *Greco-Roman Literature and the New Testament. Selected Forms and Genres*. Edited by David E. Aune. SBLSP 21. Atlanta: Scholars Press, 1988.
———. *Light from Ancient Letters*. Philadelphia: Fortress Press, 1986.
———. "New Testament Epistolary Literature in the Framework of Ancient Epistolography," *ANRW* II 25.2. Berlin and New York: de Gruyter, 1984.
———. *The Form and Function of the Body of the Greek Letter: A Study of the Letter-Body in the Non-Literary Papyri and in Paul the Apostle*. SBLDS 2. Missoula, MT: Scholars Press, 1972.
———. "The Greek Documentary Letter Tradition Third Century B.C.E. to Third Century C. E.," pages 89–106 in idem, ed., *Studies in Ancient Letter Writing*. *Semeia* 22 (1982).
Whiteley, Denys E. *Thessalonians in the Revised Standard Version: With Introduction and Commentary*. Oxford: Oxford University Press, 1969.
Whitton, J. "A Neglected Meaning for *skeuos* in 1 Thessalonians 4:4," *NTS* 28 (1982), 142–43.
Wichmann, Wolfgang. *Die Leidenstheologie. Eine Form der Leidensdeutung im Spätjudentum*. BWANT 53. Stuttgart: Kohlhammer, 1930.
Wick, Peter. "Ist I Thess 2,13-16 antijüdisch? Der rhetorische Gesamtzusammenhang des Briefes als Interpretationshilfe für eine einzelne Perikope," *TZ* 38 (1994), 9–23.
Wiefel, Wolfgang. "Die Hauptrichtung des Wandels im eschatologischen Denken des Paulus," *TZ* 30 (1974), 65–81.

Wilckens, Ulrich. *Der Brief an die Römer*. 3 vols. EKK 6. Zürich: Benziger; Neukirchen-Vluyn: Neukirchener Verlag, 1978–1982.

———. *Die Missionsreden der Apostelgeschichte. Form- und traditionsgeschichtliche Untersuchungen*. WMANT 5. Neukirchen-Vluyn: Neukirchener Verlag, 1961; 3d ed. 1974.

Williams, David J. *1 and 2 Thessalonians*. NIC. Peabody, MA: Hendrickson, 1992.

Wilson, Stephen G., ed. *Anti-Judaism in Early Christianity*. Vol. 2: *Separation and Polemic*. Studies in Christianity and Judaism 2. Waterloo, ON: Wilfrid Laurier University Press, 1986.

———. *Luke and the Law*. SNTSMS 50. Cambridge: Cambridge University Press, 1983.

———. "The Jews and the Death of Jesus in Acts," pages 155–64 in idem, ed., *Anti-Judaism in Earliest Christianity* (1986).

Wimmer, Anselm. "Trostworte des Apostels Paulus an Hinterbliebene in Thessalonich (1 Thess 4,13-17)," *Bib* 36 (1955), 173–286.

Windisch, Hans. "Der Untergang Jerusalems (Anno 70) im Urteil der Christen und Juden," *Theologisch Tijdschrift* 48 (1914), 519–50.

Winninge, Mikael. *Sinners and the Righteous. A Comparative Study of the Psalms of Solomon and Paul's Letters*. ConBNT 26. Stockholm: Almqvist & Wiksell, 1995.

Winter, Bruce W. "'If a man does not wish to work . . .' A cultural and historical setting for 2 Thessalonians 3:6-16," *TynBul* 40 (1989), 303–15.

———. "The entries and ethics of orators and Paul (1 Thess 2:1-12)," *TynBul* 44 (1993), 55–74.

Wire, Antoinette Clark. *The Corinthian Women Prophets. A Reconstruction through Paul's Rhetoric*. Minneapolis: Fortress Press, 1990.

Witherington, Ben III. *1 and 2 Thessalonians. A Socio-Rhetorical Commentary*. Grand Rapids: Eerdmans, 2006.

Witmer, Stephen E. "θεοδίδακτοι in 1 Thessalonians 4.9: A Pauline Neologism," *NTS* 52 (2006), 239–50.

Wlosok, Antonie. *Rom und die Christen. Zur Auseinandersetzung zwischen Christentum und römischem Staat*. Stuttgart: Klett, 1970.

Wohlenberg, Gustav. *Der erste und zweite Thessalonicherbrief ausgelegt*. Kommentar zum Neuen Testament 12. Leipzig: Deichert, 1903.

Wolff, Christian. *Der zweite Brief des Paulus an die Korinther*. THKNT 8. Berlin: Evangelische Verlagsanstalt, 1989, 2011.

Wolter, Michael. art. "Pseudonymität II. Kirchengeschichtlich," *TRE* 27 (1997), 662–70.

———. "Die anonymen Schriften des Neues Testaments. Annäherungsversuch an ein literarisches Phänomen," *ZNW* 79 (1988), 1–16.

Woyke, Johannes. *Götter, "Götzen," Götterbilder. Aspekte einer paulinischen "Theologie der Religionen."* BZNW 132. Berlin and New York: de Gruyter, 2005.

Wrede, William. *Die Echtheit des zweiten Thessalonicherbriefs untersucht*. Leipzig: Hinrichs, 1903.

Wuellner, Wilhelm. "The Argumentative Structure of 1 Thessalonians as Paradoxical Encomium," pages 117–38 in *The Thessalonian Correspondence* (1990).

———. "Der vorchristliche Paulus und die Rhetorik," pages 133–65 in *Tempelkult und Tempelzerstörung (70 n. Chr.). Festschrift für Clemens Thoma*. Edited by Simon Lauer and Hanspeter Ernst. JudChr 15. Bern: Peter Lang, 1995.

Xavier, Aloysius. "A study of 'theodídaktoi' (1Thessalonians 4,9). Source and theology," Dissertation Pontifical University Gregoriana, Rome, 1991.

Yarbrough, O. Larry. *Not Like the Gentiles. Marriage Rules in the Letters of Paul.* SBLDS 80. Atlanta: Scholars Press, 1985.
Yavetz, Zvi. *Judenfeindschaft in der Antike. Die Münchener Vorträge, eingeleitet von Christian Meier.* Beck'sche Reihe 1222. Munich: Beck, 1997.
———. "Judeophobia in Classical Antiquity: A Different Approach," *JJS* 44 (1993), 1–22.
Zahn, Theodor. *Einleitung in das Neue Testament*, vol. 1. Leipzig: G. Böhme (1897); Deichert, 1906. English: *Introduction to the New Testament.* Translated by John Moore Trout, et al. under the direction of Melanchthon Williams Jacobus. Edinburgh: T & T Clark, 1909.
Zeitlin, Solomon. "The Names Hebrew, Jew and Israel: A Historical Study," *JQR* 43 (1952/53), 365–79.
Zeller, Dieter. "Christus, Skandal und Hoffnung. Die Juden in den Briefen des Paulus," pages 256–78 in *Gottesverächter und Menschenfeinde? Juden zwischen Jesus und frühchristlicher Kirche.* Edited by Horst Goldstein. Düsseldorf: Patmos, 1979.
Zeller, Eduard. "Das *odium generis humani* der Christen," *ZWT* 34 (1891), 356–67.
Zimmer, Friedrich. "I Thess 2,3-8 erklärt," pages 248–73 in *Theologische Studien: Herrn wirkl. Oberkonsistorialrath Prof. D. B. Weiss zu seinem 70. Geburtstage dargebracht.* Edited by Caspar René Gregory, et al. Göttingen: Vandenhoeck & Ruprecht, 1897.
Zimmermann, Ruben. art. "Pseudepigraphie/Pseudonymität." *RGG*[4] 6 (2003), 1786–88.
———. "Unecht—und doch wahr? Pseudepigraphie im Neuen Testament als theologisches Problem," *ZNT* 12 (2003), 27–38.

INDEX

Index of Passages Referenced

INDEX